Public expenditure on education (percentage of GDP, 1995)	Student enrollment ratio, 1995 (percentage of age group)		Adult illiteracy rate, 1995 (percentage 15 and over)		Public expenditure on health (percent of GDP 1990–95)	Life expectancy at birth, 1996 (years)		Mortality			Technnology, per 1,000 people, 1996				Internet access (per 10,000 people, July, 1997)	Country
	Primary	Secondary	Males	Females		Males	Females	Infants, 1996 (per 1,000 live births)	Under 5, 1996 (per 1,000)	Maternal ratio 1990–1996 (per 100,000 live births)	Television sets	Telephone main lines	Mobile telephones	Personal computers		
na	na	na	55	82	na	35	38	174	284	1,800	17	4	na	na	na	Sierra Leone
na	40	6	42	77	4.6	44	46	123	214	1,500	3	3	0	0.8	0.02	Mozambique
na	na	na	33	53	0.3	51	55	78	130	1,000	55	4	0	4.1	0.00	Nigeria
na	na	na	26	50	1.6	43	43	99	141	550	26	2	0	0.5	0.01	Uganda
2.3	na	na	51	74	1.2	57	59	77	112	850	7	3	0	na	0.00	Bangladesh
7.4	na	na	14	30	1.9	57	60	57	90	300	19	8	0	1.6	0.16	Kenya
na	na	na	50	76	0.8	62	65	88	123	340	24	18	0	1.2	0.07	Pakistan
3.5	na	na	35	62	0.7	63	67	65	85	437	64	15	0	1.5	0.05	India
7.7	na	na	na	na	5.0	62	73	14	17	30	341	181	1	5.6	2.09	Ukraine
9.5	na	na	na	na	3.5	66	72	24	35	24	190	76	0	na	0.06	Uzbekistan
5.6	89	65	36	61	1.6	64	67	53	66	170	126	50	0	5.8	0.31	Egypt
na	97	42	10	22	0.7	63	67	49	60	390	232	21	3	4.8	0.54	Indonesia
2.3	99	na	10	27	2.1	68	71	33	39	115	252	45	6	3.0	0.21	China
2.2	94	60	5	6	1.3	64	68	37	44	208	125	25	13	9.3	0.59	Philippines
4.1	100	na	na	na	4.1	60	73	17	25	53	386	175	2	23.7	5.51	Russian Fed.
3.2	92	73	na	na	3.6	65	73	22	28	41	226	140	1	5.3	2.66	Romania
na	95	56	26	51	3.3	68	72	32	39	140	68	44	0	3.4	0.01	Algeria
na	90	19	17	17	2.7	63	71	36	42	160	289	96	16	18.4	4.2	Brazil
4.6	97	83	na	na	4.8	68	77	12	15	10	418	169	6	36.2	11.22	Poland
3.4	96	50	8	28	2.7	66	71	42	47	180	309	224	13	13.8	3.60	Turkey
4.2	na	na	4	8	1.4	67	72	34	38	200	167	70	28	16.7	2.11	Thailand
3.5	85	50	9	8	3.0	67	73	25	58	100	188	118	13	23.3	1.81	Colombia
5.3	100	na	8	13	2.8	69	75	32	36	110	193	95	11	29.0	3.72	Mexico
4.5	na	59	4	4	4.3	69	77	22	25	100	347	174	16	24.6	5.32	Argentina
5.3	91	na	11	22	1.4	70	74	11	14	43	28	183	74	42.8	19.30	Malaysia
3.7	99	96	1	3	1.8	69	76	9	11	30	326	430	70	131.7	28.77	Korea, Rep.
5.0	100	94	na	na	6.0	73	81	5	6	7	509	392	33	94.2	31.00	Spain
4.9	97	na	19	11	5.4	75	81	6	7	12	436	440	112	92.3	36.91	Italy
5.6	98	89	na	na	6.0	75	81	6	7	9	666	519	208	311.3	382.44	Australia
5.5	100	92	na	na	5.8	74	80	6	7	9	612	528	122	192.6	149.06	United Kingdom
4.7	100	88	na	na	8.2	73	80	5	6	22	493	538	71	233.2	106.68	Germany
5.9	99	88	na	na	8.0	74	82	5	6	15	598	564	42	150.7	49.86	France
7.3	95	92	na	na	6.8	76	82	6	7	6	709	602	114	192.5	228.05	Canada
3.8	100	96	na	na	5.7	77	83	4	6	8	700	489	214	128.0	75.80	Japan
5.3	96	89	na	na	6.6	74	80	7	8	12	806	640	165	362.4	442.11	United States
3.0	na	na	4	14	1.3	74	79	4	5	10	361	513	141	216.8	196.30	Singapore
na	na	na	na	na	na	77	77	na	na	na	na	na	na	na	na	Luxembourg
5.2	na	na	21	38	3.2	65	69	54	73	na	211	133	28	50.0	34.75	World*

Source: World Bank, *World Development Report 1998/99* (New York: Oxford University Press); percentage annual growth in population (1970–1980) is from 1995 edition of the *Report*. na = not available

microeconomics

About the Artist: Laura Bryant lives and works in St. Petersburg, Florida. She has won numerous awards for her woven art, including fellowships from the National Endowment for the Arts and the State of Florida. Her work is found in major public and private collections, including those of Mobil Oil Corporation and Xerox Corporation.

microeconomics

Second Edition

Timothy Tregarthen
University of Colorado
Colorado Springs

Libby Rittenberg
The Colorado College
Colorado Springs

Worth Publishers

To our children

Microeconomics, Second Edition

Manufactured in the United States of America
ISBN: 1-57259-420-9
Printing: 1 2 3 4 5 03 02 01 00

Consulting Editor: Richard Alston
Weber State University

Executive Editor: Alan McClare
Development Editor: Judith Kromm
Project Director: Scott Hitchcock
Production Editor: Margaret Comaskey
Designer: Barbara Rusin
Design Assistant: Lee Ann Mahler
Cover and Chapter Opening Art: Laura Bryant
Production Manager: Barbara Anne Seixas
Photo Researcher: Deborah Goodsite
Composition and Separations: TSI Graphics Inc.
Printing and Binding: Von Hoffmann Press, Inc.

Library of Congress Cataloging-in-Publication Data
Tregarthen, Timothy D.
Microeconomics / Timothy Tregarthen, Libby Rittenberg. —2nd ed. p. cm.
Includes index.
ISBN 1-57259-420-9
1. Microeconomics. I. Rittenberg, Libby. II. Title.
HB172.T738 1999 99-43479
338.5—dc21 CIP

Worth Publishers
41 Madison Avenue
New York, NY 10010
http://www.worthpublishers.com

About the Authors

Timothy Tregarthen is Professor of Economics at the University of Colorado at Colorado Springs. He has taught at the University since 1971 and has served as Chairman of the Department of Economics from 1974 to 1985. He received two outstanding teaching awards at the university and in 1987 he received the Chancellor's Award as the university's outstanding professor.

Dr. Tregarthen completed his graduate work in economics at the University of California at Davis, where he was a Woodrow Wilson National Fellow and a Regents Fellow. He received his M.A. in economics in 1970 and his Ph.D. in 1972. He was student body president at California State University at Chico and received his B.A. in economics *magna cum laude* from that institution in 1967.

He was Founder and Executive Editor of *The Margin* magazine from 1985 to 1994. He has written two books, hundreds of articles on a wide range of economic issues, and a nationally syndicated humor column on economics from 1980 to 1985.

Libby Rittenberg is Professor of Economics at Colorado College in Colorado Springs. She received her B.A. in economics-mathematics and Spanish from Simmons College in 1973, her M.A. in economics from Rutgers University in 1978, and her Ph.D. in economics from Rutgers University in 1980.

Prior to joining the faculty at Colorado College, she taught at Lafayette College and at the Rutgers University Graduate School of Management. She served as a Fulbright Scholar in Istanbul, Turkey, and worked as a research economist at Mathematica, Inc., in Princeton, New Jersey.

She specializes in the internationally oriented areas of economics, with numerous articles in journals and books on comparative and development economics. Recent publications include two edited volumes, *The Political Economy of Turkey in the Post-Soviet Era: Going West and Looking East?* and *The Economic Transformation of Eastern Europe: Views From Within.*

Contents in Brief

Contents

Part six

Issues in Microeconomic Analysis

Preface

The preface to the first edition of *Microeconomics* noted not very long ago that recent developments—new trade agreements, the transition of many countries to market-based economic systems, and improvements in communications technology—were transforming the world at breathtaking speed. The pace of change has certainly not slowed down. The explosive development of the internet, the transformation of perennial U.S. federal budget deficits into surpluses, the difficulties encountered by some countries of the former Soviet bloc in converting to market-based economic systems, and a series of financial crises in Asia are but a few of the events that have had a direct impact on our lives since 1996, when *Microeconomics* was first published. The economic way of thinking provides a set of powerful tools that we can use to understand the world—regardless of how much and how fast it changes.

The goal of this edition of *Microeconomics* is to teach the basic principles of economics and to emphasize their relevance in today's world. We use applications from sports, politics, campus life, and other familiar settings to illustrate the links between theoretical principles and common experiences. Because of the increasingly global nature of economic activity, we also recognize the need for a clear and consistent international focus throughout an economics text. Therefore, we have broadened the scope of the book to include even more examples and applications from all over the world. Finally, we have tried to provide a sense of the intellectual excitement of the field and an appreciation for the gains it has made, as well as an awareness of the challenges that lie ahead.

Unifying Theme

To be sure that students realize that economics is a unified discipline and not a bewildering array of seemingly unrelated topics, we develop the presentation of microeconomics around an integrating theme.

The integrating theme for microeconomics is the marginal decision rule, a simple approach to choices that maximize the value of some objective. The marginal decision rule is presented in an intuitive manner in Chapter 6 and applied as an integrating device throughout the discussion of microeconomics. Instead of a hodgepodge of rules for different market conditions, we give a single rule that can be applied within any market setting. Chapter 6 also investigates conditions under which maximizing choices will—and will not—lead to desirable outcomes. This chapter provides a clear perspective on the strengths and limitations of markets, as well as on the role of government in the economy.

Organization

While we have ordered the chapters in a way that we believe makes sense, we recognize that others may want to present topics in a different sequence and to pick and choose among various topics. We have carefully written the chapters so that, after covering the core introductory chapters (Chapters 1–4), an instructor can assign chapters out of numerical order. Within *Microeconomics,* the sequence can be varied once the basic tools have been introduced in Parts 1 and 2, so that it is possible, say, to cover competitive product and factor markets

(Chapters 9, 12, and 13) before discussing imperfectly competitive product and factor markets (Chapters 10, 11, and 14). Thus the text allows a great deal of flexibility.

The Core Chapters

First impressions are critical, so we've devoted great energy to making the core chapters of the text (Chapters 1–4) as clear and as engaging as possible.

Continuing the tradition of the first edition, we begin Chapter 1 with *A Day in the Life of a Nation*. As we were getting the manuscript ready to go to press, we picked a single day in February 1999 and selected events reported in newspapers from all over the country. Those events provide lively and relevant examples of how economics applies to everyone. Students will see how stories ranging from Nike Corporation's treatment of workers at its factories in southeast Asia to a $3.3 billion charitable donation by Bill and Melinda Gates relate to economics and to the material they will be studying in the course. Economics is the study of choice, and we use these examples to focus on the choices that individuals make and on the opportunity costs of those choices. This chapter also looks at careers in economics, the benefits of an undergraduate major in economics, and the usefulness of even a little study of economics.

The appendix to Chapter 1 provides a comprehensive explanation of essentially all the graphical and mathematical tools used throughout the text. Some students are quite comfortable with these tools, but many are not. This thorough appendix will be extremely helpful to those students who are anxious about the course. It will enable them to overcome their trepidation about the way economics is presented so that they can focus better on the content and significance of the new ideas and ways of thinking they will encounter throughout the text.

Chapter 2 explains the production possibilities model and Chapter 3 presents the model of demand and supply. To make these central chapters clear *and* exciting, we have incorporated many real examples that will engage students. To introduce the topic of production possibilities, we talk about Fort Ord, a former military base that was recently converted to a university campus: California State University, Monterey Bay. We explain the production possibilities model with a sustained example using snowboards and skis. To open the discussion of demand and supply in Chapter 3, we talk about the way in which Starbucks changed the coffee-drinking habits of Americans and then continue using coffee as an example throughout the chapter to flesh out the model of demand and supply.

To complete the core, we include a new chapter on applications of demand and supply (Chapter 4). Our goal in this chapter is to show the wide range of applications of the demand and supply model. We chose the market for personal computers, the stock market, and the market for health care services to demonstrate the relevance of the model and the breadth of its application. Price floors and price ceilings also provide excellent examples of the power of the model of demand and supply.

The Plan of *Microeconomics*

After explaining how maximizing behavior in general leads to the marginal decision rule in Chapter 6, we complete our coverage of the basic tools of microeconomics with a chapter on consumer behavior (Chapter 7) and one on production and cost (Chapter 8). Chapter 7 contains an optional section on indifference curve analysis. An appendix to Chapter 8 on the use of isocost curves and isoquants to understand how firms choose efficient levels of factors of production is available at the book's web site: <http://www.worthpublishers.com/tregarthen>.

Part 3 (Chapters 9 through 11) examines product market structures and Part 4 (Chapters 12 through 14) covers markets for factors of production. Although the relationship of government to the private sector is discussed in many places throughout microeconomics, Part 5 is devoted specifically to this topic. These chapters discuss public finance and public choice (Chapter 15) and antitrust policy and business regulation (Chapter 16). The four chapters in Part 6 apply microeconomic analysis to international trade (Chapter 17), environment issues (Chapter 18), inequality, poverty, and discrimination (Chapter 19), and economies in transition (Chapter 20).

Features and Learning Aids

Recognizing that a course in economics may seem daunting to some students, we've tried hard to make *Microeconomics* a clear and engaging text. Clarity comes in part from the intuitive presentation style, but we've also integrated a number of pedagogical features that we believe make learning economic concepts and principles easier and more fun. These features, like the rest of the text, are very student-focused.

Getting Started chapter introductions set the stage for each chapter with an example that we hope will motivate readers to study the material that follows. These essays on topics such as the value of a college degree in the labor market and the government's lawsuit against Microsoft present issues or events that lend themselves to the type of analysis explained in the chapter. We refer to these examples later in the text to demonstrate the link between theory and reality.

Case in Point essays within the chapter illustrate the influence of economic forces on real issues and real people. When students read about the Oprah Winfrey book club and about the lawsuit brought against Ms. Winfrey by a group of cattlemen, they see her not just as a television star, but also as a possible demand shifter. In another chapter, a distributor of kitchen appliances to building contractors talks about what it means to be a price taker in a competitive market.

Highlighting of key terms and definitions within the text enables students to review them in context, a process that enhances learning. A list of key terms with page references to the definition appears at the back of each chapter and all highlighted terms are included in the **Dictionary of Economic Terms** at the back of the book.

Checklists at the conclusion of major sections of each chapter review the key points covered in that section. At the end of each chapter, **A Look Back . . . A Look Ahead** summarizes the material covered in the chapter and briefly previews subsequent chapters.

Try It Yourself problems following most major sections of text give students the opportunity to be active learners. These problems, which are answered completely at the end of each chapter, give students a clear signal as to whether they understand the material before they go on to the next topic.

Caution! notes throughout the text warn of common errors and explain how to avoid making them. After our combined teaching experience of more than fifty years, we have seen the same mistakes made by many students. Confusing the difference between a shift in demand and movement along the demand curve is a typical one. Caution! notes, which are easily spotted in the margins of the text, provide additional clarification and show students how to avoid common mistakes.

For Discussion questions at the end of each chapter are intended to promote discussion of the issues raised in the chapter and to engage students in critical thinking about the material. This section includes not only general review questions to test basic understanding but also examples drawn from the news and from results of economics research.

Problems, which follow the discussion questions, provide numerical exercises as a further test of understanding.

Supplements for Students

Study Guide

Prepared by John Brock and Dale Deboer of the University of Colorado, Colorado Springs, the *Study Guide* reinforces the material covered in the text. For each chapter, the *Study Guide* provides chapter objectives, walks students step-by-step through the chapter, and quizzes students with pre-tests and post-tests. Many of the *Study Guide* chapters also contain a section called "Are You Confused?" to help students having difficulty with core concepts. More advanced students who want to delve a little further into the chapter's topics will find a section called "Enrichment."

Microeconomics 2e Companion Web Site

Found at <http://www.worthpublishers.com/tregarthen>, the web site to accompany *Microeconomics* 2e offers valuable tools, including online simulations, designed to help students master economic concepts. These tools include interactive exercises, graphing modules, and student quizzes. In addition, the site features *The Margin Online,* which contains timely articles on everyday economic issues, as well as frequent updates, including new web links, exercises, and developments in economics.

Student Activities CD-ROM

This CD-ROM contains multimedia content from the *Microeconomics* 2e companion web site, including basic drill and practice exercises, interactive simulations, graphing modules, and student quizzes. This CD-ROM is ideal for students with limited web access or for use in a lab setting.

Supplements for Instructors

Instructor's Resources Manual

The *Instructor's Resources* manual by Virginia Lee Owen of Illinois State University includes chapter overviews and outlines, learning objectives, common student difficulties, suggestions for active learning, such as annotated web sites, and lecture supplements. The manual also includes complete instructions for 12 in-class experiments, provided by John Brock, that provide hands-on learning experiences for students. A section called "Theory in Focus" presents Cases in Point not included in the text. Instructors will also find in this manual a list of readings, audio/video aids, and software to aid in class preparation and presentation.

Solutions Manual

The *Solutions Manual* contains answers for all discussion questions and problems found at the end of each text chapter.

Test Bank

Written by Paul Ballantyne of the University of Colorado, Colorado Springs, the print *Test Bank* for *Microeconomics* 2e offers over 2,000 multiple choice, true/false, and short essay questions that test comprehension, interpretation, analysis, and synthesis.

Computerized Test Bank

The *Test Bank* is also available in CD-ROM format for both Windows and Mac users. Instructors can download the test bank and then edit, add, and resequence questions to suit their needs.

Online Testing

The *Test Bank* CD-ROM allows instructors to create and administer exams on paper, over a network, and over the internet as well. Multimedia, graphics, movies, sound, and interactive activities can be included in the questions. Security features allow instructors to restrict tests to specific computers or time blocks. The CD also includes a suite of grade book and question analysis features.

Q & A Online

The *Microeconomics* 2e companion web site allows instructors to conduct and evaluate quizzes on the web at <http://www.worthpublishers.com/tregarthen>.

PowerPoint Slides

This PowerPoint set includes each figure from *Microeconomics* 2e, enhanced with a text outline. Available from the companion web site, the slides can be used directly or customized.

WebCT

On request from instructors, the text's media content is available in WebCT format for use in creating course web sites and/or online courses. WebCT includes content, threaded discussions, quizzing, a grade book, a course calendar, and a number of other specialized features.

The Margin Online

Beginning with *The Best of The Margin,* a selection of classic articles, games, and puzzles from *The Margin,* the popular periodical founded and edited by Timothy and Suzanne Tregarthen, has been relaunched. New articles will be posted to the *Microeconomics* 2e companion web site <http://www.worthpublishers.com/tregarthen>.

Transparencies

Instructors can obtain more than 100 vivid color acetates of text figures, enlarged for superior projection quality.

Videos

Microeconomics is the text chosen to accompany the economics telecourse developed by the Dallas County Community College District. For use in class, instructors have access to videos produced by the DCCCD, the nation's leading developer of distance learning materials. These videos dramatize key economics concepts.

Acknowledgments

A text is truly the joint product of the efforts of hundreds of people. We have been humbled and gratified by the enormous contributions of colleagues around the country and the staff at Worth Publishers that have made this book possible. With pleasure, we acknowledge our debt to them.

We are most grateful to Richard Alston of Weber State University. He's been with us from beginning to end, and we could not have completed this book without him. He has been our consultant, advisor, partner, co-conspirator, collaborator, prodder, and friend. His contributions and ideas have enriched this book greatly. In addition, he has played a major role in the development of the *Study Guide,* the *Test Bank,* and the *Instructor's Resources* manual to ensure their coordination with the text. We cannot thank him enough (and we mean it, Dick!).

Our colleagues who reviewed various drafts of *Microeconomics*, 1e and 2e, have made tremendous contributions to its development. We gratefully acknowledge them here. Early in the development of the second edition we held a two-day conference to discuss a variety of issues. We were joined there by the authors of the supplements and a group of peer reviewers. They told us what they thought and we took their comments to heart. We learned much from their insights. We note those who participated in the focus group with an asterisk (*) in the list below.

Jack Adams
University of Arkansas, Little Rock
Carlos Aguilar
El Paso Community College
Rasheed Al-Hmoud
Texas Tech University
Christine Amsler
Michigan State University
James Q. Aylsworth
Lakeland Community College
Andrew H. Barnett
Auburn University
Peter S. Barth
University of Connecticut
Kari Battaglia
University of North Texas
Randall Bennett
Gonzaga University
Cynthia Benzing
West Chester University
Herbert Bernstein
Drexel University
Margot Biery
Tarrant Junior College
Scott Bloom
North Dakota State University
Bruce Bolnick
Northeastern University
Frank Bonello
University of Notre Dame
M. Neil Browne
Bowling Green State University
Neil Buchanan
University of Wisconsin, Milwaukee
Michael R. Butler
Texas Christian University
Steven T. Call
Metropolitan State College of Denver
Arthur Caplan
Weber State University
Charles Capone
U.S. Department of Housing and Urban Development
Tony Caporale
Ohio University, Athens
***Robert Carlsson**
University of South Carolina
Shirley Cassing
University of Pittsburgh
Steven L. Cobb
University of North Texas
Donald Coffin
Indiana University Northwest
Francis Colella
Simpson College
Mary Cookingham
Michigan State University
James Peery Cover
Culverhouse College of Commerce, University of Alabama
Jerry Crawford
Arkansas State University
Lawrence Daellenbach
University of Wisconsin, La Crosse
John P. Dahlquist
College of Alameda
Edward Day
University of Central Florida
Ed Deak
Fairfield University
Smile Dube
California State University, Sacramento
Donald H. Dutkowsky
Syracuse University
***Harry Ellis**
University of North Texas
Steffany Ellis
University of Michigan
Mona El Shazly
Columbia College
Alejandra Edwards
California State University, Long Beach
Sherman Folland
Oakland University
Richard Fowles
University of Utah
Ralph Gamble
Fort Hays State University
Doris Geide-Stevenson
Weber State University

E. B. Gendel
Woodbury University
Frank Gertcher
University of Colorado, Colorado Springs
Kathie S. Gilbert
Western New Mexico University
***Lynn G. Gillette**
Houston Baptist University
Otis W. Gilley
Lousiana Tech University
Lisa Grobar
California State University, Long Beach
John Groesbeck
Southern Utah University
Robert Harris
University of Indianapolis
***Gus Herring**
Brookhaven College
Robert Stanley Herren
North Dakota State University
Dean Hiebert
Illinois State University
Hank Hilton
Loyola College, Baltimore
Daniel Himarios
University of Texas at Arlington
Jim Holcomb
University of Texas at El Paso
Solomon Honig
Montclair State University
Nancy A. Jianakoplos
Colorado State University
Bruce Johnson
Centre College
Walter Johnson
University of Missouri
Martin Judd
St. Mary's University of Minnesota
James Kahiga
Georgia Perimeter College
Walter Kemmsies
Memphis State University
Bill Kerby
California State University, Sacramento
Van Kolpin
University of Oregon
Edward Clifford Koziara
Drexel University
Michael Kupilik
University of Montana
Maureen Lage
Miami University of Ohio
Patrick Lenihan
Eastern Illinois State University
Jane Lillydahl
University of Colorado at Boulder
Susan Linz
Michigan State University
Roger Mack
DeAnza College
Michael Magura
University of Toledo
Henry N. McCarl
University of Alabama at Birmingham
Judith A. McDonald
Lehigh University
James McGowen
Belleville Area College
Ann McPherren
Huntington College
Dayle Mandelson
University of Wisconsin, Stout
Victor Matheson
Lake Forest College
Perry Mehrling
Barnard College
Ronald Merchant
Spokane Community College
David Molina
University of North Texas
W. Douglas Morgan
University of California, Santa Barbara
Richard Moss
Ricks College
Peter Naylor
Santa Barbara City College
James Nordyke
New Mexico State University
Frank O'Connor
Eastern Kentucky University
Valentine Okonkowo
Winston-Salem State University
John Pharr
Cedar Valley College
John G. Pomery
Purdue University
Thomas Potiowsky
Portland State University
Edward Price
Oklahoma State University
James F. Ragan
Kansas State University
Jaishankar Raman
Valparaiso University
W. Gregory Rhodus
Bentley College
Malcolm Robinson
University of North Carolina, Greensboro
Greg S. Rose
Sacramento City College
Robert Rycroft
Mary Washington College
David St. Clair
California State University, Hayward
***Allen Sanderson**
University of Chicago
***Christine Sauer**
University of New Mexico
Richard Schimming
Mankato State University
Gerald Scott
Florida Atlantic University
Terri A. Sexton
California State University, Sacramento

***Alden Shiers**
California State Polytechnic University

Chuck Sicotte
Rock Valley College

John L. Solow
University of Iowa

John Somers
Portland Community College

Gary W. Sorenson
Oregon State University

Charles Staelin
Smith College

Wendy Stock
Montana State University

Michael K. Taussig
Rutgers University

Sarah Tinkler
Weber State University

Steven G. Ullman
University of Miami

Mike Walden
North Carolina State University

Donald A. Wells
University of Arizona

Ron Whitfield
Northeastern University

***Kathryn Wilson**
Kent State University

Leslie Wolfson
The Pingry School

Louise B. Wolita
University of Texas at Austin

William C. Wood
James Madison University

***Ranita Wyatt**
North Texas State University

Darrell Young
University of Texas at Austin

Alina Zapalska
Marshall University

We are very grateful for the support we received from the entire staff at Worth Publishers. Susan Driscoll was president when this edition began and she got us launched. Liz Widdicombe, president since 1998, has been actively involved in the later stages of the project. They both provided leadership at critical stages. Catherine Woods, the publisher, and Alan McClare, the executive editor for economics, were always looking ahead and keeping us on track. Scott Hitchcock, project director, Barbara Rusin, senior designer, Stacey Alexander, supplements manager, and Barbara Anne Seixas, production manager, were masterful at pulling the project together.

We also thank those who tried to make us better writers. Judith Kromm, the Worth development editor, stayed with us from beginning to end. ("Can't you clarify this?" "Make that more exciting?" "Add one more Case in Point?") We benefited greatly from her care and concern and were often heartened by her enthusiasm. Ann Grogg and Marjorie Anderson, freelance development editors, also provided many insights. Margaret Comaskey, project editor, was invaluable in the final stages of the project. Shannon Capanna and Jordan Scott provided very able research assistance. We are grateful to them all.

We also want to thank our families. It is they who have had to live with this project as long as we have. They have all put up cheerfully with this invasion into their lives. We love them.

tregarthen@aol.com

lrittenberg@cc.colorado.edu

A Special Note to Students

"Life ain't going to be like anything you ever heard of before."[1] Forecasting is tricky business, but this statement strikes us as being as safe a bet as one can make in anticipating the changes that lie ahead, the changes we all will face. Change—rapid change—underlies all our lives.

However rapid the change, though, the principles of economics that you will learn in this book will help you to understand it. You'll learn an approach to thinking about choices that is likely to be quite different from any you've encountered before. But we think you'll find that this approach will be useful to you in all sorts of ways:

In Your Daily Life Life is a series of choices, and economics is the study of choice. As you learn about economics, you'll learn a framework for decisionmaking that applies to choosing whether to pay cash or use a credit card, how to evaluate a financial investment, or what to do this weekend.

In Your Campus Life Should you buy your texts in the campus bookstore or online? How should you choose between riding the bus or driving your car to school? Should you park in the prime (and often expensive) lot or in the shuttle lot away from campus? What factors should you consider in choosing a major? This course won't give you answers to these questions, but it will give you a useful vantage point from which to consider the alternatives.

In Your Career Whatever career you choose, your study of economics will help you. It won't pick out a career for you, but it will give you a framework for thinking about choosing one. And, once you've chosen a career, application of the economic principles you'll learn will make you more successful in it.

In Your Political Life As a participant in the political process, you will be expected to take positions on all sorts of issues. Should there be an increase in the minimum wage? Should universities have different entrance standards for different groups? Should producers be protected from foreign competition? You will want to know how such policies are likely to affect you and your fellow citizens. The economic principles you study in this course will give you insights that will help you form reasoned positions on these and a wide range of other issues.

These are ambitious goals, and we've set them with you in mind. We want you to share our excitement about economics and its power to frame your choices in a way that will make those choices better ones. We want to help you prepare for a life about which the only thing we know for certain is that it will be full of change.

[1]Lane Kirkland, former president of the AFL-CIO used this line in a commencement address to the University of South Carolina in 1985. He was paraphrasing a line from the western movie, *Missouri Breaks.*

1 Economics: The Study of Choice

Getting Started: A Look at Economics

What is economics? Here's a quick answer: Economics is the study of the choices people make.

Would you like better grades? More time to relax? More spending money for entertainment? Those things you want require that you make choices. Should you spend the next few hours studying, or should you take in a movie instead? Should you increase your work hours to boost income and give up study time—or time for movies or sleep? You've got to choose.

Not only must we make choices as individuals, we must make choices as a society. Do we want a cleaner environment? Do we want the economy to grow faster? Those goals may conflict; we've got to make a choice.

Because choices range over every imaginable aspect of human experience, so does economics. Economists have investigated the nature of family life, the arts, education, crime, sports, job creation—the list is virtually endless because so much of our lives involves making choices.

Economics is defined less by the subjects economists investigate than by the way in which economists investigate them. Economists have a way of looking at the world that differs from the way other scholars look at the world. We often call it the economic way of thinking. This chapter introduces that way of thinking.

Economics: An Introduction

Economics is a social science that examines how people choose among the alternatives available to them. It's social because it involves people and their behavior. It uses, as much as possible, a scientific approach in its investigation of choices.

The next section gives you a preview of the field of economics by surveying some of the events that occurred on February 5, 1999, from the perspective of economics. We've chosen that date because it came just before we had to get this chapter off for final editing before it was prepared for publication.

The Scope of Economics: A Day in the Life of the Nation

If economics is about making choices, it must be relevant to virtually the whole range of human behavior. Here's an economist's-eye view of some events of a single day, February 5, 1999.

> Item: A Superior Court judge in San Francisco dismissed a lawsuit that charged Nike Corporation with making misleading claims in its advertising concerning the firm's factory operations in Southeast Asia.[1]

Economic perspective: Nike was under attack by those who charged that the firm exploited its workers in Southeast Asia by forcing them to work long hours, paying substandard wages, and subjecting them to dangerous working conditions. Nike denied the charges and contended that its advertising was protected by constitutional guarantees of free speech.

[1]The case was reported in Bob Egelko, "Suit Over Defense of Nike Factory Conditions Dismissed," SacBee, the electronic news service of the *Sacramento Bee,* 6 February 1999. The service may be reached on the Internet at www.sacbee.com

Economists are interested in a host of questions raised by this case. Among them: Why do firms shift some of their operations to other countries? How does foreign production affect workers in a firm's home country? How does it affect workers in the countries where the factories operate? What forces determine wages and working conditions in those countries? Why do firms advertise, and how does that advertising affect the marketplace?

Item: The Department of Labor announced that unemployment in January 1999 had remained unchanged at 4.3 percent as the economy added 245,000 jobs during the month, far more than had been expected.[2]

Economic perspective: U.S. economic performance in the final years of the twentieth century was simply dazzling. The economy grew faster, generated more jobs and more income, and produced lower inflation than many economists had thought possible (including, quite frankly, the authors of this book).

"This is an economy with significant momentum," said Diane Swonk, deputy chief economist at Bank One Corp. in Chicago. "Everyone was expecting a slowdown, and now they may have to revise up their growth forecasts."

The first question raised by all of this is simple to ask and hard to answer: Why were many economists so surprised by the economy's performance in the late 1990s? What determines how fast an economy grows and how fast it generates jobs? What determines the rates of inflation and unemployment?

Item: The president of one of the two foundations established by Bill Gates and his wife, Melinda, announced that the couple had just given an additional $3.3 billion to the two funds.[3]

Economic perspective: The gift brought the total assets of the two foundations to $5.3 billion. Bill Gates has given away more money than any other living philanthropist.

Gates can certainly afford the gift. His fortune consists largely of his 515 million shares of Microsoft stock, the company he founded. On the day the gift was announced, that stock was worth more than $80 billion. Gates is not just the wealthiest person in the world; he is the wealthiest man who ever lived. Even adjusting for inflation, Gates's fortune stands at the top of the all-time list.

Gates's wealth reflects the extraordinary profitability of his company. Economists are interested in the role of profits in general. In the case of Microsoft, they study the effect of the firm on consumers and on rival firms, and the reasons its profits are so high. When the Gateses made the gift, Microsoft was in federal court, charged by the U.S. Justice Department with unfairly competing in the market for web browsers, software packages that help users to navigate the Internet.

The gift by Bill and Melinda Gates raises another question economists examine: Why do individuals make gifts to others? What accounts for charitable acts?

Item: The Indiana Pacers defeated the Washington Wizards 96–81 in a National Basketball Association game in Indiana.[4]

Economic perspective: This was a special game; it was the first played after a battle between the Players Association and team owners resulted in the cancellation of much of the 1998–1999 season.

[2]"Job Growth Rises; Unemployment Steady at 4.3 Percent," *Dallas Morning News* electronic edition, 6 February 1999. The electronic edition may be reached on the Internet at www.dallasnews.com
[3]Katie Hafner, "Gates and Wife Give $3.3 Billion to Their 2 Foundations," *New York Times,* electronic edition, 6 February 1999. This edition may reached on the Internet at www.nyt.com
[4]Mark Montieth, "Pacers Win Season Opener Over Wizards," *Indianapolis Star/News,* 6 February 1999, electronic edition. This edition may be reached on the Internet at www.starnews.com

One obvious question for economists to examine is the reason some professional athletes enjoy the high salaries they receive. Why were players willing to give up these high salaries while they battled owners over a labor agreement? Why were owners willing to give up the revenues they would have received had so many games not been canceled?

There was, of course, a lot more going on February 5, 1999, than this brief survey reveals. The point is that nearly everything that happened that day was the outcome of a set of choices. Those choices are the stuff of economics. We can use economic analysis to study choices people make.

Scarcity, Choice, and Cost

Nike's decision to produce shoes and other goods in Southeast Asia meant not producing them somewhere else—including, of course, the United States. When U.S. firms added 245,000 jobs at the beginning of 1999, they had to decide first that it made sense to add those jobs; second, what jobs to add; and third, whom to hire. The Gates's gift meant that the couple chose to give up the use of a tremendous amount of wealth—and chose the organizations to which to give it. NBA players and owners gave up hundreds of millions of dollars in salaries and revenues while negotiating terms of a labor agreement.

All choices mean that one alternative is selected over another. Selecting among alternatives involves three ideas central to economics: scarcity, choice, and opportunity cost.

Scarcity Our resources are limited. At any one time, we have only so much land, so many factories, so much oil, so many people. But our wants, our desires for the things that we can produce with those resources, are unlimited. We would always like more and better housing, more and better education—more and better of practically everything.

If our resources were also unlimited, we could say yes to each of our wants—and there would be no economics. Because our resources are limited, we can't say yes to everything. To say yes to one thing requires that we say no to another. Whether we like it or not, we must make choices.

Our unlimited wants are continually colliding with the limits of our resources, forcing us to pick some activities and to reject others. **Scarcity** is the condition of having to choose among alternatives. A **scarce good** is one for which the choice of one alternative requires that another be given up.

Consider a parcel of land. The parcel presents us with several alternative uses. We could build a house on it. We could put a gas station on it. We could create a small park on it. We could leave the land undeveloped in order to be able to make a decision later as to how it should be used.

Suppose we've decided the land should be used for a house. Should it be a large and expensive house or a modest one? Suppose it is to be a modest single-family house. Who should live in the house? If the Lees live in it, the Nguyens cannot. There are alternative uses of the land both in the sense of the type of use and also in the sense of who gets to use it. The fact that land is scarce means that society must make choices concerning its use.

Virtually everything is scarce. Consider the air we breathe, which is available in huge quantity at no charge to us. Could it possibly be scarce?

The test of whether air is scarce is whether it has alternative uses. What uses can we make of the air? We breathe it. We pollute it when we drive our cars, heat our houses, or operate our factories. We certainly need the air to breathe. But just as certainly, we choose to pollute it. Those two uses are clearly alternatives to each other. The more we pollute the air, the less desirable—and healthy—it will be to breathe. If we decide we want to breathe cleaner air, we must limit pollution. Air is a scarce good because it has alternative uses.

Case in Point Searching for Grizzlies

Rumors about sightings of grizzly bears in Colorado's San Juan Mountains have been around for decades, despite the fact that the bears are officially extinct in the state. Recent evidence suggesting the rumors may be true has spurred renewed efforts by conservationists to find proof that the big bears still roam in Colorado. A lot of loggers and ranchers hope the conservationists don't succeed.

Colorado's Department of Wildlife declared in 1952 that there were no grizzlies left in the state. But in 1979, a bow hunter was attacked and mauled in the area by a grizzly; the man managed to kill the bear with an arrow. The Department of Wildlife declared that this bear was the last grizzly. Jim Tolisano, a conservation biologist from Santa Fe, New Mexico, found what he thought were grizzly droppings in 1993. Tests of the droppings by the Montana Fish and Wildlife Service confirmed that they were from grizzlies.

"We also found a 10½-inch paw print," says Mr. Tolisano. "That had to be from a grizzly."

The grizzly is on the federal government's list of endangered species. If conclusive evidence of the bears' presence is established, the Forest Service and other agencies will be required by the Endangered Species Act of 1973 to take measures to protect the bears' habitat. That would almost certainly mean a reduction or elimination of grazing by sheep and a reduction in logging operations in the area. It would also mean a ban on bear hunting in the region, which stretches across the Rocky Mountains in southern Colorado and northern New Mexico.

Undeveloped mountain regions are a scarce resource. They can be left in their natural state to preserve habitat for wildlife. An alternative is to subject them to increased logging, grazing, and hunting, all of which mean reducing the habitat for wildlife. The alternatives of increased logging, hunting, and grazing have already been chosen. If the grizzlies' presence is proven, that choice will change.

Source: David Petersen, "Ghost Grizzlies," *E Magazine: The Environmental Magazine* 8 (1) (Jan–Feb 1997): 19–22; and a 1999 interview with Jim Tolisano.

Goods that are scarce force us to make choices. Not all goods, however, force such choices. A **free good** is one for which the choice of one use does not require that we give up another.

There aren't many free goods. Outer space, for example, was a free good when the only use we made of it was to gaze at it. But now, our use of space has reached the point where one use can be an alternative to another. Conflicts have already arisen over the allocation of orbital slots for communications satellites. Thus, even parts of outer space are scarce. Space will surely become more scarce in the twenty-first century as we find new ways to use it. Scarcity characterizes virtually everything. Consequently, the scope of economics is wide indeed.

Scarcity and the Fundamental Economic Questions The choices forced on us by scarcity raise three sets of issues. Every economy must answer the following questions:

1. **What should be produced?** Using the economy's scarce resources to produce one thing requires giving up another. Producing better education, for example, may require cutting back on other services, such as health care. A decision to preserve a wilderness area requires giving up other uses of the land. Every society must decide what it will produce with its scarce resources.

2. **How should goods and services be produced?** There are all sorts of choices to be made in determining how goods and services should be produced. Should a firm employ

skilled or unskilled workers? Should it produce in its own country or, as Nike does, should it use foreign plants? Should manufacturing firms use new or recycled raw materials to make their products?

3. **For whom should goods and services be produced?** If a good or service is produced, a decision must be made about who will get it. A decision to have one person or group receive a good or service usually means it won't be available to someone else. For example, representatives of the poorest nations on earth often complain that energy consumption per person in the United States is 20 times greater than energy consumption per person in the world's 49 poorest countries. Critics argue that the world's energy should be more evenly allocated. Should it? That's a "for whom" question.

Every economy must determine what should be produced, how it should be produced, and for whom it should be produced. We shall return to these questions again and again.

Opportunity Cost It is within the context of scarcity that economists define what is perhaps the most important concept in all of economics, the concept of opportunity cost. **Opportunity cost** is the value of the best alternative forgone in making any choice.

The opportunity cost to you of reading the remainder of this chapter will be the value of the best other use to which you could have put your time. If you choose to spend $10 on a potted plant, you have simultaneously chosen to give up the benefits of spending the $10 on a pizza or a paperback book or a night at the movies. If the book is the most valuable of those alternatives, then the opportunity cost of the plant is the value of the enjoyment you expect to receive from the book.

The concepts of scarcity, choice, and opportunity cost are at the heart of economics. A good is scarce if the choice of one alternative requires that another be given up. The existence of alternative uses forces us to make choices. The opportunity cost of any choice is the value of the best alternative use forgone in making it.

Checklist

- Economics is the study of how people choose among the alternatives available to them.
- Scarcity means that the choice of one alternative requires that another be given up.
- Given scarcity, a society must make choices about what to produce, how to produce it, and for whom it should be produced.
- Every choice has an opportunity cost, the value of the best alternative forgone in making a choice. Opportunity costs affect the choices people make.

Try It Yourself 1-1

Identify the elements of scarcity, choice, and opportunity cost in each of the following:

a. The Environmental Protection Agency is considering an order that a 500-acre area on the outskirts of a large city be preserved in its natural state, because the area is home to a rodent that is considered an endangered species. Developers had planned to build a housing development on the land.

b. A young man who went to work as a nurses' aide after graduating from high school leaves his job to go to college, where he will obtain training as a registered nurse.

c. The manager of an automobile assembly plant is considering whether to produce cars or sport utility vehicles (SUVs) next month. Assume that the quantities of labor and other materials required would be the same for either type of production.

The Field of Economics

We've examined the basic concepts of scarcity, choice, and opportunity cost in economics. In this section, we'll look at economics as a field of study. We begin with the characteristics that distinguish economics from other social sciences.

The Economic Way of Thinking

Economists study choices that scarcity requires us to make. This fact is not what distinguishes economics from other social sciences; all social scientists are interested in choices. An anthropologist might study the choices of ancient peoples; a political scientist might study the choices of legislatures; a psychologist might study how people choose a mate; a sociologist might study the factors that have led to a rise in single-parent households. Economists study such questions as well. What is it about the study of choices by economists that makes economics different from these other social sciences?

Three features distinguish the economic approach to choice from the approaches taken in other social sciences:

1. Economists give special emphasis to the role of opportunity costs in their analysis of choices.
2. Economists assume that individuals make choices that seek to maximize the value of some objective, and that they define their objectives in terms of their own self-interest.
3. Individuals maximize by deciding whether to do a little more or a little less of something. Economists argue that individuals pay attention to the consequences of small changes in the levels of the activities they pursue.

The emphasis economists place on opportunity cost, the idea that people make choices that maximize the value of objectives that serve their self-interest, and a focus on the effects of small changes are ideas of great power. They constitute the core of economic thinking. The next three sections examine these ideas in greater detail.

Opportunity Costs Are Important If doing one thing requires giving up another, then the expected benefits of the alternatives we face will affect the ones we choose. Economists argue that an understanding of opportunity cost is crucial to the examination of choices.

As the set of available alternatives changes, we expect that the choices individuals make will change. A rainy day could change the opportunity cost of reading a good book; we might expect more reading to get done in bad than in good weather. A high income can make it very costly to take a day off; we might expect highly paid individuals to work more hours than those who aren't paid as well. If individuals are maximizing their level of satisfaction and firms are maximizing profits, then a change in the set of alternatives they face may affect their choices in a predictable way.

The emphasis on opportunity costs is an emphasis on the examination of alternatives. One benefit of the economic way of thinking is that it pushes us to think about the value of alternatives in each problem involving choice.

Individuals Maximize in Pursuing Self-Interest What motivates people as they make choices? Perhaps more than anything else, it is the economist's answer to this question that distinguishes economics from other fields.

Economists assume that individuals make choices that they expect will create the maximum value of some objective, given the constraints they face. Furthermore, economists assume that people's objectives will be those that serve their own self-interest.

Economists assume, for example, that the owners of business firms seek to maximize profit. Given the assumed goal of profit maximization, economists can predict how firms in an industry will respond to changes in the markets in which they operate. As labor costs in the United States rise, for example, economists aren't surprised to see firms such as Nike move some of their manufacturing operations overseas.

Similarly, economists assume that maximizing behavior is at work when they examine the behavior of consumers. In studying consumers, economists assume that individual consumers make choices aimed at maximizing their level of satisfaction. In the next chapter, we'll look at the results of the shift from skiing to snowboarding; that's a shift that reflects the pursuit of self-interest by consumers.

In assuming that people pursue their self-interest, economists are not assuming people are selfish. People clearly gain satisfaction by helping others, as suggested by the charitable contributions of Bill and Melinda Gates. Pursuing one's own self-interest means pursuing the things that give one satisfaction. It need not imply greed or selfishness.

Choices Are Made at the Margin Economists argue that most choices are made "at the margin." The **margin** is the current level of an activity. Think of it as the edge from which a choice is to be made. A **choice at the margin** is a decision to do a little more or a little less of something.

Assessing choices at the margin can lead to extremely useful insights. Consider, for example, the problem of curtailing water consumption when the amount of water available falls short of the amount people now use. Economists argue that one way to induce people to conserve water is to raise its price. A common response to this recommendation is that a higher price would have no effect on water consumption, because water is a necessity. Many people assert that prices don't affect water consumption because people "need" water.

But choices in water consumption, like virtually all choices, are made at the margin. Individuals don't make choices about whether they should or should not consume water. Rather, they decide whether to consume a little more or a little less water. Household water consumption in the United States totals about 175 gallons per person per day. Think of that starting point as the edge from which a choice at the margin in water consumption is made. Could a higher price cause you to use less water brushing your teeth, take shorter showers, or water your lawn less? Could a higher price cause people to reduce their use, say, to 174 gallons per person per day? To 173? When we examine the choice to consume water at the margin, the notion that a higher price would reduce consumption seems much more plausible. Prices affect our consumption of water because choices in water consumption, like other choices, are made at the margin.

The elements of opportunity cost, maximization, and choices at the margin can be found in each of two broad areas of economic analysis: microeconomics and macroeconomics. Your economics course, for example, may be designated as a "micro" or as a "macro" course. We'll look at these two areas of economic thought in the next section.

Microeconomics and Macroeconomics

Microeconomics is the branch of economics that focuses on the choices made by consumers and firms and the impacts those choices have on individual markets. **Macroeconomics** is the branch of economics that focuses on the impact of choices on the total, or aggregate, level of economic activity.

How does the weather in Argentina affect the producers and consumers of eggs? Why do women end up doing most of the housework? Why do senior citizens get discounts on public transit systems? These questions are generally regarded as microeconomic because they focus on individual units or markets in the economy.

Is the total level of economic activity rising or falling? Is the rate of inflation increasing or decreasing? What's happening to the unemployment rate? These are questions that deal with aggregates, or totals, in the economy; they are problems of macroeconomics. The question about the level of economic activity, for example, refers to the total value of all goods and services produced in the economy. Inflation is a measure of the rate of change in the average price level for the entire economy; it is a macroeconomic problem. The total levels of employment and unemployment in the economy represent the aggregate of all labor markets; unemployment is also a topic of macroeconomics.

Both microeconomics and macroeconomics give attention to individual markets. But in microeconomics that attention is an end in itself; in macroeconomics it is aimed at explaining the movement of major economic aggregates—the level of total output, the level of employment, and the price level.

We've now examined the characteristics that define the economic way of thinking and the two branches of this way of thinking: microeconomics and macroeconomics. In the next section, we'll have a look at what one can do with training in economics.

1994–1995 rank	Major	Average score	1991–1992 rank
1	Economics	155.3	1
2	History	154.0	3
3	English	153.7	4
4	Engineering	152.7	2
5	Journalism/foreign language	152.5	7
6	Finance	152.2	5
7	Psychology	151.9	8
8	Accounting	151.8	6
9	Political science	151.6	9
10	Communications/arts	150.7	10
11	Management	149.4	11
12	Sociology/social work	149.3	13
13	Business administration	148.6	12
14	Criminology	145.8	14

Source: Michael Nieswiadomy, "LSAT Scores of Economics Majors," *Journal of Economic Education* 29 (4) (Fall 1998): 377–379.

Exhibit 1-1

LSAT Scores and Undergraduate Majors

Here are the average LSAT scores and rankings for the 14 undergraduate majors with more than 2,000 students taking the test during the 1994–1995 academic year. Rankings for the 1991–1992 academic year are also given.

Putting Economics to Work

Economics is one way of looking at the world. Because the economic way of thinking has proven quite useful, training in economics can be put to work in a wide range of fields. One, of course, is in work as an economist. Undergraduate work in economics can be applied to other careers as well.

Careers in Economics Economists work in three types of organizations. Most U.S. economists—about 60 percent—work for business firms. The remainder work for government agencies or in colleges and universities.

Economists working for business firms and government agencies sometimes forecast economic activity to assist their employers in planning. They also apply economic analysis to the activities of the firms or agencies for which they work. Economists employed at colleges and universities teach and conduct research.

Teachers at the elementary, junior, and senior high school levels aren't classified as economists, but many of them teach economics. Roughly half the nation's high school students are required to take an economics course to graduate. In many school districts economics is taught even earlier. The ideas of scarcity, choice, and opportunity cost, for example, are incorporated today in many kindergarten curricula! Even more of the basic concepts of economics are being introduced by the third grade. A career in economics may thus involve teaching at any grade level.

The accompanying profiles in the Cases in Point introduce you to three economists working in each of three major areas: business, government, and academe.

The Economics Major as Preparation for Other Careers Suppose you don't intend to pursue a career in economics. Would training in economics help you?

The evidence suggests it may. Suppose, for example, that you're considering law school. The study of law requires keen analytical skills; studying economics sharpens such skills. Economists have traditionally argued that undergraduate work in economics serves as excellent preparation for law school. Economist Michael Nieswiadomy of the University of North Texas collected data on Law School Admittance Test (LSAT) scores for 14 undergraduate majors listed by 2,000 or more students taking the test during the academic years 1991–1992 and 1994–1995. Exhibit 1-1 gives the scores, as well as the ranking for each of these majors. Economics majors recorded the highest scores, followed by history and English majors.

Did the strong performance by economics majors mean that training in economics sharpens analytical skills tested in the LSAT, or that students with good analytical skills are more likely to major in economics? Both factors were probably at work. Economics clearly attracts students with good analytical skills—and studying economics helps develop those skills.

Economics majors shine in other areas as well. According to the Bureau of Labor Statistics *Occupational Outlook Handbook,* a strong background in economic theory, mathematics, and statistics provides the basis for competing for the best job opportunities, particularly research assistant positions, in a broad range of fields. Many graduates with bachelor's degrees will find good jobs in industry and business as management or sales trainees or as administrative assistants. Because economists are concerned with understanding and interpreting financial matters, among other subjects, they will also be attracted to and qualified for jobs as financial managers, financial analysts, underwriters, actuaries, securities and financial services sales workers, credit analysts, loan and budget officers, and urban and regional planners.

Exhibit 1-2 shows average yearly salary offers for bachelor degree candidates for January 1999 and the outlook for related occupations to 2006.

One's choice of a major, or minor, isn't likely to be based solely on considerations of potential earnings or the prospect of landing a spot in law school. You'll also consider your interests and abilities in making a decision about whether to pursue further study in economics. And, of course, you'll consider the expected benefits of alternative courses of study. But, should you decide to pursue a major or minor in economics, you should know that a background in this field is likely to serve you well in a wide range of careers.

Exhibit 1-2

Average Yearly Salary Offers, January 1999 and Occupational Outlook 1996–2006, Selected Majors/Occupations

Undergraduate major	Average offer, January 1999	Projected % change in total employment in occupation 1996–2006
Electrical/electronic engineering	$44,216	28.5
Computer engineering	44,098	109.1
Management information systems	41,877	117.8
Computer programming	41,312	22.8
Geology and geological services	36,317	14.6
Economics and finance	35,016	18.6
Accounting	33,477	12.4
Business administration	31,803	20.0
Other business majors	30,493	na
Environmental sciences (incl. forestry and conservation sciences)	29,600	17.4
Other humanities	29,279	na
Foreign languages	28,619	na
Political science/government	28,318	na
Psychology	28,019	na
Other social sciences (incl. criminal justice, history, and sociology)	27,803	na
Public relations	26,745	27.2
Letters (including English)	26,425	21.2
Human resources (including labor relations)	26,228	17.9
Elementary education	24,692	10.3
Special education	24,288	59.1
Visual and performing arts	23,334	na
Pre-elementary education	21,000	19.6
Social work	19,333	32.1

Source: National Association of Colleges and Employers, *Salary Survey,* January 1999 38(1): 4–5; Bureau of Labor Statistics, *Occupational Employment, Training, and Earnings: Educational Level Report* (March 1998), URL: http://stats.bls.gov/oep/noeted/empoptd.asp

Note. Selection of specific bachelor degree majors for inclusion in this table was guided in part by requiring a corresponding occupation in the BLS report; na = not reported, that is, no specific occupation was reported in the BLS report. Other business majors and Other social sciences are weighted averages of the other disciplines, calculated by the authors.

Case in Point Three Economists: In Business, in Government, and in Academe

Lucinda Vargas—An Economist in Business

Firms in the United States, Japan, and other countries use factories in Mexico to carry out part of their manufacturing process. Many of these businesses get help from Lucinda Vargas, an economist for the El Paso branch of the Federal Reserve Bank of Dallas. Ms. Vargas specializes in issues related to Mexico's economy.

The Texas economist says that the Mexican plants, called maquiladoras, represent a classic response to differences in scarcity in various countries. "Firms that use maquiladoras carry out stages of the manufacturing process that use relatively more machinery and equipment, and less labor, in countries like the United States and Japan, where labor is relatively scarce. For manufacturing that uses more labor, they shift to Mexico, where labor is much less scarce," she says.

Ms. Vargas is one of about 30,000 business economists in the United States. These economists interpret and forecast economic conditions relevant to a firm's market and use the tools of economic analysis to help their firms operate more efficiently. The median annual base salary for business economists in 1996, according to a survey by the National Association of Business Economists, was $85,000 for economists with a Ph.D., $65,000 for those with a master's degree, and $60,000 for those with a bachelor's degree. Most business economists also earn additional income from writing, consulting, or lecturing; this income averaged about $15,000 per year in 1996.

Steve Haugen: An Economist in Government

We hear about Steve Haugen's work every month when the national statistics for unemployment are released. Mr. Haugen is an economist for the U.S. Bureau of Labor Statistics, the agency that compiles the official monthly estimate of the nation's unemployment rate.

Mr. Haugen is involved in other efforts for the Bureau as well. He has worked on studies of the number and characteristics of minimum wage workers. More recently, he worked on a project that examined the nature of growth in workers' earnings over the last decade. He says that the thing he

Checklist

- The economic way of thinking stresses opportunity costs, assumes that individuals make decisions that seek to maximize objectives defined in terms of self-interest, and focuses on decisions at the margin.
- Economics is divided into two main branches, microeconomics and macroeconomics.
- Careers in economics include work with business firms, government agencies, and educational institutions. Training in economics can also be useful in developing the analytical skills needed for other careers.

Try It Yourself 1-2

The Department of Agriculture estimated that the expenditures a middle-income, husband–wife family of three would incur to raise one additional child from birth in 1997 to likes best about his job is that it allows him to conduct research in "a totally objective and apolitical environment."

Mr. Haugen received his bachelor's degree in economics and in history at Western Maryland College and his M.B.A. at Mount Saint Mary's College in Maryland.

Economists work for the federal, state, and local governments. The average salary for economists working for the federal government was $63,870 in 1997.

Wendy Stock: An Economist in Academe

People are living—and working—longer than just a few decades ago. The 1965 Age Discrimination in Employment Act (ADEA) sought to promote employment of older persons and to prohibit arbitrary age discrimination in employment. Was it successful? "Perhaps," says Wendy Stock, an economist at Kansas State University, "but the evidence is complex and sometimes contradictory. Often, well-meaning legislation has unintended and unforeseen consequences." Ms. Stock's research focuses on how such legislation affects labor markets in general and markets for older workers in particular.

Ms. Stock, who received her bachelor's degree in economics at Weber State University and her master's and Ph.D. degrees at Michigan State University, is one of about 10,000 academic economists in the United States. Economists at colleges and universities conduct research and teach graduate and undergraduate courses. Ms. Stock teaches courses in microeconomics, econometrics, and labor economics.

Although economists in every arena are engaged in research, it is in academe that people have the most freedom to define their own projects. Ms. Stock reports that it is that freedom to do

what she wants in terms of research, along with the challenge of teaching, that she values most in her career.

The College and University Personnel Association reports that average salaries for university economics professors in the 1998–1999 academic year were as shown in the table.

	Professor	Associate Professor	Assistant Professor	New Assistant Professor
Public	$74,262	$57,448	$49,787	$48,259
Private	83,044	56,577	48,565	45,065

Source: College and University Personnel Association survey information for 1998–1999.

age 17 would be $242,890. In what way does this estimate illustrate the economic way of thinking? Would the Department's estimate be an example of microeconomic or of macroeconomic analysis? Why?

Economics and the Scientific Method

Economics differs from other social sciences because of its emphasis on opportunity cost, the assumption of maximization in terms of one's own self-interest, and the analysis of choices at the margin. But certainly much of the basic methodology of economics and many of its difficulties are common to every social science—indeed, to every science. This section explores the application of the scientific method to economics.

Researchers often examine relationships between variables. A **variable** is something whose value can change. By contrast, a **constant** is something whose value doesn't change. The speed at which a car is traveling is an example of a variable. The number of minutes in an hour is an example of a constant.

Research is generally conducted within a framework called the **scientific method,** a systematic set of procedures through which knowledge is created. In the scientific method, hypotheses are suggested and then tested. A **hypothesis** is an assertion of a relationship between two or more variables that could be proven to be false. A statement is not a hypothesis if no conceivable test could show it to be false. The statement "Plants like sunshine" is not a hypothesis; there is no way to test whether plants like sunshine or not, so it is impossible to prove the statement false. The statement "Increased solar radiation increases the rate of plant growth" is a hypothesis; experiments could be done to show the relationship between solar radiation and plant growth. If solar radiation were shown to be unrelated to plant growth or to retard plant growth, then the hypothesis would be demonstrated to be false.

If a test reveals that a particular hypothesis is false, then the hypothesis is rejected or modified. In the case of the hypothesis about solar radiation and plant growth, we would probably find that more sunlight increases plant growth over some range but that too much can actually retard plant growth. Such results would lead us to modify our hypothesis about the relationship between solar radiation and plant growth.

If the tests of a hypothesis yield results consistent with it, then further tests are conducted. A hypothesis that has not been rejected after widespread testing and that wins general acceptance is commonly called a **theory.** A theory that has been subjected to even more testing and that has won virtually universal acceptance becomes a **law.** We'll examine two economic laws in the next two chapters.

Even a hypothesis that has achieved the status of a law can't be proven true. There is always a possibility that someone may find a case that invalidates the hypothesis. That possibility means that nothing in economics, or in any other social science, or in any science, can ever be *proven* true. We can have great confidence in a particular proposition, but it is always a mistake to assert that it is "proven."

Models in Economics

All scientific thought involves simplifications of reality. The real world is far too complex for the human mind—or the most powerful computer—to consider. Scientists use models instead. A **model** is a set of simplifying assumptions about some aspect of the real world. Models are always based on assumed conditions that are simpler than those of the real world, assumptions that are necessarily false. A model of the real world cannot *be* the real world.

We'll encounter our first economic model in the next chapter. For this model, we'll assume that an economy can produce only two goods. In Chapter 3, we'll explore the model of demand and supply. One of the assumptions we'll make there is that all the goods produced by firms in a particular market are identical. Of course, real economies and real markets aren't that simple. Reality is never as simple as a model; one point of a model is to simplify the world to improve our understanding of it.

Models in economics also help us to generate hypotheses about the real world. In the next section, we'll examine some of the problems we encounter in testing those hypotheses.

Testing Hypotheses in Economics

Here's a hypothesis suggested by the model of demand and supply: A reduction in the price of gasoline will increase the quantity of gasoline consumers demand. How might we test such a hypothesis?

Economists try to test hypotheses such as this one by observing actual behavior and using empirical (that is, real-world) data. The retail price of unleaded gasoline in the United States fell from an average of $1.18 per gallon in December 1997 to $0.99 per gallon a year later. The number of gallons of gasoline consumed by U.S. motorists rose 4.2 percent during the same period.

Although the increase in the quantity of gasoline demanded by consumers as its price fell was consistent with the hypothesis that a reduced price will lead to an increase in that quantity, we must be cautious in assessing this evidence. Several problems exist in interpreting any set of economic data. One problem is that several things may be changing at once; another is that the initial event may be unrelated to the event that follows. The next two sections examine these problems in detail.

The All-Other-Things-Unchanged Problem The hypothesis that a reduction in the price of gasoline produces an increase in the quantity demanded by consumers carries with it the assumption that there are no other changes that might also affect consumer demand. A better statement of the hypothesis would be: A reduction in the price of gasoline will increase the quantity consumers demand, ceteris paribus. **Ceteris paribus** is a Latin phrase that means "all other things unchanged."

But many things changed between December 1997 and December 1998. Incomes rose sharply in the United States, and people with higher incomes are likely to buy more gasoline. Employment rose as well, and people with jobs use more gasoline as they drive to work. Population in the United States grew during the period. People bought more sport utility vehicles and other high-performance vehicles; those cars gobble up a great deal more gasoline per mile driven than do conventional cars. In short, many things happened during the period, all of which tended to increase the quantity of gasoline people purchased.

Our observation of the gasoline market between December 1997 and December 1998 did not offer a conclusive test of the hypothesis that a reduction in the price of gasoline would lead to an increase in the quantity demanded by consumers. Other things changed, and affected gasoline consumption. Such problems are likely to affect any analysis of economic events. We can't ask the world to stand still while we conduct experiments in economic phenomena. Economists employ a variety of statistical methods to allow them to isolate the impact of single events such as price changes, but they can never be certain that they have accurately isolated the impact of a single event in a world in which virtually everything is changing all the time.

In laboratory sciences such as chemistry and biology, it is relatively easy to conduct experiments in which only selected things change and all other factors are held constant. The economists' laboratory is the real world; thus, economists don't generally have the luxury of conducting controlled experiments.

The Fallacy of False Cause Hypotheses in economics typically specify a relationship in which a change in one variable causes another to change. We call the variable that responds to the change the **dependent variable;** the variable that induces a change is called the **independent variable.** Sometimes the fact that two variables move together can suggest the false conclusion that one of the variables has acted as an independent variable that has caused the change we observe in the dependent variable.

Consider the following hypothesis: The Dow Jones Industrial Average, a common measure of stock market performance, will rise in years in which a team from the National Football Conference (NFC) wins the Super Bowl and will fall when a team from the American Football Conference (AFC) wins.[5] This hypothesis seems preposterous. Yet the evidence is largely consistent with it. From 1967, when the Super Bowl was first played, to 1999, there have been only four years in which the Super Bowl rule has failed to predict the direction of stock prices. This book went to press before the end of 1999, so we won't know if the 1999 victory by the Denver Broncos (an AFC team) will lead to a slump in the market in 1999. We

[5]The hypothesis has an exception: If an AFC team that was part of the old National Football League (NFL) before it merged with the American Football League wins, stock prices will also rise.

Case in Point Smoking, Health, and Murder

It is well established that smoking contributes to cancer, heart disease, and a host of other ailments. But does smoking make a person more likely to be murdered?

We can state the proposition as a hypothesis: Smoking increases the likelihood that a person will be murdered.

The hypothesis can be tested; let's have a look at the evidence.

As it turns out, three medical researchers have reported that the observation of real-world behavior gives us data that are consistent with the hypothesis. People who smoke two packs of cigarettes per day are twice as likely to be murdered than are nonsmokers, according to the researchers. Smoking is closely associated with being murdered.

The researchers were not, however, asserting that smoking will get you killed. Their research, reported in *Lancet,* is an effort to illustrate the fallacy of false cause. The fact that two series of numbers tend to move together does not prove that one causes the other. There is simply no reason to believe that smoking makes it more likely that a person will be the target of a murder attempt. And it certainly would be awkward to conclude that being murdered causes a person to smoke!

A more likely explanation for the fact that smokers are more likely to be murdered than nonsmokers lies in income levels. People with lower incomes are more likely to be victims of murder than people with higher incomes. And smoking is much more common among low-income individuals than among high-income individuals. Thus, smokers may be more likely to be murdered than nonsmokers, but that doesn't suggest that smoking causes murders. In this case, it suggests that a third factor, income, may link smoking and murder.

Source: George Davy Smith, Andrew N. Phillips, and James D. Neaton, "Smoking as an 'Independent Risk Factor' for Suicide: Illustration of an Artifact from Observational Epidemiology?" *Lancet* 340 (8821) (19 September 1992): 709–712.

do know that the Dow Jones average rose in 1998 despite Denver's 1998 win—that year is one of the four exceptions to the Super Bowl rule.

Despite impressive evidence consistent with the hypothesis, it has won no support as an explanation of stock market prices. That's because there isn't any reason to believe that there should be a relationship between the team that wins the Super Bowl and stock prices. In general, economists first look to see whether a hypothesis is consistent with a model that makes sense and then examine the evidence that either lends support to or refutes the hypothesis. The simple fact that a hypothesis is consistent with a body of evidence is seldom sufficient to cause economists to believe it.

Sometimes there is a logical reason to expect two events to be related, but an error is made in deciding that one causes the other. We observe, for example, that more people walk under umbrellas when it's raining than when it isn't. It would be incorrect to infer from this that people cause rain by opening their umbrellas.

Reaching the incorrect conclusion that one event causes another because the two events tend to occur together is called the **fallacy of false cause.** The accompanying Case in Point on smoking and murder suggests an example of this fallacy.

Because of the danger of the fallacy of false cause, economists use special statistical tests that are designed to determine whether changes in one thing actually do cause changes observed in another. Given the inability to perform controlled experiments, however, these tests do not always offer convincing evidence that persuades all economists that one thing does, in fact, cause changes in another.

In the case of gasoline prices and consumption between December 1997 and December 1998, there is good theoretical reason to believe the price reduction should lead to an increase in the quantity consumers demand. And economists have tested the hypothesis about price and the quantity demanded quite extensively. They have developed elaborate statistical tests aimed at ruling out problems of the fallacy of false cause. While we can't prove that a reduction in price will, ceteris paribus, lead to an increase in the quantity consumers demand, we can have considerable confidence in the proposition.

Normative and Positive Statements Two kinds of assertions in economics can be subjected to testing. We've already examined one, the hypothesis. Another testable assertion is a statement of fact, such as "It is raining outside" or "Microsoft is the largest producer of operating systems for personal computers in the world." Like hypotheses, such assertions can be demonstrated to be false. Unlike hypotheses, they can also be shown to be correct. A statement of fact or a hypothesis is a **positive statement.**

Although people often disagree about positive statements, such disagreements can ultimately be resolved through investigation. There is another category of assertions, however, for which investigation can never resolve differences. A **normative statement** is one that makes a value judgment. Such a judgment is the opinion of the speaker; no one can "prove" that the statement is or is not correct. Here are some examples of normative statements in economics: "We ought to do more to help the poor." "People in the United States should save more." "Corporate profits are too high." The statements are based on the values of the person who makes them. They can't be proved false.

Because people have different values, normative statements often provoke disagreement. An economist whose values lead him or her to conclude that we should provide more help for the poor will disagree with one whose values lead to a conclusion that we should not. Because no test exists for these values, these two economists will continue to disagree, unless one persuades the other to adopt a different set of values. Many of the disagreements among economists are based on such differences in values and therefore are unlikely to be resolved.

Checklist

- Economists try to employ the scientific method in their research.
- Scientists cannot prove a hypothesis to be true; they can only fail to prove it false.
- Economists, like other social scientists and scientists, use models to assist them in their analyses.
- Two problems inherent in tests of hypotheses in economics are the all-other-things-unchanged problem and the fallacy of false cause.
- Positive statements are factual and can be tested. Normative statements are value judgments that cannot be tested. Many of the disagreements among economists stem from differences in values.

Try It Yourself 1-3

Look again at the data in Exhibit 1-1. Now consider the hypothesis: "Majoring in economics will result in a higher LSAT score." Are the data given consistent with this hypothesis? Do the data prove that this hypothesis is correct? What fallacy might be involved in accepting the hypothesis?

A Look Back

Choices are forced on us by scarcity; economists study the choices that people make. Scarce goods are those for which the choice of one alternative requires giving up another. The opportunity cost of any choice is the value of the best alternative forgone in making that choice.

Some key choices assessed by economists include what to produce, how to produce it, and for whom it should be produced. Economics is distinguished from other academic disciplines that also study choices by an emphasis on the central importance of opportunity costs in evaluating choices, the assumption of maximizing behavior that serves the interests of individual decision-makers, and a focus on evaluating choices at the margin.

Economic analyses may be aimed at explaining individual choice or choices in an individual market; such investigations are largely the focus of microeconomics. The analysis of the aggregate impact of those individual choices on total output, level of employment, and the price level is the concern of macroeconomics.

Working within the framework of the scientific method, economists formulate hypotheses and then test them. These tests can only refute a hypothesis; hypotheses in science cannot be proved. A hypothesis that has been widely tested often comes to be regarded as a theory; one that has won virtually universal acceptance is a law. Because of the complexity of the real world, economists rely on models that rest on a series of simplifying assumptions. The models are used to generate hypotheses about the economy that can be tested using real-world data.

Statements of fact and hypotheses are positive statements. Normative statements, unlike positive statements, can't be tested and provide a source for potential disagreement.

A Look Ahead The remaining chapters in Part One continue the discussion of the study of choices in economics. Chapter 2 examines choices in production; Chapter 3 explores the nature of market choices and introduces the model of demand and supply. Chapter 4 discusses several applications of this model. The Chapter 1 Appendix explains an important tool in economics: the graph.

Terms and Concepts for Review

economics, **1**
scarcity, **3**
scarce good, **3**
free good, **4**
opportunity cost, **5**
margin, **7**
choice at the margin, **7**
microeconomics, **8**
macroeconomics, **8**
variable, **11**
constant, **11**
scientific method, **12**
hypothesis, **12**
theory, **12**
law, **12**
model, **12**
ceteris paribus, **13**
dependent variable, **13**
independent variable, **13**
fallacy of false cause, **14**
positive statement, **15**
normative statement, **15**

For Discussion

1. Why does the fact that something is scarce require that we make choices?
2. Does the fact that something is abundant mean it isn't scarce in the economic sense? Why or why not?
3. In some countries, such as Cuba and North Korea, the government makes most of the decisions about what will be produced, how it will be produced, and for whom. Does the fact that these choices are made by the government eliminate scarcity in these countries? Why or why not?
4. Explain what is meant by the opportunity cost of a choice.
5. What is the approximate dollar cost of the tuition and other fees associated with the economics course you're taking? Does this dollar cost fully reflect the opportunity cost to you of taking the course?
6. In the Case in Point "Searching for Grizzlies," what would be some of the things that would be included in an estimate of the opportunity cost of preserving part of the San Juans as a habitat for grizzlies?
7. Indicate whether each of the following is a topic of microeconomics or macroeconomics:
   a. The impact of lower oil prices on the production of steel
   b. The increased demand in the 1990s for exotic dietary supplements such as pau d'arco and spirulina
   c. The slump in aggregate economic activity that hit much of Asia late in the 1990s
   d. The sharp increases in U.S. employment and total output during the second half of the 1990s
   e. The impact of preservation of wilderness areas on the logging industry and on the price of lumber
8. Determine whether each of the following raises a "what," "how," or "for whom" issue. Are the statements normative or positive?
   a. A requirement that aluminum used in cars be made from recycled materials will raise the price of automobiles.
   b. The federal government doesn't spend enough for children.
   c. An increase in police resources provided to the inner city will lower the crime rate.
   d. Automation destroys jobs.
   e. Efforts to improve the environment tend to reduce production and employment.
   f. Japanese firms should be more willing to hire additional workers when production rises and to lay off workers when production falls.
   g. Access to health care should not be limited by income.
9. Your time is a scarce resource. What if the quantity of time were increased, say to 48 hours per day, and everyone still lived as many days as before. Would time still be scarce?
10. Most college students are under age 25. Give two explanations for this—one based on the benefits people of different ages are likely to receive from higher education and one based on the opportunity costs of a college education to students of different ages.
11. Some municipal water companies charge customers a flat fee each month, regardless of the amount of water they consume. Others meter water use and charge according to the quantity of water customers use. Compare the way the two systems affect the cost of water use at the margin.
12. How might you test each of the following hypotheses? Suggest some problems that might arise in each test due to the ceteris paribus (all-other-things-unchanged) problem and the fallacy of false cause.

a. Reducing the quantity of heroin available on the street will increase total spending on heroin and increase the crime rate.
b. Higher incomes make people happier.
c. Higher incomes make people live longer.

13. Many models in physics and in chemistry assume the existence of a perfect vacuum (that is, a space entirely empty of matter). Yet we know that a perfect vacuum doesn't exist. Are such models valid? Why are models based on assumptions that are essentially incorrect?
14. Suppose you were asked to test the proposition that publishing students' teacher evaluations causes grade inflation. What evidence might you want to consider? How would the inability to carry out controlled experiments make your analysis more difficult?
15. Referring to the Case in Point "Smoking, Health, and Murder," explain the possible fallacy of false cause in concluding that smoking makes a person more likely to be murdered.
16. In 1997 the Food and Drug Administration ordered that two popular diet drugs be withdrawn from the market. The order resulted from a finding that people taking the drug had a higher rate of heart disease than the rest of the population; the FDA was concerned that the drugs might contribute to heart disease. Some researchers criticized the government's action, arguing that concluding that the diet drugs cause heart disease represented an example of the fallacy of false cause. Can you think of any reason why this might be the case?

Answers to Try It Yourself Problems

Try It Yourself 1-1

a. The 500-acre area is scarce because it has alternative uses: preservation in its natural state or a site for homes. A choice must be made between these uses. The opportunity cost of preserving the land in its natural state is the forgone value of the land as a housing development. The opportunity cost of using the land as a housing development is the forgone value of preserving the land.

b. The man can devote his time to his current career or to an education; his time is a scarce resource. He must choose between these alternatives. The opportunity cost of continuing as a nurses' aide is the forgone benefit he expects from training as a registered nurse; the opportunity cost of going to college is the forgone income he could have earned working full-time as a nurses' aide.

c. The scarce resources are the plant and the labor at the plant. The manager must choose between producing cars and producing SUVs. The opportunity cost of producing cars is the profit that could be earned from producing SUVs; the opportunity cost of producing SUVs is the profit that could be earned from producing cars.

Try It Yourself 1-2

The information given suggests one element of the economic way of thinking: assessing the choice at the margin. The estimate reflects the cost of one more child for a family that already has one. It isn't clear from the information given how close the estimate of cost comes to the economic concept of opportunity cost. The Department of Agriculture's estimate included such costs as housing, food, transportation, clothing, health care, child care, and education. An economist would add the value of the best alternative use of the additional time that will be required for the child. If the couple is looking far ahead, it may want to consider the opportunity cost of sending a child to college. And, if it's looking *very* far ahead, it may want to consider the fact that nearly half of all parents over the age of 50 support at least one child over the age of 21. This is a problem in microeconomic analysis, because it focuses on the choices of individual households.

Try It Yourself 1-3

The data are consistent with the hypothesis, but it is never possible to prove that a hypothesis is correct. Accepting the hypothesis could involve the fallacy of false cause; students who major in economics may already have the analytical skills needed to do well on the exam.

Appendix 1 Graphs in Economics

A glance through the pages of this book should convince you that there are a lot of graphs in economics. The language of graphs is one means of presenting economic ideas. If you're already familiar with graphs, you'll have no difficulty with this aspect of your study. If you've never used graphs or haven't used them in some time, this appendix will help you feel comfortable with the graphs you'll encounter in this text.

How to Construct and Interpret Graphs

Much of the analysis in economics deals with relationships between variables. A variable is simply a quantity whose value can change. A **graph** is a pictorial representation of the relationship between two or more variables. The key to understanding graphs is knowing the rules that apply to their construction and interpretation. This section defines those rules and explains how to draw a graph.

Drawing a Graph

To see how a graph is constructed from numerical data, we'll consider a hypothetical example. Suppose a college campus has a ski club that organizes day-long bus trips to a ski area about 100 miles from the campus. The club leases the bus and charges $10 per passenger for a round trip to the ski area. In addition to the revenue the club collects from passengers, it also receives a grant of $200 from the school's student government for each day the bus trip is available. The club thus would receive $200 even if no passengers wanted to ride on a particular day.

The table in Exhibit 1A-1 shows the relationship between two variables: the number of students who ride the bus on a particular day and the revenue the club receives from a trip. In the table, each combination is assigned a letter (A, B, etc.); we'll use these letters when we transfer the information from the table to a graph.

We can illustrate the relationship shown in the table with a graph. The procedure for showing the relationship between two variables, like the ones in Exhibit 1A-1, on a graph is illustrated in Exhibit 1A-2. Let's look at the steps involved.

Exhibit 1A-1

Ski Club Revenues

The ski club receives $10 from each passenger riding its bus for a trip to and from the ski area plus a payment of $200 from the student government for each day the bus is available for these trips. The club's revenues from any single day thus equal $200 plus $10 times the number of passengers. The table relates various combinations of the number of passengers and club revenues.

Combination	Number of passengers	Club revenue
A	0	$200
B	10	300
C	20	400
D	30	500
E	40	600

Step 1. Draw and Label the Axes The two variables shown in the table are the number of passengers taking the bus on a particular day and the club's revenue from that trip. We begin our graph in Panel (a) of Exhibit 1A-2 by drawing two axes to form a right angle. Each axis will represent a variable. The axes should be carefully labeled to reflect what is being measured on each axis.

It is customary to place the independent variable on the horizontal axis and the dependent variable on the vertical axis. Recall that, when two variables are related, the dependent variable is the one that changes in response to changes in the independent variable. Passengers generate revenue, so we can consider the number of passengers as the independent variable and the club's revenue as the dependent variable. The number of passengers thus goes on the horizontal axis; the club's revenue from a trip goes on the vertical axis. In some cases, the variables in a graph can't be considered independent or dependent. In those cases, the variables may be placed on either axis; we'll encounter such a case in the next chapter. In other cases, economists simply ignore the rule; we'll encounter that case in Chapter 3. The rule that the independent variable goes on the horizontal axis and the dependent variable goes on the vertical usually holds, but not always.

The point at which the axes intersect is called the **origin** of the graph. Notice that in Exhibit 1A-2 the origin has a value of zero for each variable.

In drawing a graph showing numeric values, we also need to put numbers on the axes. For the axes in Panel (a), we have chosen numbers that correspond to the values in the table. The number of passengers ranges up to 40 for a trip; club revenues from a trip range from $200 (the payment the club receives from student government) to $600. We've extended the vertical axis to $800 to allow some changes we'll consider below. We've chosen intervals of 10 passengers on the horizontal axis and $100 on the vertical axis. The choice of particular intervals is mainly a matter of convenience in drawing and reading the graph; we've chosen the ones here because they correspond to the intervals given in the table.

We have drawn vertical lines from each of the values on the horizontal axis and horizontal lines from each of the values on the vertical axis. These lines, called gridlines, will help us in Step 2.

Step 2. Plot the Points Each of the rows in the table in Exhibit 1A-1 gives a combination of the number of passengers on the bus and club revenue from a particular trip. We can plot these values in our graph.

We begin with the first row, A, corresponding to zero passengers and club revenue of $200, the payment from student government. We read up from zero passengers on the horizontal axis to $200 on the vertical axis and mark point A. This point shows that zero passengers result in club revenues of $200.

The second combination, B, tells us that if 10 passengers ride the bus, the club receives $300 in revenue from the trip—$100 from the $10-per-passenger charge plus the $200 from student government. We start at 10 passengers on the horizontal axis and follow the gridline up. When we travel up in a graph, we are traveling with respect to values on the vertical axis. We travel up by $300 and mark point B.

Points in a graph have a special significance. They relate the values of the variables on the two axes to each other. Reading to the left from point B, we see that it shows $300 in club revenue. Reading down from point B, we see that it shows 10 passengers. Those values are, of course, the values given for combination B in the table.

We repeat this process to obtain points C, D, and E. Check to be sure that you see that each point corresponds to the values of the two variables given in the corresponding row of the table.

The graph in Panel (b) is called a scatter diagram. A **scatter diagram** shows individual points relating values of the variable on one axis to values of the variable on the other.

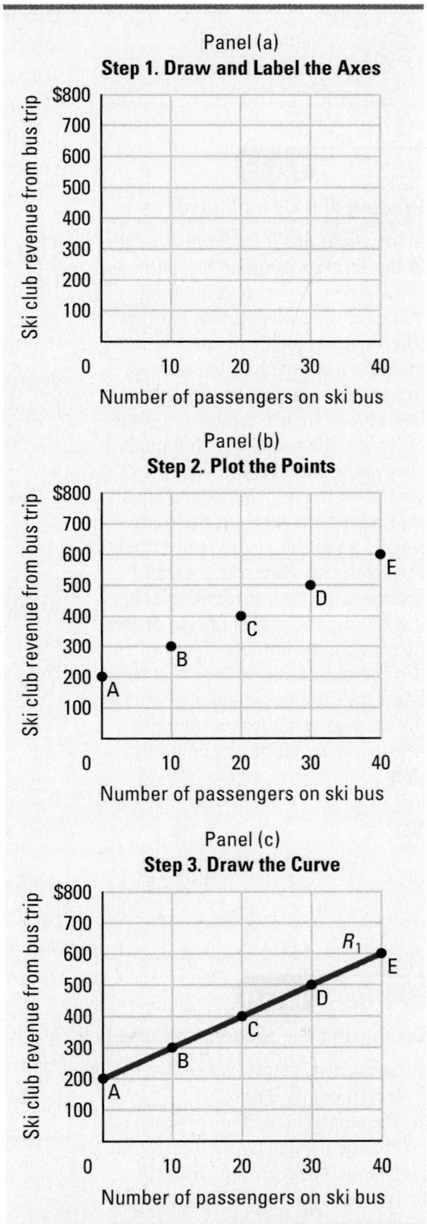

Exhibit 1A-2

Plotting a Graph

Here we see how to show the information given in Exhibit 1A-1 in a graph. Each step is explained in detail in the text.

Step 3. Draw the Curve The final step is to draw the curve that shows the relationship between the number of passengers who ride the bus and the club's revenues from the trip. The term "curve" is used for any line in a graph that shows a relationship between two variables.

We draw a line that passes through points A through E. Our curve shows club revenues; we shall call it R_1. Notice that R_1 is an upward-sloping straight line. Notice also that R_1 intersects the vertical axis at $200 (point A). The point at which a curve intersects an axis is called

$$\text{Slope} = \frac{\text{vertical change}}{\text{horizontal change}} \quad (1)$$

Exhibit 1A-3

Reading and Using Equations

Many equations in economics begin in the form of Equation (1), with the statement that one thing (in this case the slope) equals another (the vertical change divided by the horizontal change). In this example, the equation is written in words. Sometimes we use symbols in place of words. The basic idea though, is always the same: the term represented on the left side of the equals sign equals the term on the right side. In equation (1) there are three variables: the slope, the vertical change, and the horizontal change. If we know the values of two of the three, we can compute the third. In the computation of slopes that follow, for example, we will use values for the two variables on the right side of the equation to compute the slope.

the **intercept** of the curve. We often refer to the vertical or horizontal intercept of a curve; such intercepts can play a special role in economic analysis. The vertical intercept in this case shows the revenue the club would receive on a day it offered the trip and no one rode the bus.

To check your understanding of these steps, we recommend that you try plotting the points and drawing R_1 for yourself in Panel (a). Better yet, draw the axes for yourself on a sheet of graph paper and plot the curve.

The Slope of a Curve

In this section, we'll see how to compute the slope of a curve. The slopes of curves tell an important story: they show the rate at which one variable changes with respect to another.

The **slope** of a curve equals the ratio of the change in the value of the variable on the vertical axis to the change in the value of the variable on the horizontal axis, measured between two points on the curve. You may have heard this called "the rise over the run." In equation form, we can write the definition of the slope as

$$\text{Slope} = \frac{\text{vertical change}}{\text{horizontal change}} \quad (1)$$

Equation (1) is the first equation in this text. Exhibit 1A-3 provides a short review of working with equations. The material in this text relies much more heavily on graphs than on equations, but we will use equations from time to time. It's important that you understand how to use them.

Exhibit 1A-4 shows R_1 and the computation of its slope between points B and D. Point B corresponds to 10 passengers on the bus; point D corresponds to 30. The change in the horizontal axis when we go from B to D thus equals 20 passengers. Point B corresponds to club revenues of \$300; point D corresponds to club revenues of \$500. The change in the vertical axis equals \$200. The slope thus equals \$200/20 passengers, or \$10/passenger.

We've applied the definition of the slope of a curve to compute the slope of R_1 between points B and D. That same definition is given in Equation (1). Applying the equation, we have:

$$\text{Slope} = \frac{\text{vertical change}}{\text{horizontal change}} = \frac{\$200}{20 \text{ passengers}} = \$10/\text{passenger}$$

The slope of this curve tells us the amount by which revenues rise with an increase in the number of passengers. It should come as no surprise that this amount equals the price per passenger. Adding a passenger adds \$10 to the club's revenues.

Exhibit 1A-4

Computing the Slope of a Curve

1. Select two points; we've selected points B and D.
2. The slope equals the vertical change divided by the horizontal change between the two points.
3. Between points B and D, the slope equals \$200/20 passengers = \$10/passenger.
4. The slope of this curve is the price per passenger. The fact that it is positive suggests a positive relationship between revenue per trip and the number of passengers riding the bus. Because the slope of this curve is \$10/passenger between any two points on the curve, the relationship between club revenue per trip and the number of passengers is linear.

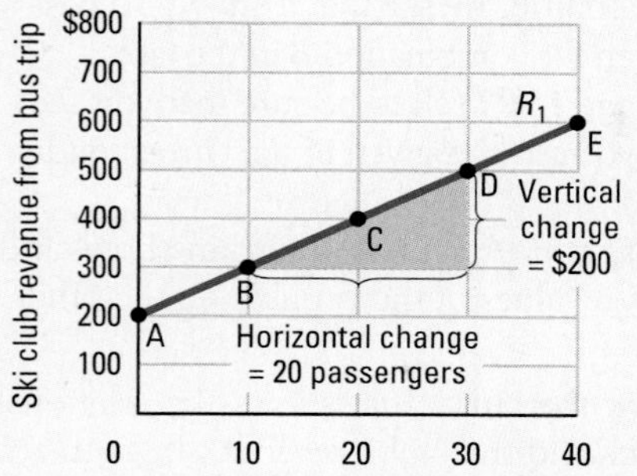

$$\text{Slope} = \frac{\text{vertical change}}{\text{horizontal change}} = \frac{\$200}{20 \text{ passengers}} = \$10/\text{passenger}$$

Notice that we can compute the slope of R_1 between any two points on the curve and get the same value; the slope is constant. Consider, for example, points A and E. The vertical change between these points is \$400 (we go from revenues of \$200 at A to revenues of \$600 at E). The horizontal change is 40 passengers (from zero passengers at A to 40 at E). The slope between A and E thus equals \$400/(40 passengers) = \$10/passenger. We get the same slope regardless of which pair of points we pick on R_1 to compute the slope. The slope of R_1

can be considered a constant, which suggests that it is a straight line. When the curve showing the relationship between two variables has a constant slope, we say there is a **linear relationship** between the variables. A **linear curve** is a curve with constant slope.

The fact that the slope of our curve equals \$10/passenger tells us something else about the curve—\$10/passenger is a positive, not a negative, value. A curve whose slope is positive is upward sloping. As we travel up and to the right along R_1, we travel in the direction of increasing values for both variables. A **positive relationship** between two variables is one in which both variables move in the same direction. Positive relationships are sometimes called direct relationships. There is a positive relationship between club revenues and passengers on the bus. We'll look at a graph showing a negative relationship between two variables in the next section.

A Graph Showing a Negative Relationship

A **negative relationship** is one in which two variables move in opposite directions. A negative relationship is sometimes called an inverse relationship. The slope of a curve describing a negative relationship is always negative. A curve with a negative slope is always downward sloping.

As an example of a graph of a negative relationship, let's look at the impact of the cancellation of games by the National Basketball Association during the 1998–1999 labor dispute on the earnings of one player: Shaquille O'Neal. During the 1998–1999 season, O'Neal headed the NBA Players Association and was the center for the Los Angeles Lakers.

O'Neal's salary with the Lakers in 1998–1999 would have been about \$17,220,000 had the 82 scheduled games of the regular season been played. But a contract dispute between owners and players resulted in the cancellation of 32 games. Mr. O'Neal's salary worked out to roughly \$210,000 per game, so the labor dispute cost him well over \$6 million. Presumably, he was able to eke out a living on his lower income, but the cancellation of games cost him a great deal.

We show the relationship between the number of games canceled and O'Neal's 1998–1999 basketball earnings graphically in Exhibit 1A-5. Canceling games reduced his earnings, so the number of games canceled is the independent variable and goes on the horizontal axis. O'Neal's earnings are the dependent variable and go on the vertical axis. The graph assumes that his earnings would have been \$17,220,000 had no games been canceled (point A, the vertical intercept). Assuming that his earnings fell by \$210,000 per game canceled, his earnings for the season were reduced to \$10,500,000 by the cancellation of 32 games (point B). We can draw a line between these two points to show the relationship between games canceled and O'Neal's 1998–1999 earnings from basketball. In this graph, we have inserted a break in the vertical axis near the origin. This allows us to expand the scale of the axis over the range from \$10,000,000 to \$18,000,000. It also prevents a large blank space between the origin and an income of \$10,500,000—there are no values below this amount.

What is the slope of the curve in Exhibit 1A-5? We have data for two points, A and B. At A, O'Neal's basketball salary would have been \$17,220,000. At B, it is \$10,500,000. The vertical

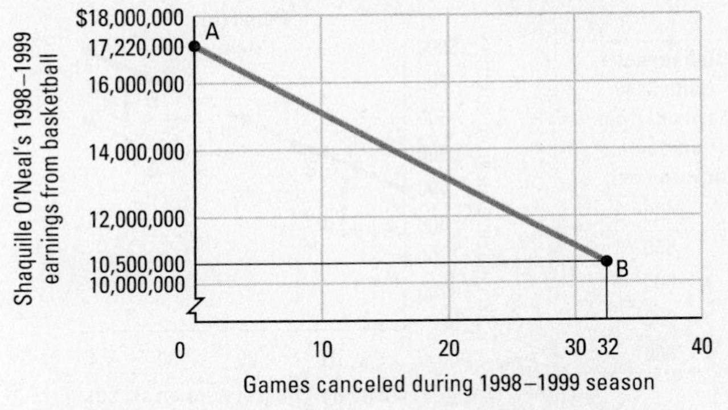

Exhibit 1A-5

Canceling Games and Reducing Shaquille O'Neal's Earnings

If no games had been canceled during the 1998–1999 basketball season, Shaquille O'Neal would have earned \$17,220,000 (point A). Assuming that his salary for the season fell by \$210,000 for each game canceled, the cancellation of 32 games during the dispute between NBA players and owners reduced O'Neal's earnings to \$10,500,000 (point B).

change between points A and B equals –$6,720,000. The change in the horizontal axis is from zero games canceled at A to 32 games canceled at B. The slope is thus

$$\text{Slope} = \frac{\text{vertical change}}{\text{horizontal change}} = \frac{-\$6{,}720{,}000}{32\text{ games}} = -\$210{,}000/\text{game}$$

Notice that this time the slope is negative, hence the downward-sloping curve. As we travel down and to the right along the curve, the number of games canceled rises and O'Neal's salary falls. In this case, the slope tells us the rate at which O'Neal lost income as games were canceled.

The slope of O'Neal's salary curve is also constant. That means there was a linear relationship between games canceled and his 1998–1999 basketball earnings.

Shifting a Curve

When we draw a graph showing the relationship between two variables, we make an important assumption. We assume that all other variables that might affect the relationship between the variables in our graph are unchanged. When one of those other variables changes, the relationship changes, and the curve showing that relationship shifts.

Consider, for example, the ski club that sponsors bus trips to the ski area. The graph we drew in Exhibit 1A-2 shows the relationship between club revenues from a particular trip and the number of passengers on that trip, assuming that all other variables that might affect club revenues are unchanged. Let's change one. Suppose the school's student government increases the payment it makes to the club to $400 for each day the trip is available. The payment was $200 when we drew the original graph. Panel (a) of Exhibit 1A-6 shows how the increase in the payment affects the table we had in Exhibit 1A-1; Panel (b) shows how the curve shifts. Each of the new observations in the table has been labeled with a prime: A′, B′, etc. The curve R_1 shifts upward by $200 as a result of the increased payment. A **shift in a curve** implies new values of one variable at each value of the other variable. The new curve is labeled R_2. With 10 passengers, for example, the club's revenue was $300 at point B on R_1. With the increased payment from the student government, its revenue with 10 passengers rises to $500 at point B′ on R_2. We have a shift in the curve.

It's important to distinguish between shifts in curves and movements along curves. A **movement along a curve** is a change from one point on the curve to another that occurs when the dependent variable changes in response to a change in the independent variable. If, for example, the student government is paying the club $400 each day it makes the ski bus available and 20 passengers ride the bus, the club is operating at point C′ on R_2. If the number of passengers increases to 30, the club will be at point D′ on the curve. This is a movement along a curve; the curve itself doesn't shift.

Now suppose that, instead of increasing its payment, the student government eliminates its payments to the ski club for bus trips. The club's only revenue from a trip now comes from its $10/passenger charge. We've again changed one of the variables we were holding unchanged, so we get another shift in our revenue curve. The table in Panel (a) of Exhibit 1A-7

Exhibit 1A-6

Shifting a Curve: An Increase in Revenues

The table in Panel (a) shows the new level of revenues the ski club receives with varying numbers of passengers as a result of the increased payment from student government. The new curve is shown in dark purple in Panel (b). The old curve is shown in light purple.

Panel (a)

Combination	Number of passengers	Club revenue (with $400 payment from student government)
A'	0	$400
B'	10	500
C'	20	600
D'	30	700
E'	40	800

Panel (b)

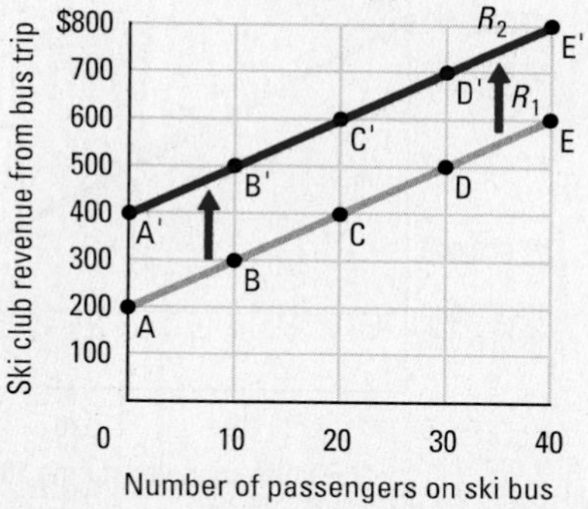

shows how the reduction in the student government's payment affects club revenues. The new values are shown as combinations A″ through E″ on the new curve, R_3, in Panel (b). Once again we have a shift in a curve, this time from R_1 to R_3.

The shifts in Exhibits 1A-6 and 1A-7 left the slopes of the revenue curves unchanged. That's because the slope in all these cases equals the price per ticket, and the ticket price remains unchanged. Next, we shall see how the slope of a curve changes when we rotate it about a single point.

Panel (a)

Combination	Number of passengers	Club revenue (with no payment from student government)
A"	0	0
B"	10	100
C"	20	200
D"	30	300
E"	40	400

Panel (b)

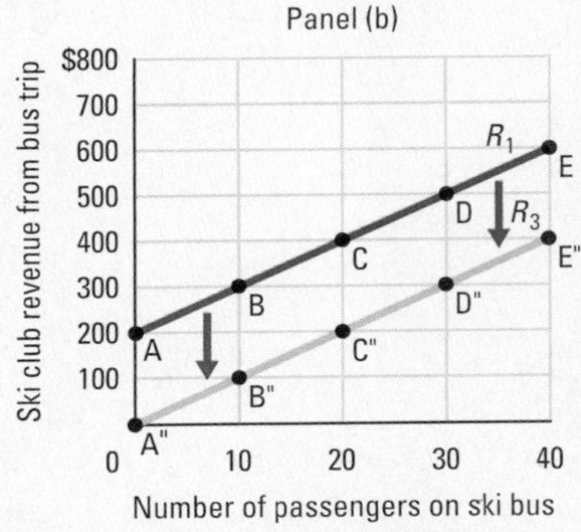

Exhibit 1A-7

Shifting a Curve: A Reduction in Revenues

The table in Panel (a) shows the impact on ski club revenues of an elimination of support from the student government for ski bus trips. The club's only revenue now comes from the $10 it charges to each passenger. The new combinations are shown as A"–E". In Panel (b) we see that the original curve relating club revenue to the number of passengers has shifted down.

Rotating a Curve

A **rotation of a curve** occurs when we change its slope, with one point on the curve fixed. Suppose, for example, the ski club changes the price of its bus rides to the ski area to $30 per trip, and the payment from the student government remains $200 for each day the trip is available. This means the club's revenues will remain $200 if it has no passengers on a particular trip. Revenue will, however, be different when the club has passengers. Because the slope of our revenue curve equals the price per ticket, the slope of the revenue curve changes.

Panel (a) of Exhibit 1A-8 shows what happens to the original revenue curve, R_1, when the price per ticket is raised. Point A doesn't change; the club's revenue with zero passengers is unchanged. But with 10 passengers, the club's revenue would rise from $300 (point B on R_1) to $500 (point B′ on R_4). With 20 passengers, the club's revenue will now equal $800 (point C′ on R_4).

The new revenue curve R_4 is steeper than the original curve. Panel (b) shows the computation of the slope of the new curve between points B′ and C′. The slope increases to $30 per passenger—the new price of a ticket. The greater the slope of a positively sloped curve, the steeper it will be.

We've now seen how to draw a graph of a curve, how to compute its slope, and how to shift and rotate a curve. We've examined both positive and negative relationships. Our work so far has been with linear relationships. Next we'll turn to nonlinear ones.

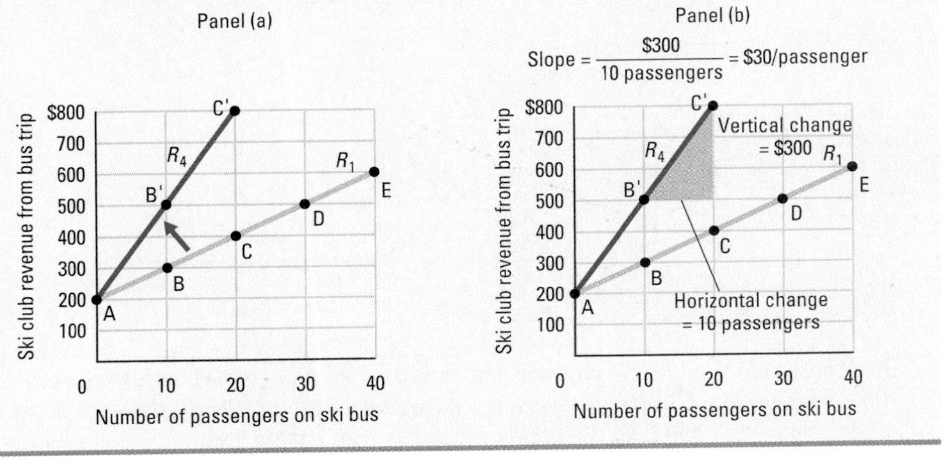

Exhibit 1A-8

Rotating a Curve

A curve is said to rotate when a single point remains fixed while other points on the curve move; a rotation always changes the slope of a curve. Here an increase in the price per passenger to $30 would rotate the revenue curve from R_1 to R_4 in Panel (a). The slope of R_4 is $30 per passenger.

Checklist

- A graph shows a relationship between two or more variables.
- An upward-sloping curve suggests a positive relationship between two variables. A downward-sloping curve suggests a negative relationship between two variables.
- The slope of a curve is the ratio of the vertical change to the horizontal change between two points on the curve. A curve whose slope is constant suggests a linear relationship between two variables.
- A change from one point on the curve to another produces a movement along the curve in the graph. A shift in the curve implies new values of one variable at each value of the other variable. A rotation in the curve implies that one point remains fixed while the slope of the curve changes.

Try It Yourself 1A-1

The following table shows the relationship between the number of gallons of gasoline people in a community are willing and able to buy per week and the price per gallon. Plot these points in the grid provided and label each point with the letter associated with the combination. Notice that there are breaks in both the vertical and horizontal axes of the grid. Draw a line through the points you've plotted. Does your graph suggest a positive or a negative relationship? What is the slope between A and B? Between B and C? Between A and C? Is the relationship linear?

Combination	Price per gallon	Number of gallons (per week)
A	$1.00	1,000
B	1.20	900
C	1.40	800

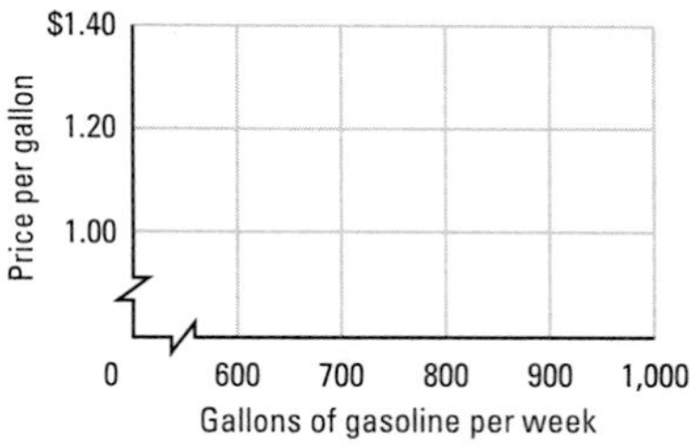

Now suppose you are given the following information about the relationship between price per gallon and the number of gallons per week gas stations in the community are willing to sell.

Combination	Price per gallon	Number of gallons (per week)
D	$1.00	800
E	1.20	900
F	1.40	1,000

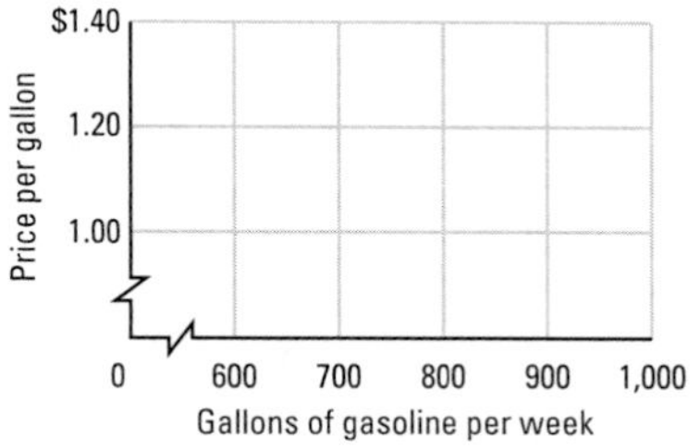

Plot these points in the grid provided and draw a curve through the points you've drawn. Does your graph suggest a positive or a negative relationship? What is the slope between D and E? Between E and F? Between D and F? Is this relationship linear?

Nonlinear Relationships and Graphs Without Numbers

In this section we'll extend our analysis of graphs in two ways: first, we'll explore the nature of nonlinear relationships; then we'll have a look at graphs drawn without numbers.

Graphs of Nonlinear Relationships

In the graphs we've examined so far, adding a unit to the independent variable on the horizontal axis always has the same effect on the dependent variable on the vertical axis. When we add a passenger riding the ski bus, the ski club's revenues always rise by the price of a ticket. The cancellation of one more game in the 1998–1999 basketball season would always reduce Shaquille O'Neal's earnings by $210,000. The slopes of the curves describing the relationships we have been discussing were constant; the relationships were linear.

Many relationships in economics are nonlinear. A **nonlinear relationship** between two variables is one for which the slope of the curve showing the relationship changes as the value of one of the variables changes. A **nonlinear curve** is a curve whose slope changes as the value of one of the variables changes.

Consider an example. Suppose Felicia Alvarez, the owner of a bakery, has recorded the relationship between her firm's daily output of bread and the number of bakers she employs. The relationship she has recorded is given in the table in Panel (a) of Exhibit 1A-9.

Panel (a)

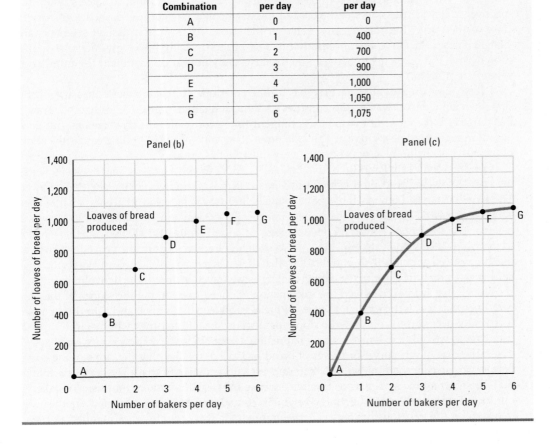

Combination	Bakers per day	Loaves of bread produced per day
A	0	0
B	1	400
C	2	700
D	3	900
E	4	1,000
F	5	1,050
G	6	1,075

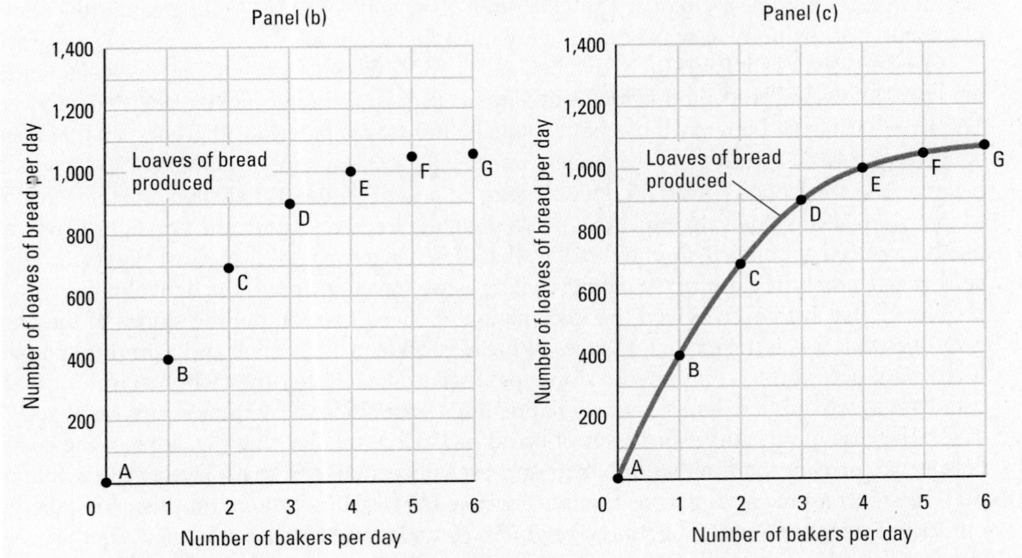

Exhibit 1A-9

A Nonlinear Curve

The table in Panel (a) shows the relationship between the number of bakers Felicia Alvarez employs per day and the number of loaves of bread produced per day. This information is plotted in Panel (b). This is a nonlinear relationship; the curve connecting these points in Panel (c) (Loaves of bread produced) has a changing slope.

Exhibit 1A-10

Estimating Slopes for a Nonlinear Curve

We can estimate the slope of a nonlinear curve between two points. Here, slopes are computed between points A and B, C and D, and E and F. When we compute the slope of a nonlinear curve between two points, we are computing the slope of a straight line between those two points. Here the lines whose slopes are computed are the dashed lines between the pairs of points.

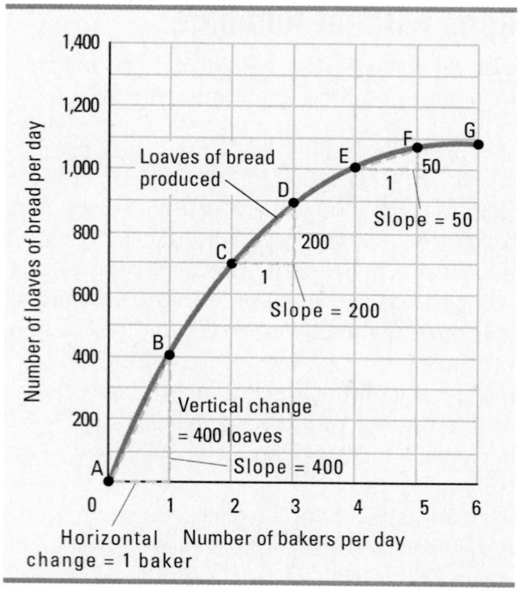

The corresponding points are plotted in Panel (b). Clearly, we can't draw a straight line through these points. Instead, we shall have to draw a nonlinear curve like the one shown in Panel (c).

Inspecting the curve for loaves of bread produced, we see that it is upward sloping, suggesting a positive relationship between the number of bakers and the output of bread. But we also see that the curve becomes flatter as we travel up and to the right along it; it is nonlinear and describes a nonlinear relationship.

How can we estimate the slope of a nonlinear curve? After all, the slope of such a curve changes as we travel along it. We can deal with this problem in two ways. One is to consider two points on the curve and to compute the slope between those two points. Another is to compute the slope of the curve at a single point.

When we compute the slope of a curve between two points, we are really computing the slope of a straight line drawn between those two points. In Exhibit 1A-10, we've computed slopes between pairs of points A and B, C and D, and E and F on our curve for loaves of bread produced. These slopes equal 400 loaves/baker, 200 loaves/baker, and 50 loaves/baker, respectively. They are the slopes of the dashed-line segments shown. These dashed segments lie close to the curve, but they clearly aren't on the curve. After all, the dashed segments are straight lines. Our curve relating the number of bakers to daily bread production is not a straight line; the relationship between the bakery's daily output of bread and the number of bakers is nonlinear.

Every point on a nonlinear curve has a different slope. To get a precise measure of the slope of such a curve, we need to consider its slope at a single point. To do that, we draw a line tangent to the curve at that point. A **tangent line** is a straight line that touches, but does not intersect, a nonlinear curve at only one point. The slope of a tangent line equals the slope of the curve at the point at which the tangent line touches the curve.

Consider point D in Panel (a) of Exhibit 1A-11. We've drawn a tangent line that just touches the curve showing bread production at this point. It passes through points labeled M and N. The vertical change between these points equals 300 loaves of bread; the horizontal change equals two bakers. The slope of the tangent line equals 150 loaves of bread/baker (300 loaves/2 bakers). The slope of our bread production curve at point D equals the slope of the line tangent to the curve at this point. In Panel (b), we've sketched lines tangent to the curve for loaves of bread produced at points B, D, and F. Notice that these tangent lines get successively flatter, suggesting again that the slope of the curve is falling as we travel up and to the right along it.

Notice that we haven't given the information we need to compute the slopes of the tangent lines that touch the curve for loaves of bread produced at points B and F. In this text, we won't have occasion to compute the slopes of tangent lines. Either they will be given or we'll use them as we did here—to see what's happening to the slopes of nonlinear curves.

In the case of our curve for loaves of bread produced, the fact that the slope of the curve falls as we increase the number of bakers suggests a phenomenon that plays a central role in both microeconomic and macroeconomic analysis. As we add workers (in this case bakers), output (in this case loaves of bread) rises, but by smaller and smaller amounts. Another way to describe the relationship between the number of workers and the quantity of bread

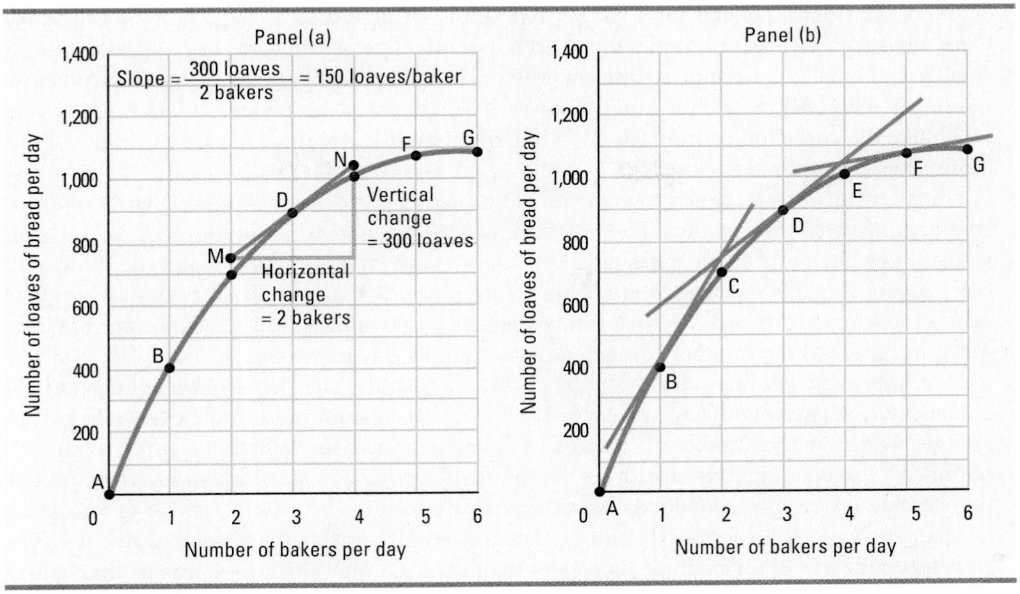

Exhibit 1A-11

Tangent Lines and the Slopes of Nonlinear Curves

Because the slope of a nonlinear curve is different at every point on the curve, the precise way to compute slope is to draw a tangent line; the slope of the tangent line equals the slope of the curve at the point the tangent line touches the curve. In Panel (a), the slope of the tangent line is computed for us: it equals 150 loaves/baker. Generally, we won't have the information to compute slopes of tangent lines. We'll use them as in Panel (b), to observe what happens to the slope of a nonlinear curve as we travel along it. We see here that the slope falls (the tangent lines become flatter) as the number of bakers rises.

produced is to say that as the number of workers increases, the output increases at a decreasing rate. In Panel (b) of Exhibit 1A-11 we express this idea with a graph, and we can gain this understanding by looking at the tangent lines, even though we don't have specific numbers. Indeed, much of our work with graphs won't require numbers at all.

We turn next to look at how we can use graphs to express ideas even when we don't have specific numbers.

Graphs Without Numbers

We know that a positive relationship between two variables can be shown with an upward-sloping curve in a graph. A negative or inverse relationship can be shown with a downward-sloping curve. Some relationships are linear and some are nonlinear. We illustrate a linear relationship with a curve whose slope is constant; a nonlinear relationship is illustrated with a curve whose slope changes. Using these basic ideas, we can illustrate hypotheses graphically even in cases in which we don't have numbers with which to locate specific points.

Exhibit 1A-12

Graphs Without Numbers

We often use graphs without numbers to suggest the nature of relationships between variables. The graphs in the four panels correspond to the relationships described in the text.

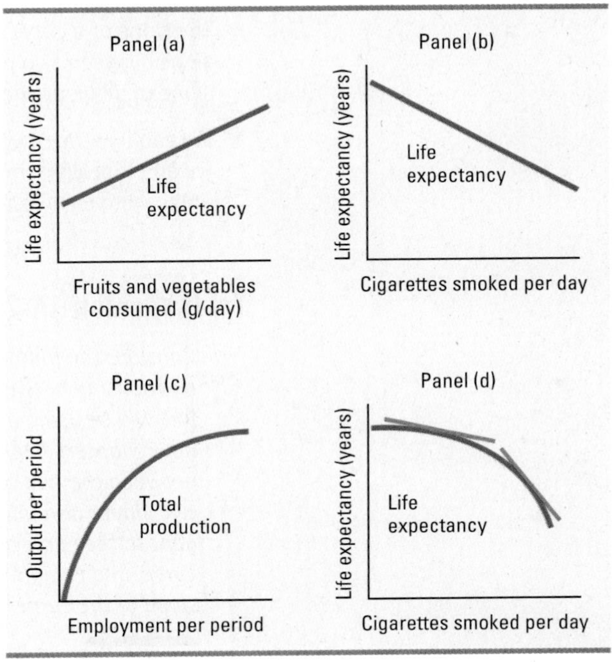

Consider first a hypothesis suggested by recent medical research: eating more fruits and vegetables each day increases life expectancy. We can show this idea graphically. Daily fruit and vegetable consumption (measured, say, in grams per day) is the independent variable; life expectancy (measured in years) is the dependent variable. Panel (a) of Exhibit 1A-12 shows the hypothesis, which suggests a positive relationship between the two variables. Notice the vertical intercept on the curve we've drawn; it implies that even people who eat no fruit or vegetables can expect to live at least a while!

Panel (b) illustrates another hypothesis we hear often: smoking cigarettes reduces life expectancy. Here the number of cigarettes smoked per day is the independent variable; life expectancy is the dependent variable. The hypothesis suggests a negative relationship. Hence, we have a downward-sloping curve.

Now consider a general form of the hypothesis suggested by the example of Felicia Alvarez's bakery: increasing employment each period increases output each period, but by smaller and smaller amounts. As we saw in Exhibit 1A-9, this hypothesis suggests a positive, nonlinear relationship. We've drawn a curve in Panel (c) of Exhibit 1A-12 that looks very much like the curve for bread production in Exhibit 1A-11. It is upward sloping, and its slope diminishes as employment rises.

Finally, consider a refined version of our smoking hypothesis. Suppose we assert that smoking cigarettes does reduce life expectancy, and that increasing the number of cigarettes smoked per day reduces life expectancy by a larger and larger amount. Panel (d) shows this case. Again, our life expectancy curve slopes downward. But now it suggests that smoking only a few cigarettes per day reduces life expectancy only a little, but life expectancy falls by more and more as the number of cigarettes smoked per day increases.

We have sketched lines tangent to the curve in Panel (d). The slopes of these tangent lines are negative, suggesting the negative relationship between smoking and life expectancy. They also get steeper as the number of cigarettes smoked per day rises. Whether a curve is linear or nonlinear, a steeper curve is one for which the absolute value of the slope rises as the value of the variable on the horizontal axis rises. When we speak of the absolute value of a negative number such as −4, we ignore the minus sign and simply say that the absolute value is 4. The absolute value of −8, for example, is greater than the absolute value of −4, and a curve with a slope of −8 is steeper than a curve whose slope is −4.

Thus far our work has focused on graphs that show a relationship between variables. We turn finally to an examination of graphs and charts that show values of one or more variables, either over a period of time or at a single point in time.

Checklist

- The slope of a nonlinear curve changes as the value of one of the variables in the relationship shown by the curve changes.
- A nonlinear curve may show a positive or a negative relationship.
- The slope of a curve showing a nonlinear relationship may be estimated by computing the slope between two points on the curve. The slope at any point on such a curve equals the slope of a line drawn tangent to the curve at that point.
- We can illustrate hypotheses about the relationship between two variables graphically, even if we aren't given numbers for the relationships. We need only draw and label the axes and then draw a curve consistent with the hypothesis.

Try It Yourself 1A-2

Consider the following curve drawn to show the relationship between two variables, A *and* B *(we will be using a curve like this one in the next chapter). Explain whether the relationship between the two variables is positive or negative, linear or nonlinear. Sketch two lines tangent to the curve at different points on the curve, and explain what is happening to the slope of the curve.*

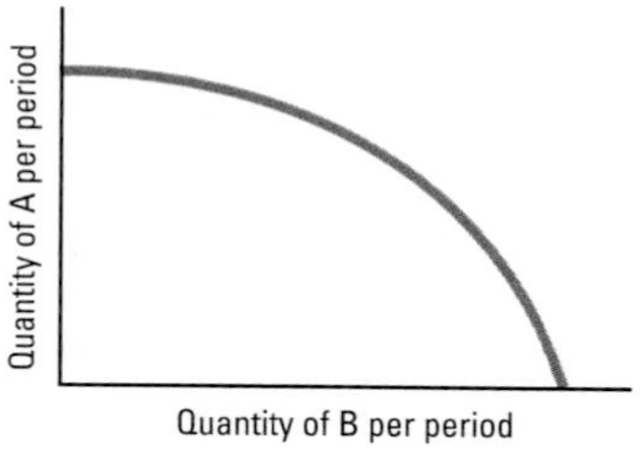

Using Graphs and Charts to Show Values of Variables

You often see pictures representing numerical information. These pictures may take the form of graphs that show how a particular variable has changed over time, or charts that show values of a particular variable at a single point in time. We'll close our introduction to graphs by looking at both ways of conveying information.

Time-Series Graphs

One of the most common types of graphs used in economics is called a time-series graph. A **time-series graph** shows how the value of a particular variable or variables has changed over some period of time. One of the variables in a time-series graph is time itself. Time is typically placed on the horizontal axis in time-series graphs. The other axis can represent any variable whose value changes over time.

The table in Panel (a) of Exhibit 1A-13 shows annual values of the unemployment rate, a measure of the percentage of workers who are available for work but aren't working, in the United States from 1990 to 1998. The grid with which these values are plotted is given in Panel (b). Notice that the vertical axis is scaled from 4 to 8 percent, instead of beginning with zero. Time-series graphs are often presented with the vertical axis scaled over a certain range. The result is the same as introducing a break in the vertical axis, as we did in Exhibit 1A-5.

The values for the U.S. unemployment rate are plotted in Panel (b) of Exhibit 1A-13. The points plotted are then connected with a line in Panel (c). Notice that unemployment rose early in the decade and fell after 1992.

Scaling the Vertical Axis in Time-Series Graphs The scaling of the vertical axis in time-series graphs can give very different views of economic data. We can make a variable appear to change a great deal, or almost not at all, depending on how we scale the axis. For that reason, it's important to note carefully how the vertical axis in a time-series graph is scaled.

Consider, for example, the issue of whether an increase or decrease in income tax rates has a significant effect on federal government revenues. This became a big issue in 1993, when President Clinton proposed an increase in income tax rates. The measure was intended to boost federal revenues. Critics of the president's proposal argued that changes in tax rates have little or no effect on federal revenues. Higher tax rates, they said, would cause some people to scale back their income-earning efforts and thus produce only a small gain—or even a loss—in revenues. Op-ed essays in the *Wall Street Journal*, for example,

Exhibit 1A-13

A Time-Series Graph

Panel (a) gives values of the U.S. unemployment rate from 1990 to 1998. These points are then plotted in Panel (b). To draw a time-series graph, we connect these points, as in Panel (c).

Panel (a)

Year	Unemployment rate (percent)
1990	5.5
1991	6.7
1992	7.4
1993	6.8
1994	6.1
1995	5.6
1996	5.4
1997	5.0
1998	4.5

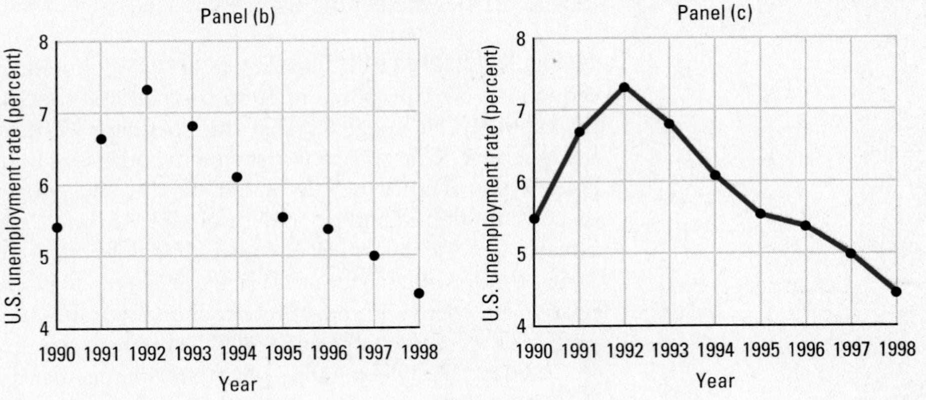

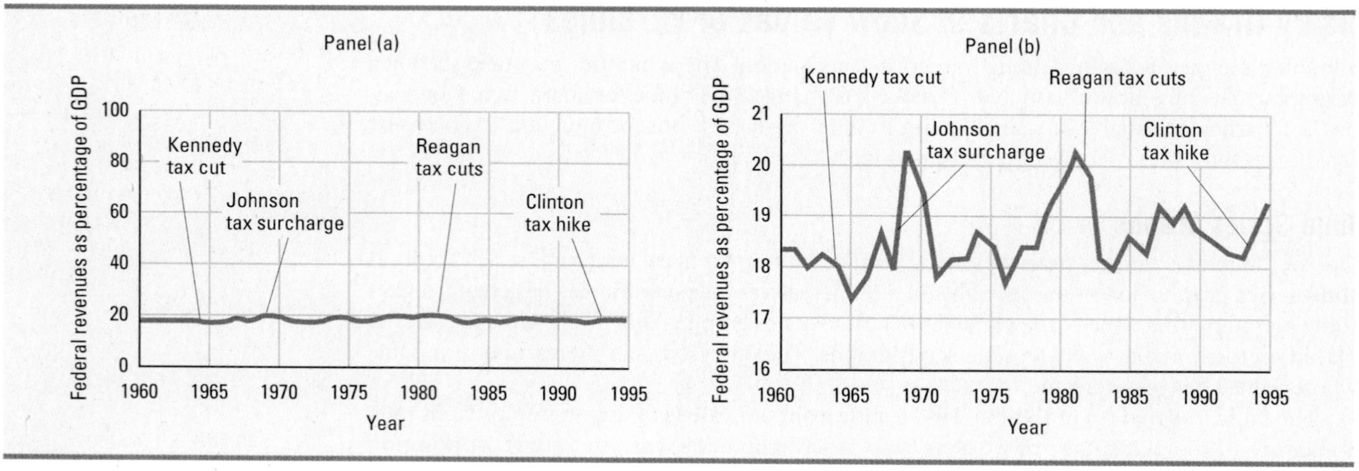

Exhibit 1A-14

Two Tales of Taxes and Income

A graph of federal revenues as a percentage of GDP emphasizes the stability of the relationship when plotted with the vertical axis scaled from 0 to 100, as in Panel (a). Scaling the vertical axis from 16 to 21 percent, as in Panel (b), stresses the short-term variability of the percentage and suggests that major tax rate changes have affected federal revenues.

often showed a graph very much like that presented in Panel (a) of Exhibit 1A-14. It shows federal revenues as a percentage of gross domestic product (GDP), a measure of total income in the economy, since 1960. Various tax reductions and increases were enacted during that period, but Panel (a) appears to show they had little effect on federal revenues relative to total income.

Laura Tyson, then President Clinton's chief economic adviser, charged that those graphs were misleading. In a *Wall Street Journal* piece, she noted the scaling of the vertical axis used by the president's critics. She argued that a more reasonable scaling of the axis shows that federal revenues tend to increase relative to total income in the economy and that cuts in taxes reduce the federal government's share. Her alternative version of these events does, indeed, suggest that federal receipts have tended to rise and fall with changes in tax policy, as shown in Panel (b) of Exhibit 1A-14.

Which version is correct? Both are. Both graphs show the same data. It's certainly true that federal revenues, relative to economic activity, have been remarkably stable over the past several decades, as emphasized by the scaling in Panel (a). But it is also true that the federal share has varied between about 17 and 20 percent. And a small change in the federal share translates into a large amount of tax revenue. A 1-percentage-point change in the federal share of total income in today's economy equals more than $80 billion.

It's easy to be misled by time-series graphs. Large changes can be made to appear trivial and trivial changes to appear large through an artful scaling of the axes. The best advice for a careful consumer of graphical information is to note carefully the range of values shown and then to decide whether the changes are really significant.

Testing Hypotheses with Time-Series Graphs John Maynard Keynes, one of the most famous economists ever, proposed in 1936 a hypothesis about total spending for consumer goods in the economy. He suggested that this spending was positively related to the income households receive. One way to test such a hypothesis is to draw a time-series graph of both variables to see whether they do, in fact, tend to move together. Exhibit 1A-15 shows the values of consumption spending and disposable income, which is after-tax income received by households. Annual values of consumption and disposable income are plotted for the period 1960–1998. Notice that both variables have tended to move quite closely together. The close relationship between consumption and disposable income is consistent with Keynes's hypothesis that there is a positive relationship between the two variables.

The fact that two variables tend to move together in a time series does not by itself prove that there is a systematic relationship between the two. Exhibit 1A-16 shows a time-series

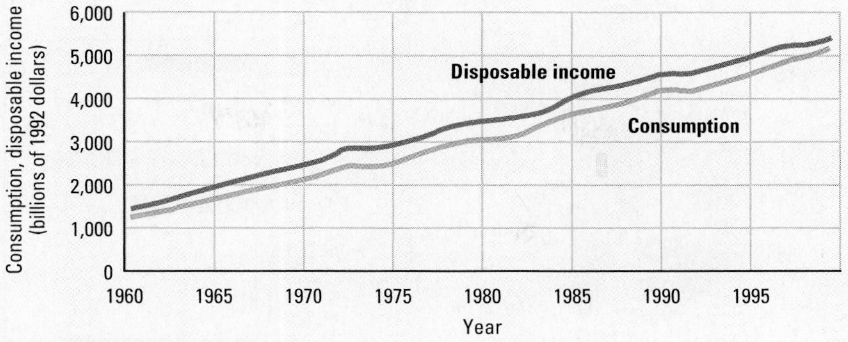

Source: Department of Commerce.

Exhibit 1A-15

A Time-Series Graph of Disposable Income and Consumption

Plotted in a time-series graph, disposable income and consumption appear to move together. This is consistent with the hypothesis that the two are directly related.

graph of monthly values in 1987 of the Dow Jones Industrial Average, an index that reflects the movement of the prices of common stock. The worst stock crash in history happened that year; notice the steep decline in the index beginning in October.

It would be useful, and certainly profitable, to be able to predict such declines. Exhibit 1A-16 also shows the movement of monthly values of a "mystery variable," *X*, for the same period. The mystery variable and stock prices appear to move closely together. Was the plunge in the mystery variable in October responsible for the stock crash? The answer is: Not likely. The mystery value is monthly average temperatures in San Juan, Puerto Rico. Attributing the stock crash in 1987 to the weather in San Juan would be an example of the fallacy of false cause.

Notice that Exhibit 1A-16 has two vertical axes. The left-hand axis shows values of temperature; the right-hand axis shows values for the Dow Jones Industrial Average. Two axes are used here because the two variables, San Juan temperature and the Dow Jones Industrial Average, are scaled in different units.

Exhibit 1A-16

Stock Prices and a Mystery Variable

The movement of the monthly average of the Dow Jones Industrial Average, a widely reported index of stock values, corresponded closely to changes in a mystery variable, *X*. Did the mystery variable contribute to the crash?

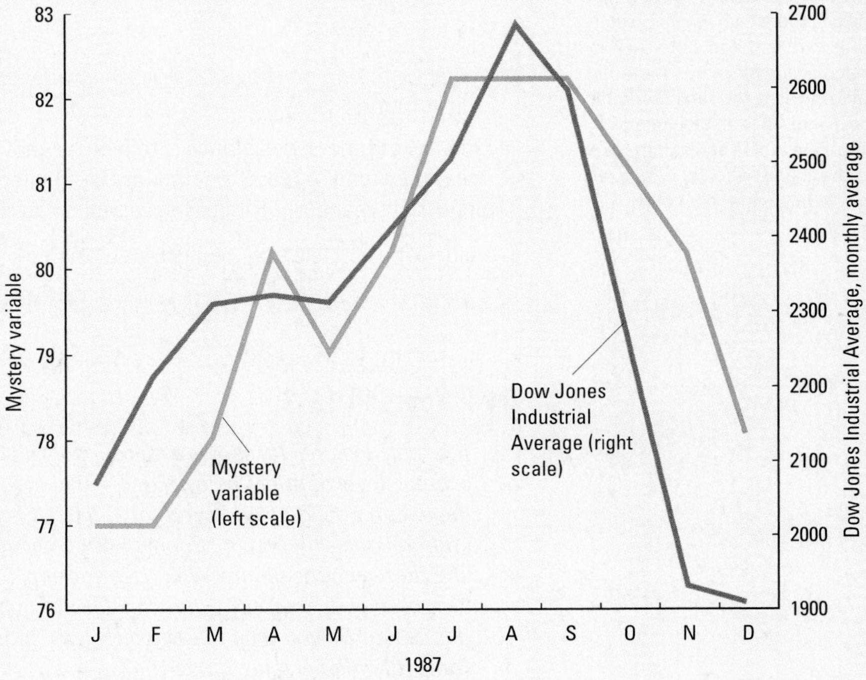

Descriptive Charts

We can use a table to show data. Consider, for example, the information compiled each year by the Higher Education Research Institute (HERI) at UCLA. HERI conducts a survey of first-year college students throughout the United States and asks what their intended academic majors are. The table in Panel (a) of Exhibit 1A-17 shows the results of the 1998 survey. In the groupings given, economics is included among the social sciences; 0.3 percent of first-year students in 1998 expressed an intention to major in economics.

Panels (b) and (c) of Exhibit 1A-17 present the same information in two

Panel (a)

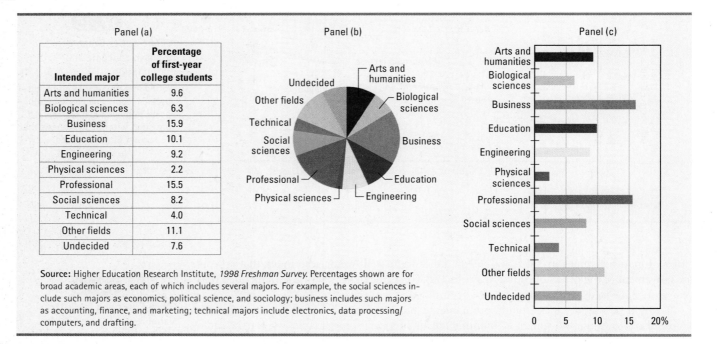

Intended major	Percentage of first-year college students
Arts and humanities	9.6
Biological sciences	6.3
Business	15.9
Education	10.1
Engineering	9.2
Physical sciences	2.2
Professional	15.5
Social sciences	8.2
Technical	4.0
Other fields	11.1
Undecided	7.6

Panel (b)

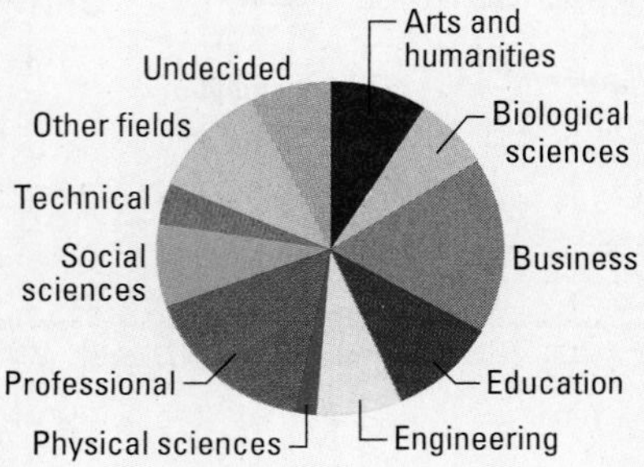

Panel (c)

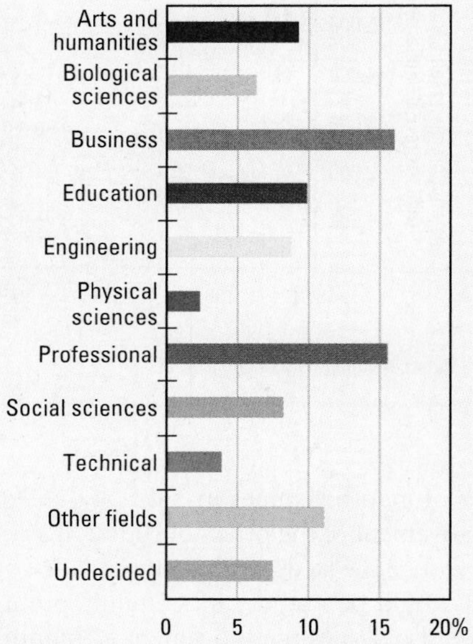

Source: Higher Education Research Institute, *1998 Freshman Survey.* Percentages shown are for broad academic areas, each of which includes several majors. For example, the social sciences include such majors as economics, political science, and sociology; business includes such majors as accounting, finance, and marketing; technical majors include electronics, data processing/computers, and drafting.

Exhibit 1A-17

Intended Academic Major Area, 1998 Survey of First-Year College Students

Panels (a), (b), and (c) show the results of a 1998 survey of first-year college students in which respondents were asked to state their intended academic major. All three panels present the same information. Panel (a) is an example of a table, Panel (b) is an example of a pie chart, and Panel (c) is an example of a horizontal bar chart.

types of charts. Panel (b) is an example of a pie chart; Panel (c) gives the data in a bar chart. The bars in this chart are horizontal; they may also be drawn as vertical. Either type of graph may be used to provide a picture of numeric information.

Check*list*

- A time-series graph shows changes in a variable over time; one axis is always measured in units of time.
- One use of time-series graphs is to plot the movement of two or more variables together to see if they tend to move together or not. The fact that two variables move together does not prove that changes in one of the variables cause changes in the other.
- Values of a variable may be illustrated using a pie or a bar chart.

Try It Yourself 1A-3

The table in Panel (a) shows a measure of the inflation rate, the percentage change in the average level of prices below. Panels (b) and (c) provide blank grids. We have already labeled the axes on the grids in Panels (b) and (c). It is up to you to plot the data in Panel (a) on the grids in Panels (b) and (c). Connect the points you have marked in the grid using straight lines between the points. What relationship do you observe? Has the inflation rate generally increased or decreased? What can you say about the trend of inflation over the course of the 1990s? Do you tend to get a different "interpretation" depending on whether you use Panel (b) or Panel (c) to guide you?

Panel (a)

Year	Inflation rate (percent)
1990	6.1
1991	3.1
1992	2.9
1993	2.7
1994	2.7
1995	2.5
1996	3.3
1997	1.7
1998	1.6

Panel (b)
Inflation Rate, 1990–1998

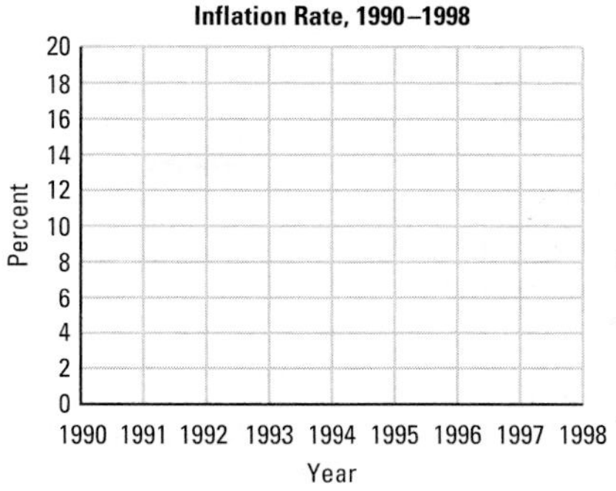

Panel (c)
Inflation Rate, 1990–1998

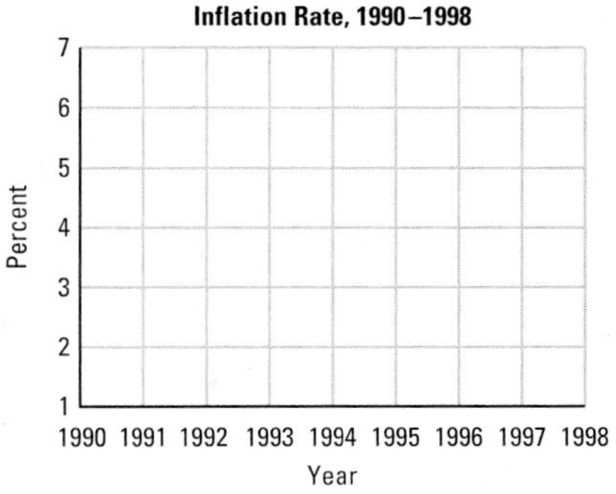

Terms and Concepts for Review

graph, **20**
origin, **21**
scatter diagram, **21**
intercept, **22**
slope, **22**
linear relationship, **23**
linear curve, **23**
positive relationship, **23**
negative relationship, **23**
shift in a curve, **24**
movement along a curve, **24**
rotation of a curve, **25**
nonlinear relationship, **27**
nonlinear curve, **27**
tangent line, **28**
time-series graph, **31**

Problems

1. Panel (a) shows a graph of a positive relationship; Panel (b) shows a graph of a negative relationship. Decide whether each proposition below demonstrates a positive or negative relationship, and decide which graph you would expect to illustrate each proposition. In each statement, identify which variable is the independent variable and thus goes on the horizontal axis, and which variable is the dependent variable and goes on the vertical axis.

Panel (a)

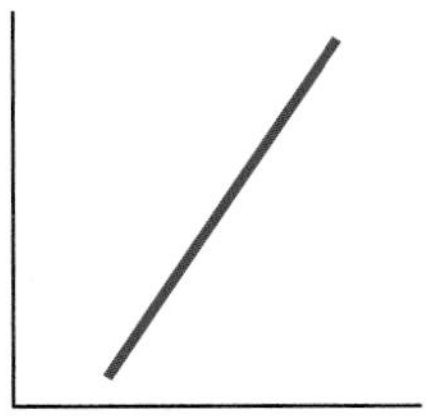

Panel (b)

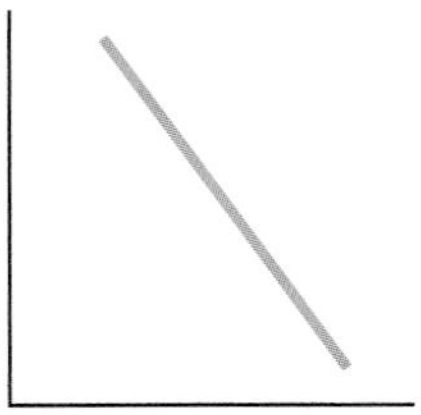

   a. An increase in national income in any one year increases the number of people killed in highway accidents.
   b. An increase in the poverty rate causes an increase in the crime rate.
   c. As the income received by households rises, they purchase fewer beans.
   d. As the income received by households rises, they spend more on home entertainment equipment.
   e. The warmer the day, the less soup people consume.

2. Suppose you have a graph showing the results of a survey asking people how many left and right shoes they owned. The results suggest that people with one left shoe had, on average, one right shoe. People with seven left shoes had, on average, seven right shoes. Put left shoes on the vertical axis and right shoes on the horizontal axis; plot the following observations:

Left shoes	1	2	3	4	5	6	7
Right shoes	1	2	3	4	5	6	7

Is this relationship positive or negative? What is the slope of the curve?

3. Suppose your assistant inadvertently reversed the order of numbers for right shoe ownership in the survey above. You thus have the following table of observations:

Left shoes	1	2	3	4	5	6	7
Right shoes	7	6	5	4	3	2	1

Is the relationship between these numbers positive or negative? What's implausible about that?

4. Suppose some of Ms. Alvarez's kitchen equipment breaks down. The following table gives the values of bread output that were shown in Exhibit 1A-9. It also gives the new l evels of bread output that Ms. Alvarez's bakers produce following the breakdown. Plot the two curves. What has happened?

	A	B	C	D	E	F	G
Bakers/day	0	1	2	3	4	5	6
Loaves/day	0	400	700	900	1,000	1,050	1,075
Loaves/day after breakdown	0	380	670	860	950	990	1,005

5. Steven Magee has suggested that there is a relationship between the number of lawyers per capita in a country and the country's rate of economic growth. The relationship is described with the following Magee curve.

   What do you think is the argument made by the curve? What kinds of countries do you think are on the upward-sloping region of the curve? Where would you guess the United States is? Japan? Does the Magee curve seem plausible to you?

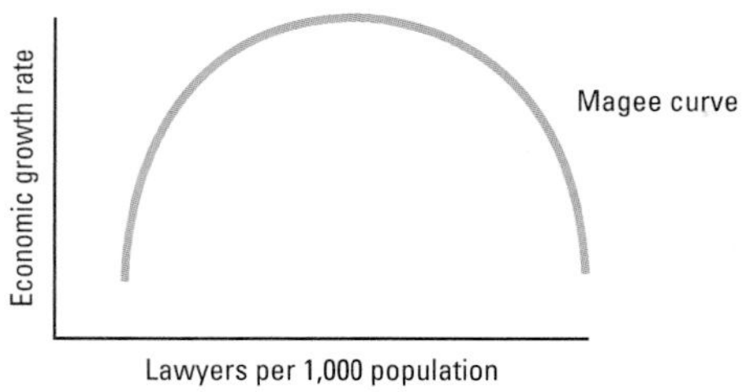

6. Draw graphs showing the likely relationship between each of the following pairs of variables. In each case, put the first variable mentioned on the horizontal axis and the second on the vertical axis.
   a. The amount of time a student spends studying economics and the grade he or she receives in the course
   b. Per capita income and total expenditures on health care
   c. Alcohol consumption by teenagers and academic performance
   d. Household income and the likelihood of being the victim of a violent crime

Answers to Try It Yourself Problems

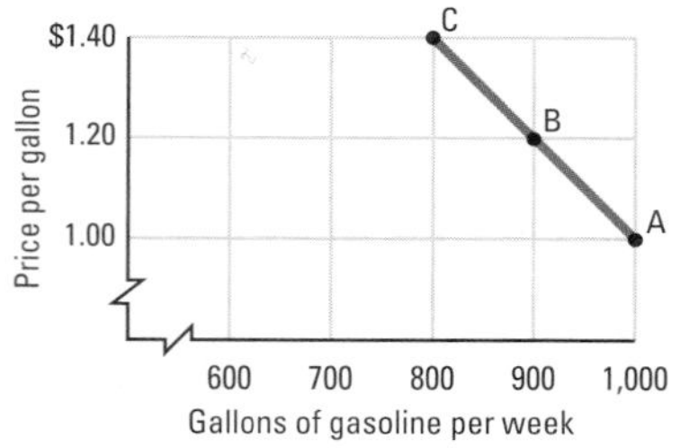

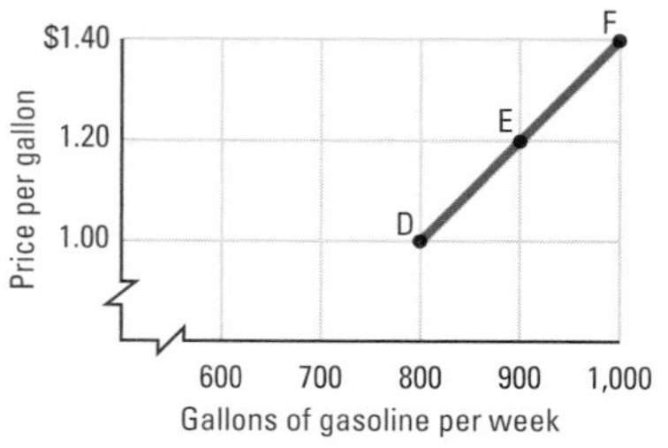

Try It Yourself 1A-1

Here is the first graph. The curve's downward slope tells us there is a negative relationship between price and the quantity of gasoline people are willing and able to buy. This curve, by the way, is a demand curve (the next one is a supply curve). We'll study demand and supply in Chapter 3; you'll be using these curves a great deal. The slope between A and B is −0.002 (slope = vertical change/horizontal change = −0.20/100). The slope between B and C and between A and C is the same. That tells us the curve is linear, which, of course, we can see—it's a straight line.

Here is the supply curve. Its upward slope tells us there is a positive relationship between price per gallon and the number of gallons per week gas stations are willing to sell. The slope between D and E is 0.002 (slope equals vertical change divided by horizontal change = 0.20/100). Because the curve is linear, the slope is the same between any two points, for example, between E and F and between D and F.

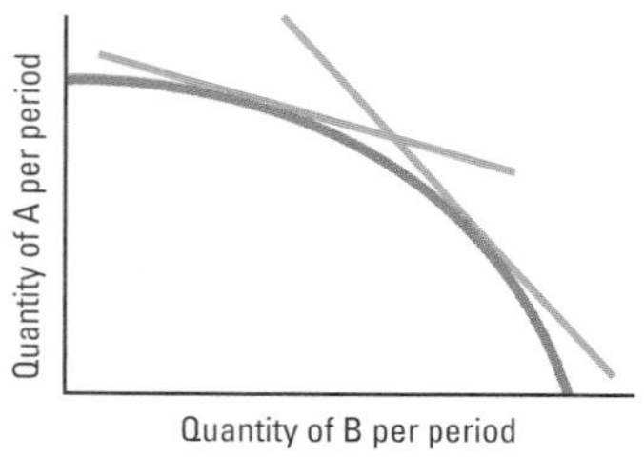

Try It Yourself 1A-2

The relationship between variable A shown on the vertical axis and variable B shown on the horizontal axis is negative. This is sometimes referred to as an inverse relationship. Variables that give a straight line with a constant slope are said to have a linear relationship. In this case, however, the relationship is nonlinear. The slope changes all along the curve. In this case the slope becomes steeper as we move downward to the right along the curve, as shown by the two tangent lines that have been drawn. As the quantity of B increases, the quantity of A decreases at an increasing rate.

Try It Yourself 1A-3

Here are the time-series graphs, Panels (b) and (c), for the information in Panel (a). The first thing you should notice is that both graphs show that the inflation rate generally declined throughout the 1990s (with the exception of 1996, when it increased). The generally downward direction of the curve suggests that the trend of inflation was downward. Notice that in this case we don't say negative, since in this instance it is not the slope of the line that matters. Rather, inflation itself is still positive (as indicated by the fact that all the points are above the origin) but is declining. Finally, comparing Panels (b) and (c) suggests that the general downward trend in the inflation rate is emphasized less in Panel (b) than in Panel (c). This impression would be emphasized even more if the numbers on the vertical axis were increased in Panel (b) from 20 to 100. Just as in Exhibit 1A-14, it is possible to make large changes appear trivial by simply changing the scaling of the axes.

Panel (a)

Year	Inflation rate (percent)
1990	6.1
1991	3.1
1992	2.9
1993	2.7
1994	2.7
1995	2.5
1996	3.3
1997	1.7
1998	1.6

Panel (b)
Inflation Rate, 1990–1998

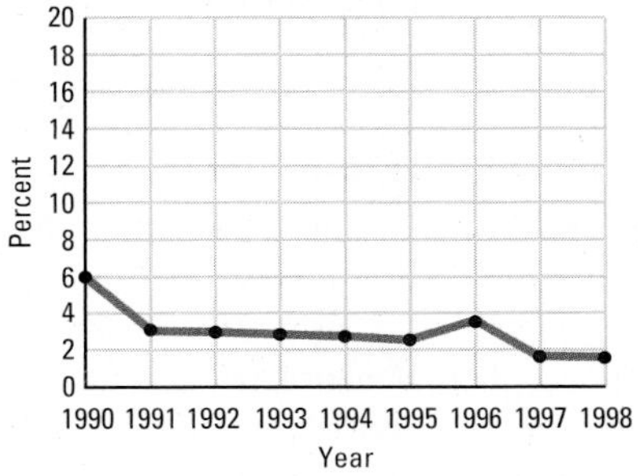

Panel (c)
Inflation Rate, 1990–1998

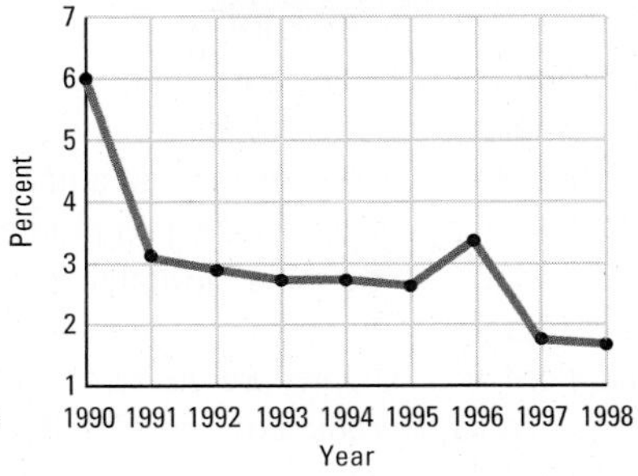

2 Confronting Scarcity: Choices in Production

Getting Started: An Army Base Becomes a College Campus

Students at California State University, Monterey Bay, can tell you about the topic of this chapter: the choices made in an economy concerning what to produce. Their school, which opened in 1995, sits on the site of a former army base, Fort Ord.

The closure of the base and the shift of its resources to civilian uses came as part of the U.S. response to the 1991 demise of the Soviet Union and the end of the Cold War. After more than four decades in which Americans had sacrificed to provide a defense they regarded as adequate to meet the military challenge posed by the Soviet Union, they suddenly found themselves willing to spend less for defense and more for civilian goods and services. They transformed military facilities, including Fort Ord, into civilian facilities such as California State University at Monterey Bay.

Economists often speak of the choice between guns and butter. In the words of that metaphor, after 1991 the United States chose to produce more butter—civilian goods and services—and fewer guns—defense goods and services. The production of military goods and services, which averaged 7.4 percent of U.S. output between 1950 and 1990, had fallen to 4.0 percent by 1998.

We saw in Chapter 1 that "What to produce?" is a fundamental economic question. Every economy must answer this question. Should it produce more education, better health care, improved transportation, a cleaner environment? There are limits to what a nation can produce; deciding to produce more of one thing inevitably means producing less of something else. In this chapter we use our first model, the production possibilities model, to examine the nature of such choices. As its name suggests, the **production possibilities model** shows the goods and services that an economy is capable of producing—its possibilities—given the factors of production and the technology it has available. The model specifies what it means to use resources fully and efficiently and suggests some important implications for international trade. We can also use the model to explain the nature and causes of economic growth, a process that expands the set of production possibilities available to an economy.

We then turn to an examination of the type of economic system in which choices are made. An **economic system** is the set of rules that define how an economy's resources are to be owned and how decisions about their use are to be made. We'll see that economic systems differ in terms of how they answer the fundamental economic questions. Many economic systems, including the systems that prevail in North America, Europe, and much of Asia and Central and South America, rely on individuals operating in a market economy to make those choices. Other economic systems, including those of Cuba and North Korea, rely on government to make these choices. Different economic systems result in different sets of choices and thus different outcomes; this fact helps to explain the dramatic shift from government-dominated toward market-dominated economic systems that has occurred throughout the world in the past decade. The chapter concludes with an examination of the role of government in an economy that relies chiefly on markets to allocate goods and services.

Factors of Production

Choices concerning what goods and services to produce are choices about an economy's use of its **factors of production,** the resources available to it for the production of goods and services. The value, or satisfaction, that people derive from the goods and services they consume and the activities they pursue is called **utility.** Ultimately, then, an economy's factors of production create utility; they serve the interests of people.

The factors of production in an economy are its labor, capital, and natural resources. **Labor** is the human effort that can be applied to the production of goods and services. **Capital** is a factor of production that has been produced for use in the production of other goods and services. Office buildings, machinery, and tools are examples of capital. **Natural resources** are the resources of nature that can be used for the production of goods and services.

In the next three sections, we'll take a closer look at the factors of production we use to produce the goods and services we consume. The three basic building blocks of labor, capital, and natural resources may be used in different ways to produce different goods and services, but they still lie at the core of production. As economists began to grapple with the problems of scarcity, choice, and opportunity cost two centuries ago, they focused on these same three factors, just as they surely will two centuries hence.

Labor

Labor is human effort that can be applied to production. People who work to repair tires, pilot airplanes, teach children, or enforce laws are all part of the economy's labor. People who would like to work but haven't found employment—who are unemployed—are also considered part of the labor available to the economy.

In some contexts, it is useful to distinguish two forms of labor. The first is the human equivalent of a natural resource. It is the natural ability an untrained, uneducated person brings to a particular production process. But most workers bring far more. The skills a worker has as a result of education, training, or experience that can be used in production are called **human capital.** Students who are attending a college or university are acquiring human capital. Workers who are gaining skills through experience or through training are acquiring human capital. Children who are learning to read are acquiring human capital.

The amount of labor available to an economy can be increased in two ways. One is to increase the total quantity of labor, either by increasing the number of people available to work or by increasing the average number of hours of work per week. The other is to increase the average amount of human capital possessed by workers. In the United States and in many other countries, economists have found that during the last 50 years increases in human capital have played a more important role in expanding the economy's ability to produce goods and services than have increases in the quantities of labor or capital or gains in technology.

Capital

A few million years ago, when the first human beings walked the earth, they produced food by picking leaves or fruit off a plant or by catching an animal and eating it. We know that very early on, however, they began shaping stones into tools, apparently for use in butchering animals. Those tools were the first capital because they were produced for use in producing other goods—food and clothing.

Modern versions of the first stone tools include saws, meat cleavers, hooks, and grinders; all are used in butchering animals. Tools such as hammers, screwdrivers, and wrenches are also capital. Transportation equipment, such as cars and trucks, is capital. Facilities such as roads, bridges, ports, and airports are capital. Buildings, too, are capital; they help us to produce goods and services.

Capital does not consist solely of physical objects. The score for a new symphony is capital because it will be used to produce concerts. Computer software used by business firms or government agencies to produce goods and services is capital. Capital may thus include physical goods and intellectual discoveries.

Any resource is capital if it satisfies two criteria:

1. The resource must have been produced.
2. The resource can be used to produce other goods and services.

One thing that is not considered capital is money. A firm can't use money directly to produce other goods, so money doesn't satisfy the second criterion for capital. Firms can, however, use money to acquire capital. Money is a form of financial capital. **Financial capital** includes money and other "paper" assets (such as stocks and bonds) that represent claims on future payments. These financial assets aren't capital, but they can be used directly or indirectly to purchase factors of production or goods and services.

Natural Resources

There are two essential characteristics of natural resources. The first is that they are found in nature—that no human effort has been used to make or alter them. The second is that they can be used for the production of goods and services. That requires knowledge; we must know how to use the things we find in nature before they become resources.

Consider oil. Oil in the ground is a natural resource because it is found (not manufactured) and can be used to produce goods and services. Two hundred years ago, however, oil was a nuisance, not a natural resource. Pennsylvania farmers in the eighteenth century who found oil oozing up through their soil were dismayed, not delighted. No one knew what could be done with the oil. It wasn't until the mid-nineteenth century that a method was found for refining oil into kerosene that could be used to generate energy, transforming oil into a natural resource. Oil is now used to make all sorts of things, including clothing, drugs, gasoline, and plastic. It became a natural resource because people discovered a way to use it.

Defining something as a natural resource only if it can be used to produce goods and services does not mean that a tree has value only for its wood or that a mountain has value only for its minerals. If people gain utility from the existence of an unspoiled wilderness, then that wilderness provides a service. The wilderness is thus a natural resource.

The natural resources available to us can be expanded in three ways. One is the discovery of new natural resources, such as the discovery of a deposit of uranium. The second is the discovery of new uses for resources, as happened when new techniques allowed oil to be put to productive use or sand to be used in manufacturing computer chips. The third is the discovery of new ways to extract natural resources in order to use them. For example, new methods of extracting gold are turning what were once piles of waste from old mines into natural resources.

Technology and the Entrepreneur

Goods and services are produced using the factors of production available to the economy. Two things play a crucial role in putting these factors of production to work. First, **technology** is the knowledge that can be applied to the production of goods and services. The second is an individual who fills a key role in a market economy: the entrepreneur. An **entrepreneur** is a person who seeks to earn profits by finding new ways to organize factors of production.

The interplay of entrepreneurs and technology affects all our lives. Entrepreneurs put new technologies to work every day, changing the way factors of production are used. Farmers and factory workers, engineers and electricians, technicians and teachers all work differently than they did just a few years ago, using new technologies introduced by entrepreneurs. The music you enjoy, the books you read, the athletic equipment with which you play are produced differently than they were five years ago. The book you're reading was written and manufactured using technologies that didn't exist when the first edition appeared in 1996. We can dispute whether all the changes have made our lives better. What we can't dispute is that they have made our lives different.

Case in Point Technology Cuts Costs, Boosts Productivity and Profits

Technology can seem an abstract force in the economy—important, but invisible.

It isn't invisible to Donald Paul. Mr. Paul, who is a vice president for Chevron Corporation, says that technology is the key to profits in the oil business. "The industry has learned to make money at prices that are about the same as they were in the '50s and '60s," he told the *Wall Street Journal*. "The reason is technology."

Chevron, like other oil companies, uses new computer technology to generate three-dimensional maps from seismic surveys of potential deposits of oil and natural gas. The new methods have helped the company reduce dramatically the number of wells it drills to find oil. Before the new mapping techniques became available, Chevron drilled 10 to 12 "dry holes" for every well that actually hit oil. Now, it hits oil roughly once in every five tries. At costs as high as $4 million per well, that translates into big savings. That kind of approach had reduced 1999 oil-industry production costs by 16 percent from their 1991 levels.

Technology, of course, marches on. In 1999, Chevron and other companies were experimenting with new "4-D" computer models that add a fourth dimension to the mapping process. The new maps will allow companies to predict how oil fields will change over time. That new technology may reduce production costs even further.

Technology is doing more than help energy companies track deposits of oil and gas. It's changing the way McDonald's franchises handle food. The restaurants now use computer systems that transfer order information at the counter instantly to the cooks who fry the hamburgers and to the machines that make the french fries. A new system, being introduced to restaurants in 1999, will forecast supply needs during the day. That will, company officials say, result in restaurants throwing away less food—and will save each restaurant about $15,000 per year. It will also allow restaurants to provide better service.

New technology is also saving the lives of tropical fish, and boosting profits, at PetsMart stores. Computer-controlled monitors can track water temperatures, acidity, and chlorine levels in as many as 160 fish tanks in a store at a time. That has reduced fish deaths at the stores by 10 percent since 1997, when PetsMart stores began applying the new technology.

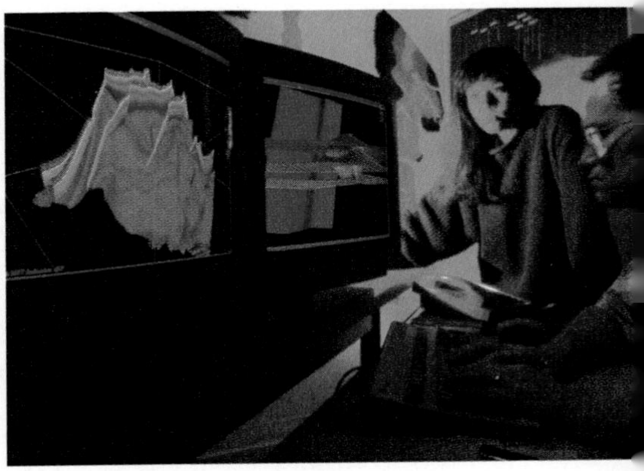

Who benefits from technological progress? Consumers gain from lower prices and better service. Workers gain: Their greater ability to produce goods and services translates into higher wages. And firms gain: Lower production costs mean higher profits. Of course, some people lose as technology advances. Some jobs are eliminated, and some firms find their services are no longer needed. But for people in general, technological gains mean real gains and real progress in the way we live and work.

Source: George Anders and Scott Thurm, "The Rocket Under the Tech Boom: Big Spending by Basic Industries," *Wall Street Journal*, 30 March 1999, p. A1.

Checklist

- Factors of production are the resources the economy has available to produce goods and services.
- Labor is the human effort that can be applied to the production of goods and services. Labor's contribution to an economy's output of goods and services can be increased either by increasing the quantity of labor or by increasing human capital.
- Capital is a factor of production that has been produced for use in the production of other goods and services.
- Natural resources are those things found in nature that can be used for the production of goods and services.
- Two keys to the utilization of an economy's factors of production are technology and, in the case of a market economic system, the efforts of entrepreneurs.

Try It Yourself 2-1

Explain whether each of the following is labor, capital, or a natural resource.

a. An unemployed factory worker

b. A college professor

c. The library building on your campus

d. Yellowstone National Park

e. An untapped deposit of natural gas

f. The White House

g. The local power plant

The Production Possibilities Curve

An economy's factors of production are scarce; they cannot produce an unlimited quantity of goods and services. A **production possibilities curve** is a graphical representation of the alternative combinations of goods and services an economy can produce. It illustrates the production possibilities model. In drawing the production possibilities curve, we shall assume that the economy can produce only two goods and that the quantities of factors of production and the technology available to the economy are fixed.

Constructing a Production Possibilities Curve

To construct a production possibilities curve, we will begin with the case of Alpine Sports, Inc., a specialized sports equipment manufacturer. Christie Rider began the business 5 years ago with a single ski production facility near Killington ski resort in central Vermont. Ski sales grew, and she also saw demand for snowboards rising. She added a second plant in a nearby town. The second plant, while smaller than the first, was designed to produce snowboards as well as skis. She also modified the first plant so that it could produce both snowboards and skis. Two years later she added a third plant in another town. While even smaller than the second plant, the third was primarily designed for snowboard production but could also produce skis.

Ms. Rider isn't ready to build a fourth plant, and is taking a cautious approach to expansion. Her business is growing, but she chooses to limit the financial capital she will commit this early in the life of her firm.

We can think of each of Ms. Rider's plants as a miniature economy and analyze it using the production possibilities model. We assume that the factors of production and technology available to each of the plants operated by Alpine Sports are unchanged.

Suppose the first plant, Plant 1, can produce 200 pairs of skis per month when it produces only skis. When devoted solely to snowboards, it produces 100 snowboards per month. It can produce skis and snowboards simultaneously as well.

The table in Exhibit 2-1 gives three combinations of skis and snowboards that Plant 1 can produce each

	Pairs of skis per month	Snowboards per month
A	200	0
B	100	50
C	0	100

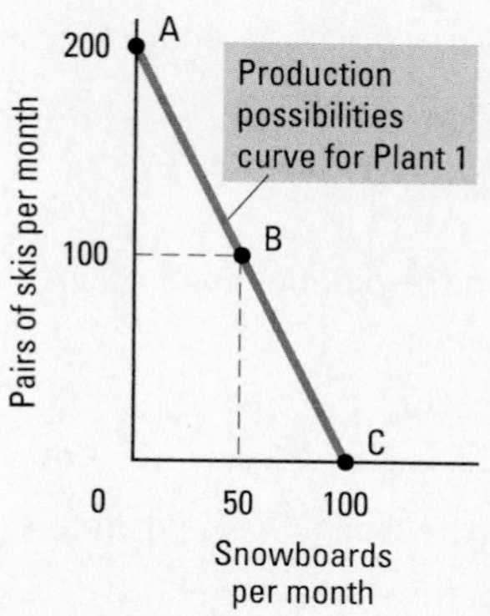

Exhibit 2-1

A Production Possibilities Curve

The table shows the combinations of pairs of skis and snowboards that Plant 1 is capable of producing each month. These are also illustrated with a production possibilities curve. Notice that this curve is linear.

month. Combination A involves devoting the plant entirely to ski production; combination C means shifting all of the plant's resources to snowboard production; combination B involves the production of both goods. These values are plotted in a production possibilities curve for Plant 1. The curve is a downward-sloping straight line, indicating that there is a linear, negative relationship between the production of the two goods.

Neither skis nor snowboards is an independent or a dependent variable in the production possibilities model; we can assign either one to the vertical or to the horizontal axis. Here, we have placed the number of pairs of skis produced per month on the vertical axis and the number of snowboards produced per month on the horizontal axis.

The negative slope of the production possibilities curve reflects the scarcity of the plant's capital and labor. Producing more snowboards requires shifting resources out of ski production and thus producing fewer skis. Producing more skis requires shifting resources out of snowboard production and thus producing fewer snowboards.

The slope of Plant 1's production possibilities curve measures the rate at which Alpine Sports must give up ski production to produce additional snowboards. Because the production possibilities curve for Plant 1 is linear, we can compute the slope between any two points on the curve and get the same result. Between points A and B, for example, the slope equals −2 pairs of skis/snowboard (−100 pairs of skis/50 snowboards). We get the same value between points B and C, and between points A and C.

To see this relationship more clearly, examine Exhibit 2-2. Suppose Plant 1 is producing 100 pairs of skis and 50 snowboards per month at point B. Now consider what would happen if Ms. Rider decided to produce 1 more snowboard per month. The segment of the curve around point B is magnified in Exhibit 2-2. The slope between points B and B′ is −2 pairs of skis/snowboard. Producing 1 additional snowboard at point B′ requires giving up 2 pairs of skis. We can think of this as the opportunity cost of producing an additional snowboard at Plant 1. This opportunity cost equals the absolute value of the slope of the production possibilities curve.

The absolute value of the slope of any production possibilities curve equals the opportunity cost of an additional unit of the good on the horizontal axis. It's the amount of the good on the vertical axis that must be given up to produce one more unit of the good on the horizontal axis. We'll make use of this important fact as we continue our investigation of the production possibilities curve.

Exhibit 2-3 shows production possibilities curves for each of the firm's three plants. Each of the plants, if devoted entirely to snowboards, could produce 100 snowboards. Plants 2 and 3, if devoted exclusively to ski production, can produce 100 and 50 pairs of skis per month, respectively.

The exhibit gives the slopes of the production possibilities curves for each plant. The opportunity cost of an additional snowboard at each plant equals the absolute values of these slopes.

The greater the absolute value of the slope of the production possibilities curve, the greater that opportunity cost will be. The plant for which the opportunity cost of an additional snowboard is greatest is thus the plant with the steepest production possibilities curve; the plant for which the opportunity cost is lowest is the plant with the flattest production possibilities curve. The plant with the lowest opportunity cost of producing snowboards is Plant 3; its slope of −0.5 means that Ms. Rider must give up half a pair of skis in that plant to produce an additional

Exhibit 2-2

The Slope of a Production Possibilities Curve

The slope of the linear production possibilities curve in Exhibit 2-1 is constant; it is −2 pairs of skis/snowboard. In the magnified section of the curve shown here, the slope can be calculated between points B and B′. Expanding snowboard production to 51 snowboards per month from 50 snowboards requires a reduction in ski production to 98 pairs of skis per month from 100 pairs. The slope equals −2 pairs of skis/snowboard. To shift from B′ to B″, Alpine Sports must give up 2 more pairs of skis. The absolute value of the slope of a production possibilities curve measures the opportunity cost of an additional unit of the good on the horizontal axis.

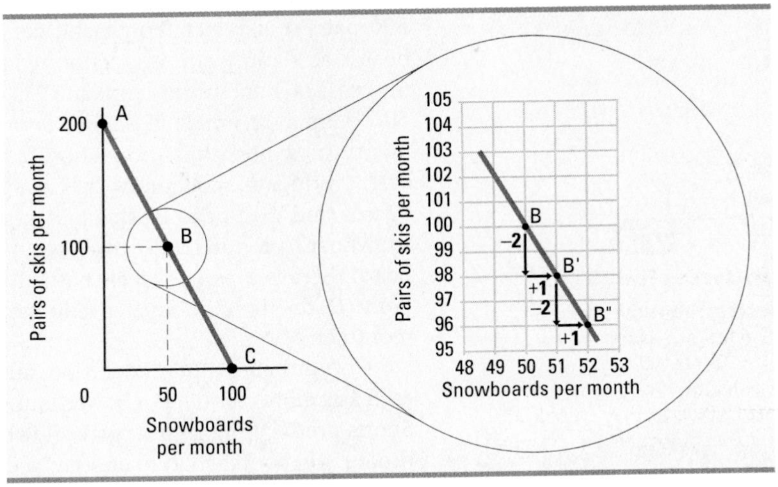

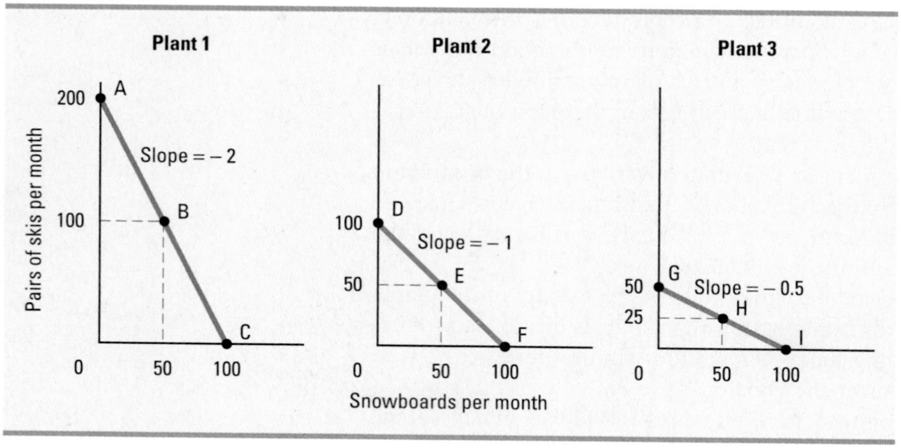

Exhibit 2-3

Production Possibilities at Three Plants

The slopes of the production possibilities curves for each plant differ. The steeper the curve, the greater the opportunity cost of an additional snowboard. Here, the opportunity cost is lowest at Plant 3 and greatest at Plant 1.

snowboard. In Plant 2, she must give up 1 pair of skis. We've already seen that an additional snowboard requires giving up 2 pairs of skis in Plant 1.

Comparative Advantage and the Production Possibilities Curve

To construct a combined production possibilities curve for all three plants, we can begin by asking how many pairs of skis Alpine Sports could produce if it were producing only skis. To find this quantity, we add up the values at the vertical intercepts of each of the production possibilities curves in Exhibit 2-3. These intercepts tell us the maximum number of pairs of skis each plant can produce. Plant 1 can produce 200 pairs of skis per month, Plant 2 can produce 100 pairs of skis per month, and Plant 3 can produce 50 pairs. Alpine Sports can thus produce 350 pairs of skis per month if it devotes its resources exclusively to ski production. In that case, it produces no snowboards.

Now suppose the firm decides to produce 100 snowboards. That will require shifting one of its plants out of ski production. Which one will it choose to shift? The sensible thing for it to do is to choose the plant in which snowboards have the lowest opportunity cost—Plant 3. It has an advantage not because it can produce more snowboards than the other plants (all the plants in this example are capable of producing up to 100 snowboards per month) but because it is the least productive plant for making skis. Producing a snowboard in Plant 3 requires giving up just half a pair of skis.

Economists say that an economy has a **comparative advantage** in producing a good or service if the opportunity cost of producing that good or service is lower for that economy than for any other. Plant 3 has a comparative advantage in snowboard production because it is the plant for which the opportunity cost of additional snowboards is lowest. To put this in terms of the production possibilities curve, Plant 3 has a comparative advantage in snowboard production (the good on the horizontal axis) because its production possibilities curve is the flattest of the three curves.

The combined production possibilities curve for the firm's three plants is shown in Exhibit 2-4. We begin at point A, with all three plants producing only skis. Production totals 350 pairs of skis per month and zero snowboards. If the firm were to produce 100 snowboards at Plant 3, ski production would fall by 50 pairs per month (recall that the opportunity cost of 1 snowboard at Plant 3 is half a pair of skis). That would bring ski production to 300 pairs, at point B. If Alpine Sports were to produce still more snowboards in a single month, it would shift production to Plant 2, the facility with the next-lowest opportunity cost. Producing 100 snowboards at Plant 2 would leave Alpine Sports producing 200 snowboards and 200 pairs of skis per month, at point C. If the firm were to switch entirely to snowboard production, Plant 1 would be the last to switch because the cost of each snowboard there is 2 pairs of skis. With all three plants producing only snowboards, the firm is at point D on the combined production possibilities curve, producing 300 snowboards per month and no skis.

Notice that this production possibilities curve, which is made up of linear segments from each assembly plant, has a bowed-out shape; the absolute value of its slope increases as Alpine Sports produces more and more snowboards. This is a result of transferring resources from the production of one good to another according to comparative advantage. We shall examine the significance of the bowed-out shape of the curve in the next section.

The Law of Increasing Opportunity Cost

We see in Exhibit 2-4 that, beginning at point A and producing only skis, Alpine Sports experiences higher and higher opportunity costs as it produces more snowboards. The fact that the opportunity cost of additional snowboards increases as the firm produces more of them is a reflection of an important economic law. The **law of increasing opportunity cost** holds that as an economy moves along its production possibilities curve in the direction of producing more of a particular good, the opportunity cost of additional units of that good will increase.

We've seen the law of increasing opportunity cost at work traveling from point A toward point D on the production possibilities curve in Exhibit 2-4. The opportunity cost of each of the first 100 snowboards equals half a pair of skis; each of the next 100 snowboards has an opportunity cost of 1 pair of skis, and each of the last 100 snowboards has an opportunity cost of 2 pairs of skis. The law also applies as the firm shifts from snowboards to skis. Suppose it begins at point D, producing 300 snowboards per month and no skis. It can shift to ski production at a relatively low cost at first. The opportunity cost of the first 200 pairs of skis is just 100 snowboards at Plant 1, a movement from point D to point C, or 0.5 snowboards per pair of skis. We would say that Plant 1 has a comparative advantage in ski production. The next 100 pairs of skis would be produced at Plant 2, where snowboard production would fall by100 snowboards per month. The opportunity cost of skis at Plant 2 is 1 snowboard per pair of skis. Plant 3 would be the last plant converted to ski production. There, 50 pairs of skis could be produced per month at a cost of 100 snowboards, or an opportunity cost of 2 snowboards per pair of skis.

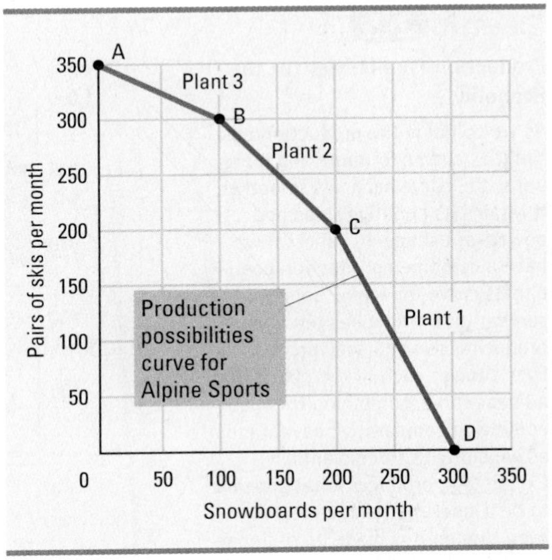

Exhibit 2-4

The Combined Production Possibilities Curve for Alpine Sports

The curve shown combines the production possibilities curves for each plant. At point A, Alpine Sports produces 350 pairs of skis per month and no snowboards. If the firm wishes to increase snowboard production, it will first use Plant 3, which has a comparative advantage in snowboards.

The bowed-out production possibilities curve for Alpine Sports illustrates the law of increasing opportunity cost. Scarcity implies that a production possibilities curve is downward sloping; the law of increasing opportunity cost implies that it will be bowed out, or concave, in shape.

The bowed-out curve of Exhibit 2-4 becomes smoother as we include more production facilities. Suppose Alpine Sports expands to ten plants, each with a linear production possibilities curve. Panel (a) of Exhibit 2-5 shows the combined curve for the expanded firm, constructed as we did in Exhibit 2-4. This production possibilities curve includes 10 linear segments and is almost a smooth curve. As we include more and more production units, the curve will become smoother and smoother. We will generally draw production possibilities curves for the economy as smooth, bowed-out curves, like the one in Panel (b). This production possibilities curve shows an economy that produces only skis and snowboards. Notice the curve still has a bowed-out shape; it still has a negative slope. Notice also that this curve has no numbers. Economists often use models such as the production possibilities model with graphs that show the general shapes of curves but that do not include numbers.

Movements Along the Production Possibilities Curve

We can use the production possibilities model to examine choices in the production of goods and services. In applying the model, we assume that the economy can produce two goods and we assume that technology and the factors of production available to the economy remain unchanged. In this section, we shall assume that the economy operates on its production possibilities curve so that an increase in the production of one good in the model implies a reduction in the production of the other.

Consider, for example, the choice to convert production from guns to butter that we examined in the chapter introduction. In this case we have categories of goods rather than specific goods. The categories are guns (defense goods and services) and butter (civilian goods and services). A choice to produce fewer guns is a choice to produce more butter. In the

Exhibit 2-5

Production Possibilities for the Economy

As we combine the production possibilities curves for more and more units, the curve becomes smoother. It retains its negative slope and bowed-out shape. In Panel (a) we have a combined production possibilities curve for Alpine Sports, assuming that it now has ten plants producing skis and snowboards. Even though each of the plants has a linear curve, combining them according to comparative advantage, as we did with three plants in Exhibit 2-4, produces what appears to be a smooth, nonlinear curve, even though it is made up of linear segments. In drawing production possibilities curves for the economy, we shall generally assume they are smooth and bowed out, as in Panel (b). This curve depicts an entire economy that produces only skis and snowboards.

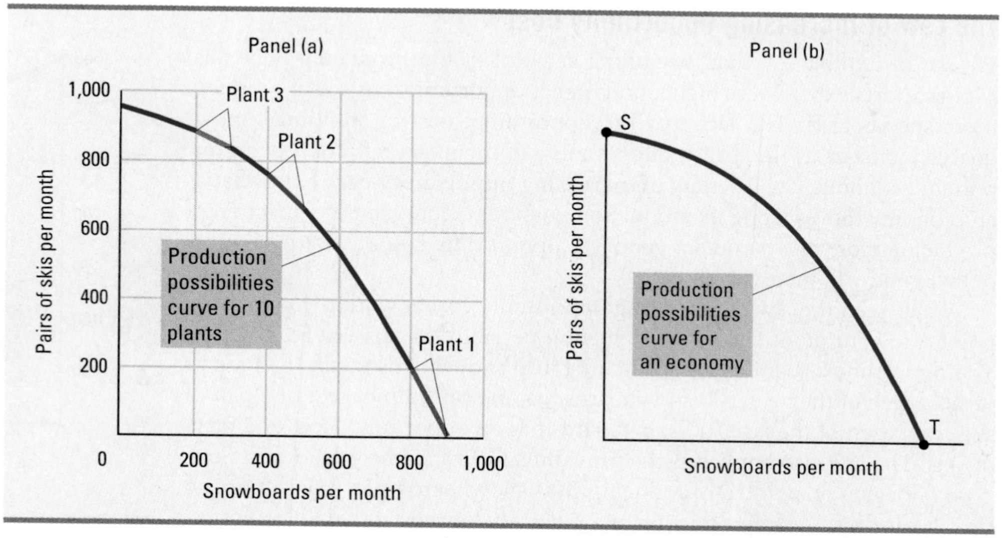

graph shown in Exhibit 2-6, this choice is a movement from point C to point D on the curve. The economy reduces gun production from GC to GD and increases butter production from BC to BD. The opportunity cost of this increased butter production thus equals GC - GD units of guns.

The law of increasing opportunity cost tells us that, as the economy moves along the production possibilities curve in the direction of more of one good, its opportunity cost will increase. We may conclude that, as the economy moved along this curve in the direction of greater production of civilian goods and services in the last decade, the opportunity cost of the additional butter began to increase. That's because the resources transferred from guns to butter had a greater and greater comparative advantage in producing guns.

The production possibilities model does not tell us where on the curve a particular economy will operate. Instead, it lays out the possibilities facing the economy. The United States, for example, chose to move along its production possibilities curve to produce more butter and fewer guns after its old enemy, the Soviet Union, collapsed. We'll see in Chapter 3 how choices about what to produce are made in the marketplace.

Exhibit 2-6

From Guns to Butter

Here an economy that can produce two categories of goods, guns and butter, begins at point C on its production possibilities curve. It produces G_C units of guns and B_C units of butter per period. A movement from C to D requires shifting resources out of gun production and into butter production. The gain in butter production, to B_D units of butter per period, has an opportunity cost of reduced gun production. Gun production falls by $G_C - G_D$ units per period.

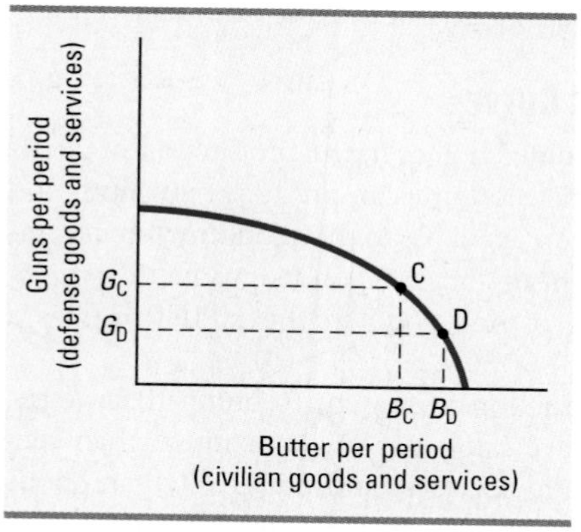

Producing On Versus Producing Inside the Production Possibilities Curve

An economy that is operating inside its production possibilities curve could, by moving onto it, produce more of all the goods and services that people value, such as food, housing, education, medical care, and music. Increasing the availability of these goods would improve the standard of living. Economists conclude that it's better to be on the production possibilities curve than inside it.

Two things could leave an economy operating at a point inside its production possibilities curve. First, the economy might fail to use fully the resources available to it. Second, it might not allocate resources on the basis of comparative advantage. In either case, production within the production possibilities curve implies the economy could improve its performance.

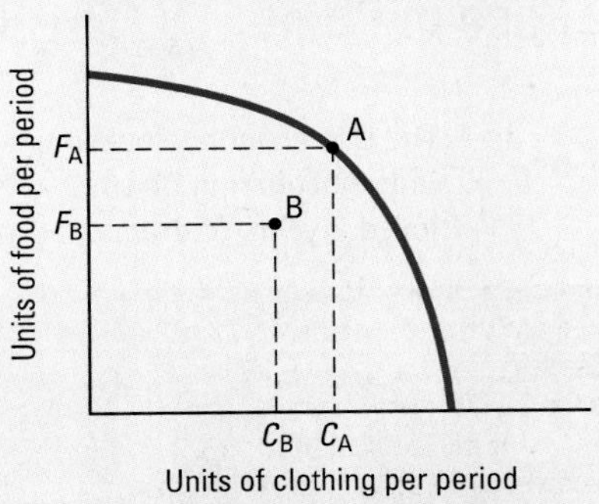

Exhibit 2-7

Idle Factors and Production

The production possibilities curve shown suggests an economy that can produce two goods, food and clothing. As a result of a failure to achieve full employment, the economy operates at a point such as B, producing F_B units of food and C_B units of clothing per period. Putting its factors of production to work allows a move to the production possibilities curve, to a point such as A. The production of both goods rises.

Idle Factors of Production Suppose an economy fails to put all its factors of production to work. Some workers are without jobs, some buildings are without occupants, some fields are without crops. Because an economy's production possibilities curve assumes the full use of the factors of production available to it, the failure to use some factors results in a level of production that lies inside the production possibilities curve.

If all the factors of production that are available for use under current market conditions are being utilized, the economy has achieved **full employment.** An economy can't operate on its production possibilities curve unless it has full employment.

Exhibit 2-7 shows an economy that can produce food and clothing. If it chooses to produce at point A, for example, it can produce F_A units of food and C_A units of clothing. Now suppose that a large fraction of the economy's workers lose their jobs, so the economy no longer makes full use of one factor of production: labor. In this example, production moves to point B, where the economy produces less food (F_B) and less clothing (C_B) than at point A. We often think of the loss of jobs in terms of the workers; they've lost a chance to work and to earn income. But the production possibilities model points to another loss: goods and services the economy could have produced that aren't being produced.

Inefficient Production Now suppose Alpine Sports is fully employing its factors of production. Could it still operate inside its production possibilities curve? Could an economy that is using all its factors of production still produce less than it could? The answer is "Yes," and the key lies in comparative advantage. An economy achieves a point on its production possibilities curve only if it allocates its factors of production on the basis of comparative advantage. If it fails to do that, it will operate inside the curve.

Suppose that, as before, Alpine Sports has been producing only skis. With all three of its plants producing skis, it can produce 350 pairs of skis per year. The firm then starts producing snowboards. This time, however, imagine that Alpine Sports switches plants from skis to snowboards in numerical order: Plant 1 first, Plant 2 second, and then Plant 3. Exhibit 2-8 illustrates the result. Instead of the bowed-out production possibilities curve ABCD, we get a bowed-in curve, AB′C′D. Suppose that Alpine Sports is producing 100 snowboards and 150 pairs of skis at point B′. Had the firm based its production choices on comparative advantage, it would have switched Plant 3 to snowboards and then Plant 2, so it would have operated at point C. It would be producing more snowboards and more pairs of skis—and using the same quantities of factors of production it was using at B′. When an economy is operating on its production possibilities curve, we say that it is engaging in **efficient production.** If it is using the same quantities of factors of production but is operating inside its production possibilities curve, it is engaging in **inefficient production.** Inefficient production implies that the economy could be producing more goods without using additional labor, capital, or natural resources.

Points on the production possibilities curve thus satisfy two conditions: the economy is making full use of its factors of production, and it is making efficient use of its factors of production. If there are idle or inefficiently allocated factors of production, the economy will operate inside the production possibilities curve. Thus, the production possibilities curve not only shows what can be produced; it provides insight into how goods and services should be produced. It suggests that to obtain efficiency in production, factors of production should be allocated on the basis of comparative advantage. Further, the economy must make full use of its factors of production if it is to produce the goods and services it is capable of producing.

Case in Point: The Cost of the Great Depression

The U.S. economy looked very healthy in the beginning of 1929. It had enjoyed 7 years of dramatic growth and unprecedented prosperity. Its resources were fully employed; it was operating quite close to its production possibilities curve.

In the summer of 1929, however, things started going wrong. Production and employment fell. They continued to fall for several years. By 1933, more than 25 percent of the nation's workers had lost their jobs. Production had plummeted by almost 30 percent. The economy had moved well within its production possibilities curve.

Output began to grow after 1933, but the economy continued to have vast numbers of idle workers, idle factories, and idle farms. These resources were not put back to work fully until 1942, after the U.S. entry into World War II demanded mobilization of the economy's factors of production.

Between 1929 and 1942, the economy produced 25 percent fewer goods and services than it would have if its resources had been fully employed. That was a loss, measured in today's dollars, of nearly $3 trillion. In material terms, the forgone output represented a greater cost than the United States would ultimately spend in World War II. The Great Depression was a costly experience indeed.

Specialization

The production possibilities model suggests that specialization will occur. **Specialization** implies that an economy is producing the goods and services in which it has a comparative advantage. If Alpine Sports selects point C in Exhibit 2-8, for example, it will assign Plant 1 exclusively to ski production and Plants 2 and 3 exclusively to snowboard production.

Such specialization is typical in an economic system. Workers, for example, specialize in particular fields in which they have a comparative advantage. People work and use the income they earn to buy goods and services from people who have a comparative advantage in doing other things. The result is a far greater quantity of goods and services than would be available without this specialization.

Exhibit 2-8

Efficient Versus Inefficient Production

When factors of production are allocated on a basis other than comparative advantage, the result is inefficient production. Suppose Alpine Sports operates the three plants we examined in Exhibit 2-3. Suppose further that all three plants are devoted exclusively to ski production; the firm operates at A. Now suppose that, to increase snowboard production, it transfers plants in numerical order: Plant 1 first, then Plant 2, and finally Plant 3. The result is the bowed-in curve AB′C′D. Production on the production possibilities curve ABCD requires that factors of production be transferred according to comparative advantage.

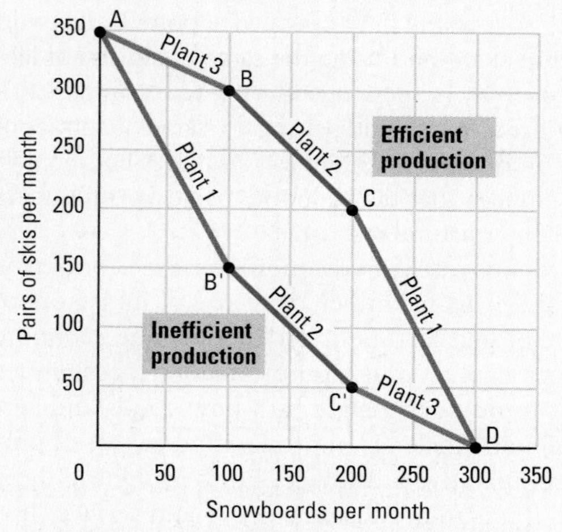

Think about what life would be like without specialization. Imagine that you are suddenly completely cut off from the rest of the economy. You must produce everything you consume; you obtain nothing from anyone else. Would you be able to consume what you consume now? Clearly not. It's hard to imagine that most of us could even survive in such a setting. The gains we achieve through specialization are enormous.

Nations specialize as well. Much of the land in the United States has a comparative advantage in agricultural production and is devoted to that activity. Hong Kong, with its huge population and tiny endowment of land, allocates virtually none of its land to agricultural use;

that option would be too costly. Its land is devoted largely to manufacturing and the provision of housing for manufacturing workers.

Checklist

- A production possibilities curve shows the combinations of two goods an economy is capable of producing.
- The downward slope of the production possibilities curve is an implication of scarcity.
- The bowed-out shape of the production possibilities curve results from allocating resources based on comparative advantage. Such an allocation implies that the law of increasing opportunity cost will hold.
- An economy that fails to make full and efficient use of its factors of production will operate inside its production possibilities curve.
- Specialization means that an economy is producing the goods and services in which it has a comparative advantage.

Try It Yourself 2-2

Suppose a manufacturing firm is equipped to produce radios or calculators. It has two plants, Plant R and Plant S, at which it can produce these goods. Given the labor and the capital available at both plants, it can produce the combinations of the two goods at the two plants shown at the right.

Put calculators on the vertical axis and radios on the horizontal axis. Draw the production possibilities curve for Plant R. On a separate graph, draw the production possibilities curve for Plant S. Which plant has a comparative advantage in calculators? In radios? Now draw the combined curves for the two plants. Suppose the firm decides to produce 100 radios. Where will it produce them? How many calculators will it be able to produce? Where will it produce the calculators?

Output per day, Plant R

Combination	Calculators	Radios
A	100	0
B	50	25
C	0	50

Output per day, Plant S

Combination	Calculators	Radios
D	50	0
E	25	50
F	0	100

Applications of the Production Possibilities Model

The production possibilities curve gives us a model of an economy. The model provides powerful insights about the real world, insights that help us to answer some important questions: How does trade between two countries affect the quantities of goods available to people? What determines the rate at which production will increase over time? What is the role of economic freedom in the economy? In this section we explore applications of the model to questions of international trade, economic growth, and the choice of an economic system.

Comparative Advantage and International Trade

One of the most powerful implications of the concepts of comparative advantage and the production possibilities curve relates to international trade. We can think of different nations as being equivalent to Christie Rider's plants. Each will have a comparative advantage in certain activities, and efficient world production requires that each nation specialize in those activities in which it has a comparative advantage. A failure to allocate resources in this way means that world production falls inside the production possibilities curve; more of each good could be produced by relying on comparative advantage.

If nations specialize, then they must rely on each other. They will sell the goods in which they specialize and purchase other goods from other nations. Suppose, for example, that the world consists of two countries that can each produce two goods: the United States and Japan can produce steel and robots used in manufacturing. Suppose they can produce the two goods according to the tables in Panels (a) and (b) of Exhibit 2-9. We have simplified this example by assuming that each country has a linear production possibilities curve; the curves are plotted below the tables in Panels (a) and (b). Each country has a separate production possibilities curve; the two have been combined to illustrate a world production possibilities curve in Panel (c) of the exhibit.

The world production possibilities curve assumes that resources are allocated between robot and steel production based on comparative advantage. Notice that, even with only two economies and the assumption of linear production possibilities curves for each, the combined curve still has a bowed-out shape. At point H, for example, the United States specializes in robots, while Japan produces only steel. World production equals 400 units of each good. In this situation, we would expect the United States to export robots to Japan while Japan exports steel to the United States.

But suppose the countries refuse to trade; each insists on producing its own steel and robots. Suppose further that each chooses to produce at the midpoint of its own production possibilities curve. The United States produces 100 units of steel and 200 robots per period, while Japan produces 200 units of steel and 100 robots per period. World production thus totals 300 units of each good per period; the world operates at point Q in Exhibit 2-9. If the two countries were willing to move from isolation to trade, the world could achieve an increase in the production of both goods. Producing at point H requires no more resources, no more effort than production at Q. It does, however, require that the world's resources be allocated on the basis of comparative advantage.

The implications of our model for trade are powerful indeed. First, we see that trade allows the production of more of all goods and services. Restrictions on trade thus reduce production of goods and services. Second, we see a lesson often missed in discussions of trade: a nation's trade policy has nothing to do with its level of employment of its factors of pro-

Exhibit 2-9

Production Possibility Curves and Trade

Suppose the world consists of two countries: Japan and the United States. They can each produce two goods: steel and robots. In this example, we assume that each country has a linear production possibilities curve, as shown in Panels (a) and (b). The United States has a comparative advantage in robot production; Japan has a comparative advantage in steel production. With free trade, the world can operate on the bowed-out curve GHI, shown in Panel (c). If the countries refuse to trade, the world will operate inside its production possibilities curve. If, for example, each country operates at the midpoint of its production possibilities curve, the world will produce 300 units of steel and 300 robots per period at point Q. If each country were to specialize in the good in which it has a comparative advantage, world production could move to a point such as H, with more of both goods produced.

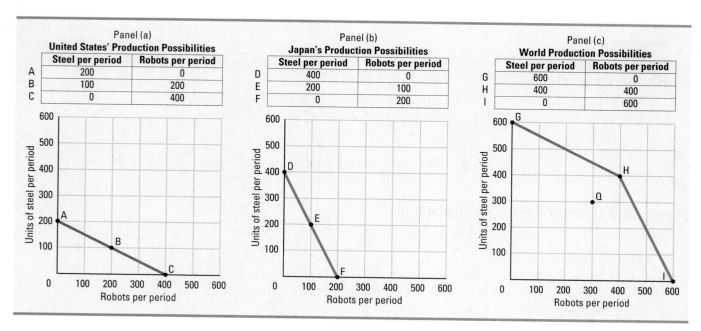

Panel (a)
United States' Production Possibilities

	Steel per period	Robots per period
A	200	0
B	100	200
C	0	400

Panel (b)
Japan's Production Possibilities

	Steel per period	Robots per period
D	400	0
E	200	100
F	0	200

Panel (c)
World Production Possibilities

	Steel per period	Robots per period
G	600	0
H	400	400
I	0	600

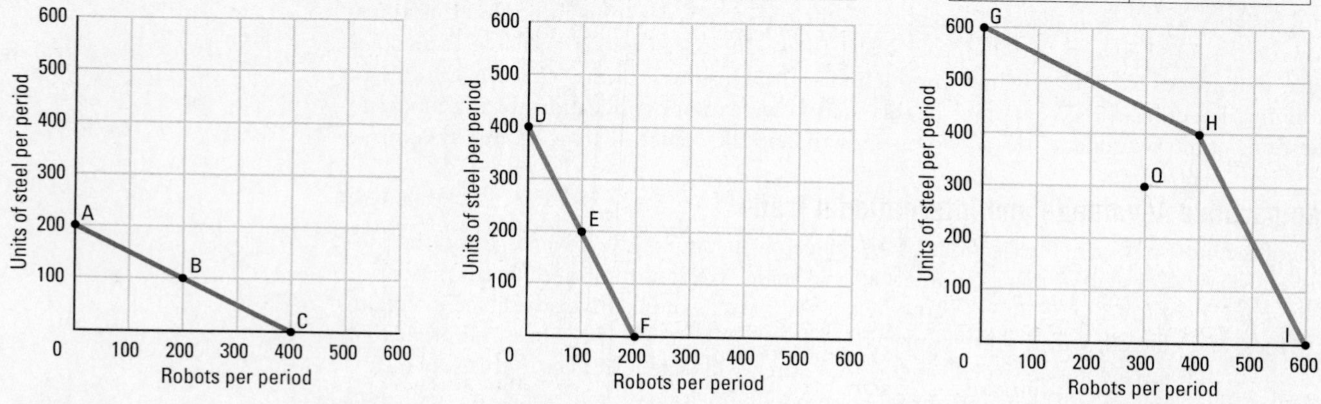

Case in Point The Expansion of Free Trade

The proposition that free trade will improve living standards has proved to be one of the most important ideas ever produced by economists. Powerful interest groups in every country seek to block trade if it hurts them. Yet, in the face of such pressures, the world has generally moved to freer and freer trade over the last two centuries.

One example of the power of free trade has been the success of the United States. The framers of the U.S. Constitution explicitly barred states from trying to limit the import of goods and services produced in other states. In effect, the constitution establishes a free trade zone within the borders of this country. That feature has prevented trade wars from breaking out among the states. It has prevented actions that would force the United States to operate inside, rather than on, its production possibilities curve.

Recent progress toward free trade has been dramatic. A trade agreement between the United States and Canada was signed in 1987; it allows virtually unrestricted movement of goods and services between the two countries. The North American Free Trade Agreement (NAFTA) added Mexico in 1993 to a free trade zone that incorporated all of North America. Preliminary discussions are under way to extend the concept throughout the western hemisphere. By the beginning of 1993, members of the European Union (EU) had taken a giant step toward creating the same situation in Europe as they removed restrictions limiting the flow of goods and services among member countries. However, substantial restrictions still limit imports of goods and services from countries outside the EU. In 1994, nations of the Pacific Rim, including the United States, Japan, and China, agreed to create a free trade zone for the Pacific Rim early in the next century.

Even among countries that restrict trade, the barriers have been coming down. Countries all over the world are moving in the direction of free trade—trade that will allow the world to move closer to its production possibilities curve.

duction. In our example, when the United States and Japan do not engage in trade and produce at the midpoints of each of their respective production possibilities curves, *they each have full employment.* With trade, the two nations still operate on their respective production possibilities curves: *they each have full employment.* Trade certainly redistributes employment in the two countries. In the United States, employment shifts from steel to robots. In Japan, it shifts from robots to steel. Once the shift is made, though, there is no effect on employment in either country.

Nearly all economists agree that largely unrestricted trade between countries is desirable; restrictions on trade generally force the world to operate inside its production possibilities curve. In some cases restrictions on trade could be desirable, but in the main, free trade promotes greater production of goods and services for the world's people. The role of international trade is explored in greater detail in subsequent chapters of this book.

Economic Growth

An increase in the physical quantity or in the quality of factors of production available to an economy or a technological gain will allow the economy to produce more goods and services; it will shift the economy's production possibilities curve outward. The process through which an economy achieves an outward shift in its production possibilities curve is called **economic growth.** An outward shift in a production possibilities curve is illustrated in Exhibit 2-10. In Panel (a), a point such as N is not attainable; it lies outside the production possibilities curve. Growth shifts the curve outward, as in Panel (b), making previously unattainable levels of production possible.

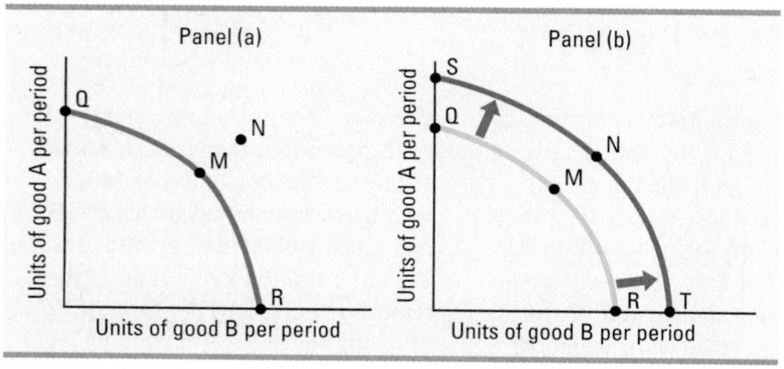

Exhibit 2-10

Economic Growth and the Production Possibilities Curve

An economy capable of producing two goods, A and B, is initially operating at point M on production possibilities curve QMR in Panel (a). Given this production possibilities curve, the economy could not produce a combination such as that shown by point N, which lies outside the curve. An increase in the factors of production available to the economy would shift the curve outward to SNT, allowing the choice of a point such as N, at which more of both goods will be produced.

The Sources of Economic Growth Economic growth implies an outward shift in an economy's production possibilities curve. Recall that when we draw such a curve, we assume that the economy's factors of production and its technology are unchanged. Changing these will shift the curve. Anything that increases the quantity or quality of the factors of production available to the economy or that improves the technology available to the economy contributes to economic growth.

Consider, for example, the dramatic gains in human capital that have occurred in the United States during the past century. In 1900, about 3.5 percent of U.S. workers had completed a high school education. By 2000, that percentage rose almost to 90. Fewer than 1 percent of the workers in 1900 had graduated from college; as late as 1940 only 3.5 percent had graduated from college. By 2000, nearly 30 percent had graduated from college. In addition to being better educated, today's workers have received more and better training on the job. They bring far more economically useful knowledge and skills to their work than did workers a century ago.

Moreover, the technological changes that have occurred within the past 100 years have greatly reduced the time and effort required to produce most goods and services. Automated production has become commonplace. Innovations in transportation (automobiles, trucks, and airplanes) have made the movement of goods and people cheaper and faster. Computers have transformed the workplace. A dizzying array of new materials is available for manufacturing.

Look again at the technological changes of the last few years described in the Case in Point on recent advances in technology. Those examples of technological progress through applications of computer technology—from new ways of mapping oil deposits to new methods to cut food wastes at McDonald's—helped propel the U.S. economy to dramatic gains in its ability to produce goods and services. They have helped shift the U.S. production possibilities curve outward. They have helped fuel economic growth.

Exhibit 2-11 summarizes the factors that have contributed to U.S. economic growth in the past century. We see that, in the first half of the century, increases in the quantities of capital and of labor were the most important factors in economic growth. In the second half of the century, though, increases in human capital and advances in technology have played the most important roles.

Waiting for Growth One key to growth is, in effect, the willingness to wait, to postpone current consumption in order to enhance future productive capability. When Stone Age people fashioned the first tools, they were spending time building capital rather than engaging in consumption. They delayed current consumption to enhance their future consumption; the tools they made would make them more productive in the future.

Resources society could have used to produce consumer goods are being used to produce new capital goods and new knowledge for production instead—all to enhance future production. As we saw in Exhibit 2-11, an even more important source of growth in the United States has been increased human capital. Increases in human capital often require the postponement of consumption. If you're a college student, you're engaged in precisely this effort. You are devoting time to study that could have been spent working, earning income, and thus engaging in a higher level of consumption. If you're like most students, you're making this choice to postpone consumption because you expect it will allow you to earn more income, and thus enjoy greater consumption, in the future.

Think of an economy as being able to produce two goods, capital and consumer goods (those destined for immediate use by consumers). By focusing on the production of consumer goods, the people in the economy will be able to enjoy a higher standard of

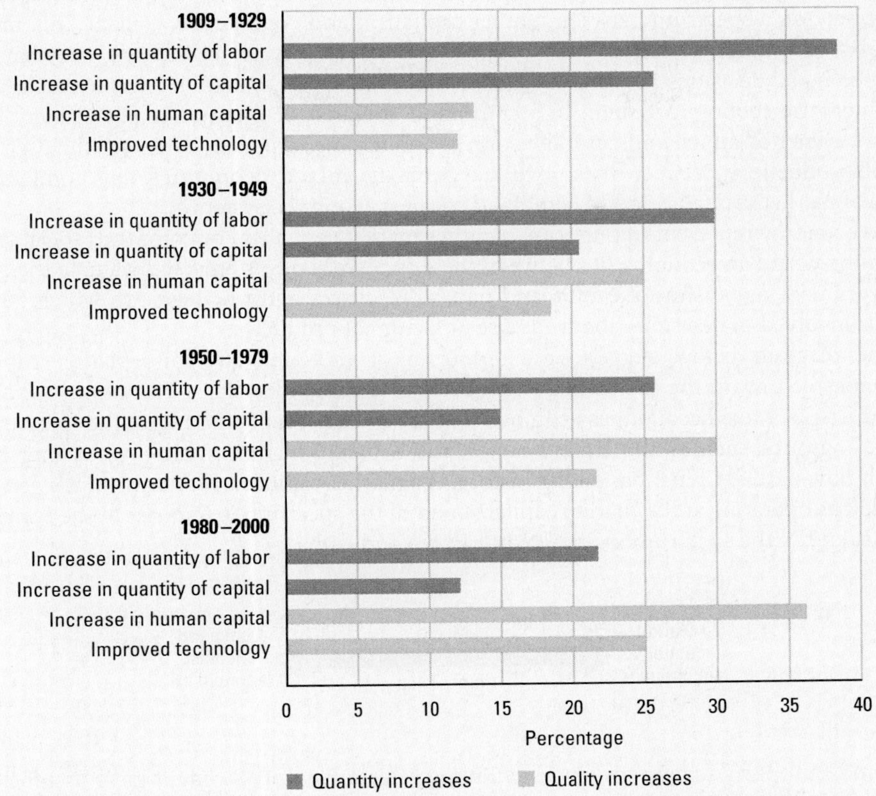

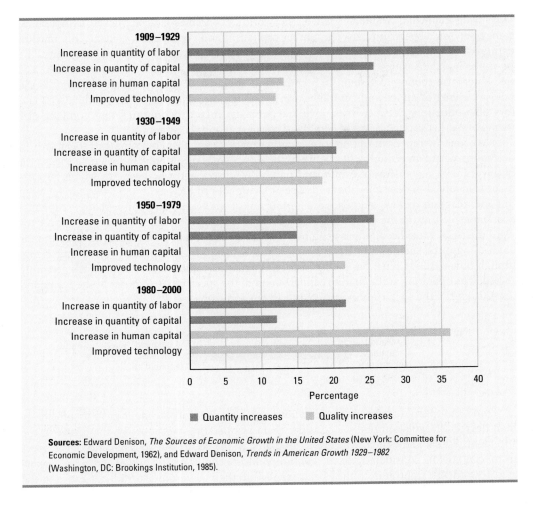

Sources: Edward Denison, *The Sources of Economic Growth in the United States* (New York: Committee for Economic Development, 1962), and Edward Denison, *Trends in American Growth 1929–1982* (Washington, DC: Brookings Institution, 1985).

Exhibit 2-11

Sources of U.S. Economic Growth, 1909–2000

Total output during the period shown increased 13-fold. The chart shows the percentage of this increase accounted for by increases in the quantity of labor and of capital and by increases in human capital and improvements in technology. In the first half of the twentieth century, gains in the quantities of these inputs were most important. In the second half of the century, qualitative changes dominated.

living today. If they reduce their consumption—and their standard of living—today to enhance their ability to produce goods and services in the future, they will be able to shift their production possibilities curve outward. That may allow them to produce even more consumer goods. A decision for greater growth typically involves the sacrifice of present consumption.

Arenas for Choice: A Comparison of Economic Systems

Under what circumstances will a nation achieve efficiency in the use of its factors of production? The discussion above suggested that Christie Rider would have an incentive to allocate her plants efficiently because by doing so she could achieve greater output of skis and snowboards than would be possible from inefficient production. But why would she want to produce more of these two goods—or of any goods? Why would decisionmakers throughout the economy want to achieve such efficiency?

Economists assume that privately owned firms seek to maximize their profits. The drive to maximize profits will lead firms such as Alpine Sports to allocate resources efficiently to gain as much production as possible from their factors of production. But whether firms will seek to maximize profits depends on the nature of the economic system within which they operate.

Classifying Economic Systems Each of the world's economies can be viewed as operating somewhere on a spectrum between market capitalism and command socialism. In a **market capitalist economy,** resources are generally owned by private individuals who have the power to make decisions about their use. A market capitalist system is often referred to as a free enterprise economic system. In a **command socialist economy,** the government is the primary owner of capital and natural resources and has broad power to allocate the use of factors of production. Between these two categories lie **mixed economies** that combine elements of market capitalist and of command socialist economic systems.

No economy represents a pure case of either market capitalism or command socialism. To determine where an economy lies between these two types of systems, we evaluate the extent of government ownership of capital and natural resources and the degree to which government is involved in decisions about the use of factors of production.

The diagram below suggests the spectrum of economic systems. Market capitalist economies lie toward the left end of this spectrum; command socialist economies appear toward the right. Mixed economies lie in between. The market capitalist end of the spectrum includes countries such as the United States, the United Kingdom, and Chile. Hong Kong, though now part of China, has a long history as a market capitalist economy, and is generally regarded as operating at the market capitalist end of the spectrum. Countries at the command socialist end of the spectrum include North Korea and Cuba.

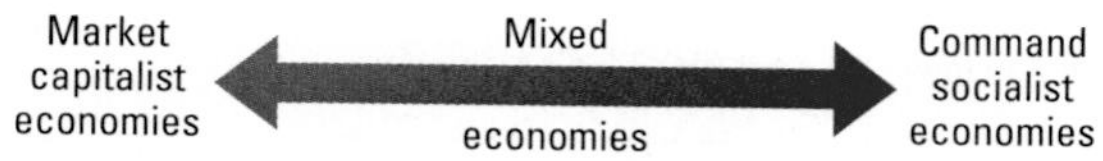

Some European economies, such as France, Germany, and Sweden, have a sufficiently high degree of regulation that we consider them as operating more toward the center of the spectrum. Russia and China, which long operated at the command socialist end of the spectrum, can now be considered mixed economies. Most economies in Latin America once operated toward the right end of the spectrum. While their governments did not exercise the extensive ownership of capital and natural resources that are one characteristic of command socialist systems, their governments did impose extensive regulations. Many of these nations are in the process of carrying out economic reforms that will move them further in the direction of market capitalism.

The global shift toward market capitalist economic systems that occurred in the 1980s and 1990s was in large part the result of three important features of such economies. First, the emphasis on individual ownership and decisionmaking power has generally yielded greater individual freedom than has been available under command socialist or some more heavily regulated mixed economic systems that lie toward the command socialist end of the spectrum. People seeking political, religious, and economic freedom have thus gravitated toward market capitalism. Second, market economies are more likely than other systems to allocate resources on the basis of comparative advantage. They thus tend to generate higher levels of production and income than do other economic systems. Third, market capitalist-type systems appear to be the most conducive to entrepreneurial activity.

Suppose Christie Rider had the same three plants we considered earlier in this chapter but was operating in a mixed economic system with extensive government regulation. In such a system, she might be prohibited from transferring resources from one use to another to achieve the gains possible from comparative advantage. If she were operating under a command socialist system, she wouldn't be the owner of the plants and thus would be unlikely to profit from their efficient use. If that were the case, there is no reason to believe she would make any effort to assure the efficient use of the three plants. Generally speaking, it is economies toward the market capitalist end of the spectrum that offer the greatest inducement to allocate resources on the basis of comparative advantage. They tend to be more productive and to deliver higher material standards of living than do economies that operate at or near the command socialist end of the spectrum.

Market capitalist economies rely on economic freedom. Indeed, one way we can assess the degree to which a country can be considered market capitalist is by the degree of economic freedom it permits. Several organizations have attempted to compare economic freedom in various countries. One of the most extensive comparisons is a joint annual effort by the Heritage Foundation and the *Wall Street Journal*. The 1998 rating was based on policies in effect in 161 nations early that year. The report ranked each nation on the basis of such things as the degree of regulation of firms, tax levels, and restrictions on international trade. Hong Kong ranked as the freest economy in the world. Cuba and North Korea tied for the dubious distinction of being the least free.

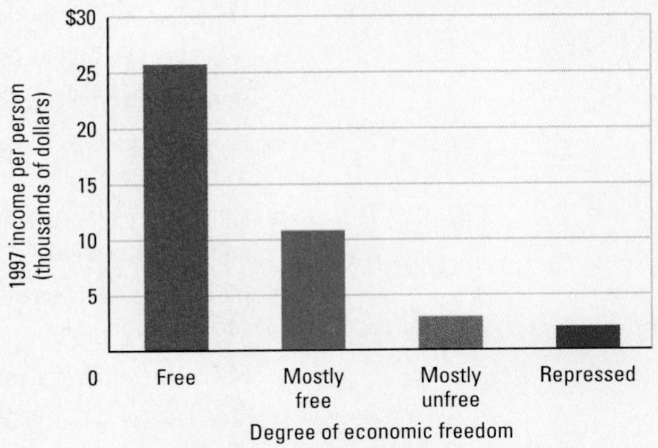

Sources: Income figures are from the World Bank, *World Development Report 1998/1999,* Table 1, and *Data Sources,* Table 1, pp. 191-192, 251; freedom rankings are given in Bryan T. Johnson, Kim R. Bolling, and Melanie Kirkpatrick, "Freedom Is the Surest Path to Prosperity," *Wall Street Journal,* 1 December 1998, p. A22.

Exhibit 2-12

Economic Freedom and Income

The chart gives 1997 figures for income per person for countries whose degree of economic freedom was rated "free," "mostly free," "mostly unfree," and "repressed" by the Heritage Foundation and the *Wall Street Journal.* Countries with higher degrees of economic freedom tended to have higher incomes.

It seems reasonable to expect that the greater the degree of economic freedom a country permits, the greater the amount of income per person it will generate. This proposition is illustrated in Exhibit 2-12. The group of countries categorized as "free" generated the highest incomes as estimated by the World Bank; those rated as "repressed" had the lowest. We must be wary of slipping into the fallacy of false cause by concluding from this evidence that economic freedom generates higher incomes. It could be that higher incomes lead nations to opt for greater economic freedom. But in this case, it seems reasonable to conclude that, in general, economic freedom does lead to higher incomes.

Government in a Market Economy

The production possibilities model provides a menu of choices among alternative combinations of goods and services. Given those choices, which combinations will be produced?

In a market economy, this question is answered in large part through the interaction of individual buyers and sellers. We will examine that interaction in Chapter 3. As we have already seen, government plays a role as well. It may seek to encourage greater consumption of some goods and discourage consumption of others. In the United States, for example, taxes imposed on cigarettes discourage smoking, while special treatment of property taxes and mortgage interest in the federal income tax encourages home ownership. Government may try to stop the production and consumption of some goods altogether, as many governments do with drugs such as heroin and cocaine. Government may supplement the private consumption of some goods by producing more of them itself, as many U.S. cities do with golf courses and tennis courts. In other cases, there may be no private market for a good or service at all. In the guns versus butter choice outlined at the beginning of this chapter, the U.S. government is virtually the sole provider of national defense.

All nations also rely on government to provide defense, enforce laws, and redistribute income. Even market economies rely on government to regulate the activities of private firms, to protect the environment, to provide education, and to produce a wide range of other goods and services. Government's role may be limited in a market economy, but it remains fundamentally important.

Checklist

- The ideas of comparative advantage and specialization suggest that restrictions on international trade are likely to reduce production of goods and services.
- Economic growth is the result of increasing the quantity or quality of an economy's factors of production and of advances in technology.
- Policies to encourage growth generally involve postponing consumption to increase capital and human capital.
- Market capitalist economies have generally proved more productive than mixed or command socialist economies.
- Government plays a crucial role in any market economy.

Try It Yourself 2-3

Draw a production possibilities curve for an economy that can produce two goods, CD players and jackets. You don't have numbers for this one—just draw a curve with the usual bowed-out shape. Put the quantity of CD players per period on the vertical axis and the quantity of jackets per period on the horizontal axis. Now mark a point A *on the curve you have drawn; extend dotted lines from this point to the horizontal and vertical axes. Mark the initial quantities of the two goods as* CD_A *and* J_A*, respectively. Explain why, in the absence of economic growth, an increase in jacket production requires a reduction in the production of CD players. Now show how economic growth could lead to an increase in the production of both goods.*

A Look Back

In Chapter 1 we saw that economics deals with choices. In Chapter 2 we have examined more carefully the range of choices in production that must be made in any economy. In particular, we looked at choices involving the allocation of an economy's factors of production: labor, capital, and natural resources.

In any economy, the level of technology plays a key role in determining how productive the factors of production will be. In a market economy, entrepreneurs organize factors of production and act to introduce technological change.

The production possibilities model is a device that assists us in thinking about many of the choices about resource allocation in an economy. The model assumes that the economy has factors of production that are fixed in both quantity and quality. When illustrated graphically, the production possibilities model typically limits our analysis to two goods. Given the economy's factors of production and technology, the economy can produce various combinations of the two goods. If it uses its factors of production efficiently and has full employment, it will be operating on the production possibilities curve.

Two characteristics of the production possibilities curve are particularly important. First, it is downward sloping. This reflects the scarcity of the factors of production available to the economy; producing more of one good requires giving up some of the other. Second, the curve is bowed out. Another way of saying this is to say that the curve gets steeper as we move from left to right; the absolute value of its slope is increasing. Producing each additional unit of the good on the horizontal axis requires a greater sacrifice of the good on the vertical axis than did the previous units produced. This fact, called the law of increasing opportunity cost, is the inevitable result of efficient choices in production—choices based on comparative advantage.

The production possibilities model has important implications for international trade. It suggests that free trade will allow countries to specialize in the production of goods and services in which they have a comparative advantage. This specialization increases the production of all goods and services.

Increasing the quantity or quality of factors of production and/or improving technology will shift the production possibilities curve outward. This process is called economic growth. In the last 50 years, economic growth in the United States has resulted chiefly from increases in human capital and from technological advance.

Choices concerning the use of scarce resources take place within the context of a set of institutional arrangements that define an economic system. The principal distinctions between systems lie in the degree to which ownership of capital and natural resources and decision-making authority over scarce resources are held by government or by private individuals. Economic systems include market capitalist, mixed, and command socialist economies. An increasing body of evidence suggests that market capitalist economies tend to be most productive; many command socialist and mixed economies are moving in the direction of market capitalist systems.

The presumption in favor of market-based systems does not preclude a role for government. Government is necessary to provide the system of laws on which market systems are founded. It may also be used to provide certain goods and services, to help individuals in need, and to regulate the actions of individuals and firms.

A Look Ahead The production possibilities model suggests the set of answers to the "what to produce" question. It also provides insights into how goods and services should be produced. Chapter 3 suggests how the "what" and "for whom" questions are answered in a market economy.

Terms and Concepts for Review

production possibilities model, **38**
economic system, **38**
factors of production, **38**
utility, **38**
labor, **39**
capital, **39**
natural resources, **39**
human capital, **39**
financial capital, **40**
technology, **40**
entrepreneur, **40**
production possibilities curve, **42**
comparative advantage, **44**
law of increasing opportunity cost, **45**
full employment, **47**
efficient production, **47**
inefficient production, **47**
specialization, **48**
economic growth, **51**
market capitalist economy, **54**
command socialist economy, **54**
mixed economies, **54**

For Discussion

1. How does a college education increase one's human capital?
2. Why does a downward-sloping production possibilities curve imply that factors of production are scarce?
3. In what way are the bowed-out shape of the production possibilities curve and the law of increasing opportunity cost related?

4. What is the relationship between the concept of comparative advantage and the law of increasing opportunity cost?
5. Suppose an economy can produce two goods, A and B. It is now operating at point E on production possibilities curve RT. An improvement in the technology available to produce good A shifts the curve to ST, and the economy selects point E′. How does this change affect the opportunity cost of producing an additional unit of good B?

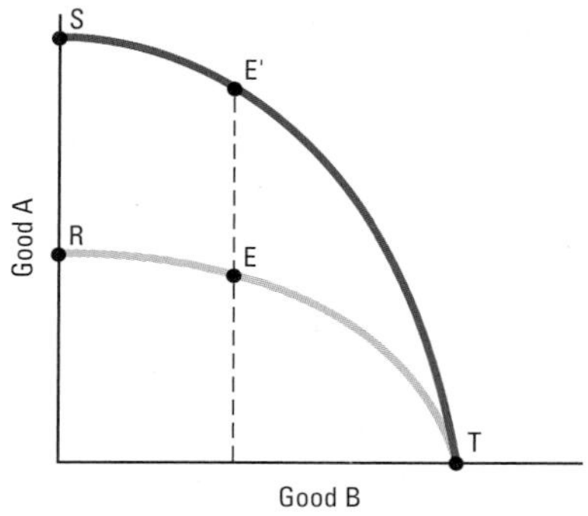

6. Could a nation's production possibilities curve ever shift inward? Explain what such a shift would mean, and discuss events that might cause such a shift to occur.
7. Suppose blue-eyed people were banned from working. How would this affect a nation's production possibilities curve?
8. Evaluate this statement: "The U.S. economy could achieve greater growth by devoting fewer resources to consumption and more to investment; it follows that such a shift would be desirable."
9. Two countries, Sportsland and Foodland, have similar total quantities of labor, capital, and natural resources. Both can produce two goods, figs and footballs. Sportsland's resources are particularly well suited to the production of footballs but are not very productive in producing figs. Foodland's resources are very productive when used for figs but aren't capable of producing many footballs. In which country is the cost of additional footballs generally greater? Explain.
10. Suppose a country is committed to using its resources based on the reverse of comparative advantage doctrine: it first transfers those resources for which the cost is greatest, not lowest. Describe this country's production possibilities curve.
11. The U.S. Constitution bans states from restricting imports of goods and services from other states. Suppose this restriction didn't exist, and that states were allowed to limit imports of goods and services produced in other states. How do you think this would affect U.S. output? Explain.
12. By 1993, nations in the European Union (EU) had eliminated all barriers to the flow of goods, services, labor, and capital across their borders. Even such things as consumer protection laws and the types of plugs required to plug in appliances have been standardized to ensure that there will be no barriers to trade. How do you think this elimination of trade barriers affected EU output?
13. How did the technological changes described in the Case in Point "Technology Cuts Costs, Boosts Productivity and Profits" affect the production possibilities curve for the United States?

Problems

1. The nation of Leisureland can produce two goods, bicycles and bowling balls. The western region of Leisureland can, if it devotes all its resources to bicycle production, produce 100 bicycles per month. Alternatively, it could devote all its resources to bowling balls and produce 400 per month—or it could produce any combination of bicycles and bowling balls lying on a straight line between these two extremes. Draw a production possibilities curve for western Leisureland (with bicycles on the vertical axis). What it is the opportunity cost of producing an additional bowling ball in western Leisureland?
2. Suppose that eastern Leisureland can, if it devotes all its resources to the production of bicycles, produce 400. If it devotes all its resources to bowling ball production, though, it can produce only 100. Draw the production possibilities curve for eastern Leisureland (assume it is linear). What is the opportunity cost of producing an additional bowling ball in eastern Leisureland? Explain the difference in cost between western and eastern Leisureland. Which region has a comparative advantage in producing bowling balls? Bicycles?
3. Draw the production possibilities curve for Leisureland, one that combines the curves for western and eastern Leisureland. Suppose it is determined that 400 bicycles must be produced. How many bowling balls can be produced? Where will these goods be produced?

Answers to Try It Yourself Problems

Try It Yourself 2-1

a. An unemployed factory worker could be put to work; he or she counts as labor.
b. A college professor is labor.
c. The library building on your campus is part of capital.

d. Yellowstone National Park. Those areas of the park left in their natural state are a natural resource. Facilities such as visitors centers, roads, and campgrounds are capital.
e. An untapped deposit of natural gas is a natural resource. Once extracted and put in a storage tank, natural gas is capital.
f. The White House is capital.
g. The local power plant is capital.

Try It Yourself 2-2

The production possibilities curves for the two plants are shown, along with the combined curve for both plants. Plant R has a comparative advantage in producing calculators. Plant S has a comparative advantage in producing radios, so, if the firm goes from producing 150 calculators and no radios to producing 100 radios, it will produce them at Plant S. In the production possibilities curve for both plants, the firm would be at M, producing 100 calculators at Plant R.

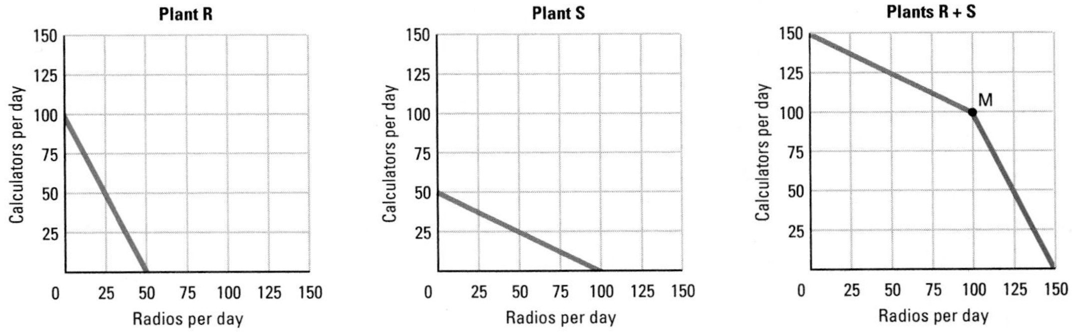

Try It Yourself 2-3

Your first production possibilities curve should resemble the one in Panel (a). Starting at point A, an increase in jacket production requires a move down and to the right along the curve, as shown by the arrow, and thus a reduction in the production of CD players. Alternatively, if there is economic growth, it shifts the production possibilities curve outward, as in Panel (b). This shift allows an increase in production of both goods, as suggested by the arrow.

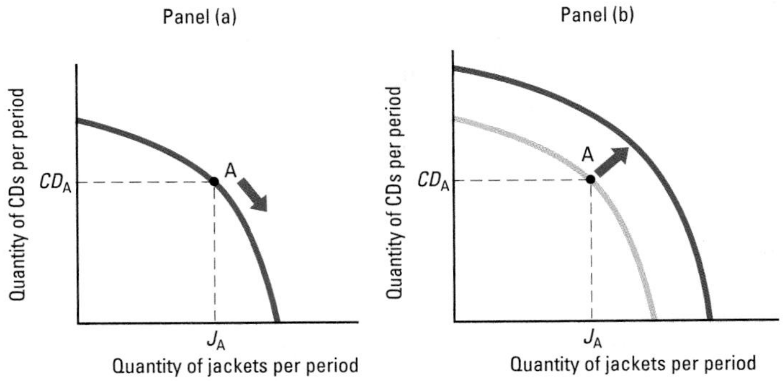

3 Demand and Supply

Getting Started: Crazy for Coffee

Starbucks Coffee Company revolutionized the coffee-drinking habits of millions of Americans. Starbucks, whose bright green-and-white logo is almost as familiar as the golden arches of McDonald's, began in Seattle in 1971. Fifteen years later it had grown into a chain of four stores in the Seattle area. Then in 1987 Howard Schultz, a former Starbucks employee, who had become enamored with the culture of Italian coffee bars during a trip to Italy, bought the company from its founders for $3.8 million. A decade later there were nearly 1,400 Starbucks stores across the country, and Americans were willingly paying $3 or more for a cappucino or a latté. The change in American consumers' taste for coffee allowed coffee retailers to charge more. Copycat retailers, such as Gourmet Bean and Gloria Jean's Coffees, were encouraged to enter the market, and today there are thousands of coffee bars, carts, drive-throughs, and kiosks in downtowns, malls, and airports all around the country.

Just as consumers were growing accustomed to their cappuccinos and lattés, the price of coffee beans shot up in 1997. Excessive rain and labor strikes in coffee-growing areas of South America had reduced the supply of coffee. Retail coffee shops began raising their prices.

The marketplace is always responding to events, such as bad harvests and changing consumer tastes that affect the prices and quantities of particular goods. The demand for some goods increases, while the demand for others decreases. The supply of some goods rises, while the supply of others falls. As such events unfold, prices adjust to keep markets in balance. This chapter explains how the market forces of demand and supply interact to determine equilibrium prices and equilibrium quantities of goods and services. We'll see how prices and quantities adjust to changes in demand and supply, and we'll also see how changes in prices serve as signals to buyers and sellers.

The model of demand and supply that we shall develop in this chapter is one of the most powerful tools in all of economic analysis. You'll be using it throughout your study of economics. We'll look first at the variables that influence demand. Then we'll turn to supply, and finally we'll put demand and supply together to explore how the model of demand and supply operates. As we examine the model, bear in mind that demand is a representation of the behavior of buyers, and supply is a representation of the behavior of sellers. Buyers may be consumers purchasing groceries or producers purchasing iron ore to make steel. Sellers may be firms selling cars or households selling their labor services. We shall see that the ideas of demand and supply apply, whatever the identity of the buyers or sellers and whatever the good or service being exchanged in the market. In this chapter, we shall focus on buyers and sellers of goods and services.

Demand

How many pizzas will people eat this year? How many doctor visits will people make? How many houses will people buy?

Each good or service has its own special characteristics that determine the quantity people are willing and able to consume. One is the price of the good or service itself. Other independent variables that are important determinants of demand include consumer preferences, prices of related goods and services, income, demographic characteristics such as population size, and buyer expectations. The number of pizzas people will purchase, for example, depends very much on whether they like pizza. It also depends on the prices for alternatives such as hamburgers or spaghetti. The number of doctor visits is likely to vary with income—people with higher incomes are likely to see a doctor more often than people with lower incomes. The demands for pizza, for doctor visits, and for housing are certainly affected by the age distribution of the population and its size.

While different variables play different roles in influencing the demands for different goods and services, economists pay special attention to one: the price of the good or service. Given the values of all the other variables that affect demand, a higher price tends to reduce the quantity people demand, and a lower price tends to increase it. A medium pizza typically sells for $5 to $10. Suppose the price were $30. Chances are, you'd buy fewer pizzas at that price than you do now. Suppose pizzas typically sold for $2 each. At that price, people would be likely to buy more pizzas than they do now.

We will discuss first how price affects the quantity demanded of a good or service and then how other variables affect demand.

Price and the Demand Curve

Because people will purchase different quantities of a good or service at different prices, economists must be careful when speaking of the "demand" for something. They have therefore developed some specific terms for expressing the general concept of demand.

The **quantity demanded** of a good or service is the quantity buyers are willing and able to buy at a particular price during a particular period, all other things unchanged. (As we learned in Chapter 1, we can substitute the Latin phrase "ceteris paribus" for "all other things unchanged.") Suppose, for example, that 100,000 movie tickets are sold each month in a particular town at a price of $8 per ticket. That quantity—100,000—is the quantity of movie admissions demanded per month at a price of $8. If the price were $12, we would expect the quantity demanded to be less. If it were $4, we would expect the quantity demanded to be greater. The quantity demanded at each price would be different if other things that might affect it, such as the population of the town, were to change. That's why we add the qualifier that other things have not changed to the definition of quantity demanded.

A **demand schedule** is a table that shows the quantities of a good or service demanded at different prices during a particular period, all other things unchanged. To introduce the concept of a demand schedule, let's consider the demand for coffee in the United States.We'll ignore differences among types of coffee beans and roasts, and speak simply of coffee. The table in Exhibit 3-1 shows quantities of coffee that will be demanded each month at prices ranging from $9 to $4 per pound; the table is a demand schedule. We see that the higher the price, the lower the quantity demanded.

The information given in a demand schedule can be presented with a **demand curve**, which is a graphical representation of a demand schedule. A demand curve thus shows the relationship between the price and quantity demanded of a good or service during a particular period, all other things unchanged. The demand curve in Exhibit 3-1 shows the prices and quantities of coffee demanded that are given in the demand schedule. At point A, for example, we see that 25 million pounds of coffee per month are demanded at a price of $6 per pound. By convention, economists graph price on the vertical axis and quantity on the horizontal axis.

Exhibit 3-1

A Demand Schedule and a Demand Curve

The table is a demand schedule; it shows quantities of coffee demanded per month in the United States at particular prices, all other things unchanged. These data are then plotted on the demand curve. At point A on the curve, 25 million pounds of coffee per month are demanded at a price of $6 per pound. At point B, 30 million pounds of coffee per month are demanded at a price of $5 per pound.

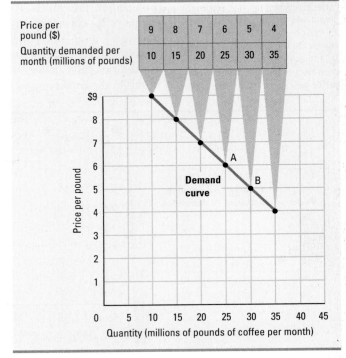

Price per pound ($)	9	8	7	6	5	4
Quantity demanded per month (millions of pounds)	10	15	20	25	30	35

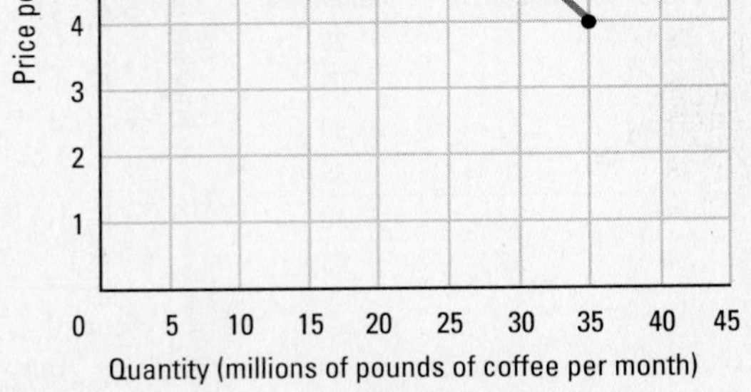

Price alone does not determine the quantity of coffee or any other good that people buy. To isolate the effect of changes in price on the quantity of a good or service demanded, however, we show the quantity demanded at each price, assuming that those other variables remain unchanged. We do the same thing in drawing a graph of any relationship between two variables; we assume that the values of other variables that may affect the variables shown in the graph (such as income or population) remain unchanged for the period under consideration.

A change in price, with no change in any of the other variables that affect demand, results in a movement *along* the demand curve. For example, if the price of coffee falls from $6 to $5 per pound, consumption rises from 25 million pounds to 30 million pounds per month. That's a movement from point A to point B along the demand curve in Exhibit 3-1. A movement along a demand curve that results from a change in price is called a **change in quantity demanded.** Note that a change in quantity demanded is not a change or shift in the demand curve; it is a movement *along* the demand curve.

The negative slope of the demand curve in Exhibit 3-1 suggests a key behavioral relationship of economics. All other things unchanged, the **law of demand** holds that, for virtually all goods and services, a higher price induces a reduction in quantity demanded and a lower price induces an increase in quantity demanded.

The law of demand is called a law because the results of countless studies are consistent with it. Undoubtedly, you've observed one manifestation of the law. When a store finds itself with an overstock of some item, such as running shoes or tomatoes, and needs to sell these items quickly, what does it do? It typically has a sale, expecting that a lower price will increase the quantity demanded. In general, we expect the law of demand to hold. Given the values of other variables that influence demand, a higher price reduces the quantity demanded. A lower price increases the quantity demanded. Demand curves, in short, slope downward.

Changes in Demand

Of course, price alone does not determine the quantity of a good or service that people consume. Coffee consumption, for example, will be affected by such variables as income and population. Preferences will play a role—the introduction to this chapter alleges that per capita coffee consumption has risen in the United States due to the Starbucks phenomenon. We also expect other prices to affect coffee consumption. People often eat doughnuts or bagels with their coffee, so a reduction in the price of doughnuts or bagels might induce people to drink more coffee. An alternative to coffee is tea, so a reduction in the price of tea might result in the consumption of more tea and less coffee. Thus, a change in any one of the variables held constant in constructing a demand schedule will change the quantities demanded at each price. The result will be a *shift* in the demand curve rather than a movement along the demand curve. A *shift* in a demand curve is called a **change in demand.**

Suppose, for example, that something happens to increase the quantity of coffee demanded at each price. Several events could produce such a change: an increase in incomes, an increase in population, or an increase in the price of tea would each be likely to increase the quantity of coffee demanded at each price. Any such change produces a new demand schedule. Exhibit 3-2 shows

Exhibit 3-2

An Increase in Demand

An increase in the quantity of a good or service demanded at each price is shown as an increase in demand. Here, the original demand curve D_1 shifts to D_2. Point A on D_1 corresponds to a price of $6 per pound and a quantity demanded of 25 million pounds of coffee per month. On the new demand curve D_2, the quantity demanded at this price rises to 35 million pounds of coffee per month (point A′).

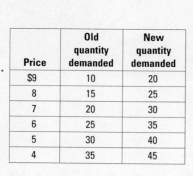

Price	Old quantity demanded	New quantity demanded
$9	10	20
8	15	25
7	20	30
6	25	35
5	30	40
4	35	45

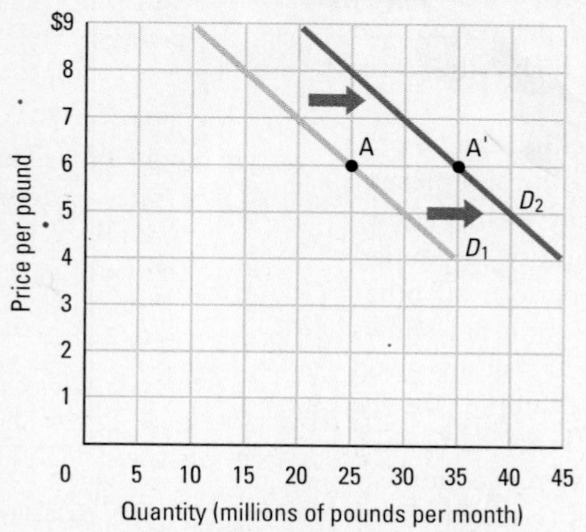

such a change in the demand schedule for coffee. We see that the quantity of coffee demanded per month is greater at each price than before. We show that graphically as a shift in the demand curve. The original curve, labeled D_1, shifts to the right to D_2. At a price of $6 per pound, for example, the quantity demanded rises from 25 million pounds per month (point A) to 35 million pounds per month (point A′).

Just as demand can increase, it can decrease. In the case of coffee, demand might fall as a result of events such as a reduction in population, a reduction in the price of tea, or a change in preferences. A discovery that the caffeine in coffee contributes to heart disease, for example, could change preferences and reduce the demand for coffee.

Price	Old quantity demanded	New quantity demanded
$9	10	0
8	15	5
7	20	10
6	25	15
5	30	20
4	35	25

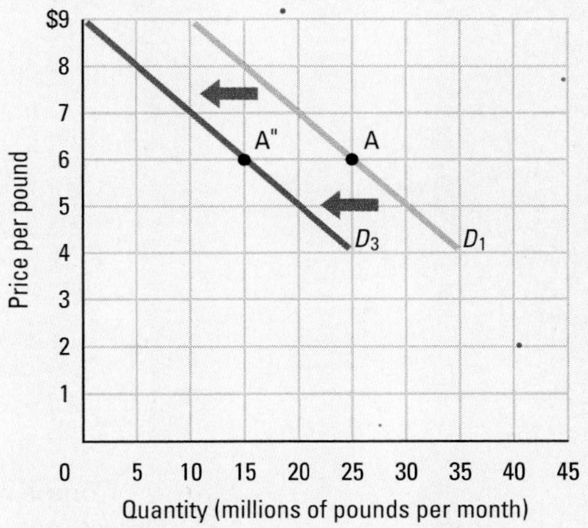

Exhibit 3-3

A Reduction in Demand

A reduction in demand occurs when the quantities of a good or service demanded fall at each price. Here, the demand schedule shows a lower quantity of coffee demanded at each price than we had in Exhibit 3-1. The reduction shifts the demand curve for coffee to D_3 from D_1. The quantity demanded at a price of $6 per pound, for example, falls from 25 million pounds per month (point A) to 15 million pounds of coffee per month (point A″).

A reduction in the demand for coffee is illustrated in Exhibit 3-3. The demand schedule shows that less coffee is demanded at each price than in Exhibit 3-1. The result is a shift in demand from the original curve D_1 to D_3. The quantity of coffee demanded at a price of $6 per pound falls from 25 million pounds per month (point A) to 15 million pounds per month (point A″). Note, again, that a change in quantity demanded, ceteris paribus, refers to a movement *along* the demand curve, while a change in demand refers to a *shift* in the demand curve.

A variable that can change the quantity of a good or service demanded at each price is called a **demand shifter.** When these other variables change, the all-other-things-unchanged conditions behind the original demand curve no longer hold. Although different goods and services will have different demand shifters, the demand shifters are likely to include (1) consumer preferences, (2) the prices of related goods and services, (3) income, (4) demographic characteristics, and (5) buyer expectations. Let's look at each of these.

Preferences Changes in preferences of buyers can have important consequences for demand. We've already seen how Starbucks supposedly increased the demand for coffee. Another example is a reduced demand for eggs caused by concern about cholesterol.

A change in preferences that makes one good or service more popular will shift the demand curve to the right. A change that makes it less popular will shift the demand curve to the left.

Prices of Related Goods and Services Suppose the price of doughnuts were to fall. Many people who drink coffee enjoy dunking doughnuts in their coffee; the lower price of doughnuts might therefore increase the demand for coffee, shifting the demand curve for coffee to the right. A lower price for tea, however, would be likely to reduce coffee demand, shifting the demand curve for coffee to the left.

In general, if a reduction in the price of one good increases the demand for another, the two goods are called **complements.** If a reduction in the price of one good reduces the demand for another, the two goods are called **substitutes.** These definitions hold in reverse as well: Two goods are complements if an increase in the price of one reduces the demand for the other, and they are substitutes if an increase in the price of one increases the demand for the other. Doughnuts and coffee are complements; tea and coffee are substitutes.

Complements (coffee and doughnuts)	
↓ *Reducing* the price of one . . .	↑ *increases* the demand for the other.
↑ *Increasing* the price of one . . .	↓ *reduces* the demand for the other.

Substitutes (coffee and tea)	
↑ *Increasing* the price of one . . .	↑ *increases* the demand for the other.
↓ *Reducing* the price of one . . .	↓ *reduces* the demand for the other.

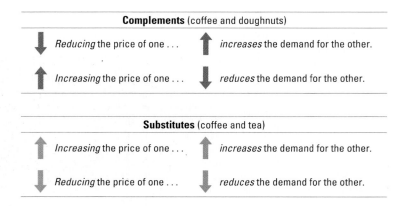

Complementary goods are goods used in conjunction with one another. Tennis rackets and tennis balls, eggs and bacon, and stationery and postage stamps are complementary goods. Substitute goods are goods used instead of one another. Cassettes, for example, are likely to be substitutes for compact discs. Breakfast cereal is a substitute for eggs. A file attachment to an e-mail is a substitute for both a fax machine and postage stamps.

Income As incomes rise, people increase their consumption of many goods and services, and as incomes fall, their consumption of these goods and services falls. For example, an increase in income is likely to raise the demand for ski trips, new cars, and jewelry. There are, however, goods and services for which consumption falls as income rises—and rises as income falls. As incomes rise, for example, people tend to consume more fresh fruit but less canned fruit.

A good for which demand increases when income increases is called a **normal good.** A good for which demand decreases when income increases is called an **inferior good.** An increase in income shifts the demand curve for fresh fruit (a normal good) to the right; it shifts the demand curve for canned fruit (an inferior good) to the left.

Demographic Characteristics The number of buyers affects the total quantity of a good or service that will be bought; in general, the greater the population, the greater the demand. Other demographic characteristics can affect demand as well. As the share of the population over age 65 increases, the demand for medical services, ocean cruises, and motor homes increases. The birth rate in the United States fell sharply between 1955 and 1975 but has gradually increased since then. That increase has raised the demand for such things as infant supplies, elementary school teachers, soccer coaches, and in-line skates. It caused the demand for higher education in the second half of the 1990s to increase and should continue to increase demand for the next several years. Demand can thus shift as a result of changes in both the number and characteristics of buyers.

Buyer Expectations The consumption of goods that can be easily stored, or whose consumption can be postponed, is strongly affected by buyer expectations. The expectation of digital TV could slow down sales of large home entertainment systems. If people expect gasoline prices to rise tomorrow, they'll fill up their tanks today to try to beat the price increase. The same will be true for goods such as automobiles and washing machines: an expectation of higher prices in the future will lead to more purchases today. If the price of a good is expected to fall, however, people are likely to reduce their purchases today and await tomorrow's lower prices. The expectation that computer prices will fall, for example, can reduce current demand.

Case in Point The Oprah Effect

"As a novelist there are three phone calls you never expect to receive in your lifetime because if you waited for them you would grow despairing—one calling from Stockholm with a Swedish accent [informing you that you'd just won a Nobel Prize], one from the NBA and one from Oprah Winfrey," declared Chris Bohjalian, author of *Midwives,* the October 1998 selection of Oprah's Book Club. Bohjalian had reason to be pleased. Begun in September 1996, Oprah's Book Club has turned more than a dozen books into bestsellers. The format is familiar to viewers of Oprah's daytime talk show. Oprah selects a book each month and invites the author and a few viewers to dinner to discuss it. Excerpts of the mealtime conversation are subsequently broadcast on the show. Like so many Oprah selections before it, *Midwives* instantly jumped onto the bestseller lists.

It doesn't seem to matter whether the Oprah pick is by a well-known author, such as Toni Morrison, or an obscure one, such as Sheri Reynolds. The result is the same: increased demand due to what publishers now call the Oprah effect. Oprah can be credited with saving Reynolds's career. Her book, *The Rapture of Canaan,* was selling so poorly that her publisher had already rejected her second novel. After getting the nod from Oprah in April 1997, *Canaan* became an instant bestseller and seven publishing houses offered Reynolds a contract on her second novel.

Oprah has also been accused of causing a decrease in demand. "It has just stopped me cold from eating another burger," declared Oprah Winfrey when a guest on her show on April 16, 1996, suggested that the practice in the United States of letting cattle by-products be included in cattle feed could lead to mad cow disease. The guest, food safety activist Howard

Lyman, said that the United States was "following the exact path they followed in England." In England, the human version of the disease, Creutzfeldt–Jakob, was linked to the similar disease in cattle that makes a brain look like a sponge. The hypothesized connection resulted in the slaughter of thousands of cattle in Britain and a ban on beef exports from that country. Feeding cattle ground cattle flesh and cattle by-products has since been halted in both England and the United States.

After Winfrey's interview with Lyman was broadcast, the two became the first people to be sued under Texas's food disparagement law. More than a dozen states have perishable food libel laws, which make it illegal to knowingly make false statements in order to manipulate food and animal markets. The rationale for imposing this limit on free speech is that, because food is perishable, a false or unsubstantiated statement means lost revenue that can never be recovered. In this case, a Texas rancher claimed that Oprah's pronouncements caused a reduction in demand that had cost him over $6 million. Other ranchers joined in the suit.

Oprah moved her TV show to Amarillo, Texas, in January 1998 for the trial. In the course of the six-week trial, the judge ruled that cattle do not constitute a perishable food product, so the case that was sent to the jurors was decided on whether Winfrey's and Lyman's statements were knowingly false and aimed specifically at the *plaintiff's* cattle—a much more rigid standard. The jury decided they were not. The jury left unanswered the question of whether Oprah and Lyman had shifted demand for cattle overall.

Sources: Amy Boaz, "Chris Bohjalian: On the Fringes of Modern Life," *Publisher's Weekly,* 246(1) (4 January 1999), p. 67. T. Evan Schaeffer "Boycott Oprah's Book Club to Protect Literary Variety," *Houston Chronicle,* 22 September 1997, p. A23.

Caution!

It's crucial to distinguish between a change in quantity demanded, which is a movement along the demand curve caused by a change in price, and a change in demand, which implies a shift of the demand curve itself. A change in demand is caused by a change in a demand shifter. An increase in demand is a shift of the demand curve to the right. A decrease in demand is a shift in the demand curve to the left. This drawing of a demand curve highlights the difference.

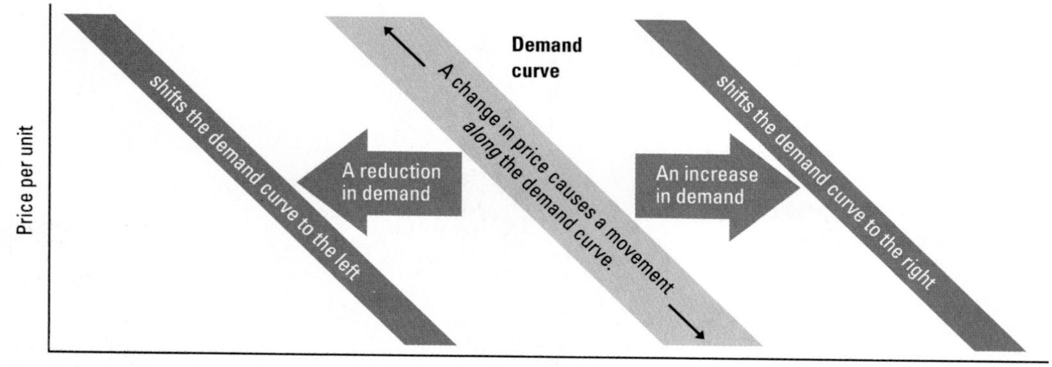

Checklist

- The quantity demanded of a good or service is the quantity buyers are willing and able to buy at a particular price during a particular period, all other things unchanged.
- A demand schedule is a table that shows the quantities of a good or service demanded at different prices during a particular period, all other things unchanged.
- A demand curve shows graphically the quantities of a good or service demanded at different prices during a particular period, all other things unchanged.
- A change in the price of a good or service causes a change in the quantity demanded—a movement *along* the demand curve.
- A change in a demand shifter causes a change in demand, which is shown as a *shift* of the demand curve. Demand shifters include preferences, the prices of related goods and services, income, demographic characteristics, and buyer expectations.
- Two goods are substitutes if an increase in the price of one causes an increase in the demand for the other. Two goods are complements if an increase in the price of one causes a decrease in the demand for the other.
- A good is a normal good if an increase in income causes an increase in demand. A good is an inferior good if an increase in income causes a decrease in demand.

Try It Yourself 3-1

All other things unchanged, what happens to the demand curve for video rentals if there is (a) an increase in the price of movie theater tickets, (b) a decrease in family income, or (c) an increase in the price of video rentals? In answering this and other "Try It Yourself" problems in this chapter, draw and carefully label a set of axes. On the horizontal axis of your graph, show the quantity of video rentals. It is necessary to specify the time period to which your quantity pertains (e.g., "per period," "per week," or "per year"). On the vertical axis show the price per video rental. Since you don't have specific data on prices and quantities demanded, make a "free-hand" drawing of the curve or curves you are asked to examine. Focus on the general shape and position of the curve(s) before and after events occur. Draw new curve(s) to show what happens in each of the circumstances given. The curves could shift to the left or to the right, or stay where they are.

Supply

What determines the quantity of a good or service sellers are willing to offer for sale? Price is one factor; ceteris paribus, a higher price is likely to induce sellers to offer a greater quantity of a good or service. Production cost is another determinant of supply. Variables that affect production cost include the prices of factors used to produce the good or service, returns from alternative activities, technology, the expectations of sellers, and natural events such as weather changes. Still another factor affecting the quantity of a good that will be offered for sale is the number of sellers—the greater the number of sellers of a particular good or service, the greater will be the quantity offered at any price per time period.

Price and the Supply Curve

The **quantity supplied** of a good or service is the quantity sellers are willing to sell at a particular price during a particular period, all other things unchanged. Ceteris paribus, the receipt of a higher price increases profits and induces sellers to increase the quantity they supply.

In general, we expect higher prices to increase the quantity supplied, but there is no law of supply corresponding to the law of demand. There are cases in which a higher price will not induce an increase in quantity supplied. Goods that can't be produced, such as additional land on the corner of Park Avenue and 56th Street in Manhattan, are fixed in supply—a higher price can't induce an increase in the quantity supplied. There are even cases, which we investigate in microeconomic analysis, in which a higher price induces a reduction in the quantity supplied.

Generally speaking, however, when there are many sellers of a good, an increase in price results in a greater quantity supplied. The relationship between price and quantity supplied is suggested in a **supply schedule,** a table that shows quantities supplied at different prices during a particular period, all other things unchanged. Exhibit 3-4 gives a supply schedule for the quantities of coffee that will be supplied per month at various prices, ceteris paribus. At a price of $4 per pound, for example, producers are willing to supply 15 million pounds of coffee per month. A higher price, say $6 per pound, induces sellers to supply a greater quantity—25 million pounds of coffee per month.

A **supply curve** is a graphical representation of a supply schedule. It shows the relationship between price and quantity supplied during a particular period, all other things unchanged. Because the relationship between price and quantity supplied is generally positive, supply curves are generally upward sloping. The supply curve for coffee in Exhibit 3-4 shows graphically the values given in the supply schedule.

Exhibit 3-4

A Supply Schedule and a Supply Curve

The supply schedule shows the quantity of coffee that will be supplied in the United States each month at particular prices, all other things unchanged. The same information is given graphically in the supply curve. The values given here suggest a positive relationship between price and quantity supplied.

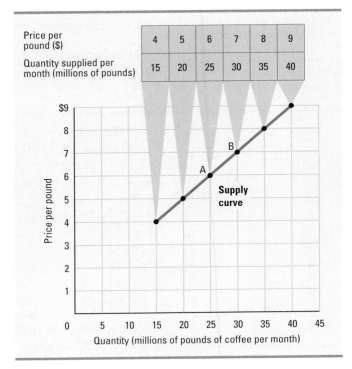

Price per pound ($)	4	5	6	7	8	9
Quantity supplied per month (millions of pounds)	15	20	25	30	35	40

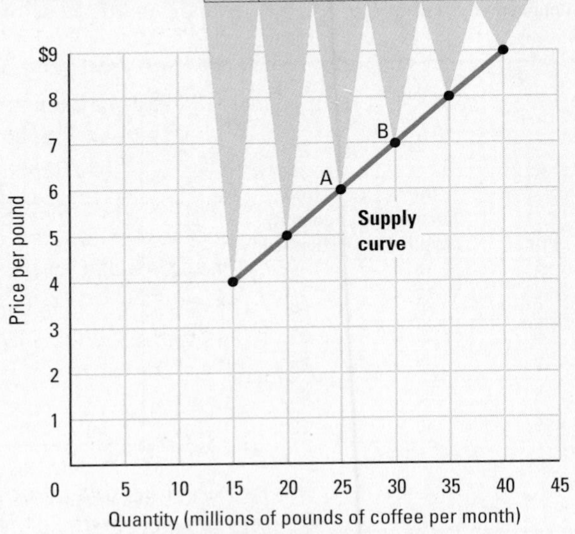

A change in price causes a movement along the supply curve; such a movement is called a **change in quantity supplied.** As is the case with a change in quantity demanded, a change in quantity supplied does not shift the supply curve. By definition, it is a movement along the supply curve. For example, if the price rises from $6 per pound to $7 per pound, the quantity supplied rises from 25 million pounds to 30 million pounds. That's a movement from point A to point B along the supply curve in Exhibit 3-4.

Changes in Supply

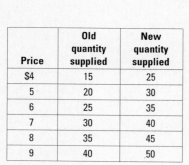

When we draw a supply curve, we assume that other variables that affect the willingness of sellers to supply a good or service are unchanged. It follows that a change in any of those variables will cause a **change in supply,** which is a shift in the supply curve. A change that increases the quantity of a good or service supplied at each price shifts the supply curve to the right. Suppose, for example, that the price of fertilizer falls. That will reduce the cost of producing coffee and thus increase the quantity of coffee producers will offer for sale at each price. The supply schedule in Exhibit 3-5 shows an increase in the quantity of coffee supplied at each price. We show that increase graphically as a shift in the supply curve from S_1 to S_2. We see that the quantity supplied at each price increases by 10 million pounds of coffee per month. At point A on the original supply curve S_1, for example, 25 million pounds of coffee per month are supplied at a price of $6 per pound. After the increase in supply, 35 million pounds per month are supplied at the same price (point A′ on curve S_2).

An event that reduces the quantity supplied at each price shifts the supply curve to the left. An increase in production costs and excessive rain that reduces the yields from coffee plants are examples of events that might reduce supply. Exhibit 3-6 shows a reduction in the supply of coffee. We see in the supply schedule that the quantity of coffee supplied falls by 10 million pounds of coffee per month at each price. The supply curve thus shifts from S_1 to S_3.

A variable that can change the quantity of a good or service supplied at each price is called a **supply shifter.** Supply shifters include (1) prices of factors of production, (2) returns from alternative activities, (3) technology, (4) seller expectations, (5) natural events, and (6) the number of sellers. When these other variables change, the all-other-things-unchanged conditions behind the original supply curve no longer hold. Let's look at each of the supply shifters.

Prices of Factors of Production A change in the price of labor or some other factor of production will change the cost of producing any given quantity of the good or service. This change in the cost of production will change the quantity that suppliers are willing to offer at any price. An increase in factor prices should decrease the quantity suppliers will offer at any price, shifting the supply curve to the left. A reduction in factor prices increases the quantity suppliers will offer at any price, shifting the supply curve to the right.

Suppose coffee growers must pay a higher wage to the workers they hire to harvest coffee or must pay more for fertilizer. Such increases in production cost will cause them to produce a smaller quantity at each price, shifting the supply curve for coffee to the left. A reduction in any of these costs increases supply, shifting the supply curve to the right.

Exhibit 3-5

An Increase in Supply

If there is a change in supply that increases the quantity supplied at each price, as is the case in the supply schedule here, the supply curve shifts to the right. At a price of $6 per pound, for example, the quantity supplied rises from the previous level of 25 million pounds per month on supply curve S_1 (point A) to 35 million pounds per month on supply curve S_2 (point A′).

Price	Old quantity supplied	New quantity supplied
$4	15	25
5	20	30
6	25	35
7	30	40
8	35	45
9	40	50

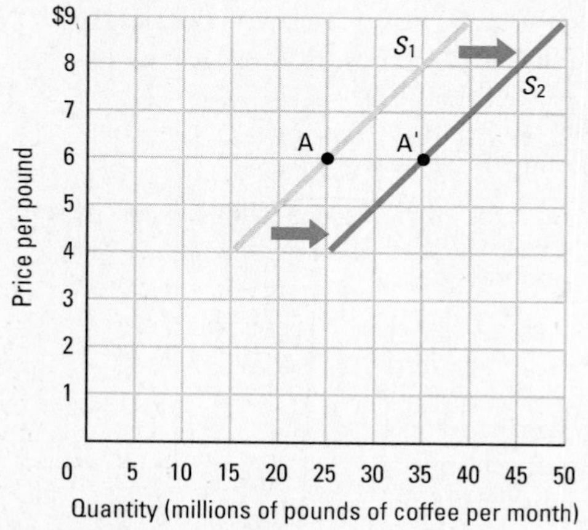

Returns from Alternative Activities To produce one good or service means forgoing the production of another. The concept of opportunity cost in economics suggests that the value of the activity forgone is the opportunity cost of the activity chosen; this cost should affect supply. For example, one opportunity cost of producing eggs is not selling chickens. An increase in the price people are willing to pay for fresh chicken would make it more profitable to sell chickens and would thus increase the opportunity cost of producing eggs. It would shift the supply curve for eggs to the left, reflecting a decrease in supply.

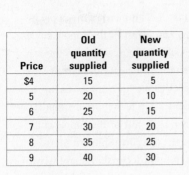

Price	Old quantity supplied	New quantity supplied
$4	15	5
5	20	10
6	25	15
7	30	20
8	35	25
9	40	30

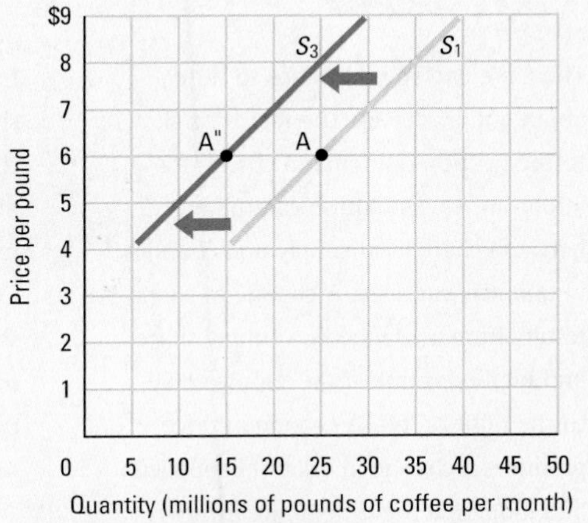

Exhibit 3-6

A Reduction in Supply

A change in supply that reduces the quantity supplied at each price shifts the supply curve to the left. At a price of $6 per pound, for example, the original quantity supplied was 25 million pounds of coffee per month (point A). With a new supply curve S_3, the quantity supplied at that price falls to 15 million pounds of coffee per month (point A″).

Technology A change in technology alters the combinations of inputs or the types of inputs required in the production process. An improvement in technology usually means that fewer and/or less costly inputs are needed. If the cost of production is lower, the profits available at a given price will increase, and producers will produce more. With more produced at every price, the supply curve will shift to the right, meaning an increase in supply.

Impressive technological changes have occurred in the computer industry in recent years. Computers are much smaller and are far more powerful than they were only a few years ago—and they are much cheaper to produce. The result has been a huge increase in the supply of computers, shifting the supply curve to the right.

While we usually think of technology as enhancing production, declines in production due to problems in technology are also possible. Outlawing the use of certain equipment without pollution-control devices has increased the cost of production for many goods and services, thereby reducing profits available at any price and shifting these supply curves to the left.

Seller Expectations All supply curves are based in part on seller expectations about future market conditions. Many decisions about production and selling are typically made long before a product is ready for sale. Those decisions necessarily depend on expectations. Changes in seller expectations can have important effects on price and quantity.

Consider, for example, the owners of oil deposits. Oil pumped out of the ground and used today will be unavailable in the future. If a change in the international political climate leads many owners to expect that oil prices will rise in the future, they may decide to leave their oil in the ground, planning to sell it later when the price is higher. Thus, there will be a decrease in supply; the supply curve for oil will shift to the left.

Natural Events Storms, insect infestations, and drought affect agricultural production and thus the supply of agricultural goods. If something destroys a substantial part of an agricultural crop, the supply curve will shift to the left. If there is an unusually good harvest, the supply curve will shift to the right. In the introduction to this chapter we described the impact on the coffee market of too much rain in South America in 1997. This reduced the supply of coffee, thereby shifting the supply curve for coffee to the left.

The Number of Sellers The supply curve for an industry, such as coffee, includes all the sellers in the industry. A change in the number of sellers in an industry changes the quantity available at each price and thus changes supply. An increase in the number of sellers

Caution!

There are two special things to note about supply curves. The first is similar to the caution on demand curves: it's important to distinguish carefully between changes in supply and changes in quantity supplied. A change in supply results from a change in a supply shifter and implies a shift of the supply curve to the right or left. A change in price produces a change in quantity supplied and induces a movement along the supply curve. A change in price does not shift the supply curve.

The second caution relates to the interpretation of increases and decreases in supply. Notice that in Exhibit 3-5 an increase in supply is shown as a shift of the supply curve to the right; the curve shifts in the direction of increasing quantity with respect to the horizontal axis. In Exhibit 3-6 a reduction in supply is shown as a shift of the supply curve to the left; the curve shifts in the direction of decreasing quantity with respect to the horizontal axis.

Because the supply curve is upward sloping, a shift to the right produces a new curve that in a sense lies "below" the original curve. Students sometimes make the mistake of thinking of such a shift as a shift "down" and therefore as a reduction in supply. Similarly, it's easy to make the mistake of showing an increase in supply with a new curve that lies "above" the original curve. But that's a *reduction* in supply!

To avoid such errors, focus on the fact that an increase in supply is an increase in the quantity supplied at each price and shifts the supply curve in the direction of increased quantity on the horizontal axis. Similarly, a reduction in supply is a reduction in the quantity supplied at each price and shifts the supply curve in the direction of a lower quantity on the horizontal axis.

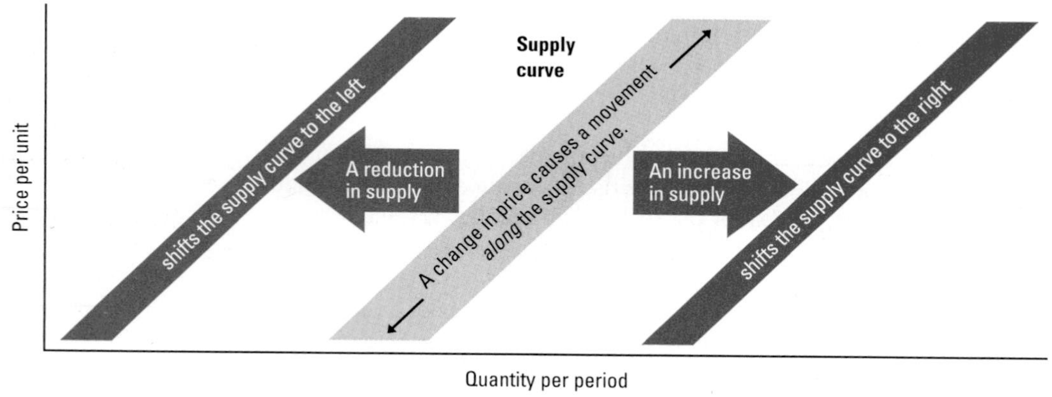

supplying a good or service shifts the supply curve to the right; a reduction in the number of sellers shifts the supply curve to the left.

The market for cellular phone service has been affected by an increase in the number of firms offering the service. Over the past decade, new cellular phone companies emerged, shifting the supply curve for cellular phone service to the right.

Checklist

- The quantity supplied of a good or service is the quantity sellers are willing to sell at a particular price during a particular period, all other things unchanged.
- A supply schedule shows the quantities supplied at different prices during a particular period, all other things unchanged. A supply curve shows this same information graphically.
- A change in the price of a good or service causes a change in the quantity supplied—a movement *along* the supply curve.

Case in Point The Monks of St. Benedict's Get Out of the Egg Business

It was cookies that lured the monks of St. Benedict's out of the egg business, and now private retreat sponsorship is luring them away from cookies.

St. Benedict's is a Benedictine monastery, nestled on a ranch high in the Colorado Rockies, about 20 miles down the road from Aspen. The monastery's 15 monks operate the ranch to support themselves and to provide help for poor people in the area. They lease out about 3,500 acres of their land to cattle and sheep grazers, produce cookies, and sponsor private retreats. They used to produce eggs.

Attracted by potential profits and the peaceful nature of the work, the monks went into the egg business in 1967. They had 10,000 chickens producing their Monastery Eggs brand. For a while, business was good. Very good. Then, in the late 1970s, the price of chicken feed started to rise rapidly.

"When we started in the business, we were paying $60 to $80 a ton for feed—delivered," recalls the monastery's abbot, Father Joseph Boyle. "By the late 1970s, our cost had more than doubled. We were paying $160 to $200 a ton. That really hurt, because feed represents a large part of the cost of producing eggs."

The monks adjusted to the blow. "When grain prices were lower, we'd pull a hen off for a few weeks to molt, then return her to laying. After grain prices went up, it was 12 months of laying and into the soup pot," Father Joseph says.

Grain prices continued to rise in the 1980s and increased the costs of production for all egg producers. It caused the supply of eggs to fall. Demand fell at the same time, as Americans worried about the cholesterol in eggs. Times got tougher in the egg business.

"We were still making money in the financial sense," Father Joseph says. "But we tried an experiment in 1985 producing cookies, and it was a success. We finally decided that devoting our time and energy to the cookies would pay off better than the egg business, so we quit the egg business in 1986."

The mail-order cookie business was good to the monks. They sold 200,000 ounces of Monastery Cookies in 1987.

By 1998, however, they had limited their production of cookies, selling only locally and to gift shops. In the past five years, they have switched to "providing private retreats for individuals and groups—about 40 people per month," according to Brother Charles.

The monks' calculation of their opportunity costs revealed that they would earn a higher return through sponsorship of private retreats than in either cookies or eggs. This projection has proved correct.

And there is another advantage as well.

"The chickens didn't stop laying eggs on Sunday," Father Joseph chuckles. "When we shifted to cookies we could take Sundays off. We weren't hemmed in the way we were with the chickens." The move to providing retreats is even better in this regard. Since guests provide their own meals, most of the monastery's effort goes into planning and scheduling, which frees up even more of their time for other worldly as well as spiritual pursuits.

Source: Personal interviews.

- A change in a supply shifter causes a change in supply, which is shown as a *shift* of the supply curve. Supply shifters include prices of factors of production, returns from alternative activities, technology, seller expectations, natural events, and the number of sellers.
- An increase in supply is shown as a shift to the right of a supply curve; a decrease in supply is shown as a shift to the left.

Try It Yourself 3-2

If all other things are unchanged, what happens to the supply curve for video rentals if there is (a) an increase in wages paid to video store clerks, (b) an increase in the price of video rentals, or (c) an increase in the number of video rental stores? Draw a graph that shows what happens to the supply curve in each circumstance. The supply curve can shift to the left or to the right, or stay where it is. Remember to label the axes and curves, and remember to specify the time period (e.g., "Videos rented per week").

Demand, Supply, and Equilibrium

In this section we combine the demand and supply curves we've just studied into a new model. The **model of demand and supply** uses demand and supply curves to explain the determination of price and quantity in a market.

The Determination of Price and Output

The logic of the model of demand and supply is simple. The demand curve shows the quantities of a particular good or service that buyers will be willing and able to purchase at each price during a specified period. The supply curve shows the quantities that sellers will offer for sale at each price during that same period. By putting the two curves together, we should be able to find a price at which the quantity buyers are willing and able to purchase equals the quantity sellers will offer for sale.

Exhibit 3-7 combines the demand and supply data introduced in Exhibits 3-1 and 3-4. Notice that the two curves intersect at a price of $6 per pound—at this price the quantities demanded and supplied are equal. Buyers want to purchase, and sellers are willing to offer for sale, 25 million pounds of coffee per month. The market for coffee is in equilibrium. Unless the demand or supply curve shifts, there will be no tendency for price to change. The **equilibrium price** in any market is the price at which quantity demanded equals quantity supplied. The equilibrium price in the market for coffee is thus $6 per pound. The **equilibrium quantity** is the quantity demanded and supplied at the equilibrium price.

With an upward-sloping supply curve and a downward-sloping demand curve, there is only a single price at which the two curves intersect. This means there is only one price at which equilibrium is achieved. It follows that at any price other than the equilibrium price, the market will not be in equilibrium. Let's examine what happens at prices other than the equilibrium price.

Exhibit 3-7

The Determination of Equilibrium Price and Quantity

When we combine the demand and supply curves for a good in a single graph, the point at which they intersect is called the equilibrium price. Here, the equilibrium price is $6 per pound. Consumers demand, and suppliers supply, 25 million pounds of coffee per month at this price.

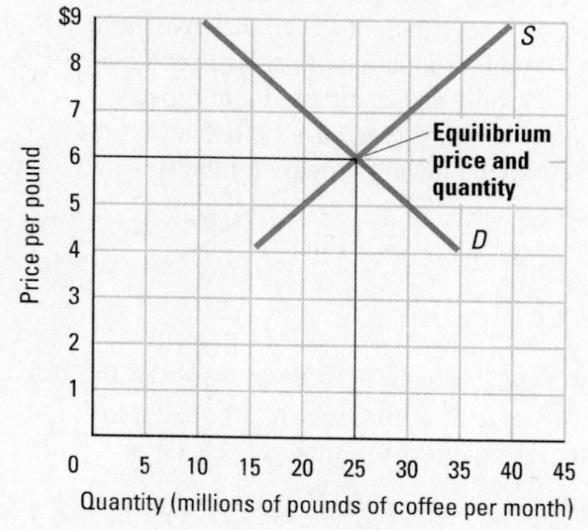

Surpluses Exhibit 3-8 shows the same demand and supply curves we have just examined, but this time the initial price is $8 per pound of coffee. Because we no longer have a balance between quantity demanded and quantity supplied, this price is not the equilibrium price. At a price of $8, we read over to the demand curve to determine the quantity of coffee consumers will be willing to buy—15 million pounds per month. The supply curve tells us what sellers will offer for sale—35 million pounds per month. The difference, 20 million pounds of coffee per month, is called a surplus. More generally, a **surplus** is the amount by which the quantity supplied exceeds the quantity demanded at the current price. There is, of course, no surplus at the equilibrium price; a surplus occurs only if the current price exceeds the equilibrium price.

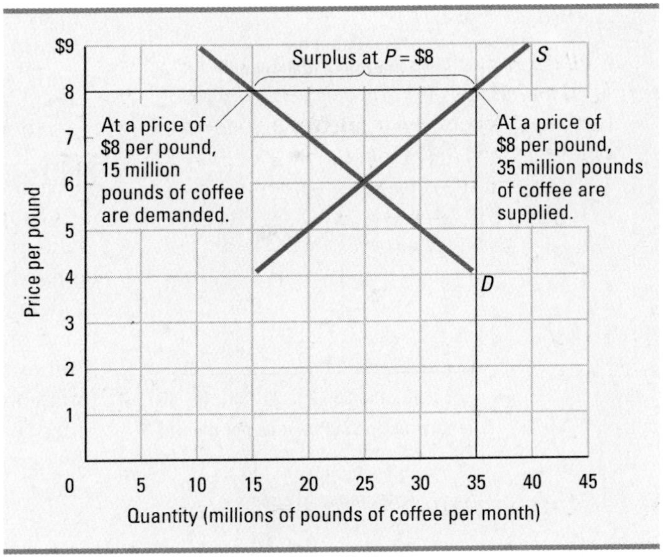

Exhibit 3-8

A Surplus in the Market for Coffee

At a price of $8, the quantity supplied is 35 million pounds of coffee per month and the quantity demanded is 15 million pounds per month; there is a surplus of 20 million pounds of coffee per month. Given a surplus, the price will fall quickly toward the equilibrium level of $6.

A surplus in the market for coffee won't last long. With unsold coffee on the market, sellers will begin to reduce their prices to clear out unsold coffee. As the price of coffee begins to fall, the quantity of coffee supplied begins to decline. At the same time, the quantity of coffee demanded begins to rise. Remember that the reduction in quantity supplied is a movement *along* the supply curve—the curve itself doesn't shift in response to a reduction in price. Similarly, the increase in quantity demanded is a movement *along* the demand curve—the demand curve doesn't shift in response to a reduction in price. Price will continue to fall until it reaches its equilibrium level, at which the demand and supply curves intersect. At that point, there will be no tendency for price to fall further. In general, surpluses in the marketplace are short-lived. The prices of most goods and services adjust quickly, eliminating the surplus. Later on, we'll discuss some markets where adjustment of price to equilibrium may occur only very slowly or not at all.

Shortages Just as a price above the equilibrium price will cause a surplus, a price below equilibrium will cause a shortage. A **shortage** is the amount by which the quantity demanded exceeds the quantity supplied at the current price.

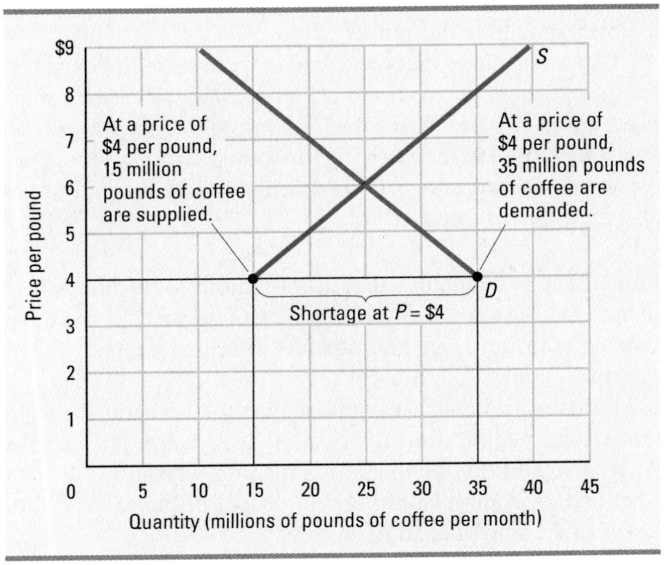

Exhibit 3-9

A Shortage in the Market for Coffee

At a price of $4 per pound, the quantity of coffee demanded is 35 million pounds per month and the quantity supplied is 15 million pounds per month. The result is a shortage of 20 million pounds of coffee per month.

Exhibit 3-9 shows a shortage in the market for coffee. Suppose the price is $4 per pound. At that price, 15 million pounds of coffee would be supplied per month and 35 million pounds would be demanded per month. When more coffee is demanded than supplied, there is a shortage.

In the face of a shortage, sellers are likely to begin to raise their prices. As the price rises, there will be an increase in the quantity supplied (but not a change in

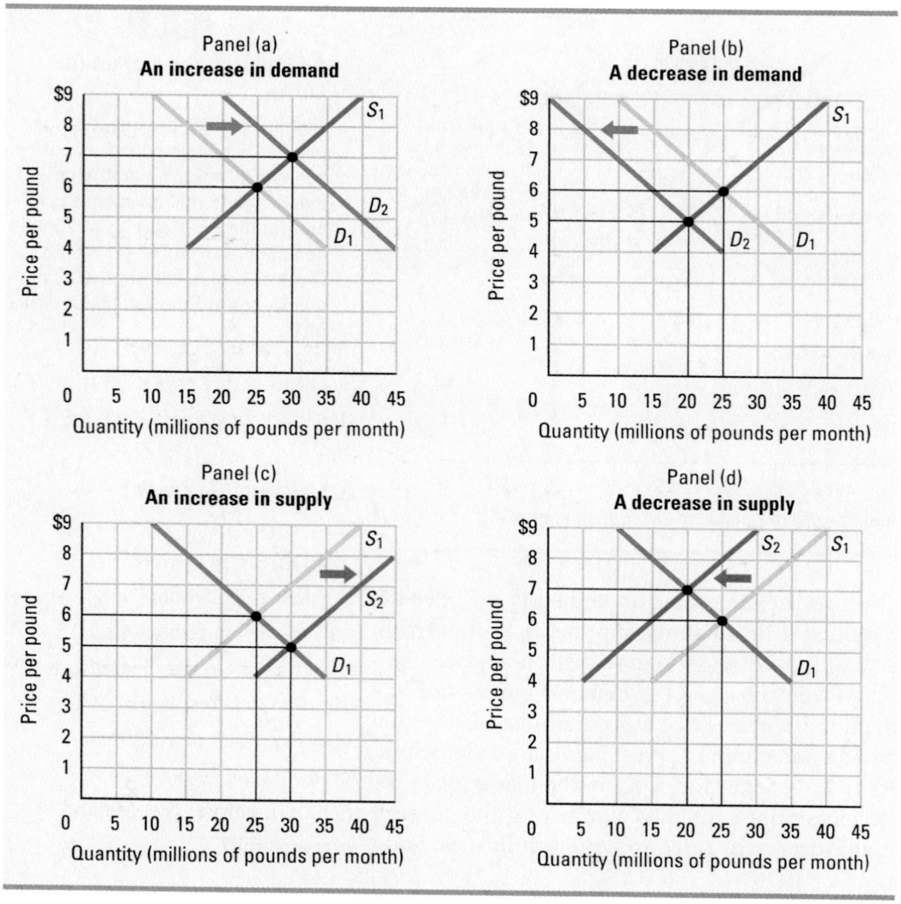

Exhibit 3-10

Changes in Demand and Supply

A change in demand or in supply changes the equilibrium solution in the model. Panels (a) and (b) show an increase and a decrease in demand, respectively; Panels (c) and (d) show an increase and a decrease in supply, respectively.

supply) and a reduction in the quantity demanded (but not a change in demand) until the equilibrium price is achieved.

Shifts in Demand and Supply

A change in one of the variables (shifters) held constant in any model of demand and supply will create a change in demand or supply. A shift in a demand or supply curve changes the equilibrium price and equilibrium quantity for a good or service. Exhibit 3-10 combines the information about changes in the demand and supply of coffee presented in Exhibits 3-2, 3-3, 3-5, and 3-6. In each case, the original equilibrium price is $6 per pound and the corresponding equilibrium quantity is 25 million pounds of coffee per month. Exhibit 3-10 shows what happens with an increase in demand, a reduction in demand, an increase in supply, and a reduction in supply. We then look at what happens if both curves shift simultaneously. Each of these possibilities is discussed in turn below.

An Increase in Demand An increase in demand for coffee shifts the demand curve to the right, as shown in Panel (a) of Exhibit 3-10. The equilibrium price rises to $7 per pound. As the price rises to the new equilibrium level, the quantity supplied increases to 30 million pounds of coffee per month. Notice that the supply curve doesn't shift; rather there is a movement along the supply curve.

Demand shifters that could cause an increase in demand include a shift in preferences that leads to greater coffee consumption; a lower price for a complement to coffee, such as doughnuts; a higher price for a substitute for coffee, such as tea; an increase in income; and an increase in population. A change in buyer expectations, perhaps due to predictions of bad weather lowering expected yields on coffee plants and increasing future coffee prices, could also increase current demand.

A Decrease in Demand Panel (b) of Exhibit 3-10 shows that a decrease in demand shifts the demand curve to the left. The equilibrium price falls to $5 per pound. As the price falls to the new equilibrium level, the quantity supplied decreases to 20 million pounds of coffee per month.

Demand shifters that could reduce the demand for coffee include a shift in preferences that makes people want to consume less coffee; an increase in the price of a complement, such as doughnuts; a reduction in the price of a substitute, such as tea; a reduction in income; a reduction in population; and a change in buyer expectations that leads people to expect lower prices for coffee in the future.

Caution!

You're likely to be given problems in which you'll have to shift a demand or supply curve. Suppose you are told that an invasion of pod-crunching insects has gobbled up half the crop of fresh peas, and you are asked to use demand and supply analysis to predict what will happen to the price and quantity of peas demanded and supplied. Here are some suggestions.

Put the quantity of the good you're asked to analyze on the horizontal axis and its price on the vertical axis. Draw a downward-sloping line for demand and an upward-sloping line for supply. The initial equilibrium price is determined by the intersection of the two curves. Label the equilibrium solution. You may find it helpful to use a number for the equilibrium price instead of the letter "P." Pick a price that seems plausible, say, 79 cents per pound. Don't worry about the precise positions of the demand and supply curves; you can't be expected to know what they are.

Step 2 can be the most difficult step; the problem is to decide which curve to shift. The key is to remember the difference between a change in demand or supply and a change in quantity demanded or supplied. At each price, ask yourself whether the given event would change the quantity demanded. Would the fact that a bug has attacked the pea crop change the quantity demanded at a price of say, 79 cents per pound? Clearly not; none of the demand shifters have changed. The event would, however, reduce the quantity supplied at this price, and the supply curve would shift to the left. There is a change in supply and a reduction in the quantity demanded. There is no change in demand.

Next check to see whether the result you've obtained makes sense. The graph in Step 2 makes sense; it shows price rising and quantity demanded falling.

It's easy to make a mistake such as the one shown below. One might, for example, reason that when fewer peas are available, fewer will be demanded, and therefore the demand curve will shift to the left. This suggests the price of peas will fall—but that doesn't make sense. If only half as many fresh peas were available, their price would surely rise. The error here lies in confusing a change in quantity demanded with a change in demand. Yes, buyers will end up buying fewer peas. But no, they won't demand fewer peas at each price than before; the demand curve does not shift.

1. Set up the Graph

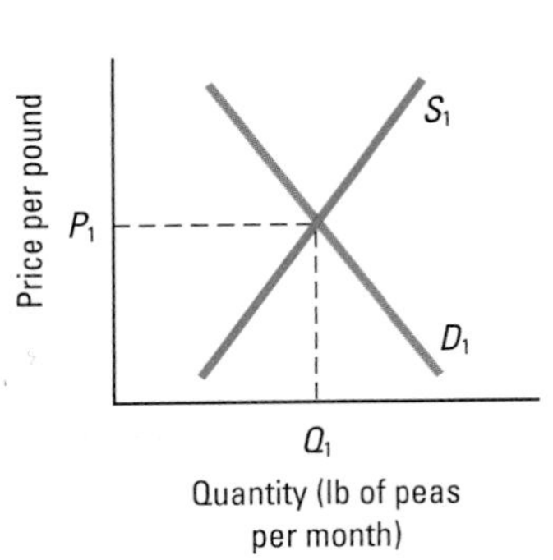

2. Shift the Curve

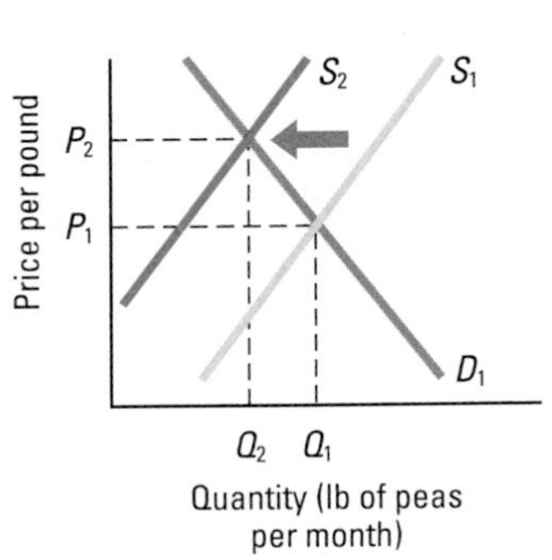

3. Troubleshoot

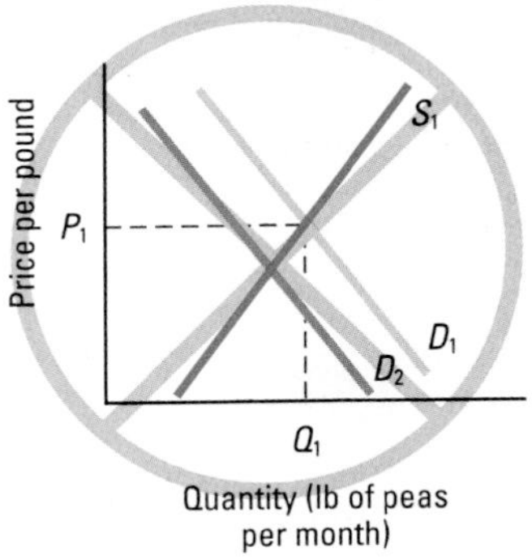

An Increase in Supply An increase in the supply of coffee shifts the supply curve to the right, as shown in Panel (c) of Exhibit 3-10. The equilibrium price falls to $5 per pound. As the price falls to the new equilibrium level, the quantity of coffee demanded increases to 30 million pounds of coffee per month. Notice that the demand curve doesn't shift; rather there is movement along the demand curve.

Possible supply shifters that could increase supply include a reduction in the price of an input such as labor, a decline in the returns available from alternative uses of the

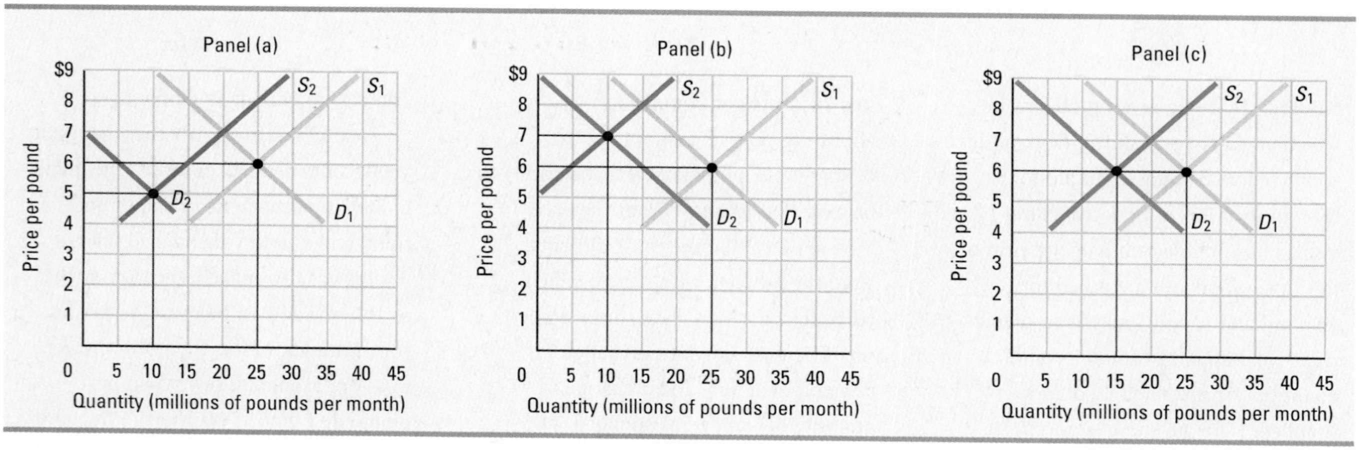

Exhibit 3-11

Simultaneous Decreases in Demand and Supply

Both the demand and the supply of coffee decrease. Since decreases in demand and supply, considered separately, each cause equilibrium quantity to fall, the impact of both decreasing simultaneously means that a new equilibrium quantity of coffee must be less than the old equilibrium quantity. In Panel (a), the demand curve shifts further to the left than does the supply curve, so equilibrium price falls. In Panel (b), the supply curve shifts further to the left than does the demand curve, so the equilibrium price rises. In Panel (c), both curves shift to the left by the same amount, so equilibrium price stays the same.

inputs that produce coffee, an improvement in the technology of coffee production, good weather, and an increase in the number of coffee-producing firms.

A Decrease in Supply Panel (d) of Exhibit 3-10 shows that a decrease in supply shifts the supply curve to the left. The equilibrium price rises to $7 per pound. As the price rises to the new equilibrium level, the quantity demanded decreases to 20 million pounds of coffee per month.

Possible supply shifters that could reduce supply include an increase in the prices of inputs used in the production of coffee, an increase in the returns available from alternative uses of these inputs, a decline in production because of problems in technology (perhaps caused by a restriction on pesticides used to protect coffee beans), a reduction in the number of coffee-producing firms, or a natural event, such as excessive rain.

Simultaneous Shifts As we have seen, when *either* the demand or the supply curve shifts, the results are unambiguous; that is, we know what will happen to both equilibrium price and equilibrium quantity, so long as we know whether demand or supply increased or decreased. However, in practice, several events may occur at around the same time that cause *both* the demand and supply curves to shift. To figure out what happens to equilibrium price and equilibrium quantity we must know not only in which direction the demand and supply curves have shifted, but also the relative amount by which each curve shifts. Of course, the demand and supply curves could shift in the same direction or in opposite directions, depending on the specific events causing them to shift.

For example, all three panels of Exhibit 3-11 show a decrease in demand for coffee (caused perhaps by a decrease in the price of a substitute good, such as tea) and a simultaneous decrease in the supply of coffee (caused perhaps by bad weather). Since reductions in demand and supply, considered separately, each cause the equilibrium quantity to fall, the impact of both curves shifting simultaneously to the left means that the new equilibrium quantity of

Exhibit 3-12

Simultaneous Shifts in Demand and Supply

If simultaneous shifts in demand and supply cause equilibrium price or quantity to move in the same direction, then equilibrium price or quantity clearly moves in that direction. If the shift in one of the curves causes equilibrium price or quantity to rise while the shift in the other curve causes equilibrium price or quantity to fall, then the relative amount by which each curve shifts is critical to figuring out what happens to that variable.

Shift in Demand \ Shift in Supply	Decrease in supply	Increase in supply
Decrease in demand	Equilibrium price ? Equilibrium quantity ↓	Equilibrium price ↓ Equilibrium quantity ?
Increase in demand	Equilibrium price ↑ Equilibrium quantity ?	Equilibrium price ? Equilibrium quantity ↑

Case in Point "El Niño" Meant More Work for Roofers

When it rains, it pours, and the demand for new roofs and roof repairs goes up. Such was the case in southern California after the drenching summer of 1997. The unusually heavy rainfall was brought on by "El Niño," a condition created by a warm water mass that periodically develops in the Pacific Ocean and disrupts normal weather patterns. By September, roofing contractors were trying to figure out how to keep up with what seemed to be an ever-growing backlog of work. The increase in demand had driven prices and profits up, and Champion Roofs, Inc., a local company, was considering doubling its 100-person work force in order to increase its quantity of roofs and roof repairs supplied.

How did Champion and other roofers actually respond to this surge in demand? According to Matt Canale, production manager at Champion, the lure of profits attracted new roofing contractors, who suddenly appeared in the Los Angeles area offering to do the repair and replacement work for about 25–30 percent more than Champion had been charging. Homeowners and businesses that were in a hurry to have the work done accepted the higher price.

The heavy rains damaged roofs in southern California, thereby shifting the demand curve for roofs and roof repairs to the right. When new roofing contractors swiftly entered the market, the number of sellers increased and the supply curve shifted to the right as well. The shift in demand (from D_1 to D_2) and the shift in supply (from S_1 to S_2) taken individually would lead to an increase in the quantity of new roofs and roof repairs. Since equilibrium price rose, the increase in demand must have been greater than the increase in supply, as shown.

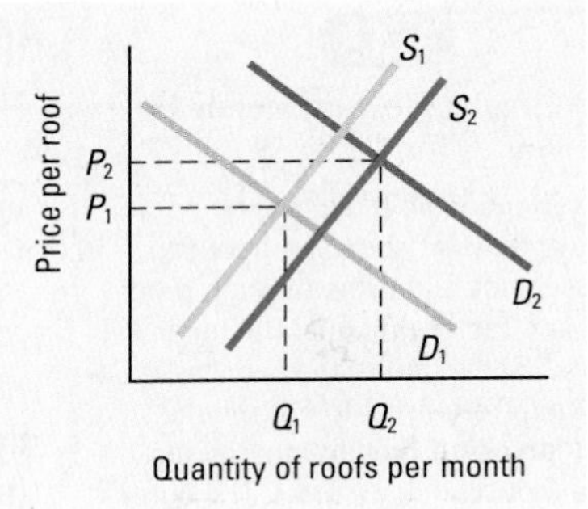

Sources: "Inundated With Business, Roofers Are on Top of the World," *Wall Street Journal*, 30 September 1997, p. A1; and personal interview.

coffee is less than the old equilibrium quantity. The effect on the equilibrium price, though, is ambiguous. Whether the equilibrium price is higher, lower, or unchanged depends on the extent to which each curve shifts.

If the demand curve shifts further to the left than does the supply curve, as shown in Panel (a) of Exhibit 3-11, then the equilibrium price will be lower than it was before the curves shifted. In this case the new equilibrium price falls from $6 per pound to $5 per pound. If the shift to the left of the supply curve is greater than that of the demand curve, the equilibrium price will be higher than it was before, as shown in Panel (b). In this case, the new equilibrium price rises to $7 per pound. In Panel (c), since both curves shift to the left by the same amount, equilibrium price does not change; it remains $6 per pound.

Regardless of the scenario, changes in equilibrium price and equilibrium quantity resulting from two different events need to be considered separately. If both events cause equilibrium price or quantity to move in the same direction, then clearly price or quantity can be expected to move in that direction. If one event causes price or quantity to rise while the other causes it to fall, the extent by which each curve shifts is critical to figuring out what happens. Exhibit 3-12 summarizes what may happen to equilibrium price and quantity when demand and supply both shift.

As demand and supply curves shift, prices adjust to maintain a balance between the quantity of a good demanded and the quantity supplied. If prices did not adjust, this balance could not be maintained.

Notice that the demand and supply curves that we have examined in this chapter have all been drawn as linear. This simplification of the real world makes the graphs a bit easier to read without sacrificing the essential point: whether the curves are linear or nonlinear, demand curves are downward sloping and supply curves are generally upward sloping. As circumstances that shift the demand curve or the supply curve change, we can analyze what will happen to price and what will happen to quantity.

Try It Yourself 3-3

What happens to the equilibrium price and the equilibrium quantity of video rentals if the price of movie theater tickets increases and wages paid to video store clerks increases, all other things unchanged? Be sure to show all possible scenarios, as was done in Exhibit 3-11. Again, you don't need actual numbers to arrive at an answer. Just focus on the general position of the curve(s) before and after events occurred.

An Overview of Demand and Supply: The Circular Flow Model

Implicit in the concepts of demand and supply is a constant interaction and adjustment that economists illustrate with the circular flow model. The **circular flow model** provides an overview of how markets work and how they are related to each other. It shows flows of spending and income through the economy.

A great deal of economic activity can be thought of as a process of exchange between households and firms. Firms supply goods and services for households. Households buy these goods and services from firms. Households supply factors of production—labor, capital, and natural resources—that firms require. The payments firms make in exchange for these factors represent the incomes households earn.

The flow of goods and services, factors of production, and the payments they generate is illustrated in Exhibit 3-13. This circular flow model of the economy shows the interaction of households and firms as they exchange goods and services and factors of production. For simplicity, the model here shows only the private domestic economy; it omits the government and foreign sectors.

Exhibit 3-13

The Circular Flow of Economic Activity

This simplified circular flow model shows flows of spending between households and firms through product and factor markets. The inner arrows show goods and services flowing from firms to households and factors of production flowing from households to firms. The outer flows show the payments for goods, services, and factors of production. These flows, in turn, represent millions of individual markets for products and factors of production.

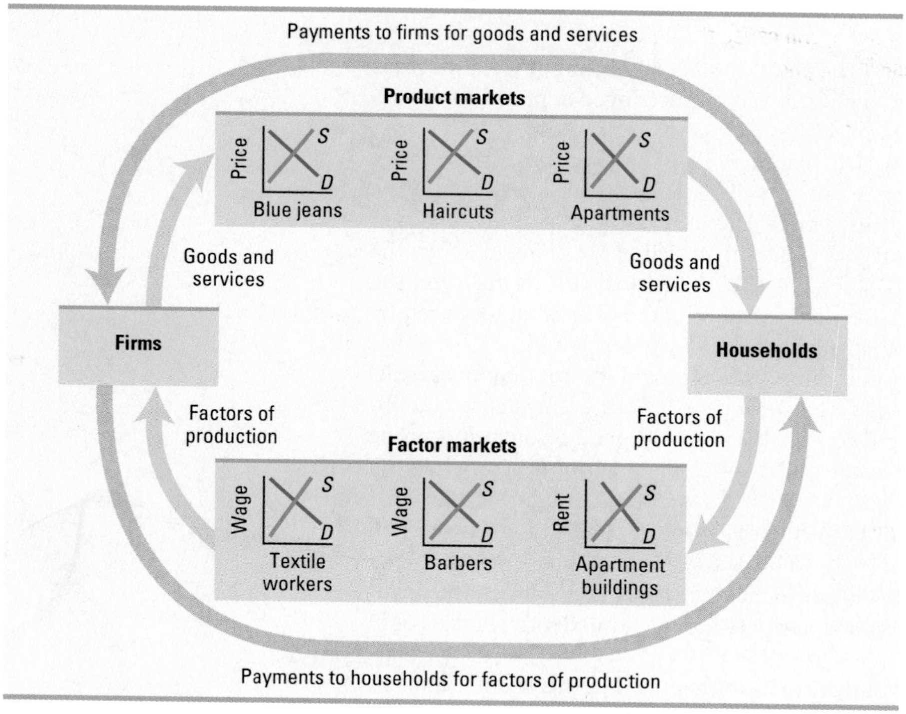

The circular flow model shows that goods and services that households demand are supplied by firms in **product markets.** The exchange for goods and services is shown in the top half of Exhibit 3-13. The bottom half of the exhibit illustrates the exchanges that take place in factor markets. **Factor markets** are markets in which households supply factors of production—labor, capital, and natural resources—demanded by firms.

Our model is called a circular flow model because households use the income they receive from their supply of factors of production to buy goods and services from firms. Firms, in turn, use the payments they receive from households to pay for their factors of production.

The demand and supply model developed in this chapter gives us the basic tool for understanding what is happening in each of these product or factor markets and also allows us to see how these markets are interrelated. In Exhibit 3-13, markets for three goods and services that households want—blue jeans, haircuts, and apartments—create demands by firms for textile workers, barbers, and apartment buildings. The equilibrium of supply and demand in each market determines the price and quantity of that item. Moreover, a change in equilibrium in one market will affect equilibrium in related markets. For example, an increase in the demand for haircuts would lead to an increase in demand for barbers. Equilibrium price and quantity could rise in both markets. For some purposes, it will be adequate to simply look at a single market, whereas at other times we will want to look at what happens in related markets as well.

In either case, the model of demand and supply is one of the most widely used tools of economic analysis. That widespread use is no accident. The model yields results that are, in fact, broadly consistent with what we observe in the marketplace. Your mastery of this model will pay big dividends in your study of economics.

Checklist

- The equilibrium price is the price at which the quantity demanded equals the quantity supplied. It is determined by the intersection of the demand and supply curves.
- A surplus exists if the quantity of a good or service supplied exceeds the quantity demanded at the current price; it causes downward pressure on price. A shortage exists if the quantity of a good or service demanded exceeds the quantity supplied at the current price; it causes upward pressure on price.
- An increase in demand, all other things unchanged, will cause the equilibrium price to rise; quantity supplied will increase. A decrease in demand will cause the equilibrium price to fall; quantity supplied will decrease.
- An increase in supply, all other things unchanged, will cause the equilibrium price to fall; quantity demanded will increase. A decrease in supply will cause the equilibrium price to rise; quantity demanded will decrease.
- To determine what happens to equilibrium price and equilibrium quantity when both the supply and demand curves shift, you must know in which direction each of the curves shifts and the extent to which each curve shifts.
- The circular flow model provides an overview of demand and supply in product and factor markets and suggests how these markets are linked to one another.

A Look Back

In this chapter we have examined the model of demand and supply. We found that a demand curve shows the quantity demanded at each price, all other things unchanged. The law of demand asserts that an increase in price reduces the quantity demanded and a decrease in price increases the quantity demanded, all other things unchanged. The supply curve shows the quantity of a good or service that sellers will offer at various prices, all other things unchanged. Supply curves are generally upward sloping: an increase in price generally increases the quantity supplied, all other things unchanged.

The equilibrium price occurs where the demand and supply curves intersect. At this price, the quantity demanded equals the quantity supplied. A price higher than the equilibrium price increases the quantity supplied and reduces the quantity demanded, causing a surplus. A price lower than the equilibrium price increases the quantity demanded and reduces the quantity supplied, causing a shortage. Usually, market surpluses and shortages are short-lived. Changes in demand or supply, caused by changes in the determinants of demand and supply otherwise held constant in the analysis, change the equilibrium price and output. The circular flow model allows us to see how demand and supply in various markets are related to one another.

A Look Ahead In the next chapter, we'll look at more applications of the model of demand and supply. We'll look at cases where markets work well in the sense that shortages or surpluses are quickly eliminated and at cases where the government imposes rules that keep markets out of equilibrium, leading to shortages and surpluses that may persist for extended periods of time. We'll also look at the market for health-care services in order to see how the tools of demand and supply can be used to analyze this market, which has received much special attention in recent years.

Terms and Concepts for Review

quantity demanded, **61**
demand schedule, **61**
demand curve, **61**
change in quantity demanded, **62**
law of demand, **62**
change in demand, **62**
demand shifter, **63**
complements, **63**
substitutes, **63**
normal good, **64**
inferior good, **64**
quantity supplied, **67**
supply schedule, **67**
supply curve, **67**
change in quantity supplied, **68**
change in supply, **68**
supply shifter, **68**
model of demand and supply, **72**
equilibrium price, **72**
equilibrium quantity, **72**
surplus, **73**
shortage, **73**
circular flow model, **78**
product markets, **78**
factor markets, **78**

For Discussion

1. What do you think happens to the demand for pizzas during the Super Bowl? Why?
2. Which of the following goods are likely to be classified as normal goods or services? Inferior? Defend your answer.
   a. Beans
   b. Tuxedos
   c. Used cars
   d. Used clothing
   e. Computers
   f. Books reviewed in the *New York Times*
   g. Macaroni and cheese
   h. Calculators
   i. Cigarettes
   j. Caviar
   k. Legal services
3. Which of the following pairs of goods are likely to be classified as substitutes? Complements? Defend your answer.
   a. Peanut butter and jelly
   b. Eggs and ham
   c. Nike brand and Reebok brand sneakers
   d. IBM and Apple Macintosh brand computers
   e. Dress shirts and ties
   f. Airline tickets and hotels
   g. Gasoline and tires
   h. Beer and wine
   i. Faxes and first-class mail
   j. Cereal and milk
   k. Cereal and eggs
4. A study found that lower airfares led some people to substitute flying for driving to their vacation destinations. This reduced the demand for car travel and led to reduced traffic fatalities, since air travel is safer per passenger mile than car travel. Using the logic suggested by that study, suggest how each of the following events would affect the number of highway fatalities in any one year.

a. An increase in the price of gasoline
b. A large reduction in rental rates for passenger vans
c An increase in airfares

5. Children under age 2 are now allowed to fly free on U.S. airlines; they usually sit in their parents' laps. Some safety advocates have urged that they be required to be strapped in infant seats, which would mean their parents would have to purchase tickets for them. Some economists have argued that such a measure would actually increase infant fatalities. Can you say why?

6. The graphs below show four possible shifts in demand or in supply that could occur in particular markets. Relate each of the events described below to one of them.

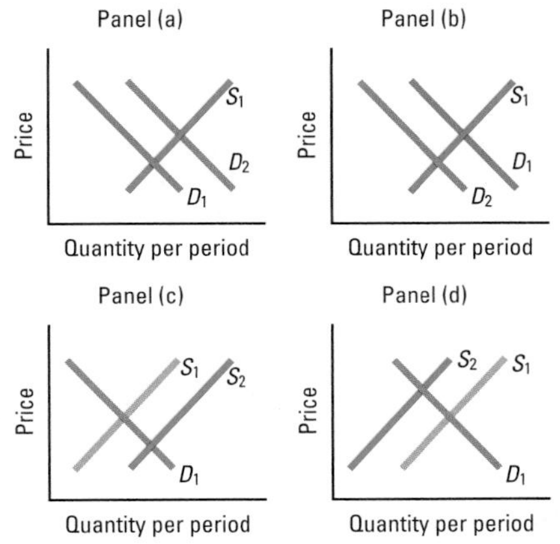

a. How did the heavy rains in South America in 1997 affect the market for coffee?
b. The Surgeon General decides french fries aren't bad for your health after all and issues a report endorsing their use. What happens to the market for french fries?
c. How do you think rising incomes affect the market for ski vacations?
d. A new technique is discovered for manufacturing computers that greatly lowers their production cost. What happens to the market for computers?
e. How would a ban on smoking in public affect the market for cigarettes?

7. Suppose egg prices rise sharply and most people expect them to remain high. How might this affect the monks' supply of cookies or private retreats? (See the Case in Point on the Monks of St. Benedict's.)

8. Gasoline prices typically rise in Colorado during the summer, a time of heavy tourist traffic. A "street talk" feature on a radio station in Colorado Springs sought tourist reaction to higher gasoline prices. Here was one response: "I don't like 'em [the higher prices] much. I think the gas companies just use any excuse to jack up prices, and they're doing it again now." How does this tourist's perspective differ from that of economists who use the model of demand and supply?

9. The introduction to the chapter argues that preferences for coffee changed in the 1990s and that excessive rain hurt yields from coffee plants. Show and explain the effects of these two circumstances on the coffee market.

10. A Conference Board report in 1993 predicted that the 1990s would see a sharp increase in the number of high-income households. It predicted, for example, that the number of households earning $100,000 or more would double by the year 2000. Much of the boom in high-income households, the organization said, would be the result of gains in income for women, who entered the ranks of professional workers in large numbers in the 1980s and 1990s. Name some goods and services for which this development is likely to increase demand. Are there any for which it will reduce demand?

11. Gary Jacobson, a stock analyst for Kidder Peabody, has some bad news for manufacturers of fitness products. "We're all a bunch of lazy slobs," he told the *Wall Street Journal* in 1993. In somewhat more analytical terms, he said that "the market for fitness products is flattening." The *Journal* reported evidence that backs Mr. Jacobson's claim. American Sports Data reported that the number of "frequent fitness participants" declined 4.8 percent in 1991 and 2.7 percent in 1992. The firm reported that for every person who exercises regularly, there are three couch potatoes who don't. Show what all this means for the market for fitness products.

12. For more than a century, milk producers have produced skim milk, which contains virtually no fat, along with regular milk, which contains 4 percent fat. But a century ago, skim milk accounted for only about 1 percent of total production, and much of it was fed to hogs. Today, skim and other reduced-fat milks make up the bulk of milk sales. What curve shifted, and what factor shifted it?

13. Iowa State agricultural economics professor Marvin Hayenga argued that a drop in beef consumption in southeast Asia due to an economic slump there had far more impact on the slump in cattle prices than did negative comments on the Oprah Winfrey Show. (See the Case in Point on the Oprah Effect.) Use the model of demand and supply to explain how changes in southeast Asia could affect the cattle market in the United States.

14. Suppose firms in the economy were to produce fewer goods and services. How do you think this would affect household spending on goods and services? (*Hint:* Use the circular flow model to analyze this question.)

Problems

The following problems are based on the model of demand and supply for coffee as shown in Exhibit 3-7. You can graph the initial demand and supply curves by using the following values, with all quantities in millions of pounds of coffee per month:

Price	Quantity demanded	Quantity supplied
$4	35	15
5	30	20
6	25	25
7	20	30
8	15	35
9	10	40

1. Suppose the quantity demanded rises by 20 million pounds of coffee per month at each price. Draw the initial demand and supply curves based on the values given in the table above. Then draw the new demand curve given by this change, and show the new equilibrium price and quantity.
2. Suppose the quantity demanded falls, relative to the values given in the above table, by 20 million pounds per month at prices between $4 and $6 per pound; at prices between $7 and $9 per pound, the quantity demanded becomes zero. Draw the new demand curve and show the new equilibrium price and quantity.
3. Suppose the quantity supplied rises by 20 million pounds per month at each price, while the quantities demanded retain the values shown in the table above. Draw the new supply curve and show the new equilibrium price and quantity.
4. Suppose the quantity supplied falls, relative to the values given in the table above, by 20 million pounds per month at prices above $5; at a price of $5 or less per pound, the quantity supplied becomes zero. Draw the new supply curve and show the new equilibrium price and quantity.

Answers to Try It Yourself Problems

Try It Yourself 3-1

Since going to the movies is a substitute for watching a video at home, an increase in the price of going to the movies should cause more people to switch from going to the movies to staying at home and renting videos. Thus, the demand curve for video rentals will shift to the right when the price of movie theater tickets increases [Panel (a)].

A decrease in family income will cause the demand curve to shift to the left, if video rentals are a normal good, but to the right if video rentals are an inferior good. The latter may be the case for some families since staying at home and watching videos is a cheaper form of entertainment than taking the family to the movies. For most others, however, video rentals are probably a normal good [Panel (b)].

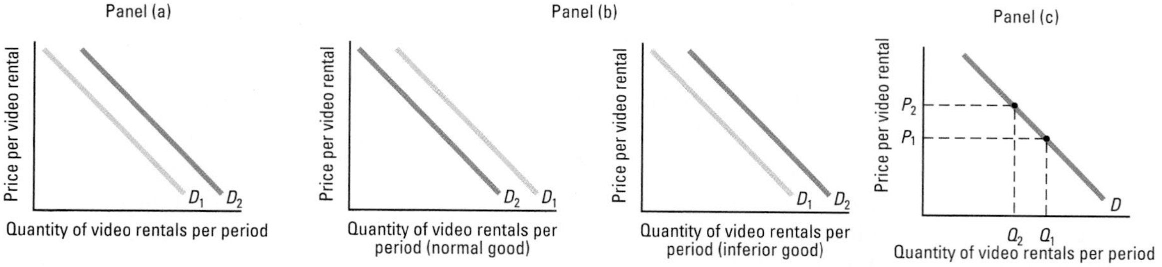

An increase in the price of video rentals does not shift the demand curve for video rentals at all; rather an increase in price, say from P_1 to P_2, is a movement upward to the left along the demand curve. At a higher price, people will rent fewer videos, say Q_2 instead of Q_1, ceteris paribus [Panel (c)].

Try It Yourself 3-2

Video store clerks are a factor of production in the video rental market. An increase in their wages raises the cost of production, thereby causing the supply curve of video rentals to shift to the left [Panel (a)]. (*Caution*: It is possible that you thought of the wage increase as an increase in income, a demand shifter, that would lead to an increase in demand, but this would be incorrect. The question refers only to wages of video store clerks. They may rent some videos, but their impact on total demand would be negligible. Besides, we have no information on what has happened overall to incomes of people who rent videos. We do know, however, that the cost of a factor of production, which is a supply shifter, increased.)

An increase in the price of video rentals does not shift the supply curve at all; rather, it corresponds to a movement upward to the right along the supply curve. At a higher price of P_2 instead of P_1, a greater quantity of video rentals, say Q_2 instead of Q_1, will be supplied [Panel (b)].

An increase in the number of stores renting videos will cause the supply curve to shift to the right [Panel (c)].

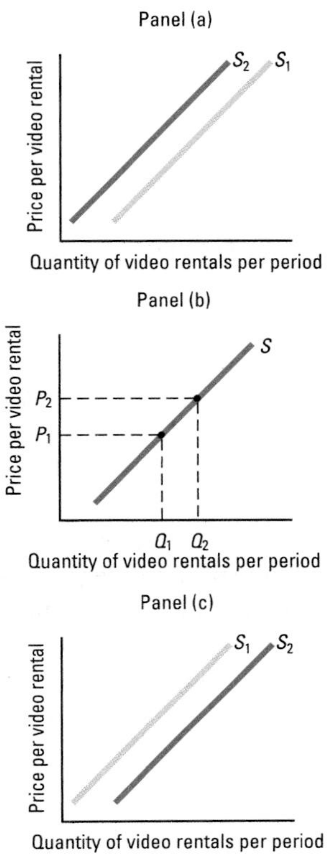

Try It Yourself 3-3

An increase in the price of movie theater tickets (a substitute for video rentals) will cause the demand curve for video rentals to shift to the right. An increase in the wages paid to video store clerks (an increase in the cost of a factor of production) shifts the supply curve to the left. Each event taken separately causes equilibrium price to rise. Whether equilibrium quantity will be higher or lower depends on which curve shifted more.

If the demand curve shifted more, then the equilibrium quantity of video rentals will rise [Panel (a)].

If the supply curve shifted more, then the equilibrium quantity of video rentals will fall [Panel (b)].

If the curves shifted by the same amount, then the equilibrium quantity of video rentals would not change [Panel (c)].

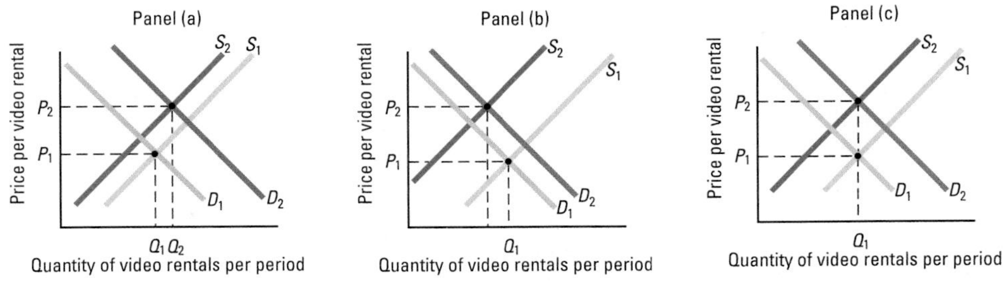

4 Applications of Demand and Supply

Getting Started: A Composer Logs On

"Since the age of seven, I knew that I would be a musician. And from age 14, I knew that I would be a composer," says Israeli-born Ofer Ben-Amots. What he did not know was that he would use computers to carry out his work. He is now a professor of music at Colorado College and Dr. Ben-Amots's compositions and operas have been performed in the United States, Europe, and Japan.

Since 1989, he has used musical notation software to help in composing music. "The output is extremely elegant. Performers enjoy looking at such a clear and clean score. The creation of parts out of a full score is as easy as pressing the <ENTER> key on the keyboard." Changes can easily be inserted into the notation file, which eliminates the need for recopying. In addition, Dr. Ben-Amots uses computers for playback. "I can listen to a relatively accurate 'digital performance' of the score at any given point, with any tempo or instrumentation I choose." He can also produce CDs on his own, and in recent years he has engaged in self-publication of scores and self-marketing. "In my case, I get to keep the copyrights on all of my music. This would have been impossible ten to twelve years ago when composers transferred their rights to publishers. Home pages on the World Wide Web allow me to promote my own work."

Dr. Ben-Amots started out in 1989 with a Macintosh SE30 that had 4 megabytes of random access memory (RAM) and an 80-megabyte hard drive. It cost him about $3,000. Today, he uses a Power Macintosh 7300/200 for which he paid only $2,300. Its operating system has 16 times more RAM and its hard drive 25 times the storage capacity of his old computer.

How personal computers came to play such an integral part in our lives is just one of the stories about markets we will tell in this chapter, which aims to help you understand how the model of market demand and supply, introduced in Chapter 3, applies to the real world.

First we'll look at two markets that you are likely to have participated in or been affected by—the market for personal computers and the stock market. You may have agonized over buying a computer, and stock market earnings may be helping to pay your college tuition. The concepts of demand and supply go a long way in explaining the behavior of equilibrium prices and quantities in both markets.

In the second part of the chapter we'll look at markets in which the government has historically played a large role in regulating prices. By legislating maximum or minimum prices, the government has kept the prices of certain goods below or above equilibrium. We'll look at the rationales for direct government intervention in controlling prices as well as the consequences of such policies. As we shall see, not allowing the price of a good to find its own equilibrium often has unexpected consequences, some of which may be at odds with the intentions of the policymakers.

In the third section of the chapter we'll look at the market for health care. This market is interesting because how well (or poorly) it works can be a matter of life and death, and because it has special characteristics. In particular, markets in which participants do not pay for goods directly, but rather pay insurers who then pay the suppliers of the goods, operate somewhat differently from those in which participants pay directly for their purchases. This extension of demand and supply analysis reveals much about how such markets operate. To see the power of demand and supply in analyzing such a complex issue—one that has become an area of national concern—is the major goal of this section.

Putting Demand and Supply to Work

In Chapter 3 we learned that a shift in either demand or supply, or in both, would lead to a change in equilibrium price and equilibrium quantity. We begin this chapter by examining two markets—the market for personal computers and the stock market—where, in response to such shifts, equilibrium is restored rather quickly. These markets are thus direct applications of the model of demand and supply.

Vendor	U.S. (% of shipments)	Worldwide (% of shipments)
Compaq	16.0	13.7
Dell	9.4	6.0
Packard Bell-NEC	8.8	4.6
IBM	8.7	8.2
Gateway 2000	6.9	—
Hewlett-Packard	—	5.8
Others	50.2	61.7

Source: Dataquest, Inc. [as reported by *Chicago Tribune*, 27 January 1998, p. 5, and *Interactive Week* 4(39), 10 (November 1997)] worldwide data reflect share of shipments in third quarter, 1997.

Exhibit 4-1

Personal Computer Unit Shipments, by Vendor, United States and Worldwide, 1997

The Personal Computer Market

In the 1960s, to speak of computers was to speak of IBM, the dominant maker of large mainframe computers used by businesses and government agencies. Then between 1976, when Apple Computer introduced its first desktop computer, and 1981, when IBM produced its first PCs, the old world was turned upside down. The latest official data provided by the U.S. Census Bureau show that the percentage of households with personal computers rose rapidly from 8.2 percent in 1984 to 36.7 percent 1997, with fully 18 percent of households buying new computers in 1996 or 1997. Today personal computers are as common in offices as typewriters once were. The tools of demand and supply tell the story from an economic perspective.

Technological change has been breathtakingly swift in the computer industry. The invention of the microchip in the 1970s reduced both the size and cost of computers. Regular improvements in microchip technology have continued ever since.

Initially, most personal computers were manufactured by Apple or Compaq and both companies were very profitable. The potential for profits attracted IBM and other firms to the industry. Unlike large mainframe computers, personal computer clones turned out to be fairly easy things to manufacture. As shown in Exhibit 4-1, the top 5 of a total of 89 personal computer manufacturers produced about half of the personal computers sold in the United States in 1997, and the largest manufacturer, Compaq, sold only about 16 percent of the total in 1997. This is a far cry from the more than 90 percent of the mainframe computer market that IBM once held. The market has become far more competitive.

Exhibit 4-2 illustrates the effects of technological improvement and the increase in the number of sellers in the personal computer market over the last 20 years. Both of these factors led to an increase in supply, thereby shifting the supply curve to the right. The horizontal axis shows the quantity of computers adjusted for quality. This adjustment recognizes that a computer that you might buy today is different from a computer you would have bought in the past. It is likely to have a faster microprocessor, more memory, and more peripherals, such as internal modems and CD-ROM drives. To analyze the behavior of the market over time, it is necessary to have a common unit of measurement. Thus, the quantity axis can be thought of as a unit of computing power. Similarly, the price axis can be thought of as a price per unit of computing power.

As shown, the supply curve shifted markedly to the right and caused a large drop in price, from P_1 to P_2, and a large increase in quantity, from Q_1 to Q_2. This shift in supply led to a movement along the demand curve. That is, consumers responded to falling computing prices by increasing the quantity demanded. (To simplify the analysis, we ignore other factors, such as increases in income, which caused the demand curve to shift to the right, since the primary change in this market has been a shifting supply curve.)

Exhibit 4-2

The Personal Computer Market

The supply curve of computing power has shifted markedly to the right, causing a large decrease in price and a large increase in quantity.

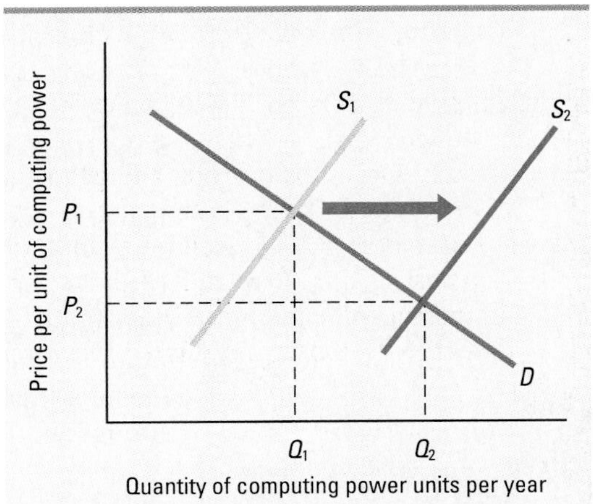

In 1990, approximately 27 million personal computers were sold at an average price of about $2,000. In 1997, about 87 million personal computers were sold worldwide at an average price of about $1,400. In quality-adjusted terms, the increase in the amount of computing power sold would be even greater than the increase in the number of computers. Similarly, the decline in price per unit of computing power has fallen even more markedly than the price of computers. Indeed, since 1970, the price per unit of computing power has fallen about 15 percent per year. With no end to technological change in sight, this downward trend in computer prices is expected to continue. The power of market forces has led to dramatic changes in price and quantity that have, in turn, dramatically affected the way we live and work.

The Stock Market

The circular flow model introduced in Chapter 3 suggests that capital, like other factors of production, is supplied by households to firms. Firms, in turn, pay income to those households for the use of their capital. Generally speaking, however, capital is actually owned by firms themselves. General Motors owns its assembly plants, and Wal-Mart owns its stores; these firms therefore own their capital. But the firms, in turn, are owned by people—and those people, of course, live in households. It is through their ownership of firms that households own capital.[1]

A firm may be owned by one individual (a **sole proprietorship**), by several individuals (a **partnership**), or by shareholders who own stock in the firm (a **corporation**). Although most firms in the United States are sole proprietorships or partnerships, the bulk of the nation's total output (about 90 percent) is produced by corporations. Corporations also own most of the capital (machines, plants, buildings, and the like). This section describes how the prices of shares of **corporate stock,** shares in the ownership of a corporation, are determined. Ultimately, the same forces that determine the value of a firm's stock determine the value of a sole proprietorship or partnership.

When a corporation needs funds to increase its capital, one means at its disposal is to issue new stock in the corporation. (Other means include borrowing funds or using past profits.) Once the new shares have been sold in what is called an initial public offering (IPO), the corporation receives no further funding as shares of its stock are bought and sold on the secondary market. The secondary market is the market for stocks that have been issued in the past, and the daily news reports about stock prices almost always refer to activity in the secondary market. Generally, the corporations whose shares are traded are not involved in these transactions.

The **stock market** is the set of institutions in which shares of stock are bought and sold. The New York Stock Exchange (NYSE) is one such institution. There are many others all over the world, such as the DAX in Germany and the Bolsa in Mexico. To buy or sell a share of stock, you place an order with a stockbroker who relays your order to one of the traders at the NYSE or at some other exchange.

The process through which shares of stock are bought and sold can seem chaotic. At many exchanges, traders with orders from customers who want to buy stock shout out the prices those customers are willing to pay. Traders with orders from customers who want to sell shout out offers of prices at which their customers are willing to sell. Some exchanges use electronic trading, but the principle is the same: if the price someone is willing to pay matches the price at which someone else is willing to sell, the trade is made. The most recent price at which a stock has traded is reported almost instantaneously throughout the world.

[1]Some capital is owned by government agencies and by nonprofit institutions. In addition, owner-occupied homes are considered part of the nation's capital. Our focus here is on the capital used by private firms.

Exhibit 4-3 applies the model of demand and supply to the determination of stock prices. Suppose the demand curve for shares in Intel Corporation is given by D_1 and the supply by S_1 and that these curves intersect at a price of $75, at which Q_1 shares are traded each day. If the price were higher, more shares would be offered for sale than would be demanded, and the price would quickly fall. If the price were lower, more shares would be demanded than would be supplied, and the price would quickly rise. In general, we can expect the prices of shares of stock to move quickly to their equilibrium levels.

The intersection of the demand and supply curves for shares of stock in a particular company determines the equilibrium price for a share of stock. But what determines the demand and supply for shares of a company's stock?

The owner of a share of a company's stock owns a share of the company, and, hence, a share of its profits; typically, a corporation will retain and reinvest its profits to increase its future profitability. Because a share of stock gives its owner a claim on part of a company's future profits, it follows that the expected level of future profits plays a role in determining the value of its stock.

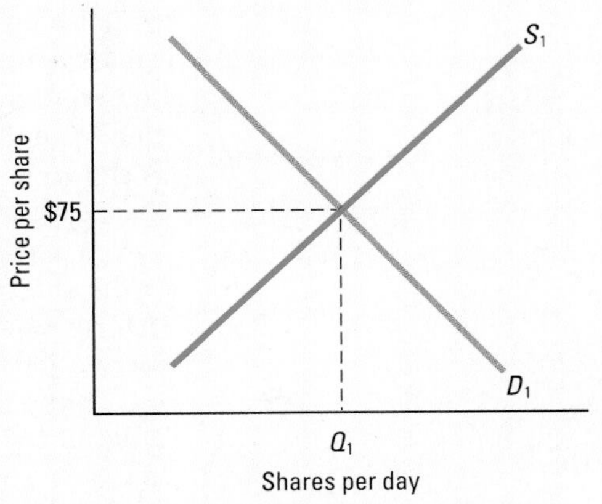

Exhibit 4-3

Demand and Supply in the Stock Market

The equilibrium price of stock shares in Intel Corporation is initially $75, determined by the intersection of demand and supply curves D_1 and S_1, at which Q_1 million shares are traded each day.

Of course, those future profits cannot be known with certainty; investors can only predict what they might be, based on information about future demand for the company's products, future costs of production, information about the soundness of a company's management, and so on. Stock prices in the real world thus reflect guesses about a company's profits projected into the future.

The downward slope of the demand curve suggests that at lower prices for the stock, more people calculate that the firm's future earnings will justify the stock's purchase. The upward slope of the supply curve tells us that as the price of the stock rises, more people conclude that the firm's future earnings don't justify holding the stock and therefore offer to sell it. At the equilibrium price, the number of shares supplied by people who think holding the stock no longer makes sense just balances the number of shares demanded by people who think it does.

What factors, then, cause the demand or supply curves for shares of stocks to shift? The most important factor is a change in the expectations of a company's future profits. Suppose Intel announces a new generation of computer chips that will lead to faster computers with larger memories. Current owners of Intel stock would adjust upward their estimates of what the value of a share of Intel stock should be. At the old equilibrium price of $75 fewer owners of Intel stock would be willing to sell. Since this would be true at every possible share price, the supply curve for Intel stock would shift to the left, as shown in Exhibit 4-4. Among the reasons that supply curves shift, which were presented in Chapter 3, this shift in the supply curve corresponds to a change in seller expectations.

What about potential buyers of Intel stock? At each possible stock price, more people would be willing to buy Intel stock because the information from Intel about the new generation of computer chips is likely to also make some potential buyers believe that Intel's profit picture has brightened. Thus the demand curve shifts to the right, as shown in Exhibit 4-4. The reason for the demand curve to shift, among those discussed in Chapter 3, is a change in buyer expectations.

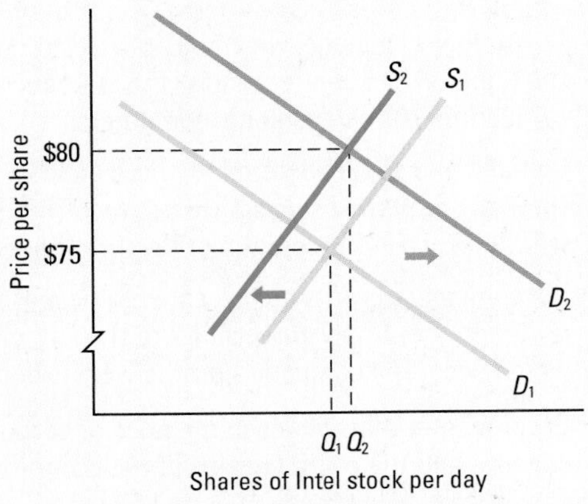

Exhibit 4-4

Effect of Higher Expected Profits on Corporate Stock Price

When expectations of a company's future profits rise, the supply curve for its stock shifts to the left and the demand curve shifts to the right, causing the equilibrium price to rise from $75 to $80.

The overall effect of higher expected profits on the market for Intel stock is a higher price for its stock. As we learned in Chapter 3, the shift in each curve considered separately causes the equilibrium price to rise, since in this case the demand curve for Intel stock has shifted to the right and the supply curve has shifted to the left. What happens to equilibrium quantity depends on which curve shifts more. In Exhibit 4-4 the equilibrium quantity is shown to have increased because the demand curve is shown to have shifted farther to the right than the supply curve has shifted to the left. Had the extent of the shifts been reversed, equilibrium quantity would have fallen. Had the demand and supply curves shifted to the same extent, equilibrium quantity would not have changed. Regardless, the model of demand and supply clearly predicts that the price of a share of Intel stock will rise, in this case to $80.

Unlike the market for coffee analyzed in the last chapter, in the stock market and in other financial markets, changes in expectations are likely to affect both suppliers and demanders. Expectations that cause the demand curve to shift in one direction are generally associated with a shift in the supply curve in the opposite direction. For example, what happens in the market for a firm's output (computer chips in the case of Intel) affects expectations of both potential buyers (the possible future owners) and potential sellers (current owners) of the firm's stock.

Other factors may alter the price of an individual corporation's share of stock or the level of stock prices in general. For example, demographic change and rising incomes have affected the demand for stocks in recent years. As the baby boomers have moved into the period in their lives when their earnings are fairly high and as they begin to think about and plan for retirement, the demand for stocks has risen.

Information on the economy as a whole is also likely to affect stock prices. If the economy overall is doing well and people expect that to continue, they may become more optimistic about how profitable companies will be in general, and thus the prices of stocks will rise. Conversely, expectations of a sluggish economy could cause stock prices in general to fall.

The stock market is bombarded with new information every minute of every day. Firms announce their profits of the previous quarter. They announce that they plan to move into a new product line or sell their goods in another country. We learn that the price of Company A's good, which is a substitute for one sold by Company B, has risen. We learn that countries sign trade agreements, launch wars, or make peace. All of this information may affect stock prices because any information can affect how buyers and sellers value companies.

Check*list*

- Technological change, which has caused the supply curve for personal computers to shift to the right, is the main reason for the rapid increase in equilibrium quantity and decrease in equilibrium price in personal computers.
- Demand and supply determine prices of shares of corporate stock. The equilibrium price of a share of stock strikes a balance between those who think the stock is worth more and those who think it's worth less than the current price.
- If a company's profits are expected to increase, the demand curve for its stock shifts to the right and the supply curve shifts to the left, causing equilibrium price to rise. The opposite would occur if a company's profits were expected to decrease.
- Other factors that influence the price of corporate stock include demographic and income changes and the overall health of the economy.

Case in Point Internet Stock Prices Soar on News of Falling Personal Computer Prices

Stock prices are affected by information on what's happening in markets for the goods and services related to them. With personal computer prices falling in 1998, analysts projected that the quantity of personal computers demanded by households would increase substantially. One of the main uses of household computers is to get on the internet.

Thus the prospect of more internet surfers sent the stock prices of internet search providers, such as Yahoo!, and of companies that conduct business over the internet, such as Amazon.com, soaring during the first week of March 1998.

These companies provide services that are complementary to personal computers. As we learned in Chapter 3, if two goods are complements, a fall in the price of one good (in this case, personal computers) increases the demand for the complementary good (in this case, internet-related services). Of course, the price increases for internet stocks were fueled by expectations. It is only with the passage of time that the participants in the market for internet stocks will learn whether their expectations were realized.

Internet stocks	% Change in stock price (March 4–10, 1998)
Yahoo!	+22.2
Infoseek	+17.5
Excite	+14.8
Amazon.com	+13.2
America Online	+ 8.8
Earthlink Network	+ 8.2
NZKNK	+ 6.6
Lycos	+ 6.0

Source: Susan Pulliam, "Internet Stocks Surf on Fears of PC Pricing," *Wall Street Journal*, 11 March 1998, p. C1.

Try It Yourself 4-1

Suppose an airline announces that its earnings this year are lower than expected due to reduced ticket sales. The airline spokesperson gives no information on how the company plans to turn things around. Use the model of demand and supply to show and explain what is likely to happen to the price of the airline's stock.

Government Intervention in Market Prices: Price Floors and Price Ceilings

So far in this chapter and in the previous chapter, we have learned that markets tend to move toward their equilibrium prices and quantities. Surpluses and shortages of goods are short-lived as prices adjust so as to equate quantity demanded with quantity supplied.

In some markets, however, governments have been called on by groups of citizens to intervene to keep prices of certain items higher or lower than what would otherwise result from the market finding its own equilibrium price. In this section we'll examine agricultural markets and apartment rental markets—two markets that have often been subject to price controls. Through these examples, we will identify the effects of controlling prices. In each case, we'll look at reasons why governments have chosen to control prices in these markets and the consequences of these policies.

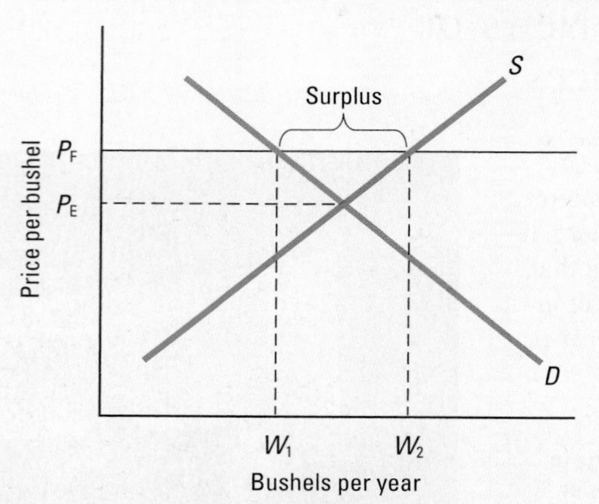

Exhibit 4-5

Effect of a Price Floor on the Market for Wheat

A price floor for wheat that is set above the equilibrium price creates a surplus of wheat equal to ($W_2 - W_1$) bushels.

Agricultural Price Floors

Governments often seek to assist farmers by setting price floors in agricultural markets. A minimum allowable price is a **price floor.** With a price floor, the government forbids a price below the minimum. A price floor that is set above the equilibrium price creates a surplus.

Exhibit 4-5 shows the market for wheat. Suppose the government sets the price of wheat at P_F. Notice that P_F is above the equilibrium price of P_E. At P_F, we read over to the demand curve to find that the quantity of wheat that buyers will be willing and able to buy is W_1 bushels. Reading over to the supply curve, we find that sellers will offer W_2 bushels of wheat at the price floor of P_F. Because P_F is above the equilibrium price, there is a surplus of wheat equal to ($W_2 - W_1$) bushels. The surplus persists because legally the price cannot fall.

Why have many governments around the world set price floors in agricultural markets? Farming has changed dramatically over the past two centuries. Technological improvements in the form of new equipment, fertilizers, pesticides, and new varieties of crops have led to dramatic increases in crop output per acre. Worldwide production capacity has expanded markedly. As we have learned, technological improvements cause the supply curve to shift to the right.

Demand for agricultural products has increased as well, but rather more slowly. One reason why the demand curve has shifted to the right has been rising incomes. Farm products are, for the most part, normal goods for which increases in income produce increases in demand. However, empirical evidence suggests that as people get richer, food expenditures constitute a decreasing percentage of their income. Thus, the shift in demand to the right is not very pronounced. Population increases are another reason that the demand curve has shifted to the right. Exhibit 4-6 shows that the supply curve has shifted much farther to the right, from S_1 to S_2, than the demand curve has, from D_1 to D_2. As a result, equilibrium quantity has risen dramatically, from Q_1 to Q_2, and equilibrium price has plummeted, from P_1 to P_2.

On top of this long-term historical trend in agriculture, agricultural prices are subject to wide swings over shorter periods. Droughts or freezes can sharply reduce supplies of particular crops, causing sudden increases in prices. Demand for agricultural goods of one country can suddenly dry up if the government of another country imposes trade restrictions against its products, and prices can fall. Such dramatic shifts in prices and quantities make incomes of farmers erratic.

The Great Depression of the 1930s led to a huge federal role in agriculture. The Depression affected the entire economy, but it hit farmers particularly hard. Prices received by farmers plunged nearly two-thirds from 1930 to 1933. Many farmers had a tough time keeping up mortgage payments. By 1932, more than half of all farm loans were in default.

Farm legislation passed during the Great Depression has been modified many times, but the federal government has continued its direct involvement in agricultural markets. This has meant a variety of government programs that guarantee a minimum price for some types of agricultural products. These programs have been accompanied by government purchases of any surplus, by requirements to restrict acreage in order to limit those surpluses, by crop restrictions, and the like.

Exhibit 4-6

Supply and Demand Shifts for Agricultural Products

A relatively large increase in the supply of agricultural products, accompanied by a relatively small increase in the demand for agricultural products, has reduced the price received by farmers and increased the quantity of agricultural goods.

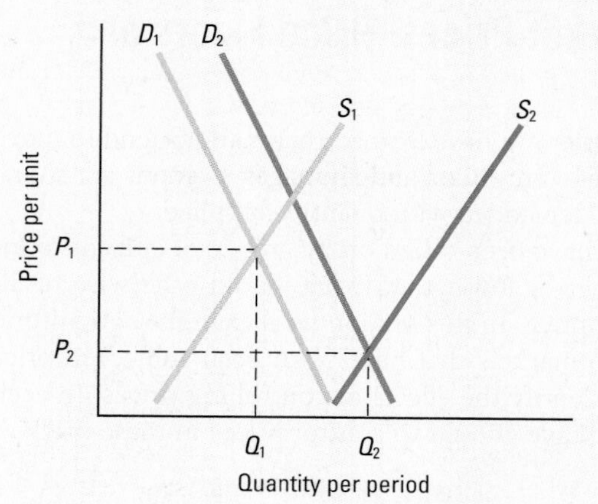

Case in Point Dairy Floor Milked Consumers, Boosted Producers: Where Will It End?

Every year from 1949 until 1997, the federal government went to the market to buy milk, butter, and cheese—a *lot* of milk, butter, and cheese. In a typical year, the government snapped up about $3 billion worth of these dairy products.

The government's spending spree wasn't a result of a particular enthusiasm for dairy products on the part of Washington bureaucrats. In fact, most of the milk, butter, and cheese the government bought wasn't used. Although some of it was distributed to low-income people, most sat unused in government warehouses. In 1994 the government had more than 5 billion pounds of milk, butter, and cheese in storage.

The government's purchase program was part of an effort to prop up dairy prices. The government set a minimum price for raw milk; it was illegal for a dairy to pay dairy farmers less. Because the price floor exceeded the equilibrium price, the program produced a surplus. By itself, such a program might not have been particularly helpful to dairy farmers; it raised the price they received but lowered the quantity they could sell. However, the federal government guaranteed that it would purchase any surplus the program created, thus assuring producers not only of a higher price but of a greater quantity sold as well.

The federal program affected consumers in two ways. As taxpayers, they paid to buy and store surplus milk, butter, and cheese. The more important cost, however, was the higher prices consumers faced. University of Maryland economist Bruce Gardner estimated that the program boosted the prices consumers paid by about 30 percent—for example, a gallon of milk that sold for $3 would have sold for about $2.30 in the absence of federal intervention.

Mr. Gardner, for one, didn't think much of the government's effort. "I see no justification whatever for government support of the industry," he said. But many dairy farmers, to whom the federal support made the difference between making money and losing it, felt quite differently: "Without the dairy program, I'd lose money, and that means I'd get out of the business," said Wisconsin dairy farmer Bob Henshaw. "If you want milk, you've got to pay for it."

As part of Federal Agriculture Improvement and Reform Act of 1996, or FAIR, dairy price supports were replaced with standard payments to farmers that are unconnected to prices. These payments were set to decline each year and to expire in 1999. Many people, economists included, are skeptical that the government will actually get out of the farm business at that time.

When prices for many crops fell in 1998, Congress responded by passing an emergency aid package for farmers. Even though dairy prices at that time were at record high levels, the industry still received an extra $200 million shot in the arm, netting every dairy farmer in the country a bonus of about $2,000. And in the first quarter of the 1999 market year, supposedly the last year of the program, the government had already purchased 328,000 pounds of butter, 29,775,000 pounds of cheese, and 728,000 pounds of nonfat dry milk.

Sources: Laurent Belsie "Harvest with Help from Congress," *Christian Science Monitor,* 23 October 1998, p. 3; Sam Walker, "Wild New Agricultural Markets Curdle Some Dairy Farmers," *Christian Science Monitor,* 14 August 1997, p. 1; Personal interviews.

To see generally how such policies work, look back at Exhibit 4-5. At P_F, W_2 bushels of wheat will be supplied. With that much wheat on the market, there is market pressure on the price of wheat to fall. To prevent price from falling, the government buys the surplus wheat of $(W_2 - W_1)$ bushels, so that only W_1 bushels are actually available to private consumers for purchase on the market. The government can store the surpluses or find special uses for them. For example, surpluses generated in the United States have been shipped to developing countries as grants-in-aid or distributed to local school lunch programs. As a variation on this scheme, the government can require farmers who want to participate in the price support program to reduce acreage in order to limit the size of the surpluses.

After 1973, the government stopped buying the surpluses (with some exceptions) and simply guaranteed farmers a "target price." If the average market price for a crop fell below the crop's target price, the government paid the difference. If, for example, a crop had a market price of $3 per unit and a target price of $4 per unit, the government would give farmers a payment of $1 for each unit sold. Farmers would thus receive the market price of $3 plus a government payment of $1 per unit. For farmers to receive these payments, they had to agree to remove acres from production and to comply with certain conservation provisions. These restrictions sought to reduce the size of the surplus generated by the target price, which acted as a kind of price floor.

What are the effects of such farm support programs? The intention is to boost and stabilize farm incomes. But, with price floors, consumers pay more for food than they would otherwise, and governments spend heavily to finance the programs. With the target price approach, consumers pay less but government financing of the program continues. For example, direct government payments to farmers peaked at $16.7 billion in 1987, but cost U.S. taxpayers over $7 billion in each year between 1983 and 1997.

Help to farmers has sometimes been justified on the grounds that it boosts incomes of "small" farmers. However, since farm aid has generally been allotted on the basis of how much farms produce rather than on a per farm basis, most federal farm support has gone to the largest farms. If the goal is to eliminate poverty among farmers, farm aid could be redesigned to supplement the incomes of small or poor farmers directly rather than to undermine the functioning of agricultural markets.

In 1996, the U.S. Congress passed the Federal Agriculture Improvement and Reform Act of 1996, or FAIR. The thrust of the new legislation was to do away with the various programs of price support for most crops and hence provide incentives for farmers to respond to market price signals. To protect farmers through a transition period, the act provided for continued payments that were scheduled to decline over a seven-year period. However, with prices for many crops falling in 1998, the U.S. Congress passed an emergency aid package that increased payments to farmers. The bill also mandated the establishment an 11-member commission to monitor the agricultural economy and make recommendations to Congress about the appropriate role of the federal government in agriculture by January 1, 2001. Whether the changes in agricultural policy will become permanent remains to be seen.

Rental Price Ceilings

The purpose of rent control is to make rental units cheaper for tenants than they would otherwise be. Unlike agricultural price controls, rent control in the United States has been largely a local phenomenon, although there were national rent controls in effect during World War II. Currently, about 200 cities and counties have some type of rent control provisions, and about 10 percent of rental units in the United States are now subject to price controls. New York City's rent control program, which began in 1943, is among the oldest in the country. Many other cities in the United States adopted some form of rent control in the 1970s. Rent controls have been pervasive in Europe since World War I, and many large cities in poorer countries have also adopted rent controls.

Rent controls in different locales differ in terms of their flexibility. Some forms allow rent increases for specified reasons, such as to make improvements in apartments or to allow rents to keep pace with price increases elsewhere in the economy. Often, rental housing constructed after the imposition of the rent control ordinances is exempted. Apartments that are vacated may also be decontrolled. For simplicity, the model presented here assumes that apartment rents are controlled at a price that does not change.

Exhibit 4-7 shows the market for rental apartments. Notice that the demand and supply curves are drawn to look like all the other demand and supply curves you've encountered so far in this text: the demand curve is downward sloping and the supply curve is upward sloping.

The demand curve shows that a higher price (rent) reduces the quantity of apartments demanded. For example, with higher rents, more young people will choose to live at home. With lower rents, more will choose to live in apartments. Higher prices may encourage more apartment sharing; lower prices would induce more people to live alone.

The supply curve is drawn to show that as price increases, property owners will be encouraged to offer more apartments to rent. Even though an aerial shot of a city would show apartments to be fixed at a point in time, owners of those properties will decide how many to rent depending on the amount of rent they anticipate. Higher rents may also induce some homeowners to rent out apartment space. In addition, renting out apartments implies a certain level of service to renters, so that low rents may lead some property owners to keep some apartments vacant.

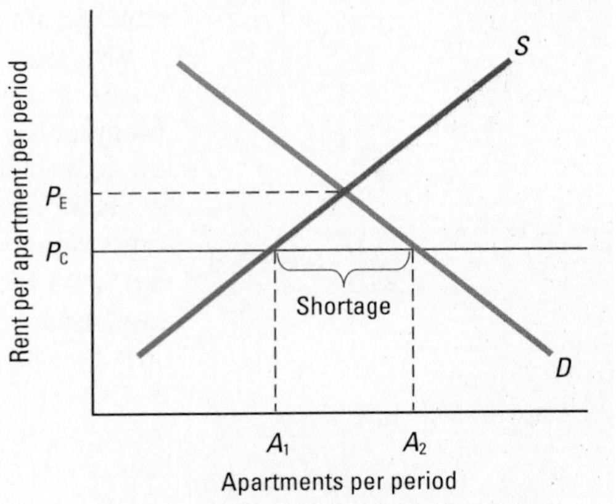

Exhibit 4-7

Effect of a Price Ceiling on the Market for Apartments

A price ceiling on apartment rents that is set below the equilibrium rent creates a shortage of apartments equal to $(A_2 - A_1)$ apartments.

Rent control is an example of a **price ceiling,** a maximum allowable price. With a price ceiling, the government forbids a price above the maximum. A price ceiling that is set below the equilibrium price creates a shortage that will persist.

Suppose the government sets the price of an apartment at P_C in Exhibit 4-7. Notice that P_C is below the equilibrium price of P_E. At P_C, we read over to the supply curve to find that sellers are willing to offer A_1 apartments. Reading over to the demand curve, we find that consumers would like to rent A_2 apartments at the price ceiling of P_C. Because P_C is below the equilibrium price, there is a shortage of apartments equal to $(A_2 - A_1)$.

If rent control creates a shortage of apartments, why do some citizens nonetheless clamor for rent control and why do governments often acquiesce? The rationale generally given for rent control is to keep apartments affordable for low- and middle-income tenants.

But the reduced quantity of apartments supplied must be rationed in some way, since, at the price ceiling, the quantity demanded would exceed the quantity supplied. Current occupants may be reluctant to leave their dwellings because finding other apartments will be difficult. As apartments do become available, there will be a line of potential renters waiting to fill them, any of whom is willing to pay the controlled price of P_C or more. In fact, reading up to the demand curve in Exhibit 4-8 from A_1 apartments, the quantity available at P_C, you can see that for A_1 apartments, there are many potential renters willing and able to pay P_B. This often leads to various "back-door" payments to apartment owners, such as large security deposits, payments for things renters may not want (such as furniture), so-called "key" payments ("The monthly rent is $500 and the key price is $3,000"), or simple bribes.

In the end, rent controls, and other price ceilings, often end up hurting some of the people they are intended to help. Many people will have trouble finding apartments to rent. Ironically, some of those who do find apartments may actually end up paying more than they would have paid in the absence of rent control. And many of the people that the rent controls do help (primarily current occupants, regardless of their income, and those lucky enough to find apartments)

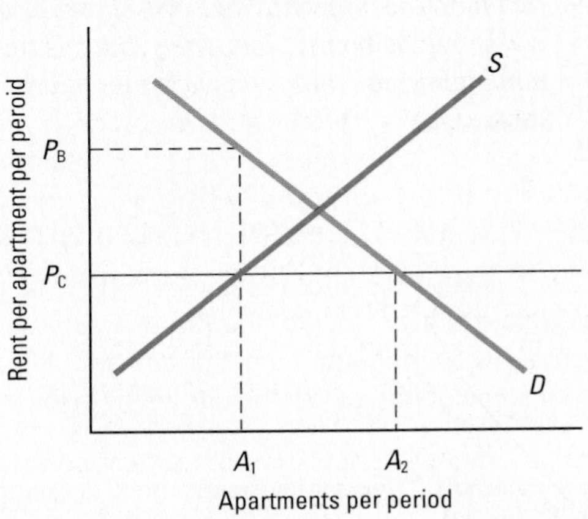

Exhibit 4-8

The Unintended Consequence of Rent Control

Controlling apartment rents at P_C creates a shortage of $(A_2 - A_1)$ apartments. For A_1 apartments, consumers are willing and able to pay P_B, which leads to various "back-door" payments to apartment owners.

are not those they are intended to help (the poor). There are also costs in government administration and enforcement.

Because New York City has the longest history of rent controls of any city in the United States, its program has been widely studied. There is general agreement that the rent control program has reduced tenant mobility, led to a substantial gap between rents on controlled and uncontrolled units, and favored long-term residents at the expense of newcomers to the city.[2]

A more direct means of helping poor tenants, one that would avoid interfering with the functioning of the market, would be to subsidize their incomes. As with price floors, interfering with the market mechanism may solve one problem, but creates many others at the same time.

Checklist

- Government-imposed price floors that are set above the equilibrium price create surpluses, and government-imposed price ceilings that are set below the equilibrium price create shortages.
- Over much of the period since the Great Depression, the U.S. government has supported farm incomes in various ways, including guaranteeing minimum prices to farmers and imposing limits on agricultural production. Such government programs have increased prices to consumers, and most farm support has gone to the largest farms.
- The 1996 Federal Agricultural Improvement and Reform Act (FAIR) sought to phase out agricultural price supports for most crops. The act provided transition payments to farmers and set up a commission to make recommendations on long-term agricultural policy.
- Many local governments have instituted rent control to keep the price of rental units below equilibrium.
- Rent controls make it more difficult for people to find rental apartments, lead to various "back-door" payments to apartment owners, favor current occupants, and generate administrative and enforcement costs.

Try It Yourself 4-2

A minimum wage law is another example of a price floor. Draw demand and supply curves for labor. The horizontal axis will show the quantity of labor per period and the vertical axis will show the hourly wage rate, which is the price of labor. Show and explain the effect of a minimum wage that is above the equilibrium wage.

The Market for Health-Care Services

There has been much discussion over the past two decades about the health-care "problem" in the United States. Much of this discussion has focused on rising spending for health care. In this section, we'll apply the model of demand and supply to health care to see what we can learn about some of the reasons behind rising spending in this important sector of the economy.

[2]Richard Arnott, "Time for Revisionism on Rent Control," *Journal of Economic Perspectives* 9: 1(Winter, 1995): 99–120.

One way to express health-care spending is to show the share of a nation's total output devoted to health care. The greater this share, the greater the fraction of a nation's factors of production devoted to producing health-care goods and services—and the smaller the share devoted to the production of other goods and services. Thinking of spending this way gives us a good idea of the opportunity cost of providing health care. Exhibit 4-9 shows the share of U.S. output devoted to health care since 1960. In 1960, about 5 percent of total output was devoted to health care; by 1997 this share had risen to 13.5 percent. Although the share has been stable in the last few years, when viewed over the last three decades, the opportunity cost of health care has soared. That has meant that we're devoting more of our spending to health care, and less to other goods and services, than we would be had health-care spending not risen so much.

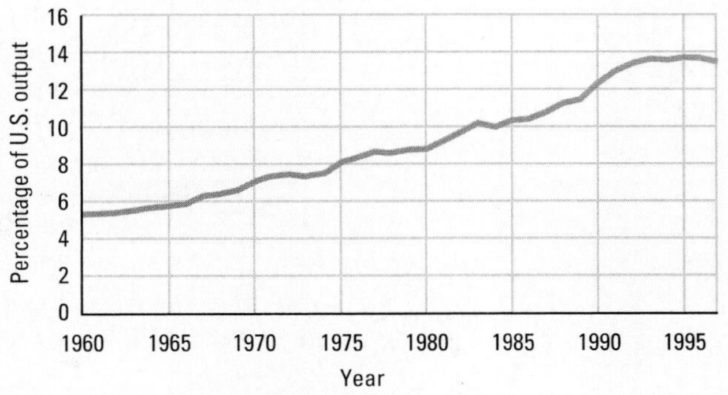

Source: Health Care Finance Association at www.hcfa.gov/stats/nhe-oact/tables/t10.htm

Exhibit 4-9

Health-Care Spending as a Percentage of U.S. Output, 1960–1997

Health care's share of total U.S. output rose from about 5 percent in 1960 to 13.5 percent in 1997.

Why were Americans willing to increase their spending on health care so dramatically? The model of demand and supply gives us part of the answer. As we apply the model to this problem, we'll also gain a better understanding of the role of prices in a market economy.

The Demand and Supply of Health Care

When we speak of "health care," we're speaking of the entire health-care industry. This industry produces services ranging from heart transplant operations to therapeutic massages; it produces goods ranging from X-ray machines to aspirin tablets. Clearly each of these goods and services is exchanged in a particular market. To assess the market forces affecting health care, we'll focus first on just one of these markets: the market for physician office visits. When you go to the doctor, you're part of the demand for these visits. Your doctor, by seeing you, is part of the supply.

Exhibit 4-10 shows the market, assuming that it operates in a fashion similar to other markets. The demand curve D_1 and the supply curve S_1 intersect at point E, with an equilibrium price of $30 per office visit. The equilibrium quantity of office visits per week is 1,000,000.

We can use the demand and supply graph to show total spending, which equals the price per unit (in this case, $30 per visit) times the quantity consumed (in this case, 1,000,000 visits per week). Total spending for physician office visits thus equals $30,000,000 per week ($30 times 1,000,000 visits). We show total spending as the area of a rectangle bounded by the price and the quantity. It is the shaded region in Exhibit 4-10.

Exhibit 4-10

Total Spending for Physician Office Visits

Total spending on physician office visits is $30 per visit multiplied by 1,000,000 visits per week, which equals $30,000,000. It is the shaded area bounded by price and quantity.

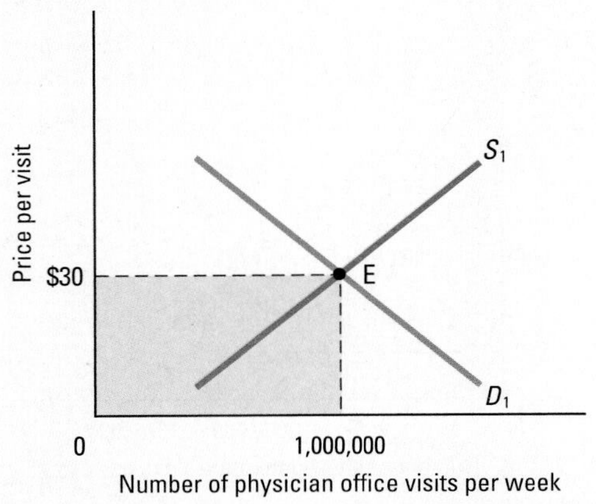

The picture in Exhibit 4-10 misses a crucial feature of the market. Most people in the United States have health insurance, provided either by private firms or by the government. People seek insurance to protect themselves from the possibility that an accident or illness could require them to spend a very large amount of money to pay for their care. With health insurance, people agree to pay a fixed amount to the insurer in exchange for the insurer's agreement to pay for most of the health-care expenses they incur. In the United States, employers make most private purchases of insurance for their employees. The federal government also provides insurance through Medicare (health insurance for the elderly) and Medicaid (health insurance for the poor).

Insurance plans differ in their specific provisions. They may require that subscribers to the insurance plan pay a small percentage of the costs of the health-care services they consume. Many require that subscribers pay a small payment each time they visit the doctor in addition to the fixed fee, or premium, subscribers pay. Let us suppose that all individuals have plans that require them to pay $10 for an office visit; the insurance company will pay the rest.

How will this insurance affect the market for physician office visits? If it costs only $10 for a visit instead of $30, people will visit their doctors more often. The quantity of office visits demanded will increase.

Think about your own choices. When you get a cold, do you go to the doctor? You probably don't if it's a minor cold. But if you feel like you're dying, or wish you were, you probably head for the doctor. Clearly, there are lots of colds in between these two extremes. Whether you drag yourself to the doctor will depend on the severity of your cold and what you'll pay for a visit. At a lower price, you're more likely to go to the doctor; at a higher price, you're less likely to go.

Exhibit 4-11 shows how our hypothetical insurance plan affects the market for physician office visits. The quantity of visits demanded increases. In the case shown, it rises to 1,500,000 per week. But that suggests a potential problem. The quantity of visits supplied at a price of $30 per visit was 1,000,000. According to supply curve S_1, it will take a price of $50 per visit to increase the quantity supplied to 1,500,000 visits (Point F on S_1). But consumers—patients—pay only $10.

Insurers make up the difference between the fees doctors receive and the price patients pay. In our example, insurers pay $40 per visit of insured patients to supplement the $10 that patients pay. When an agent other than the seller or the buyer pays part of the price of a good or service, we say that the agent is a **third-party payer**.

Notice how the presence of a third-party payer affects total spending on office visits. When people paid for their own visits, and the price equaled $30 per visit, total spending equaled $30 million per week. Now doctors receive $50 per visit and provide 1,500,000 visits per week. Total spending has risen to $75 million per week ($50 times 1,500,000 visits, shown by the darkly shaded region plus the lightly shaded region).

The response described in Exhibit 4-11 holds for all health-care services covered by insurance. The availability of health insurance increases the quantity of health-care services consumed and increases total spending for health care.

We've seen in Exhibit 4-9 that spending for health care is not just high, but has grown over the decades. It has grown in terms of its total value, and it has grown relative to total output—it accounts for more than two and a half times the share of total output that it did in 1960. Insurance has clearly played a role in this increasing share. In 1960 people paid, on average, $0.56 of each dollar's worth of health-care services consumed themselves. By 1997, they paid only $0.19. As the fraction people pay falls, their quantity of health-care services consumed rises.

Exhibit 4-11

Total Spending for Physician Office Visits Covered by Insurance

With insurance, the quantity of physician office visits demanded rises to 1,500,000. The supply curve shows that it takes a price of $50 per visit to increase the quantity supplied to 1,500,000 visits. Patients pay $10 per visit and insurance pays $40 per visit. Total spending rises to $75,000,000 per week, shown by the darkly shaded region plus the lightly shaded region.

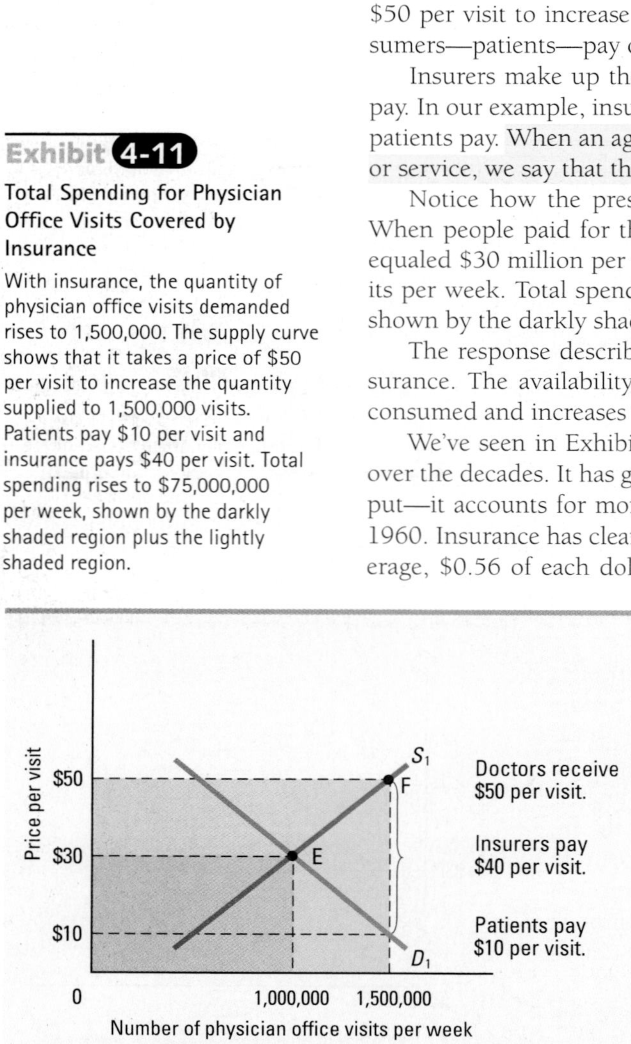

Consider again the example in Exhibit 4-11. Suppose the amount people are required to pay for visits to their doctors falls to $5. That would increase the quantity demanded still further, increase the price doctors receive, and increase total spending on visits to doctors. Certainly the increased coverage available from health insurance has been an important factor in rising spending for health care.

While the increased share of health-care costs borne by third-party payers has increased total spending on health care, other forces have played a role as well. Rising income over time and the aging of the population in the United States have contributed to increased demand for health-care services. After all, health care is a normal good, for which higher income increases demand, and the elderly are more likely to be sick than the

Case in Point The Oregon Plan

Like all other states, Oregon has wrestled with the problem of soaring Medicaid costs. Its solution to the problem illustrates some of the choices society might make in seeking to reduce health-care costs.

Oregon used to have a plan similar to plans in many other states. Households whose incomes were lower than 50 percent of the poverty line qualified for Medicaid. In 1987, the state began an effort to manage its Medicaid costs. It decided that it would no longer fund organ transplants and that it would use the money saved to give better care to pregnant women. The decision turned out to be a painful one; the first year, a 7-year-old boy with leukemia, who might have been saved with a bone marrow transplant, died. But state officials argued that the shift of expenditures to pregnant women would ultimately save more lives.

The state gradually expanded its concept of determining what services to fund and what services not to fund. It collapsed a list of 10,000 different diagnoses that had been submitted to its Medicaid program in the past into a list of more than 700 condition-treatment pairs. One such pair, for example, is appendicitis-appendectomy. Health-care officials then ranked these pairs in order of priority. The rankings were based on such factors as the seriousness of a particular condition and the cost and efficacy of treatments. The state announced that it would provide Medicaid to all households below the poverty line, but that it would not fund any procedure ranked below a certain level, initially 588 on its list. Among the treatments no longer funded are surgery for low back pain, treatment for extremely premature babies, liver transplants for alcoholic cirrhosis, and treatment of viral warts. The plan also sets a budget limit for any one year; if spending rises above that limit, the legislature must appropriate additional money or drop additional procedures from the list of those covered by the plan.

While the Oregon plan has been applied only for households below the poverty line that are not covered by other programs, it suggests a means of reducing health-care spending. Clearly, if part of the health-care problem is excessive provision of services, a system designed to cut services must determine what treatments not to fund.

Subscribers to the plan lose because they have a less generous range of covered services than people under other Medicaid programs. However, by limiting coverage, Oregon has been able to include more people in the program, given its budgetary limitations.

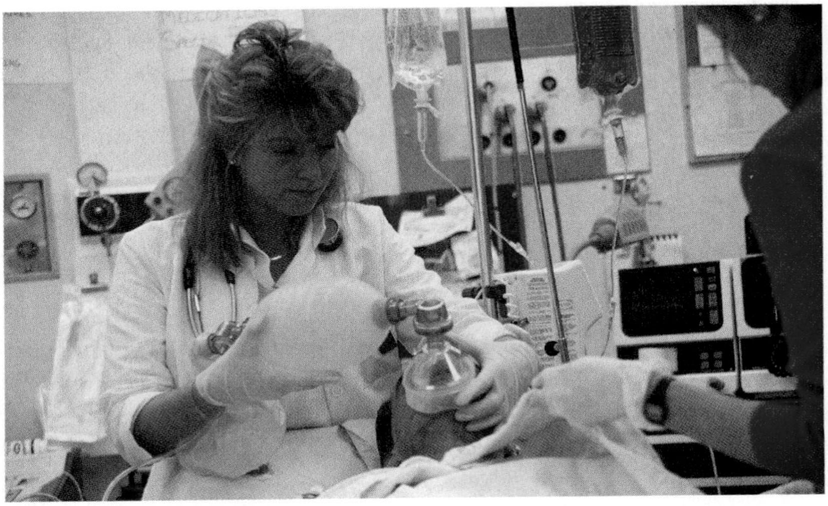

young. New technologies, such as organ transplant procedures, save lives; they are also very expensive. All these things contribute to an increased demand for health-care services, and thus a further increase in total spending.

The Health-Care Spending Dilemma

We've seen that prices help to balance quantities demanded and supplied. In most cases, the price buyers pay is the price sellers receive. The equilibrium price then is one that balances the interests of buyers and of sellers. The same price that limits the quantity buyers demand also determines the quantity sellers supply.

In a market such as the health-care market, we've seen that an equilibrium is achieved, but it is not at the intersection of the demand and supply curves. The effect of third-party payers is to decrease the price that consumers directly pay for the health-care services they consume and to increase the price that health-care providers receive for the services they supply. Consumers use more than they would in the absence of third-party payers, and providers are encouraged to supply more than they otherwise would. The result is increased total health-care spending. That increased spending became a topic of considerable concern in the last two decades, as health-care spending gobbled up a larger and larger share of the nation's output.

To many observers, health-care spending had gotten out of control. In 1993, President Clinton proposed federal regulation that would force a reduction in the quantity of health-care services consumed, and thus a reduction in total spending. Congress rejected that proposal, questioning the federal government's ability to manage so large a share of a market economy's output.

But pressure to rein in health-care spending continued. Today, spending restraint is accomplished more and more through insurance companies, which are, in turn, responding to pressure from the payers of the bulk of the insurance premiums: business firms and the government. They seek to force the demand curve to the left by limiting patients' choices in consuming health care. They may, for example, restrict the doctors and other health-care providers patients may select. In addition, insurers refuse to pay for some services.

The health-care industry presents us with a dilemma. Clearly, it makes sense for people to have health insurance. Just as clearly, health insurance generates a substantial increase in spending for health care. If that spending is to be limited, some mechanism must be chosen to do it. One mechanism would be to require patients to pay a larger share of their own health-care consumption directly, reducing the payments made by third-party payers. Another is government regulation; the accompanying Case in Point describes how Oregon has chosen to limit health-care spending by Medicaid patients. A third option is to continue the current trend toward using insurance companies as the agents that limit spending.

Check*list*

- The rising share of the output of the United States devoted to health care represents a rising opportunity cost. More spending on health care means less spending on other goods and services, compared to what would have transpired had health-care spending not risen so much.
- The U.S. health-care system is characterized by third-party payers, principally private insurance companies, but there are also government-sponsored health insurance programs, such as Medicare and Medicaid.
- The model of demand and supply can be used to show the effect of third-party payers on health-care spending. With third-party payers (health insurers), the quantity of health-care services consumed rises, as does health-care spending.
- Mechanisms to limit spending on health care include pressure from insurance companies to force reductions in demand, requiring patients to pay a larger share of their health-care consumption directly, and government regulation.

Try It Yourself 4-3

Using the model of demand and supply, show and explain how an increase in the share individuals must pay directly for medical care they consume would address the issue of controlling health-care spending.

A Look Back

In this chapter we used the tools of demand and supply to understand a wide variety of market outcomes. We learned that technological change and the entry of new sellers has caused the supply curve of personal computers to shift markedly to the right, thereby reducing equilibrium price and increasing equilibrium quantity. Market forces have made personal computers a common item in offices and homes.

Prices of shares of corporate stock were also explained by demand and supply. The price per share of corporate stock reflects the market's estimate of the expected profitability of the firm. Any information about the firm that causes potential buyers or current owners of corporate stock to reevaluate how profitable they think the firm is, or will be, will cause the equilibrium price of the stock to change.

We then examined markets in which some form of government price control keeps price permanently above or below equilibrium. A price floor leads to persistent surpluses when it is set above the equilibrium price, whereas a price ceiling, when it is set below the equilibrium price, leads to persistent shortages. We saw that interfering with the market mechanism may solve one problem, but often creates other problems at the same time. We discussed what some of these unintended consequences might be. For example, agricultural price floors aimed at boosting farm income have also raised prices for consumers and cost taxpayers dearly, and the bulk of government payments have gone to large farms. Rent controls have lowered rents, but they have also reduced the quantity of rental housing supplied, created shortages, and sometimes led to various forms of "back-door" payments.

Finally, we looked at the market for health care and a special feature behind demand and supply in this market that helps to explain why the share of output of the United States that is devoted to health care has risen. Health care is an example of a market in which there are third-party payers (primarily private insurers and the government). With third-party payers the quantity of health-care services consumed rises, as does health-care spending. Rising incomes, the aging of the population, and new technologies have also contributed to the increase in spending on health care. There are ways to limit spending on this item; whether or not to employ them is a choice that society and individuals much make.

A Look Ahead This chapter concludes our introduction to the field of economics and to the models of production possibilities and of demand and supply. With this foundation, you can go on to study either microeconomics or macroeconomics.

Terms and Concepts for Review

sole proprietorship, **86**
partnership, **86**
corporation, **86**
corporate stock, **86**
stock market, **86**
price floor, **90**
price ceiling, **93**
third-party payer, **96**

For Discussion

1. Like personal computers, camcorders have become a common household item. Camcorder prices have plunged in the last decade. Use the model of demand and supply to explain the fall in price and increase in quantity.
2. In 1999, Microsoft was charged with violating antitrust laws (laws designed to encourage competition in the marketplace and prevent abuse of market power). If convicted, it faced fines or other forms of punishment. Use the model of demand and supply to explain the possible impact of the trial on the price of a share of Microsoft stock.
3. During World War II there was a freeze on wages, and employers found that they could evade the limit by providing

nonsalary benefits, particularly employer-paid (and therefore untaxed) health-care insurance. The IRS has allowed the benefits (with some exceptions) to remain untaxed ever since. Employer-based health insurance was thus an unintended consequence of wage controls that were in effect during World War II. Are wage controls an example of a price ceiling or a price floor? Use the tools of demand and supply to explain why employers at the time might have begun to offer health insurance to their employees.

4. We learned in Chapter 3 that technological improvements lower the cost of production. In Chapter 4 we learned that technology is a factor in driving up the cost of health care. Reconcile these seemingly conflicting statements.
5. The provision of university education through taxpayer-supported state universities is another example of a third-party payer system. Use the tools of demand and supply to discuss the impact this has on the higher education market.
6. "During most of the past 50 years the United States has had a surplus of farmers, and this has been the root of the farm problem." Comment.
7. Suppose the Department of Agriculture ordered all farmers to reduce the acreage they plant by 10 percent. Would you expect a 10 percent reduction in food production? Why or why not?
8. Given that people pay premiums for their health insurance, how can we say that insurance lowers the prices people pay for health-care services?
9. Suppose that physicians now charge $30 for an office visit and insurance policies require patients to pay 33⅓ percent of the amount they pay the physicians, so the out-of-pocket cost to consumers is $10 per visit. In an effort to control costs, the government imposes a price ceiling of $27 per office visit. Using a demand and supply model, show how this policy would affect the market for health care.
10. Do you think the U.S. health-care system requires reform? Why or why not? If you think reform is in order, explain the approach to reform you advocate.

Problems

Problems 1–4 are based on the following demand and supply schedules for corn (all quantities are in millions of bushels per year).

Price per bushel	Quantity demanded	Quantity supplied
$0	6	0
1	5	1
2	4	2
3	3	3
4	2	4
5	1	5
6	0	6

1. Draw the demand and supply curves for corn. What is the equilibrium price? The equilibrium quantity?
2. Suppose the government now imposes a price floor at $4 per bushel. Show the effect of this program graphically. How large is the surplus of corn?
3. With the price floor, how much do farmers receive for their corn? How much would they have received if there were no price floor?
4. If the government buys all the surplus wheat, how much will it spend?

Answers to Try It Yourself Problems

Try It Yourself 4-1

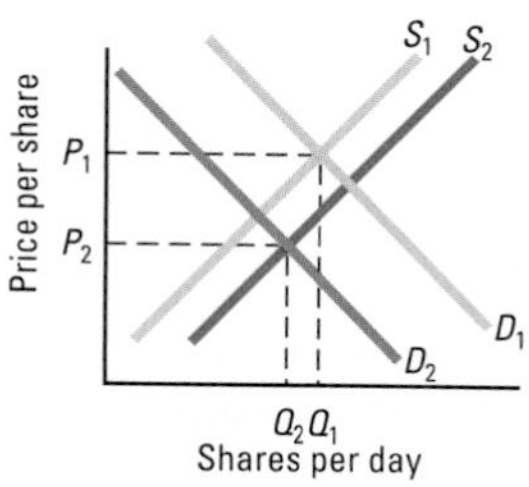

The information given in the problem suggests that the airline's profits are likely to fall below expectations. Current owners of the airline's stock and potential buyers of the stock would adjust downward their estimates of what the value of the corporation's stock should be. As a result the supply curve for the stock would increase, thereby shifting it to the right, while the demand curve for the stock would decrease, thereby shifting it to the left. As a result, equilibrium price of the stock falls from P_1 to P_2. What happens to equilibrium quantity depends on the extent to which each curve shifts. In the diagram, equilibrium quantity is shown to decrease from Q_1 to Q_2.

Try It Yourself 4-2

A minimum wage (W_{min}) that is set above the equilibrium wage would create a surplus of labor equal to $(L_2 - L_1)$. That is, L_2 units of labor are offered at the minimum wage but companies only want to use L_1 units at that wage.

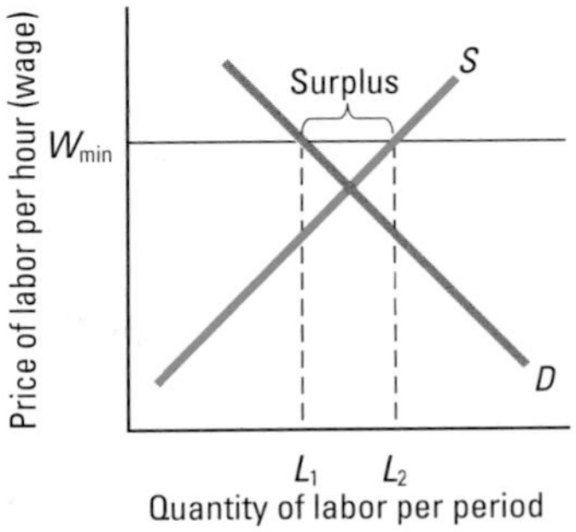

Try It Yourself 4-3

An increase in the share individuals pay directly for the health care they consume lowers the quantity demanded. For example, if the fee they pay rises from P_1 to P_2, the quantity demanded of health-care services falls from Q_1 to Q_2. To compare total spending at a price to individuals of P_1 to total spending at a price to individuals of P_2, read up to the supply curve at each quantity and then over to the vertical axis. Total health-care spending falls from $0ABQ_1$ to $0CDQ_2$.

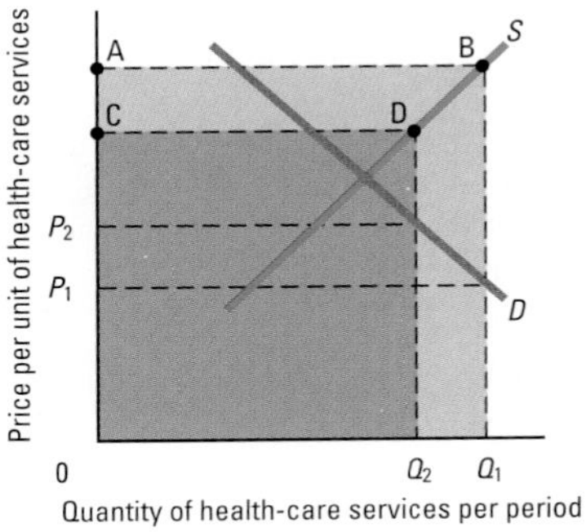

5 Elasticity: A Measure of Response

Getting Started: Raise Fares? Lower Fares? What's a Public Transit Manager To Do?

Imagine that you're the manager of the public transportation system for a metropolitan area. Operating costs for the system have soared in the last few years, and you're under pressure to boost revenues. What do you do?

An obvious choice would be to raise fares. That will make your customers angry, but at least it will generate the extra revenue you need—or will it? The law of demand says that raising fares will reduce the number of passengers riding on your system. If the number of passengers falls only a little, then the higher fares that your remaining passengers are paying might produce the higher revenues you need. But, what if the number of passengers falls by so much that your higher fares actually reduce your revenues? If that happens, you'll have made your customers mad and your financial problem worse!

Maybe you should recommend *lower* fares. After all, the law of demand also says that lower fares will increase the number of passengers. Having more people use the public transportation system could more than offset a lower fare you collect from each person. But it might not. What *will* you do?

Your job and the health of the public transit system are riding on your making the correct decision. To do so, you need to know just how responsive the quantity demanded is to a price change. You need a measure of responsiveness.

Economists use a measure of responsiveness called elasticity. **Elasticity** is the ratio of the percentage change in a dependent variable to a percentage change in an independent variable. A dependent variable is said to be more elastic (responsive) if the percentage change in the dependent variable is large relative to the percentage change in the independent variable. It is less elastic if the reverse is true.

The concept of elasticity will help you solve your public transit pricing problem, and a great many other issues in economics. We'll examine several elasticities in this chapter—all will tell us how responsive one variable is to a change in another. We begin with the responsiveness of quantity demanded to a change in price.

The Price Elasticity of Demand

We know from the law of demand how the quantity demanded will respond to a price change: it will change in the opposite direction. But how *much* will it change? It seems reasonable to expect, for example, that a 10-percent change in the price charged for a visit to the doctor would yield a different percentage change in quantity demanded than a 10-percent change in the price of an Oldsmobile. But how much is this difference?

To show how responsive quantity demanded is to a change in price, we apply the concept of elasticity. The **price elasticity of demand** for a good or service, e_P, is the percentage change in quantity demanded divided by the percentage change in the price of the good or service, all other things unchanged. Thus we can write

$$e_P = \frac{\text{Percentage change in quantity demanded}}{\text{Percentage change in price}} \qquad (1)$$

Because it reports the responsiveness of quantity demanded to a price change, assuming that other factors that influence demand are unchanged, the price elasticity of demand reflects movements along a demand curve. With a downward-sloping demand curve, price and quantity demanded move in opposite directions,

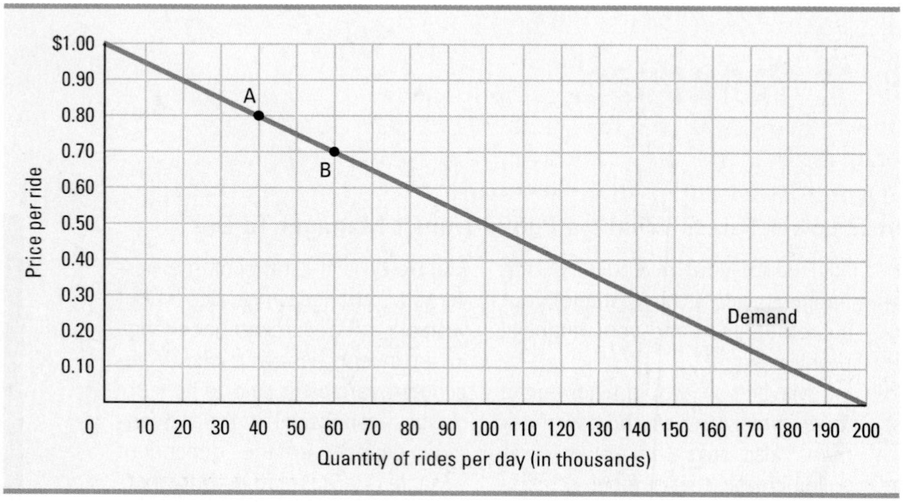

so the price elasticity of demand is negative. A positive percentage change in price implies a negative percentage change in quantity demanded, and vice versa. Sometimes you will see the absolute value of the price elasticity measure reported. In essence, the minus sign is ignored because it is expected that there will be a negative (inverse) relationship between quantity demanded and price. In this text, however, we will retain the minus sign in reporting price elasticity of demand and will say "the absolute value of the price elasticity of demand" when that's what we are describing.

Exhibit 5-1

Responsiveness and Demand

The demand curve shows how changes in price lead to changes in the quantity demanded. A movement from point A to point B, for example, shows how a $0.10 reduction in price increases the number of rides demanded by 20,000. A movement from B to A is a $0.10 increase in price, which reduces quantity demanded by 20,000 rides.

Computing the Price Elasticity of Demand

Finding the price elasticity of demand requires that we first compute percentage changes in price and in quantity demanded. We'll calculate those changes between two points on a demand curve.

Exhibit 5-1 shows a typical demand curve, a demand curve for public transit rides. Suppose the initial price is $0.80 and the quantity demanded is 40,000 rides per day; we are at point A on the curve. Now suppose the price falls to $0.70 and we want to report the responsiveness of the quantity demanded. We see that at the new price, the quantity demanded rises to 60,000 rides per day (point B). To compute the elasticity, we need to compute the percentage changes in price and in quantity demanded between points A and B.

We measure the percentage change between two points as the change in the variable divided by the *average* value of the variable between the two points. Thus, the percentage change in quantity between point A and point B in Exhibit 5-1 is computed relative to the *average* of the quantity values at points A and B: (60,000 + 40,000)/2 = 50,000. The percentage change in quantity, then, is 20,000/50,000, or 40 percent. Likewise, the percentage change in price is considered relative to the *average* of the two prices: ($0.80 + $0.70)/2 = $0.75, and so we have a percentage change of −0.10/0.75, or −13.33 percent. The price elasticity of demand between points A and B is thus 40%/(−13.33%) = −3.00.

This measure of elasticity, which is based on percentage changes relative to the average value of each variable between two points, is called **arc elasticity.** It is the method we shall use to compute elasticity.

For the arc elasticity method, we calculate the price elasticity of demand using the average value of price, $\overline{P}$ and the average value of quantity demanded, $\overline{Q}$. We shall use the Greek letter Δ to mean "change in," so the change in quantity between two points is ΔQ and the change in price is ΔP. Now we can write the formula for the price elasticity of demand as

$$e_P = \frac{\Delta Q/\overline{Q}}{\Delta P/\overline{P}} \tag{2}$$

The price elasticity of demand between points A and B is thus

$$e_P = \frac{20{,}000/50{,}000}{-0.10/0.75} = \frac{40\%}{-13.33\%} = 3.00$$

With the arc elasticity formula, the elasticity is the same whether we move from point A to point B or from point B to point A. If we start at point B and move to point A, we have

$$e_P = \frac{-20{,}000/50{,}000}{0.10/0.75} = \frac{-40\%}{13.33\%} = -3.00$$

The arc elasticity method gives us an estimate of elasticity. It gives the value of elasticity at the midpoint over a range of change, such as the movement between points A and B.[1] For a precise computation of elasticity, we would need to consider the response of a dependent variable to an extremely small change in an independent variable. The fact that arc elasticities are approximate suggests an important practical rule in calculating elasticities: we should consider only small changes in independent variables. We cannot apply the concept of arc elasticity to large changes.

Another argument for considering only small changes in computing price elasticities of demand will become evident in the next section. We'll investigate what happens to price elasticities as we move from one point to another along a linear demand curve.

Price Elasticities Along a Linear Demand Curve

What happens to the price elasticity of demand when we travel along the demand curve? The answer depends on the nature of the demand curve itself. On a linear demand curve, such as the one in Exhibit 5-2, elasticity becomes smaller (in absolute value) as we travel downward and to the right.

Exhibit 5-2 shows the same demand curve we saw in Exhibit 5-1. We've already calculated the price elasticity of demand between points A and B; it equals −3.00. Notice, however, that when we use the same method to compute the price elasticity of demand between other sets of points, our answer varies. For each of the pairs of points shown, the changes in price and quantity are the same (a $0.10 decrease and a 20,000-unit increase, respectively). But at the high prices and low quantities on the upper part of the demand curve, the

Exhibit 5-2

Price Elasticities of Demand for a Linear Demand Curve

The price elasticity of demand varies between different pairs of points along a linear demand curve. The lower the price and the greater the quantity demanded, the lower the absolute value of the price elasticity of demand.

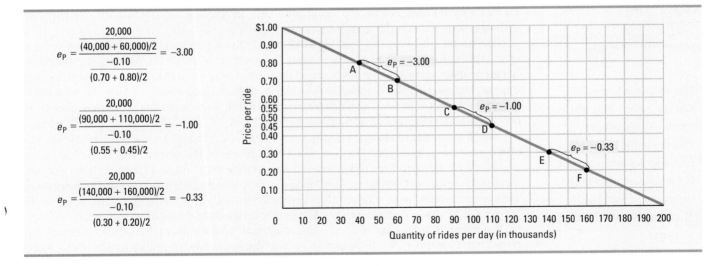

$$e_P = \frac{\dfrac{20{,}000}{(40{,}000 + 60{,}000)/2}}{\dfrac{-0.10}{(0.70 + 0.80)/2}} = -3.00$$

$$e_P = \frac{\dfrac{20{,}000}{(90{,}000 + 110{,}000)/2}}{\dfrac{-0.10}{(0.55 + 0.45)/2}} = -1.00$$

$$e_P = \frac{\dfrac{20{,}000}{(140{,}000 + 160{,}000)/2}}{\dfrac{-0.10}{(0.30 + 0.20)/2}} = -0.33$$

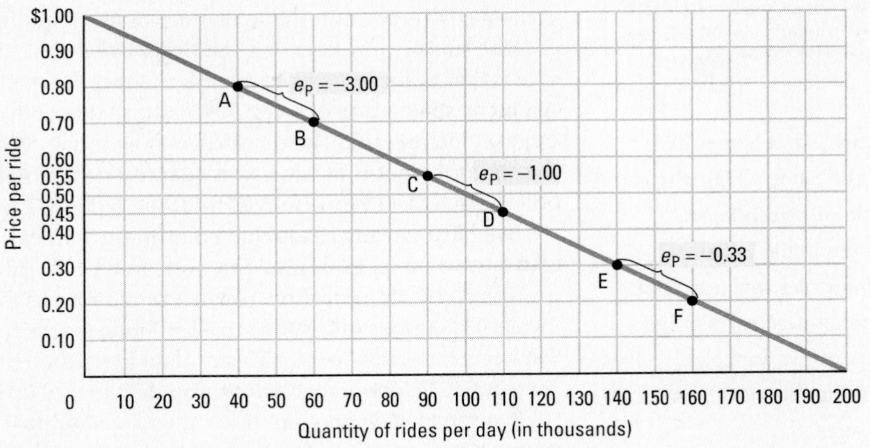

[1]Notice that in the arc elasticity formula, the method for computing a percentage change differs from the standard method that you may be familiar with, which measures the percentage change in a variable relative to the original value. For example, using the standard method, if the price of a good rises from $4 to $5, the good is said to have increased in price by 25 percent: (5 − 4)/4 = 0.25, or a 25-percent price increase. If the price falls from $5 to $4, the price is said to have decreased by 20 percent: (4 − 5)/5 = −0.20, or a 20-percent price decrease. Using the average price of $4.50 in the denominator of the formula for percentage change gives us a change of 22.22 percent whether price increases or decreases over the range. In economics, we are often interested in the elasticity over a range of values in variables—for example, between points A and B in Exhibit 5-1. With the arc elasticity formula, which uses the average values of the variables in calculating percentage changes, we accommodate changes from A to B and changes from B to A.

percentage change in quantity is relatively large while the percentage change in price is relatively small. The absolute value of the price elasticity of demand is thus relatively large. As we move down the demand curve, equal changes in quantity represent smaller and smaller percentage changes while equal changes in price represent larger and larger percentage changes, and the absolute value of the elasticity measure declines. Between points C and D, for example, the price elasticity of demand is −1.00, and between points E and F the price elasticity of demand is −0.33.

On a linear demand curve, the price elasticity of demand varies depending on the arc, or interval, over which we are measuring it. For any linear demand curve, the absolute value of the price elasticity of demand will fall as we move down and to the right along the curve.

The Price Elasticity of Demand and Changes in Total Revenue

Suppose the public transit authority is considering raising fares. Will its total revenues go up or down? **Total revenue** is the price per unit times the number of units sold.[2] In this case, it is the fare times the number of riders. The transit authority will certainly want to know whether a price increase will cause its total revenue to rise or fall. In fact, determining the impact of a price change on total revenue is crucial to the analysis of many problems in economics.

Let's do two quick calculations before generalizing the principle involved. Given the demand curve shown in Exhibit 5-2, we see that at a price of $0.80, the transit authority will sell 40,000 rides. Total revenue would be $32,000 ($0.80 times 40,000). If the price were lowered by $0.10 to $0.70, quantity demanded would increase to 60,000 rides and total revenue would increase to $42,000 ($0.70 times 60,000). It appears that a reduction in the fare will *increase* total revenue. However, if the initial price had been $0.30 and the transit authority reduced it by $0.10 to $0.20, total revenue would *decrease* from $42,000 ($0.30 times 140,000) to $32,000 ($0.20 times 160,000). So it appears that the impact of a price change on total revenue depends on the initial price and, by implication, the original elasticity. We generalize this point in the remainder of this section.

The problem in assessing the impact of a price change on total revenue of a good or service is that a change in price always changes the quantity demanded in the opposite direction. An increase in price reduces the quantity demanded, and a reduction in price increases the quantity demanded. The question is how much. Because total revenue is found by multiplying the price per unit times the quantity demanded, it isn't clear whether a change in price will cause total revenue to rise or fall.

We have already made this point in the context of the transit authority. Consider the following additional examples. Suppose that 1,000 gallons of gasoline per day are demanded at a price of $1.25 per gallon. Total revenue for gasoline thus equals $1,250 per day. If an increase in the price of gasoline to $1.40 reduces the quantity demanded to 950 gallons per day, total revenue rises to $1,330 per day. Even though people consume less gasoline at $1.40 than at $1.25, the higher price more than makes up for the drop in consumption.

Now consider another price increase. Suppose 1,000 cans of frozen orange juice per month are demanded at a price of $1 per can. Total revenue for orange juice equals $1,000 per month. If an increase in the price of orange juice to $1.10 reduces quantity demanded to 880 cans per month, total revenue for orange juice falls to $968 per month. As in the case of gasoline, people will buy less orange juice when the price rises from $1.00 to $1.10, but in this example total revenue drops.

Caution!

Elasticity and Slope Are Not the Same Elasticity is a ratio of *percentage changes* in the values of two variables, whereas slope is a ratio of *changes* in the values of two variables. Thus, they are not the same measures.

For example, price elasticity of demand falls (in absolute value) as we travel along the linear demand curve shown in Exhibit 5-2. The slope of a linear demand curve, however, is the same all along it.

[2]Notice that since the number of units sold of a good is the same as the number of units bought, the definition for total revenue could also be used to define total spending. Which term we use depends on the question at hand. If we are trying to determine what happens to revenues of sellers, then we are asking about total revenue. If we are trying to determine what happens to spending (as was the case in Chapter 4 when we were interested in spending on health care), then we are asking about total spending.

Consider yet one more price increase. Suppose 1,000 pounds of hamburger per week are demanded at a price of $2 per pound. Total revenue for hamburger equals $2,000. If an increase in the price of hamburger to $2.50 per pound reduces quantity demanded to 800 pounds per week, total revenue will still be $2,000. Again, when price goes up, consumers buy less, but this time there is no change in total revenue.

In our first example, an increase in price increased total revenue. In the second, a price hike reduced total revenue. In the third example, the price rise had no effect on total revenue. Is there a way to predict how a price change will affect total revenue? The answer is yes: The effect depends on the value of the price elasticity of demand.

Elastic, Unit Elastic, and Inelastic Demand To determine how a price change will affect total revenue, economists place price elasticities of demand in three categories, based on their absolute value. If the absolute value of the price elasticity of demand is greater than 1, demand is termed **price elastic.** If it is equal to 1, demand is **unit price elastic.** And if it is less than 1, demand is **price inelastic.**

Relating Elasticity to Total Revenue When the price of a good or service changes, the quantity demanded changes in the opposite direction. Total revenue will move in the direction of the variable that changes by the larger percentage. If the variables move by the same percentage, total revenue stays the same. If quantity demanded changes by a larger percentage than price, total revenue will change in the direction of the quantity change. If price changes by a larger percentage than quantity demanded, total revenue will move in the direction of the price change. If price and quantity demanded change by the same percentage, then total revenue does not change.

When demand is price inelastic, a given percentage change in price results in a smaller percentage change in quantity demanded. That implies that total revenue will move in the direction of the price change: a reduction in price will reduce total revenue, and an increase in price will increase it.

Consider the price elasticity of demand for gasoline. We calculate this value for the price and quantity changes already given:

$$e_P = \frac{-50/975}{0.15/1.325} = \frac{-5.13\%}{11.32\%} = -0.45$$

The demand for gasoline is price inelastic, and total revenue moves in the direction of the price change. When price rises, total revenue rises.

When demand is price elastic, a given percentage change in price results in a larger percentage change in quantity demanded. That implies that total revenue will move in the direction of the quantity change: a reduction in price will increase total revenue, and an increase in price will reduce it.

Now consider the case of orange juice. Using the price and quantity changes already given, we can compute the price elasticity of demand for orange juice as

$$e_P = \frac{-120/940}{0.10/1.05} = \frac{-12.77\%}{9.52\%} = -1.34$$

Demand is price elastic, and total revenue moves in the direction of the quantity change. Quantity demanded and total revenue fall.

When demand is unit elastic, price and quantity demanded change by the same percentage, so total revenue stays the same when the price changes. Using the price and quantity changes for hamburger that were already given, we can compute the price elasticity of demand for hamburger as

$$e_P = \frac{-200/900}{0.50/2.25} = \frac{-0.22\%}{0.22\%} = -1.00$$

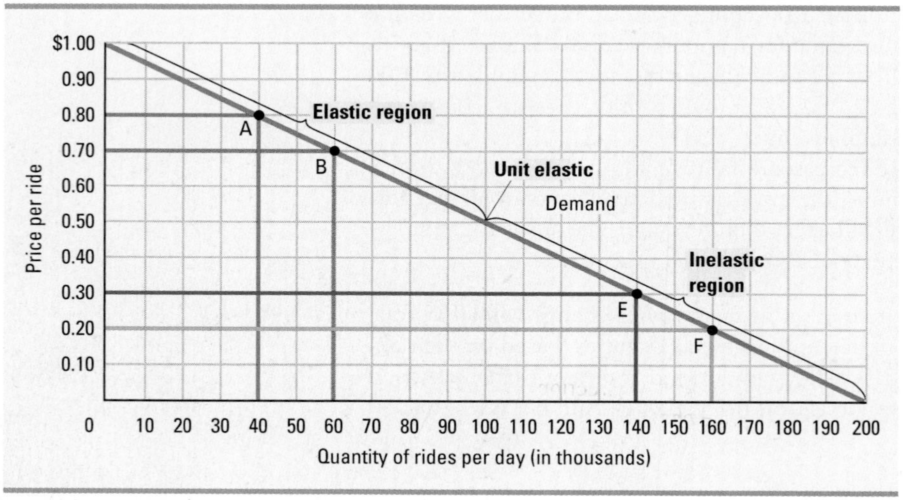

Exhibit 5-3

Changes in Total Revenue and a Linear Demand Curve

Moving from point A to point B implies a reduction in price and an increase in the quantity demanded. Demand is elastic between these two points. Total revenue, shown by the areas of the rectangles drawn from points A and B to the origin, rises. When we move from point E to point F, which is in the inelastic region of the demand curve, total revenue falls.

A demand curve can also be used to show changes in total revenue. Exhibit 5-3 shows the demand curve from Exhibits 5-1 and 5-2. At point A, total revenue from public transit rides is given by the area of a rectangle drawn with point A in the upper right-hand corner and the origin in the lower left-hand corner. The height of the rectangle is price; its width is quantity. (We've already seen that total revenue at point A is $32,000.) When we reduce the price and move to point B, the rectangle showing total revenue becomes shorter and wider. Notice that the area gained in moving to the rectangle at B is greater than the area lost; total revenue rises to $42,000. Recall from Exhibit 5-2 that demand is elastic between points A and B. In general, demand is elastic in the upper half of any linear demand curve, so total revenue moves in the direction of the quantity change.

A movement from point E to point F also shows a reduction in price and an increase in quantity demanded. This time, however, we are in an inelastic region of the demand curve. Total revenue now moves in the direction of the price change—it falls. Notice that the rectangle drawn from point F is smaller in area than the rectangle drawn from point E, once again confirming our earlier calculation.

We've noted the reason a linear demand curve is more elastic in its upper half, where prices are relatively high and quantities relatively low, than in its lower half, where prices are

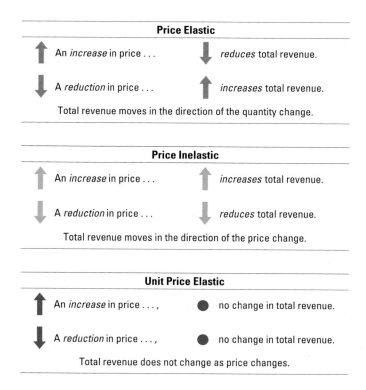

Price Elastic	
↑ An *increase* in price . . .	↓ *reduces* total revenue.
↓ A *reduction* in price . . .	↑ *increases* total revenue.
Total revenue moves in the direction of the quantity change.	

Price Inelastic	
↑ An *increase* in price . . .	↑ *increases* total revenue.
↓ A *reduction* in price . . .	↓ *reduces* total revenue.
Total revenue moves in the direction of the price change.	

Unit Price Elastic	
↑ An *increase* in price . . . ,	● no change in total revenue.
↓ A *reduction* in price . . . ,	● no change in total revenue.
Total revenue does not change as price changes.	

Case in Point — Bad Weather Boosts Farm Revenue; Good Weather Lowers It

In 1988 wheat farmers suffered the worst drought since the Great Depression—and had a record year for total farm revenue. A decade later, good weather increased wheat yields and total farm revenue plummeted.

In terms of the model of demand and supply, the drought reduced supply. It shifted the supply curve from S_1 to S_2, raising the equilibrium price from P_1 to P_2 and reducing the quantity of wheat demanded from Q_1 to Q_2. The opposite occurred in the late 1990s. The supply curve shifted from S_2 to S_1, lowering equilibrium price from P_2 to P_1 and increasing equilibrium quantity from Q_2 to Q_1.

The demand for wheat is inelastic. Estimates of the price elasticity of demand for wheat range between −0.3 and −0.7. When demand is inelastic and price rises, total revenue rises. An increase in price thus boosts farm revenues. Inelastic demand also means that a decrease in price depresses farm revenues. As stated in the text, when demand is inelastic, total revenue moves in the direction of the price change.

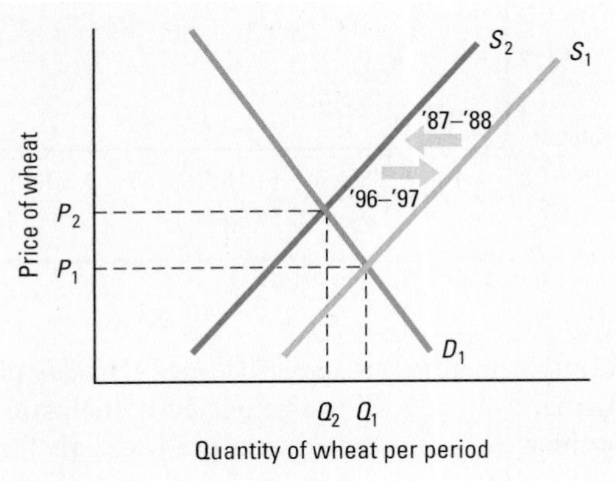

The drought shifted the supply curve for wheat to the left. Wheat production plunged 15 percent in 1988. Inelastic demand meant prices rose by an even greater percentage; the average price per bushel of wheat soared from $2.57 in 1987 to $3.72 in 1988, an increase of 37 percent (obtained by calculating percentage change in price as the change in price divided by the average price between the two periods). The larger percentage increase in prices raised total revenues for wheat farmers.

The situation for wheat farmers was the opposite 10 years later. The supply curve shifted to the right. Wheat production rose about 9 percent between 1996 and 1997 and wheat prices plunged from $4.30 per bushel in 1996 to $3.38 per bushel in 1997, a decrease of 24 percent.

Of course, farmers whose crops were wiped out by the 1988 drought didn't have a good year. Similarly, in 1997, farmers who had especially large harvests did well, even at the lower price. But for farmers taken as a group, a bad year for production meant a good year for farm revenues; a good year for production meant a bad year for farm revenues.

The year 1998 was an even worse year for farm revenues. In that year, however, the main reason for the continued decline in farm revenues was a leftward shift in the demand curve for U. S. farm products, as many Asian countries, in the midst of an economic downturn, demanded fewer U.S. farm goods. Since the ceteris paribus conditions for calculating elasticity didn't hold between 1997 and 1998, we cannot use the elasticity concept to explain that drop in revenues.

Source: Department of Agriculture data, www.nass.usda.gov/ipedb

relatively low and quantities relatively high. We can be even more specific. *For any linear demand curve, demand will be price elastic in the upper half of the curve and price inelastic in its lower half. At the midpoint of a linear demand curve, demand is unit price elastic.*

Constant Elasticity Demand Curves

Exhibit 5-4 shows four demand curves over which price elasticity of demand is the same at all points. The demand curve in Panel (a) is vertical. This means that price changes have no effect on quantity demanded. The numerator of the formula given in Equation (2) for the price

Exhibit 5-4

Demand Curves With Constant Price Elasticities

The demand curve in Panel (a) is perfectly inelastic. The demand curve in Panel (b) is perfectly elastic. Price elasticity of demand is −1.00 all along the demand curve in Panel (c), while it is –0.50 all along the demand curve in Panel (d).

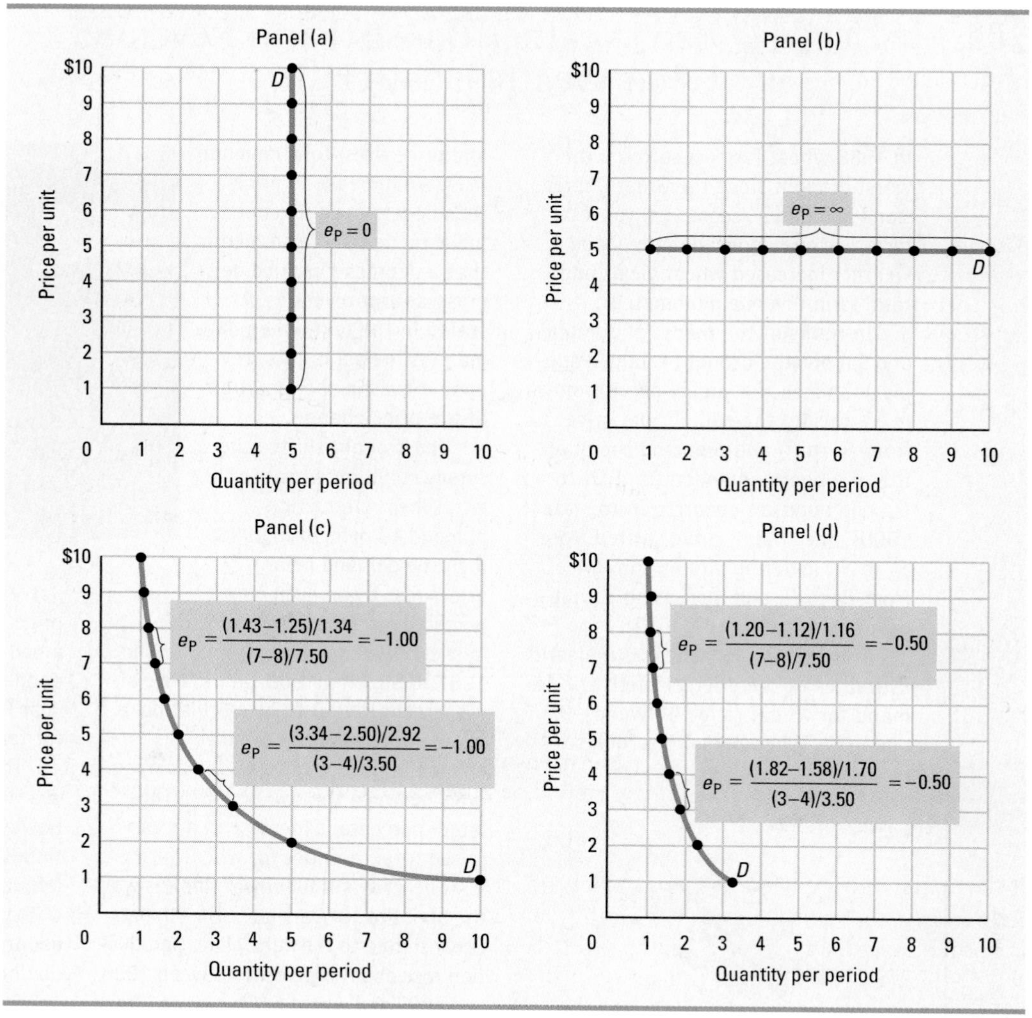

elasticity of demand (percentage change in quantity demanded) is zero. The price elasticity of demand in this case is therefore zero and the demand curve is said to be **perfectly inelastic.** This is a theoretically extreme case, and no good that has been studied empirically exactly fits it. A good that comes close, at least over a specific price range, is insulin. A diabetic will not consume more insulin as its price falls but, over some price range, will consume the amount needed to control the disease.

The demand curve in Panel (b) is horizontal. This means that even the smallest price changes have enormous effects on quantity demanded. The denominator of the formula given in Equation (2) for the price elasticity of demand (percentage change in price) approaches zero. The price elasticity of demand in this case is therefore infinite and the demand curve is said to be **perfectly elastic.**[3] This curve is what the demand for a single farm's corn could look like. If the corn of other farms is selling at $5 per bushel, a typical farm can sell as much corn as it wants to at $5, but nothing at $5.01.

[3]Division by zero results in an undefined solution. Saying that the price elasticity is infinite requires that we say the denominator "approaches" zero.

The nonlinear demand curves in Panels (c) and (d) have price elasticities of demand that are negative; but, unlike the linear demand curve discussed above, the value of the price elasticity is constant all along each demand curve. The demand curve in Panel (c) has price elasticity of demand equal to −1.00 throughout its range; in Panel (d) the price elasticity of demand is equal to −0.50 throughout its range.

Determinants of the Price Elasticity of Demand

The greater the absolute value of the price elasticity of demand, the greater the responsiveness of quantity demanded to a price change. Depending on whether demand is price elastic, unit price elastic, or price inelastic, total revenue may rise, remain unchanged, or fall in response to a price change. What determines whether demand is more or less price elastic? The most important determinants of the price elasticity of demand for a good or service are the availability of substitutes, the importance of the item in household budgets, and time.

Availability of Substitutes The price elasticity of demand for a good or service will be greater in absolute value if many close substitutes are available for it. If there are lots of substitutes for a particular good or service, then it's easy for consumers to switch to those substitutes when there is a price increase for that good or service. Suppose, for example, that the price of Ford automobiles goes up. There are many close substitutes for Fords—Chevrolets, Chryslers, Toyotas, and so on. The availability of close substitutes tends to make the demand for Fords more price elastic.

If a good has no close substitutes, its demand is likely to be somewhat less price elastic. There are no close substitutes for cigarettes, for example. The price elasticity of demand for cigarettes is generally estimated to be about −0.4. Since the absolute value of price elasticity is less than 1, it is price inelastic. We would expect, though, that the demand for a particular brand of cigarettes will be much more price elastic than the demand for cigarettes in general.

Importance in Household Budgets One reason price changes affect quantity demanded is that they change how much a consumer can buy; a change in the price of a good or service affects the purchasing power of a consumer's income and thus affects the amount of a good the consumer will buy. This effect is stronger when a good or service is important in a typical household's budget.

A change in the price of jeans, for example, is probably more important in your budget than a change in the price of buttons. Suppose the prices of both were to double. You'd planned to buy four pairs of jeans this year, but now you might decide to make do with two new pairs. The change in button prices, in contrast, might lead to very little reduction in quantity demanded. The greater the importance of an item in household budgets, the greater the absolute value of the price elasticity of demand is likely to be.

While the price elasticity of demand for cigarettes for the population at large is −0.4, it is −0.7 for teenagers. One reason for the higher teen elasticity is that cigarettes constitute a larger portion of teenagers' budgets.

Time Suppose the price of electricity rises tomorrow morning. What will happen to the quantity demanded?

The answer depends in large part on how much time we allow for a response. If we're interested in the reduction in quantity demanded by tomorrow afternoon, we can expect that the response will be very small. But if we give consumers a year to respond to the price change, we can expect the response to be much greater. We expect that the absolute value of the price elasticity of demand will be greater when more time is allowed for consumer responses.

Caution!

Inelastic Demand Versus Perfectly Inelastic Demand
Don't confuse price inelastic demand and perfectly inelastic demand. Perfectly inelastic demand means that the change in quantity is zero for any percentage change in price; the demand curve in this case is vertical. Price inelastic demand means only that the percentage change in quantity is less than the percentage change in price, not that the change in quantity is zero. With price inelastic (as opposed to perfectly inelastic) demand, the demand curve itself is still downward sloping.

Case in Point Elasticity and the Drug War

We don't have good data on the market for illegal drugs, but economists who study this market have reached some tentative conclusions about the nature of demand elasticities for various drugs.

In the case of marijuana, for example, demand is generally thought to be price inelastic. This presumption is based partly on estimates of the impact of price changes on marijuana consumption and partly on the fact that the drug's low price makes it a minor item in the budgets of casual users. Harvard University economist Mark Kleiman, a leading expert on the economics of illegal drugs, estimates that the price elasticity of demand for marijuana is no greater than −0.4.

Professor Kleiman suggests that the elasticity for cocaine, however, is much greater. Part of the reason for that greater elasticity is the drug's higher price; a "hit" of cocaine costs about 5 times as much as a hit of marijuana. Expenditures on cocaine thus make up a bigger share of the budgets of its consumers than expenditures on marijuana. Professor Kleiman estimates that the demand for cocaine is unit price elastic, or −1.

Professor Kleiman thinks the different elasticities suggest very different strategies for enforcement efforts aimed at restricting the supply of the two drugs. If law enforcement officials succeeded in reducing the supply of a drug, the supply curve would shift to the left, raising price. That would increase total expenditures on marijuana, increasing the revenues earned by dealers. Unit price elastic demand for cocaine, however, means total expenditures would be unchanged. Since the enforcement efforts would also increase the costs to cocaine dealers, their profits would fall. Professor Kleiman concludes that enforcement efforts aimed at restricting marijuana sales should be reduced, whereas those aimed at cocaine should be increased.

Source: Mark A. R. Kleiman, *Marijuana: Costs of Abuse, Costs of Control* (Westport, CT: Greenwood Press, 1989).

Consider the price elasticity of gasoline demand. Economists James M. Griffin of Texas A&M University and Henry B. Steele of the University of Houston estimate that the price elasticity of demand for gasoline is −0.1 when consumers are given no more than a month to respond to a price change. Demand is very inelastic because a short period of time doesn't give consumers much of a chance to respond. Over longer periods, with higher fuel prices, they may switch to more fuel-efficient cars and make greater use of car pools and public transit systems. Over very long periods, some people may even move. If gasoline is getting cheaper, consumers may move farther from work to escape city congestion; if gasoline prices are rising, they may move closer to work to economize on gasoline. Professors Griffin and Steele estimate that over a period of several years, the demand for gasoline becomes elastic, with a price elasticity of −1.5.[4]

Check*list*

- The price elasticity of demand measures the responsiveness of quantity demanded to changes in price; it is calculated by dividing the percentage change in quantity demanded by the percentage change in price.
- Demand is price inelastic if the absolute value of the price elasticity of demand is less than 1; it is unit price elastic if the absolute value is equal to 1; and it is price elastic if the absolute value is greater than 1.

[4]James M. Griffin and Henry B. Steele, *Energy Economics and Policy* (New York: Academic Press, 1980), p. 232.

- Demand is price elastic in the upper half of any linear demand curve and price inelastic in the lower half. It is unit price elastic at the midpoint.
- When demand is price inelastic, total revenue moves in the direction of a price change. When demand is unit price elastic, total revenue doesn't change in response to a price change. When demand is price elastic, total revenue moves in the direction of a quantity change.
- The absolute value of the price elasticity of demand is greater when substitutes are available, when the good is important in household budgets, and when buyers have more time to adjust to changes in the price of the good.

Try It Yourself 5-1

You're now ready to play the part of the manager of the public transit system. Your finance officer has just advised you that the system faces a deficit. Your board doesn't want you to cut service, which means that you can't cut costs. Your only hope is to increase revenue. Would a fare increase boost revenue?

You consult the economist on your staff who has researched studies on public transportation elasticities. She reports that the estimated price elasticity of demand for the first few months after a price change is about −0.5, but that after several years, it will be about −1.5.

a. Explain why the estimated values for price elasticity of demand differ.

b. Compute what will happen to ridership over the next few months if you decide to raise fares by 5 percent.

c. Compute what will happen to ridership over the next few years if you decide to raise fares by 5 percent.

d. What happens to total revenue now and after several years if you choose to raise fares?

Responsiveness of Demand to Other Factors

Although the response of quantity demanded to changes in price is the most widely used measure of elasticity, economists are interested in the response to changes in the demand shifters as well. Two of the most important measures show how demand responds to changes in income and to changes in the prices of related goods and services.

Income Elasticity of Demand

We saw in Chapter 3 that the demand for a good or service is affected by income. We measure the **income elasticity of demand,** e_Y, as the percentage change in quantity demanded *at a specific price* divided by the percentage change in income that produced the demand change, all other things unchanged:

$$e_Y = \frac{\text{Percentage change in } Q}{\text{Percentage change in } Y}$$

The symbol Y is often used in economics to represent income. Because income elasticity of demand reports the responsiveness of quantity demanded to a change in income, all other things unchanged (including the price of the good), it reflects a shift in the demand curve at a given price. Remember that price elasticity of demand reflects movements along a demand curve.

A positive income elasticity of demand means that income and demand move in the same direction—an increase in income increases demand, and a reduction in income reduces demand. As we learned in Chapter 3, a good whose demand rises as income rises is called a normal good.

Studies show that most goods and services are normal, and thus their income elasticities are positive. Goods and services for which demand is likely to move in the same direction as income include housing, seafood, rock concerts, and medical services.

In an examination of the demand for state colleges in New York, New Jersey, and Pennsylvania, for example, four economists found a strong link between family income and the number of students seeking to attend school. The economists estimated that the income elasticity of demand for enrollment in public colleges and universities in the three states was 1.67. That means that a 10-percent increase in incomes could be expected to increase the demand for public institutions of higher education in the three states by 16.7 percent.[5] The positive income elasticity implies that a college education is a normal good.

Normal Good	
↑ An *increase* in income . . .	↑ *increases* demand.
↓ A *decrease* in income . . .	↓ *decreases* demand.

Inferior Good	
↑ An *increase* in income . . .	↓ *decreases* demand.
↓ A *decrease* in income . . .	↑ *increases* demand.

If a good or service is inferior, then an increase in income reduces demand for the good. That implies a negative income elasticity of demand. Goods and services for which the income elasticity of demand is likely to be negative include used clothing, beans, and intercity bus service.

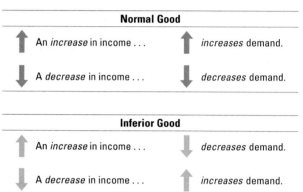

When we compute the income elasticity of demand, we are looking at the change in the quantity demanded at a specific price. We are thus dealing with a change that shifts the demand curve. An increase in income shifts the demand for a normal good to the right; it shifts the demand for an inferior good to the left.

Cross Price Elasticity of Demand

We saw in Chapter 3 that the demand for a good or service is affected by the prices of related goods or services. A reduction in the price of stereo speakers, for example, would increase the demand for CD players, suggesting that speakers are a complement of CD players. A reduction in the price of CD players, however, would reduce the demand for cassette players, suggesting that CD players are a substitute for cassette players.

The measure economists use to describe the responsiveness of demand for a good or service to a change in the price of another good or service is called the **cross price elasticity of demand,** e_{AB}. It equals the percentage change in the quantity demanded of one good or service *at a specific price* divided by the percentage change in the price of a related good or service. We are varying the price of a related good when we consider the cross price elasticity of demand, so the response of quantity demanded is shown as a shift in the demand curve.

The cross price elasticity of the demand for good A with respect to the price of good B is given by

$$e_{AB} = \frac{\text{Percentage change in } Q_A}{\text{Percentage change in } P_B}$$

Cross price elasticities of demand define whether two goods are substitutes, complements, or unrelated. If two goods are substitutes, an increase in the price of one will lead to an increase in the demand for the other—the cross price elasticity of demand is posi-

[5]Jules M. Levine et al., "The Demand for Higher Education in Three Mid-Atlantic States," *New York Economic Review* 18 (Fall 1988): 3–20.

tive. If two goods are complements, an increase in the price of one will lead to a reduction in the demand for the other—the cross price elasticity of demand is negative. If two goods are unrelated, a change in the price of one will not affect the demand for the other—the cross price elasticity of demand is zero.

For example, one might expect natural and artificial Christmas trees to be substitutes for each other. Indeed, their cross price elasticity is estimated to be about 0.2. The positive number tells us that the two goods are substitutes. The numerical value tells us that a 10-percent increase (decrease) in the price of artificial Christmas trees leads to a 2-percent increase (decrease) in the demand for natural Christmas trees at the going price.

Substitutes	
↑ An *increase* in P_B . . .	↑ *increases* demand for good A.
↓ A *decrease* in P_B . . .	↓ *decreases* demand for good A.

Complements	
↑ An *increase* in P_B . . .	↓ *decreases* demand for good A.
↓ A *decrease* in P_B . . .	↑ *increases* demand for good A.

The cross price elasticity of alcohol with respect to the price of food is estimated to be –0.16. The negative value of the estimate of the cross price elasticity means that food and alcohol are complements. The specific numerical estimate means that a 10-percent increase (decrease) in the price of food leads to a 1.6-percent decrease (increase) in the demand for alcohol at the going price of alcohol.

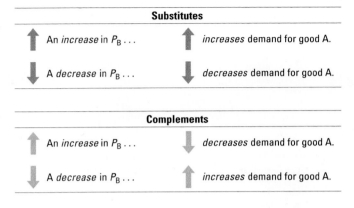

Check list

- The income elasticity of demand reflects the responsiveness of demand to changes in income. It is the percentage change in quantity demanded *at a specific price* divided by the percentage change in income, ceteris paribus.
- Income elasticity is positive for normal goods and negative for inferior goods.
- The cross price elasticity of demand measures the way demand for one good or service responds to changes in the price of another. It is the percentage change in the quantity demanded of one good or service *at a specific price* divided by the percentage change in the price of another good or service, all other things unchanged.
- Cross price elasticity is positive for substitutes, negative for complements, and zero for goods or services whose demands are unrelated.

Caution!

Notice that with income elasticity of demand and cross price elasticity of demand we are primarily concerned with whether the measured value of these elasticities is positive or negative. In the case of income elasticity of demand this tells us whether the good or service is normal or inferior. In the case of cross price elasticity of demand it tells us whether two goods are substitutes or complements. With price elasticity of demand we were concerned with whether the measured absolute value of this elasticity was greater than, less than, or equal to 1, because this gave us information about what happens to total revenue as price changes. The terms elastic and inelastic apply to price elasticity of demand. They are not used to describe income elasticity of demand or cross price elasticity of demand.

Case in Point Cigarette Taxes and Teen Smoking

The harmful effects of smoking cigarettes have been well known and well publicized for many years, yet the number of teen smokers continues to climb. Between 1993 and 1996, the number of high school seniors who smoke grew by 14 percent and the number of eighth- and tenth-grade smokers rose by over 22 percent. Recent Food and Drug Administration (FDA) regulations are aimed toward reducing access by youth and teens to cigarettes and reducing the appeal of cigarettes by curbing advertising in various ways.

Another way to reduce teen smoking would be to raise the tax on cigarettes. The 1997 Hatch–Kennedy bill would have increased the federal tax on cigarettes and raised the price of cigarettes by about 23 percent. Based on the estimate given in the text of a teen price elasticity of demand for cigarettes of –0.7, this tax would reduce the quantity of cigarettes demanded by teen smokers by about 16 percent. Assuming a similar reduction in the number of teen smokers, this translates into over 2.6 million fewer smokers and over 850,000 fewer smoking-related premature deaths among the current U.S. population that is younger than 18 years old. In the words of John D. Giglio, manager of tobacco control advocacy for the American Cancer Society, "Raising tobacco taxes is our number one strategy to damage the tobacco industry. The . . . industry has found ways around everything else we have done, but they can't repeal the laws of economics."

There are, however, several caveats in evaluating the impact of a tax hike. The price of a pack of cigarettes might not rise by the full amount of the tax if manufacturers lower the price of cigarettes to wholesalers. Also, teens might switch from cigarettes to smokeless tobacco, which is associated with higher risk of oral cancer. It is estimated that for young males the cross price elasticity of smokeless tobacco with respect to the price of cigarettes is 1.2—a 10-percent increase in cigarette prices leads to a 12-percent increase in young males using smokeless tobacco.

Source: Michael Grossman, "Cigarette Taxes," *Public Health Reports* 112(4) (July/August 1997): 290–297.

Try It Yourself 5-2

Suppose that when the price of bagels rises by 10 percent, the demand for cream cheese falls by 3 percent at the current price, and that when income rises by 10 percent, the demand for bagels increases by 1 percent at the current price. Calculate the cross price elasticity of demand for cream cheese with respect to the price of bagels and tell whether bagels and cream cheese are substitutes or complements. Calculate the income elasticity of demand and tell whether bagels are normal or inferior.

Price Elasticity of Supply

The elasticity measures encountered so far in this chapter all relate to the demand side of the market. It is also useful to know how responsive quantity supplied is to a change in price.

Suppose the demand for apartments rises. There will be a shortage of apartments at the old level of apartment rents and pressure on rents to rise. All other things unchanged, the more responsive the quantity of apartments supplied is to changes in monthly rents, the lower the increase in rent required to eliminate the shortage and to bring the market back to equilibrium. Conversely, if quantity supplied is less responsive to price changes, price will have to rise more to eliminate a shortage caused by an increase in demand.

This is illustrated in Exhibit 5-5. Suppose the rent for a typical apartment had been R_0 and the quantity Q_0 when the demand curve was D_1 and the supply curve was either S_1 (a supply curve in which quantity supplied is less responsive to price changes) or S_2 (a supply curve in which quantity supplied is more responsive to price changes). Note that with either supply curve, equilibrium price and quantity are initially the same. Now suppose that demand increases to D_2, perhaps due to population growth. With supply curve S_1, the price (rent in this case) will rise to R_1 and the quantity of apartments will rise to Q_1. If, however, the supply curve had been S_2, the rent would only have to rise to R_2 to bring the market back to equilibrium. In addition, the new equilibrium number of apartments would be higher at Q_2. Supply curve S_2 shows greater responsiveness of quantity supplied to price change than does supply curve S_1.

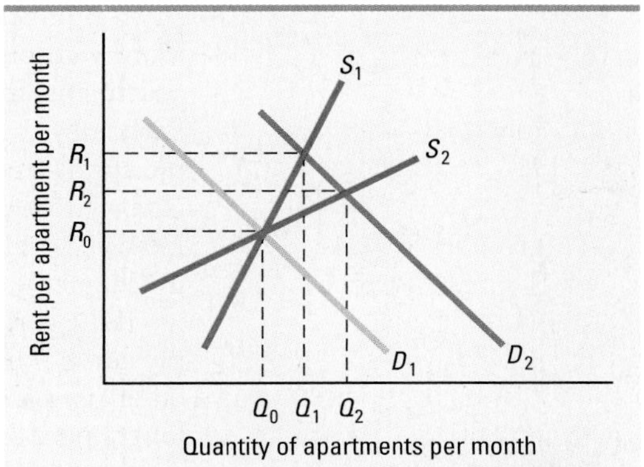

Exhibit 5-5

Increase in Apartment Rents Depends on How Responsive Supply Is

The more responsive the supply of apartments is to changes in price (rent in this case), the less rents rise when the demand for apartments increases.

We measure the **price elasticity of supply** (e_S) as the ratio of the percentage change in quantity supplied of a good or service to the percentage change in its price, all other things unchanged:

$$e_S = \frac{\text{Percentage change in quantity supplied}}{\text{Percentage change in price}}$$

Because price and quantity supplied usually move in the same direction, the price elasticity of supply is usually positive. The larger the price elasticity of supply, the more responsive the firms that supply the good or service are to a price change.

Like demand, supply is said to be price elastic if the price elasticity of supply is greater than 1, unit price elastic if it is equal to 1, and price inelastic if it is less than 1. A vertical supply curve, as shown in Panel (a) of Exhibit 5-6, is said to be perfectly inelastic; its price elasticity of supply is zero. The supply of Beatles songs is perfectly inelastic because the band no longer exists. A horizontal supply curve, as shown in Panel (b) of Exhibit 5-6, is said to be perfectly elastic; its price elasticity of supply is infinite. It corresponds to the case where suppliers are willing to supply any amount at a certain price.

Time: An Important Determinant of the Elasticity of Supply

Time plays a very important role in the determination of the price elasticity of supply. Let's look again at the effect of rent increases on the supply of apartments. Suppose apartment rents in a city rise. If we're looking at a supply curve of apartments over a short period of a few months, the rent increase is likely to induce apartment owners to rent out a relatively

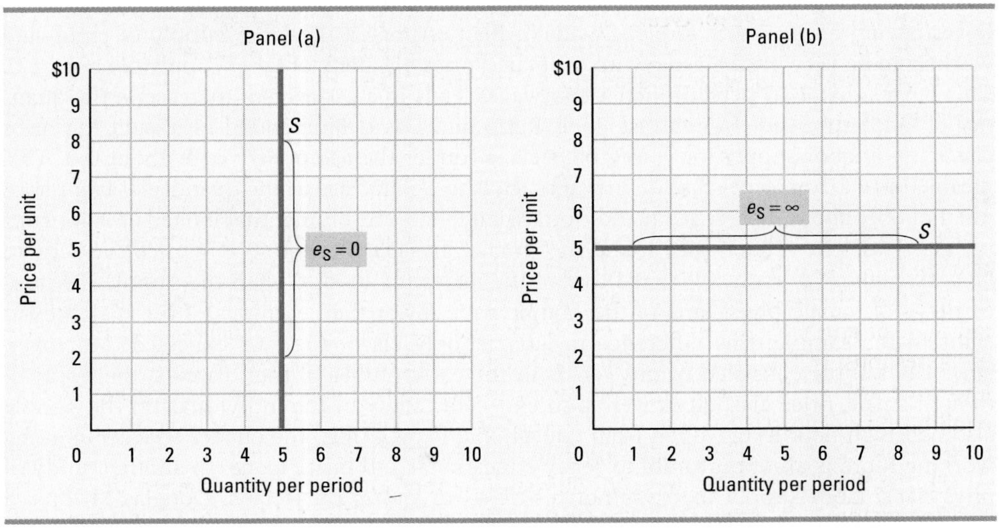

Exhibit 5-6

Supply Curves and Their Price Elasticities

The supply curve in Panel (a) is perfectly inelastic. In Panel (b), the supply curve is perfectly elastic.

small number of additional apartments. With the higher rents, apartment owners may be more vigorous in reducing their vacancy rates and indeed, with more people looking for apartments to rent, this should be fairly easy to accomplish. Attics and basements might be fairly easy to renovate and rent out as additional units. In a short period of time, however, the supply response is likely to be fairly modest, implying that the price elasticity of supply is fairly low. A supply curve corresponding to a short period of time would look like S_1 in Exhibit 5-5. It is during such periods that there may be calls for rent controls, as discussed in Chapter 4.

If the period of time under consideration is a few years rather than a few months, the supply curve is likely to be much more price elastic. Over time, buildings can be converted from other uses and new apartment complexes can be built. A supply curve corresponding to a longer period of time would look like S_2 in Exhibit 5-5.

As another example, consider the price elasticity of milk supply. When looking at dairy farms' response to price change within a year, Professor Adesoji O. Adelaja of Rutgers University found that the price elasticity of supply is about 0.36. The increased milk supplied comes from higher yields, that is, from getting more milk from the cows that are on the farms at the time of the price change. If you consider price response over a period of 4 years, the price elasticity of supply rises to 0.51. The additional milk supplied over the longer period comes from adjustments in average herd size and from an increase in the number of dairy farms.

Elasticity of Labor Supply: A Special Application

The concept of price elasticity of supply can be applied to labor to show how the quantity of labor supplied responds to changes in wages or salaries. What makes this case interesting is that it has sometimes been found that the measured elasticity is negative, that is, that an increase in the wage rate is associated with a reduction in the quantity of labor supplied.

In most cases, labor supply curves have their normal upward slope: higher wages induce people to work more. For them, having the additional income from working more is preferable to having more leisure time. However, wage increases may lead some people in very highly paid jobs to cut back on the number of hours they work because their incomes are already high and they'd rather have more time for leisure activities. In this case, the labor supply curve would have a negative slope. The reasons for this phenomenon are explained more fully in Chapter 12.

Studies support the idea that labor supply is less elastic in high-paying jobs than in lower-paying ones. For example, David M. Blau estimated the labor supply of child-care workers to be very price elastic, with estimated price elasticity of labor supply of about 2.0. This means that a 10-percent increase in wages leads to a 20-percent increase in the quantity of labor supplied. In contrast, John Rizzo and David Blumenthal estimated the price elasticity of labor supply for young physicians (under the age of 40) to be about 0.3. This means that a 10-percent increase in wages leads to an increase in the quantity of labor supplied of only about 3 percent. In addition, when Rizzo and Blumenthal looked at labor supply elasticities by gender, they found the female physicians' labor supply price elasticity to be a bit higher (at about 0.5) than that of the males (at about 0.2) in the sample. Because earnings of female physicians in the sample were lower than earnings of the male physicians in the sample, this difference in labor supply elasticities was expected. Moreover, since the sample consisted of physicians in the early phases of their careers, the positive, though small, price elasticities were also expected. Many of the individuals in the sample also had high debt levels, often from educational loans. Thus, the chance to earn more by working more is an opportunity to repay educational and other loans. In another study of physicians' labor supply that was not restricted to young physicians, Douglas M. Brown

Product	Elasticity
Price elasticity of demand	
Gasoline*	–0.1
Cabbage	–0.25
Peanuts	–0.38
Marijuana	–0.4
Cigarettes	–0.4
Milk (two different estimates)	–0.49; –0.63
Soft drinks	–0.55
Transportation*	–0.6
Cigarettes (teenagers)	–0.7
Food*	–0.7
Beer	–0.7 to –0.9
Cocaine	–1.0
Ground Beef	–1.0
Gasoline**	–1.5
Coke	–1.71
Transportation**	–1.9
Pepsi	–2.08
Fresh tomatoes	–2.22
Food**	–2.3
Lettuce	–2.58
Fresh peas	–2.83

Note: * = short run; ** = long run.

Product	Elasticity
Cross price elasticity of demand	
Fuel with respect to price of transport	–0.48
Alcohol with respect to price of food	–0.16
Pork with respect to price of poultry	0.06
Poultry with respect to price of pork	0.16
Pork with respect to price of ground beef	0.03
Fresh Christmas trees with respect to price of artificial Christmas trees	0.2
Poultry with respect to price of ground beef	0.23
Ground beef with respect to price of poultry	0.24
Ground beef with respect to price of pork	0.35
Coke with respect to price of Pepsi	0.61
Pepsi with respect to price of Coke	0.80
Price elasticity of supply	
Physicians (specialists)	–0.3
Physicians (primary care)	0.0
Physicians (young male)	0.2
Physicians (young female)	0.5
Milk*	0.36
Milk**	0.51
Child care labor	2.0

Product	Elasticity
Income elasticity of demand	
Lottery: instant game sales in Colorado	–0.06
Ground beef	–0.197
Potatoes	0.15
Food**	0.2
Clothing**	0.3
Beer	0.4
Eggs	0.57
Coke	0.60
Shelter**	0.7
Beef (table cuts—not ground)	0.81
Oranges	0.83
Apples	1.32
Leisure**	1.4
Peaches	1.43
Health care**	1.6
Education**	1.6
Higher education	1.67
Pepsi	1.70
Cream	1.72

Sources: See footnotes 4, 5, and 7 and the following: Robert W. Fogel, "Catching Up With the Economy," *American Economic Review* 89(1) (March 1999): 1–21; Michael Grossman, "A Survey of Economic Models of Addictive Behavior," *Journal of Drug Issues* 28:3 (Summer 1998): 631–643; Sanjib Bhuyan and Rigoberto A. Lopez, "Oligopoly Power in the Food and Tobacco Industries," *American Journal of Agricultural Economics* 79 (August 1997): 1035–1043; Ann Hansen, "The Tax Incidence of the Colorado State Lottery Instant Game," *Public Finance Quarterly* 23(3) (July 1995): 385–398; Daniel B. Suits, "Agriculture," pp. 1–33, and Kenneth G. Elzinga, "Beer," pp. 119–151, in Walter Adams and James Brock, eds, *The Structure of American Industry*, 9th ed. (Englewood Cliffs, NJ: Prentice Hall, 1995); Douglas M. Brown, "The Rising Price of Physicians' Services: A Correction and Extension on Supply," *Review of Economics and Statistics* 76(2) (May 1994): 389–393; John A. Rizzo and David Blumenthal, "Physical Labor Supply: Do Income Effects Matter?" *Journal of Health Economics* 13(4) (December 1994): 433–453; George C. Davis and Michael K. Wohlgenant, "Demand Elasticities from a Discrete Choice Model: The Natural Christmas Tree Market," *Journal of Agricultural Economics* 75(3) (August 1993): 730–738; David M. Blau, "The Supply of Child Care Labor," *Journal of Labor Economics* 2(11) (April 1993): 324–347; Richard Blundell et al., "What Do We Learn About Consumer Demand Patterns from Micro Data?" *American Economic Review* 83(3) (June 1993): 570–597; F. Gasmi et al., "Econometric Analysis of Collusive Behavior in a Soft-Drink Market," *Journal of Economics and Management Strategy* (Summer 1992): 277–311; M. R. Baye, D. W. Jansen, and J.W. Lee, "Advertising Effects in Complete Demand Systems," *Applied Economics* 24 (1992): 1087–1096; Gary W. Brester and Michael K. Wohlgenant, "Estimating Interrelated Demands for Meats Using New Measures for Ground and Table Cut Beef," *American Journal of Agricultural Economics* 73 (November 1991): 1182–1194; Mark A. R. Kleinman, *Marijuana: Costs of Abuse, Costs of Control* (Westport, CT: Greenwood Press, 1989); Michael Grossman and Henry Saffer, "Beer Taxes, the Legal Drinking Age, and Youth Motor Vehicle Fatalities," *Journal of Legal Studies* 16(2) (June 1987): 351–374.

Exhibit 5-7

Selected Elasticity Estimates

found the labor supply price elasticity for primary care physicans to be close to zero, and that of specialists to be negative, at about –0.3. Thus, for this sample of physicians, increases in wages have little or no effect on the amount the primary care doctors work, while a 10-percent increase in wages for specialists *reduces* their quantity of labor supplied by about 3 percent. Because the earnings of specialists exceed those of primary care doctors, this elasticity differential also makes sense.

This chapter has covered a variety of elasticity measures. Exhibit 5-7 provides some estimates of these elasticities for a variety of goods.

Checklist

- The price elasticity of supply measures the responsiveness of quantity supplied to changes in price. It is the percentage change in quantity supplied divided by the percentage change in price. It is usually positive.
- Supply is price inelastic if the price elasticity of supply is less than 1; it is unit price elastic if the price elasticity of supply is equal to 1; and it is price elastic if the price elasticity of supply is greater than 1. A vertical supply curve is said to be perfectly inelastic. A horizontal supply curve is said to be perfectly elastic.
- Price elasticity of supply is greater when the length of time under consideration is longer because over time producers have more options for adjusting to the change in price.
- When applied to labor supply, the price elasticity of supply is usually positive but can be negative. If higher wages induce people to work more, the labor supply curve is upward sloping and the price elasticity of supply is positive. In some very high-paying professions, the labor supply curve may have a negative slope, which leads to a negative price elasticity of supply.

Try It Yourself 5-3

It was reported on April 3, 1998, on the Nightly News with Jim Lehrer *that the high-tech industry is worried about being able to find enough workers with computer-related expertise. Job offers for recent college graduates with degrees in computer science have been as high as $50,000, it was reported. A computer science professor at Stanford University also reported that enrollments in computer science courses are higher than ever and that new professors are being hired. What will happen to the price elasticity of supply of computer scientists over time and how will this affect salaries in this field?*

A Look Back

This chapter introduced a new tool: the concept of elasticity. Elasticity is a measure of the degree to which one variable, a dependent variable, responds to a change in an independent variable. It is the percentage change in a dependent variable divided by the percentage change in an independent variable, all other things unchanged.

The most widely used elasticity measure is the price elasticity of demand, which reflects the responsiveness of quantity demanded to changes in price. Demand is said to be price elastic if the absolute value of the price elasticity of demand is greater than 1, unit price elastic if it is equal to 1, and price inelastic if it is less than 1. The price elasticity of demand is useful in forecasting the response of quantity demanded to price changes; it is also useful for predicting the impact a price change will have on total revenue. Total revenue moves in the direction of the quantity change if demand is price elastic, it moves in the direction of the price change if demand is price inelastic, and it does not change if demand is unit price elastic. The most important determinants of the price elasticity of demand are the availability of substitutes, the importance of the item in household budgets, and time.

Two other elasticity measures commonly used in conjunction with demand are income elasticity and cross price elasticity. The signs of these elasticity measures play important roles. A positive income elasticity tells us that a good is normal; a negative income elasticity tells us the good is inferior. A positive cross price elasticity tells us that two goods are substitutes; a negative cross price elasticity tells us they are complements.

Elasticity of supply measures the responsiveness of quantity supplied to changes in price. The value of price elasticity of supply is generally positive. Supply is classified as being price elastic, unit price elastic, or price inelastic if price elasticity if greater than 1, equal to 1, or less than 1, respectively. The length of time over which supply is being considered is an important determinant of the price elasticity of supply.

A Look Ahead This chapter is the first in a series on basic tools of microeconomic analysis. In Chapter 6, we'll examine the nature of maximizing behavior and explore its relationship to economic efficiency. Then in Chapters 7 and 8 we'll turn to the theory of consumer behavior and the theory of production and cost. Later, we'll apply the tools to various types of markets in the economy.

Terms and Concepts for Review

elasticity, **103**
price elasticity of demand, **103**
arc elasticity, **104**
total revenue, **106**
price elastic, **107**
unit price elastic, **107**
price inelastic, **107**
perfectly inelastic, **110**
perfectly elastic, **110**
income elasticity of demand, **113**
cross price elasticity of demand, **114**
price elasticity of supply, **117**

For Discussion

1. Explain why the price elasticity of demand is a negative number, except in the cases where the demand curve is perfectly elastic or perfectly inelastic.
2. Explain why the sign (positive or negative) of the cross price elasticity of demand is important.
3. Explain why the sign (positive or negative) of the income elasticity of demand is important.
4. Economist David Romer found that in introductory economics classes a 10-percent increase in class attendance is associated with a 4-percent increase in course grade.[6] What is the elasticity of course grade with respect to class attendance? Do you think it is worth it to go to class or not?
5. Economists Dale Heien and Cathy Roheim Wessells found that the price elasticity of demand for fresh milk is –0.63 and the price elasticity of demand for cottage cheese is –1.1.[7] Why do you think the elasticity estimates differ?
6. The price elasticity of demand for health care has been estimated to be –0.2. Characterize this demand as price elastic, unit price elastic, or price inelastic. The text argues that the greater the importance of an item in consumer budgets, the greater its elasticity. Health-care costs account for a relatively large share of household budgets. How could the price elasticity of demand for health care be such a small number?
7. Suppose you are able to organize an alliance that includes all farmers. They agree to follow the group's instructions with respect to the quantity of agricultural products they produce. What might the group seek to do? Why?
8. Suppose you're the chief executive officer of a firm, and you have been planning to reduce your prices. Your marketing manager reports that the price elasticity of demand for your product is –0.65. How will this news affect your plans?
9. Suppose the income elasticity of the demand for beans is –0.8. Interpret this number.
10. Transportation economists generally agree that the cross price elasticity of demand for automobile use with respect to the price of bus fares is about 0. Explain what this number means.
11. Suppose the price elasticity of supply of tomatoes as measured on a given day in July is 0. Interpret this number.

[6]David Romer, "Do Students Go to Class? Should They?" *Journal of Economic Perspectives* 7(3) (Summer 1993): 167–174.
[7]Dale M. Heien and Cathy Roheim Wessells, "The Demand for Dairy Products: Structure, Prediction, and Decomposition," *American Journal of Agricultural Economics* 70(2) (May 1988): 219–228.

12. The price elasticity of supply for child-care workers was reported to be quite high, about 2. What will happen to the wages of child-care workers as demand for them increases, compared to what would happen if the measured price elasticity of supply were lower?

13. The Case in Point on cigarette taxes and teen smoking suggests that a higher tax on cigarettes would reduce teen smoking and premature deaths. Should cigarette taxes therefore be raised?

Problems

1. Compute the price elasticity of demand between points B and C and between points D and E in Exhibit 5-2. How do the values of price elasticity of demand compare?
2. Consider the following quote from the July 8, 1993 issue of the *Wall Street Journal:* "A bumper crop of oranges in Florida last year drove down orange prices. As juice marketers' costs fell, they cut prices by as much as 15%. That was enough to tempt some value-oriented customers: unit volume of frozen juices actually rose about 6% during the quarter." Given these numbers, and assuming there were no changes in demand shifters for frozen orange juice, what was the price elasticity of demand for frozen orange juice? What do you think happened to total spending on frozen orange juice? Why?
3. Suppose you are the manager of a restaurant that serves an average of 400 meals per day at an average price per meal of $20. On the basis of a survey, you've determined that reducing the price of an average meal to $18 would increase the quantity demanded to 450 per day. Compute the price elasticity of demand between these two points. Would you expect total revenues to rise or fall? Explain.
4. The text notes that, for any linear demand curve, demand is price elastic in the upper half and price inelastic in the lower half. Consider the following demand curves:

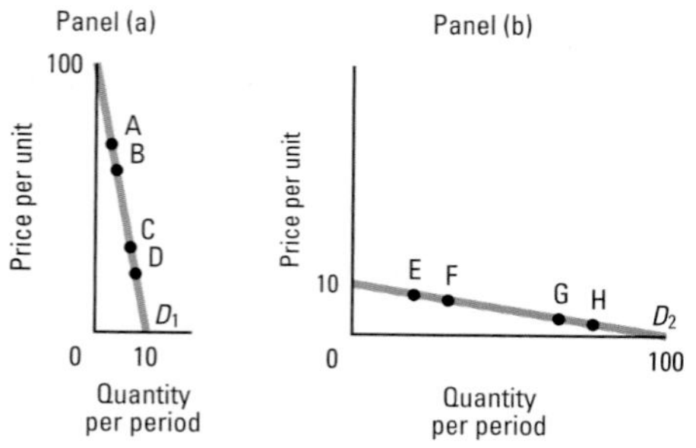

The tables below give the prices and quantities corresponding to each of the points shown on the two demand curves:

Demand curve D_1 [Panel (a)]			Demand curve D_1 [Panel (b)]		
	Price	Quantity		Price	Quantity
A	80	2	E	8	20
B	70	3	F	7	30
C	30	7	G	3	70
D	20	8	H	2	80

a. Compute the price elasticity of demand between points A and B and between points C and D on demand curve D_1 in Panel (a). Are your results consistent with the notion that a linear demand curve is price elastic in its upper half and price inelastic in its lower half?

b. Compute the price elasticity of demand between points E and F and between points G and H on demand curve D_2 in Panel (b). Are your results consistent with the notion that a linear demand curve is price elastic in its upper half and price inelastic in its lower half?

5. a. Compare total spending at points A and B on D_1 in Panel (a) of Problem 4. Is your result consistent with your finding about the price elasticity of demand between those two points?

b. Compare total spending at points C and D on D_1 in Panel (a) of Problem 4. Is your result consistent with your finding about the price elasticity of demand between those two points?

c. Compare total spending at points E and F on D_2 in Panel (b) of Problem 4. Is your result consistent with your finding about the price elasticity of demand between those two points?

d. Compare total spending at points G and H on D_2 in Panel (b) of Problem 4. Is your result consistent with your finding about the price elasticity of demand between those two points?

Answers to Try It Yourself Problems

Try It Yourself 5-1

a. The absolute value of price elasticity of demand tends to be greater when more time is allowed for consumers to respond. Over time, riders of the commuter rail system can organize car pools, move, or otherwise adjust to the fare increase.

b. Using the formula for price elasticity of demand and plugging in values for the estimate of price elasticity (–0.5) and the percentage change in price (5%) and then rearranging terms, we can solve for the percentage change in quantity demanded as: $e_P = \%\ \Delta$ in $Q/\%\ \Delta$ in P; $-0.5 = \%\ \Delta$ in $Q/5\%$; $(-0.5)(5\%) = \%\ \Delta$ in $Q = -2.5\%$. Ridership falls by 2.5 percent in the first few months.

c. Using the formula for price elasticity of demand and plugging in values for the estimate of price elasticity over a few years (–1.5) and the percentage change in price (5%), we can solve for the percentage change in quantity demanded as $e_P = \%\ \Delta$ in $Q/\%\ \Delta$ in P; $-1.5 = \%\ \Delta$ in $Q/5\%$; $(-1.5)(5\%) = \%\ \Delta$ in $Q = -7.5\%$. Ridership falls by 7.5 percent over a few years.

d. Total revenue rises immediately after the fare increase, since demand over the immediate period is price inelastic. Total revenue falls after a few years, since demand changes and becomes price elastic.

Try It Yourself 5-2

Using the formula for cross price elasticity of demand, we find that $e_{AB} = (-3\%)/(10\%) = -0.3$. Since the e_{AB} is negative, bagels and cream cheese are complements. Using the formula for income elasticity of demand, we find that $e_Y = (+1\%)/(10\%) = +0.1$. Since e_Y is positive, bagels are a normal good.

Try It Yourself 5-3

While currently the supply of people with degrees in computer science is very price inelastic, over time the elasticity should rise. That the number of students at Stanford who are deciding to major in computer science is growing lends credence to this prediction. As supply becomes more price elastic, salaries in this field should rise more slowly or perhaps even fall.

6 Markets, Maximizers, and Efficiency

Getting Started: A Drive in the Country

Suppose you decide to take a drive. This will be a hypothetical drive, so you're free to make it as pleasant as you wish. You might want to imagine a gorgeous day, that you have a new convertible, and that there is some lovely countryside nearby to explore.

Your decision to take this drive is a choice. Since economics deals with choices, we can put economics to work in thinking about it. Economists assume that people make choices that maximize the value of some objective. You are a consumer; we assume that taking a drive is a choice that maximizes your utility—the satisfaction you obtain from your use of goods and services and from the activities you pursue.

You certainly plan to enjoy the drive; that enjoyment is the benefit you expect from it. But you'll give up some things as well. Your drive will take some time, time you could have spent doing something else. It will take some gasoline; what you spend for the gasoline could have been used for something else. The drive will also generate some wear and tear on your car. That will cost you the price of repair and maintenance and reduced resale value of your car. The opportunity cost of your drive will thus include the value of the best other use of your time and the value of the best other use of the funds your drive will require. To maximize utility you will weigh the benefits of the drive against the cost of the drive and maximize the difference between those benefits and costs.

This chapter introduces the method through which maximizing choices can be made. This method applies not just to your decision to take a drive, but also can be applied to Wal-Mart's decision to hire extra workers and to USX Corporation's to produce extra steel. The method we will learn can be applied to the analysis of any choice; we will use it throughout our investigation of microeconomics.

We'll also see how maximizing choices by individuals and by firms can lead to an allocation of resources that generates the greatest gains possible for the economy as a whole. In this analysis, we'll put a new item in our toolkit, the method through which individuals and firms maximize, together with the demand and supply analysis we learned in Chapter 3, to see how the marketplace can guide resources to their best uses.

We'll also examine cases in which maximizing choices don't guide resources to their best uses. That possibility is suggested by another aspect of your choice to take a drive. In addition to the costs you will consider, there will be costs imposed on others. Your drive will pollute the air, so part of the opportunity cost of the drive will be the value of the slightly cleaner air people in your area might have had. Resources such as the air we breathe will almost certainly be misallocated as the result of maximizing choices. We'll see just how misallocation of an economy's resources can occur, and we'll see how this misallocation could be fixed.

The Logic of Maximizing Behavior

To say that individuals maximize is to say that they pick some objective and then seek to maximize its value. A sprinter might want to maximize his or her speed; a politician might want to maximize the probability that he or she will win the next election. Economists place special attention on two groups of maximizers: consumers and firms. We assume that consumers seek to maximize **utility**, the satisfaction derived from the consumption of goods and services and from other activities pursued. We also assume that firms seek to maximize **economic profit**, which is the difference between total revenue and total cost. The costs involved in this concept of economic profit are computed in the economic sense—as the opportunity costs, or value of the best opportunity forgone.

The assumption of maximizing behavior lies at the heart of economic analysis. As we explore its implications, however, we must keep in mind the distinction between models and the real world. Our model assumes that individuals make choices in a way that achieves a maximum value for some clearly defined objective. In using such a model, economists don't assume that people actually go through the calculations we will describe. What economists do argue is that people's behavior is broadly consistent with such a model. People may not consciously seek to maximize anything, but they behave as though they do.

The Analysis of Maximizing Behavior

The activities of consumers and firms have benefits, and they also have opportunity costs. We assume that given these benefits and costs, consumers and firms will make choices that maximize the **net benefit** of each activity—the total benefit of the activity minus its opportunity cost. The specific measures of benefit and cost vary with the kind of choice being made. In the case of a firm's choices in production, for example, the total benefit of production is the revenue a firm receives from selling the product; the total cost is the opportunity cost the firm incurs by producing it. The net benefit is thus total revenue minus total opportunity cost, or economic profit.

Economists maintain that in order to maximize net benefit, consumers and firms evaluate each activity at the margin—they consider the additional benefit and the additional cost of another unit of the activity. Should you "super-size" your order at McDonald's? Will the additional beverage and the additional french fries be worth the extra cost? Should a firm hire one more worker? Will the benefits to the firm of hiring this worker be worth the cost of hiring him or her?

The **marginal benefit** is the amount by which an additional unit of an activity increases its total benefit. It's the amount by which the extra french fries increase your satisfaction, or the extra revenue the firm expects to bring in by hiring another worker. The **marginal cost** is the amount by which an additional unit of an activity increases its total cost. You'll pay more to super-size your McDonald's order; the firm's labor costs will rise when it hires another worker.

To determine the quantity of any activity that will maximize its net benefit, we apply the **marginal decision rule:** If the marginal benefit of an additional unit of an activity exceeds the marginal cost, the quantity of the activity should be increased. If the marginal benefit is less than the marginal cost, the quantity should be reduced. Net benefit is maximized at the point at which marginal benefit equals marginal cost.

The marginal decision rule basically says this: If the additional benefit of one more unit exceeds the extra cost, do it; if it doesn't, don't. This simple logic gives us a powerful tool for the analysis of choice.

Maximizing choices must be made within the parameters imposed by some **constraint,** which is a boundary that limits the range of choices that can be made. We assume that a consumer seeks the greatest satisfaction possible within the limits of his or her income. A firm can't produce beyond the limits of its production capacity.

The marginal decision rule forms the foundation for the structure economists use to analyze all choices. At first glance, it may seem that a consumer seeking satisfaction from, say, jelly beans, has little in common with an entrepreneur seeking profit from the production of custom-designed semiconductors. But maximizing choices always follow the marginal decision rule—and that rule holds regardless of what is being maximized or who is doing the maximizing.

To see how the logic of maximizing choices works, we'll examine a specific problem. We'll then extend that problem to the general analysis of maximizing choices.

A Problem in Maximization Suppose a college student, Laurie Phan, faces two midterms tomorrow, one in economics and another in accounting. She has already decided to spend 5 hours studying for the two examinations. This decision imposes a constraint on the problem. Suppose that Ms. Phan's goal is to allocate her 5 hours of study so that she increases her total score for the two exams by as much as possible.

Ms. Phan expects the relationship between the time she spends studying for the economics exam and the total gain in her score to be as given by the second row of the table in Panel (a) of Exhibit 6-1. We interpret the expected total gain in her score as the total benefit of study. She expects that 1 hour of study will raise her score by 18 points; 2 hours will raise it by a total of 32 points, and so on. These values are plotted in Panel (b). Notice that the total benefit curve rises, but by smaller and smaller amounts, as she studies more and more. The slope of the curve, which in this case tells us the rate at which her expected score rises with increased study time, falls as we travel up and to the right along the curve.

Now look at the third row in the table in Panel (a). It tells us the amount by which each additional hour of study increases her expected score; it gives the marginal benefit of studying for the economics exam. Marginal benefit equals the amount by which total benefit rises with each additional hour of study. Because these marginal benefits are given by the changes in total benefits from additional hours of study, they equal the slope of the total benefit curve. We see this in the relationship between Panels (b) and (c) of Exhibit 6-1. The changing slope of the total benefit curve in Panel (b) gives us the downward-sloping marginal benefit curve in Panel (c).

The marginal benefit curve tells us what happens when we pass from one point to another on the total benefit curve, so we have plotted marginal benefits at the midpoints of the hourly intervals in Panel (c). For example, the total benefit curve in Panel (b) tells us that, when Ms. Phan increases her time studying for the economics exam from 2 hours to 3 hours, her total benefit rises from 32 points to 42 points. The increase of 10 points is the marginal benefit of increasing study time from 2 hours to 3 hours. We mark the point for a marginal benefit of 10 midway between 2 and 3 hours. Because marginal values tell us what happens as we pass from one quantity to the next, we shall always plot them at the midpoints of intervals of the variable on the horizontal axis.

We can perform the same kind of analysis to obtain the marginal benefit curve for studying for the accounting exam. Exhibit 6-2 presents this curve. Like the marginal benefit curve for studying economics, it slopes downward. Once again, we have plotted marginal values at the midpoints of the intervals. Increasing study time in accounting from 0 to 1 hour increases Ms. Phan's expected accounting score by 14 points.

Ms. Phan's marginal benefit curves for studying typify a general phenomenon in economics. Marginal benefit curves for virtually all activities, including the activities of consumers and of firms, slope downward. Think about your own experience with studying. On a given day, the first hour spent studying a certain subject probably generates a greater marginal benefit than the second, and the second

Exhibit 6-1

The Benefits of Studying Economics

The table in Panel (a) shows the total benefit and marginal benefit of the time Laurie Phan spends studying for her economics exam. Panel (b) shows the total benefit curve. Panel (c) shows the marginal benefit curve, which is given by the slope of the total benefit curve in Panel (b).

Panel (a)

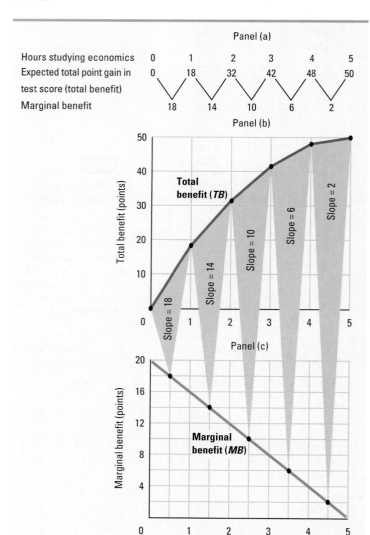

Hours studying economics	0		1		2		3		4		5
Expected total point gain in test score (total benefit)	0		18		32		42		48		50
Marginal benefit		18		14		10		6		2	

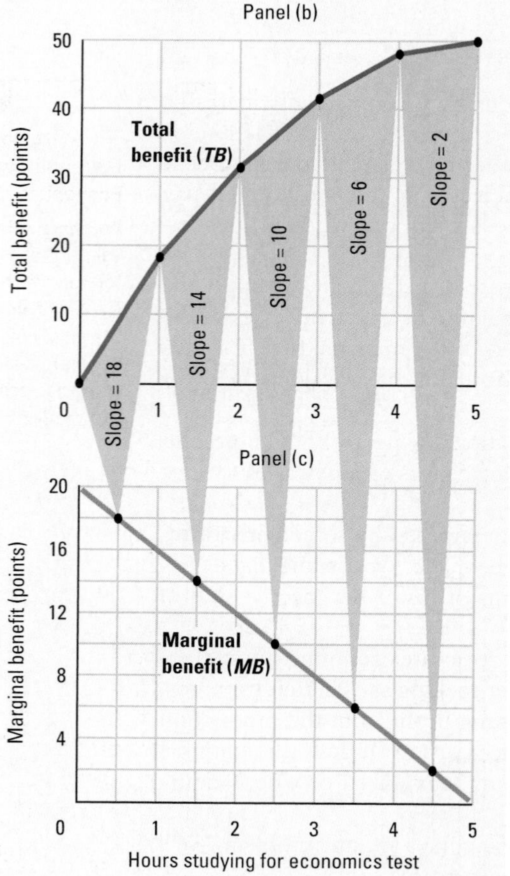

hour probably generates a greater marginal benefit than the third. You may reach a point at which an extra hour of study doesn't seem likely to yield any benefit at all.

The nature of marginal benefits can change with different applications. For a restaurant, the marginal benefit of serving one more meal can be defined as the revenue that meal produces. For a consumer, the marginal benefit of one more slice of pizza can be considered in terms of the additional satisfaction the pizza will create. But whatever the nature of the benefit, marginal benefits generally fall as quantities increase.

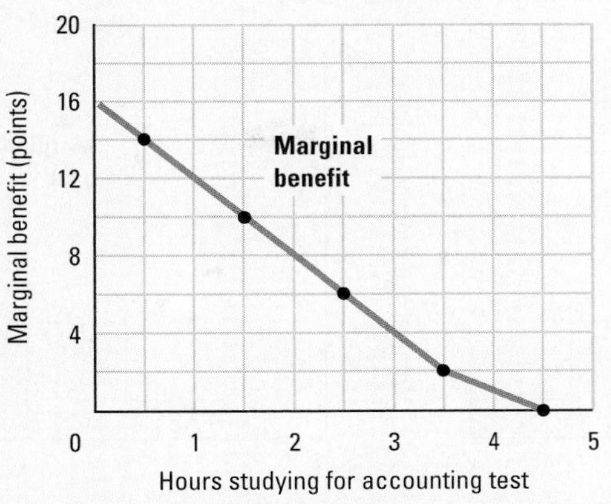

Exhibit 6-2

The Benefits of Studying Accounting

The marginal benefit Laurie Phan expects for studying for her accounting exam is shown by the marginal benefit curve. The first hour of study increases her expected score on the accounting exam by 14 points, the second by 10 points, the third by 6 points, and so on.

Ms. Phan's falling marginal benefit from hours spent studying accounting has special significance for our analysis of her choice concerning how many hours to devote to economics. In our problem, she had decided to devote 5 hours to studying the two subjects. That means that the opportunity cost of an hour spent studying economics equals the benefit she would have gotten spending that hour studying accounting.

Suppose, for example, that she were to consider spending all 5 hours studying accounting. The marginal benefit curve for studying for her accounting exam tells us that she expects that the fifth hour will add nothing to her score. Shifting that hour to economics would cost nothing. We can say that the marginal cost of the first hour spent studying economics is zero. We obtained this value from the marginal benefit curve for studying accounting in Exhibit 6-2.

Similarly, we can find the marginal cost of the second hour studying economics. That requires giving up the fourth hour spent on accounting. Exhibit 6-2 tells us that the marginal benefit of that hour equals 2—that's the marginal cost of spending the second hour studying economics.

Exhibit 6-3 shows the marginal cost curve of studying economics. We see that at first, time devoted to studying economics has a low marginal cost. As time spent studying economics increases, however, it requires her to give up study time in accounting that she expects will be more and more productive. The marginal cost curve for studying economics can thus be derived from the marginal benefit curve for studying accounting. Exhibit 6-3 also shows the marginal benefit curve for studying economics that we derived in Panel (c) of Exhibit 6-1.

Just as marginal benefit curves generally slope downward, marginal cost curves generally slope upward, as does the one in Exhibit 6-3. In the case of allocating time, the phenomenon of rising marginal cost results from the simple fact that, the more time a person devotes to one activity, the less time is available for another. And the more one reduces the second activity, the greater the forgone marginal benefits are likely to be. That means the marginal cost curve for that first activity rises.

Because we now have marginal benefit and marginal cost curves for studying economics, we can apply the marginal decision rule. This rule says that, to maximize the net benefit of an activity, a decisionmaker should increase an activity up to the point at which marginal benefit equals marginal cost. That occurs where the marginal benefit and marginal cost curves intersect, with 3 hours spent studying economics and 2 hours spent studying accounting.

Using Marginal Benefit and Marginal Cost Curves to Find Net Benefits We can use marginal benefit and marginal cost curves to show the total benefit, the total cost, and the net benefit of an activity. We'll see that equating marginal benefit to marginal cost does, indeed, maximize net benefit. We'll also develop another tool to use in interpreting marginal benefit and cost curves.

Exhibit 6-3

The Marginal Benefits and Marginal Costs of Studying Economics

The marginal benefit curve from Panel (c) of Exhibit 6-1 is shown together with the marginal cost curve of studying economics. The marginal cost curve is derived from the marginal benefit curve for studying accounting shown in Exhibit 6-2.

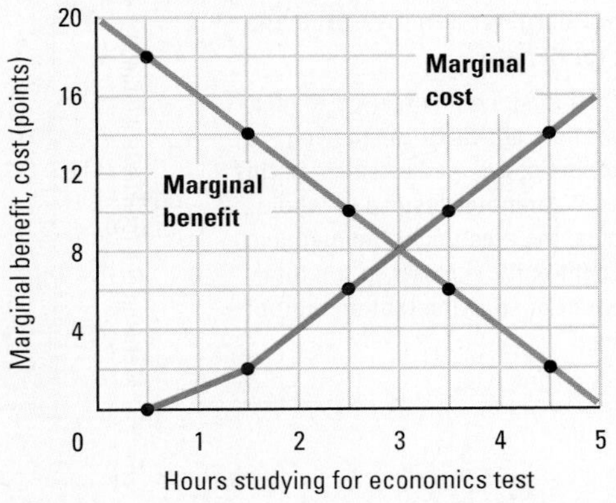

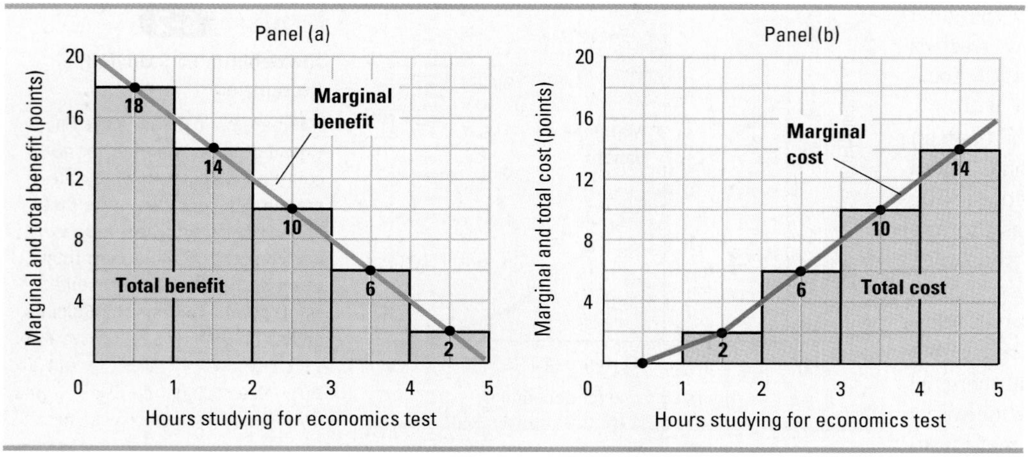

Exhibit 6-4

The Benefits and Costs of Studying Economics

Panel (a) shows the marginal benefit curve of Exhibit 6-1. The total benefit of studying economics at any given quantity of study time is given approximately by the shaded area below the marginal benefit curve up to that level of study. Panel (b) shows the marginal cost curve from Exhibit 6-3. The total cost of studying economics at any given quantity of study time is given approximately by the shaded area below the marginal cost curve up to that level of study.

Panel (a) of Exhibit 6-4 shows the marginal benefit curve we derived in Panel (c) of Exhibit 6-1. The corresponding point on the marginal benefit curve gives the marginal benefit of the first hour of study for the economics exam, 18 points. This same value equals the area of the rectangle bounded by 0 and 1 hour of study and the marginal benefit of 18. Similarly, the marginal benefit of the second hour, 14 points, is shown by the corresponding point on the marginal benefit curve and by the area of the shaded rectangle bounded by 1 and 2 hours of study. The total benefit of 2 hours of study equals the sum of the areas of the first two rectangles, 32 points. We continue this procedure through the fifth hour of studying economics; the areas for each of the shaded rectangles are shown in the graph.

Two features of the curve in Panel (a) of Exhibit 6-4 are particularly important. First, note that the sum of the areas of the five rectangles, 50 points, equals the total benefit of 5 hours of study given in the table in Panel (a) of Exhibit 6-1. Second, notice that the shaded areas are approximately equal to the area under the marginal benefit curve between 0 and 5 hours of study. We can pick any quantity of study time, and the total benefit of that quantity equals the sum of the shaded rectangles between zero and that quantity. Thus, the total benefit of 2 hours of study equals 32 points, the sum of the areas of the first two rectangles.

Now consider the marginal cost curve in Panel (b) of Exhibit 6-4. The areas of the shaded rectangles equal the values of marginal cost. The marginal cost of the first hour of study equals zero; there is thus no rectangle under the curve. The marginal cost of the second hour of study equals 2 points; that is the area of the rectangle bounded by 1 and 2 hours of study and a marginal cost of 2. The marginal cost of the third hour of study is 6 points; this is the area of the shaded rectangle bounded by 2 and 3 hours of study and a marginal cost of 6.

Looking at the rectangles in Panel (b) over the range of 0 to 5 hours of study, we see that the areas of the 5 rectangles total 32, the total cost of spending all 5 hours studying economics. And looking at the rectangles, we see that their area is approximately equal to the area under the marginal cost curve between 0 and 5 hours of study.

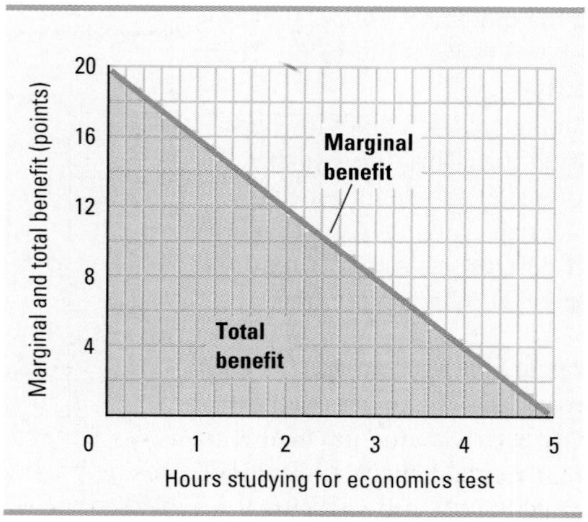

Exhibit 6-5

The Marginal Benefit Curve and Total Benefit

When the increments used to measure time allocated to studying economics are made smaller, in this case 12 minutes instead of whole hours, the area under the marginal benefit curve is closer to the total benefit of studying that amount of time.

We've seen that the areas of the rectangles we've drawn with Laurie Phan's marginal benefit and marginal cost curves equal the total benefit and total cost of studying economics. We've also seen that these areas are roughly equal to the areas under the curves themselves. We can make this last statement much stronger. Suppose, instead of thinking in intervals of whole hours, we think in terms of smaller intervals, say, of 12 minutes. Then each rectangle would be only one-fifth as wide as the rectangles we drew in Exhibit 6-4. Their areas would still equal the total benefit and total cost of study, and the sum of those areas would be closer to the area under the curves. We've done this for Ms. Phan's marginal benefit curve in Exhibit 6-5; notice that the areas of the rectangles closely approximate the area under the curve. They still "stick out" from either side of the curve as did the rectangles we drew in Exhibit 6-4, but you almost need a magnifying glass to see that. The smaller the interval we choose, the closer the areas under the marginal benefit and marginal cost curves will be to total benefit and total cost. For purposes of our model, we can imagine that the intervals are as small as we like. Over a particular range of quantity, the area under a marginal benefit curve equals the total benefit of that quantity, and the area under the marginal cost curve equals the total cost of that quantity.

Panel (a) of Exhibit 6-6 shows marginal benefit and marginal cost curves for studying economics, this time without numbers. We have the usual downward-sloping marginal benefit curve and upward-sloping marginal cost curve. The marginal decision rule tells us to choose D hours to study economics, the quantity at which marginal benefit equals marginal cost at point C. We know that the total benefit of study equals the area under the marginal benefit curve over the range from A to D hours of study, the area ABCD. Total cost equals the area under the marginal cost curve over the same range, or ACD. The difference between total benefit and total cost equals the area between marginal benefit and marginal cost between A and D hours of study; it is the green-shaded triangle ABC. This difference is the net benefit of time spent studying economics.

Now consider the situation in Panel (b). A person spending only E hours studying economics receives a total benefit equal to the area under the marginal benefit curve for this number of hours, ABGE. The total cost is the area under the marginal cost curve, AFE, for a net benefit given by the shaded region ABGF. This is a smaller net benefit than was achieved by expanding study to the intersection of the marginal benefit and marginal cost curves. A person spending only E hours studying economics would be sacrificing the net benefit, FGC,

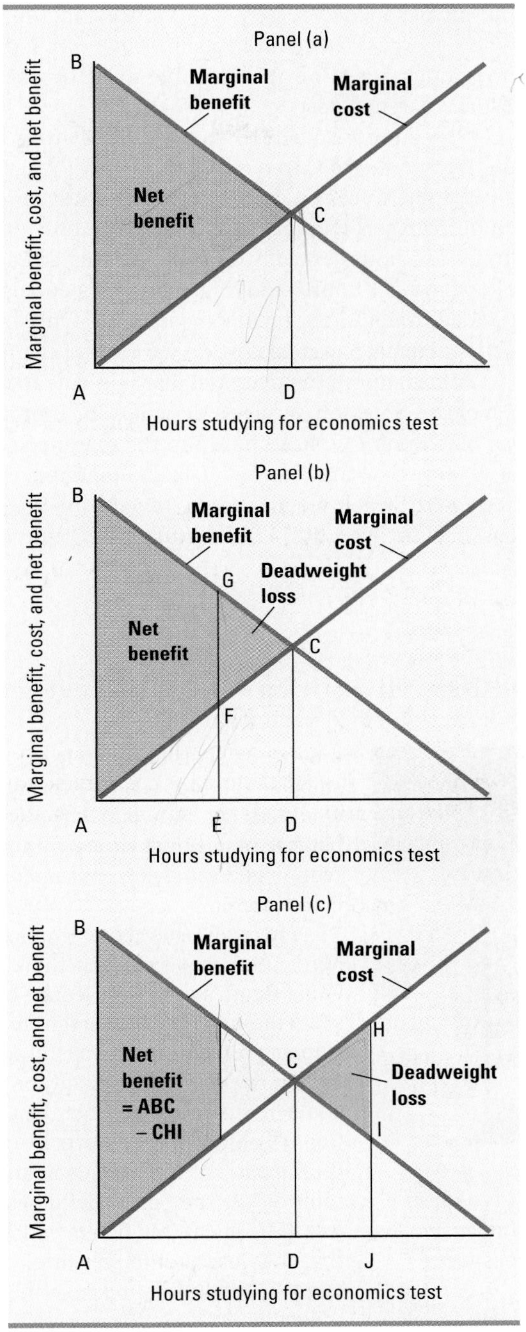

Exhibit 6-6

Using Marginal Benefit and Marginal Cost Curves to Determine Net Benefit

In Panel (a) net benefits are given by the difference between total benefits (as measured by the area under the demand curve, up to any given level of activity) and total costs (as measured by the area under the marginal cost curve, up to any given level of activity). Maximum net benefits are found at the level of activity where the marginal benefit curve intersects the marginal cost curve, at activity level D. Panel (b) shows that if the level of activity is restricted to activity level E, net benefits are reduced from the light-green shaded triangle ABC in Panel (a) to the smaller area ABGF. The forgone net benefits or deadweight loss is given by the purple shaded area FGC. If the activity level is increased from D to J, as shown in Panel (c), net benefits decline by the deadweight loss measured by the area CHI.

the purple shaded region. We call the amount of net benefit given up by failing to operate where marginal benefit equals marginal cost a **deadweight loss.** The deadweight loss tells us how much better off it is possible to be by choosing the solution at which marginal benefit equals marginal cost.

Now suppose a person increases study time from D to J hours in Panel (c). The area under the marginal cost curve between D and J gives the total cost of increasing study time; it is DCHJ. The total benefit of increasing study time equals the area under the marginal benefit curve between D and J; it is DCIJ. The cost of increasing study time in economics from D hours to J hours exceeds the benefit. This gives us a deadweight loss of CHI. The net benefit of spending J hours studying economics equals the net benefit of studying for D hours less the deadweight loss, or ABC *minus* CHI. Only by studying up to the point at which marginal benefit equals marginal cost do we achieve the maximum net benefit shown in Panel (a).

We can apply the marginal decision rule to the problem in Exhibit 6-6 in another way. In Panel (b), a person studies economics for E hours. Reading up to the marginal benefit curve, we reach point G. Reading up to the marginal cost curve, we reach point F. Marginal benefit at G exceeds marginal cost at F; the marginal decision rule says economics study should be increased, which would take us toward the intersection of the marginal benefit and marginal cost curves. Spending J hours studying economics as shown in Panel (c) is too much. Reading

Case in Point Preventing Oil Spills

Do we have enough oil spills in our oceans and waterways? It is a question that perhaps only economists would ask—and as economists we should ask it.

There is, of course, no virtue in an oil spill. It destroys wildlife and fouls shorelines. Cleanup costs can be tremendous. However, preventing oil spills has costs as well—greater enforcement expenditures and higher costs to shippers of oil, and therefore higher costs of goods such as gasoline to consumers. The only way to prevent oil spills completely is to stop shipping oil; that is a cost few people would accept. But what is the right balance between environmental protection and satisfying consumer demands for oil?

Vanderbilt University economist Mark Cohen has examined the U.S. Coast Guard's efforts to reduce oil spills through its enforcement of shipping regulations in coastal waters and on rivers. He focused on the costs and benefits resulting from the Coast Guard's enforcement efforts in 1981. On the basis of the frequency of oil spills before the Coast Guard began its enforcement, Mr. Cohen estimated that the Coast Guard prevented 1,159,352 gallons of oil from being spilled in 1981.

Given that there was a total of 824,921 gallons of oil actually spilled in 1981, should the Coast Guard have attempted to prevent even more spillage? Mr. Cohen estimated that the marginal benefit of preventing one more gallon from being spilled was $7.27 ($3.42 in avoided cleanup cost, $3 less in environmental damage, and $0.85 worth of oil saved). The marginal cost of preventing one more gallon from being spilled was $5.50. Mr. Cohen suggests that because the marginal benefit of more vigorous enforcement exceeded the marginal cost, even more vigorous Coast Guard efforts would have been justified.

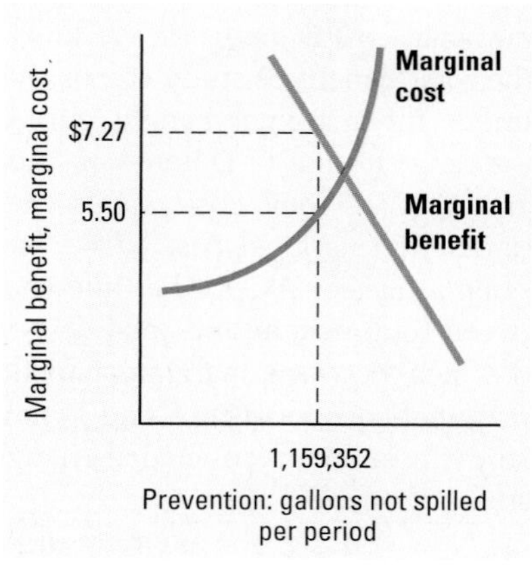

Source: Mark A. Cohen, "The Costs and Benefits of Oil Spill Prevention and Enforcement," *Journal of Environmental Economics and Management* 13(2) (June 1986): 167–188.

up to the marginal benefit and marginal cost curves, we see that marginal cost exceeds marginal benefit, suggesting that study time be reduced.

This completes our introduction to the marginal decision rule and the use of marginal benefit and marginal cost curves. We will spend the remainder of the chapter applying the model. First, though, let's review what we've learned:

1. The marginal benefit curve for most activities slopes downward, while the marginal cost curve slopes upward.

2. The marginal benefit rule tells us that we can maximize the net benefit of any activity by choosing the quantity at which marginal benefit equals marginal cost. At this quantity, the net benefit of the activity is maximized.

3. The total benefit of an activity equals the area under the marginal benefit curve up to the quantity of the activity. The area under the marginal cost curve gives total cost. Net benefit equals total benefit minus total cost.

4. If the marginal benefit of an activity exceeds the marginal cost, the activity should be expanded. If the marginal cost exceeds the marginal benefit, the activity should be reduced.

Caution!

It's easy to make the following mistake in thinking about the marginal decision rule: "Because marginal benefit equals marginal cost, total benefit equals total cost and there is no net benefit." It's crucial to avoid this error. In fact, when marginal benefit equals marginal cost, net benefit (the *difference* between total benefits and total costs) is maximized.

Checklist

- Economists assume that decisionmakers make choices in a way that maximizes the value of some objective.
- Maximization involves determining the change in total benefit and the change in total cost associated with each unit of an activity. These changes are called marginal benefit and marginal cost, respectively.
- If the marginal benefit of an activity exceeds the marginal cost, the decisionmaker will gain by increasing the activity.
- If the marginal cost of an activity exceeds the marginal benefit, the decisionmaker will gain by reducing the activity.
- The area under the marginal benefit curve for an activity gives its total benefit; the area under the marginal cost curve gives the activity's total cost. Net benefit equals total benefit less total cost.
- The net gain from an activity is maximized at the point at which the marginal benefit of the activity equals the marginal cost.

Try It Yourself 6-1

Suppose Ms. Phan still faces the exams in economics and in accounting, and she still plans to spend a total of 5 hours studying for the two exams. However, she revises her expectations about the degree to which studying economics and accounting will affect her scores

Hours Studying Economics and Expected Benefits and Costs

Hours studying economics	0	1	2	3	4	5
Total benefit	0	14	24	30		32
Total cost	0	2	8		32	50
Net benefit	0	12		12	0	−18

Hours studying economics	0		1		2		3		4		5
Total benefit	0		14		24		30		—		32
Marginal benefit		—		—		—		—		—	
Total cost	0		2		8		—		32		50
Marginal cost		—		—		—		—		—	

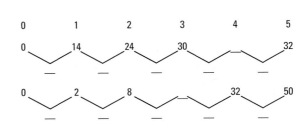

on the two exams. She expects studying economics will add somewhat less to her score and she expects studying accounting will add more. The result is the table at left on page 131 of expected total benefits and total costs of hours spent studying economics. Notice that several values in the table have been omitted. Fill in the three missing values in the table. How many hours of study should Ms. Phan devote to economics to maximize her net benefit? Now compute the marginal benefits and costs of hours devoted to studying economics, completing the table at the right.

Draw the marginal benefit and marginal cost curves for studying economics (remember to plot marginal values at the midpoints of the respective hourly intervals). Do your curves intersect at the "right" number of hours of study—the number that maximizes the net benefit of studying economics?

Maximizing in the Marketplace

In perhaps the most influential book in economics ever written, *An Inquiry Into the Nature and Causes of the Wealth of Nations,* published in 1776, Adam Smith argued that the pursuit of self-interest in a marketplace would promote the general interest. He said resources would be guided, as if by an "invisible hand," to their best uses. That invisible hand was the marketplace.

Smith's idea was radical for its time; he saw that the seemingly haphazard workings of the marketplace could promote the common good. In this section, we'll use the tools we have developed thus far to see the power of Smith's invisible hand. Efforts by individuals to maximize net benefit can maximize net benefit for the economy as a whole.

When the net benefits of all economic activities are maximized, economists say the allocation of resources is **efficient.** This concept of efficiency is broader than the notion of efficient production that we encountered in Chapter 2. There, we saw that the economy's factors of production would be efficient *in production* if they were allocated according to the principle of comparative advantage. That meant producing as much as possible with the factors of production available. The concept of an efficient allocation of resources incorporates both the production and consumption of goods and services.

Achieving Efficiency

Imagine yourself arriving at the store to purchase tomatoes. In your choice, you'll weigh your own benefits and costs to maximize your own net benefit. The farmers, distributors, and the grocer have sought to maximize their net benefits as well. How can we expect that all those efforts will maximize net benefits for the economy as a whole? How can we expect the marketplace to achieve an efficient allocation of tomatoes, or of anything else?

One condition that must be met if the market's allocation is to be efficient is that the marketplace must be competitive. We'll have a great deal more to say about competitive markets versus not-so-competitive ones in subsequent chapters. For now, we can simply note that a competitive market is one with many buyers and sellers in each market. No one controls the price; the forces of demand and supply determine price.

The second condition that must hold if the market is to achieve an efficient allocation concerns property rights. We turn to that topic in the next section.

The Role of Property Rights A smoothly functioning market requires that producers possess property rights to the goods and services they produce and that consumers possess property rights to the goods and services they buy. **Property rights** are a set of rules that specify the ways in which an owner can use a resource.

Consider the tomato market. Farmers who grow tomatoes have clearly defined rights to their land and to the tomatoes they produce and sell. Distributors who purchase tomatoes from farmers and sell them to grocers have clear rights to the tomatoes until they sell them to grocers. The grocers who purchase the tomatoes retain rights to them until they sell them to consumers. When you buy a tomato, you have the exclusive right to its use.

A system of property rights forms the basis for all market exchange. Before exchange can begin, there must be a clear specification of who owns what. The system of property rights must also show what purchasers are acquiring when they buy rights to particular resources. Because property rights must exist if exchange is to occur, and because exchange is the process through which economic efficiency is achieved, a system of property rights is essential to the efficient allocation of resources.

Imagine what would happen in the market for tomatoes if property rights weren't clearly defined. Suppose, for example, that grocers couldn't legally prevent someone from simply

Case in Point Saving the Elephant Through Exchange

The African elephant, the world's largest land mammal, is in danger of being hunted into extinction. The elephant population of Central and East Africa, which numbered more than 1.3 million in 1980, fell to 580,000 by 1995 according to statistics from the World Wildlife Fund. Kenya's elephant population fell most precipitously, from 167,000 at the beginning of the 1970s to about 26,000 in 1997.

Elephants are killed chiefly for their ivory. The tusks from a single elephant can fetch more than $2,000 in the black market—almost twice the annual per capita income of Kenya.

To combat the slaughter, the Central African countries of Kenya, Zambia, Tanzania, and Somalia have imposed bans on killing elephants. Government patrols trained in guerrilla warfare roam the countryside with orders to shoot poachers on sight. But the elephants continue to be slaughtered at a rate of 200 per day. Bans on the export of ivory and international bans on trade in ivory instituted in 1989 have failed to stop the massacre.

The basic problem is that no one in Central Africa owns property rights in elephants. Elephants in these countries are a common property resource. There is thus no one who can profit from efforts to preserve or expand the population of elephants.

Although prospects are not encouraging in the central part of the continent, there is good news to the south. Elephant populations in Botswana, Namibia, South Africa, and Zimbabwe increased during the 1980s and 1990s. Botswana's herd, for example, increased from 20,000 at the beginning of the 1980s to more than 100,000 by the end of the 1990s. What's the secret of countries in which herds are increasing?

Each of the four countries of southern Africa has established exclusive, transferable licenses to hunt elephants. Each license allows a hunter to kill a single elephant. The licenses are typically granted to villages or regional parks, which can sell them to hunters. A village or park that succeeds in increasing its own herd qualifies for additional licenses. The village of Masoka, in Zimbabwe, earns more than $40,000 a year by selling licenses, which in 1999 went for a hefty fee of about $12,000 to $15,000 per animal. That's more than the ivory was worth; presumably hunters were paying a premium for the opportunity to hunt for elephants.

In April 1999, the first legal sale of ivory (from stockpiles held in warehouses) took place in Botswana, Zimbabwe, and Namibia after a 10-year ban. It remains to be seen whether the opening of trade in ivory brings back the

slaughter by poachers. But because the property rights now belong to the villagers who have an interest in increasing the size of their herds, poachers will have a more difficult time of it. According to Jacomea Nare, a spokesperson for the Communal Areas Management Program for Indigenous Resources (CAMPFIRE), "the poaching and illegal hunting has stopped completely [in Zimbabwe], because everyone in the community is a policeman now."

Sources: Lisa Graingerr, "Are They Safe in Our Hands?" *The Times of London*, 16 July 1994, p. 18; Tracey C. Rembert, "Opening the Ivory Door: An Exercise in Democracy Pits Conservation Against Animal Rights," at *www.emagazine.com/july-august_1998/0798curr_ivory.html;* and Lettie Gaelesiwe, "Botswana Auctions Ivory," *Mmegi/The Reporter* (Gaborone), 16 April 1999, at www.africanews.org/south/botswana/stories/19990416_feat1.html

grabbing some tomatoes and leaving without paying for them. If that were the case, grocers wouldn't be likely to offer tomatoes for sale. If it were the case for all grocery items, there wouldn't be grocery stores.

Although property rights vary for different resources, two characteristics are required if the marketplace is to achieve an efficient allocation of resources:

1. Property rights must be exclusive. An **exclusive property right** is one that allows its owner to prevent others from using the resource. The owner of a house, for example, has the right to exclude others from the use of the house. If this right did not exist, ownership would have little value; it isn't likely that the property could be exchanged in a market.

2. Property rights must be transferable. A **transferable property right** is one that allows the owner of a resource to sell or lease it to someone else. In the absence of transferability, no exchange could occur.

Markets and the Efficiency Condition A competitive market with well-defined and transferable property rights satisfies the **efficiency condition.** If met, we can assume that the market's allocation of resources will be efficient.

Consider again your purchase of tomatoes. Suppose the curves of demand and supply for tomatoes are those given in Exhibit 6-7; the equilibrium price equals $1.50 per pound. Suppose further that the market satisfies the efficiency condition. With that assumption, we can relate the model of demand and supply to our analysis of marginal benefits and costs.

The demand curve tells us that the last pound of tomatoes was worth $1.50; we can think of that as the marginal benefit of the last pound of tomatoes. We can say that about any price on a market demand curve; a demand curve can be considered as a marginal benefit curve. Similarly, the supply curve can be considered the marginal cost curve. In the case of the tomato market, for example, the price tells us that the marginal cost of producing the last pound of tomatoes is $1.50. This marginal cost is considered in the economic sense—other goods and services worth $1.50 weren't produced in order to make an additional pound of tomatoes available.

On what basis can we presume that the price of a pound of tomatoes equals its marginal cost? The answer lies in our marginal decision rule. Profit-maximizing tomato producers will produce more tomatoes as long as their marginal benefit exceeds their marginal cost. What is the marginal benefit to a producer of an extra pound of tomatoes? It is the price that the producer will receive. What is the marginal cost? It is the value that must be given up to produce an extra pound of tomatoes.

Producers maximize profit by expanding their production up to the point at which their marginal cost equals their marginal benefit, which is the market price. The price of $1.50 thus reflects the marginal cost to society of making an additional pound of tomatoes available. In terms of the marginal benefit–marginal cost framework we've already developed, we can think of the supply curve as a marginal cost curve.

At the equilibrium price and output of tomatoes, then, the marginal benefit of tomatoes to consumers, as reflected by the price they are willing to pay, equals the marginal cost of producing tomatoes. Where marginal benefit equals marginal cost, net benefit is maximized. The equilibrium quantity of tomatoes, as determined by demand and supply, is efficient.

Exhibit 6-7

Demand and Supply and the Efficiency Condition

In a competitive market with exclusive and transferable property rights, such as the market for tomatoes, the efficiency condition is met. Buyers and sellers are faced with all of the relevant costs and benefits, and the equilibrium price equals the marginal cost to society of producing that output, here $1.50 per pound. We can interpret the market demand and supply curves as marginal benefit and marginal cost curves, respectively.

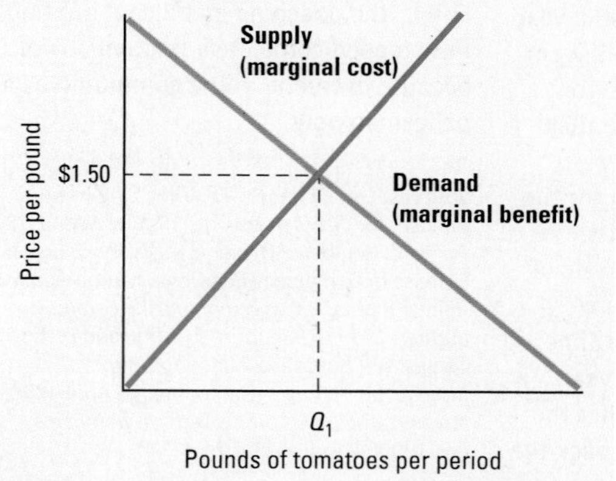

Producer and Consumer Surplus

Think about the last thing you purchased. You bought it because you expected that its benefits would exceed its opportunity cost; you expected that the purchase would make you better off. The seller sold it to you because he

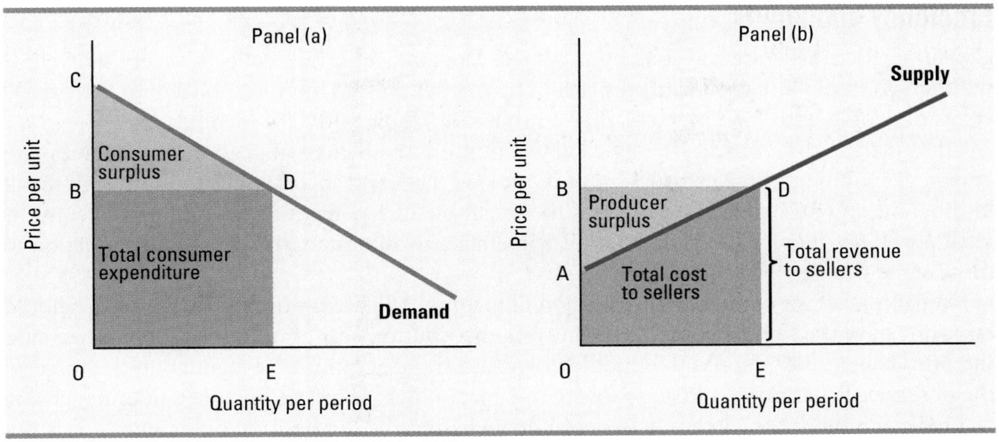

Exhibit 6-8

Consumer and Producer Surplus

Consumer surplus [Panel (a)] measures the difference between total benefits of consuming a given quantity of output and the total expenditures consumers pay to obtain them. Here, total benefits are given by the rectangle OCDE, total expenditures are given by the rectangle OBDE. The difference, shown by the triangle BCD, is consumer surplus. Producer surplus [Panel (b)] measures the difference between total revenue received by firms at a given quantity of output and the total cost of producing it. Here, total revenue is given by the rectangle OADE, and total costs are given by the area OBDE. The difference, shown by the triangle ABD, is producer surplus.

or she expected that the money you paid would be worth more than the value of keeping the item. The seller expected to be better off as a result of the sale. Exchanges in the marketplace have a remarkable property: Both buyers and sellers expect to emerge from the transaction better off.

Panel (a) of exhibit 6-8 shows a market demand curve for a particular good. Suppose the price equals OB and the quantity equals OE. The area under the demand curve over the range of quantities from the origin at O to the quantity at E equals the total benefit of consuming OE units of the good. Consumers pay for this benefit; their total expenditures equal the rectangle OBDE, which is the dark shaded region in the graph.

But the benefit to consumers is greater than the rectangle that shows what they spend; it's the entire area under the demand curve. The amount by which the total benefit to consumers exceeds their total expenditure is called **consumer surplus.** It's the light-shaded triangle BCD in Panel (a). Consumer surplus gives us the net gain to consumers from buying goods and services.

Now consider the sellers' side of transactions. Panel (b) Exhibit 6-8 shows a market supply curve; recall that it gives us marginal cost. Suppose the market price equals OB and quantity supplied is OE; those are the same values we had in Panel (a). The price times the quantity equals the total revenue received by sellers. It is shown as the entire shaded rectangle OBDE. The total revenue received by sellers equals total expenditures by consumers.

The total cost to sellers is the area under the marginal cost curve; it is the area OADE. That cost is less than revenue. The difference between the total revenue received by sellers and their total cost is called **producer surplus.** In Panel (b) it is the light-shaded triangle ABD.

We put the demand and supply curves of Exhibit 6-8 Panels (a) and (b) together in Exhibit 6-9. The intersection of the two curves determines the equilibrium price, OB, and the equilibrium quantity, OE. The shaded regions give us consumer and producer surplus. The sum of these two surpluses is net benefit. This net benefit is maximized where the demand and supply curves intersect.

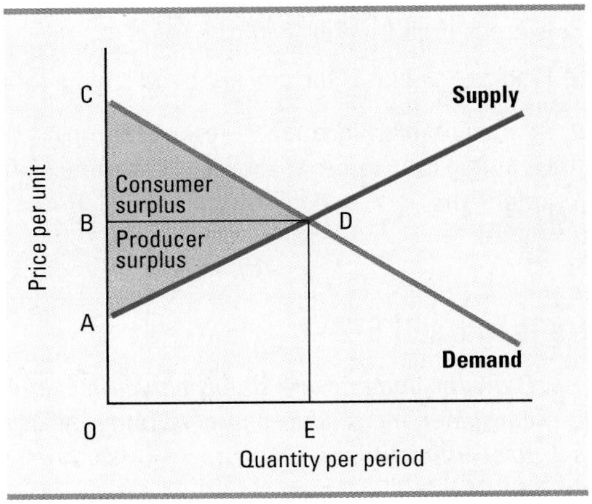

Exhibit 6-9

Net Benefit—The Sum of Consumer and Producer Surplus

The sum of consumer surplus and producer surplus measures the net benefit to society of any level of economic activity. Net benefit is maximized when production and consumption are carried out at the level where the demand and supply curves intersect.

Efficiency and Equity

Consumer demands are affected by incomes. Demand, after all, reflects ability as well as willingness to pay for goods and services. The market will be more responsive to the preferences of people with high incomes than to those of people with low incomes.

In a market that satisfies the efficiency condition an efficient allocation of resources will emerge from any particular distribution of income. Different income distributions will result in different, but still efficient, outcomes. For example, if 1 percent of the population controls virtually all the income, then the market will efficiently allocate virtually all its production to those same people.

What *is* a fair, or equitable, distribution of income? What is an unfair distribution? Should everyone have the same income? Is the current distribution fair? Should the rich have less and the poor have more? Should the middle class have more? Equity is very much in the mind of the observer. What may seem equitable to one person may seem inequitable to another. There is, however, no test we can apply to determine whether the distribution of income is or is not equitable. As you learned in Chapter 1, that question requires a normative judgment.

Determining whether the allocation of resources is or is not efficient is one problem. Determining whether the distribution of income is fair is another. The governments of all nations act in some way to redistribute income. That fact suggests that people generally have concluded that leaving the distribution of income solely to the market would not be fair, and that some redistribution is desirable. This may take the form of higher taxes for people with higher incomes than for those with lower incomes. It may take the form of special programs, such as welfare programs, for low-income people.

Whatever distribution society chooses, an efficient allocation of resources is still preferred to an inefficient one. Because an efficient allocation maximizes net benefits, the gain in net benefits could be distributed in a way that leaves all people better off than they would be at any inefficient allocation. If an efficient allocation of resources seems unfair, it must be because the distribution of income is unfair.

Check*list*

- In a competitive system in which demand and supply determine prices, the demand and supply curves can be considered as marginal benefit and marginal cost curves, respectively.
- An efficient allocation of resources is one that maximizes the net benefits of each activity. We expect it to be achieved in markets that satisfy the efficiency condition, which requires a competitive market and well-defined, transferable property rights.
- Consumer surplus is the amount by which the total benefit to consumers from some activity exceeds their total expenditure for it.
- Producer surplus is the amount by which the total revenues of producers exceed their total costs.
- An inequitable allocation of resources implies that the distribution of income and wealth is inequitable. Judgments about equity in the distribution of income and wealth are normative judgments.

Try It Yourself 6-2

Draw the demand and supply curves in Exhibit 3-7 in Chapter 3. Now show the areas of consumer and producer surplus. Under what circumstances is the market for coffee likely to be efficient?

Market Failure

Private decisions in the marketplace may not be consistent with the maximization of the net benefit of a particular activity. The failure of private decisions in the marketplace to achieve an efficient allocation of scarce resources is called **market failure.** Markets will not generate an efficient allocation of resources if they are not competitive or if property rights are not well defined and fully transferable. Either condition will mean that decisionmakers are not faced with the marginal benefits and costs of their choices.

Think about the imaginary drive that we had you take at the beginning of this chapter. You faced some, but not all, of the opportunity costs involved in that choice. In particular, your choice to go for a drive would increase air pollution and might increase traffic congestion. That means that, in weighing the marginal benefits and marginal costs of going for a drive, not all of the costs would be counted. As a result, the net benefit of the allocation of resources such as the air might not be maximized.

Noncompetitive Markets

The model of demand and supply assumes that markets are competitive. No one in these markets has any power over the equilibrium price; each consumer and producer takes the market price as given and responds to it. Under such conditions, price is determined by the intersection of demand and supply.

In some markets, however, individual buyers or sellers are powerful enough to influence the market price. In subsequent chapters, we will study cases in which producers or consumers are in a position to affect the prices they charge or must pay, respectively. We shall find that when individual firms or groups of firms have market power, which is the ability to change the market price, the price will be distorted—it will not equal marginal cost.

Public Goods

Some goods are unlikely to be produced and exchanged in a market because of special characteristics of the goods themselves. The benefits of these goods are such that exclusion is not feasible. Once they are produced, anyone can enjoy them; there is no practical way to exclude people who haven't paid for them from consuming them. Furthermore, the marginal cost of adding one more consumer is zero. A good for which the cost of exclusion is prohibitive and for which the marginal cost of an additional user is zero is a **public good.** A good for which exclusion is possible and for which the marginal cost of another user is positive is a **private good.**

National defense is a public good. Once defense is provided, it is not possible to exclude people who haven't paid for it from its consumption. Further, the cost of an additional user is zero—an army doesn't cost any more if there is one more person to be protected. Other examples of public goods include law enforcement, fire protection, and efforts to preserve species threatened with extinction.

Free Riders Suppose a private firm, Star Wars, Inc., develops a completely reliable system to intercept any missiles that might be launched toward the United States from anywhere in the world. This service is a public good. Once it is provided, no one can be excluded from the system's protection on grounds that he or she hasn't paid for it, and the cost of adding one more person to the group protected is zero. Suppose that the system, by eliminating a potential threat to U.S. security, makes the average person in the United States better off; the benefit to each household from the added security is worth $40 per month. There are roughly 104 million households in the United States, so the total benefit of the system is $4.16 billion per month. Assume that it will cost Star Wars $1 billion per month to operate. The benefits of the system far outweigh the cost.

Suppose that Star Wars installs its system and sends a bill to each household for $20 for the first month of service—an amount equal to half of each household's benefit. If each household pays its bill, Star Wars will enjoy a tidy profit; it will receive revenues of more than $2 billion per month.

But will each household pay? Once the system is in place, each household would recognize that it enjoys the benefits of the security provided by Star Wars whether it pays its bill or not. Although some households will voluntarily pay their bills, it seems unlikely that very many will. Recognizing the opportunity to consume the good, most would be free riders. **Free riders** are people or firms that consume a public good without paying for it. Even though the total benefit of the system is $4 billion, Star Wars won't be faced by the marketplace with a signal that suggests that the system is worthwhile. It's unlikely that it will recover its cost of $1 billion per month. Star Wars isn't likely to get off the ground.

The bill for $20 from Star Wars sends the wrong signal, too. An efficient market requires a price equal to marginal cost. But the marginal cost of protecting one more household is zero; adding one more household adds nothing to the cost of the system. A household that decides not to pay Star Wars anything for its service is paying a price equal to its marginal cost. But doing that, being a free rider, is precisely what prevents Star Wars from operating.

Because no household can be excluded and because the cost of an extra household is zero, the efficiency condition will not be met in a private market. What is true of Star Wars, Inc., is true of public goods in general; they simply do not lend themselves to private market provision.

Public Goods and the Government Because many individuals who benefit from public goods won't pay for them, private firms will produce a smaller quantity of public goods than is efficient, if they produce them at all. In such cases, it may be desirable for government agencies to step in. Government can supply a greater quantity of the good by direct provision, by purchasing the public good from a private agency, or by subsidizing consumption. In any case, the cost is financed through taxation and thus avoids the free-rider problem.

Most public goods are provided directly by government agencies. Governments produce national defense and law enforcement, for example. Private firms under contract with government agencies produce some public goods. Park maintenance and fire services are public goods that are sometimes produced by private firms. In other cases, the government promotes consumption by subsidizing some activities. Private charitable contributions often support activities that are public goods; federal and state governments subsidize these by allowing taxpayers to reduce their tax payments by a fraction of the amount they contribute.

While the market will produce some level of public goods in the absence of government intervention, we do not expect that it will produce the quantity that maximizes net benefit. Exhibit 6-10 illustrates the problem. Suppose that provision of a public good such as national defense is left entirely to private firms. It's likely that some defense services would be produced; suppose that equals Q_1 units per period. The efficient quantity occurs where demand, or marginal benefit, equals marginal cost, at Q^*. The deadweight loss is the shaded area ABC; we can think of this as the net benefit of government intervention to increase the production of national defense.

Exhibit 6-10

Public Goods and Market Failure

Because free riders will prevent firms from being able to require consumers to pay for the benefits received from consuming a public good, output will likely be less than the efficient level. In the absence of government intervention in such markets, restricted output at Q_1 will result in a deadweight loss to society, shown here as the area ABC.

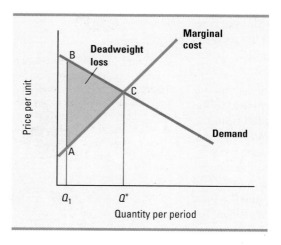

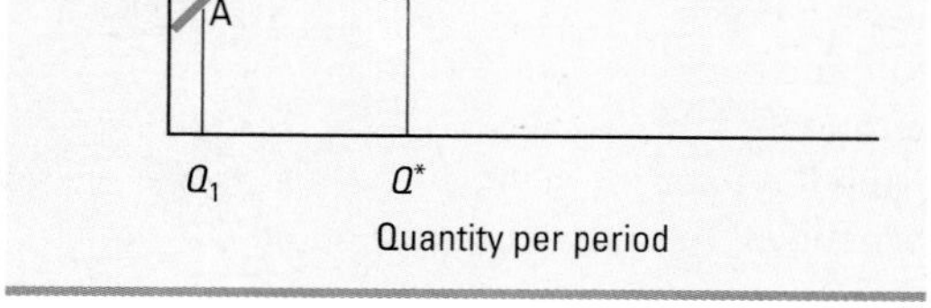

External Costs and Benefits

Suppose that in the course of production, the firms in a particular industry generate air pollution. These firms thus impose costs on others, but they do so outside the context of any market exchange—no agreement has been made between the firms and the people affected by the pollution. The firms thus won't be faced with the costs of their action. A cost imposed on others outside of any market exchange is an **external cost.**

We saw an example of an external cost in your imaginary decision to go for a drive. Here's another: violence on television, in the movies, and in other media such as video games. Many critics argue that the violence that pervades these media fosters the kind of violent behavior that took 15 lives in 1999 at Columbine High School in Littleton, Colorado. Two students at the school killed classmates, a teacher, and themselves in a tragedy that shook the nation. Some media critics argue that violent entertainment contributes to such disasters, and thus puts everyone at greater risk. This risk is a cost not faced by the producers of this entertainment, and thus constitutes an external cost.

An action taken by a person or firm can also create benefits for others, again in the absence of any market agreement; such a benefit is called an **external benefit.** A firm that builds a beautiful building generates benefits to everyone who admires it; such benefits are external.

Caution!

Note that the definitions of public and private goods are based on characteristics of the goods themselves, not on whether they are provided by the public or the private sector. Postal services are a private good provided by the public sector. The fact that these goods are produced by a government agency doesn't make them a public good. Private individuals or firms sometimes provide public goods such as parks. These parks may satisfy the criteria for public goods, despite the fact that they're provided by the private sector.

External Costs and Efficiency The case of the polluting firms is illustrated in Exhibit 6-11. The industry supply curve S_1 reflects private marginal costs, MC_p. The market price is P_p for a quantity Q_p. If the external costs generated by the pollution were added, the new supply curve S_2 would reflect higher marginal costs, MC_e. Faced with those costs, the market would generate a lower equilibrium quantity, Q_e. That quantity would command a higher price, P_e. The failure to confront producers with the cost of their pollution means that consumers do not pay the full cost of the good they are purchasing. The level of output and the level of pollution are therefore higher than would be economically efficient. If a way could be found to confront producers with the full cost of their choices, then consumers would be faced with a higher cost as well. Exhibit 6-11 shows that consumption would be reduced to the efficient level, Q_e, at which demand and the full marginal cost curve (MC_e) intersect. The deadweight loss generated by allowing the external cost to be generated with an output of Q_p is given as the shaded region in the graph.

External Costs and Government Intervention If an activity generates external costs, the decisionmakers generating the activity will not be faced with its full costs. As a result, they will carry out an excessive quantity of the activity. In such cases, government may try to intervene to reduce the level of the activity toward the efficient quantity. In the case shown in Exhibit 6-11, for example, firms generating an external cost have a supply curve S_1 that reflects their private marginal costs, MC_p. A per-unit pollution fee imposed on the firms would increase their marginal costs to MC_e, thus shifting the supply curve to S_2, and the efficient level of production would emerge. Taxes or other restrictions may be imposed on the activity that generates the external cost in an effort to confront decisionmakers with the costs that they are imposing. In many areas, firms and consumers that pollute rivers and lakes are required to pay fees based on the amount they pollute. Firms in many areas are required to purchase permits in order to pollute the air; the permits serve to confront the firms with the costs of their choices.

Another approach to dealing with problems of external costs is direct regulation. For example, a firm may be ordered to reduce its pollution. A person who turns his or her front yard into a garbage dump may be ordered to clean it up. Participants at a raucous party may be told to be quiet. Alternative ways of dealing with external costs are discussed in more detail in Chapter 18.

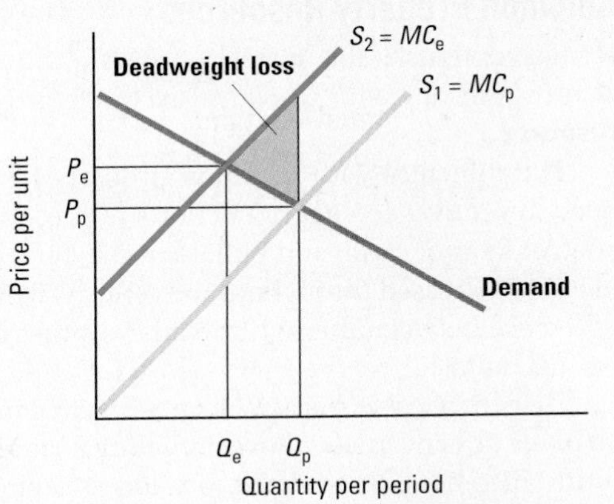

Exhibit 6-11

External Costs

When firms in an industry generate external costs, the supply curve S_1 reflects only their private marginal cost, MC_p. Forcing firms to pay the external costs they impose shifts the supply curve to S_2, which reflects the full marginal cost of the firms' production, MC_e. Output is reduced and price goes up. The deadweight loss is the shaded area in the graph.

Case in Point Externalities, Cigarettes, and Alcohol

Smokers and heavy drinkers impose substantial costs on themselves. Do they impose external costs as well? A 1989 Rand Corporation study, directed by University of Michigan economist Willard G. Manning, suggests that they do. The Rand study concluded that smokers more than pay for their external costs through the taxes they pay, but that heavy drinkers do not.

The private costs of smoking are huge. Health experts estimate that each pack of cigarettes smoked reduces a smoker's life expectancy by more than 2 hours. Smoking-related illnesses kill more than 300,000 people per year in the United States alone. The Rand study estimated that the value of life expectancy lost was about $5 per pack smoked. But that is a private cost—a cost smokers impose on themselves.

Smokers generate external costs in three ways. First, they impose costs on others by forcing health-care costs up, and thus raising health insurance premiums. It is these costs that many states have used as the basis for lawsuits against tobacco companies. Cigarettes also cause fires that destroy more than $300 million worth of property each year. Finally, smokers may kill nonsmokers with their smoke. An estimated 2,400 people die each year from so-called passive smoking. The Rand researchers estimated that the total value of external costs generated by smokers was $0.53 per pack.

In an important way, however, smokers also generate external benefits. Smokers contribute to retirement programs and to Social Security, then die sooner than nonsmokers. They thus subsidize the retirement costs of the rest of the population. According to the Rand study, that produces a benefit of $0.24 per pack. The net external cost of smoking was thus $0.29 per pack. Given that state and federal excise taxes averaged $0.37 per pack in 1989, the Rand researchers concluded that smokers more than paid their own way.

The Rand study defined heavy drinking as alcohol consumed in excess of an equivalent of two drinks per day. Heavy drinking, like smoking, increases health insurance costs for the rest of the population. Heavy drinkers also account for most highway fatalities.

Like smokers, heavy drinkers die earlier than those in the rest of the population. But unlike smokers, they also leave the work force earlier, so drinkers don't yield the same retirement benefits to society that smokers do.

The Rand researchers estimated that the total external cost of alcohol consumption was $1.19 per excess ounce consumed. The average of federal, state, and local excise taxes per ounce of alcohol was $0.23 per ounce in 1985. The study concluded that increases in alcohol taxes were justified on grounds of external costs.

Source: Willard G. Manning, Emmett B. Keeler, Joseph P. Newhouse, Elizabeth M. Sloss, and Jeffrey Wasserman, "The Taxes of Sin: Do Smokers and Drinkers Pay Their Way?" *Journal of the American Medical Association* 261 (17 March 1989): 1604–1609.

Common Property Resources

Exclusive, transferable property rights give owners an incentive to use their resources efficiently. A resource for which no exclusive property rights exist is called a **common property resource.**

The difficulty with common property resources is that individuals may not have adequate incentives to engage in efforts to preserve or protect them. Consider, for example, the relative fates of cattle and buffalo in the United States in the nineteenth century. Cattle populations increased throughout the century, while the buffalo nearly became extinct. The chief difference between the two animals was that exclusive property rights existed for cattle but not for buffalo.

Owners of cattle had an incentive to maintain herd sizes. A cattle owner who slaughtered all of his or her cattle without providing for replacement of the herd wouldn't have a source of future income. Cattle owners not only maintained their herds, but engaged in extensive efforts to breed high-quality livestock. They invested time and effort in the efficient management of the resource on which their livelihoods depended.

Buffalo hunters surely had similar concerns about the maintenance of buffalo herds, but they had no individual stake in doing anything about them—the animals were a common property resource. Thousands of individuals hunted buffalo for a living. Anyone who cut back on hunting in order to help to preserve the herd would lose income—and face the likelihood that other hunters would go on hunting at the same rate as before.

Today, exclusive rights to buffalo have been widely established. The demand for buffalo meat, which is lower in fat than beef, has been increasing, but the number of buffalo in the United States is rising rapidly. If buffalo were still a common property resource, that increased demand would, in the absence of other restrictions on hunting of the animals, surely result in the elimination of the animal.

When a species is threatened with extinction, it is likely that no one has exclusive property rights to it. Whales, condors, grizzly bears, elephants in Central Africa—whatever the animal that is threatened—are common property resources. In such cases a government agency may impose limits on the killing of the animal or destruction of its habitat. Such limits can prevent the excessive private use of a common property resource. Alternatively, as was done in the case of the buffalo, private rights can be established, giving resource owners the task of preservation.

Checklist

- Public sector intervention to increase the level of provision of public goods may improve the efficiency of resource allocation by overcoming the problem of free riders.
- Activities that generate external costs are likely to be carried out at levels that exceed those that would be efficient; the public sector may seek to intervene to confront decisionmakers with the full costs of their choices.
- Some private activities generate external benefits.
- A common property resource is unlikely to be allocated efficiently in the marketplace.

Try It Yourself 6-3

The manufacture of memory chips for computers generates pollutants that generally enter rivers and streams. Use the model of demand and supply to show the equilibrium price and output of chips. Assuming chip manufacturers don't have to pay the costs these pollutants impose, what can you say about the efficiency of the quantity of chips produced? Show the area of deadweight loss imposed by this external cost. Show how a requirement that firms pay these costs as they produce the chips would affect the equilibrium price and output of chips. Would such a requirement help to satisfy the efficiency condition? Explain.

A Look Back

Economists insist that individuals do not make choices willy-nilly. Rather, economists assume that individuals make those choices in a purposeful way, one that seeks the maximum value for some objective. Economists assume that consumers seek to maximize utility and that firms seek to maximize profits.

Whatever is being maximized, choices are based on the marginal decision rule. Following the marginal decision rule results in an allocation that achieves the greatest degree of individual utility or profit possible.

If utility- and profit-maximizing choices are made in the context of a price system that confronts decisionmakers with all the costs and all the benefits of their choices, the allocation of resources in the economy is efficient. An efficient allocation is one that maximizes the net benefit of an activity. The concepts of consumer and producer surplus show us how this net benefit is shared. Equity is a separate issue, one that calls for a normative evaluation of the fairness of the distribution of income.

The allocation of resources will be inefficient in the absence of competitive markets. It will also be inefficient if property rights are not exclusive and transferable. These two conditions break down when there are public goods, common property resources, or external benefits or costs. In each of those cases, public sector intervention may improve the efficiency of resource allocation. When a market fails to achieve the efficient solution, net benefit falls short of the maximum possible. Deadweight loss is the amount by which net benefit falls below the net benefit possible at the efficient solution.

A Look Ahead We shall apply the marginal decision rule throughout the remainder of our examination of microeconomics. We shall explore markets that satisfy the efficiency condition as well as markets that do not.

Terms and Concepts for Review

utility, **124**
economic profit, **124**
net benefit, **125**
marginal benefit, **125**
marginal cost, **125**
marginal decision rule, **125**
constraint, **125**
deadweight loss, **130**
efficient, **132**
property rights, **132**
exclusive property right, **134**
transferable property right, **134**
efficiency condition, **134**
consumer surplus, **135**
producer surplus, **135**
market failure, **137**
public good, **137**
private good, **137**
free riders, **138**
external cost, **138**
external benefit, **139**
common property resource, **140**

For Discussion

1. What is achieved by selecting the quantity of an activity at which marginal benefit equals marginal cost?
2. Suppose the marginal benefit of an activity exceeds the marginal cost. What does the marginal decision rule say a maximizing decisionmaker will do?
3. Suppose you are a discus hurler and your goal is to maximize the distance you achieve. You "produce" discus hurls by practicing. The total benefit of practice is distance achieved, and the input that achieves this distance is hours of practice. Describe the total benefit curve of practice. What point on the curve would you select?
4. This chapter argues that consumers maximize utility and firms maximize profits. What do you suppose each of the following might be presumed to maximize?
   a. A minister or rabbi
   b. A United States Senator
   c. The manager of a major league baseball team
   d. The owner of a major league baseball team
   e. The director of a charitable organization
5. For each of the following goods, indicate whether exclusive, transferable property rights exist and whether the good poses a problem for public policy. If it does, does the problem relate to a problem of property rights?
   a. Clean air
   b. Tomatoes
   c. Housing
   d. Blue whales

6. The dry-cleaning industry is a major source of air pollution. What can you conclude about the price and output of dry-cleaning services?
7. Economists often recommend that polluters such as dry-cleaning establishments be charged fees for the pollution they emit. Critics of this idea respond that the establishments would simply respond by passing these charges on to their customers. Comment on this objection.
8. Government agencies often require that children be inoculated against communicable diseases such as polio and measles. From the standpoint of economic efficiency, is there any justification for such a requirement?
9. Which of the following goods or services are public?
   a. Libraries
   b. Fire protection
   c. Television programs
   d. Health care
   e. Water for household consumption
10. If a village in Botswana is granted several licenses to kill elephants, how does this give it an incentive to preserve elephants and increase the size of the herd? How does the international ban on ivory sales affect the incentive in Botswana to preserve the elephant?
11. The number of fish caught in the ocean has fallen in recent years despite more intensive fishing efforts and the use of more sophisticated equipment. Fish in the ocean are a common property resource. How might this fact be related to declining fish catches? How do you think this drop in the catch affects the price of seafood?

Problems

1. Joe Higgins is thinking about how much time to spend studying for an exam tomorrow in biology. Using "utility units" he measures the benefits and costs of study; his calculations are shown in the following table.

Hours spent studying	0	1	2	3	4	5	6
Total benefit	0	100	180	240	280	300	300
Total cost	0	50	100	150	200	250	350
Net benefit							

   a. Fill in the fourth row for net benefit in the table.
   b. Using a graph to similar to Panel (a) of Exhibit 6-4, show the marginal benefit curve and verify that the area under the curve at 3 hours of study corresponds to the total benefit of that much study. (*Hint:* Remember that marginal values are plotted at the midpoints of the corresponding intervals on the horizontal axis.)
   c. Use a graph similar to Exhibit 6-4, Panel (b), to show the marginal cost curve and verify that the area under the curve at 3 hours of study corresponds to the total cost of that much study.
   d. Use a graph similar to Panel (a) of Exhibit 6-6 to combine the marginal benefit and marginal cost curves you drew in parts (a) and (b). Based on the marginal decision rule, how many hours should Joe spend studying for his biology exam?
2. Now suppose some friends of Joe's call to say they're having a party tonight. Joe calculates that the party is now his best alternative to study, and he increases his estimate of the cost of each hour of study. One hour of study now costs 70; two hours cost 140; three hours 200, four hours 280; five hours 350; and six hours 470. Draw the new marginal benefit and marginal cost curves as in Problem 1, part (d), and identify the new solution that maximizes the net benefit of study time.
3. The local gasoline market in a particular community has demand and supply curves given by the following data. (All quantities are in millions of gallons per month.)

Price per gallon	$0.50	$0.75	$1.00	$1.25	1.50	1.75	2.00
Quantity demanded	6	5	4	3	2	1	0
Quantity supplied	0	1	2	3	4	5	6

   a. Plot the demand and supply curves, and determine the equilibrium price and quantity.
   b. Show the areas of consumer and producer surplus.
   c. Now suppose that the community determines that each gallon of gasoline consumed imposes $0.50 in pollution costs. Accordingly, a $0.50-per-gallon tax is imposed. The tax is imposed on sellers of gasoline, and it has the effect of increasing by $0.50 the price required to induce the quantities supplied in the table. For example, a price of $1.25 is now required for a quantity of 1 million gallons to be supplied each month. Plot the new supply curve, and determine the new equilibrium price and output. Does the price increase by the full amount of the tax? If not, explain why. Would your answer be different if the demand for gasoline were perfectly inelastic?

4. Given the following information about the supply and demand for apples, draw a graph similar to Exhibit 6-9. Assuming the market for apples meets the efficiency condition, show the equilibrium price and quantity that maximizes net benefit to society. Identify the area of consumer surplus and the area of producer surplus.

Price per pound	Quantity demanded (pounds per month)	Quantity supplied (pounds per month)
$0.50	12,000	0
0.75	10,000	2,000
1.00	8,000	4,000
1.25	6,000	6,000
1.50	4,000	8,000
1.75	2,000	10,000
2.00	0	12,000

Answers to Try It Yourself Problems

Try It Yourself 6-1

Here are the completed data table and the table showing total and marginal benefit and cost.

Hours Studying Economics and Expected Benefits and Costs

Hours studying economics	0	1	2	3	4	5
Total benefit	0	14	24	30	32	32
Total cost	0	2	8	18	32	50
Net benefit	0	12	16	12	0	−18

Hours studying economics	0		1		2		3		4		5
Total benefit	0		14		24		30		32		32
Marginal benefit		14		10		6		2		0	
Total cost	0		2		8		18		32		50
Marginal cost		2		6		10		14		18	

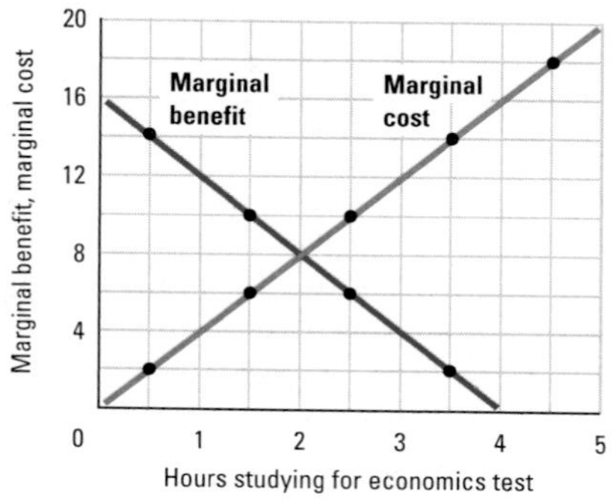

Ms. Phan maximizes her net benefit by reducing her time studying economics to 2 hours. The change in her expectations reduced the benefit and increased the cost of studying economics. The completed graph of marginal benefit and marginal cost is at the far left. Notice that answering the question using the marginal decision rule gives the same answer.

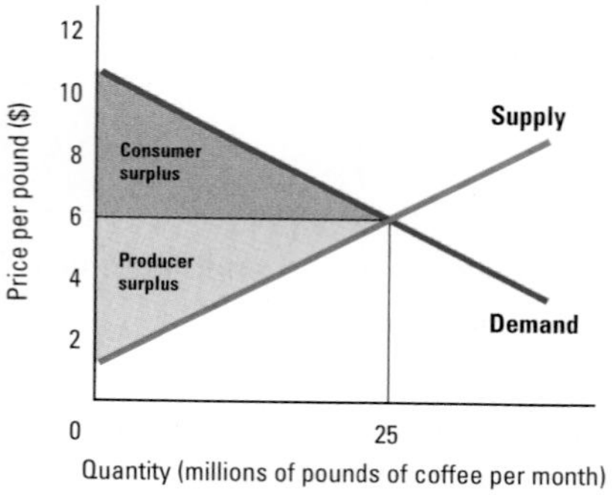

Try It Yourself 6-2

On the assumption that the coffee market is competitive and that it is characterized by well-defined exclusive and transferable property rights, the coffee market meets the efficiency condition. That means that the allocation of resources shown at the equilibrium (left) will be the one that maximizes the net benefit of all activities. The net benefit is shared by coffee consumers (as measured by consumer surplus) and coffee producers (as measured by producer surplus).

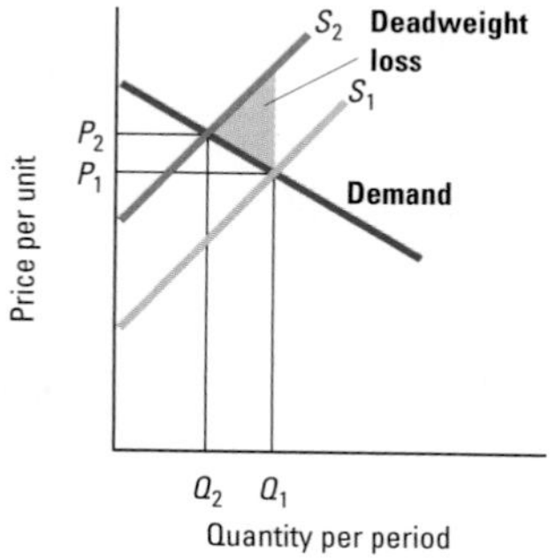

Try It Yourself 6-3

In the absence of any regulation, chip producers aren't faced with the costs of the pollution their operations generate. The market price is thus P_1 and the quantity Q_1. The efficiency condition is not met; the price is lower and the quantity greater than would be efficient. If producers were forced to face the cost of their pollution as well as other production costs, the supply curve would shift to S_2, the price would rise to P_2, and the quantity would fall to Q_2. The new solution satisfies the efficiency condition.

7 The Analysis of Consumer Choice

Getting Started: A Day at the Grocery Store

You're in the checkout line at the grocery store when your eyes wander over to the ice cream display. It's a hot day and you could use something to cool you down before you get into your hot car. The problem is that you've left your checkbook and credit and debit cards at home—*on purpose*, actually, because you have decided that you only want to spend $20 today at the grocery store. You're uncertain whether or not you've brought enough cash with you to pay for the items that are already in your cart. You put the ice cream bar into your cart and tell the clerk to let you know if you go over $20 because that's all you have. He rings it up and it comes to $22. You have to make a choice. You decide to keep the ice cream and ask the clerk if he would mind returning a box of cookies to the shelf.

We all engage in these kinds of choices every day. We have budgets and must decide how to spend them. The model of utility theory that economists have constructed to explain consumer choice assumes that consumers will try to maximize their utility. For example, when you decided to keep the ice cream bar and return the cookies, you, consciously or not, applied the marginal decision rule to the problem of maximizing your utility: You bought the ice cream because you expect that eating it will give you greater satisfaction than would consuming the box of cookies.

Utility theory provides insights into demand. It lets us look behind demand curves to see how utility-maximizing consumers can be expected to respond to price changes. While the focus of this chapter is on consumers making decisions about what goods and services to buy, the same model can be used to understand how individuals make other types of decisions, such as how much to work and how much of their incomes to spend now or to sock away for the future. The model is also applied to the labor supply decision (Chapter 12) and to the consumption-saving decision (Chapter 13).

We can approach the analysis of utility maximization in two ways. The first two sections of the chapter cover the marginal utility concept, while the final section examines an alternative approach using indifference curves.

The Concept of Utility

Why do you buy the goods and services you do? It must be because they provide you with satisfaction—you feel better off because you have purchased them. Economists call this satisfaction *utility*.

The concept of utility is an elusive one. A person who consumes a good such as peaches gains utility from eating the peaches. But we can't measure this utility the same way we can measure a peach's weight or calorie content. There is no scale we can use to determine the quantity of utility a peach generates.

Francis Edgeworth, one of the most important contributors to the theory of consumer behavior, imagined a device he called a *hedonimeter* (after hedonism, the pursuit of pleasure):

> [*L*]et there be granted to the science of pleasure what is granted to the science of energy; to imagine an ideally perfect instrument, a psychophysical machine, continually registering the height of pleasure experienced by an individual. . . . From moment to moment the hedonimeter varies; the delicate index now flickering with the flutter of passions, now steadied by intellectual activity, now sunk whole hours in the neighborhood of zero, or momentarily springing up towards infinity.[1]

[1]Francis Y. Edgeworth, *Mathematical Psychics: An Essay on the Application of Mathematics to the Moral Sciences* (New York: Augustus M. Kelley, 1967), p. 101. First published 1881.

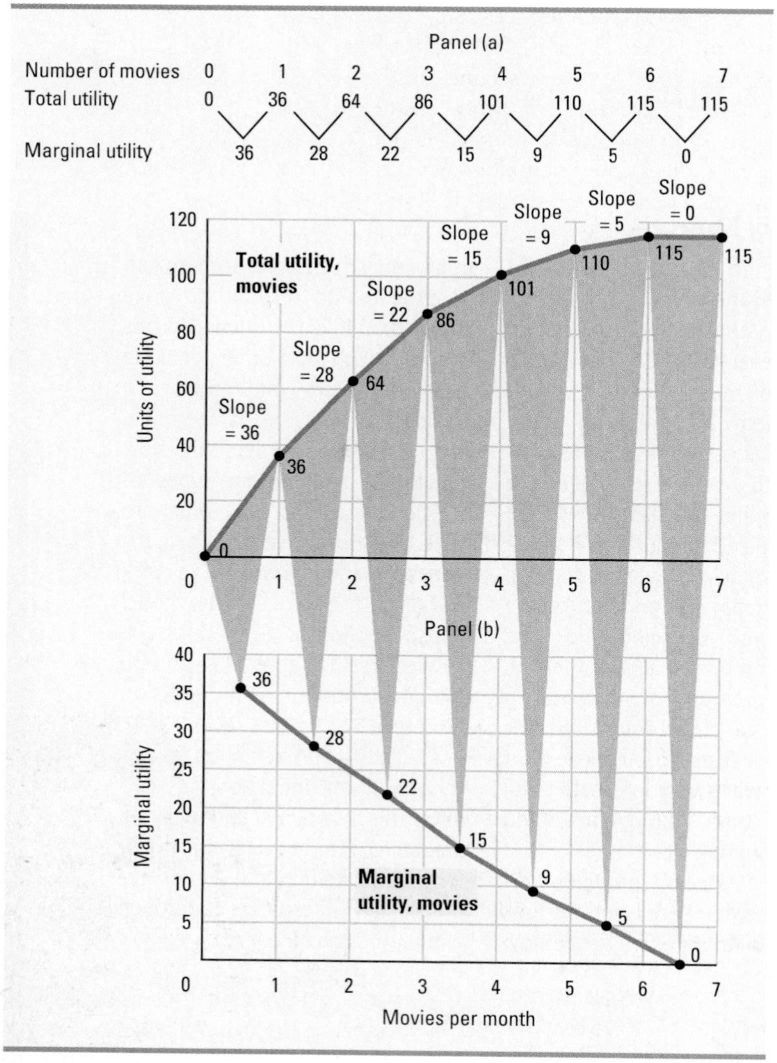

Exhibit 7-1

Total Utility and Marginal Utility Curves

Panel (a) shows Henry Higgins's total utility curve for attending movies. It rises as the number of movies increases, reaching a maximum of 115 units of utility at 6 movies per month. Marginal utility is shown in Panel (b); it is the slope of the total utility curve. Because the slope of the total utility curve declines as the number of movies increases, the marginal utility curve is downward sloping.

Perhaps some day a hedonimeter will be invented. The utility it measures will not be a characteristic of particular goods, but rather of each consumer's reactions to those goods. The utility of a peach exists not in the peach itself, but in the preferences of the individual consuming the peach. One consumer may wax ecstatic about a peach; another may say it tastes OK.

When we speak of maximizing utility, then, we are speaking of the maximization of something we can't measure. We assume, however, that each consumer acts as if he or she can measure utility and arranges consumption so that the utility gained is as high as possible.

Total Utility

If we could measure utility, **total utility** would be the number of units of utility that a consumer gains from consuming a given quantity of a good, service, or activity during a particular time period. The higher a consumer's total utility, the greater that consumer's level of satisfaction.

Panel (a) of Exhibit 7-1 shows the total utility Henry Higgins obtains from attending movies. In drawing his total utility curve, we are imagining that he can measure his total utility. The total utility curve shows that when Mr. Higgins attends no movies during a month, his total utility from attending movies is zero. As he increases the number of movies he sees, his total utility rises. When he consumes 1 movie, he obtains 36 units of utility. When he consumes 4 movies, his total utility is 101. He achieves the maximum level of utility possible, 115, by seeing 6 movies per month. Seeing a seventh movie adds nothing to his total utility.

Mr. Higgins's total utility rises at a decreasing rate. The rate of increase is given by the slope of the total utility curve, which is reported in Panel (a) of Exhibit 7-1 as well. The slope of the curve between 0 movies and 1 movie is 36. It is 28 between 1 and 2 movies, 22 between 2 and 3, and so on. The slope between 6 and 7 movies is zero; the total utility curve between these two quantities is horizontal.

Marginal Utility

The amount by which total utility rises with consumption of an additional unit of a good, service, or activity, all other things unchanged, is **marginal utility**. The first movie Mr. Higgins sees increases his total utility by 36 units. Hence, the marginal utility of the first movie is 36. The second increases his total utility by 28 units; its marginal utility is 28. The seventh movie does not increase his total utility; its marginal utility is zero. Notice that in the table marginal utility is listed between the columns for total utility because, similar to other marginal concepts, marginal utility is the change in utility as we go from one quantity to the next. Mr. Higgins's marginal utility curve is plotted in Panel (b) of Exhibit 7-1. The values for marginal utility are plotted midway between the numbers of movies attended. The marginal utility curve is downward sloping; it shows that Mr. Higgins's marginal utility for movies declines as he consumes more of them.

Mr. Higgins's marginal utility from movies is typical of all goods and services. Suppose that you're *really* thirsty and you decide to consume a soft drink. Consuming the drink increases your utility, probably by a lot. Suppose now you have another. That second drink probably increases your utility by less than the first. A third would increase your utility by still less. This tendency of marginal utility to decline beyond some level of consumption during a period is called the **law of diminishing marginal utility.** This law implies that all goods and services eventually will have downward-sloping marginal utility curves. It is the law that lies behind the negatively sloped marginal benefit curve for consumer choices that we examined in Chapter 6.

One way to think about this effect is to remember the last time you ate at an "all you can eat" cafeteria-style restaurant. Did you eat only one type of food? Did you consume food without limit? No, because of the law of diminishing marginal utility. As you consumed more of one kind of food, its marginal utility fell. You reached a point at which the marginal utility of another dish was greater, and you switched to that. Eventually, there was no food whose marginal utility was great enough to make it worth eating, and you stopped.

What if the law of diminishing marginal utility didn't hold? That is, what would life be like in a world of constant or increasing marginal utility? Let's go back to the cafeteria and imagine that you have rather unusual preferences: Your favorite food is creamed spinach. You start with

Case in Point Channel Zapping

Zenith Corporation introduced the remote control to television in 1956. The device, called Space Command, enjoyed a modest success. It allowed viewers to turn their sets on and off, adjust the volume, and select from among the available offerings of ABC, CBS, and NBC. Some cities boasted a handful of independent stations, but it was rare that a viewer couldn't count the available options on one hand.

The blossoming of cable systems and cable networks in the late 1980s changed the role of the remote. Suddenly there were scores, even hundreds, of channels available to viewers. The wider range of choice has spawned a new phenomenon among television viewers: the channel zapper. The popularity of the remote, which not only allows viewers to zap one channel in favor of another but to make selections on a videocassette recorder, has soared.

As recently as 1985, fewer than 20 percent of U.S. households with television sets owned remote-control devices. By 1995, 85 percent did.

Channel zappers sit down at the television not to watch a particular program but to browse. They switch from one channel to another when their interest fades. It can fade quickly: A 1992 study by the Cable Television Administration and Marketing Society found that particularly active zappers change channels an average of once every 30 seconds. The study classed 23 percent of cable system viewers as "restless viewers" who routinely zap one program in favor of another.

Because they now need not only to attract viewers but also to hold them, broadcasters have changed the way they deliver programming. In 1968, for example, television news programs ran excerpts ("sound bites") of the statements of political leaders that were 42.5 seconds long, on average. By 1992, the average bite was just 7.3 seconds long—newscasters try to cut to something else before the zappers do.

Zapping (also known as channel surfing, grazing, or prowling) has a straightforward economic explanation. Zappers, like everyone else, experience diminishing marginal utility. For them, however, utility doesn't just taper off slowly—it collapses. With more alternatives, the probability of obtaining greater marginal utility somewhere else is high. Is the marginal utility of the news declining? *Zap!* Is MTV growing stale? *Zap!* Is the football game getting dull? *Zap!* The remote control allows viewers to respond to diminishing marginal utility with the squeeze of a thumb. And squeeze they do. *Zap!*

Source: "The Zapper! All About the Remote Control," *TV Guide* 40(33) (15 Aug. 1992): 8–13.

that because its marginal utility is highest of all the choices before you in the cafeteria. As you eat more, however, its marginal utility doesn't fall; it remains higher than the marginal utility of any other option. Unless eating more creamed spinach somehow increases your marginal utility for some other food, you will eat only creamed spinach. And until you've reached the limit of your body's capacity (or the restaurant manager's patience), you won't stop. Failure of marginal utility to diminish would thus lead to extraordinary levels of consumption of a single good to the exclusion of all others. Since we don't observe that happening, it seems reasonable to assume that marginal utility falls beyond some level of consumption.

Maximizing Utility

Economists assume that consumers behave in a manner consistent with the maximization of utility. To see how consumers do that, we'll put the marginal decision rule to work. First, however, we must reckon with the fact that the ability of consumers to purchase goods and services is limited by their budgets.

The Budget Constraint The total utility curve in Exhibit 7-1 shows that Mr. Higgins achieves the maximum total utility possible from movies when he sees six of them each month. It's likely that his total utility curves for other goods and services will have much the same shape, reaching a maximum at some level of consumption. We assume that the goal of each consumer is to maximize total utility. Does that mean a person will consume each good at a level that yields the maximum utility possible?

The answer, in general, is no. Our consumption choices are constrained by the income available to us and by the prices we must pay. Suppose, for example, that Mr. Higgins can spend just $25 per month for entertainment and that the price of going to see a movie is $5. To achieve the maximum total utility from movies, Mr. Higgins would have to exceed his entertainment budget. Since we assume that he cannot do that, Mr. Higgins must arrange his consumption so that his total expenditures do not exceed his **budget constraint:** a restriction that total spending cannot exceed the budget available.

Suppose that in addition to movies, Mr. Higgins enjoys concerts, and the average price of a concert ticket is $10. He must select the number of movies he sees and concerts he attends so that his monthly spending on the two goods doesn't exceed his budget.

Individuals may, of course, choose to save or to borrow. When we allow this possibility, we consider the budget constraint not just for a single period of time but for several periods. For example, economists often examine budget constraints over a consumer's lifetime. A consumer may in some years save for future consumption and in other years borrow on future income for present consumption. Whatever the time period, a consumer's spending will be constrained by his or her budget.

To simplify our analysis, we shall assume that a consumer's spending in any one period is based on the budget available in that period. In this analysis consumers neither save nor borrow. We could extend the analysis to cover several periods and generate the same basic results that we shall establish using a single period. We'll also carry out our analysis by looking at the consumer's choices about buying only two goods. Again, the analysis could be extended to cover more goods and the basic results would still hold.

Applying the Marginal Decision Rule Because consumers can be expected to spend the budget they have, utility maximization is a matter of arranging that spending to achieve the highest total utility possible. If a consumer decides to spend more on one good, he or she must necessarily spend less on another in order to satisfy the budget constraint.

The marginal decision rule states that an activity should be expanded if its marginal benefit exceeds its marginal cost. The marginal benefit of this activity is the utility gained by spending an additional $1 on the good. The marginal cost is the utility lost by spending $1 less on another good.

How much utility is gained by spending another $1 on a good? It is the marginal utility of the good divided by its price. The utility gained by spending an additional dollar on good X, for example, is

$$\frac{MU_X}{P_X}$$

This additional utility is the *marginal benefit* of spending another $1 on the good.

Suppose that the marginal utility of good X is 4 and that its price is $2. Then an extra $1 spent on X buys 2 additional units of utility ($MU_X/P_X = 4/2 = 2$). If the marginal utility of good X is 1 and its price is $2, then an extra $1 spent on X buys 0.5 additional units of utility ($MU_X/P_X = 1/2 = 0.5$).

The loss in utility from spending $1 less on another good or service is calculated the same way: as the marginal utility divided by the price. The *marginal cost* to the consumer of spending $1 less on a good is the loss of the additional utility that could have been gained from spending that $1 on the good.

Suppose a consumer derives more utility by spending an additional $1 on good X rather than on good Y:

$$\frac{MU_X}{P_X} > \frac{MU_Y}{P_Y} \tag{1}$$

The marginal benefit of shifting $1 from good Y to the consumption of good X exceeds the marginal cost. In terms of utility, the gain from spending an additional $1 on good X exceeds the loss in utility from spending $1 less on good Y. The consumer can increase utility by shifting spending from Y to X.

As the consumer buys more of good X and less of good Y, however, the marginal utilities of the two goods will change. The law of diminishing marginal utility tells us that the marginal utility of good X will fall as the consumer consumes more of it; the marginal utility of good Y will rise as the consumer consumes less of it. The result is that the value of the left-hand side of Equation (1) will fall and the value of the right-hand side will rise as the consumer shifts spending from Y to X. When the two sides are equal, total utility will be maximized. In terms of the marginal decision rule, the consumer will have achieved a solution at which the marginal benefit of the activity (spending more on good X) is equal to the marginal cost:

$$\frac{MU_X}{P_X} = \frac{MU_Y}{P_Y} \tag{2}$$

We can extend this result to all goods and services a consumer uses. Utility maximization requires that the ratio of marginal utility to price be equal for all of them, as suggested in Equation (3):

$$\frac{MU_A}{P_A} = \frac{MU_B}{P_B} = \frac{MU_C}{P_C} = \cdots = \frac{MU_n}{P_n} \tag{3}$$

Equation (3) states the **utility-maximizing condition:** Utility is maximized for a given budget when total outlays equal the budget and when the ratios of marginal utilities to prices are equal for all goods and services.

Consider, for example, the shopper introduced in the opening of this chapter. In shifting from cookies to ice cream, the shopper must have felt that the marginal utility of spending an additional dollar on ice cream exceeded the marginal utility of spending an additional dollar on cookies. In terms of Equation (1), if good X is ice cream and good Y is cookies, the shopper will have lowered the value of the left-hand side of the equation and moved toward the utility-maximizing condition, as expressed by Equation (2).

The Problem of Divisibility If we are to apply the marginal decision rule to utility maximization, goods must be divisible; that is, it must be possible to buy them in any amount. Otherwise we can't meaningfully speak of spending $1 more or $1 less on them. Strictly speaking, however, few goods are completely divisible.

Even a small purchase, such as an ice cream bar, fails the strict test of being divisible; grocers generally frown on requests to purchase one-half of a $2 ice cream bar if the consumer wants to spend an additional dollar on ice cream. Can a consumer buy a little more movie admission, to say nothing of a little more car?

In the case of a car, we can think of the quantity as depending on characteristics of the car itself. A car with a compact disc player could be regarded as containing "more car" than one that has only a cassette player. Stretching the concept of quantity in this manner doesn't entirely solve the problem. It's still difficult to imagine that one could purchase "more car" by spending $1 more.

Remember, though, that we are dealing with a model. In the real world, consumers may not be able to satisfy Equation (3) precisely. The model predicts, however, that they will come as close to doing so as possible.

Checklist

- The utility of a good or service is determined by how much satisfaction a particular consumer obtains from it. Utility is not a quality inherent in the good or service itself.
- Total utility is a conceptual measure of the number of units of utility a consumer gains from consuming a good, service, or activity. Marginal utility is the increase in total utility obtained by consuming one more unit of a good, service, or activity.
- As a consumer consumes more and more of a good or service, its marginal utility falls.
- Utility maximization requires seeking the greatest total utility from a given budget.
- Utility is maximized when total outlays equal the budget available and when the ratios of marginal utility to price are equal for all goods and services a consumer consumes; this is the utility-maximizing condition.

Try It Yourself 7-1

A college student, Ramón Juarez, often purchases candy bars or bags of potato chips between classes; he tries to limit his spending on these snacks to $8 per week. A bag of chips costs $0.75 and a candy bar costs $0.50 from the vending machines on campus. He has been purchasing an average of 6 bags of chips and 7 candy bars each week. Mr. Juarez is a careful maximizer of utility, and he estimates that the marginal utility of an additional bag of chips during a week is 6.

a. *How much is he spending on snacks? How does this amount compare to his budget constraint?*

b. *What is the marginal utility of an additional candy bar during the week?*

Utility Maximization and Demand

Choices that maximize utility—that is, choices that follow the marginal decision rule—generally produce downward-sloping demand curves. This section shows how an individual's utility-maximizing choices can lead to a demand curve.

Deriving an Individual's Demand Curve

Suppose, for simplicity, that Mary Andrews consumes only apples and oranges. Apples cost \$2 per pound and oranges cost \$1 per pound, and her budget allows her to spend \$20 per month on the two goods. We assume that Ms. Andrews will adjust her consumption so that the utility-maximizing condition given in Equation (2) holds for the two goods: The ratio of marginal utility to price is the same for apples and oranges. That is,

$$\frac{MU_A}{\$2} = \frac{MU_O}{\$1} \tag{4}$$

Here MU_A and MU_O are the marginal utilities of apples and oranges, respectively. Her spending equals her budget of \$20 per month; suppose she buys 5 pounds of apples and 10 of oranges.

Now suppose that an unusually large harvest of apples lowers their price to \$1 per pound. The lower price of apples increases the marginal utility of each \$1 Ms. Andrews spends on apples, so that at her current level of consumption of apples and oranges

$$\frac{MU_A}{\$1} > \frac{MU_O}{\$1} \tag{5}$$

Ms. Andrews will respond by purchasing more apples. As she does so, the marginal utility she receives from apples will decline. If she regards apples and oranges as substitutes, she will also buy fewer oranges. That will cause the marginal utility of oranges to rise. She will continue to adjust her spending until the marginal utility per \$1 spent is equal for both goods:

$$\frac{MU_A}{\$1} = \frac{MU_O}{\$1} \tag{6}$$

Suppose that at this new solution, she purchases 12 pounds of apples and 8 pounds of oranges. She is still spending all of her budget of \$20 on the two goods.

It is through a consumer's reaction to different prices that we trace the consumer's demand curve for a good. When the price of apples was \$2 per pound, Ms. Andrews maximized her utility by purchasing 5 pounds of apples, as illustrated in Exhibit 7-2. When the price of apples fell, she increased the quantity of apples she purchased to 12 pounds.

Exhibit 7-2

Utility Maximization and an Individual's Demand Curve

Mary Andrews's demand curve for apples, *d*, can be derived by determining the quantities of apples she will buy at each price. Those quantities are determined by the application of the marginal decision rule to utility maximization. At a price of \$2 per pound, Ms. Andrews maximizes utility by purchasing 5 pounds of apples per month. When the price of apples falls to \$1 per pound, the quantity of apples at which she maximizes utility increases to 12 pounds per month.

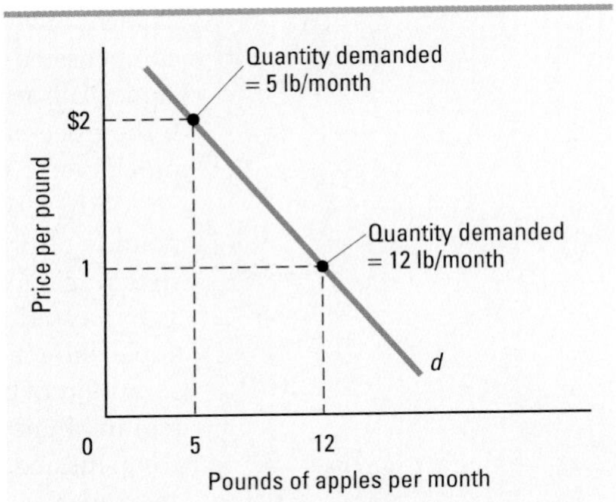

From Individual to Market Demand

The market demand curves we studied in previous chapters are derived from individual demand curves such as the one depicted in Exhibit 7-2. Suppose that in addition to Ms. Andrews, there are two other consumers in our particular market—Ellen Smith and Koy Keino. The quantities each consumes at various prices are given in Exhibit 7-3, along with the quantities that Ms. Andrews consumes at each price. The demand curves for each are shown in Panel (a). The market demand curve for all three consumers, shown in Panel (b), is then found by adding the quantities demanded at each price for all three consumers. At a price of \$2 per pound, for example, Ms. Andrews demands 5 pounds of apples per month, Ms. Smith demands 3 pounds, and Mr. Keino demands 8 pounds. A total of 16 pounds of apples are demanded per month at this price. Adding the individual quantities demanded at \$1 per pound yields market demand of 40 pounds per month.

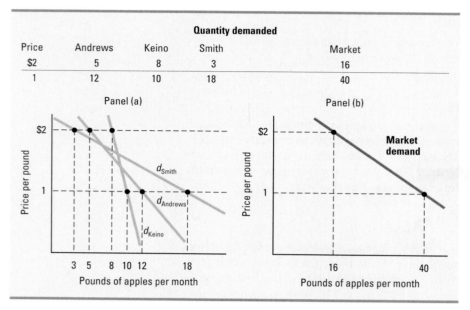

	Quantity demanded			
Price	Andrews	Keino	Smith	Market
$2	5	8	3	16
1	12	10	18	40

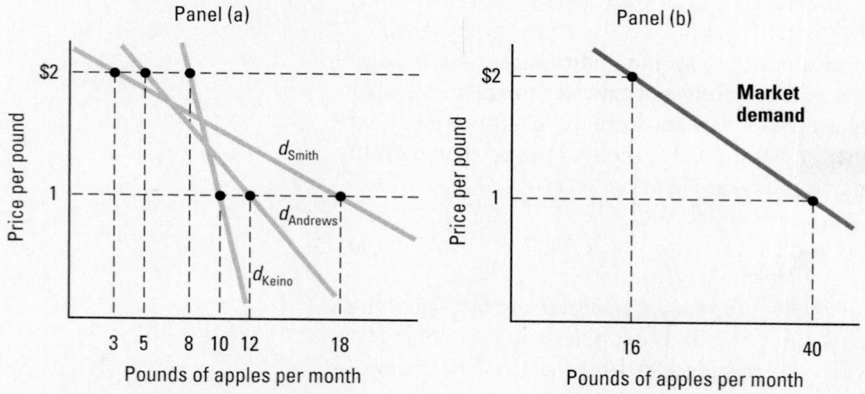

Exhibit 7-3

Deriving a Market Demand Curve

The demand schedules for Mary Andrews, Ellen Smith, and Koy Keino are given in the table. Their individual demand curves are plotted in Panel (a). The market demand curve for all three is shown in Panel (b).

Individual demand curves, then, reflect utility-maximizing adjustment by consumers to various market prices. Once again, we see that as the price falls, consumers tend to buy more of a good. Demand curves are downward-sloping.

Substitution and Income Effects

We saw that when the price of apples fell from $2 to $1 per pound, Mary Andrews increased the quantity of apples she demanded. Behind that adjustment, however, lie two distinct effects. It's important to distinguish these effects, because they can have quite different implications for the elasticity of the demand curve.

First, the reduction in the price of apples made them cheaper relative to oranges. Before the price change, it cost the same amount to buy 2 pounds of oranges or 1 pound of apples. After the price change, it cost the same amount to buy 1 pound of either oranges or apples. In effect, 2 pounds of oranges would exchange for 1 pound of apples before the price change, and 1 pound of oranges would exchange for 1 pound of apples after the price change.

Second, the price reduction essentially made consumers of apples richer. Before the price change, Ms. Andrews was purchasing 5 pounds of apples and 10 pounds of oranges at a total cost to her of $20. At the new lower price of apples, she could purchase this same combination for $15. In effect, the price reduction for apples was equivalent to handing her a $5 bill, thereby increasing her purchasing power. Purchasing power refers to the quantity of goods and services that can be purchased with a given budget.

To distinguish these two effects, economists consider first the impact of a price change with no change in the consumer's ability to purchase goods and services. An **income-compensated price change** is an imaginary exercise in which we assume that when the price of a good or service changes, the consumer's income is adjusted so that he or she has just enough to purchase the original combination of goods and services at the new set of prices. Ms. Andrews was purchasing 5 pounds of apples and 10 pounds of oranges before the price change. Buying that same combination after the price change would cost $15. The income-compensated price change thus requires us to take $5 from Ms. Andrews when the price of apples falls to $1 per pound. She can still buy 5 pounds of apples and 10 pounds of oranges. If the price of apples increased, we would give Ms. Andrews more money so that she could purchase the same combination of goods.

With $15 and cheaper apples, Ms. Andrews *could* buy 5 pounds of apples and 10 pounds of oranges. But would she? The answer lies in comparing the marginal benefit of spending another $1 on apples to the marginal benefit of spending another $1 on oranges, as expressed in Equation (5). It shows that the extra utility per $1 she could obtain from apples now exceeds the extra utility per $1 from oranges. She will thus increase her consumption of apples. If she had only $15, any increase in her consumption of apples would require a reduction in her consumption of oranges. In effect, she responds to the income-compensated price change for apples by substituting apples for oranges. The change in a consumer's consumption of a good in response to an income-compensated price change is called the **substitution effect**.

Suppose that with an income-compensated reduction in the price of apples to $1 per pound, Ms. Andrews would increase her consumption of apples to 9 pounds per month and reduce her consumption of oranges to 6 pounds per month. The substitution effect of the price reduction is an increase in apple consumption of 4 pounds per month.

The substitution effect always involves a change in consumption in a direction opposite that of the price change. When a consumer is maximizing utility, the ratio of marginal utility to price is the same for all goods as shown in Equation (3). An income-compensated price reduction increases the extra utility per dollar available from the good whose price has fallen; a consumer will thus purchase more of it. An income-compensated price increase reduces the extra utility per dollar from the good; the consumer will purchase less of it.

In other words, when the price of a good falls, people react to the lower price by substituting or switching toward that good, buying more of it and less of other goods *if* we artificially hold the consumer's ability to buy goods constant. When the price of a good goes up, people react to the higher price by substituting or switching away from that good, buying less of it and instead buying more of other goods. By examining the impact of consumer purchases of an income-compensated price change, we are looking at *just* the change in relative prices of goods and eliminating any impact on consumer buying that comes from the effective change in the consumer's ability to purchase goods and services (that is, we hold the consumer's purchasing power constant).

To complete our analysis of the impact of the price change, we must now consider the $5 that Ms. Andrews effectively gained from it. After the price reduction, it cost her just $15 to buy what cost her $20 before. She has, in effect, $5 more than she did before. Her additional income may also have an effect on the number of apples she consumes. The change in consumption of a good resulting from the implicit change in income because of a price change is called the **income effect** of a price change. When the price of a good rises, there is an implicit reduction in income. When the price of a good falls, there is an implicit increase. When the price of apples fell, Ms. Andrews (who was consuming 5 pounds of apples per month) received an implicit increase in income of $5.

Suppose Ms. Andrews uses her implicit increase in income to purchase 3 more pounds of apples and 2 more pounds of oranges per month. She has already increased her apple consumption to 9 pounds per month because of the substitution effect, so the added 3 pounds brings her consumption level to 12 pounds per month. That's precisely what we observed when we derived her demand curve; it's the change we would observe in the marketplace. We see now, however, that her increase in quantity demanded consists of a substitution effect and an income effect. Exhibit 7-4 shows the combined effects of the price change.

The size of the substitution effect depends on the rate at which the marginal utilities of goods change as the consumer adjusts consumption to a price change. As Ms. Andrews buys more apples and fewer oranges, the marginal utility of apples will fall and the marginal utility of oranges will rise. If relatively small changes in quantities consumed produce large changes in marginal utilities, the substitution effect that is required to restore the equality of marginal-utility-to-price ratios will be small. If much larger changes in quantities consumed are needed to produce equivalent changes in marginal utilities, then the substitution effect will be large.

The magnitude of the income effect of a price change depends on how responsive the demand for a good is to a change in income and on how important the good is in a consumer's budget. When the price changes for a good that makes up a substantial fraction of a consumer's budget, the change in the consumer's ability to buy things is substantial. A change in the price of a good that makes up a trivial fraction of a consumer's budget, however, has little effect on his or her purchasing power; the income effect of such a price change is small.

Exhibit 7-4

The Substitution and Income Effects of a Price Change

This demand curve for Ms. Andrews was presented in Exhibit 7-3. It shows that a reduction in the price of apples from $2 to $1 per pound increases the quantity Ms. Andrews demands from 5 pounds of apples to 12. This graph shows that this change consists of a substitution effect and an income effect. The substitution effect increases the quantity demanded by 4 pounds, the income effect by 3, for a total increase in quantity demanded of 7 pounds.

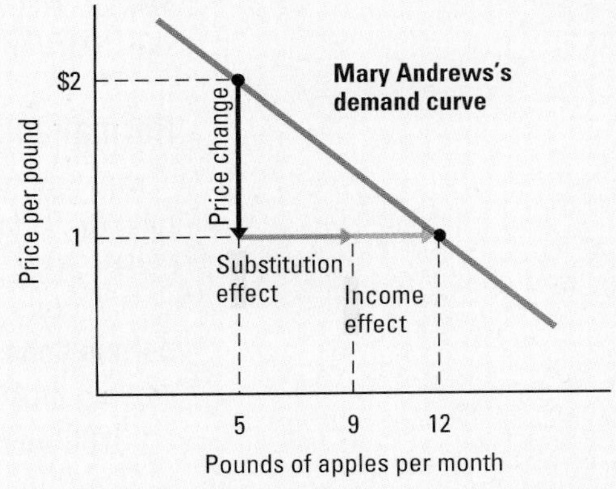

Case in Point Found! An Upward-Sloping Demand Curve (For Rats Only)

The fact that income and substitution effects move in opposite directions in the case of inferior goods raises a tantalizing possibility: What if the income effect were the *stronger* of the two? Could demand curves be upward sloping?

The answer, from a theoretical point of view, is yes. If the income effect in Exhibit 7-5 were larger than the substitution effect, it would reduce the quantity demanded below q_1. The result would be a reduction in quantity demanded in response to a reduction in price. The demand curve would be upward sloping!

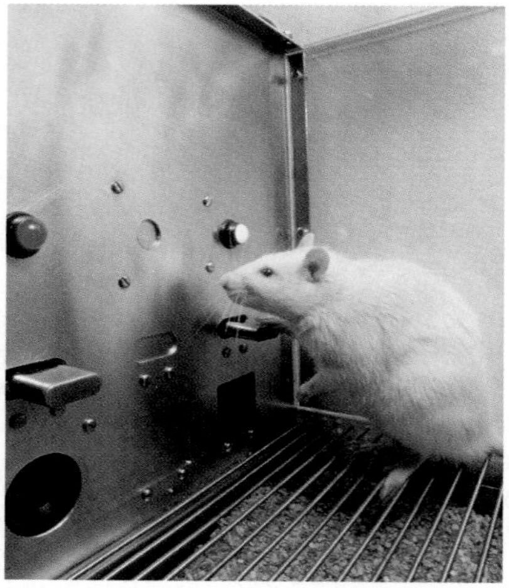

The suggestion that a good could have an upward-sloping demand curve is generally attributed to Robert Giffen, a British journalist who wrote widely on economic matters late in the nineteenth century. Such goods are thus called Giffen goods. To qualify as a Giffen good, a good must be inferior and must have an income effect strong enough to overcome the substitution effect.

Although Giffen goods are a theoretical possibility, no one has ever found one—at least for humans. Some thirsty little Texas rats, however, have blazed their way into the annals of economic history. They have an upward-sloping demand curve for quinine water.

Researchers at Texas A&M University and at the University of Houston have led the way in conducting economic experiments using laboratory animals. In one set of experiments, they have used rats to test the propositions of the theory of consumer behavior.

In one experiment, rats were given all the water they wanted, plus soft drinks (root beer and collins mix). The water was free, but they had to "pay" for root beer and collins mix by pushing two levers. Pushing the root beer lever earned a rat a squirt of root beer; pushing the collins mix lever earned a squirt of collins mix. The "prices" of root beer and collins mix were set by adjusting the quantity of each drink the rats received for a single push. A reduction in the quantity per push was equivalent to a price increase. The rats were put on a budget; they got only so many lever pushes per day. The number of pushes was, in effect, the rat's income.

Once rats were confronted with an income and prices, they quickly settled into their own equilibrium solutions for the two soft drinks. When prices or the rats' incomes were changed, the animals adjusted their consumption in ways that were consistent with eco-

Because each consumer's response to a price change depends on the sizes of the substitution and income effects, these effects play a role in determining the price elasticity of demand. All other things unchanged, the larger the substitution effect, the greater the absolute value of the price elasticity of demand. When the income effect moves in the same direction as the substitution effect, a greater income effect contributes to a greater price elasticity of demand as well. There are, however, cases in which the substitution and income effects move in opposite directions. We shall explore these ideas in the next section.

Normal and Inferior Goods

The nature of the income effect of a price change depends on whether the good is normal or inferior. The income effect reinforces the substitution effect in the case of normal goods; it works in the opposite direction for inferior goods.

Normal Goods We saw in Chapter 3 that a normal good is one whose consumption increases with an increase in income. When the price of a normal good falls, there are two effects:

1. The substitution effect contributes to an increase in the quantity demanded because consumers substitute more of the good for other goods.

nomic theory. For example, the researchers were able to confront the rats with income-compensated price changes and confirm that the substitution effect always changed consumption in a direction opposite to that of a price change.

In another experiment, the researchers tried to create a Giffen good. They reasoned that the good would have to be inferior and would have to loom large in the rats' budgets. That meant the rats had to be poor and the good cheap. It also had to be something the rats weren't crazy about. The researchers tried quinine water. Rats hate quinine water.

A group of rats were given slightly less than the minimum quantity of water that rats require. They could supplement their fluid intake with root beer or quinine water, each of which required pushes on a lever. After several adjustments of prices and budgets, the researchers found a combination of a low income, a relatively high price for root beer, and a very low price for quinine water at which the rats were willing to spend much of their incomes on quinine water.

The researchers then reduced the price of quinine water. That effectively made the rats richer—and they responded by consuming less quinine water. A Giffen good had been found! The accompanying graph shows how one rat responded to the price change. The points show actual values of rat 532's consumption at relative quinine water prices of 0.33 and 0.25. When the relative price of quinine water was reduced from 0.33 to 0.25, rat 532 consumed less quinine water. The demand curve for rat 532 is drawn so that it roughly corresponds to the four observations.

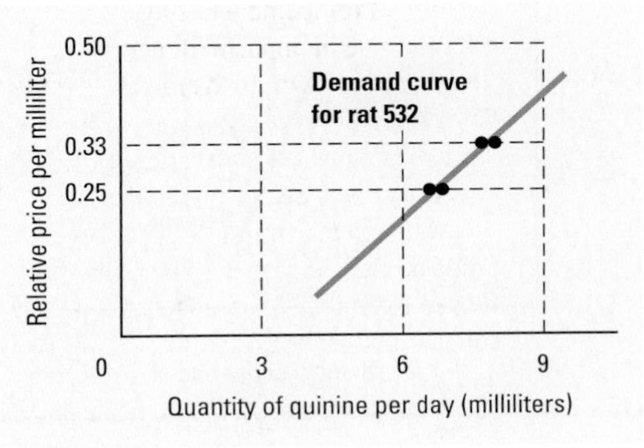

The fact that utility-maximizing behavior of humans is theoretically consistent with the existence of a Giffen good reminds us that the law of demand is an empirical proposition. We can have confidence in the law of demand because virtually all real-world experience is consistent with it. One sometimes hears people say that the law of demand is fine in theory but is not valid in the real world. The facts show quite the opposite: The law of demand can be easily violated in theory, but it is confirmed by our real-world experience.

Source: Raymond Battalio, John H. Kagel, and Carl A. Kogut, "Experimental Confirmation of the Existence of a Giffen Good," *American Economic Review* 81(4) (Sept. 1991): 961–970.

2. The reduction in price increases the consumer's ability to buy goods. Because the good is normal, this increase in purchasing power further increases the quantity of the good demanded through the income effect.

In the case of a normal good, then, the substitution and income effects reinforce each other. Ms. Andrews's response to a price reduction for apples is a typical response to a lower price for a normal good.

An increase in the price of a normal good works in an equivalent fashion. The higher price causes consumers to substitute more of other goods, whose prices are now relatively lower. The substitution effect thus reduces the quantity demanded. The higher price also reduces purchasing power, causing consumers to reduce consumption of the good via the income effect.

Inferior Goods Also in Chapter 3 we saw that an inferior good is one for which demand falls when income rises. It is likely to be a cheap good that people don't really like very much. When incomes are low, people consume the inferior good because it's what they can afford. As their incomes rise and they can afford something they like better, they consume less of the inferior good.

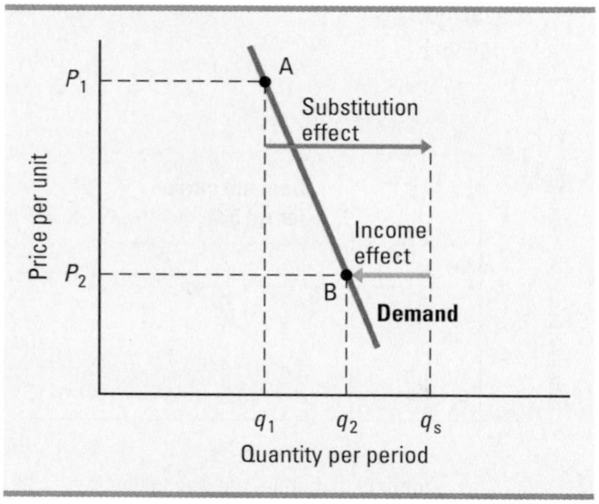

Exhibit 7-5

Substitution and Income Effects for Inferior Goods

The substitution and income effects work against each other in the case of inferior goods. The consumer begins at point A, consuming q_1 units of the good at a price P_1. When the price falls to P_2, the consumer moves to point B, increasing quantity demanded to q_2. The substitution effect increases quantity demanded to q_s, but the income effect reduces it from q_s to q_2.

When the price of an inferior good falls, two things happen:

1. Consumers will substitute more of the inferior good for other goods because its price has fallen relative to those goods. The quantity demanded increases as a result of the substitution effect.
2. The lower price effectively makes consumers richer. But, because the good is inferior, this reduces quantity demanded.

The case of inferior goods is thus quite different from that of normal goods. The income effect works in a direction *opposite* to that of the substitution effect in the case of an inferior good, whereas it reinforces the substitution effect in the case of a normal good.

Exhibit 7-5 illustrates the substitution and income effects of a price reduction for an inferior good. When the price falls from P_1 to P_2, the quantity demanded by a consumer increases from q_1 to q_2. The substitution effect increases quantity demanded from q_1 to q_s. But the income effect reduces quantity demanded from q_s to q_2; the substitution effect is stronger than the income effect. The result is consistent with the law of demand: A reduction in price increases the quantity demanded. The quantity demanded is smaller, however, than it would be if the good were normal. Inferior goods are therefore likely to have less elastic demand than normal goods.

Checklist

- Individual demand curves reflect utility-maximizing adjustment by consumers to changes in price.
- Market demand curves are found by summing the demand curves of all the consumers in the market.
- The substitution effect of a price change changes consumption in a direction opposite to the price change.
- The income effect of a price change reinforces the substitution effect if the good is normal; it moves consumption in the opposite direction if the good is inferior.

Try It Yourself 7-2

Ilana Drakulic has an entertainment budget of $200 per semester, which she divides among purchasing CDs, going to concerts, eating in restaurants, and so forth. When the price of CDs fell from $20 to $10, her purchases rose from 5 per semester to 10 per semester. When asked how many she would have bought if her budget constraint were $150 (since with $150 she could continue to buy 5 CDs and as before still have $100 for spending on other items), she said she would have bought 8 CDs. What is the size of her substitution effect? Her income effect? Are CDs normal or inferior for her? Which Exhibit, 7-4 or 7-5, depicts more accurately her demand curve for CDs?

Indifference Curve Analysis: An Alternative Approach to Understanding Consumer Choice

Economists typically use a different set of tools than those presented in the chapter up to this point to analyze consumer choices. While somewhat more complex, the tools presented in this section give us a powerful framework for assessing consumer choices.

We'll begin our analysis with an algebraic and graphical presentation of the budget constraint. We'll then examine a new concept that allows us to draw a map of a consumer's preferences. Then we can draw some conclusions about the choices a utility-maximizing consumer could be expected to make.

The Budget Line

As we've already seen, a consumer's choices are limited by the budget available. Total spending for goods and services can fall short of the budget constraint but may not exceed it.

Algebraically, we can write the budget constraint for two goods X and Y as

$$P_X Q_X + P_Y Q_Y \leq B \qquad (7)$$

where P_X and P_Y are the prices of goods X and Y and Q_X and Q_Y are the quantities of goods X and Y chosen. The total income available to spend on the two goods is B, the consumer's budget. Equation (7) states that total expenditures on goods X and Y (the left-hand side of the equation) cannot exceed B.

Suppose a college student, Janet Bain, enjoys skiing and horseback riding. A day spent pursuing either activity costs $50. Suppose she has $250 available to spend on these two activities each semester. Ms. Bain's budget constraint is illustrated in Exhibit 7-6.

For a consumer who buys only two goods, the budget constraint can be shown with a budget line. A **budget line** shows graphically the combinations of two goods a consumer can buy with a given budget.

The budget line shows all the combinations of skiing and horseback riding Ms. Bain can purchase with her budget of $250. She could also spend less than $250, purchasing combinations that lie below and to the left of the budget line in Exhibit 7-6. Combinations above and to the right of the budget line are beyond the reach of her budget.

The vertical intercept of the budget line (point D) is given by the number of days of skiing per month that Ms. Bain could enjoy if she devoted all of her budget to skiing and none to horseback riding. She has $250, and the price of a day of skiing is $50. If she spent the entire amount on skiing, she could ski 5 days per semester. She would be meeting her budget constraint, since

$$\$50 \times 0 + \$50 \times 5 = \$250$$

The horizontal intercept of the budget line (point E) is the number of days she could spend horseback riding if she devoted her $250 entirely to that sport. She could purchase 5 days of either skiing or horseback riding per semester. Again, this is within her budget constraint, since

$$\$50 \times 5 + \$50 \times 0 = \$250$$

Because the budget line is linear, we can compute its slope between any two points. Between points D and E the vertical change is −5 days of skiing; the horizontal change is 5 days of horseback riding. The slope is thus −5/5 = −1. More generally, we find the slope of the budget line by finding the vertical and horizontal intercepts and then computing the slope between those two points. The vertical intercept of the budget line is found by dividing Ms. Bain's budget, B, by the price of skiing, the good on the vertical axis (P_S). The horizontal intercept is found by dividing B by the price of horseback riding, the good on the horizontal axis, (P_H). The slope is thus

$$\text{Slope} = -\frac{B/P_S}{B/P_H} \qquad (8)$$

Exhibit 7-6

The Budget Line

The budget line shows combinations of skiing and horseback riding Janet Bain could consume if the price of each activity is $50 and she has $250 available for them each semester. The slope of this budget line is −1, the negative of the price of horseback riding divided by the price of skiing.

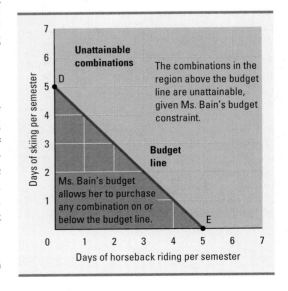

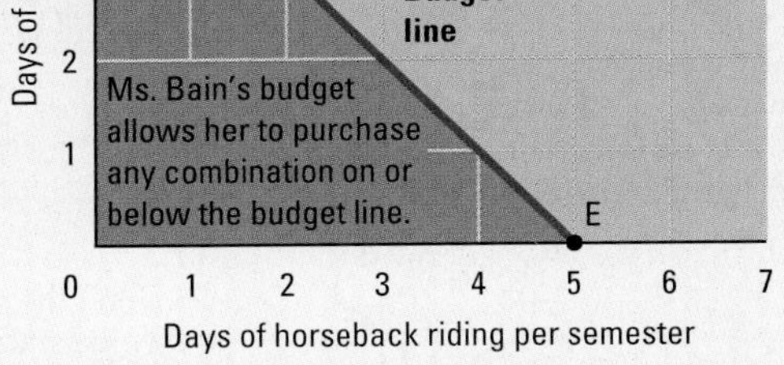

Simplifying this equation, we obtain

$$\text{Slope} = \frac{B}{P_S} \times \frac{P_H}{B} = -\frac{P_H}{P_S} \qquad (9)$$

After canceling, Equation (9) shows that the slope of a budget line is the negative of the price of the good on the horizontal axis divided by the price of the good on the vertical axis.

Caution!

It's easy to go awry on the issue of the slope of the budget line: It's the negative of the price of the good on the *horizontal* axis divided by the price of the good on the *vertical* axis. But doesn't slope equal the change in the *vertical* axis divided by the change in the *horizontal* axis? The answer, of course, is that the definition of slope hasn't changed. Notice that Equation 8 gives the vertical change divided by the horizontal change between two points. We then manipulated Equation 8 a bit to get to Equation 9 and found that slope also equaled the negative of the price of the good on the horizontal axis divided by the price of the good on the vertical axis. Price isn't the variable that's shown on the two axes. The axes show the quantities of the two goods.

Indifference Curves

Suppose Ms. Bain spends 2 days skiing and 3 days horseback riding per semester. She will derive some level of total utility from that combination of the two activities. There are other combinations of the two activities that would yield the same level of total utility. Combinations of two goods that yield equal levels of utility are shown on an **indifference curve.**[2] Because all points along an indifference curve generate the same level of utility, economists say that a consumer is *indifferent* between them.

Exhibit 7-7 shows an indifference curve for combinations of skiing and horseback riding that yield the same level of total utility. Point X marks Ms. Bain's initial combination of 2 days skiing and 3 days horseback riding per semester. The indifference curve shows that she could obtain the same level of utility by moving to point W, skiing for 7 days and going horseback riding for 1 day. She could also get the same level of utility at point Y, skiing just 1 day and spending 5 days horseback riding. Ms. Bain is indifferent among combinations W, X, and Y. We assume that the two goods are divisible, so she is indifferent between *any* two points along an indifference curve.

Now look at point T in Exhibit 7-7. It has the same amount of skiing as point X, but fewer days are spent horseback riding. Ms. Bain would thus prefer point X to point T. Similarly, she prefers X to U. What about a choice between the combinations at point W and point T? Because combinations X and W are equally satisfactory, and because Ms. Bain prefers X to T, she must prefer W to T. In general, any combination of two goods that lies below and to the left of an indifference curve for those goods yields less utility than any combination on the indifference curve. Such combinations are *inferior* to combinations on the indifference curve.

Exhibit 7-7

An Indifference Curve

The indifference curve *A* shown here gives combinations of skiing and horseback riding that produce the same level of utility. Janet Bain is thus indifferent to which point on the curve she selects. Any point below and to the left of the indifference curve would produce a lower level of utility; any point above and to the right of the indifference curve would produce a higher level of utility.

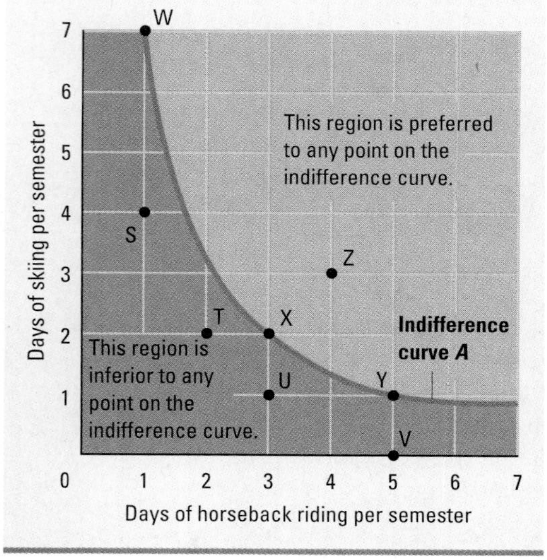

Point Z, with 3 days of skiing and 4 days of horseback riding, provides more of both activities than point X; Z therefore yields a higher level of utility. It's also superior to point W. In general, any combination that lies above and to the right of an indifference curve is preferred to any point on the indifference curve.

We can draw an indifference curve through any combination of two goods. Exhibit 7-8 shows indifference curves drawn through each of the points we have discussed. Indifference curve *A* from Exhibit 7-7 is inferior to indifference curve *B*. Ms. Bain prefers all the combinations on indifference curve *B* to those on curve

[2]Limiting the situation to two goods allows us to show the problem graphically. By stating the problem of utility maximization with equations, we could extend the analysis to any number of goods and services.

A, and she regards each of the combinations on indifference curve *C* as inferior to those on curves *A* and *B*.

Although only three indifference curves are shown in Exhibit 7-8, in principle an infinite number could be drawn. The collection of indifference curves for a consumer constitutes a kind of map illustrating a consumer's preferences. Different consumers will have different maps. We have good reason to expect the indifference curves for all consumers to have the same basic shape as those shown here: They slope downward, and they become less steep as we travel down and to the right along them.

The slope of an indifference curve shows the rate at which two goods can be exchanged without affecting the consumer's utility. Exhibit 7-9 shows indifference curve *C* from Exhibit 7-8. Suppose Ms. Bain is at point S, consuming 4 days of skiing and 1 day of horseback riding per semester. Suppose she spends another day horseback riding. This additional day of horseback riding does not affect her utility if she gives up 2 days of skiing, moving to point T. She is thus willing to give up 2 days of skiing for a second day of horseback riding. The curve shows, however, that she would be willing to give up at most 1 day of skiing to obtain a third day of horseback riding (shown by point U).

The maximum amount of one good a consumer would be willing to give up in order to obtain an additional unit of another is called the **marginal rate of substitution (*MRS*)**, which is equal to the absolute value of the slope of the indifference curve between two points. Exhibit 7-9 shows that as Ms. Bain devotes more and more time to horseback riding, the rate at which she is willing to give up days of skiing for additional days of horseback riding—her marginal rate of substitution—diminishes.

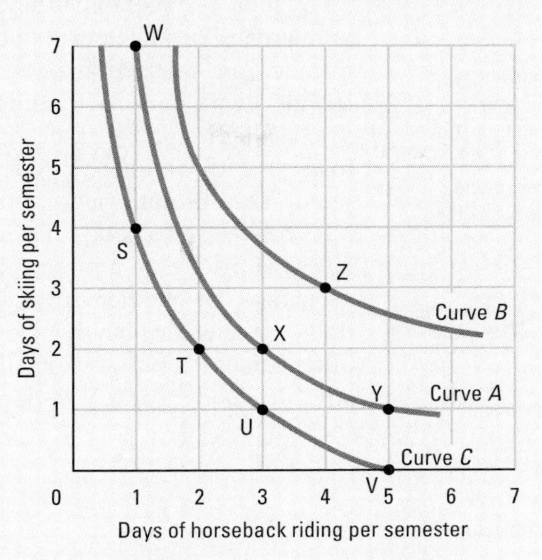

Exhibit 7-8

Indifference Curves

Each indifference curve suggests combinations among which the consumer is indifferent. Curves that are higher and to the right are preferred to those that are lower and to the left. Here, indifference curve *B* is preferred to curve *A*, which is preferred to curve *C*.

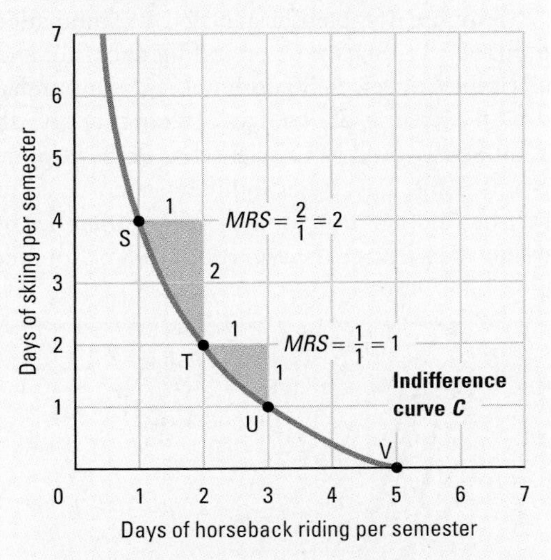

Exhibit 7-9

The Marginal Rate of Substitution

The marginal rate of substitution is equal to the absolute value of the slope of an indifference curve. It is the maximum amount of one good a consumer is willing to give up to obtain an additional unit of another. Here, it is the number of days of skiing Janet Bain would be willing to give up to obtain an additional day of horseback riding. Notice that the marginal rate of substitution (*MRS*) declines as she consumes more and more days of horseback riding.

The Utility-Maximizing Solution

We assume that each consumer seeks the highest indifference curve possible. The budget line gives the combinations of two goods that the consumer can purchase with a given budget. Utility maximization is therefore a matter of selecting a combination of two goods that satisfies two conditions:

1. The point at which utility is maximized must be within the attainable region defined by the budget line.
2. The point at which utility is maximized must be on the highest indifference curve consistent with condition 1.

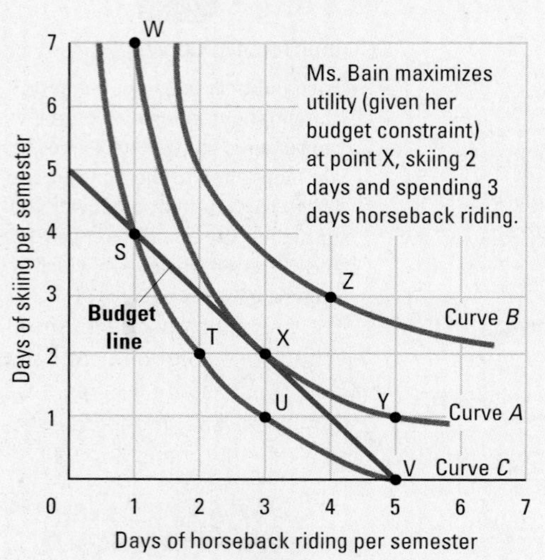

Exhibit 7-10

The Utility-Maximizing Solution

Combining Janet Bain's budget line and indifference curves from Exhibits 7-6 and 7-8, we find a point that (1) satisfies the budget constraint and (2) is on the highest indifference curve possible. That occurs for Ms. Bain at point X.

Exhibit 7-10 combines Janet Bain's budget line from Exhibit 7-6 with her indifference curves from Exhibit 7-8. Our two conditions for utility maximization are satisfied at point X, where she skis 2 days per semester and spends 3 days horseback riding.

The highest indifference curve possible for a given budget line is tangent to the line; the indifference curve and budget line have the same slope at that point. The absolute value of the slope of the indifference curve shows the *MRS* between two goods. The absolute value of the slope of the budget line gives the price ratio between the two goods; it is the rate at which one good exchanges for another in the market. At the point of utility maximization, then, the rate at which the consumer is willing to exchange one good for another equals the rate at which the goods can be exchanged in the market. For any two goods X and Y, with good X on the horizontal axis and good Y on the vertical axis,

$$MRS_{X,Y} = \frac{P_X}{P_Y} \qquad (10)$$

Utility Maximization and the Marginal Decision Rule

How does the achievement of the utility maximizing solution in Exhibit 7-10 correspond to the marginal decision rule? That rule says that additional units of an activity should be pursued if the marginal benefit of the activity exceeds the marginal cost. The observation of that rule would lead a consumer to the highest indifference curve possible for a given budget.

Suppose Ms. Bain has chosen a combination of skiing and horseback riding at point S in Exhibit 7-11. She's now on indifference curve *C*. She's also on her budget line; she's spending all of the budget, $250, available for the purchase of the two goods.

An exchange of two days of skiing for one day of horseback riding would leave her at point T, and she would be as well off as she is at point S. Her marginal rate of substitution between points S and T is 2; her indifference curve is steeper than the budget line at point S. The fact that her indifference curve is steeper than her budget line tells us that the rate at which she is *willing* to exchange the two goods differs from the rate the market asks. She would be willing to give up as many as 2 days of skiing to gain an extra day of horseback riding; the market demands that she give up only one. The marginal decision rule says that if an additional unit of an activity yields greater benefit than its cost, it should be pursued. If the benefit to Ms. Bain of one more day of horseback riding equals the benefit of 2 days of skiing, yet she can get it by giving up only 1 day of skiing, then the benefit of that extra day of horseback riding is clearly greater than the cost.

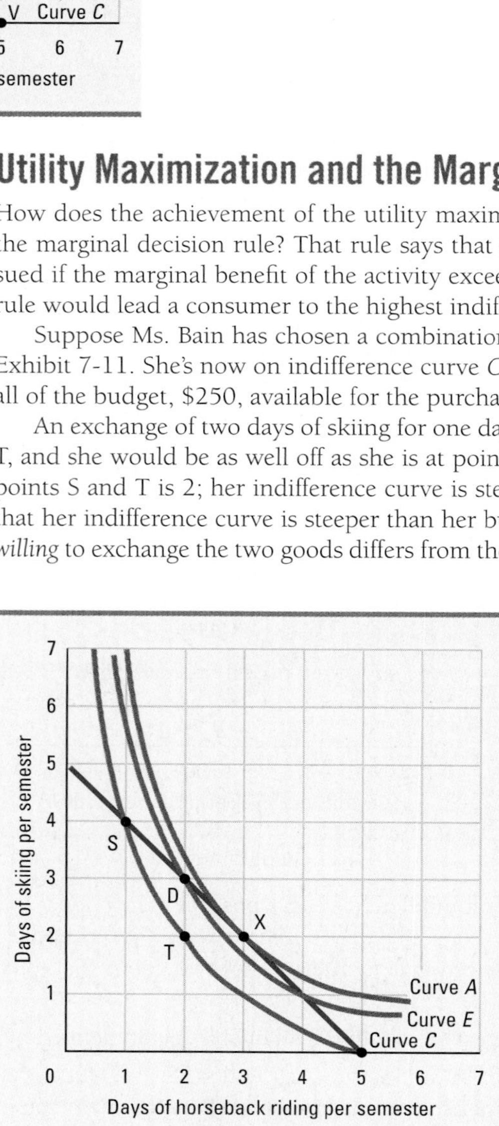

Exhibit 7-11

Applying the Marginal Decision Rule

Suppose Ms. Bain is initially at point S. She is spending all of her budget, but she isn't maximizing utility. Because her marginal rate of substitution exceeds the rate at which the market asks her to give up skiing for horseback riding, she can increase her satisfaction by moving to point D. Now she's on a higher indifference curve, *E.* She'll continue exchanging skiing for horseback riding until she reaches point X, at which she's on curve *A*, the highest indifference curve possible.

Because the market asks that she give up less than she is willing to give up for an additional day of horseback riding, she'll make the exchange. Beginning at point S, she'll exchange a day of skiing for a day of horseback riding. That moves her along her budget line to point D. Recall

Case in Point Preferences Prevail in P.O.W. Camps

Economist R. A. Radford spent time in prisoner of war (P.O.W.) camps in Italy and Germany during World War II. He put this unpleasant experience to good use by testing a number of economic theories there. Relevant to this chapter, he consistently observed utility-maximizing behavior.

In the P.O.W. camps where he stayed, prisoners received rations, provided by their captors and the Red Cross, including tinned milk, tinned beef, jam, butter, biscuits, chocolate, tea, coffee, cigarettes, and other items. While all prisoners received approximately equal official rations (though some did manage to receive private care packages as well), their marginal rates of substitution between goods in the ration packages varied. To increase utility, prisoners began to engage in trade.

Prices of goods tended to be quoted in terms of cigarettes. Some camps had better organized markets than others but, in general, even though prisoners of each nationality were housed separately, so long as they could wander from bungalow to bungalow, the "cigarette" prices of goods were equal across bungalows. Trade allowed the prisoners to maximize their utility.

Consider coffee and tea. Panel (a) shows the indifference curves and budget line for typical British prisoners and Panel (b) shows the indifference curves and budget line for typical French prisoners. Suppose the price of an ounce of tea is 2 cigarettes and the price of an ounce of coffee is 1 cigarette. The slopes of the budget lines in each panel are identical; all prisoners faced the same prices. The price ratio is 1/2.

Suppose the ration packages given to all prisoners contained the same amounts of both coffee and tea. But notice that for typical British prisoners, given indifference curves which reflect their general preference for tea, the *MRS* at the initial allocation (point A) is less than the price ratio. For French prisoners, the *MRS* is greater than the price ratio (point B). By trading, both British and French prisoners can move to higher indifference curves. For the British prisoners, the utility-maximizing solution is at point E, with more tea and little coffee. For the French prisoners the utility-maximizing solution is at point E′, with more coffee and less tea. In equilibrium, both British and French prisoners consumed tea and coffee so that their *MRS*'s equal 1/2, the price ratio in the market.

Source: R. A. Radford, "The Economic Organisation of a P.O.W. Camp," *Economica* 12 (November 1945): 189–201; and Jack Hirshleifer, *Price Theory and Applications* (Englewood Cliffs, NJ: Prentice Hall, 1976): 85–86.

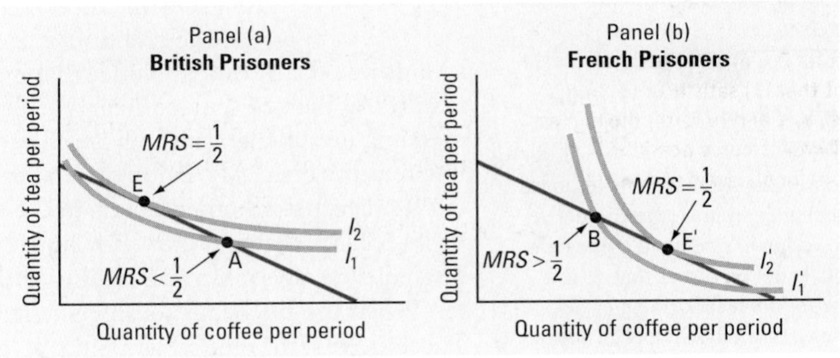

that we can draw an indifference curve through any point; she's now on indifference curve *E*. It's above and to the right of indifference curve *C*, so Ms. Bain is clearly better off. And that should come as no surprise. When she was at point S, she was willing to give up 2 days of skiing to get an extra day of horseback riding. The market asked her to give up only one; she got her extra day of riding at a bargain! Her move along her budget line from point S to point D suggests a very important principle. If a consumer's indifference curve intersects the budget line, then it will always be possible for the consumer to make exchanges along the budget line that move to a higher indifference curve. Ms. Bain's new indifference curve at point D also intersects her budget line; she's still willing to give up more skiing than the market asks for additional riding. She'll make another exchange and move along her budget line to point X, at which she attains the highest indifference curve possible with her budget. Point X is on indifference curve *A*, which is tangent to the budget line.

Having reached point X, Ms. Bain clearly wouldn't give up still more days of skiing for additional days of riding. Beyond point X, her indifference curve is flatter than the budget line—her marginal rate of substitution is less than the absolute value of the slope of the budget line. That means that the rate at which she'd be willing to exchange skiing for horseback riding is

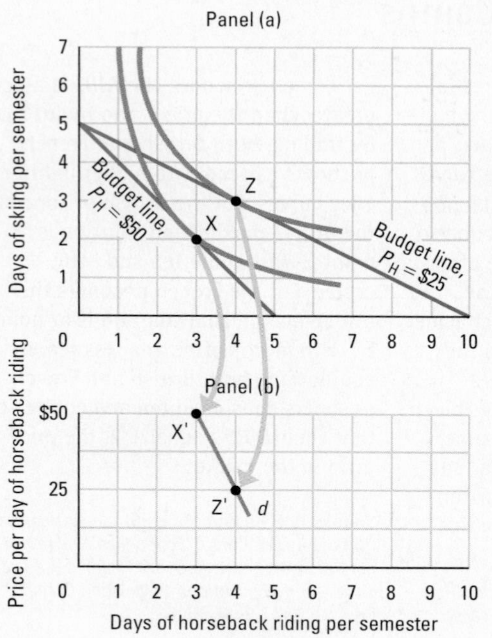

Exhibit 7-12

Utility Maximization and Demand

By observing a consumer's response to a change in price, we can derive the consumer's demand curve for a good. Panel (a) shows that at a price for horseback riding of $50 per day, Janet Bain chose to spend 3 days horseback riding per semester. Panel (b) shows that a reduction in the price to $25 increases her quantity demanded to 4 days per semester. Points X and Z, at which Ms. Bain maximizes utility at horseback riding prices of $50 and $25, respectively, become points X′ and Z′ on her demand curve, *d*, for horseback riding in Panel (b).

less than the market asks. She can't make herself better off than she is at point X by further rearranging her consumption. Point X, where the rate at which she's willing to exchange one good for another equals the rate the market asks, gives her the maximum utility possible.

Utility Maximization and Demand

Exhibit 7-11 showed Janet Bain's utility-maximizing solution for skiing and horseback riding. She achieved it by selecting a point at which an indifference curve was tangent to her budget line. A change in the price of one of the goods, however, will shift her budget line. By observing what happens to the quantity of the good demanded, we can derive Ms. Bain's demand curve.

Panel (a) of Exhibit 7-12 shows the original solution at point X, where Ms. Bain has $250 to spend and the price of a day of either skiing or horseback riding is $50. Now suppose the price of horseback riding falls by half, to $25. That changes the horizontal intercept of the budget line; if she spends all of her money on horseback riding, she can now ride 10 days per semester. Another way to think about the new budget line is to remember that its slope is equal to the negative of the price of the good on the horizontal axis divided by the price of the good on the vertical axis. When the price of horseback riding (the good on the horizontal axis) goes down, the budget line becomes flatter. Ms. Bain picks a new utility-maximizing solution at point Z.

The solution at Z involves an increase in the number of days Ms. Bain spends horseback riding. Notice that only the price of horseback riding has changed; all other features of the utility-maximizing solution remain the same. Ms. Bain's budget and the price of skiing are unchanged; this is reflected in the fact that the vertical intercept of the budget line remains fixed. Ms. Bain's preferences are unchanged; they are reflected by her indifference curves. Because all other factors in the solution are unchanged, we can determine two points on Ms. Bain's demand curve for horseback riding from her indifference curve diagram. At a price of $50, she maximized utility at point X, spending 3 days horseback riding per semester. When the price falls to $25, she maximizes utility at point Z, riding 4 days per semester. Those points are plotted as points X′ and Z′ on her demand curve for horseback riding in Panel (b) of Exhibit 7-11.

Check*list*

- A budget line shows combinations of two goods a consumer is able to consume, given a budget constraint.
- An indifference curve shows combinations of two goods that yield equal satisfaction.
- To maximize utility, a consumer chooses a combination of two goods at which an indifference curve is tangent to the budget line.
- At the utility-maximizing solution, the consumer's marginal rate of substitution (the absolute value of the slope of the indifference curve) is equal to the price ratio of the two goods.
- We can derive a demand curve from an indifference map by observing the quantity of the good consumed at different prices.

Try It Yourself 7-3

a. *Suppose a consumer has a budget for fast-food items of $20 per week and spends this money on two goods, hamburgers and pizzas. Suppose hamburgers cost $5 each and pizzas cost $10. Put the quantity of hamburgers purchased per week on the horizontal axis and the quantity of pizzas purchased per week on the vertical axis. Draw the budget line. What is its slope?*

b. *Suppose the consumer in part (a) is indifferent among the combinations of hamburgers and pizzas shown at the right. In the grid you used to draw the budget lines, draw an indifference curve passing through the combinations shown, and label the corresponding points* A, B, *and* C. *Label this curve I.*

Combination	Hamburgers/week	Pizzas/week
A	5	0
B	3	1/2
C	0	3

c. *The budget line is tangent to indifference curve I at* B. *Explain the meaning of this tangency.*

A Look Back

In this chapter we've examined the model of utility-maximizing behavior. Economists assume that consumers make choices consistent with the objective of achieving the maximum total utility possible for a given budget constraint.

Utility is a conceptual measure of satisfaction; it is not actually measurable. The theory of utility maximization allows us to ask how a utility-maximizing consumer would respond to a particular event.

By following the marginal decision rule, consumers will achieve the utility-maximizing condition: Expenditures equal consumers' budgets, and ratios of marginal utility to price are equal for all pairs of goods and services. Thus, consumption is arranged so that the extra utility per dollar spent is equal for all goods and services. The marginal utility from a particular good or service eventually diminishes as consumers consume more of it during a period of time.

Utility maximization underlies consumer demand. The amount by which the quantity demanded changes in response to a change in price consists of a substitution effect and an income effect. The substitution effect always changes quantity demanded in a manner consistent with the law of demand. The income effect of a price change reinforces the substitution effect in the case of normal goods, but it affects consumption in an opposite direction in the case of inferior goods.

An alternative approach to utility maximization uses indifference curves. This approach does not rely on the concept of marginal utility, and it gives us a graphical representation of the utility-maximizing condition.

A Look Ahead In this chapter we looked at the consumer behavior that underlies the demand curve. In Chapter 8 we'll examine the theory of production that underlies the supply curve. We'll see how a firm can minimize the cost of producing a given level of output—or achieve the maximum output possible for a given level of cost.

Terms and Concepts for Review

total utility, **146**
marginal utility, **146**
law of diminishing marginal utility, **147**
budget constraint, **148**
utility-maximizing condition, **149**
income-compensated price change, **152**
substitution effect, **152**
income effect, **153**
budget line, **157**
indifference curve, **158**
marginal rate of substitution, **159**

For Discussion

1. Suppose you really, *really* like ice cream. You *adore* ice cream. Does the law of diminishing marginal utility apply to your ice cream consumption?
2. If two commodities that you purchase on a regular basis carry the same price, does that mean they both provide the same total utility? Marginal utility?
3. If a person goes to the bowling alley planning to spend $15 but comes away with $5, what, if anything, can you conclude about the marginal utility of the alternatives (for example, bowl another line, have a soda or a sandwich) available to the person at the time he or she leaves?
4. Which do you like more—going to the movies or watching rented tapes on the videocassette recorder (VCR)? If you engage in both activities during the same period, say a week, explain why.
5. Do you tend to eat more at a fixed-price buffet or when ordering from an a la carte menu? Explain, using the marginal decision rule that guides your behavior.
6. Senators Phil Gramm of Texas (who is a former economics professor) and Pete Dominici of New Mexico introduced an amendment to the Tobacco Bill being considered in 1998. The bill called for a tax increase on cigarettes of $1.10 per pack. Senator Gramm's amendment would provide a tax cut for married working couples earning less than $50,000, a cut of up to $510 per year. Suppose such a couple smokes an average of 464 packs of cigarettes per year—and would thus face a tax increase of about $510 per year from the cigarette tax at the couple's current level of consumption. The income tax measure would increase the couple's after-tax income by $510. Would the combined measures be likely to have any effect on the couple's consumption of cigarettes? Why or why not?
7. How does an increase in income affect a consumer's budget line? His or her total utility?
8. Why can't Ms. Bain consume at point Y in Exhibit 7-10?
9. Suppose Ms. Bain is now consuming at point V in Exhibit 7-10. Use the marginal decision rule to explain why a shift to X would increase her utility.
10. Suppose that you are a utility maximizer and so is your economics instructor. What can you conclude about your respective marginal rates of substitution for movies and concerts?

Problems

1. Suppose the marginal utility of good A is 20 and its price is $4, and the marginal utility of good B is 50 and its price is $5. The individual to whom this information applies is spending $20 on each good. Is he or she maximizing satisfaction? If not, what should the individual do to increase total satisfaction? On the basis of this information, can you pick an optimum combination? Why or why not?
2. John and Marie settle down to watch the evening news. Marie is content to watch the entire program, while John continually zaps it in favor of possible alternatives. Draw the likely marginal utility curves for the two individuals.
3. Li, a very careful maximizer of utility, consumes two services, going to the movies and bowling. She has arranged her consumption of the two activities so that the marginal utility of going to a movie is 20 and the marginal utility of going bowling is 10. The price of going to a movie is $10, and the price of going bowling is $5. Show that she is satisfying the requirement for utility maximization. Now show what happens when the price of going bowling rises to $10.
4. Sid is a commuter-student at his college. During the day, he snacks on cartons of yogurt and the "house special" sandwiches at the Student Center cafeteria. A carton of yogurt costs $1.20; the Student Center often offers specials on the sandwiches, so their price varies a great deal. Sid has a budget of $36 per week for food at the Center. Five of Sid's indifference curves are given by the schedule on page 165; the points listed in the tables correspond to the points shown in the graph.
   a. Use the set of Sid's indifference curves shown as a guide in drawing your own graph grid. Draw Sid's indifference curves and budget line, assuming sandwiches cost $3.60. Identify the point at which he maximizes utility. How many sandwiches will he consume? How many cartons of yogurt? (*Hint:* All of the answers in this exercise occur at one of the combinations given in the tables on page 165.)
   b. Now suppose the price of sandwiches is cut to $1.20. Draw the new budget line. Identify the point at which Sid maximizes utility. How many sandwiches will he consume? How many cartons of yogurt?

c. Now draw the budget lines implied by a price of yogurt of $1.20 and sandwich prices of $0.90 and $1.80. With the observations you've already made for sandwich prices of $3.60 and $1.20, draw the demand curve. Explain how this demand curve illustrates the law of demand.

Curve U_1

Point on curve	Sandwiches	Yogurt
A	2	24
B	4	20
C	7	16
D	10	11

Curve U_2

Point on curve	Sandwiches	Yogurt
E	4	26
F	6	21
G	13	15
H	18	13

Curve U_3

Point on curve	Sandwiches	Yogurt
I	7	25
J	10	20
K	16	16
L	20	15

Curve U_4

Point on curve	Sandwiches	Yogurt
M	10	26
N	12	23
O	15	18
P	19	17

Curve U_5

Point on curve	Sandwiches	Yogurt
Q	10	31
R	12	26
S	20	21
T	24	20

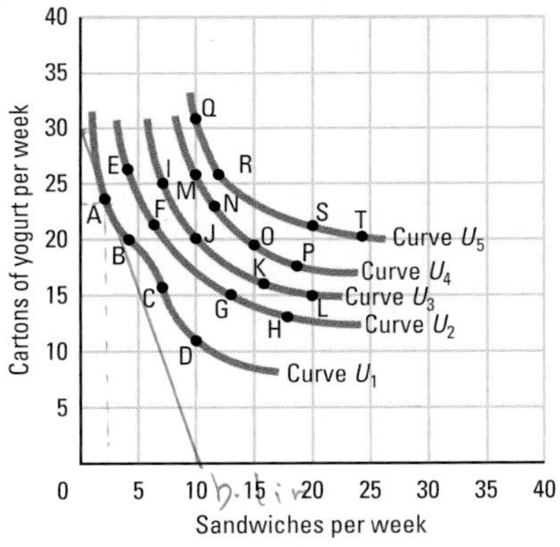

Answers to Try It Yourself Problems

Try It Yourself 7-1

a. He is spending $4.50 (= $0.75 × 6) on potato chips and $3.50 (= $0.50 × 7) on candy bars, for a total of $8. His budget constraint is $8.

b. In order for the ratios of marginal utility to price to be equal, the marginal utility of a candy bar must be 4. Let the marginal utility and price of candy bars be MU_{CB} and P_{CB}, respectively, and the marginal utility and price of a bag of potato chips be MU_{PC} and P_{PC}, respectively. Then we want

$$\frac{MU_{PC}}{P_{PC}} = \frac{MU_{CB}}{P_{CB}}$$

We know that P_{PC} is $0.75 and P_{CB} equals $0.50. We are told that MU_{PC} is 6. Thus

$$\frac{6}{0.75} = \frac{MU_{CB}}{0.50}$$

Solving the equation for MU_{CB}, we find that it must equal 4.

Try It Yourself 7-2

One hundred fifty dollars is the income that allows Ms. Drakulic to purchase the same items as before, and thus can be used to measure the substitution effect. Looking only at the income-compensated price change (that is, holding her to the same purchasing power as in the original relative price situation), we find that the substitution effect is 3 more CDs (from 5 to 8). The CDs that she buys beyond 8 constitute her income effect; it is 2 CDs. Because the income effect reinforces the substitution effect, CDs are a normal good for her and her demand curve is similar to that shown in Exhibit 7-4.

Try It Yourself 7-3

a. The budget line is shown in Panel (a). Its slope is – \$5/\$10 = – 0.5.
b. Panel (b) shows indifference curve *I*. The points A, B, and C on *I* have been labeled.
c. The tangency point at B shows the combinations of hamburgers and pizza that maximize the consumer's utility, given the budget constraint. At the point of tangency, the marginal rate of substitution (*MRS*) between the two goods is equal to the ratio of prices of the two goods. This means that the rate at which the consumer is willing to exchange one good for another equals the rate at which the goods can be exchanged in the market.

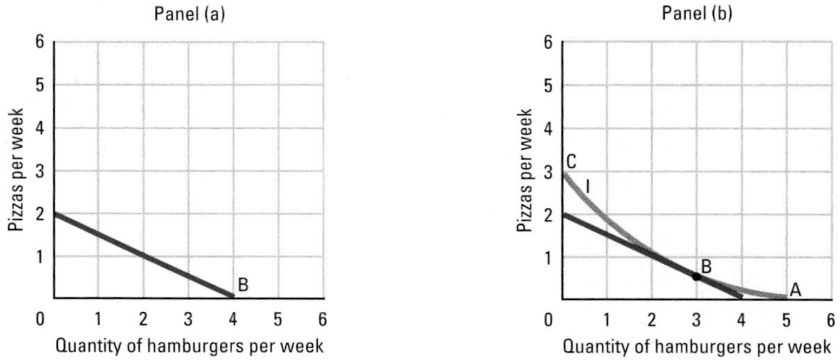

8 Production and Cost

Getting Started: Street Cleaning Around the World

It is dawn in Beijing, China. Already thousands of Chinese are out cleaning the city's streets. They are using brooms.

On the other side of the world, night falls in Washington, D.C., where the streets are also being cleaned—by a handful of giant street-sweeping machines driven by a handful of workers.

The difference in method is not the result of a greater knowledge of modern technology in the United States—the Chinese know perfectly well how to build street-sweeping machines. It is a production decision based on costs in the two countries. In China, where wages are relatively low, an army of workers armed with brooms is the least expensive way to produce clean streets. In Washington, where labor costs are high, it makes sense to use more machinery and less labor.

All types of production efforts require choices in the use of factors of production. In this chapter we examine such choices. Should a good or service be produced using relatively more labor and less capital? Or should relatively more capital and less labor be used? What about the use of natural resources?

In this chapter we'll see why firms make the production choices they do and how their costs affect their choices. We'll apply the marginal decision rule to the production process and see how this rule ensures that production is carried out at the lowest cost possible.

Just as we examined the nature of consumer behavior (in Chapter 7) in order to build a better understanding of demand, so in this chapter we examine the nature of production and costs in order to gain a better understanding of supply. We thus shift our focus to **firms,** organizations that produce goods and services. In producing goods and services, firms combine the factors of production we discussed in Chapter 2—labor, capital, and natural resources—to produce various products.

Economists assume that firms engage in production in order to earn a profit and that they seek to make this profit as large as possible. That is, economists assume that firms apply the marginal decision rule as they seek to maximize their profits. Whether we consider the operator of a shoeshine stand at an airport or the firm that produces airplanes, we'll find there are basic relationships between the use of factors of production and output levels, and between output levels and costs, that apply to all production. Just as utility maximization, covered in Chapter 7, is the foundation of demand, the production choices of firms and their associated costs are at the foundation of supply.

Production Choices and Costs: The Short Run

Our analysis of production and cost begins with a period economists call the short run. The **short run** is a planning period over which the managers of a firm must consider one or more of their factors of production as fixed in quantity. For example, a restaurant may regard its building as a fixed factor over a period of at least the next year. It would take at least that much time to find a new building or to expand or reduce the size of its present facility. Decisions concerning the operation of the restaurant during the next year must assume the building will remain unchanged. Other factors of production could be changed during the year, but the size of the building must be regarded as a constant.

When the quantity of a factor of production cannot be changed during a particular period, it is called a **fixed factor of production.** For the restaurant, its building is a fixed factor of production for at least a year. A factor of production whose quantity can be changed during a particular period is called a **variable factor of production;** factors such as labor and food are examples.

While the managers of the restaurant are making choices concerning its operation over the next year, they are also planning for longer periods. Over those periods, managers may contemplate alternatives such as modifying the building, building a new facility, or selling the building and leaving the restaurant business. The planning period over which a firm can consider *all* factors of production as variable is called the **long run.**

At any one time, a firm will be making both short-run and long-run choices. The managers may be planning what to do for the next few weeks and for the next few years. Their decisions over the next few weeks are likely to be short-run choices. Decisions that will affect operations over the next few years may be long-run choices, in which managers can consider changing every aspect of their operations. Our analysis in this section focuses on the short run. We'll examine long-run choices later in this chapter.

The Short-Run Production Function

A firm uses factors of production to produce a product. The relationship between factors of production and the output of a firm is called a **production function.** Our first task is to explore the nature of the production function.

Consider a hypothetical firm, Acme Clothing, a shop that produces jackets. Suppose that Acme has a lease on its building and equipment. During the period of the lease, Acme's capital is its fixed factor of production. Acme's variable factors of production include things such as labor, cloth, and electricity. In the analysis that follows, we shall simplify by assuming that labor is Acme's *only* variable factor of production.

Total, Marginal, and Average Products Exhibit 8-1 shows the number of jackets Acme can obtain with varying amounts of labor (in this case, tailors) and its given level of capital. A **total product curve** shows the quantities of output that can be obtained from different amounts of a variable factor of production, assuming other factors of production are fixed.

Notice what happens to the slope of the total product curve in Exhibit 8-1. Between 0 and 3 units of labor per day, the curve becomes steeper. Between 3 and 7 workers, the curve continues to slope upward, but its slope diminishes. Beyond the seventh tailor, production begins to decline and the curve slopes downward.

We measure the slope of any curve as the vertical change between two points divided by the horizontal change between the same two points. The slope of the total product curve for labor equals the change in output (ΔQ) divided by the change in units of labor (ΔL):

$$\text{Slope of the total product curve} = \Delta Q / \Delta L$$

Exhibit 8-1

Acme Clothing's Total Product Curve

The table gives output levels per day for Acme Clothing Company at various quantities of labor per day, assuming the firm's capital is fixed. These values are then plotted graphically as a total product curve.

Point on graph	A	B	C	D	E	F	G	H	I
Units of labor per day	0	1	2	3	4	5	6	7	8
Jackets per day	0.0	1.0	3.0	7.0	9.0	10.0	10.7	11.0	10.5

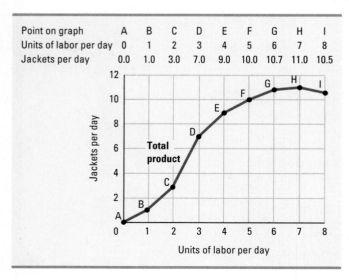

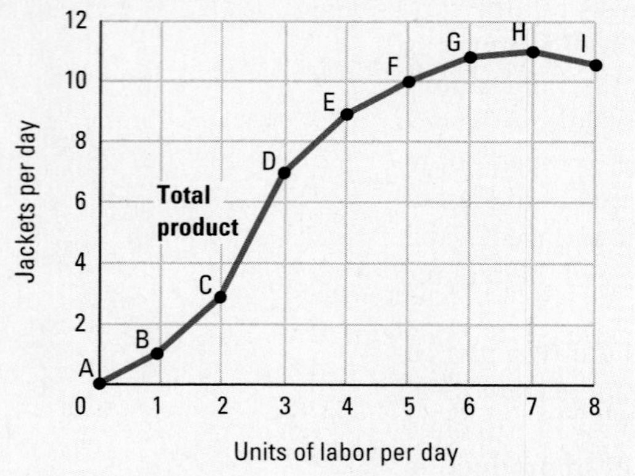

The slope of a total product curve for any variable factor is a measure of the change in output associated with a change in the amount of the variable factor, with the quantities of all other factors held constant. The amount by which output rises with an additional unit of a variable factor is the **marginal product** of the variable factor. Mathematically, marginal product is the ratio of the change in output to the change in the amount of a variable factor. The **marginal product of labor,** for example, is the amount by which output rises with an additional unit of labor. It is thus the ratio of the change in output to the change in the quantity of labor ($\Delta Q/\Delta L$), all other things unchanged. It is measured as the slope of the total product curve for labor.

In addition we can define the **average product** of a variable factor. It is the output per unit of variable factor. The **average product of labor,** for example, is the ratio of output to the number of units of labor (Q/L). The concept of average product is often used for comparing productivity levels over time or in comparing productivity levels among nations. When you read in the newspaper that productivity is rising or falling, or that productivity in the United States is nine times greater than productivity in China, the report is probably referring to some measure of the average product of labor.

The total product curve in Panel (a) of Exhibit 8-2 is repeated from Exhibit 8-1. Panel (b) shows the marginal product and average product curves. Notice that marginal product is the slope of the total product curve, and that marginal product rises as the slope of the total product curve increases, falls as the slope of the total product curve declines, reaches zero when the total product curve achieves its maximum value, and becomes negative as the total product curve slopes downward. As was done in Chapters 6 and 7, marginal products are plotted at the midpoint of each interval. The marginal product of the fifth unit of labor, for example, is plotted between 4 and 5 units of labor. Also notice that the marginal product curve intersects the average product curve at the maximum point on the average product curve. When marginal product is above average product, average product is rising. When marginal product is below average product, average product is falling.

Exhibit 8-2

From Total Product to the Average and Marginal Product of Labor

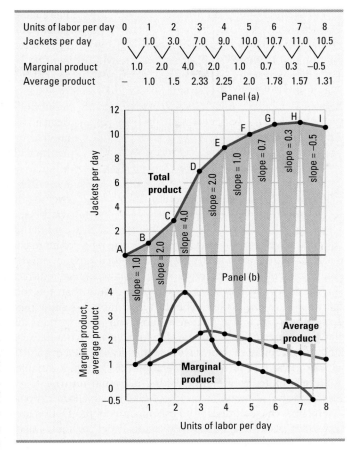

Units of labor per day	0	1	2	3	4	5	6	7	8
Jackets per day	0	1.0	3.0	7.0	9.0	10.0	10.7	11.0	10.5
Marginal product		1.0	2.0	4.0	2.0	1.0	0.7	0.3	−0.5
Average product	–	1.0	1.5	2.33	2.25	2.0	1.78	1.57	1.31

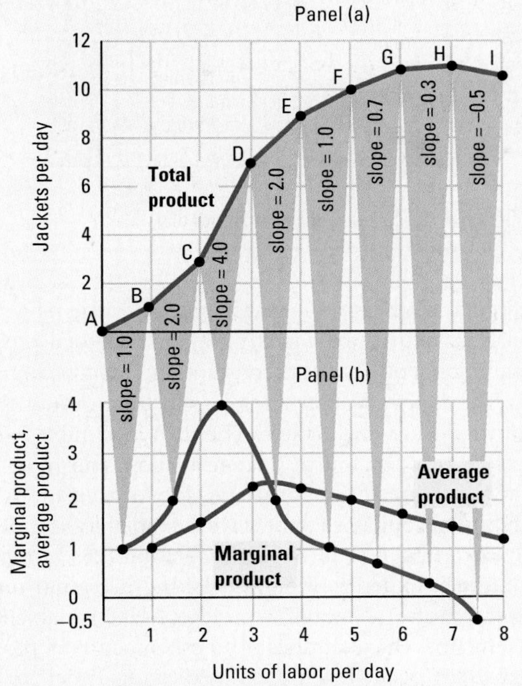

The first two rows of the table give the values for quantities of labor and total product from Exhibit 8-1. Marginal product, given in the third row, is the change in output resulting from a one-unit increase in labor. Average product, given in the fourth row, is output per unit of labor. Panel (a) shows the total product curve. The slope of the total product curve is marginal product, which is plotted in Panel (b). Values for marginal product are plotted at the midpoints of the intervals. Average product rises and falls. Where marginal product is above average product, average product rises. Where marginal product is below average product, average product falls. The marginal product curve intersects the average product curve at the maximum point on the average product curve.

As a student you can use your own experience to understand the relationship between marginal and average values. Your grade point average (GPA) represents the average grade you've earned in all your course work so far. When you take an additional course, your grade in that course represents the marginal grade. What happens to your GPA when you get a grade that's higher than your previous average? It rises. What happens to your GPA when you get a grade that's lower than your previous average? It falls.

The relationship between average product and marginal product is similar. However, unlike your course grades, which may go up and down willy-nilly, marginal product always rises and then falls, for reasons we'll explore shortly. As soon as marginal product falls below average product, the average product curve slopes downward. While marginal product is above average product, whether marginal product is increasing or decreasing, the average product curve slopes upward.

As we have learned, maximizing behavior requires focusing on making decisions at the margin. For this reason, we turn our attention now toward increasing our understanding of marginal product.

Exhibit 8-3

Increasing Marginal Returns, Diminishing Marginal Returns, and Negative Marginal Returns

This graph shows Acme's total product curve from Exhibit 8-1 with the ranges of increasing marginal returns, diminishing marginal returns, and negative marginal returns marked. Acme experiences increasing marginal returns between 0 and 3 units of labor per day, diminishing marginal returns between 3 and 7 units of labor per day, and negative marginal returns beyond the 7th unit of labor.

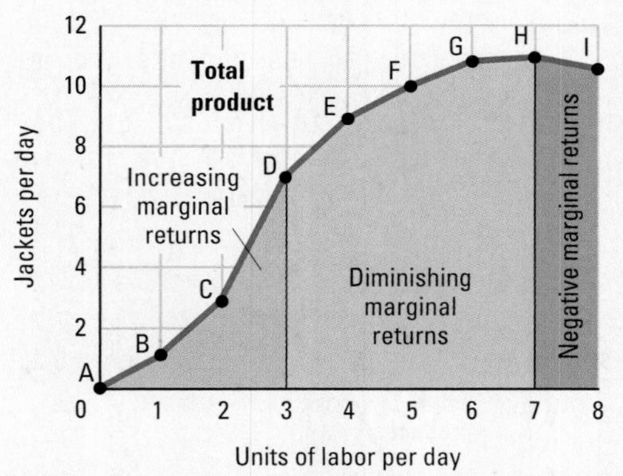

Increasing, Diminishing, and Negative Marginal Returns Adding the first worker increases Acme's output from 0 to 1 jacket per day. The second tailor adds 2 jackets to total output; the third adds 4. The marginal product goes up because when there are more workers, each one can specialize to a degree. One worker might cut the cloth, another might sew the seams, and another might sew the buttonholes. Their increasing marginal products are reflected by the increasing slope of the total product curve over the first 3 units of labor and by the upward slope of the marginal product curve over the same range. The range over which marginal products are increasing is called the range of **increasing marginal returns.** Increasing marginal returns exist in the context of a total product curve for labor, so we are holding the quantities of other factors constant. Increasing marginal returns may occur for any variable factor.

The fourth worker adds less to total output than the third; the marginal product of the fourth worker is 2 jackets. The data in Exhibit 8-2 show that marginal product continues to decline after the fourth worker as more and more workers are hired. The additional workers allow even greater opportunities for specialization, but because they are operating with a fixed amount of capital, each new worker adds less to total output. The fifth tailor adds only a single jacket to total output. When each additional unit of a variable factor adds less to total output, the firm is experiencing **diminishing marginal returns.** Over the range of diminishing marginal returns, the marginal product of the variable factor is positive but falling. Once again, we assume that the quantities of all other factors of production are fixed. Diminishing marginal returns may occur for any variable factor. Panel (b) shows that Acme experiences diminishing marginal returns between the third and seventh workers, or between 7 and 11 jackets per day.

After the seventh unit of labor, Acme's fixed plant becomes so crowded that adding another worker actually reduces output. When additional units of a variable factor reduce total output, given constant quantities of all other factors, the company experiences **negative marginal returns.** Now the total product curve is downward sloping, and the marginal product curve falls below zero. Exhibit 8-3 shows the ranges of increasing, diminishing, and negative marginal returns. Clearly, a firm will never intentionally add so much of a variable factor of production that it enters a range of negative marginal returns.

The idea that the marginal product of a variable factor declines over some range is important enough, and general enough, that economists state it as a law. The **law of diminishing marginal returns** holds that the marginal product of any variable factor of production will eventually decline, assuming the quantities of other factors of production are unchanged.

To see the logic of the law of diminishing marginal returns, imagine a case in which it does not hold. Say that you have a small plot of land for a vegetable garden, 10 feet by 10 feet in size. The plot itself is a fixed factor in the production of vegetables. Suppose you are able to hold constant all other factors—water, sunshine, temperature, fertilizer, and seed—and vary the amount of labor devoted to the garden. How much food could the garden produce? Suppose the marginal product of labor kept increasing or was constant. Then you could grow an *unlimited* quantity of food on your small plot—enough to feed the entire world! You could add an unlimited number of workers to your plot and still increase output at a constant or increasing rate. If you didn't get enough output with, say, 500 workers, you could use 5 million; the five-millionth worker would add at least as much to total output as the first. If diminishing marginal returns to labor did not occur, the total product curve would slope upward at a constant or increasing rate.

Caution!

It is easy to confuse the concept of diminishing marginal returns with the idea of negative marginal returns. To say a firm is experiencing diminishing marginal returns is *not* to say its output is falling. Diminishing marginal returns mean that the marginal product of a variable factor is declining. Output is still increasing as the variable factor is increased, but it is increasing by smaller and smaller amounts. As we saw in Exhibits 8-2 and 8-3, the range of diminishing marginal returns was between the third and seventh workers; over this range of workers, output rose from 7 to 11 jackets. Negative marginal returns started after the seventh worker.

Case in Point The Production of Fitness

How much should an athlete train?

Sports physiologists often measure the "total product" of training as the increase in an athlete's aerobic capacity—the capacity to absorb oxygen into the bloodstream. An athlete can be thought of as producing aerobic capacity using a fixed factor (his or her natural capacity) and a variable input (exercise). The chart shows how this aerobic capacity varies with the number of workouts per week. The curve has a shape very much like a total product curve—which, after all, is precisely what it is.

The data suggest that an athlete experiences increasing marginal returns from exercise for the first three days of training each week; indeed, over half the total gain in aerobic capacity possible is achieved. A person can become even more fit by exercising more, but the gains become smaller with each added day of training. The law of diminishing marginal returns applies to training.

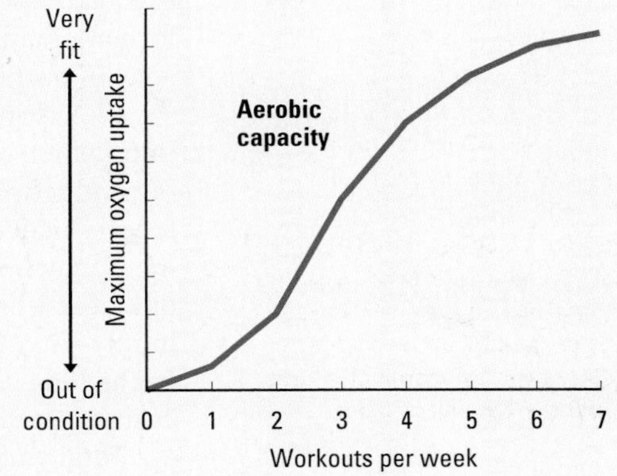

The increase in fitness that results from the sixth and seventh workouts each week is small. Studies also show that the costs of daily training, in terms of increased likelihood of injury, are high. Many trainers and coaches now recommend that athletes—at all levels of competition—take a day or two off each week.

Source: Jeff Galloway, *Galloway's Book on Running* (Bolinas, CA: Shelter Publications, 1984), p. 73.

The shape of the total product curve and the shape of the resulting marginal product curve drawn in Exhibit 8-2 are typical of *any* firm for the short run. Given its fixed factors of production, increasing the use of a variable factor will generate increasing marginal returns at first; the total product curve for the variable factor becomes steeper and the marginal product rises. The opportunity to gain from increased specialization in the use of the variable factor accounts for this range of increasing marginal returns. Eventually, though, diminishing returns will set in. The total product curve will become flatter, and the marginal product curve will fall.

Try It Yourself 8-1

Suppose Acme gets some new equipment for producing jackets. The table below gives its new production function. Compute marginal product and average product and fill in the bottom two rows of the table. Referring to Exhibit 8-2, draw a graph showing Acme's new total product curve. On a second graph, below the one showing the total product curve you drew, sketch the marginal and average product curves. Remember to plot marginal product at the midpoint between each input level. On both graphs, shade the regions where Acme experiences increasing marginal returns, diminishing marginal returns, and negative marginal returns.

Units of labor per day	0	1	2	3	4	5	6	7	8
Jackets per day	0	2	5.5	9.5	12	14	15	15.5	15
Marginal product		2	3.5	4.0	2.5	2	1	0.5	-0.5
Average product	___	___	___	___	___	___	___	___	___

Costs in the Short Run

A firm's costs of production depend on the quantities and prices of its factors of production. Because we expect a firm's output to vary with the firm's use of labor in a specific way, we can also expect the firm's costs to vary with its output in a specific way. We shall put our information about Acme's product curves to work to discover how a firm's costs vary with its level of output.

We distinguish between the costs associated with the use of variable factors of production, which are called **variable costs,** and the costs associated with the use of fixed factors of production, which are called **fixed costs.** For most firms, variable costs includes costs for raw materials, salaries of production workers, and utilities. The salaries of top management may be fixed costs; any charges set by contract over a period of time, such as Acme's one-year lease on its building and equipment, are likely to be fixed costs. A term commonly used for fixed costs is *overhead.* Notice that fixed costs exist only in the short run. In the long run, the quantities of all factors of production are variable, so that all long-run costs are variable.

Total variable cost is cost that varies with the level of output. **Total fixed cost** is cost that does not vary with output. **Total cost** is the sum of total variable cost and total fixed cost.

From Total Production to Total Cost Let's illustrate the relationship between Acme's total product curve and its total costs. Acme can vary the quantity of labor it uses each day, so the cost of this labor is a variable cost. We assume capital is a fixed factor of production in the short run, so its cost is a fixed cost.

Suppose that Acme pays a wage of $100 per worker per day. If labor is the only variable factor, Acme's total variable costs per day amount to $100 times the number of workers it employs. We can use the information given by the total product curve, together with the wage, to compute Acme's total variable costs.

We know from Exhibit 8-1 that Acme requires 1 worker working 1 day to produce 1 jacket. The total variable cost of a jacket thus equals $100. Three units of labor produce 7 jackets per day; the total variable cost of 7 jackets equals $300. Exhibit 8-4 shows Acme's total variable costs for producing each of the output levels given in Exhibit 8-1.

Exhibit 8-4 gives us costs for several quantities of jackets, but we'll need a bit more detail. We know, for example, that 7 jackets have a total variable cost of $300. What is the total variable cost of 6 jackets?

We can estimate total variable costs for other quantities of jackets by inspecting the total product curve in Exhibit 8-1. Reading over from a quantity of 6 jackets to the total product curve and then down suggests that the Acme needs about 2.8 units of labor to produce 6 jackets per day. Acme needs 2 full-time and 1 part-time tailor to produce 6 jackets. Exhibit 8-5 gives the precise total variable costs for quantities of jackets ranging from 0 to 11 per day. The numbers in boldface type are taken from Exhibit 8-4; the other numbers are estimates we've assigned to produce a total variable cost curve that is consistent with our total product curve. You should, however, be certain that you understand how the numbers in boldface type were found.

Suppose Acme's present plant, including the building and equipment, is the equivalent of 20 units of capital. Acme has signed a long-term lease for these 20 units of capital at a cost of $200 per day. In the short run, Acme can't increase or decrease its quantity of capital—it must pay the $200 per day no matter what it does. Even if the firm cuts production to zero, it must still pay $200 per day in the short run.

Exhibit 8-4

Computing Variable Costs

The points shown give the variable costs of producing the quantities of jackets given in the total product curve in Exhibits 8-1 and 8-2. Suppose Acme's workers earn $100 per day. If Acme produces 0 jackets, it will use no labor—its variable cost thus equals $0 (Point A′). Producing 7 jackets requires 3 units of labor; Acme's variable cost equals $300 (Point D′).

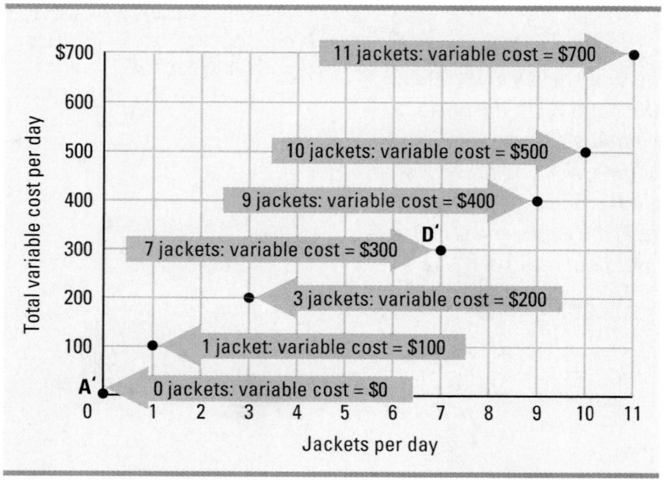

Acme's total cost is its total fixed cost of $200 plus its total variable cost. We add $200 to the total variable cost curve in Exhibit 8-5 to get the total cost curve shown in Exhibit 8- 6.

Notice something important about the shapes of the total cost and total variable cost curves in Exhibit 8-6. The total cost curve, for example, starts at $200 when Acme produces 0 jackets—that's its total fixed cost. The curve rises, but at a decreasing rate, up to the seventh jacket. Beyond the seventh jacket, the curve becomes steeper and steeper. The slope of the total variable cost curve behaves in precisely the same way.

Recall that Acme experienced increasing marginal returns to labor for the first three units of labor—or the first seven jackets. Up to the third worker, each additional worker added more and more to Acme's output. Over the range of increasing marginal returns, each additional jacket requires less and less additional labor. The first jacket required one tailor; the second required the addition of only a part-time tailor; the third required only that Acme boost that part-time tailor's hours to a full day. Up to the seventh jacket, each additional jacket requires less and less additional labor, and thus costs rise at a decreasing rate; the total cost and total variable cost curves become flatter over the range of increasing marginal returns.

Acme experiences diminishing marginal returns beyond the third unit of labor—or the seventh jacket. Notice that the total cost and total variable cost curves become steeper and steeper beyond this level of output. In the range of diminishing marginal returns, each additional unit of a factor adds less and less to total output. That means each additional unit of output requires larger and larger increases in the variable factor, and larger and larger increases in costs.

Marginal and Average Costs

Marginal and average cost curves, which will play an important role in the analysis of the firm, can be derived from the total cost curve. *Marginal cost* shows the additional cost of each

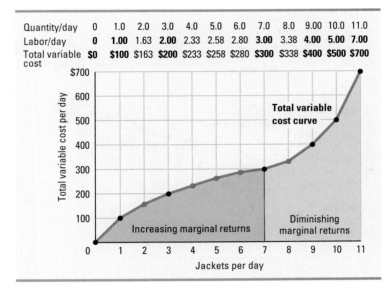

Quantity/day	0	1.0	2.0	3.0	4.0	5.0	6.0	7.0	8.0	9.00	10.0	11.0
Labor/day	**0**	**1.00**	1.63	**2.00**	2.33	2.58	2.80	**3.00**	3.38	**4.00**	**5.00**	**7.00**
Total variable cost	**$0**	**$100**	$163	**$200**	$233	$258	$280	**$300**	$338	**$400**	**$500**	**$700**

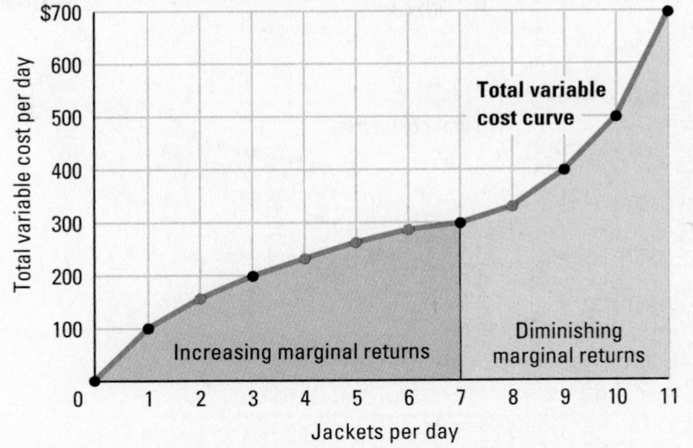

Exhibit 8-5

The Total Variable Cost Curve

Total variable costs for output levels shown in Acme's total product curve were shown in Exhibit 8-4. To complete the total variable cost curve, we need to know the variable cost for each level of output from 0 to 11 jackets per day. The variable costs and quantities of labor given in Exhibit 8-4 are shown in boldface in the table here and with black dots in the graph. The remaining values were estimated from the total product curve in Exhibits 8-1 and 8-2. For example, producing 6 jackets requires 2.8 workers, for a variable cost of $280.

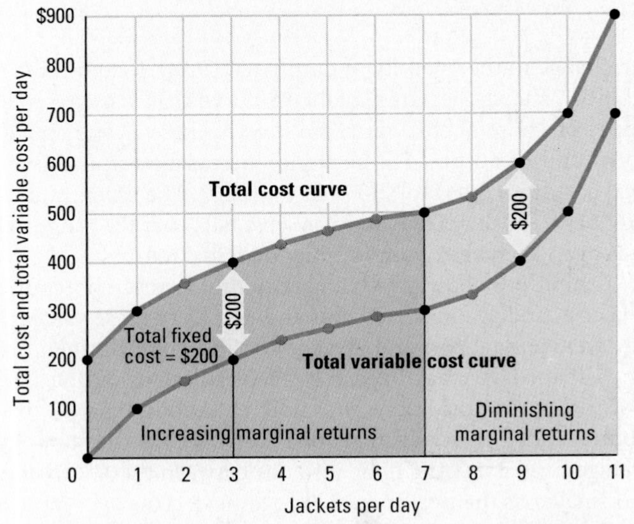

Exhibit 8-6

From Variable Cost to Total Cost

We add total fixed cost to the total variable cost to obtain total cost. In this case, Acme's total fixed cost equals $200 per day.

Exhibit 8-7

Total Cost and Marginal Cost

Marginal cost in Panel (b) is the slope of the total cost curve in Panel (a).

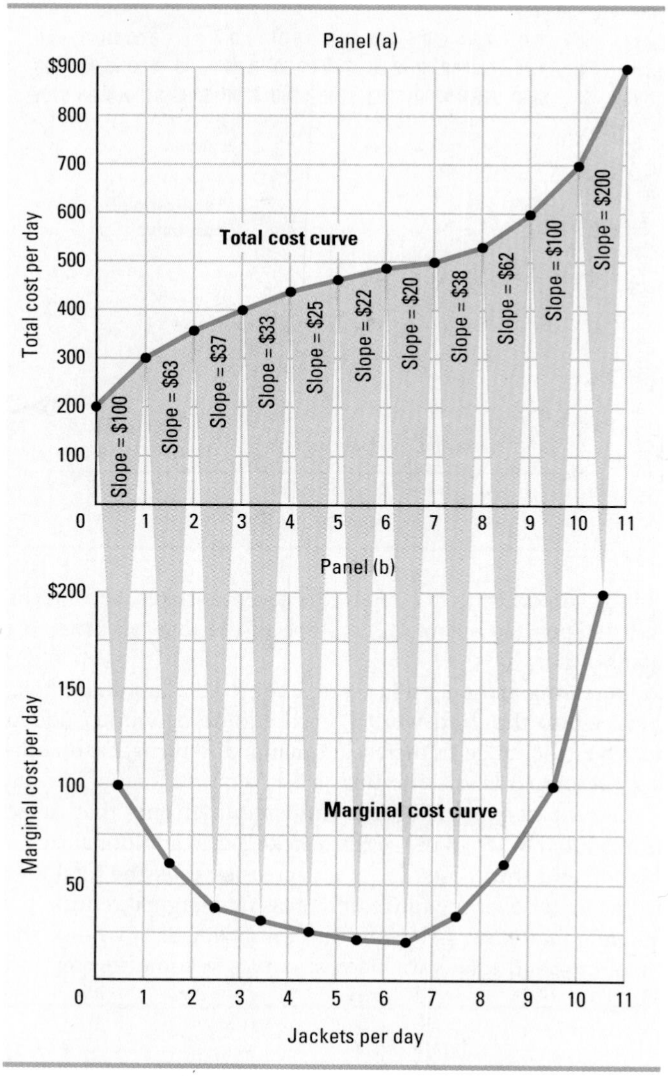

additional unit of output a firm produces. This is a specific application of the general concept of marginal cost that was presented in Chapter 6. Given the marginal decision rule's focus on evaluating choices at the margin, the marginal cost curve takes on enormous importance in the analysis of a firm's choices. The second curve we shall derive shows the firm's average total cost at each level of output. **Average total cost** is total cost divided by quantity; it is the firm's total cost per unit of output. We shall also discuss **average variable cost,** which is the firm's variable cost per unit of output; it is total variable cost divided by quantity. We are still assessing the choices facing the firm in the short run, so we assume that at least one factor of production is fixed. Finally, we'll discuss **average fixed cost,** which is total fixed cost divided by quantity.

Marginal cost is the amount by which total cost rises with an additional unit of output. It is the ratio of the change in total cost to the change in the quantity of output, $\Delta TC/\Delta Q$. It equals the slope of the total cost curve. Exhibit 8-7 shows the same total cost curve that was presented in Exhibit 8-6. This time the slopes of the total cost curve are shown; these slopes equal the marginal cost of each additional unit of output. For example, increasing output from 6 to 7 units ($\Delta Q = 1$) increases total cost from \$480 to \$500 ($\Delta TC = \$20$). The seventh unit thus has a marginal cost of \$20 ($\Delta Q/\Delta L = \$20/1 = \$20$). Marginal cost falls over the range of increasing marginal returns and rises over the range of diminishing marginal returns.

Caution!

Notice that the various cost curves are drawn with the quantity of output on the horizontal axis. The various product curves are drawn with quantity of a factor of production on the horizontal axis.

Exhibit 8-8 shows the computation of Acme's short-run average total cost, average variable cost, and average fixed cost and graphs of these values. Notice that the curves for short-run average total cost and average variable cost fall, then rise. We say that these cost curves are U-shaped. Average fixed cost keeps falling as output increases. This is because the fixed costs are spread out more and more as output expands; by definition, they do not vary as labor is added. Since average total cost (*ATC*) is the sum of average variable cost (*AVC*) and average fixed cost (*AFC*), the distance between the *ATC* and *AVC* curves keeps getting smaller and smaller as the firm spreads its overhead costs over more and more output.

Exhibit 8-8 includes the marginal cost curve from Exhibit 8-7. It intersects the average total cost and average variable cost curves at their lowest points. When marginal cost is below average total cost or average variable cost, the average total and average variable cost curves slope downward. When marginal cost is greater than short-run average total cost or average variable cost, these average cost curves slope upward. The logic behind the relationship between marginal cost and average total and variable costs is the same as it is for the relationship between marginal product and average product.

We turn next in this chapter to an examination of production and cost in the long run, a planning period in which the firm can consider changing the quantities of all factors.

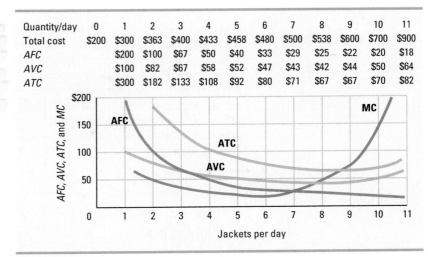

Quantity/day	0	1	2	3	4	5	6	7	8	9	10	11
Total cost	$200	$300	$363	$400	$433	$458	$480	$500	$538	$600	$700	$900
AFC		$200	$100	$67	$50	$40	$33	$29	$25	$22	$20	$18
AVC		$100	$82	$67	$58	$52	$47	$43	$42	$44	$50	$64
ATC		$300	$182	$133	$108	$92	$80	$71	$67	$67	$70	$82

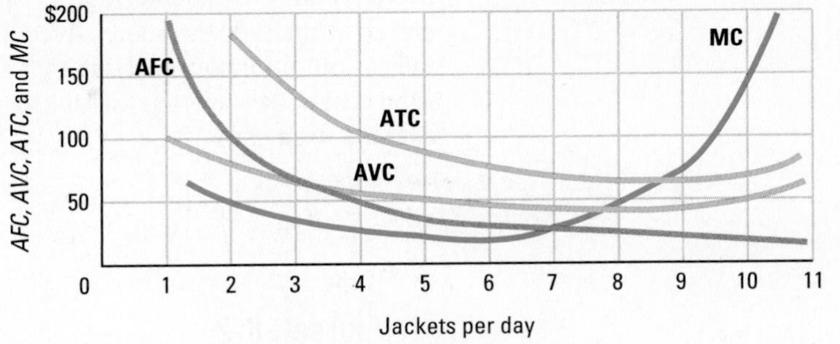

Exhibit 8-8

Marginal Cost, Average Fixed Cost, Average Variable Cost, and Average Total Cost in the Short Run

Total cost figures for Acme Clothing are taken from Exhibit 8-7. The other values are derived from these. Average total cost (*ATC*) equals total cost divided by quantity produced; it also equals the sum of the average fixed cost (*AFC*) and average variable cost (*AVC*) (exceptions in table are due to rounding to the nearest dollar); average variable cost is variable cost divided by quantity produced. The marginal cost (*MC*) curve (from Exhibit 8-7) intersects the *ATC* and *AVC* curves at the lowest points on both curves. The *AFC* curve falls as quantity increases.

Checklist

- In Panel (a), the total product curve for a variable factor in the short run shows that the firm experiences increasing marginal returns from zero to F_a units of the variable factor (zero to Q_a units of output), diminishing marginal returns from F_a to F_b (Q_a to Q_b units of output), and negative marginal returns beyond F_b units of the variable factor.

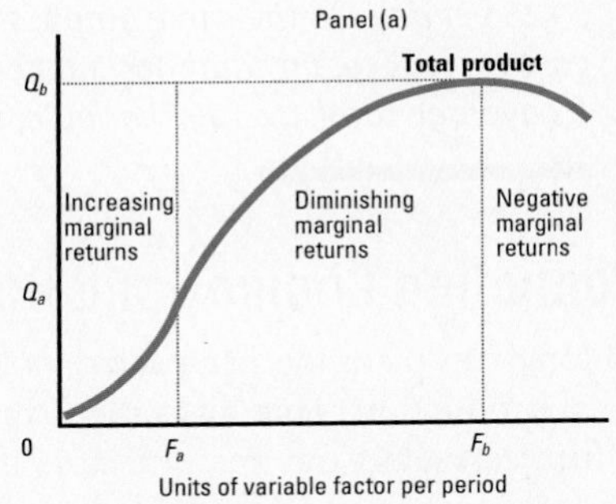

- Panel (b) shows that marginal product rises over the range of increasing marginal returns, falls over the range of diminishing marginal returns, and becomes negative over the range of negative marginal returns. Average product rises when marginal product is above it and falls when marginal product is below it.

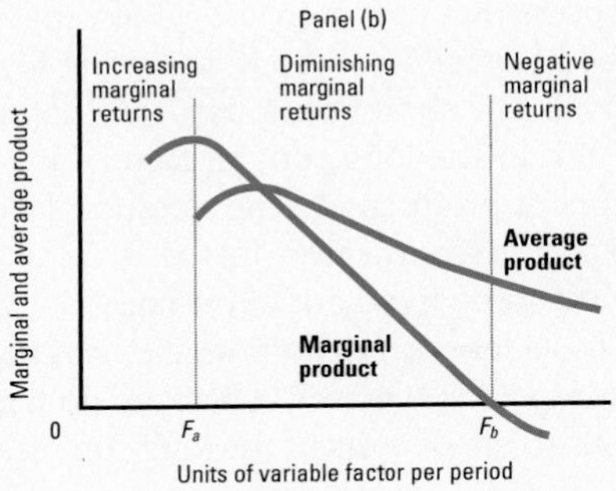

- In Panel (c), total cost rises at a decreasing rate over the range of output from zero to Q_a. This was the range of output that was shown in Panel (a) to exhibit increasing marginal returns. Beyond Q_a, the range of diminishing marginal returns, total cost at an increasing rate. The total cost at zero units of output (the vertical axis) is total fixed cost.

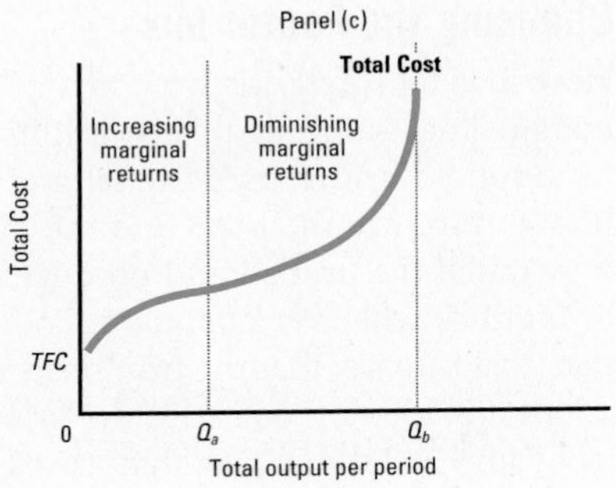

- Panel (d) shows that marginal cost falls over the range of increasing marginal returns, then rises over the range of diminishing marginal returns. The marginal cost curve intersects the average total cost and average variable cost curves at their lowest points. Average fixed cost falls as output increases. Note that average total cost equals average variable cost plus average fixed cost.

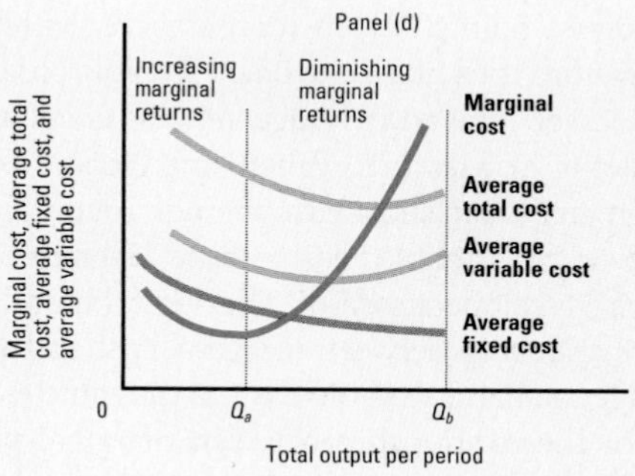

Try It Yourself 8-2

Draw the points showing total variable cost at daily outputs of 0, 1, 3, 7, 9, 10, and 11 jackets per day when Acme faced a wage of $100 per day. (Use Exhibit 8-5 as a model.) Sketch the total variable cost curve as shown in Exhibit 8-4. Now suppose that the wage rises to $125 per day. On the same graph, show the new points and sketch the new total variable cost curve. Explain what has happened. What will happen to Acme's marginal cost curve? Its average total, average variable, and average fixed cost curves? Explain.

Production Choices and Costs: The Long Run

In a long-run planning perspective, a firm can consider changing the quantities of *all* its factors of production. That gives the firm opportunities it does not have in the short run. First, the firm can select the mix of factors it wishes to use. Should it choose a production process with lots of labor and not much capital, like the street sweepers in China? Or should it select a process that uses a great deal of capital and relatively little labor, like street sweepers in the United States? The second thing the firm can select is the scale (or overall size) of its operations. In the short run, a firm can increase output only by increasing its use of a variable factor. But in the long run, all factors are variable, so the firm can expand the use of all of its factors of production. The question facing the firm in the long run is: How much of an expansion or contraction in the scale of its operations should it undertake? Alternatively, it could choose to go out of business.

In its long-run planning, the firm not only regards all factors as variable, but it regards all costs as variable as well. There are no fixed costs in the long run. Because all costs are variable, the structure of costs in the long run differs somewhat from what we saw in the short run.

Choosing the Factor Mix

How shall a firm decide what mix of capital, labor, and other factors to use? We can apply the marginal decision rule to answer this question.

Suppose a firm uses capital and labor to produce a particular good. It must determine how to produce the good and the quantity it should produce. We'll address the question of how much the firm should produce in subsequent chapters, but certainly the firm will want to produce whatever quantity it chooses at as low a cost as possible. Another way of putting that goal is to say that the firm seeks the maximum output possible at every level of total cost.

At any level of total cost, the firm can vary its factor mix. It could, for example, substitute labor for capital in a way that leaves its total cost unchanged. In terms of the marginal decision rule, we can think of the firm as considering whether to spend an additional $1 on one factor, hence $1 less on another. The marginal decision rule says that a firm will shift spending among factors as long as the marginal benefit of such a shift exceeds the marginal cost.

What is the marginal benefit, say, of an additional $1 spent on capital? An additional unit of capital produces the marginal product of capital. To determine the marginal benefit of $1 spent on capital, we divide capital's marginal product by its price: MP_K/P_K. The price of capital is the "rent" paid for the use of a unit of capital for a given period. If the firm already owns the capital, then this rent is an opportunity cost; it represents the return the firm could get by renting the capital to another user or by selling it and earning interest on the money thus gained.

If capital and labor are the only factors, then spending an additional $1 on capital while holding total cost constant means taking $1 out of labor. The cost of that action will be the output lost from cutting back $1 worth of labor. That cost equals the ratio of the marginal product of labor to the price of labor, MP_L/P_L, where the price of labor is the wage.

Suppose that a firm's marginal product of labor is 15 and the price of labor is $5 per unit; the firm gains 3 units of output by spending an additional $1 on labor. Suppose further that the marginal product of capital is 50 and the price of capital is $50 per unit, so the firm would lose 1 unit of output by spending $1 less on capital. Thus,

$$\frac{MP_L}{P_L} > \frac{MP_K}{P_K}$$

$$\frac{15}{5} > \frac{50}{50}$$

The firm achieves a net gain of 2 units of output, without any change in cost, by transferring $1 from capital to labor. It will continue to transfer funds from capital to labor as long as it gains more output from the additional labor than it loses in output by reducing capital. As the firm shifts spending in this fashion, however, the marginal product of labor will fall and the marginal product of capital will rise. At some point, the ratios of marginal product to price will be equal for the two factors. At this point, the firm will obtain the maximum output possible for a given total cost:

$$\frac{MP_L}{P_L} = \frac{MP_K}{P_K} \tag{1}$$

Suppose that a firm that uses capital and labor is satisfying Equation (1) when suddenly the price of labor rises. At the current usage levels of the factors, a higher price of labor lowers the ratio of the marginal product of labor to the price of labor:

$$\frac{MP_L}{P_L} < \frac{MP_K}{P_K} \tag{2}$$

The firm will shift funds out of labor into capital. It will continue to shift from labor to capital until the ratios of marginal product to price are equal for the two factors. In general, a profit-maximizing firm will seek a combination of factors such that

$$\frac{MP_1}{P_1} = \frac{MP_2}{P_2} = \cdots = \frac{MP_n}{P_n} \tag{3}$$

When a firm satisfies the condition given in Equation (3) for efficient use, it produces the greatest possible output for a given cost. To put it another way, the firm achieves the lowest possible cost for a given level of output.

As the price of labor rises, the firm will shift to a factor mix that uses relatively more capital and relatively less labor. As a firm increases its ratio of capital to labor, we say it is becoming more **capital intensive.** A lower price for labor will lead the firm to use relatively more labor and less capital, reducing its ratio of capital to labor. As a firm reduces its ratio of capital to labor, we say it is becoming more **labor intensive**. The notions of labor-intensive and capital-intensive production are purely relative; they imply only that a firm has a higher or lower ratio of capital to labor. Sometimes economists speak of labor-intensive versus capital-intensive countries in the same manner.

Now that we understand how to apply the marginal decision rule to the problem of choosing the mix of factors, we can answer the question that began this chapter: Why does the United States employ a capital-intensive production process to clean streets while China chooses a labor-intensive process? Given that the same technology—know-how—is available, both countries could, after all, use the same production process. Suppose for a moment that the relative prices of labor and capital are the same in China and the United States. In that case, China and the United States can be expected to use the same method to clean streets. But the price of labor relative to the price of capital is, in fact, far lower in China than in the United States. A lower relative price for labor increases the ratio of the marginal product of labor to its price, making it efficient to substitute labor for capital. China thus finds it cheaper to clean streets with lots of people using brooms, while the United States finds it efficient to clean streets with large machines and relatively less labor.

Costs in the Long Run

As in the short run, costs in the long run depend on the firm's level of output, the costs of factors, and the quantities of factors needed for each level of output. The chief difference between long- and short-run costs is there are no fixed factors in the long run. There are thus no fixed costs. All costs are variable, so we do not distinguish between total variable cost and total cost in the long run: total cost *is* total variable cost.

The **long-run average cost (*LRAC*) curve** shows the firm's cost per unit at each level of output, assuming that all factors of production are variable. The *LRAC* curve assumes that the firm has chosen the optimal factor mix, as described in the previous section, for producing any level of output. The costs it shows are therefore the lowest costs possible for each level of output.

Exhibit 8-9 shows how a firm's *LRAC* curve is derived. Suppose Lifetime Disc Co. produces compact discs (CDs) using capital and labor. We have already seen how a firm's average total cost curve can be drawn in the short run for a given quantity of a particular factor of production, such as capital. In the short run, Lifetime Disc might be limited to operating with a given amount of capital; it would face one of the short-run average total cost curves shown in Exhibit 8-9. If it has 30 units of capital, for example, its average total cost curve is ATC_{30}. In the long run the firm can examine the average total cost curves associated with varying levels of capital. Four possible short-run average total cost curves for Lifetime Disc are shown in Exhibit 8-9 for quantities of capital from 20 to 50 units. The *LRAC* curve is derived from this set of short-run curves by finding the lowest average total cost associated with each level of output.

Exhibit 8-9

Relationship Between Short-Run and Long-Run Average Total Costs

The *LRAC* curve is found by taking the lowest average total cost curve at each level of output. Here, average total cost curves for quantities of capital of 20, 30, 40, and 50 units are shown for the Lifetime Disc Co. At a production level of 10,000 CDs per week, Lifetime minimizes its cost per CD by producing with 20 units of capital (point A). At 20,000 CDs per week, an expansion to a plant size associated with 30 units of capital minimizes cost per unit (point B). The lowest cost per unit is achieved with production of 30,000 CDs per week using 40 units of capital (point C). If Lifetime chooses to produce 40,000 CDs per week, it will do so most cheaply with 50 units of capital (point D).

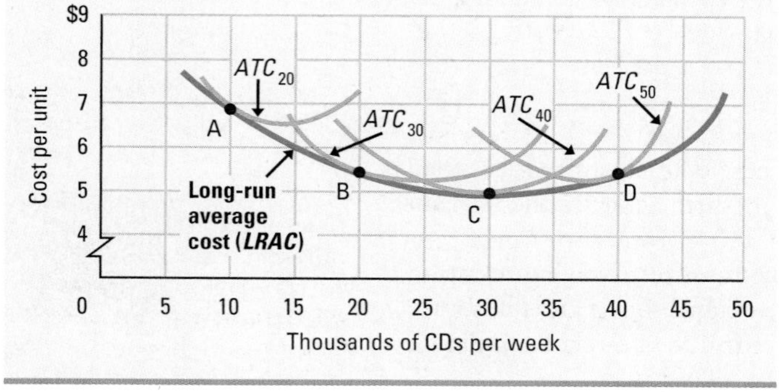

Economies and Diseconomies of Scale Notice that the long-run average cost curve in Exhibit 8-9 first slopes downward and then slopes upward. The shape of this curve tells us what is happening to average cost as the firm changes its scale of operations. A firm is said to experience **economies of scale** when long-run average cost declines as the firm expands its output. A firm is said to experience **diseconomies of scale** when long-run average cost increases as the firm expands its output. **Constant returns to scale** occur when long-run average cost stays the same over an output range.

Case in Point The *Maquiladoras*

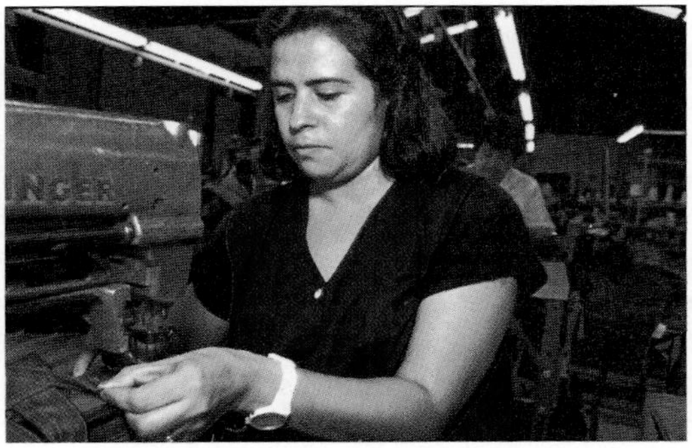

One implication of the marginal decision rule for factor use is that firms in countries where labor is relatively expensive, such as the United States, will use capital-intensive production methods. Less developed countries, where labor is relatively cheap, will use labor-intensive methods.

Some U.S. firms have it both ways. They complete part of the production process in the United States, using capital-intensive methods. They then ship the unfinished goods to *maquiladoras,* plants in Mexico where further processing is done using low-cost workers and labor-intensive methods. For example, many U.S. clothing manufacturers produce cloth at U.S. plants on large high-speed looms. They then ship the cloth to Mexico, where it is fashioned into clothing by workers using sewing machines. The resulting clothing items are shipped back to the United States, labeled "Assembled in Mexico from U.S. materials."

The *maquiladoras* have been a boon to workers in Mexico, who enjoy a higher demand for their services and receive higher wages as a result. The system also benefits the U.S. firms that participate and U.S. consumers who obtain less expensive goods than they would otherwise. It works because different factor prices imply different mixes of labor and capital. Companies are able to carry out the capital-intensive side of the production process in the United States and the labor-intensive side in Mexico.

Source: Lucinda Vargas, "El Paso's Labor Mismatch Dilemma," *Business Frontier* 1 (1998): 1–6.

Why would a firm experience economies of scale? One source of economies of scale is gains from specialization. As the scale of a firm's operation expands, it is able to use its factors in more specialized ways, increasing their productivity. Another source of economies of scale lies in the economies that can be gained from mass production methods. As the scale of a firm's operation expands, the company can begin to utilize large-scale machines and production systems that can substantially reduce cost per unit.

Why would a firm experience diseconomies of scale? At first glance, it might seem that the answer lies in the law of diminishing marginal returns, but this is not the case. The law of diminishing marginal returns, after all, tells us how output changes as a single factor is increased, with all other factors of production held constant. In contrast, diseconomies of scale describe a situation of rising average cost even when the firm is free to vary any or all of its factors as it wishes. Diseconomies of scale are generally thought to be caused by management problems. As the scale of a firm's operations expands, it becomes harder and harder for management to coordinate and guide the activities of individual units of the firm. Eventually, the diseconomies of management overwhelm any gains the firm might be achieving by operating with a larger scale of plant, and long-run average costs begin rising.

Firms experience constant returns to scale at output levels where there are neither economies nor diseconomies of scale. For the range of output over which the firm experiences constant returns to scale, the long-run average cost curve is horizontal.

Firms are likely to experience all three situations, as shown in Exhibit 8-10. At very low levels of output, the firm is likely to experience economies of scale as it expands the scale of its operations. There may follow a range of output over which the firm experiences constant returns to scale—empirical studies suggest that the range over which firms experience constant returns to scale is often very large. And certainly there must be some range of output over which diseconomies of scale occur; this phenomenon is one factor that limits the size of firms. A firm operating on the upward-sloping part of its *LRAC* curve is likely to be undercut in the market by smaller firms operating with lower costs per unit of output.

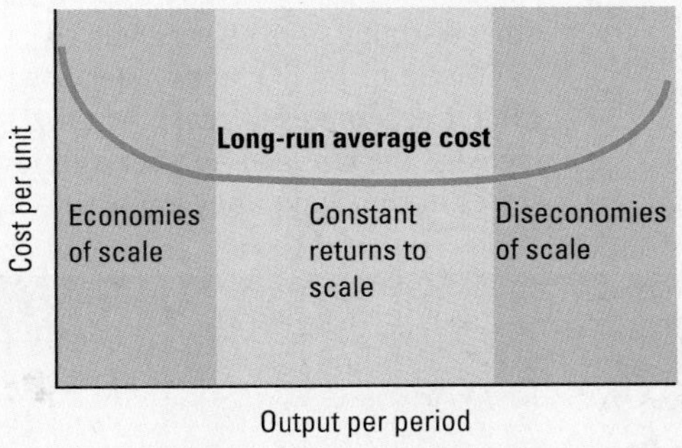

Exhibit 8-10

Economies and Diseconomies of Scale and Long-Run Average Cost

The downward-sloping region of the firm's *LRAC* curve is associated with economies of scale. There may be a horizontal range associated with constant returns to scale. The upward-sloping range of the curve implies diseconomies of scale.

The Size Distribution of Firms Economies and diseconomies of scale have a powerful effect on the sizes of firms that will operate in any market. Suppose firms in a particular industry experience diseconomies of scale at relatively low levels of output. That industry will be characterized by a large number of fairly small firms. The restaurant market appears to be such an industry. Barbers and beauticians are another example.

If firms in an industry experience economies of scale over a very wide range of output, firms that expand to take advantage of lower cost will force out smaller firms that have higher costs. Such industries are likely to have a few large firms instead of many small ones. In the refrigerator industry, for example, the size of firm necessary to achieve the lowest possible cost per unit is large enough to limit the market to only a few firms. In most cities, economies of scale leave room for only a single newspaper.

One factor that can limit the achievement of economies of scale is the demand facing an individual firm. The scale of output required to achieve the lowest unit costs possible may require sales that exceed the demand facing a firm. A grocery store, for example, could minimize unit costs with a large store and a large volume of sales. But the demand for groceries in a small, isolated community may not be able to sustain such a volume of sales. The firm is thus limited to a small scale of operation even though this might involve higher unit costs.

Case in Point Wal-Mart: Taking Advantage of Small Markets and Economies of Scale

When Sam Walton, the founder of Wal-Mart, died in 1992, he was the richest man in America. What did he know that other discount store owners didn't?

Discount retail chains appear to exhibit economies of scale. As they increase the size and number of retail stores in the chain, they enjoy substantial cost savings through high product turnover, low inventory, and more efficient management. Huge volume discounts on their merchandise reduce factor costs. So extensive are the apparent economies of scale that many discount retailers have taken the view that discount stores should locate in cities of over 100,000 people in order to justify the scale of operation.

Sam Walton disagreed. He believed that he could take advantage of Wal-Mart's falling long-run average cost curve by locating in relatively small communities. There, small mom-and-pop stores and medium-sized stores faced costs so high that he could easily undersell them, thereby attracting much of the retail business to Wal-Mart. But why didn't other retail chains follow in his path? The answer, which Sam Walton knew all along, was that many small communities were too small to support *two* big discount stores. There would not be enough business to justify such a large operation if the market were shared by more than one discount store. Sam Walton gambled that if he could beat the other retailers to the punch, he would prevent them from entering the market. By 1999, Wal-Mart had over 2,400 stores in operation and had emerged as the leading retail firm in the United States. Sam Walton gambled on his negatively sloped long-run average cost curve—and won!

Source: Robert S. Pindyck and Daniel L. Rubinfeld, *Microeconomics* (Englewood Cliffs, NJ: Prentice-Hall, 1995): pp. 475–476; http://www.walmart.com

Checklist

- A firm chooses its factor mix in the long run on the basis of the marginal decision rule; it seeks to equate the ratio of marginal product to price for all factors of production. By doing so, it minimizes the cost of producing a given level of output.
- The long-run average cost (*LRAC*) curve is derived from the average total cost curves associated with different quantities of the factor that is fixed in the short run. The *LRAC* curve shows the lowest cost per unit at which each quantity can be produced.
- A firm may experience economies of scale, constant returns to scale, or diseconomies of scale. Economies of scale imply a downward-sloping long-run average cost (*LRAC*) curve. Constant returns to scale imply a horizontal *LRAC* curve. Diseconomies of scale imply an upward-sloping *LRAC* curve.
- A firm's ability to exploit economies of scale is limited by the extent of market demand for its products.
- The range of output over which firms experience economies of scale, constant return to scale, or diseconomies of scale is an important determinant of how many firms will survive in a particular market.

Try It Yourself 8-3

a. *Suppose Acme Clothing is operating with 20 units of capital and producing 9 units of output at an average total cost of $67, as shown in Exhibit 8-8. How much labor is it using?*
b. *Suppose it finds that, with this combination of capital and labor,* $MP_K/P_K > MP_L/P_L$. *What adjustment will the firm make in the long run? Why doesn't it make this same adjustment in the short run?*

A Look Back

In this chapter we have concentrated on the production and cost relationships facing firms in the short run and in the long run.

In the short run, a firm has at least one factor of production that it cannot vary. This fixed factor limits the firm's range of factor choices. As a firm uses more and more of a variable factor (with fixed quantities of other factors of production), it is likely to experience at first increasing, then diminishing, then negative marginal returns. Thus, the short-run total cost curve has a positive value at a zero level of output (the firm's total fixed cost), then slopes upward at a decreasing rate (the range of increasing marginal returns), and then slopes upward at an increasing rate (the range of diminishing marginal returns).

In addition to short-run total product and total cost curves, we derived a firm's marginal product, average product, average total cost, average variable cost, average fixed cost, and marginal cost curves.

If the firm is to maximize profit in the long run, it must select the cost-minimizing combination of factors for its chosen level of output. Thus, the firm must try to use factors of production in accordance with the marginal decision rule. That is, it will use factors so that the ratio of marginal product to factor price is equal for all factors of production.

A firm's long-run average cost (*LRAC*) curve includes a range of economies of scale, over which the curve slopes downward, and a range of diseconomies of scale, over which the curve slopes upward. There may be an intervening range of output over which the firm experiences constant returns to scale; its *LRAC* curve will be horizontal over this range. The size of operations necessary to reach the lowest point on the *LRAC* curve has a great deal to do with determining the relative sizes of firms in an industry.

This chapter has focused on the nature of production processes and the costs associated with them. These ideas will prove useful in understanding the behavior of firms and the decisions they make concerning supply of goods and services.

A Look Ahead Our discussion of the basic tools of microeconomics ends with this chapter. We'll put our analyses of utility maximization and of production and cost to work in Parts Three and Four.

Terms and Concepts for Review

firms, **167**
short run, **167**
fixed factor of production, **167**
variable factor of production, **167**
long run, **168**
production function, **168**
total product curve, **168**
marginal product, **168**
marginal product of labor, **168**
average product, **168**
average product of labor, **168**
increasing marginal returns, **170**
diminishing marginal returns, **170**
negative marginal returns, **170**
law of diminishing marginal returns, **170**
variable costs, **172**
fixed costs, **172**
total variable cost, **172**
total fixed cost, **172**
total cost, **172**
average total cost, **174**
average variable cost, **174**
average fixed cost, **174**
capital intensive, **177**
labor intensive, **178**
long-run average cost curve, **178**
economies of scale, **178**
diseconomies of scale, **178**
constant returns to scale, **178**

For Discussion

1. Which of the following would be considered long-run choices? Which are short-run choices?
   a. A dentist hires a new part-time dental hygienist.
   b. The local oil refinery plans a complete restructuring of its production processes, including relocating the plant.
   c. A farmer increases the quantity of water applied to his or her fields.
   d. A law partnership signs a 3-year lease for an office complex.
   e. The university hires a new football coach on a 3-year contract.
2. "There are no fixed costs in the long run." Explain.
3. Business is booming at the local McDonald's restaurant. It is contemplating adding a new grill and french-fry machine. But the day supervisor suggests simply hiring more workers. How should the manager decide which alternative to pursue?
4. Suppose that the average age of students in your economics class is 23.7 years. If a new 19-year-old student enrolls in the class, will the average age in the class rise or fall? Explain how this relates to the relationship between average and marginal values.
5. Sammy Sosa's career home run average in his first nine years in major league baseball (through 1997) was 23 home runs per season. In 1998, he hit 66 home runs. What happened to his career home run average? How many home runs did he hit in 1999? (If you don't have access to the statistics, just pick a number, say, 60.) What effect did his performance in 1999 have on his career home run average? Explain how this relates to the relationship between average and marginal values.
6. Suppose a firm is operating at the minimum point of its short-run average total cost curve, so that marginal cost equals average total cost. Under what circumstances would it choose to alter the size of its plant? Explain.
7. What happens to the difference between average total cost and average variable cost as a firm's output expands? Explain.
8. How would each of the following affect average total cost, average variable cost, and marginal cost?

a. An increase in the cost of the lease of the firm's building
b. A reduction in the price of electricity
c. A reduction in wages
d. A change in the salary of the president of the company

9. Consider the following types of firms. For each one, the long-run average cost curve eventually exhibits diseconomies of scale. For which firms would you expect diseconomies of scale to set in at relatively low levels of output? Why?
   a. A copy shop
   b. A hardware store
   c. A dairy
   d. A newspaper
   e. An automobile manufacturer
   f. A restaurant

10. As car manufacturers incorporate more sophisticated computer technology in their vehicles, auto-repair shops require computerized testing equipment, which is quite expensive, in order to repair newer cars. How is this likely to affect the shape of these firms' long-run average total cost curves? How is it likely to affect the number of auto-repair firms in any market?

Problems

1. Suppose a firm is producing 1,000 units of output. Its average fixed costs are $100. Its average variable costs are $50. What is the total cost of producing 1,000 units of output?
2. The director of a nonprofit foundation that sponsors 8-week summer institutes for graduate students analyzed the costs and expected revenues for the next summer institute and recommended that the session be canceled. In her analysis she included a share of the foundation's overhead—the salaries of the director and staff and costs of maintaining the office—to the program. She estimated costs and revenues as follows:

Projected revenues (from tuition and fees)	$300,000
Projected costs	
Overhead	$ 50,000
Room and board for students	$100,000
Costs for faculty and miscellaneous	$175,000
Total costs	$325,000

   What was the error in the director's recommendation?
3. The average total cost for printing 10,000 copies of an issue of a magazine is $0.45 per copy. For 20,000 copies, the average total cost is $0.35 apiece; for 30,000, the average total cost is $0.30 per copy. The average total cost continues to decline slightly over every level of output that the publishers of the magazine have considered. Sketch the approximate shapes of the average and marginal cost curves. What are some variable costs of publishing magazines? Some fixed costs?
4. Suppose a firm finds that the marginal product of capital is 60 and the marginal product of labor is 20. If the price of capital is $6 and the price of labor is $2.50, how should the firm adjust its mix of capital and labor? What will be the result?

Answers to Try It Yourself Problems

Try It Yourself 8-1

Units of labor per day	0	1	2	3	4	5	6	7	8
Jackets per day	0	2	5.5	9.5	12	14	15	15.5	15
Marginal product		2	3.5	4.0	2.5	2.0	1.0	0.5	−0.5
Average product		2	2.75	3.17	3	2.8	2.5	2.21	1.88

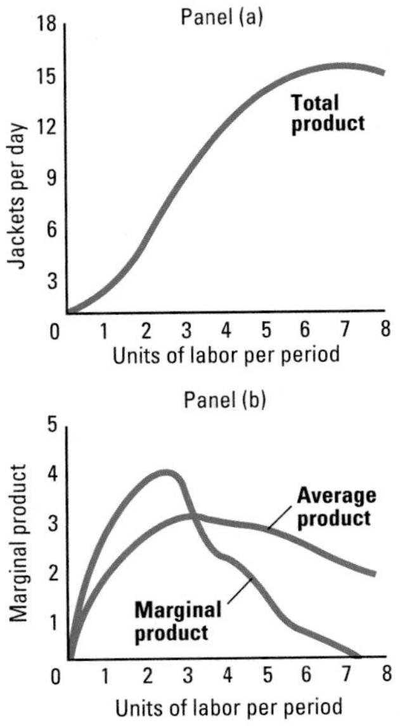

Try It Yourself 8-2

The increased wage will shift the total variable cost curve upward; the old and new points and the corresponding curves are shown at the right.

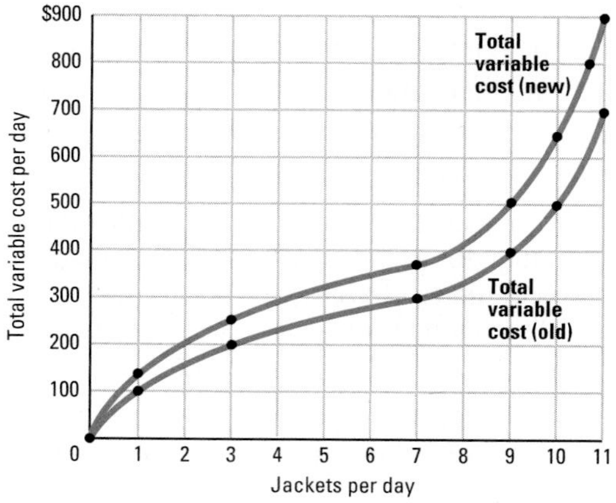

The total variable cost curve has shifted upward because the cost of labor, Acme's variable factor, has increased. The marginal cost curve shows the additional cost of each additional unit of output a firm produces. Because an increase in output requires more labor, and because labor now costs more, the marginal cost curve will shift upward. The increase in total variable cost will increase total cost; average total and average variable costs will rise as well. Average fixed cost will not change.

Try It Yourself 8-3

a. To produce 9 jackets, Acme uses 4 units of labor.

b. In the long run, Acme will substitute capital for labor. It cannot make this adjustment in the short run because its capital is fixed in the short run.

9 Competitive Markets for Goods and Services

Getting Started: Life on the Farm

They produce a commodity that is essential to our daily lives, one for which the demand is virtually assured. And yet many seem to live on the margin of failure—thousands are driven out of business each year. We provide billions of dollars in aid for them, but still we hear of the hardships they face. They are our nation's farmers.

What is it about farmers, and farming, that arouses our concern? Much of the answer probably lies in our sense that farming is fundamental to the American way of life. Our country was built, in large part, by independent men and women who made their living from the soil. Many of us perceive their plight as our plight. But part of the answer lies in the fact that farmers do, in fact, face a difficult economic environment. Most of them operate in highly competitive markets, markets that tolerate few mistakes and generally offer small rewards. Finally, perhaps our concern is stirred by our recognition that the farmers' plight is our blessing. The low prices that make life difficult for farmers are the low prices we enjoy as consumers of food.

What keeps the prices of farm goods so low? What holds many farmers in a situation in which they always seem to be just getting by? In this chapter we shall see that prices just high enough to induce firms to continue to produce are precisely what we would expect to prevail in a competitive market. We'll examine a model of how competitive markets work. Not only does this model help to explain the situation facing farmers, but it will also help us to understand the determination of price and output in a wide range of markets. A farm is a firm, and our analysis of such a firm in a competitive market will give us the tools to analyze the choices of all firms operating in competitive markets.

We'll put the concepts of marginal cost, average variable cost, and average total cost we developed in the last chapter to work to see how firms in a competitive market respond to market forces. We'll see how firms adjust to changes in demand and supply in the short run and in the long run. In all of this, we'll be examining how firms use the marginal decision rule that we introduced in Chapter 6.

The competitive model introduced in this chapter lies at one end of a spectrum of market models. At the other end is the monopoly model, which we'll examine in the next chapter. It assumes a market in which there is no competition, a market in which only a single firm operates. Then, in Chapter 11, we'll look at two models that fall between the extremes of perfect competition and monopoly.

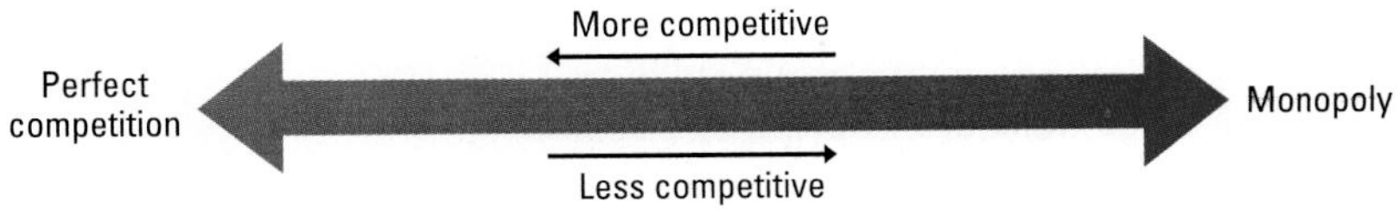

Perfect Competition: A Model

Virtually all firms in a market economy face competition from other firms. In this chapter, we'll be working with a model of a highly idealized form of competition called "perfect" by economists.

Perfect competition is a model of the market based on the assumption that a large number of firms produce identical goods consumed by a large number of buyers. The model of perfect competition also assumes that it's easy for new firms to enter the market and for existing ones to leave. And finally, it assumes that buyers and sellers have complete information about market conditions.

As we examine these assumptions in greater detail, we'll see that they allow us to work with the model more easily. No market fully meets the conditions set out in these assumptions. As is always the case with models, our purpose is to understand the way things work, not to describe them. And the model of perfect competition will prove enormously useful in understanding the world of markets.

Assumptions of the Model

The assumptions of the model of perfect competition, taken together, imply that individual buyers and sellers in a perfectly competitive market accept the market price as given. No one buyer or seller has any influence over that price. Individuals or firms who must take the market price as given are called **price takers.** A consumer or firm that takes the market price as given has no ability to influence that price. A price-taking firm or consumer is like an individual who's buying or selling stocks. He or she looks up the market price and buys or sells at that price. The price is determined by demand and supply in the market—not by individual buyers or sellers. In a perfectly competitive market, each firm and each consumer is a price taker. A price-taking consumer assumes that he or she can purchase any quantity at the market price—without affecting that price. Similarly, a price-taking firm assumes it can sell whatever quantity it wishes at the market price without affecting the price.

You're a price taker when you go into a store. You observe the prices listed and make a choice to buy or not. Your choice won't affect that price. Should you sell a textbook back to your campus bookstore at the end of a course, you are a price-taking seller. You're confronted by a market price and you decide whether to sell or not. Your decision won't affect that price.

To see how the assumptions of the model of perfect competition imply price-taking behavior, let us examine each of them in turn.

Identical Goods In a perfectly competitive market for a good or service, one unit of the good or service cannot be differentiated from any other on any basis. A bushel of, say, hard winter wheat is an example. A bushel produced by one farmer is identical to that produced by another. There are no brand preferences or consumer loyalties.

The assumption that goods are identical is necessary if firms are to be price takers. If one farmer's wheat were perceived as having special properties that distinguished it from other wheat, then that farmer would have some power over its price. By assuming that all goods and services produced by firms in a perfectly competitive market are identical, we establish a necessary condition for price-taking behavior. Economists sometimes say that the goods or services in a perfectly competitive market are ***homogeneous***, meaning that they are all alike. There are no brand differences in a perfectly competitive market.

A Large Number of Buyers and Sellers How many buyers and sellers are in our market? The answer rests on our presumption of price-taking behavior. There are so many buyers and sellers that none of the buyers or sellers have any influence on the market price regardless of how much they purchase or sell. A firm in a perfectly competitive market can react to prices, but cannot affect the prices it pays for the factors of production or the prices it receives for its output.

Ease of Entry and Exit The assumption that it's easy for other firms to enter a perfectly competitive market implies an even greater degree of competition. Firms in a market must deal not only with the large number of competing firms but with the possibility that still more firms might enter the market.

Later in this chapter, we'll see how ease of entry is related to the sustainability of economic profits. If entry is easy, then the promise of high economic profits will quickly attract new firms. If entry is difficult, it won't.

The model of perfect competition assumes easy exit as well as easy entry. The assumption of easy exit strengthens the assumption of easy entry. Suppose a firm is considering entering a particular market. Entry may be easy, but suppose that getting out is difficult. For example, suppliers of factors of production to firms in the industry might be happy to accommodate new firms but might require that they sign long-term contracts. Such contracts could make leaving the market difficult and costly. If that were the case, a firm might be hesitant to enter in the first place. Easy exit helps make entry easier.

Complete Information We assume that all sellers have complete information about prices, technology, and all other knowledge relevant to the operation of the market. No one seller has any information about production methods that isn't available to all other sellers. If one seller had an advantage over other sellers, perhaps special information about a lower-cost production method, then that seller could exert some control over market price—the seller would no longer be a price taker.

We assume also that buyers know the prices offered by every seller. If buyers didn't know about prices offered by different firms in the market, then a firm might be able to sell a good or service for a price other than the market price and thus could avoid being a price taker.

The availability of information that is assumed in the model of perfect competition implies that information can be obtained at low cost. If consumers and firms can obtain information at low cost, they're likely to do so. Information about the marketplace may come over the internet, over the airways in a television commercial, or over a cup of coffee with a friend. Whatever its source, we assume that its low cost ensures that consumers and firms have enough of it so that everyone buys or sells goods and services at market prices determined by the intersection of demand and supply curves.

The assumptions of the perfectly competitive model ensure that each buyer or seller is a price taker. The market, not individual consumers or firms, determines price in the model of perfect competition. No individual has enough power in a perfectly competitive market to have any impact on that price.

Perfect Competition and the Real World

The assumptions of identical products, a large number of buyers, easy entry and exit, and perfect information are strong assumptions. The notion that firms must sit back and let the market determine price seems to fly in the face of what we know about most real firms, which is that firms customarily do set prices. Yet this is the basis for the model of demand and supply, the power of which you've already seen.

When we use the model of demand and supply, we assume that market forces determine prices. In this model, buyers and sellers respond to the market price. They are price takers. The assumptions of the model of perfect competition underlie the assumption of price-taking behavior. Thus we are using the model of perfect competition whenever we apply the model of demand and supply.

As we've seen, the model of demand and supply allows us to understand a wide range of market outcomes. In Chapter 3, we used the model to examine the market for coffee. In Chapter 4 we used it to explain the determination of prices in the stock market and the remarkable fall in prices and increase in quantity in the market for computers. We've put the demand and supply model to work to examine the effects of price floors, such as agricultural price supports, and of price ceilings, such as rent controls.

We can understand most markets by applying the model of demand and supply. Even though those markets don't fulfill all the assumptions of the model of perfect competition, the model allows us to understand some key features of these markets.

Changes within your lifetime have made many markets more competitive. Falling costs of transportation, together with dramatic advances in telecommunications, have opened the

Case in Point A Price Taker's Lament

Bill Adams can tell you what life for a price-taking firm is like. He runs one.

Mr. Adams is president of Associated Sales, a Phoenix firm that sells household appliances to builders of custom homes. A homebuilder who wants to include a built-in refrigerator, for example, might order it from Mr. Adams's firm. The firm is a small one, with $2 million in annual sales.

After more than 20 years in business, Mr. Adams knows exactly how his prices are set. "The market tells us what we can sell a product for," he says. "Our customers want to know two things: the price and whether you can get the merchandise to them on time. And the primary factor is the price."

As president of his own company, Mr. Adams can charge any price he wants. But he has lots of competitors from which his customers can choose. If his prices drift above those of his rivals, he won't make sales. The items he sells, such as top-of-the-line refrigerators and stoves, are typically quite expensive. But even the smallest deviation of his price from the market's can doom him.

"If I could raise the price of every item I sold by $10, I'd be in good shape. But I can't," he says.

Of course, Mr. Adams could charge a lower price than his rivals. But he says that he's barely making a profit now—a lower price would create sales, but he'd suffer major losses.

As long as Mr. Adams's firm charges the market price for the items he sells, he can compete with his rivals and make sales. A highly competitive marketplace for his product makes him a price taker.

Source: Personal interview.

possibility of entering markets to firms all over the world. A company in South Korea can compete in the market for steel in the United States. A furniture maker in New Mexico can compete in the market for furniture in Japan. A firm can enter the world market simply by creating a web page to advertise its products and to take orders.

In the remaining sections of this chapter, we'll learn more about the response of firms to market prices. We'll see how firms respond, in the short run and in the long run, to changes in demand and to changes in production costs. In short, we'll be examining the forces that constitute the supply side of the model of demand and supply.

We'll also see how competitive markets work to serve consumer interests and how competition acts to push economic profits down, sometimes eliminating them entirely. When we've finished we'll have a better understanding of the market conditions facing farmers and of the conditions that prevail in any competitive industry.

Checklist

- The central characteristic of the model of perfect competition is the fact that price is determined by demand and supply; buyers and sellers are price takers.
- The model assumes a large number of firms producing identical (homogeneous) goods or services, a large number of buyers and sellers, easy entry and exit in the industry, and complete information about prices in the market.
- The model of perfect competition underlies the model of demand and supply.

Output Determination in the Short Run

Our goal in this section is to see how a firm in a perfectly competitive market determines its output level in the short run—a planning period in which at least one factor is fixed in quantity. We shall see that the firm can maximize economic profit by applying the marginal decision rule and increasing output up to the point at which the marginal benefit of an additional unit of output is just equal to the marginal cost. This fact has an important implication: Over a wide range of output, the firm's marginal cost curve is its supply curve.

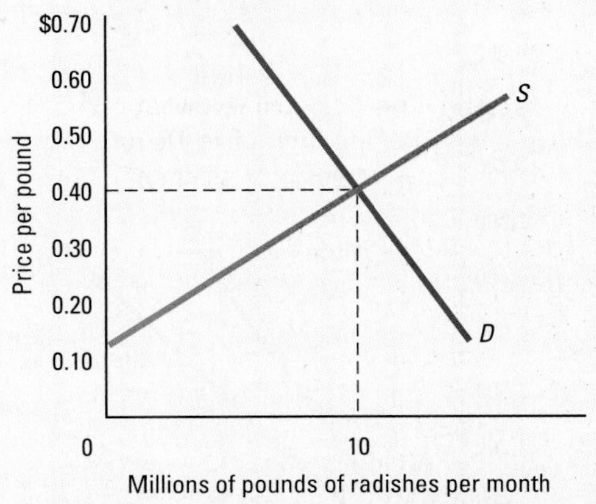

Exhibit 9-1

The Market for Radishes

Price and output in a competitive market are determined by demand and supply. In the market for radishes, the equilibrium price is $0.40 per pound; 10 million pounds per month are produced and purchased at this price.

Price and Revenue

Each firm in a perfectly competitive market is a price taker; the equilibrium price and industry output are determined by demand and supply. Exhibit 9-1 shows how demand and supply in the market for radishes, which we shall assume are produced under conditions of perfect competition, determine total output and price. The equilibrium price is $0.40 per pound; the equilibrium quantity is 10 million pounds per month.

Because it is a price taker, each firm in the radish industry assumes it can sell all the radishes it wants at a price of $0.40 per pound. No matter how many or how few radishes it produces, the firm expects to sell them all at the market price.

The assumption that the firm expects to sell all the radishes it wants at the market price is crucial. If a firm didn't expect to sell all of its radishes at the market price—if it had to lower the price to sell some quantities—the firm wouldn't be a price taker. And price-taking behavior is central to the model of perfect competition.

Radish growers—and perfectly competitive firms in general—have no reason to charge a price lower than the market price. Because buyers have complete information and because we assume each firm's product is identical to that of its rivals, firms are unable to charge a price higher than the market price. For perfectly competitive firms, the price is very much like the weather: They may complain about it, but in perfect competition there isn't anything any of them can do about it.

Total Revenue While a firm in a perfectly competitive market has no influence over its price, it does determine the output it will produce. In selecting the quantity of that output, one important consideration is the revenue the firm will gain by producing it.

A firm's **total revenue** is found by multiplying its output by the price at which it sells that output. For a perfectly competitive firm, total revenue (*TR*) is the market price (*P*) times the quantity the firm produces (*Q*), or

$$TR = P \times Q \qquad (1)$$

The relationship between market price and the firm's total revenue curve is a crucial one. Panel (a) of Exhibit 9-2 shows total revenue curves for a radish grower at three possible market prices: $0.20, $0.40, and $0.60 per pound. Each total revenue curve is a linear, upward-sloping curve. At any price, the greater the quantity a perfectly competitive firm sells, the greater its total revenue. Notice that, the greater the price, the steeper the total revenue curve is.

Price, Marginal Revenue, and Average Revenue The slope of a total revenue curve is particularly important. It equals the change in the vertical axis (total revenue) divided by the change in the horizontal axis (quantity) between any two points. The slope measures the rate at which total revenue increases as output increases. We can think of it as the increase in total revenue associated with a 1-unit increase in output. The increase in total revenue from a 1-unit increase in quantity is **marginal revenue.** Thus marginal revenue (*MR*) equals the slope of the total revenue curve.

How much additional revenue does a radish producer gain from selling one more pound of radishes? The answer, of course, is the market price for 1 pound. Marginal revenue equals

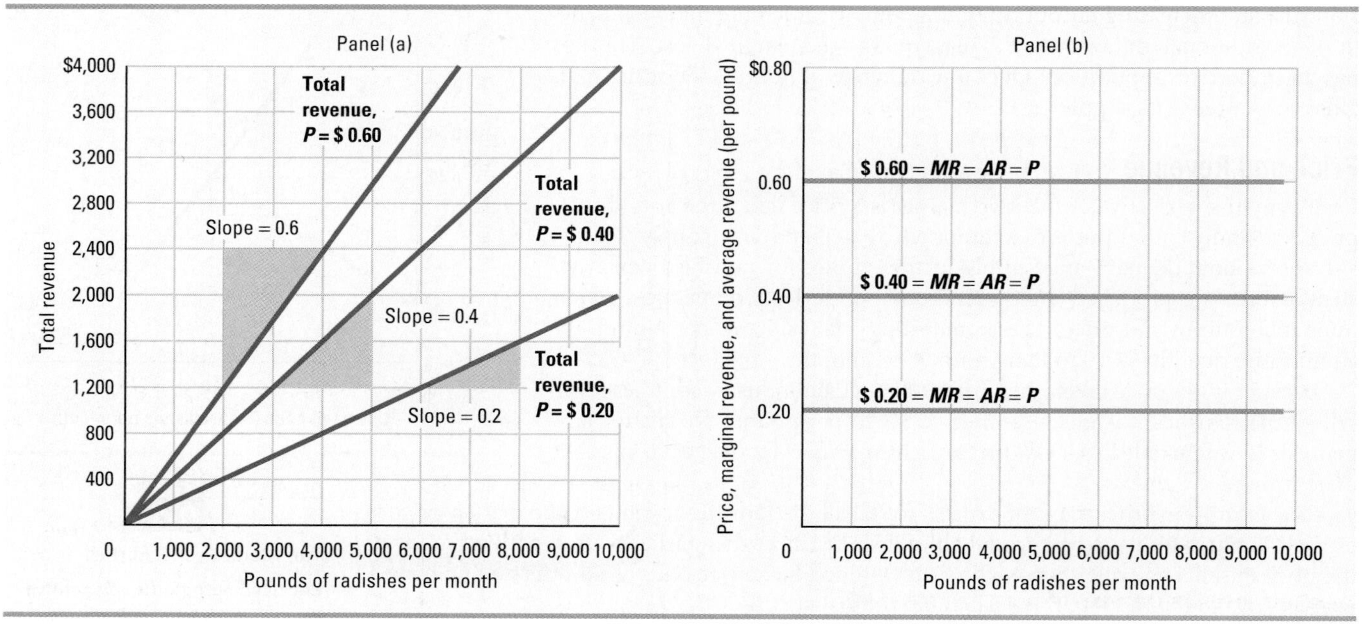

Exhibit 9-2

Total Revenue, Marginal Revenue, and Average Revenue

Panel (a) shows different total revenue curves for three possible market prices in perfect competition. A total revenue curve is a straight line coming out of the origin. The slope of a total revenue curve is *MR*; it equals the market price (*P*) and *AR* in perfect competition. Marginal revenue and average revenue are thus a single horizontal line at the market price, as shown in Panel (b). There is a different marginal revenue curve for each price.

the market price. Because the market price is not affected by the output choice of a single firm, the marginal revenue the firm gains by producing one more unit is always the market price. The marginal revenue curve shows the relationship between marginal revenue and the quantity a firm produces. For a perfectly competitive firm, the marginal revenue curve is a horizontal line at the market price. If the market price of a pound of radishes is $0.40, then the marginal revenue is $0.40. Marginal revenue curves for prices of $0.20, $0.40, and $0.60 are given in Panel (b) of Exhibit 9-2. In perfect competition, a firm's marginal revenue curve is a horizontal line at the market price.

Price also equals **average revenue,** which is total revenue divided by quantity. Equation (1) gives total revenue, *TR*. To obtain average revenue (*AR*), we divide total revenue by quantity, *Q*. Because total revenue equals price (*P*) times quantity (*Q*), dividing by quantity leaves us with price.

$$AR = \frac{TR}{Q} = \frac{P \times Q}{Q} = P \tag{2}$$

The marginal revenue curve is a horizontal line at the market price, and average revenue equals the market price. The average and marginal revenue curves are given by the same horizontal line. This is consistent with what we've learned about the relationship between marginal and average values. In Chapter 8, for example, we saw in the case of marginal and average products that when the marginal value exceeds the average value, the average value will be rising. When the marginal value is less than the average value, the average value will be falling. What happens when the average and marginal values don't change, as in the horizontal curves of Panel (b) of Exhibit 9-2? The marginal value must equal the average value; the two curves coincide.

Marginal Revenue, Price, and Demand for the Perfectly Competitive Firm We've seen that a perfectly competitive firm's marginal revenue curve is simply a horizontal line at the market price and that this same line is also the firm's average revenue curve. For the perfectly competitive firm, $MR = P = AR$. The marginal revenue curve has another meaning as well. It is the demand curve facing a perfectly competitive firm.

Consider the case of a single radish producer, Tony Gortari. We assume that the radish market is perfectly competitive; Mr. Gortari runs a perfectly competitive firm. Suppose the market price of radishes is $0.40 per pound. How many pounds of radishes can Mr. Gortari sell at this price? The answer comes from our assumption that he is a price taker: He can sell *any* quantity he wishes at this price. How many pounds of radishes will he sell if he charges a price that exceeds the market price? None. His radishes are identical to those of every other firm in the market, and everyone in the market has complete information. That means the demand curve facing Mr. Gortari is a horizontal line at the market price as illustrated in Exhibit 9-3. Notice that the curve is labeled *d* to distinguish it from the market demand curve, *D*, in Exhibit 9-1. The horizontal line in Exhibit 9-3 is also Mr. Gortari's marginal revenue curve, *MR*, and his average revenue curve, *AR*. It is also the market price, *P*.

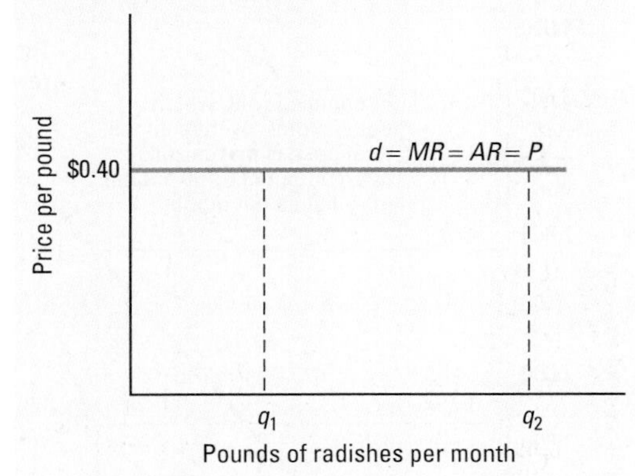

Exhibit 9-3

Price, Marginal Revenue, and Demand

A perfectly competitive firm faces a horizontal demand curve at the market price. Here, radish grower Tony Gortari faces demand curve *d* at the market price of $0.40 per pound. He could sell q_1 or q_2—or any other quantity—at a price of $0.40 per pound.

Of course, Mr. Gortari could charge a price below the market price, but why would he? We assume he can sell all the radishes he wants at the market price; there would be no reason to charge a lower price. Mr. Gortari faces a demand curve that is a horizontal line at the market price. In our subsequent analysis, we shall refer to the horizontal line at the market price simply as marginal revenue. We should remember, however, that this same line gives us the market price, average revenue, and the demand curve facing the firm.

More generally, we can say that *any* perfectly competitive firm faces a horizontal demand curve at the market price. We saw an example of a horizontal demand curve in Chapter 5. Such a curve is perfectly elastic, meaning that any quantity is demanded at a given price.

Economic Profit in the Short Run

A firm's economic profit is the difference between total revenue and total cost. Recall that total cost is the opportunity cost of producing a certain good or service. When we speak of economic profit we are speaking of a firm's total revenue less the total opportunity cost of its operations.

In Chapter 8 we found that a firm's total cost curve in the short run intersects the vertical axis at some positive value equal to the firm's total fixed costs. Total cost then rises at a decreasing rate over the range of increasing marginal returns to the firm's variable factors. It rises at an increasing rate over the range of diminishing marginal returns. Exhibit 9-4 shows the total cost curve for Mr. Gortari, as well as the total revenue curve for a price of $0.40 per pound. Suppose that his total fixed cost is $400 per month. Mr. Gortari's economic profit is the vertical distance between the total revenue curve and the total cost curve.

Let's examine the total revenue and total cost curves in Exhibit 9-4 more carefully. At zero units of output, Mr. Gortari's total cost is $400 (his total fixed cost); total revenue is zero. Total cost continues to exceed total revenue up to an output of 3,300 pounds per month, at which point the two curves intersect. At this point, economic profit equals zero. As Mr. Gortari expands output above 3,300 pounds per month, total revenue becomes greater than total cost. We see that at a quantity of 3,300 pounds per month, the total revenue curve is steeper than the total cost curve. Because revenues are rising faster than costs, profits rise with increased output. As long as the total revenue curve is steeper than the total cost curve, profit increases as the firm increases its output.

The total revenue curve's slope doesn't change as the firm increases its output. But the total cost curve becomes steeper and steeper as diminishing marginal returns set in. Eventually, the total cost and total revenue curves will have the same slope. That happens in Exhibit 9-4 at an output of 6,700 pounds of radishes per month. Notice that a line drawn tangent to the total cost curve at that quantity has the same slope as the total revenue curve.

As output increases beyond 6,700 pounds, the total cost curve continues to become steeper. It becomes steeper than the total revenue curve, and profits fall as costs rise faster

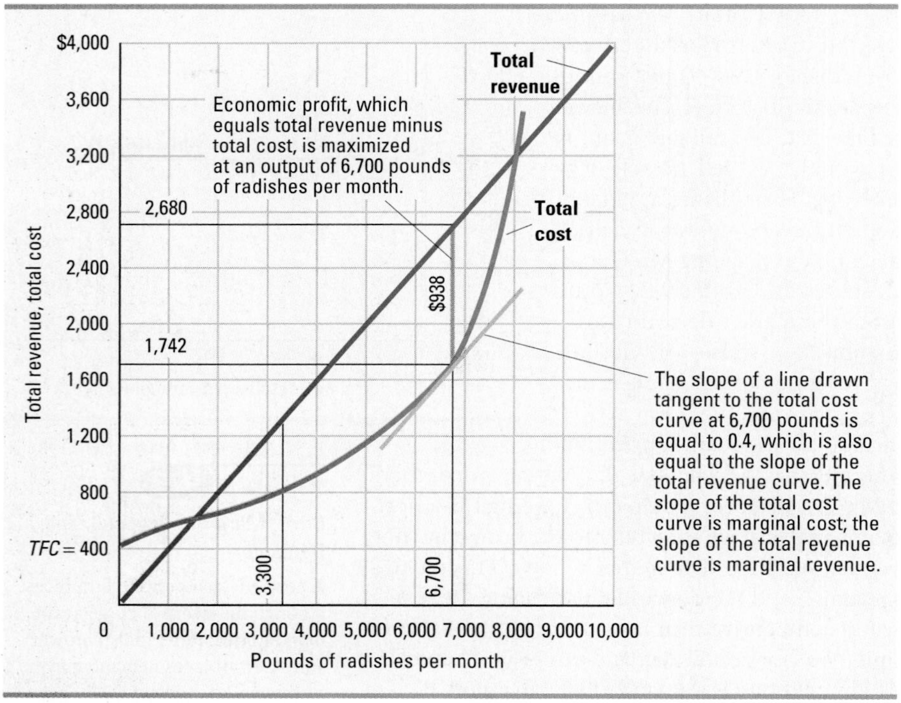

Exhibit 9-4

Total Revenue, Total Cost, and Economic Profit

Economic profit is the vertical distance between the total revenue and total cost curves (revenue minus costs). Here, the maximum profit attainable by Tony Gortari for his radish production is $938 per month at an output of 6,700 pounds.

than revenues. At an output slightly above 8,000 pounds per month, the total revenue and cost curves intersect again, and economic profit equals zero. Mr. Gortari achieves the greatest profit possible by producing 6,700 pounds of radishes per month, the quantity at which the total cost and total revenue curves have the same slope. More generally, we can conclude that a perfectly competitive firm maximizes economic profit at the output level at which the total revenue curve and the total cost curve have the same slope.

Applying the Marginal Decision Rule

The slope of the total revenue curve is marginal revenue; the slope of the total cost curve is marginal cost. Economic profit, the difference between total revenue and total cost, is maximized where marginal revenue equals marginal cost. This is consistent with the marginal decision rule, which holds that a profit-maximizing firm should increase output until the marginal benefit of an additional unit equals the marginal cost. The marginal benefit of selling an additional unit is measured as marginal revenue. Finding the output at which marginal revenue equals marginal cost is thus an application of our marginal decision rule.

Exhibit 9-5 shows how a firm can use the marginal decision rule to determine its profit-maximizing output. Panel (a) shows the market for radishes; the market demand curve (*D*), and supply curve (*S*) that we had in Exhibit 9-1; the market price is $0.40 per pound. In Panel (b), the *MR* curve is given by a horizontal line at the market price. The firm's marginal cost curve (*MC*) intersects the marginal revenue curve at the point where profit is maximized. Mr. Gortari maximizes profits by producing 6,700 pounds of radishes per month. That is, of course, the result we obtained in Exhibit 9-4, where we saw that the firm's total revenue and total cost curves differ by the greatest amount at the point at which the slopes of the curves, which equal marginal revenue and marginal cost, respectively, are equal.

We can use the graph in Exhibit 9-5 to compute Mr. Gortari's economic profit. **Economic profit per unit** is the difference between price and average total cost. At the profit-maximizing output of 6,700 pounds of radishes per month, average total cost (*ATC*) is $0.26 per pound, as shown in Panel (b). Price is $0.40 per pound, so economic profit per unit is $0.14. Economic profit is found by multiplying economic profit per unit by the number of units produced; the firm's economic profit is thus $938 ($0.14 × 6,700). It is shown graphically by the area of the shaded rectangle in Panel (b); this area equals the vertical distance between total revenue and total cost at an output of 6,700 pounds of radishes times the number of pounds of radishes produced, 6,700, in Exhibit 9-5.

Economic Losses in the Short Run

In the short run, a firm has one or more inputs whose quantities are fixed. That means that in the short run the firm can't leave its industry. Even if it cannot cover *all* of its costs, including both its variable and fixed costs, going entirely out of business is not an option in the short run. The firm may close its doors, but it must continue to pay its fixed costs. It is forced to accept an **economic loss,** the amount by which its total cost exceeds its total revenue.

Suppose, for example, that a manufacturer has signed a 1-year lease on some equipment. It must make payments for this equipment during the term of its lease, whether it produces anything or not. During the period of the lease, the payments represent a fixed cost for the firm.

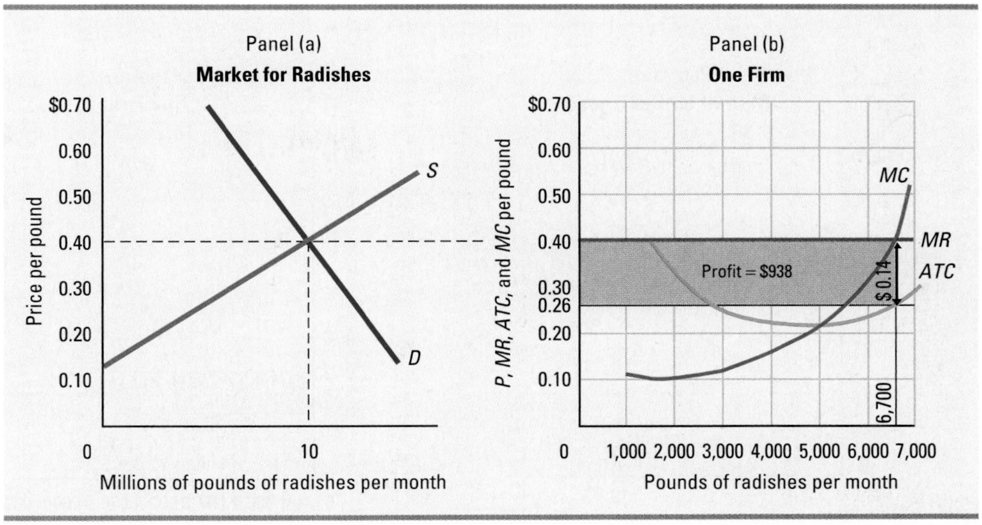

Exhibit 9-5

Applying the Marginal Decision Rule

The market price is determined by the intersection of demand and supply. As always, the firm maximizes profit by applying the marginal decision rule. It takes the market price, $0.40 per pound, as given and selects an output at which *MR* equals *MC*. Economic profit per unit is the difference between *ATC* and price (here, $0.14 per pound); economic profit is profit per unit times the quantity produced ($0.14 × 6,700 = $938).

A firm that is experiencing economic losses—whose economic profits have become negative—in the short run may either continue to produce or shut down its operations, reducing its output to zero. It will choose the option that minimizes its losses. The crucial test of whether to operate or shut down lies in the relationship between price and average variable cost.

Producing to Minimize Economic Loss Suppose the demand for radishes falls to D_2, as shown in Panel (a) of Exhibit 9-6. The market price for radishes plunges to $0.18 per pound, which is below average total cost. Consequently Mr. Gortari experiences negative economic profits—a loss. Although the new market price falls short of average total cost, it still exceeds average variable cost, shown in Panel (b) as *AVC*. Therefore, Mr. Gortari should continue to produce an output at which marginal cost equals marginal revenue. These curves (labeled *MC* and MR_2) intersect in Panel (b) at an output of 4,444 pounds of radishes per month.

Caution!

Look carefully at the rectangle that shows economic profit in Panel (b) of Exhibit 9-5. It is found by taking the profit-maximizing quantity, 6,700 pounds, then reading up to the *ATC* curve and the firm's demand curve at the market price. Economic profit per unit equals price minus average total cost (*P* – *ATC*).

The firm's economic profit equals economic profit per unit times the quantity produced. It is found by extending horizontal lines from the *ATC* and *MR* curves to the vertical axis and taking the area of the rectangle formed.

There is no reason for the profit-maximizing quantity to correspond to the lowest point on the *ATC* curve; it does not in this case. Students sometimes make the mistake of calculating economic profit as the difference between the price and the lowest point on the *ATC* curve. That gives us the maximum economic profit per unit, but we assume that firms maximize economic profit, not economic profit per unit. The firm's economic profit equals economic profit per unit times quantity. The quantity that maximizes economic profit is determined by the intersection of *MC* and *MR*.

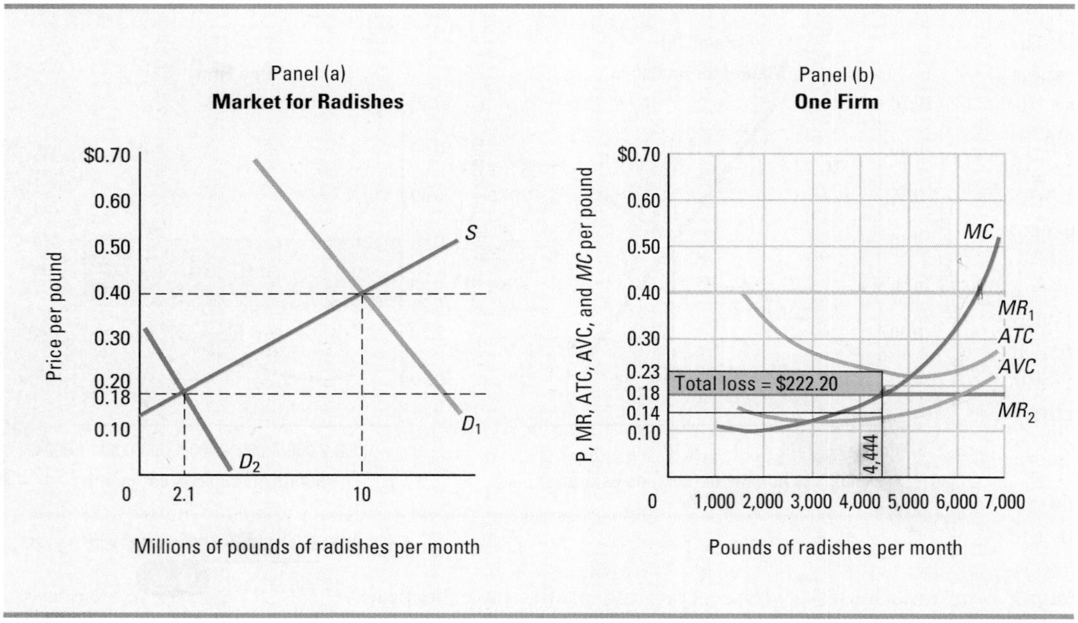

Exhibit 9-6

Suffering Economic Losses in the Short Run

Tony Gortari experiences a loss when price drops below *ATC*, as it does in Panel (b) as a result of a reduction in demand. If price is above *AVC*, however, he can minimize his losses by producing where *MC* equals MR_2. Here, that occurs at an output of 4,444 pounds of radishes per month. The price is $0.18 per pound, and average total cost is $0.23 per pound. He loses $0.05 per pound, or $222.20 per month.

When producing 4,444 pounds of radishes per month, Mr. Gortari faces an average total cost of $0.23 per pound. At a price of $0.18 per pound, he loses a nickel on each pound produced. Total economic losses at an output of 4,444 pounds per month are thus $222.20 per month (= $4,444 × $0.05).

No producer likes a loss (that is, negative economic profit), but the loss solution shown in Exhibit 9-6 is the best Mr. Gortari can attain. Any level of production other than the one at which marginal cost equals marginal revenue would produce even greater losses.

Suppose Mr. Gortari were to shut down and produce no radishes. Ceasing production would reduce variable costs to zero, but he would still face fixed costs of $400 per month (recall that $400 was the vertical intercept of the total cost curve in Exhibit 9-4). By shutting down, Mr. Gortari would lose $400 per month. By continuing to produce, he loses $222.20.

Mr. Gortari is better off producing where marginal cost equals marginal revenue because at that output price exceeds average variable cost. Average variable cost is $0.14 per pound, so by continuing to produce he covers his variable costs, with $0.04 per pound left over to apply to fixed costs. Whenever price is greater than average variable cost, the firm maximizes economic profit (or minimizes economic loss) by producing the output level at which marginal revenue and marginal cost curves intersect.

Shutting Down to Minimize Economic Loss Suppose price drops below a firm's average variable cost. Now the best strategy for the firm is to shut down, reducing its output to zero. The minimum level of average variable cost, which occurs at the intersection of the marginal cost curve and the average variable cost curve, is called the **shutdown point.** Any price below the minimum value of average variable cost will cause the firm to shut down. If the firm were to continue producing, not only would it lose its fixed costs, but it would also face an additional loss by not covering its variable costs.

Exhibit 9-7 shows a case where the price of radishes drops to $0.10 per pound. Price is less than average variable cost, so Mr. Gortari not only would lose his fixed cost but would also incur additional losses by producing. Suppose, for example, he decided to operate where marginal cost equals marginal revenue, producing 1,700 pounds of radishes per month. Average variable cost equals $0.14 per pound, so he'd lose $0.04 on each pound he produces ($68) plus his fixed cost of $400 per month. He would lose $468 per month. If he shut down, he'd lose only his fixed cost. Because the price of $0.10 falls below his average variable cost, his best course would be to shut down.

Case in Point Kitty Litter Reopens a Bentonite Plant

Dennis Walker didn't always like cats. "I guess you could say I've learned to love 'em," he says. He should. The nation's population of more than 60 million pet cats saved his job.

Mr. Walker is a plant foreman at Bentonite Corporation, a bentonite processing plant in Lovell, Wyoming. Bentonite is a clay found in soils all over the country, but deposits in Wyoming and parts of Utah are rich enough to mine. Bentonite was once used primarily as a lubricant for oil-drilling rigs. When the oil industry slumped in the 1980s, the demand for bentonite fell, and Mr. Walker's plant shut down because Bentonite's revenues no longer covered its variable costs. At that time, all of the plant's output went to the oil industry.

A new use for bentonite dramatically increased demand for the clay. Bentonite swells and clumps when wet. When used in cat litter, this property makes for easily removed clumps, and thus helps cat owners keep litter pans relatively odor-free. Cat litter containing bentonite appeared on supermarket shelves in 1987. It's now used in about half the cat litter produced in the United States.

By 1995, the demand for bentonite had risen enough to reopen Mr. Walker's plant. By 1998 the plant employed 65 people and processed more than a half-million tons of bentonite. About 40 percent of its output now goes to cat litter producers. Just 20 percent goes to oil companies, Mr. Walker says. The remaining 20 percent

is used in a variety of applications, including cleanup of environmental spills.

Sources: Tara Parker-Pope, "Cat Litter Breathes New Life Into Region of Bentonite Mines," *Wall Street Journal*, 1 April 1987, p. A1; and interview with Dennis Walker.

Shutting down is not the same thing as going out of business. A firm shuts down by closing its doors; it can reopen them whenever it expects to cover its variable costs. We can even think of a firm's decision to close at the end of the day as a kind of shutdown point; the firm makes this choice because it doesn't anticipate that it will be able to cover its variable cost overnight. It expects to cover those costs the next morning when it reopens its doors.

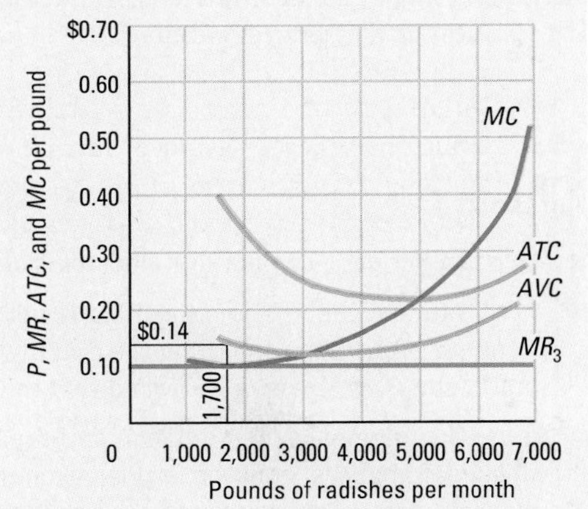

Exhibit 9-7

Shutting Down

The market price of radishes drops to $0.10 per pound, so MR_3 is below Mr. Gortari's *AVC*. Thus he would suffer a greater loss by continuing to operate than by shutting down. Whenever price falls below average variable cost, the firm will shut down, reducing its production to zero.

Marginal Cost and Supply

In the model of perfect competition, we assume that a firm determines its output by finding the point where the marginal revenue and marginal cost curves intersect. Provided that price exceeds average variable cost, the firm produces the quantity determined by the intersection of the two curves.

A supply curve tells us the quantity that will be produced at each price, and that's what the firm's marginal cost curve tells us. The firm's supply curve in the short run is its marginal cost curve for prices above the minimum value of average variable cost. At prices below average variable cost, the firm's output drops to zero.

Panel (a) of Exhibit 9-8 shows the average variable cost and marginal cost curves for a hypothetical astrologer, Madame LaFarge, who is in the business of providing astrological

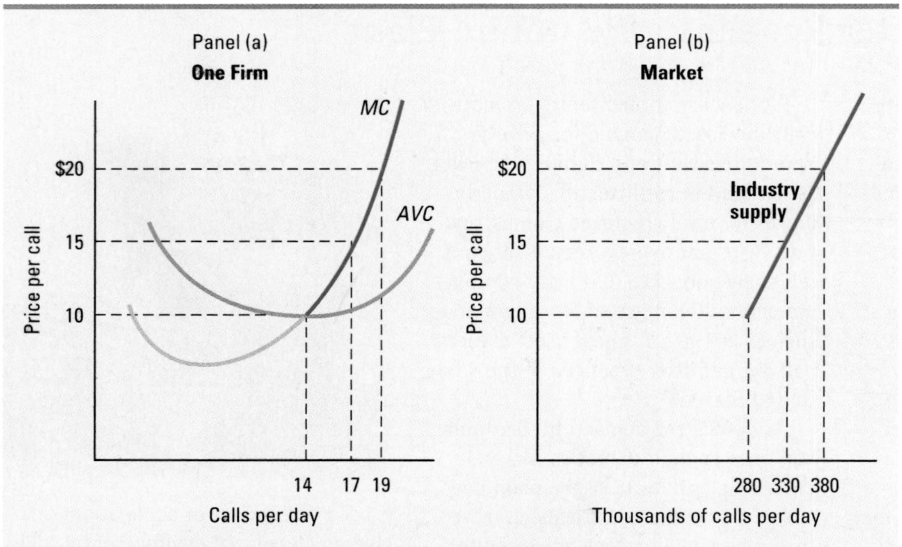

Exhibit 9-8

Marginal Cost and Supply

The supply curve for a firm is that portion of its *MC* curve that lies above the *AVC* curve, shown in Panel (a). To obtain the short-run supply curve for the industry, we add the outputs of each firm at each price. The industry supply curve is given in Panel (b).

consultations over the telephone. We shall assume that this industry is perfectly competitive. At any price below $10 per call, Madame LaFarge would shut down. If the price is $10 or greater, however, she produces an output at which price equals marginal cost. The marginal cost curve is thus her supply curve at all prices greater than $10.

Now suppose that the astrological forecast industry consists of Madame LaFarge and thousands of other firms similar to hers. The market supply curve is found by adding the outputs of each firm at each price, as shown in Panel (b) of Exhibit 9-8. At a price of $10 per call, for example, Madame LaFarge supplies 14 calls per day. Adding the quantities supplied by all the other firms in the market, suppose we get a quantity supplied of 280,000. Notice that the market supply curve we have drawn is linear; throughout the book we have made the assumption that market demand and supply curves are linear in order to simplify our analysis.

Looking at Exhibit 9-8, we see that profit-maximizing choices by firms in a perfectly competitive market will generate a market supply curve that reflects marginal cost. Provided there are no external benefits or costs in producing a good or service, a perfectly competitive market satisfies the efficiency condition.

Checklist

- Price in a perfectly competitive industry is determined by demand and supply.
- A firm's total revenue curve is a straight, upward-sloping line whose slope is the market price. Economic profit is maximized at the output level at which the slopes of the total revenue and total cost curves are equal, provided that the firm is covering its variable cost.
- To use the marginal decision rule in profit maximization, the firm produces the output at which marginal cost equals marginal revenue. Economic profit per unit is price minus average total cost; total economic profit equals economic profit per unit times quantity.
- If price falls below average total cost, but remains above average variable cost, the firm will continue to operate in the short run, producing the quantity where $MR = MC$; doing so minimizes its losses.
- If price falls below average variable cost, the firm will shut down in the short run, reducing output to zero. The lowest point on the average variable cost curve is called the shutdown point.
- The firm's supply curve in the short run is its marginal cost curve for prices greater than the minimum average variable cost.

Try It Yourself 9-1

Assume that Acme Clothing, the firm introduced in Chapter 8, produces jackets in a perfectly competitive market. Suppose the demand and supply curves for jackets intersect at a price of $81. Now, using the marginal cost and average total cost curves for Acme given in Exhibit 8-8, estimate Acme's profit-maximizing output per day (assume the firm selects a whole number). What are Acme's economic profits per day?

Perfect Competition in the Long Run

In the long run, a firm is free to adjust all of its inputs. New firms can enter any market; existing firms can leave their markets. We shall see in this section that the model of perfect competition predicts that, at a long-run equilibrium, production takes place at the lowest possible cost per unit and that all economic profits and losses are eliminated.

Economic Profit and Economic Loss

Economic profits and losses play a crucial role in the model of perfect competition. The existence of economic profits in a particular industry attracts new firms to the industry in the long run. As new firms enter, the supply curve shifts to the right, price falls, and profits fall. Firms continue to enter the industry until economic profits fall to zero. If firms in an industry are experiencing economic losses, some will leave. The supply curve shifts to the left, increasing price and reducing losses. Firms continue to leave until the remaining firms are no longer suffering losses—until economic profits are zero.

Before examining the mechanism through which entry and exit eliminate economic profits and losses, we shall examine an important key to understanding it: the difference between the accounting and economic concepts of profit and loss.

Economic Versus Accounting Concepts of Profit and Loss Economic profit equals total revenue minus total cost, where cost is measured in the economic sense as opportunity cost. An economic loss (negative economic profit) is incurred if total cost exceeds total revenue.

Accountants include only explicit costs in their computation of total cost. **Explicit costs** include charges that must be paid for factors of production such as labor and capital, together with an estimate of depreciation. Profit computed using only explicit costs is called **accounting profit.** It is the measure of profit firms typically report; firms pay taxes on their accounting profits, and a corporation reporting its profit for a particular period reports its accounting profits. To compute his accounting profits, Mr. Gortari, the radish farmer, would subtract explicit costs, such as charges for labor, equipment, and other supplies, from the revenue he receives.

Economists recognize costs in addition to the explicit costs listed by accountants. If Mr. Gortari were not growing radishes, he could be doing something else with the land and with his own efforts. Suppose the most valuable alternative use of his land would be to produce carrots, from which Mr. Gortari could earn $250 per month in accounting profits. The income he forgoes by not producing carrots is an opportunity cost of producing radishes. This cost is not explicit; the return Mr. Gortari could get from producing carrots will not appear on a conventional accounting statement of his accounting profit. A cost that is included in the economic concept of opportunity cost but that is not an explicit cost is called an **implicit cost.**

The Long Run and Zero Economic Profits Given our definition of economic profits, we can easily see why, in perfect competition, they must always ec al zero in the long run. Suppose there are two industries in the economy, a ndustry A are earning economic

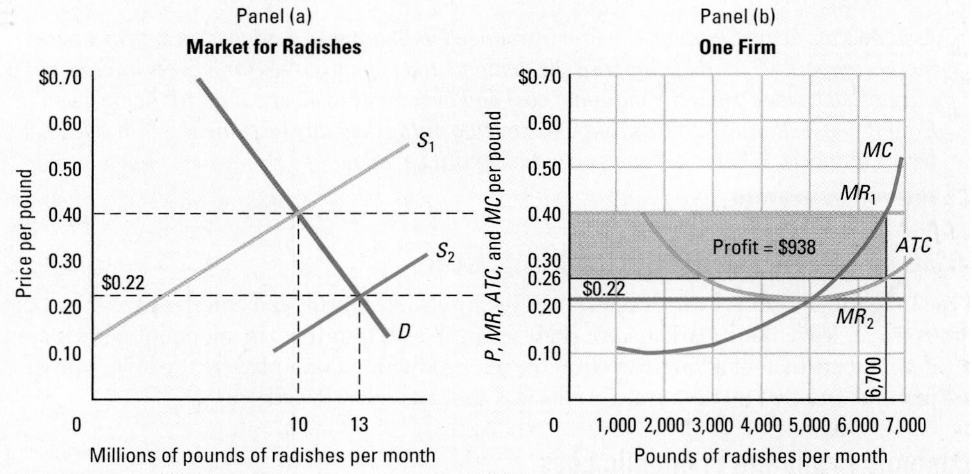

Exhibit 9-9

Eliminating Economic Profits in the Long Run

If firms in an industry are making an economic profit, entry will occur in the long run. In Panel (b), a single firm's profit is shown by the shaded area. Entry continues until firms in the industry are operating at the lowest point on their respective average total cost curves, and economic profits fall to zero.

profits. By definition, firms in Industry A are earning a return greater than the return available in Industry B. That means that firms in Industry B are earning less than they could in Industry A. Firms in Industry B are experiencing economic losses.

Given easy entry and exit, some firms in Industry B will leave it and enter Industry A to earn the greater profits available there. As they do so, the supply curve in Industry B will shift to the left, increasing prices and profits there. As former Industry B firms enter Industry A, the supply curve in Industry A will shift to the right, lowering profits in A. The process of firms leaving Industry B and entering A will continue until firms in both industries are earning zero economic profit. That suggests an important long-run result: *Economic profits in a system of perfectly competitive markets will, in the long run, be driven to zero in all industries.*

Eliminating Economic Profit: The Role of Entry The process through which entry will eliminate economic profits in the long run is illustrated in Exhibit 9-9, which is based on the situation presented in Exhibit 9-5. The price of radishes is $0.40 per pound. Mr. Gortari's average total cost at an output of 6,700 pounds of radishes per month is $0.26 per pound. Profit per unit is $0.14 ($0.40 – $0.26). Mr. Gortari thus earns a profit of $938 per month (= $0.14 × 6,700).

Profits in the radish industry attract entry in the long run. Panel (a) of Exhibit 9-9 shows that as firms enter, the supply curve shifts to the right and the price of radishes falls. New firms enter as long as there are economic profits to be made—as long as price exceeds *ATC* in Panel (b). As price falls, marginal revenue falls to MR_2 and the firm reduces the quantity it supplies, moving along the marginal cost (*MC*) curve to the lowest point on the *ATC* curve, at $0.22 per pound and an output of 5,000 pounds per month. Although the output of individual firms falls in response to falling prices, there are now more firms, so industry output rises to 13 million pounds per month in Panel (a).

Eliminating Losses: The Role of Exit Just as entry eliminates economic profits in the long run, exit eliminates economic losses. In Exhibit 9-10, Panel (a) shows the case of an industry in which the market price P_1 is below *ATC*. In Panel (b), at price P_1 a single firm produces a quantity q_1, assuming it is at least covering its average variable cost. The firm's losses are shown by the shaded rectangle bounded by its average [illegible] cost C_1 and price P_1 and by output q_1.

Because firms in the industry are losing money, some will exit. The supply curve in Panel (a) shifts to the left, and it continues shifting as long as firms are suffering losses. Eventually the supply curve shifts all the way to S_2, price rises to P_2, and economic profits return to zero.

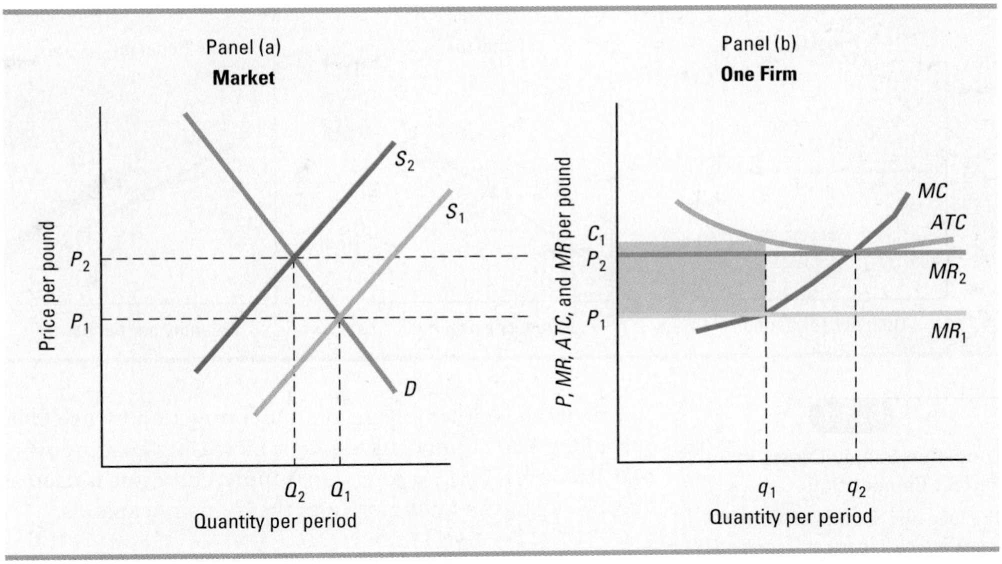

Exhibit 9-10

Eliminating Economic Losses in the Long Run

Panel (b) shows that at the initial price P_1, firms in the industry cannot cover average total cost (MR_1 is below *ATC*). That induces some firms to leave the industry, shifting the supply curve in Panel (a) to S_2, reducing industry output to Q_2 and raising price to P_2. At that price (MR_2), firms earn zero economic profit, and exit from the industry ceases. Panel (b) shows that the firm increases output from q_1 to q_2; total output in the market falls in Panel (a) because there are fewer firms. Notice that in Panel (a) quantity is designated by uppercase Q, while in Panel (b) quantity is designated by lowercase q. This convention is used throughout the text to distinguish between the quantity supplied in the market (Q) and the quantity supplied by a typical firm (q).

Entry, Exit, and Production Costs In our examination of entry and exit in response to economic profit or loss in a perfectly competitive industry, we assumed that the *ATC* curve of a single firm does not shift as new firms enter or existing firms leave the industry. That is the case when expansion or contraction doesn't affect prices for the factors of production used by firms in the industry. When expansion of the industry does not affect the prices of factors of production, it is a **constant-cost industry.** In some cases, however, the entry of new firms may affect input prices.

As new firms enter, they add to the demand for the factors of production used by the industry. If the industry is a significant user of those factors, the increase in demand could push up the market price of factors of production for all firms in the industry. If that occurs, then entry into an industry will boost average costs at the same time as it puts downward pressure on price. Long-run equilibrium will still occur at a zero level of economic profit and with firms operating on the lowest point on the *ATC* curve, but that cost curve will be somewhat higher than before entry occurred. Suppose, for example, that an increase in demand for new houses drives prices higher and induces entry. That will increase the demand for workers in the construction industry and is likely to result in higher wages in the industry, driving up costs.

An industry in which the entry of new firms bids up the prices of factors of production and thus increases production costs is called an **increasing-cost industry.** As such an industry expands in the long run, its price will rise.

Some industries may experience reductions in input prices as they expand with the entry of new firms. That may occur because firms supplying the industry experience economies of scale as they increase production, thus driving input prices down. Expansion may also induce technological changes that lower input costs. That's clearly the case of the computer industry, which has enjoyed falling input costs as it has expanded. An industry in which production costs fall as firms enter in the long run is a **decreasing-cost industry.**

Just as industries may expand with the entry of new firms, they may contract with the exit of existing firms. In a constant-cost industry, exit will not affect the input prices of remaining firms. In an increasing-cost industry, exit will reduce the input prices of remaining firms. And, in a decreasing-cost industry, input prices may rise with the exit of existing firms.

The behavior of production costs as firms in an industry expand or reduce their output has important implications for the **long-run industry supply curve,** a curve that relates the price of a good or service to the quantity produced after all long-run adjustments to a price change have been completed. Every point on a long-run supply curve therefore shows a price

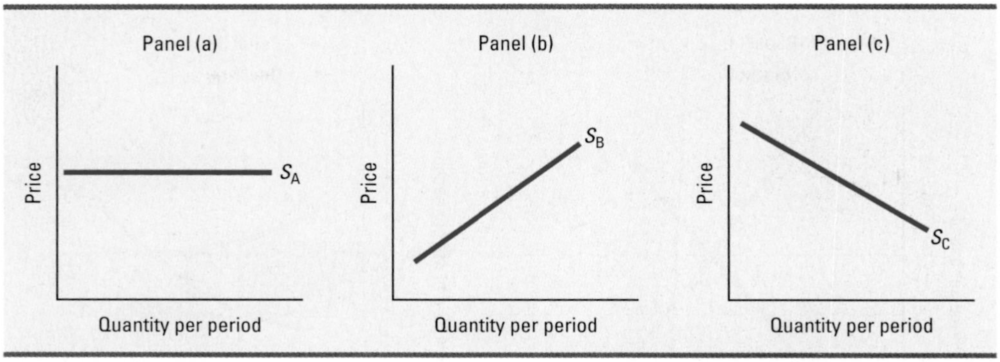

Exhibit 9-11

Long-Run Supply Curves in Perfect Competition

The long-run supply curve for a constant-cost, perfectly competitive industry is a horizontal line, S_A, shown in Panel (a). The long-run curve for an increasing-cost industry is an upward-sloping curve, S_B, as in Panel (b). The downward-sloping long-run supply curve, S_C, for a decreasing cost industry is given in Panel (c).

and quantity supplied at which firms in the industry are earning zero economic profit. Unlike the short-run market supply curve, the long-run industry supply curve does not hold factor costs and the number of firms constant.

Exhibit 9-11 shows three long-run industry supply curves. In Panel (a), S_A is a long-run supply curve for a constant-cost industry. It is horizontal. Neither expansion nor contraction by itself affects market price. In Panel (b), S_B is a long-run supply curve for an increasing-cost industry. It rises as the industry expands. In Panel (c), S_C is a long-run supply curve for a decreasing-cost industry. Its downward slope suggests a falling price as the industry expands.

Changes in Demand and in Production Cost

The primary application of the model of perfect competition is in predicting how firms will respond to changes in demand and in production costs. To see how firms respond to a particular change, we determine how the change affects demand or cost conditions and then see how the profit-maximizing solution is affected in the short run and in the long run. Having determined how the profit-maximizing firms of the model would respond, we can then predict firms' responses to similar changes in the real world.

In the examples that follow, we shall assume, for simplicity, that entry or exit do not affect the input prices facing firms in the industry. That is, we assume a constant-cost industry with a horizontal long-run industry supply curve similar to S_A in Exhibit 9-11. We shall assume that firms are covering their average variable costs, so we can ignore the possibility of shutting down.

Changes in Demand Changes in demand can occur for any of the reasons we discussed in Chapter 3. There may be a change in preferences, incomes, the price of a related good, population, or consumer expectations. A change in demand causes a change in the market price, thus shifting the marginal revenue curves of firms in the industry.

Let's consider the impact of a change in demand for oats. Suppose new evidence suggests that eating oats not only helps to prevent heart disease, but also prevents baldness in males. This will, of course, increase the demand for oats. To assess the impact of this change, we assume that the industry is perfectly competitive and that it is initially in long-run equilibrium at a price of $1.70 per bushel. Economic profits equal zero.

The initial situation is depicted in Exhibit 9-12. Panel (a) shows that at a price of $1.70, industry output is Q_1 (point A), while Panel (b) shows that the market price constitutes the marginal revenue, MR_1, facing a single firm in the industry. The firm responds to that price by finding the output level at which the MC and MR_1 curves intersect. That implies a level of output q_1 at point A'.

The new medical evidence causes demand to increase to D_2 in Panel (a). That increases the market price to $2.30 (point B), so the marginal revenue curve for a single firm rises to MR_2 in Panel (b). The firm responds by increasing its output to q_2 in the short run (point B'). Notice that the firm's average total cost is slightly higher than its original level of $1.70; that's because of the U shape of the curve. The firm is making an economic profit shown by the shaded rectangle in Panel (b). Other firms in the industry will earn an economic profit as well, which, in the long run, will attract entry by new firms. New entry will shift the supply curve to the right; entry will continue as long as firms are making an economic profit. The supply curve in Panel (a) shifts to S_2, driving the price down in the long run to the original level of $1.70 per bushel and returning economic profits to zero in long-run equilibrium. A single firm will return to its original level of output, q_1 (point A') in Panel (b), but because there are more firms in the industry, industry output rises to Q_3 (point C) in Panel (a).

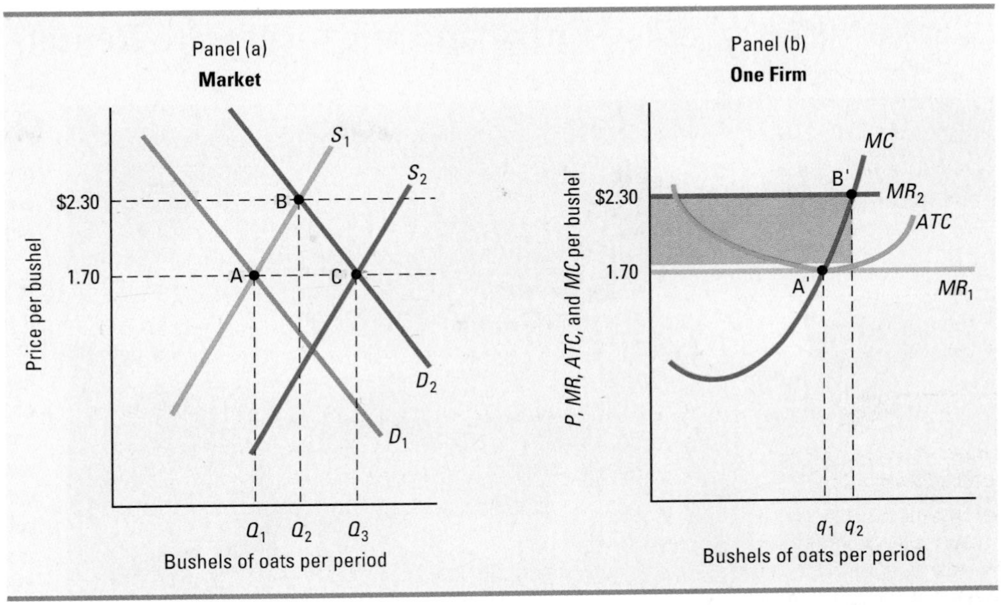

Exhibit 9-12

Short-Run and Long-Run Adjustments to an Increase in Demand

The initial equilibrium price and output are determined in the market for oats by the intersection of demand and supply at point A in Panel (a). An increase in the market demand for oats, from D_1 to D_2 in Panel (a), shifts the equilibrium solution to point B. The price increases in the short run from $1.70 per bushel to $2.30. Industry output rises to Q_2. For a single firm, the increase in price raises marginal revenue from MR_1 to MR_2; the firm responds in the short run by increasing its output to q_2. It earns an economic profit given by the shaded rectangle. In the long run, the opportunity for profit attracts new firms. In a constant-cost industry, the short-run supply curve shifts to S_2; market equilibrium now moves to point C in Panel (a). The market price falls back to $1.70. The firm's demand curve returns to MR_1, and its output falls back to the original level, q_1. Industry output has risen to Q_3 because there are more firms.

A reduction in demand would lead to a reduction in price, shifting each firm's marginal revenue curve downward. Firms would experience economic losses, thus causing exit in the long run and shifting the supply curve to the left. Eventually, the price would rise back to its original level, assuming changes in industry output did not lead to changes in input prices. There would be fewer firms in the industry, but each firm would end up producing the same output as before.

Changes in Production Cost A firm's costs change if the costs of its inputs change. They also change if the firm is able to take advantage of a change in technology. Changes in production cost shift the *ATC* curve. If a firm's variable costs are affected, its marginal cost curves will shift as well. Any change in marginal cost produces a similar change in industry supply, since it is found by adding up marginal cost curves for individual firms.

Suppose a reduction in the price of oil reduces the cost of producing oil changes for automobiles. We shall assume that the oil-change industry is perfectly competitive and that it is initially in long-run equilibrium at a price of $27 per oil change, as shown in Panel (a) of Exhibit 9-13. Suppose that the reduction in oil prices reduces the cost of an oil change by $3.

A reduction in production cost shifts the firm's cost curves down. The firm's average total cost and marginal cost curves shift down, as shown in Panel (b). In Panel (a) the supply curve shifts from S_1 to S_2. The industry supply curve is made up of the marginal cost curves of individual firms; because each of them has shifted downward by $3, the industry supply curve shifts downward by $3.

Notice that price in the short run falls to $26; it does not fall by the $3 reduction in cost. That's because the supply and demand curves are sloped. While the supply curve shifts downward by $3, its intersection with the demand curve falls by less than $3. The firm in Panel (b) responds to the lower price and lower cost by increasing output to q_2, where MC_2 and MR_2 intersect. That leaves firms in the industry with an economic profit; the economic profit for the firm is shown by the shaded rectangle in Panel (b). Profits attract entry in the

Case in Point Easy Entry and Videocassette Rentals

Michelle Sedlak remembers the good old days in the video rental business.

"When I started in the business, we were charging $8 for a 24-hour rental for the first tape, $4 for the second," she says.

That was in 1982. Videocassette recorders (VCRs) had just been introduced, and there weren't many video rental outlets. "In 1982 you had to look for a video store. The nearest competition was likely to be several miles away. Now there's a video store on practically every block. The competition has really driven the price down."

How much? By 1990 Ms. Sedlak was a store manager for Budget Video, a small chain in Baltimore, Maryland. She was charging $1.99 per night for new releases and $0.99 to $1.50 for other titles. The number of video stores had risen from just 5,000 in 1981 to 25,000 by 1990.

Rapid entry and falling prices had produced sharply lower accounting profits by 1990. "Several years ago, our profits were as high as 80 percent of sales," Ms. Sedlak recalls. "That fell pretty quickly to 50 percent. Now, we're lucky to get 10 percent. The business has gotten a lot tougher."

The video rental market continued to change in the 1990s. There was only a small increase in the number of stores in the 1990s. Blockbuster now has about 7,000 outlets, about 25 percent of the national total. Rental stores now compete not only with each other, but with stores like Wal-Mart that offer videos for sale. In 1997, consumers spent more in the purchase of videos than they did for rentals. Pay-per-view offerings on cable and on satellite outlets provide still more competition. New technologies are likely to allow consumers to receive videos on demand over the telephone within a few years.

The boom years for video rentals may have come to an end. But the experience of the 1980s shows how easy entry can drive down prices and profits. The experience of the twenty-first century may be one in which falling demand forces widespread exit.

Source: Personal interview with Ms. Sedlak; industry information from company news releases and from Kelly Johnson, "Shrinking Ranks of Independent Video Stores Dig In," *Sacramento Business Journal*, 13(51) (10 March 1997):16.

long run, shifting the supply curve to the right to S_3. Entry will continue as long as firms are making an economic profit—it will thus continue until the price falls by the full amount of the $3 reduction in cost. The price falls to $24, industry output rises to Q_3, and the firm's output returns to its original level, q_1.

An increase in variable costs would shift the average total, average variable, and marginal cost curves upward. It would shift the industry supply curve upward by the same amount. The result in the short run would be an increase in price, but by less than the increase in cost per unit. Firms would experience economic losses, causing exit in the long run. Eventually, price would increase by the full amount of the increase in production cost.

Some cost increases will not affect marginal cost. Suppose, for example, that an annual license fee of $5,000 is imposed on firms in a particular industry. The fee is a fixed cost; it does not affect marginal cost. Imposing such a fee shifts the average total cost curve upward but causes no change in marginal cost. There is no change in price or output in the short run. Because firms are suffering economic losses, there will be exit in the long run. Prices ultimately rise by enough to cover the cost of the fee, leaving the remaining firms in the industry with zero economic profit.

Price will change to reflect whatever change we observe in production cost. A change in variable cost causes price to change in the short run. In the long run, any change in average total cost changes price by an equal amount.

The message of long-run equilibrium in a competitive market is a profound one. The ultimate beneficiaries of the innovative efforts of firms are consumers. In the Case in Point on technology in Chapter 2, we noted the efforts of oil companies to lower the cost of finding oil and thus the cost of producing gasoline. The gasoline market is a relatively competitive one; finding a cheaper way to produce gasoline will result in cheaper gasoline for consumers. More generally, successful efforts to lower production costs in competitive markets will always lead to lower prices for consumers.

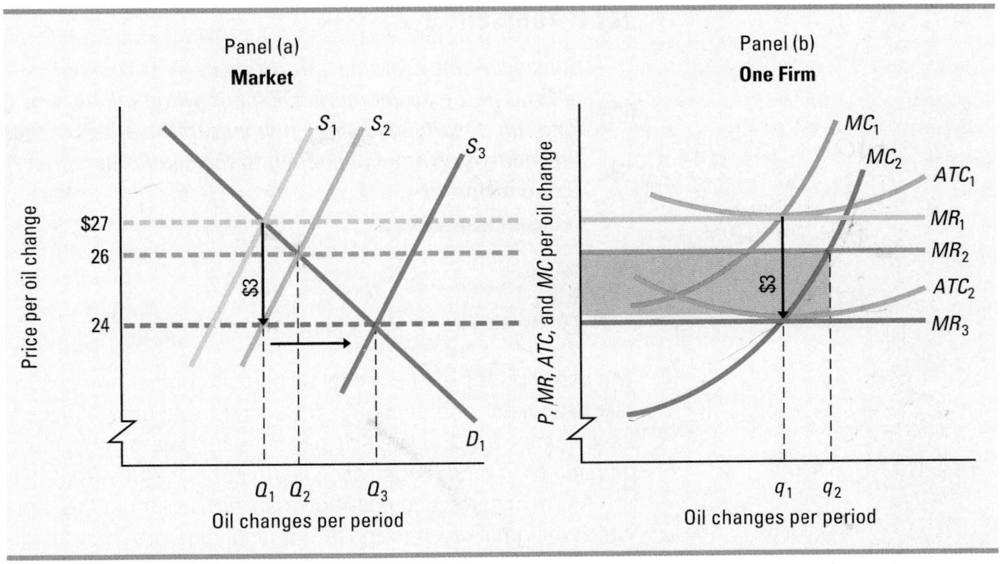

Exhibit 9-13

A Reduction in the Cost of Producing Oil Changes

The initial equilibrium price, \$27, and quantity, Q_1, of automobile oil changes are determined by the intersection of market demand, D_1, and market supply, S_1 in Panel (a). The industry is in long-run equilibrium; a typical firm, shown in Panel (b), earns zero economic profit. A reduction in oil prices reduces the marginal and average total costs of producing an oil change by \$3. The firm's marginal cost curve shifts to MC_2, and its average total cost curve shifts to ATC_2. The short-run industry supply curve shifts down by \$3 to S_2. The market price falls to \$26; the firm increases its output to q_2 and earns an economic profit given by the shaded rectangle. In the long run, the opportunity for profit shifts the industry supply curve to S_3. The price falls to \$24, and the firm reduces its output to the original level, q_1. It now earns zero economic profit once again. Industry output in Panel (a) rises to Q_3 because there are more firms; price has fallen by the full amount of the reduction in production costs.

Checklist

- The economic concept of profit differs from accounting profit. The accounting concept deals only with explicit costs, while the economic concept of profit incorporates explicit and implicit costs.
- The existence of economic profits attracts entry, economic losses lead to exit, and in long-run equilibrium, firms in a perfectly competitive industry will earn zero economic profit.
- The long-run supply curve in an industry in which expansion does not change input prices (a constant-cost industry) is a horizontal line. The long-run supply curve for an industry in which production costs increase as output rises (an increasing-cost industry) is upward sloping. The long-run supply curve for an industry in which production costs decrease as output rises (a decreasing-cost industry) is downward sloping.
- In a perfectly competitive market in long-run equilibrium, an increase in demand creates economic profit and induces entry in the long run; a reduction in demand creates economic losses (negative economic profits) in the short run and forces some firms to exit the industry in the long run.
- When production costs change, price will change by less than the change in production cost in the short run. Price will adjust to reflect fully the change in production cost in the long run.
- A change in fixed cost will have no effect on price or output in the short run. It will induce entry or exit in the long run so that price will change by enough to leave firms earning zero economic profit.

Try It Yourself! 9-2

Consider Acme Clothing's situation in Try It Yourself 9-1. Suppose this situation is typical of firms in the jacket market. Explain what will happen in the market for jackets in the long run, assuming nothing happens to the prices of factors of production used by firms in the industry. What will happen to the equilibrium price? What is the equilibrium level of economic profits?

A Look Back

The assumptions of the model of perfect competition ensure that every decisionmaker is a price taker—demand and supply in the market determine price. Although most firms in real markets have some control over their prices, the model of perfect competition suggests how changes in demand or in production cost will affect price and output in a wide range of real-world cases.

A firm in perfect competition maximizes profit in the short run by producing an output level at which marginal revenue equals marginal cost, provided marginal revenue is at least as great as the minimum value of average variable cost. For a perfectly competitive firm, marginal revenue equals price and average revenue. This implies that the firm's marginal cost curve is its short-run supply curve for values greater than average variable cost. If price drops below average variable cost, the firm shuts down.

If firms in an industry are earning economic profit, entry by new firms will drive price down until economic profit achieves its long-run equilibrium value of zero. If firms are suffering economic loss, exit by existing firms will continue until price rises to eliminate the loss and economic profits are zero. A long-run equilibrium may be changed by a change in demand or in production cost, which would affect supply. The adjustment to the change in the short run is likely to result in economic profits or losses; these will be eliminated in the long run by entry or by exit.

A Look Ahead In Chapter 10, we'll examine the opposite end of the spectrum of market types—monopoly. Where a perfectly competitive market has many firms, a monopoly has only one. Where it's easy to enter a perfectly competitive market, entry in a monopoly is blocked. In Chapter 11, we'll look at models of markets that lie between the extreme cases of perfect competition and of monopoly.

Terms and Concepts for Review

perfect competition, **185**
price takers, **186**
total revenue, **189**
marginal revenue, **189**
average revenue, **190**
economic profit per unit, **192**
economic loss, **193**
shutdown point, **194**
explicit costs, **197**
accounting profit, **197**
implicit cost, **197**
constant-cost industry, **199**
increasing-cost industry, **199**
decreasing-cost industry, **199**
long-run industry supply curve, **200**

For Discussion

1. Explain how each of the assumptions of perfect competition contributes to the fact that all decisionmakers in perfect competition are price takers.
2. Consider the following goods and services. Which are the most likely to be produced in a perfectly competitive industry? Which are not? Explain why you made the choices you did, relating your answer to the assumptions of the model of perfect competition.
   a. Coca-Cola and Pepsi
   b. Potatoes

c. Private physicians in your local community
d. Government bonds and corporate stocks
e. Taxicabs in Lima, Peru—a city that does not restrict entry or the prices drivers can charge
f. Oats

3. In the Case in Point on Associated Sales, the Phoenix supplier of appliances, the owner bemoans his inability to change the price of his goods by as much as $10. He still determines his own prices. Is it reasonable to think of him as a price taker?
4. Explain why an economic profit of zero is acceptable to a firm.
5. Explain why a perfectly competitive firm whose average total cost exceeds the market price may continue to operate in the short run. What about the long run?
6. You've decided to major in biology rather than computer science. A news report suggests that the salaries of computer science majors are increasing. How does this affect the opportunity cost of your choice?
7. Explain how each of the following events would affect the marginal cost curves of firms and thus the supply curve in a perfectly competitive market in the short run.
   a. An increase in wages
   b. A tax of $1 per unit imposed on the seller
   c. The introduction of cost-cutting technology
   d. The imposition of an annual license fee of $1,000
8. In a perfectly competitive market, who benefits from an event that lowers production costs for firms?
9. Dry-cleaning establishments generate a considerable amount of air pollution in producing cleaning services. Suppose these firms are allowed to pollute without restriction and that reducing their pollution would add significantly to their production costs. Who benefits from the fact that they pollute the air? Now suppose the government requires them to reduce their pollution. Who will pay for the cleanup? (Assume dry cleaning is a perfectly competitive industry, and answer these questions from a long-run perspective.)
10. Columnist William F. Buckley, commenting on a strike by the Teamsters Union against UPS in 1997, offered this bit of economic analysis to explain how UPS had succeeded in reducing its average total cost: "UPS has done this by 'economies of scale.' Up to a point (where the marginal cost equals the price of the marginal unit), the larger the business, the less the per-unit cost." The concept of economies of scale is discussed in Chapter 8. Use that concept, together with the information presented in this chapter, to explain the error in Mr. Buckley's statement.[1]

Problems

1. Suppose rocking-chair manufacturing is a perfectly competitive industry in which there are 1,000 identical firms. Each firm's total cost is related to output per day as follows:

Quantity	Total cost	Quantity	Total cost
0	$500	5	$2,200
1	$1,000	6	$2,700
2	$1,300	7	$3,300
3	$1,500	8	$4,000
4	$1,800		

   a. Prepare a table that shows total variable cost, average total cost, and marginal cost at each level of output.
   b. Plot the average total cost, average variable cost, and marginal cost curves for a single firm (remember that values for marginal cost are plotted at the midpoint of the respective intervals). What is the firm's supply curve? How many chairs would the firm produce at prices of $350, $450, $550, and $650? (In computing quantities, assume that a firm produces a certain number of completed chairs each day; it does not produce fractions of a chair on any one day.)
   c. Suppose the demand curve in the market for rocking chairs is given by the following table:

Price	Quantity of chairs demanded/day	Price	Quantity of chairs demanded/day
$650	5,000	$450	7,000
550	6,000	350	8,000

   Plot the market demand curve for chairs. Compute and plot the market supply curve, using the information you obtained for a single firm in part (b). What is the equilibrium price? The equilibrium quantity?
   d. Given your solution in part (c), plot the total revenue and total cost curves for a single firm. Does your graph correspond to your solution in part (b)? Explain.

[1]William F. Buckley, "Carey Took on 'Greed' as His Battle Cry," *The Gazette*, 22 August 1997, News 7 (a Universal Press Syndicate column).

2. The following table shows the total output, total revenue, total variable cost, and total fixed cost of a firm. What level of output should the firm produce? Should it shut down? Should it exit the industry? Explain.

Output	Total revenue	Total variable cost	Total fixed cost
1	$1,000	$1,500	$500
2	2,000	2,000	500
3	3,000	2,600	500
4	4,000	3,900	500
5	5,000	5,000	500

3. Suppose a rise in fuel costs increases the cost of producing oats by $0.50 per bushel. Illustrate graphically how this change will affect the oat market and a single firm in the market in the short run and in the long run.

4. Suppose the demand for car washes in Collegetown falls as a result of a cutback in college enrollment. Show graphically how the price and output for the market and for a single firm will be affected in the short run and in the long run. Assume the market is perfectly competitive and that it is initially in long-run equilibrium at a price of $12 per car wash. Assume also that input prices don't change as the market responds to the change in demand.

Answers to Try It Yourself Problems

Try It Yourself 9-1

We use the information in Exhibit 8-7. At a price of $81, Acme's marginal revenue curve is a horizontal line at $81. The firm produces the output at which marginal cost equals marginal revenue; the curves intersect at a quantity of 9 jackets per day. Acme's average total cost at this level of output equals $67, for an economic profit per jacket of $14. Acme's economic profit per day equals about $126.

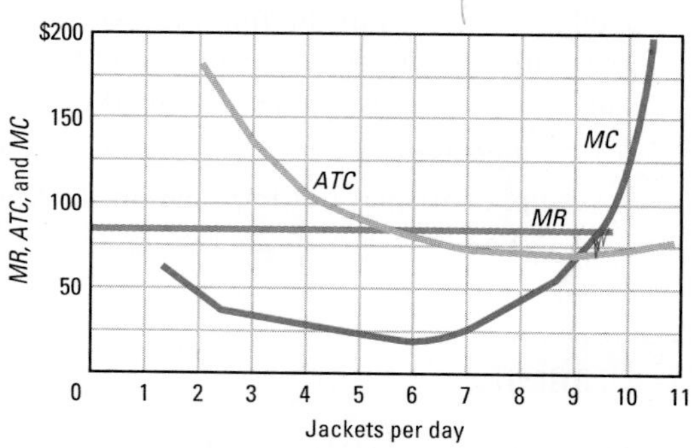

Try It Yourself 9-2

The availability of economic profits will attract new firms to the jacket industry in the long run, shifting the market supply curve to the right. Entry will continue until economic profits are eliminated. The price will fall; Acme's marginal revenue curve shifts down. The equilibrium level of economic profits in the long run is zero.

Monopoly 10

Getting Started: Surrounded by Monopolies

If your college or university is like most, you spend a lot of time, and money, dealing with firms that face very little competition. Your campus bookstore is likely to be the only local firm selling the texts that professors require you to read. Your school may have granted an exclusive franchise to a single firm for food service and to another firm for vending machines. You may face a single supplier of local telephone service. A single firm may provide your utilities—electricity, natural gas, and water.

In the last chapter we assumed that individual firms operate in a competitive market, taking the price, which is determined by demand and supply, as given. In this chapter we investigate the behavior of firms that have their markets all to themselves. As the only suppliers of particular goods or services, they face the downward-sloping market demand curve alone.

We'll find that firms that have their markets all to themselves behave in a manner that is in many respects quite different from the behavior of firms in perfect competition. Such firms continue to use the marginal decision rule in maximizing profits, but their freedom to select from the price and quantity combinations given by the market demand curve affects the ways in which they apply this rule.

We will show that a monopoly firm is likely to produce less and charge more for what it produces than firms in a competitive industry. As a result, a monopoly solution is likely to be inefficient from society's perspective. We'll explore in broad terms the policy alternatives available to government agencies in dealing with monopoly firms. First, though, we'll look at characteristics of monopoly and at conditions that give rise to monopolies in the first place.

The Nature of Monopoly

Monopoly is at the opposite end of the spectrum of market models from perfect competition. A **monopoly** firm has no rivals. It is the only firm in its industry. There are no close substitutes for the good or service a monopoly produces. Not only does a monopoly firm have the market to itself, but it also need not worry about other firms entering. In the case of monopoly, entry by potential rivals is prohibitively difficult.

A monopoly does not take the market price as given; it determines its own price. It selects from its demand curve the price that corresponds to the quantity the firm has chosen to produce in order to earn the maximum profit possible. The entry of new firms, which eliminates profit in the long run in a competitive market, cannot occur in the monopoly model.

A firm that sets or picks price based on its output decision is called a **price setter.** A firm that acts as a price setter possesses **monopoly power.** We shall see in the next chapter that monopolies are not the only firms that have this power; however, the absence of rivals in monopoly gives it much more price-setting power.

As was the case when we discussed perfect competition in the previous chapter, the assumptions of the monopoly model are rather strong. In assuming there is one firm in a market, we assume there are no other firms producing goods or services that could be considered part of the same market as that of the monopoly firm. In assuming blocked entry, we assume, for reasons we'll discuss below, that no other firm can enter that market. Such conditions are rare in the real world. As always with models, we make the assumptions that define monopoly in order to simplify our analysis, not to describe the real world. The result is a model that gives us important insights into the nature of the choices of firms and their impact on the economy.

Sources of Monopoly

Why are some markets dominated by single firms? What are the sources of monopoly power? Economists have identified a number of conditions that, individually or in combination, can lead to domination of a market by a single firm and create barriers that prevent the entry of new firms. **Barriers to entry** are characteristics of a particular market that block new firms from entering it. They include economies of scale, special advantages of location, high sunk costs, a dominant position in the ownership of some of the inputs required to produce the good, and government restrictions. These barriers may be interrelated, making entry that much more formidable. Although these barriers might allow one firm to gain and hold monopoly control over a market, there are often forces at work that can erode this control.

Economies of Scale Scale economies and diseconomies, which were explained in Chapter 8, define the shape of a firm's long-run average cost (*LRAC*) curve as it increases its output. If long-run average cost declines as the level of production increases, a firm is said to experience *economies of scale.*

A firm that confronts economies of scale over the entire range of outputs demanded in its industry is a **natural monopoly.** Utilities that distribute electricity, water, and natural gas to some markets are examples. In a natural monopoly, the *LRAC* of any one firm intersects the market demand curve where long-run average costs are falling or are at a minimum. If this is the case, one firm in the industry will expand to exploit the economies of scale available to it. Because this firm will have lower unit costs than its rivals, it can drive them out of the market and gain monopoly control over the industry.

Suppose there are 12 firms, each operating at the scale shown by ATC_1 (average total cost) in Exhibit 10-1. A firm that expanded its scale of operation to achieve an average total cost curve such as ATC_2 could produce 240 units of output at a lower cost than could the smaller firms producing 20 units each. By cutting its price below the minimum average total cost of the smaller plants, the larger firm could drive the smaller ones out of business. In this situation, the industry demand is not large enough to support more than one firm. If another firm attempted to enter the industry, the natural monopolist would always be able to undersell it.

Exhibit 10-1

Economies of Scale Lead to Natural Monopoly

A firm with falling *LRAC* throughout the range of outputs relevant to existing demand (*D*) will monopolize the industry. Here, one firm operating with a large plant (ATC_2) produces 240 units of output at a lower cost than the $7 cost per unit of the 12 firms operating at a smaller scale (ATC_1), and producing 20 units of output each.

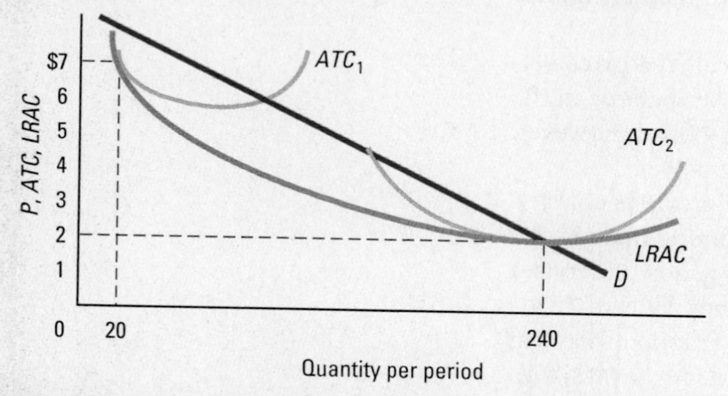

Location Sometimes monopoly power is the result of location. For example, sellers in markets isolated by distance from their nearest rivals have a degree of monopoly power. The local movie theater in a small town has a monopoly in showing first-run movies. Doctors, dentists, and mechanics in isolated towns may also be monopolists.

Sunk Costs The greater the cost of establishing a new business in an industry, the more difficult it is to enter that industry. That cost will, in turn, be greater if the outlays required to start a business are unlikely to be recovered if the business should fail.

Suppose, for example, that entry into a particular industry requires extensive advertising to make consumers aware of the new brand. Should the effort fail, there is no way to recover the expenditures for such advertising. An expenditure that has already been made and that cannot be recovered is called a **sunk cost.**

If a substantial fraction of a firm's initial outlays will be lost upon exit from the industry, exit will be costly. Difficulty of exit can make for difficulty of entry. The more firms have to lose from an unsuccessful effort to penetrate a particular market, the less likely they are to try. The potential for high sunk costs could thus contribute to the monopoly power of an established firm by making entry more difficult.

Restricted Ownership of Raw Materials and Inputs In a very few cases the source of monopoly power is the ownership of strategic inputs. If a particular firm owns all of an input required for the production of a particular good or service, then it could emerge as the only producer of that good or service.

The Aluminum Company of America (ALCOA) gained monopoly power through its ownership of virtually all the bauxite mines in the world (bauxite is the source of aluminum). The International Nickel Company of Canada at one time owned virtually all the world's nickel. De Beers has acquired rights to nearly all the world's diamond production, giving it enormous power in the market for diamonds. This power may decline, however, if Russia, which has huge diamond reserves, begins to develop this resource and sell it independently of De Beers.

Government Restrictions Another important basis for monopoly power consists of special privileges granted to some business firms by government agencies. State and local governments have commonly assigned exclusive franchises—rights to conduct business in a specific market—to taxi and bus companies, to cable television companies, and to providers of telephone services, electricity, natural gas, and water, although the trend in recent years has been to encourage competition for many of these services. Governments might also regulate entry into an industry or a profession through licensing and certification requirements. Governments also provide patent protection to inventors of new products or production methods in order to encourage innovation; these patents may afford their holders a degree of monopoly power during the 17-year life of the patent.

Patents can take on extra importance when network effects are present. **Network effects** arise in situations where products become more useful the larger the number of users of the product. For example, a fax machine is increasingly useful to a business as the number of other businesses using compatible fax machines grows. In such cases, the firm that gets in first and manages to establish and patent the standards for the product has an advantage over latecomers. In the 1880s, following the invention of the typewriter, Remington held the patent on the QWERTY keyboard. Once that keyboard (named for the position of the letters on the top row) became the industry standard, alternatives fell by the wayside. Similarly, Microsoft, with its Windows operating system for personal computers, has a near monopoly not just because Microsoft holds patents on Windows, but also because Windows has become the standard for a product where the network effect is very important.

The Fragility of Monopoly Power

Monopoly power can be a fleeting thing. Firms constantly seek out the market power that monopoly offers. When conditions are right to achieve this power, firms that succeed in carving out monopoly positions enjoy substantial profits. But the potential for high profits invites continuing attempts to break down the barriers to entry that insulate monopolies from competition.

Technological change and the pursuit of profits chip away constantly at the entrenched power of monopolies. Whether it is Sprint and MCI challenging AT&T's old monopoly in long-distance telephone service, catalog companies challenging the monopoly positions of some retailers, internet booksellers challenging the monopoly power of your university's bookstore, or Federal Express taking on the U.S. Postal Service, the assaults on monopoly power are continuous. Thus, even the monopoly firm must be on the lookout for potential competitors.

Case in Point The Stirrup and the Rise and Fall of the Roman Empire

Did the invention of the stirrup bring on the collapse of the Roman Empire?

By the first century A.D., the Roman Empire encompassed most of Europe, the Middle East, and northern Africa. Its success, argues economic historian Leonard Dudley of the University of Montreal, rested in large part on its ability to produce military force at a lower cost than its adversaries.

Until the first century A.D., military operations were conducted by foot soldiers. In general, the larger the number of soldiers, the more powerful the army. The Roman army used a strategy in which its legions of soldiers stood side by side holding large shields, forming a virtually invincible wall. Each additional soldier increased military force by providing greater protection to the other soldiers. The advantages of large numbers meant that the cost per unit of producing military force fell as the quantity of force increased.

However, between the first century and the ninth, Rome succumbed to a series of civil wars and foreign invasions. Historians attribute Rome's success largely to its ability to establish and maintain military control. Explanations of its failure range from moral laxity to high taxes to lead in the water pipes that served its ruling class; more than 400 factors have been cited to explain the fall of the greatest empire in human history. Mr. Dudley links Rome's rise—and fall—to its long-run average cost curve for the production of military force.

Mr. Dudley suggests that, during the period of Rome's expansion, there were significant economies of scale throughout its range of production of military services. That gave Rome an advantage over the peoples it conquered; it could maintain an army at a lower cost per unit of military force than could its rivals. In effect, it emerged as a natural monopolist in the "market" for military control over most of the Western world.

But economies of scale depend crucially on the nature of the technology available. Mr. Dudley argues that the introduction of the saddle in the first century and the subsequent introduction of the stirrup greatly increased the effectiveness of mounted soldiers in combat. Smaller cavalry units could now defeat much larger armies of foot soldiers. Mounted soldiers fought for the most part as individuals; they didn't rely on their fellow soldiers for protection, Mr. Dudley says. He suggests that cavalry units could produce military force at a lower cost per unit than foot soldiers. The new technology didn't generate economies of scale; if anything, Rome lost its cost advantage in military production. The result, Mr. Dudley says, was that smaller states could compete effectively with Rome, and the Empire vanished.

Source: Leonard Dudley, "Structural Change in Interdependent Bureaucracies: Was Rome's Failure Economic or Military?" *Explorations in Economic History* 27 (June 1990): 232–248.

Consider local telephone service. As of 1999, most areas had a single company providing local service. But substitutes had begun to appear. For example, while a cellular phone was not yet so close a substitute for traditional telephone service that providers of cellular service could be regarded as part of the market for residential telephone service, they were rapidly approaching that point in 1999. Technological changes in cellular phone service made it possible for multiple cellular phones to have a single phone number, coverage areas had increased, voice messaging and other phone services had become available, and so on. Already some people had decided that they could do without residential phone service if they had a cell phone.

It would be shortsighted for any phone company in this day and age to assume that it has the market for any kind of phone service to itself. Potential rivals are clearly beating at the door and thereby making its fragile market contestable (that is, open to entry, at least in the sense of rival firms producing "close enough," if not perfect, substitutes).

Checklist

- An industry with a single firm, in which entry is blocked, is called a monopoly.
- A firm that sets or picks price depending on its output decision is called a price setter. A price setter possesses monopoly power.
- The sources of monopoly power include economies of scale, locational advantages, high sunk costs associated with entry, restricted ownership of key inputs, and government restrictions, such as exclusive franchises, licensing and certification requirements, and patents.
- A firm that confronts economies of scale over the entire range of output demanded in the industry is a natural monopoly.
- The sources of monopoly power can be eroded by technological advances or other changes in the economy.

Try It Yourself 10-1

What is the source of monopoly power in each of the following situations?

a. The U.S. Food and Drug Administration granted Burroughs Wellcome exclusive rights until 2005 to manufacture and distribute AZT, a drug used in the treatment of AIDS.

b. John and Mary Doe run the only shoe repair shop in town.

c. One utility company distributes residential electricity in your town.

d. The widespread use of automatic teller machines (ATMs) has proven a boon to Diebold, the principal manufacturer of the machines.

The Monopoly Model

Analyzing choices is a more complex challenge for a monopoly firm than for a perfectly competitive firm. After all, a competitive firm takes the market price as given and determines its profit-maximizing output. Because a monopoly has its market all to itself, it can determine not only its output but its price as well. What kinds of price and output choices will such a firm make?

We will answer that question in the context of the marginal decision rule: A firm will produce additional units of a good until marginal revenue equals marginal cost. To apply that rule to a monopoly firm, we must first investigate the special relationship between demand and marginal revenue for a monopoly.

Monopoly and Market Demand

Because a monopoly firm has its market all to itself, it faces the market demand curve. Exhibit 10-2 compares the demand situations faced by a monopoly and a perfectly competitive firm. In Panel (a), the equilibrium price for a perfectly competitive firm is determined by the

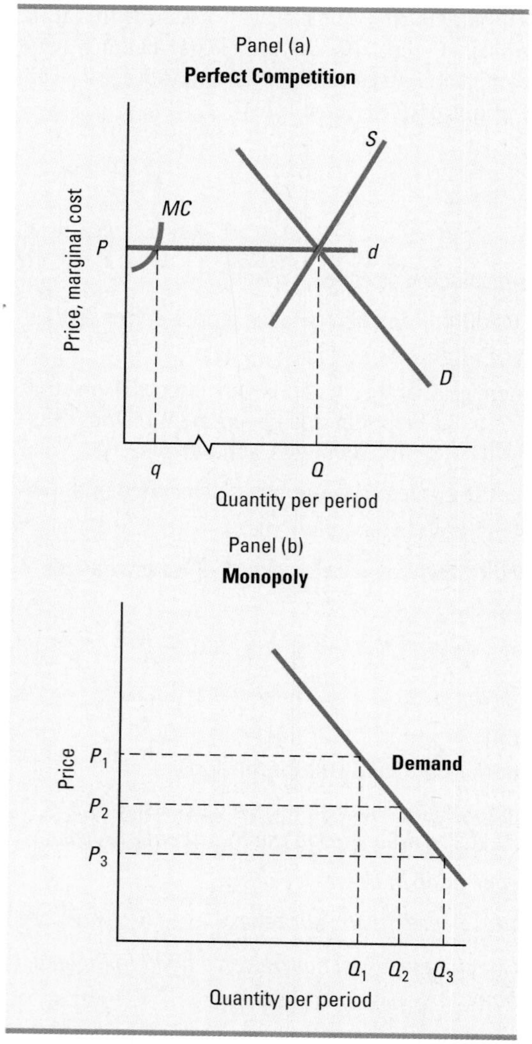

Exhibit 10-2

Perfect Competition Versus Monopoly

Panel (a) shows the determination of equilibrium price and output in a perfectly competitive market. A typical firm with marginal cost curve *MC* is a price taker, choosing to produce quantity *q* at the equilibrium price *P*. In Panel (b) a monopoly faces a downward-sloping market demand curve. As a profit maximizer, it determines its profit-maximizing output. Once it determines that quantity, however, the price at which it can sell that output is found from the demand curve. The monopoly firm can sell additional units only by lowering price. The perfectly competitive firm, by contrast, can sell any quantity it wants at the market price.

intersection of the demand and supply curves. The market supply curve is found simply by summing the supply curves of individual firms. Those, in turn, consist of the portions of marginal cost curves that lie above the average variable cost curves. The marginal cost curve, *MC*, for a single firm is illustrated. Notice the break in the horizontal axis indicating that the quantity produced by a single firm is a trivially small fraction of the whole. In the perfectly competitive model, one firm has *nothing* to do with the determination of the market price. Each firm in a perfectly competitive industry faces a horizontal demand curve defined by the market price.

Contrast the situation shown in Panel (a) with the one faced by the monopoly firm in Panel (b). Because it is the only supplier in the industry, the monopolist faces the downward-sloping market demand curve alone. It may choose to produce any quantity. But, unlike the perfectly competitive firm, which can sell all it wants at the going market price, a monopolist can sell a greater quantity only by cutting its price.

Suppose, for example, that a monopoly firm can sell quantity Q_1 units at a price P_1 in Panel (b). If it wants to increase its output to Q_2 units—and sell that quantity—it must reduce its price to P_2. To sell quantity Q_3 it would have to reduce the price to P_3. The monopoly firm may choose its price and output, but it is restricted to a combination of price and output that lies on the demand curve. It could not, for example, charge price P_1 and sell quantity Q_3 To be a price setter, a firm must face a downward-sloping demand curve.

Total Revenue and Price Elasticity

We saw in Chapter 5 that a firm's elasticity of demand with respect to price has important implications for assessing the impact of a price change on total revenue. We also saw that the price elasticity of demand can be different at different points on a firm's demand curve. In this section, we shall see why a monopoly firm will always select a price in the elastic region of its demand curve.

Suppose the demand curve facing a monopoly firm is given by Equation (1), where Q is the quantity demanded per unit of time and P is the price per unit:

$$Q = 10 - P \tag{1}$$

This demand equation implies the demand schedule shown in Exhibit 10-3. Total revenue for each quantity equals the quantity times the price at which that quantity is demanded. The monopoly firm's total revenue curve is given in Panel (b). Because a monopolist must cut the price of every unit in order to increase sales, total revenue does not always increase as output rises. In this case, total revenue reaches a maximum of $25 when 5 units are sold. Beyond 5 units, total revenue begins to decline.

The demand curve in Panel (a) of Exhibit 10-3 shows ranges of values of the price elasticity of demand. We saw in Chapter 5 that price elasticity varies along a linear demand curve in a special way: Demand is price elastic at points in the upper half of the demand curve and price inelastic in the lower half of the demand curve. If demand is price elastic, a price reduction increases total revenue. To sell an additional unit, a monopoly firm must lower its price. The sale of one more unit will increase revenue because the percentage increase in the quantity demanded exceeds the percentage decrease in the price. The elastic range of the demand curve corresponds to the range over which the total revenue curve is rising in Panel (b) of Exhibit 10-3.

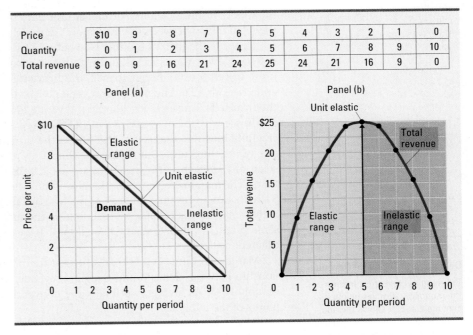

Price	$10	9	8	7	6	5	4	3	2	1	0
Quantity	0	1	2	3	4	5	6	7	8	9	10
Total revenue	$ 0	9	16	21	24	25	24	21	16	9	0

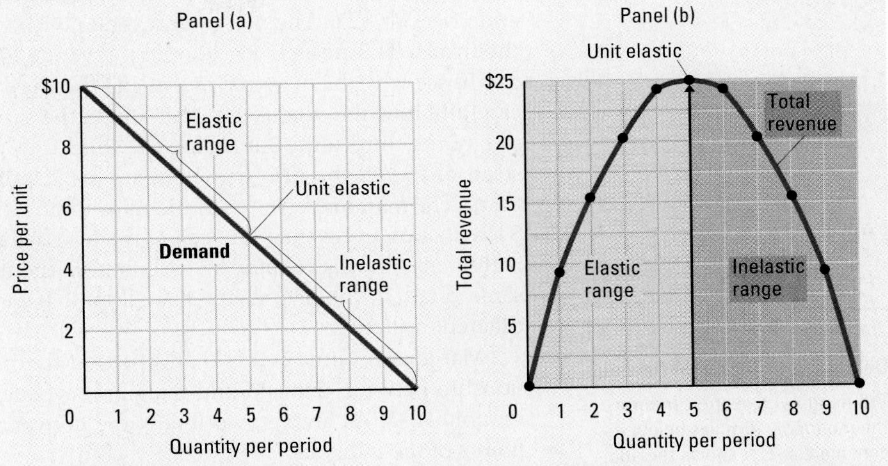

Exhibit 10-3

Demand, Elasticity, and Total Revenue

Suppose a monopolist faces the downward-sloping demand curve shown in Panel (a). In order to increase the quantity sold, it must cut the price. Total revenue is found by multiplying the price and quantity sold at each price. Total revenue, plotted in Panel (b), is maximized at $25, when the quantity sold is 5 units and the price is $5. At that point on the demand curve, the price elasticity of demand equals −1.

If demand is price inelastic, a price reduction reduces total revenue because the percentage increase in the quantity demanded is less than the percentage decrease in the price. Total revenue falls as the firm sells additional units over the inelastic range of the demand curve. The downward-sloping portion of the total revenue curve in Panel (b) corresponds to the inelastic range of the demand curve.

Finally, recall that the midpoint of a linear demand curve is the point at which demand becomes unit price elastic. That point on the total revenue curve in Panel (b) corresponds to the point at which total revenue reaches a maximum.

The relationship among price elasticity, demand, and total revenue has an important implication for the selection of the profit-maximizing price and output: A monopoly firm will not choose a price and output in the inelastic range of the demand curve. Suppose, for example, that the monopoly firm represented in Exhibit 10-3 is charging $3 and selling 7 units. Its total revenue is thus $21. Because this combination is in the inelastic portion of the demand curve, the firm could increase its total revenue by raising its price. It could, at the same time, reduce its total cost. Raising price means reducing output; a reduction in output would reduce total cost. If the firm is operating in the inelastic range of its demand curve, then it is not maximizing profits. The firm could earn a higher profit by raising price and reducing output. It will continue to raise its price until it is in the elastic portion of its demand curve. A profit-maximizing monopoly firm will therefore select a price and output combination in the elastic range of its demand curve.

Of course, the firm could choose a point at which demand is unit price elastic. At that point, total revenue is maximized. But the firm seeks to maximize profit, not total revenue. A solution that maximizes total revenue will not maximize profit unless marginal cost is zero.

Demand and Marginal Revenue

In the perfectly competitive case, the additional revenue a firm gains from selling an additional unit—its marginal revenue—is equal to the market price. The firm's demand curve, which is a horizontal line at the market price, is also its marginal revenue curve. But a monopoly firm can sell an additional unit only by lowering the price. That fact complicates the relationship between the monopoly's demand curve and its marginal revenue.

Suppose the firm in Exhibit 10-3 sells 2 units at a price of $8 per unit. Its total revenue is $16. Now it wants to sell a third unit and wants to know the marginal revenue of that unit. To sell 3 units rather than 2, the firm must lower its price to $7 per unit. Total revenue rises to $21. The marginal revenue of the third unit is thus $5. But the *price* at which the firm sells 3 units is $7. Marginal revenue is less than price.

To see why the marginal revenue of the third unit is less than its price, let's examine more carefully how the sale of that unit affects the firm's revenues. The firm brings in $7 from the sale of the third unit. But selling the third unit required the firm to charge a price of $7 instead of the $8 the firm was charging for 2 units. Now the firm receives less for the first 2 units. The marginal revenue of the third unit is the $7 the firm receives for that unit *minus* the $1 reduction in revenue for each of the first two units. The marginal revenue of the third unit is thus $5. (In this chapter we assume that the monopoly firm sells all units of output at the same price. In the next chapter, we'll look at cases in which firms charge different prices to different customers.)

Marginal revenue is less than price for the monopoly firm. Exhibit 10-4 shows the relationship between demand and marginal revenue, based on the demand curve introduced in Exhibit 10-3. As always, we follow the convention of putting marginal values at the midpoints of the intervals.

When the demand curve is linear, as in Exhibit 10-4, the marginal revenue curve can be placed according to the following rules: The marginal revenue curve is always below the demand curve and the marginal revenue curve will bisect any horizontal line drawn between the vertical axis and the demand curve. To put it another way, the marginal revenue curve will be twice as steep as the demand curve. The demand curve in Exhibit 10-4 is given by the equation $Q = 10 - P$, which can be written $P = 10 - Q$. The marginal revenue curve is given by $P = 10 - 2Q$, which is twice as steep as the demand curve.

The marginal revenue and demand curves in Exhibit 10-4 follow these rules. The marginal revenue curve lies below the demand curve, and it bisects any horizontal line drawn from the vertical axis to the demand curve. At a price of $6, for example, the quantity demanded is 4. The marginal revenue curve passes through 2 units at this price. At a price of 0, the quantity demanded is 10; the marginal revenue curve passes through 5 units at this point.

Just as there is a relationship between the firm's demand curve and the price elasticity of demand, there is a relationship between its marginal revenue curve and elasticity. Where marginal revenue is positive, demand is price elastic. Where marginal revenue is negative, demand is price inelastic. Where marginal revenue is zero, demand is unit price elastic.

When marginal revenue is . . .	then demand is . . .
positive,	price elastic.
negative,	price inelastic.
zero,	unit price elastic.

A firm wouldn't produce an additional unit of output with negative marginal revenue. And, assuming that the production

Exhibit 10-4

Demand and Marginal Revenue

The marginal revenue curve for the monopoly firm lies below its demand curve. It shows the additional revenue gained from selling an additional unit. Notice that, as always, marginal values are plotted at the midpoints of the respective intervals.

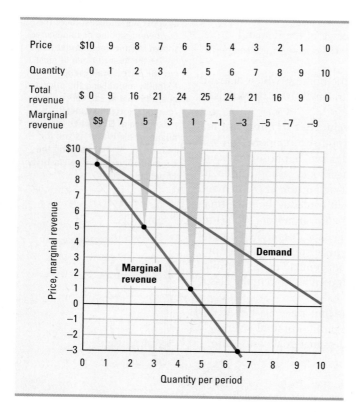

Price	$10	9	8	7	6	5	4	3	2	1	0
Quantity	0	1	2	3	4	5	6	7	8	9	10
Total revenue	$ 0	9	16	21	24	25	24	21	16	9	0
Marginal revenue	$9	7	5	3	1	−1	−3	−5	−7	−9	

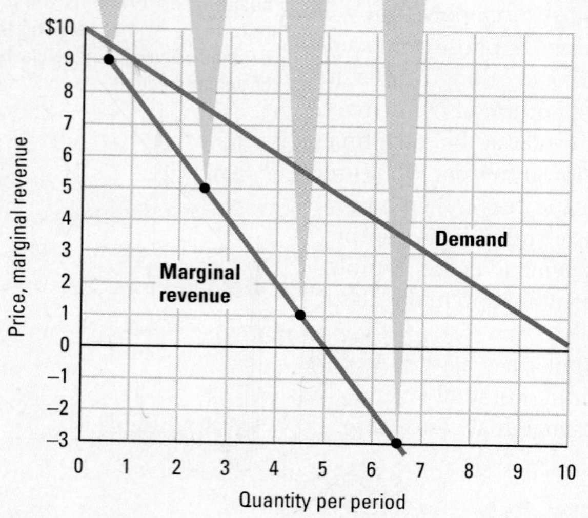

of an additional unit has some cost, a firm won't produce the extra unit if it has zero marginal revenue. Because a monopoly firm will generally operate where marginal revenue is positive, we see once again that it will operate in the elastic range of its demand curve.

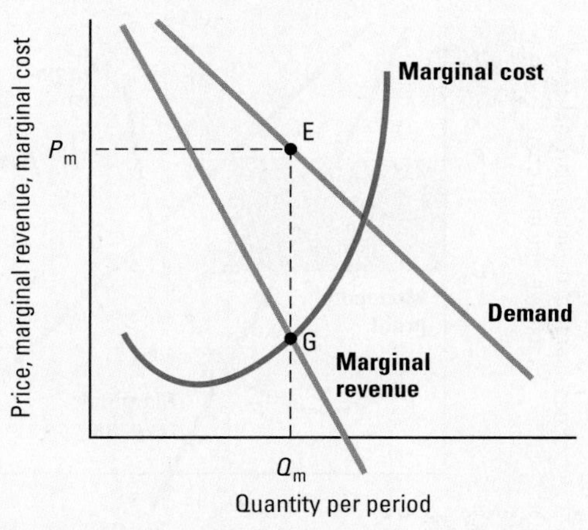

Exhibit 10-5

The Monopoly Solution

The monopoly firm maximizes profit by producing an output Q_m at point G, where the marginal revenue and marginal cost curves intersect. It sells this output at price P_m.

Monopoly Equilibrium: Applying the Marginal Decision Rule

Profit-maximizing behavior is always based on the marginal decision rule presented in Chapter 6: Additional units of a good should be produced as long as the marginal revenue of an additional unit exceeds the marginal cost. The maximizing solution occurs where marginal revenue equals marginal cost. As always, firms seek to maximize economic profit, and costs are measured in the economic sense of opportunity cost.

Exhibit 10-5 shows a demand curve and an associated marginal revenue curve facing a monopoly firm. The marginal cost curve is like those we derived in Chapter 8; it falls over the range of output in which the firm experiences increasing marginal returns, then rises as the firm experiences diminishing marginal returns.

To determine the profit-maximizing output, we note the quantity at which the firm's marginal revenue and marginal cost curves intersect (Q_m in Exhibit 10-5). We read up from Q_m to the demand curve to find the price P_m at which the firm can sell Q_m units. The profit-maximizing price and output are given by point E on the demand curve.

Caution!

Dispelling Myths About Monopoly

Three common misconceptions about monopoly are:

1. Because there are no rivals selling the products of monopoly firms, they can charge whatever they want.
2. Monopolists will charge whatever the market will bear.
3. Because monopoly firms have the market to themselves, they are guaranteed huge profits.

As Exhibit 10-5 shows, once the monopoly firm decides on the number of units of output that will maximize profit, the price at which it can sell that many units is found by "reading off" the demand curve the price associated with that many units. If it tries to sell Q_m units of output for more than P_m, some of its output will go unsold. The monopoly firm can set its price, but is restricted to price and output combinations that lie on its demand curve. It can't just "charge whatever it wants." And if it charges "all the market will bear," it will sell either 0 or, at most, 1 unit of output.

Neither is the monopoly firm guaranteed a profit. Consider Exhibit 10-6. Suppose the average total cost curve, instead of lying below the demand curve for some output levels as shown, were instead everywhere *above* the demand curve. In that case, the monopoly will incur losses no matter what price it chooses, since average total cost will always be greater than any price it might charge. As is the case for perfect competition, the monopoly firm can keep producing in the short run so long as price exceeds average variable cost. In the long run, it will stay in business only if it can cover all of its costs.

No one who has taken and passed this course will ever be overheard making such statements about monopolies!

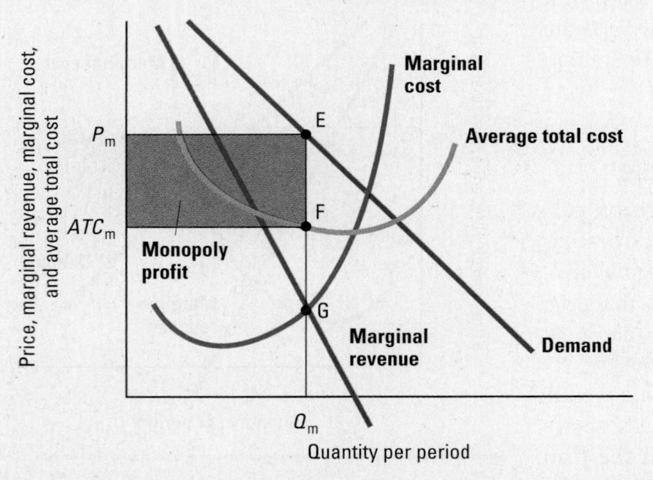

Exhibit 10-6

Computing Monopoly Profit

A monopoly firm's profit per unit is the difference between price and average total cost. Total profit equals profit per unit times the quantity produced. Total profit is given by the area of the shaded rectangle ATC_mP_mEF.

Thus we can determine a monopoly firm's profit-maximizing price and output by following three steps:

1. Determine the demand, marginal revenue, and marginal cost curves.
2. Select the output level at which the marginal revenue and marginal cost curves intersect.
3. Determine from the demand curve the price at which that output can be sold.

Once we have determined the monopoly firm's price and output, we can determine its economic profit by adding the firm's average total cost curve to the graph showing demand, marginal revenue, and marginal cost, as shown in Exhibit 10-6. The average total cost (*ATC*) at an output of Q_m units is ATC_m. The firm's profit per unit is thus $P_m - ATC_m$. Total profit is found by multiplying the firm's output, Q_m, by profit per unit, so total profit equals $Q_m(P_m - ATC_m)$, the area of the shaded rectangle in Exhibit 10-6.

Checklist

- If a firm faces a downward-sloping demand curve, marginal revenue is less than price.
- Marginal revenue is positive in the elastic range of a demand curve, negative in the inelastic range, and zero where demand is unit price elastic.
- If a monopoly firm faces a linear demand curve, its marginal revenue curve is also linear, lies below the demand curve, and bisects any horizontal line drawn from the vertical axis to the demand curve.
- To maximize profit or minimize losses, a monopoly firm produces the quantity at which marginal cost equals marginal revenue. Its price is given by the point on the demand curve that corresponds to this quantity.

Try It Yourself 10-2

The Troll Road Company is considering building a toll road. It estimates that its linear demand curve is as shown below. Assume that the fixed cost of the road is $0.5 million per year. Maintenance costs, which are the only other costs of the road, are also given in the table.

Toll per trip	$.00	0.90	0.80	0.70	0.60	0.50
Number of trips per year (in millions)	1	2	3	4	5	6
Maintenance cost per year (in millions)	$0.7	1.2	1.8	2.9	4.2	6.0

a. *Using the midpoint convention, compute the profit-maximizing level of output.*

b. *Using the midpoint convention, what price will the company charge?*

c. *What is marginal revenue at the profit-maximizing output level? How does marginal revenue compare to price?*

Case in Point Profit-Maximizing Hockey Teams

Professional hockey teams set admission prices at levels that maximize their profits, according to four economists at the University of Vancouver. They regard hockey teams as monopoly firms and use the monopoly model to examine the teams' behavior.

The economists, Donald G. Ferguson, Kenneth G. Stewart, John Colin H. Jones, and Andre Le Dressay, used data from three seasons to estimate demand and marginal revenue curves facing each team in the National Hockey League. They found that demand for a team's tickets is affected by population and income in the team's home city, the team's standing in the National Hockey League, and the number of superstars on the team.

Because a sports team's costs don't vary significantly with the number of fans who attend a given game, the economists assumed that marginal cost is zero. The profit-maximizing number of seats sold per game is thus the quantity at which marginal revenue is zero, provided a team's stadium is large enough to hold that quantity of fans. This unconstrained quantity is labeled Q_u, with a corresponding price P_u, in the graph.

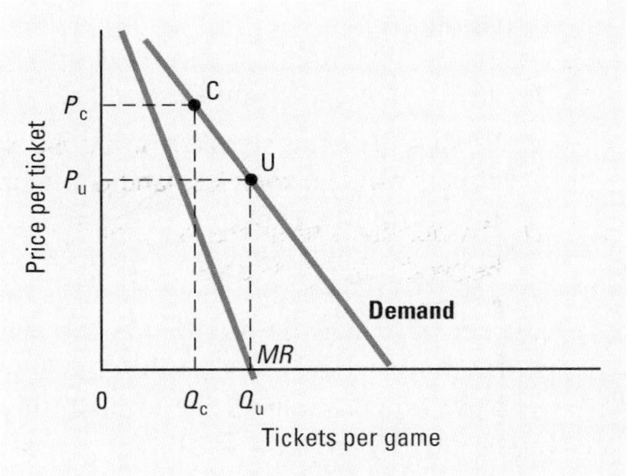

Stadium size and the demand curve facing a team might prevent the team from selling the profit-maximizing quantity of tickets. If its stadium holds only Q_c fans, for example, the team will sell that many tickets at price P_c; its marginal revenue is positive at that quantity. Economic theory thus predicts that the marginal revenue for teams that consistently sell out their games will be positive, and the marginal revenue for other teams will be zero.

The economists' statistical results were consistent with the theory. They found that teams that don't typically sell out their games operate at a quantity at which marginal revenue is about zero, and that teams with sellouts have positive marginal revenue. "It's clear that these teams are very sophisticated in their use of pricing to maximize profits," Mr. Ferguson said.

Sources: Donald G. Ferguson et al., "The Pricing of Sports Events: Do Teams Maximize Profit?" *Journal of Industrial Economics* 39(3) (March 1991): 297–310 and personal interview.

Assessing Monopoly

We have seen that for monopolies pursuing profit maximization, the outcome differs from the case of perfect competition presented in Chapter 9. Does this matter to society? In this section, we'll focus on the differences that stem from market structure and assess their implications.

Efficiency, Equity, and Concentration of Power

We have seen that a monopoly firm determines its output by setting marginal cost equal to marginal revenue. It then charges the price at which it can sell that output, a price determined

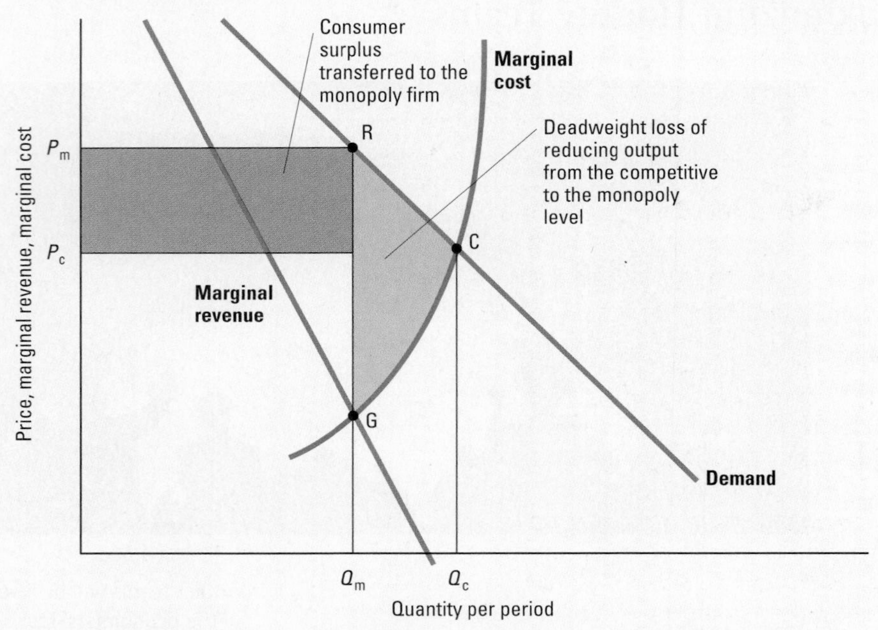

Exhibit 10-7

Perfect Competition, Monopoly, and Efficiency

Given market demand and marginal revenue, we can compare the behavior of a monopoly to that of a perfectly competitive industry. The marginal cost curve may be thought of as the supply curve of a perfectly competitive industry. The perfectly competitive industry produces quantity Q_c and sells the output at price P_c. The monopolist restricts output to Q_m and raises the price to P_m.

Reorganizing a perfectly competitive industry as a monopoly results in a deadweight loss to society given by the shaded area GRC. It also transfers a portion of the consumer surplus earned in the competitive case to the monopoly firm.

by the demand curve. That price exceeds marginal revenue; it therefore exceeds marginal cost as well. That contrasts with the case in perfect competition, in which price and marginal cost are equal. The higher price charged by a monopoly firm may allow it a profit—in large part at the expense of consumers, whose reduced options may give them little say in the matter. The monopoly solution thus raises problems of efficiency, equity, and the concentration of power.

Monopoly and Efficiency The fact that price in monopoly exceeds marginal cost suggests that the monopoly solution violates the basic condition for economic efficiency introduced in Chapter 6, that the price system must confront decisionmakers with the costs and benefits of their choices. Efficiency requires that consumers confront prices that equal marginal costs. Because a monopoly firm charges a price greater than marginal cost, consumers will consume less of the monopoly's good or service than is economically efficient.

To contrast the efficiency of the perfectly competitive outcome with the inefficiency of the monopoly outcome, imagine a perfectly competitive industry whose solution is depicted in Exhibit 10-7. The short-run industry supply curve is the summation of individual marginal cost curves; it may be regarded as the marginal cost curve for the industry. A perfectly competitive industry achieves equilibrium at point C, at price P_c and quantity Q_c.

Now suppose that all the firms in the industry merge and a government restriction prohibits entry by any new firms. Our perfectly competitive industry is now a monopoly. Assume the monopoly continues to have the same marginal cost and demand curves that the competitive industry did. The monopoly firm faces the same market demand curve, from which it derives its marginal revenue curve. It maximizes profit at output Q_m and charges price P_m. Output is lower and price higher than in the competitive solution.

Society would gain by moving from the monopoly solution at Q_m to the competitive solution at Q_c. The benefit to consumers would be given by the area under the demand curve between Q_m and Q_c; it is the area Q_mRCQ_c. An increase in output, of course, has a cost. Because the marginal cost curve measures the cost of each additional unit, we can think of the area under the marginal cost curve over some range of output as measuring the total cost of that output. Thus, the total cost of increasing output from Q_m to Q_c is the area under the marginal cost curve over that range—the area Q_mGCQ_c. Subtracting this cost from the benefit gives us the net gain of moving from the monopoly to the competitive solution; it is the shaded area GRC. That is the potential gain from moving to the efficient solution. The area GRC is a deadweight loss.

Monopoly and Equity The monopoly solution raises issues not just of efficiency but also of equity. Exhibit 10-7 shows that the monopolist charges price P_m rather than the competitive price P_c; the higher price charged by the monopoly firm reduces consumer surplus. Recall from Chapter 6 that consumer surplus is the difference between what consumers are willing to pay for a good and what they actually pay. It is measured by the area under the demand curve and above the price of the good over the range of output produced.

If the industry were competitive, consumer surplus would be the area below the demand curve and above P_cC. With monopoly, consumer surplus would be the area below the demand curve and above P_mR. Part of the reduction in consumer surplus is the area under the demand curve between Q_c and Q_m; it is contained in the deadweight loss area GRC. But consumers also lose the area of the rectangle bounded by the competitive and monopoly prices and by the monopoly output; this lost consumer surplus is transferred to the monopolist.

The fact that society suffers a deadweight loss due to monopoly is an efficiency problem. But the transfer of a portion of consumer surplus to the monopolist is an equity issue. Is such a transfer legitimate? After all, the monopoly firm enjoys a privileged position, protected by barriers to entry from competition. Should it be allowed to extract these gains from consumers? We'll see that public policy suggests that the answer is no. Regulatory efforts imposed in monopoly cases often seek to reduce the degree to which monopoly firms extract consumer surplus from consumers by reducing the prices these firms charge.

Monopoly and the Concentration of Power The objections to monopoly run much deeper than worries over economic efficiency and high prices. Because it enjoys barriers that block potential rivals, a monopoly firm wields considerable market power. For many people, that concentration of power is objectionable. A decentralized, competitive market constantly tests the ability of firms to satisfy consumers, pushes them to find new products and new and better production methods, and whittles away economic profits. Firms that operate in the shelter of monopoly may be largely immune to such pressures. Consumers are left with fewer choices, higher costs, and lower quality.

Attitudes about Microsoft reflect these concerns. Even among people who feel that its products are good and fairly priced, there is uneasiness about our seeming dependence on it. And once it has secured its position, will it charge more for its products? Will it continue to innovate?

Perhaps more important in the view of many economists is the fact that the existence of economic profits provides both an incentive and the means for monopolists to aggressively protect their position and extend it if possible. These economists point out that monopolists may be willing to spend their economic profits in attempts to influence political leaders and public authorities (including regulatory authorities) who can help them maintain or enhance their monopoly position. Graft and corruption may be the result, claim these critics. Indeed, Microsoft has been accused by its rival Netscape of bullying computer manufacturers into installing its web browser, Internet Explorer, exclusively on their computers.

Public Policy Toward Monopoly Pulling together what we have learned in this chapter on monopoly and in Chapter 9 on perfect competition, Exhibit 10-8 summarizes the differences between the models of perfect competition and monopoly. Most importantly we note that whereas the perfectly competitive firm is a price taker, the monopoly firm is a price setter. Because of this difference, we can object to monopoly on grounds of economic efficiency; monopolies produce too little and charge too much. Also, the high price and persistent profits strike many as inequitable. Others may simply see monopoly as an unacceptable concentration of power.

Public policy toward monopoly generally recognizes two important dimensions of the monopoly problem. On the one hand, the combining of competing firms into a monopoly creates an inefficient and, to many, inequitable solution. On the other hand, some industries are characterized as natural monopolies; production by a single firm allows economies of scale that result in lower costs.

Exhibit 10-8

Characteristics of Perfect Competition and Monopoly

Characteristics of Perfect Competition and Monopoly

Characteristic or Event	Perfect Competition	Monopoly
Market	Large number of sellers and buyers producing a homogeneous good or service; easy entry.	Large number of buyers, one seller. Entry is blocked.
Demand and marginal revenue curves	The firm's demand and marginal revenue curve is a horizontal line at the market price.	The firm faces the market demand curve; marginal revenue is below market demand.
Price	Determined by demand and supply; each firm is a price taker. Price equals marginal cost.	The monopoly firm determines price; it is a price setter. Price is greater than marginal cost.
Profit maximization	Firms produce where marginal cost equals marginal revenue.	Firms produce where marginal cost equals marginal revenue and charge the corresponding price on the demand curve.
Profit	Entry forces economic profit to zero in the long run.	Because entry is blocked, a monopoly firm can sustain an economic profit in the long run.
Efficiency	The equilibrium solution is efficient because price equals marginal cost.	The equilibrium solution is inefficient because price is greater than marginal cost.

The combining of competing firms into a monopoly firm or unfairly driving competitors out of business is generally forbidden in the United States. Regulatory efforts to prevent monopoly fall under the purview of the nation's antitrust laws. Such efforts are examined in Chapter 16.

At the same time, we must be careful to avoid the mistake of simply assuming that competition is the alternative to monopoly, that every monopoly can and should be replaced by a competitive market. One key source of monopoly power, after all, is economies of scale. In the case of natural monopoly, the alternative to a single firm is many small, high-cost producers. We may not like having only one local provider of water, but we might like even less having dozens of providers whose costs—and prices—are higher. Where monopolies exist because economies of scale prevail over the entire range of market demand, they may serve a useful economic role. We might want to regulate their production and pricing choices, but we may not want to give up their cost advantages.

Where a natural monopoly exists, the price charged by the firm and other aspects of its behavior may be subject to regulation.Water or natural gas, for example, is often distributed by a public utility—a monopoly firm—at prices regulated by a state or local government agency. Typically, such agencies seek to force the firm to charge lower prices, and to make less profit, than it would otherwise seek.

Although economists are hesitant to levy blanket condemnations of monopoly, they are generally sharply critical of monopoly power where no rationale for it exists. When firms have substantial monopoly power only as the result of government policies that block entry, there may be little defense for their monopoly positions.

Public policy toward monopoly aims generally to strike the balance implied by economic analysis. Where rationales exist, as in the case of natural monopoly, monopolies are permitted—and their prices are regulated. In other cases, monopoly is prohibited outright. Societies are likely to at least consider taking action of some kind against monopolies unless they appear to offer cost or other technological advantages.

Case in Point Breakin' Up Is Hard To Do

You go to your mailbox and there's a letter from AT&T, the long-distance telephone service company you switched from two months earlier. The letter contains a check for $100 that's yours *if* you'll leave your new long-distance carrier MCI and return to AT&T.

This kind of competition was unthinkable before 1984, the year in which the Department of Justice's 10-year long antitrust case against AT&T finally came to an end.

The 1984 divestiture agreement separated AT&T, which would continue to provide long-distance telecommunications services, from the regional Bell operating companies, which would continue to hold monopoly positions for local service in their respective regions of the country. The separation would eliminate the tendency of the so-called Baby Bells to give preference to AT&T as the long-distance carrier. The divestiture agreement further stipulated that the regional phone companies would be allowed to enter the long-distance business only if the local markets became competitive.

With few signs of competition for local service emerging more than a decade later, Congress passed the Telecommunications Act of 1996 to spur it on. In the ensuing two years, did local phone service become more competitive? Hardly. In 1998, local phone service was still provided almost exclusively by regional monopolies. Barriers to entry were still formidable. Clearly, it is in the self-interest of the Baby Bells to maintain their near-monopoly positions and they use every means they can muster. Moreover, there are large sunk costs, such as the cost of launching a communication satellite or laying cable, associated with market entry, and natural monopoly conditions continue in some areas. Rather than creating competition, the act unleashed two years of merger mania. For example, due to acquisitions, in 1998 Southwest Bell Company (SBC) had access to one-third of the nation's local access lines.

Mergers don't generally mean more competition. However, in the case of local phone service, each merger was approved only after conditions designed to promote competition had been met. For example, the Federal Communications Commission required the combined Bell Atlantic–NYNEX regional system to install a single back-office billing system so that potential competitors need only develop a single interface. SBC promised to use its strength to enter into local markets outside the area in which it had been operating.

The days of local monopoly telephone service may be numbered, but how large that number is remains anyone's guess. In a few areas of the country, some competition for business customers had emerged by 1999 and there were nascent signs of competition for residential customers. However, no Baby Bell had been allowed into the long-distance market at that time. Consumers continued waiting for lower prices or $100 checks in the mail.

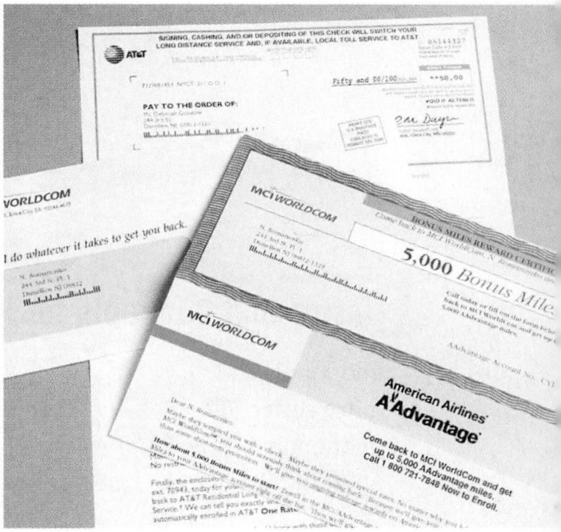

Check *list*

- A monopoly firm produces an output that is less than the efficient level. The result is a deadweight loss to society, given by the area between the demand and marginal cost curves over the range of output between the output chosen by the monopoly firm and the efficient output.
- The higher price charged by the monopoly firm compared to the perfectly competitive firm reduces consumer surplus, part of which is transferred to the monopolist. This transfer generates an equity issue.
- The monopoly firm's market power reduces consumers' choices and may result in higher prices, but there may be advantages to monopoly as well, such as economies of scale and technological innovations encouraged by the patent system.
- Public policy toward monopoly consists of antitrust laws and regulation of natural monopolies.

A Look Back

This chapter has examined the profit-maximizing behavior of monopoly firms. Monopoly occurs if an industry consists of a single firm and entry into that industry is blocked.

Potential sources of monopoly power include the existence of economies of scale over the range of market demand, locational advantages, high sunk costs associated with entry, restricted ownership of raw materials and inputs, and government restrictions such as licenses or patents. Network effects for certain products further increase the market power that patents afford.

Because the demand curve faced by the monopolist is downward sloping, the firm is a price setter. It will maximize profits by producing the quantity of output at which marginal cost equals marginal revenue. The profit-maximizing price is then found on the demand curve for that quantity.

Because a typical monopolist holds market price above marginal cost, the major impact of monopoly is a reduction in efficiency. Compared to a competitive market, the monopoly is characterized by more centralized power, potential higher profits, and less pressure to be responsive to consumer preferences. Public policy toward monopoly includes antitrust laws and, in the case of natural monopolies, regulation of price and other aspects of the firm's behavior.

A Look Ahead We've now examined the choices of firms in two market settings, perfect competition and monopoly. These two settings represent extremes on the spectrum of market models; Chapter 11 examines cases in between these two extremes.

Terms and Concepts for Review

monopoly, **207**
price setter, **207**
monopoly power, **207**
barriers to entry, **208**
natural monopoly, **208**
sunk cost, **208**
network effects, **210**

For Discussion

1. What are the necessary conditions for a monopoly position in the market to be established?
2. Suppose the government were to impose an annual license fee on a monopolist equal to its economic profits. How would such a fee affect price and output? Do you think that such a fee would be appropriate? Why or why not?
3. Name one monopoly firm you deal with. What is the source of its monopoly power? Do you think it seeks to maximize its profits?
4. "A monopolist will never produce so much output as to operate in the inelastic portion of the demand curve." Explain.
5. "A monopoly is not efficient, and its pricing behavior leads to losses to society." What does this statement mean?
6. Explain why under monopoly price is greater than marginal revenue, while under perfect competition price is equal to marginal revenue.
7. In what sense is the monopoly equilibrium inequitable?
8. What is a natural monopoly?
9. Give some examples of industries in which you think natural monopoly conditions are likely to prevail. Why do you think so?
10. Suppose a 10-percent tax is imposed on a monopoly firm's output. What happens to its price and output? Would the tax be likely to move the firm's output closer to the efficient level? Explain.

Problems

1. A university football team estimates that it faces the demand schedule shown for tickets for each game it plays. The team plays in a stadium that holds 60,000 fans. It estimates that its marginal cost of attendance, and thus for tickets sold, is zero.

Price per Ticket	Tickets per Game
$30	0
20	20,000
10	40,000
0	60,000

   a. Draw the demand and marginal revenue curves. Compute the team's profit-maximizing price and the number of tickets it will sell at that price.

   b. Determine the price elasticity of demand at the price you determined in part (a).

2. Now suppose the city in which the university in Problem 1 is located imposes a $10,000 annual license fee on all suppliers of sporting events, including the university. How does this affect the price of tickets?

3. Suppose the city in Problem 2 now imposes a tax of $10 per ticket sold. Using the demand and marginal revenue curves you drew in Problem 1, draw the new marginal cost curve and determine the profit-maximizing price and output.

Answers to Try It Yourself Problems

Try It Yourself 10-1

a. Government restriction in the form of an exclusive franchise
b. Location
c. Natural monopoly
d. Patent with strong network effects

Try It Yourself 10-2

Maintenance costs constitute the variable costs associated with building the road. In order to answer the first four parts of the question, you will need to compute total revenue, marginal revenue, and marginal cost, as shown at right:

Price per trip	$1.00	0.90	0.80	0.70	0.60	0.50
Number of trips per year (in millions)	1	2	3	4	5	6
Total variable costs per year (in millions)	$0.7	1.2	1.8	2.9	4.2	6.0
Total revenue (in millions)	$1.00	1.80	2.40	2.80	3.00	3.00
Marginal revenue		$0.80	0.60	0.40	0.20	0.00
Marginal cost		$0.50	0.60	1.10	1.30	1.80

a. Using the "midpoint" convention, the profit-maximizing level of output is 2.5 million trips per year. With that number of trips, marginal revenue ($0.60) equals marginal cost ($0.60).
b. Again, we use the "midpoint" convention. The company will charge a toll of $0.85.
c. The marginal revenue is $0.60, which is less than the $0.85 toll (price).

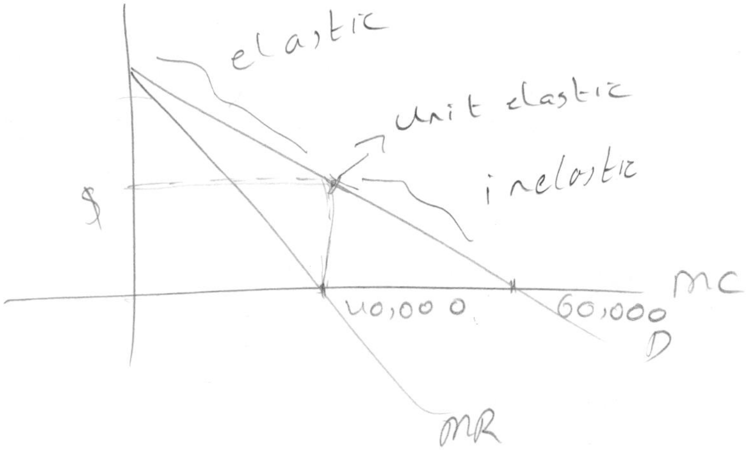

11 The World of Imperfect Competition

Getting Started: Between Idealized Extremes

Coca-Cola and Pepsi battle for greater shares of the soft-drink market. Chrysler, Ford, and General Motors compete with each other while struggling to regain ground lost to foreign-car imports. United Parcel Service attempts to muscle Federal Express aside as the leader in the overnight delivery industry. Apple Computer and IBM join forces in an effort to gain market share and to throttle Microsoft's dominance of the market for computer operating software.

This is not the aloof world of perfect competition where consumers are indifferent about which firm has produced a particular product, where each firm knows it can sell all it wants at the going market price, where firms must settle for zero economic profit in the long run. Nor is it the world of monopoly, where a single firm maximizes its profits, believing that barriers to entry will keep out would-be competitors, at least for a while. This is the world of imperfect competition, one that lies between the idealized extremes of perfect competition and monopoly. It is a world in which firms battle over market shares, in which economic profits may persist, in which rivals try to outguess each other with their pricing, advertising, and product-development strategies.

Unlike the chapters on perfect competition and monopoly, this chapter does not provide a single model to explain firms' behavior. There are too many variations on an uncertain theme for one model to explain the complexities of imperfect competition. Rather, the chapter provides an overview of some of the many different models and explanations advanced by economists. The analytical tools you have acquired in the course of studying the models of competitive and monopoly markets will be very much in evidence in this discussion.

The spectrum of business enterprise ranges from perfectly competitive firms to monopoly. Between these extremes lies the business landscape in which the vast majority of firms—those in the world of imperfect competition—actually operate. **Imperfect competition** is a market structure with more than one firm in an industry in which at least one firm is a price setter. An imperfectly competitive firm has a degree of monopoly power, either based on product differentiation that leads to a downward-sloping demand curve or resulting from the interaction of rival firms in an industry with only a few firms.

There are two broad categories of imperfectly competitive markets. The first is one in which many firms compete, each offering a slightly different product. The second is one in which the industry is dominated by a few firms. Important features of both kinds of markets are advertising and price discrimination, which we examine later in this chapter.

Monopolistic Competition: Competition Among Many

The first model of an imperfectly competitive industry that we shall investigate has conditions quite similar to those of perfect competition. The model of monopolistic competition assumes a large number of firms. It also assumes easy entry and exit. This model differs from the model of perfect competition in one key respect: It assumes that the goods and services produced by firms are differentiated. This differentiation may occur by virtue of advertising, convenience of location, product quality, reputation of the seller, or other factors. Product differentiation gives firms producing a particular version of a product some degree of price-setting or monopoly power. However, because of the availability of close substitutes, the price-setting power of monopolistically competitive firms is quite limited. **Monopolistic competition** is a model characterized by many firms producing similar but differentiated products in a market with easy entry and exit.

Restaurants are a monopolistically competitive sector; in most areas there are many firms, each is different, and entry and exit are very easy. Each restaurant has many close substitutes—these may include other restaurants, fast-food outlets, and the deli and frozen-food sections at local supermarkets. Other industries that engage in monopolistic competition are retail stores, barber and beauty shops, auto-repair shops, service stations, banks, and law and accounting firms.

Profit Maximization

Suppose a restaurant raises its prices slightly above those of similar restaurants with which it competes. Will it have any customers? Probably. Because the restaurant is different from other restaurants, some people will continue to patronize it. Within limits, then, the restaurant can set its own prices; it doesn't take the market prices as given.

Because products in a monopolistically competitive industry are differentiated, firms face downward-sloping demand curves. As we saw in Chapter 10, whenever a firm faces a downward-sloping demand curve, the graphical framework for monopoly can be used. In the short run, the model of monopolistic competition looks exactly like the model of monopoly. An important distinction between monopoly and monopolistic competition, however, emerges from the assumption of easy entry and exit. In monopolistic competition, entry will eliminate any economic profits in the long run. We begin with an analysis of the short run.

The Short Run Because a monopolistically competitive firm faces a downward-sloping demand curve, its marginal revenue curve is a downward-sloping line that lies below the demand curve, as in the monopoly model.

Exhibit 11-1 shows the demand, marginal revenue, marginal cost, and average total cost curves facing a monopolistically competitive firm, Mama's Pizza. Mama's competes with several other similar firms in a market in which entry and exit are relatively easy. Mama's demand curve D_1 is downward sloping; even if Mama's raises its prices above those of its competitors, it will still have some customers. Given the downward-sloping demand curve, Mama's marginal revenue curve MR_1 lies below demand. To sell more pizzas, Mama's must lower its price, and that means its marginal revenue from additional pizzas will be less than price.

Given the marginal revenue curve *MR* and marginal cost curve *MC*, Mama's will maximize profits by selling 2,150 pizzas per week. Mama's demand curve tells us that it can sell that quantity at a price of $10.40. Looking at the average total cost curve *ATC*, we see that the firm's cost per unit is $9.20. Its economic profit per unit is thus $1.20. Total economic profit, shown by the shaded rectangle, is $2,580 per week.

Exhibit 11-1

Short-Run Equilibrium in Monopolistic Competition

Looking at the intersection of the marginal revenue curve MR_1 and the marginal cost curve *MC*, we see that the profit-maximizing quantity is 2,150 units per week. Reading up to the average total cost curve *ATC*, we see that the cost per unit equals $9.20. Price, given on the demand curve D_1, is $10.40, so the profit per unit is $1.20. Total profit per week equals $1.20 times 2,150, or $2,580; it is shown by the shaded rectangle.

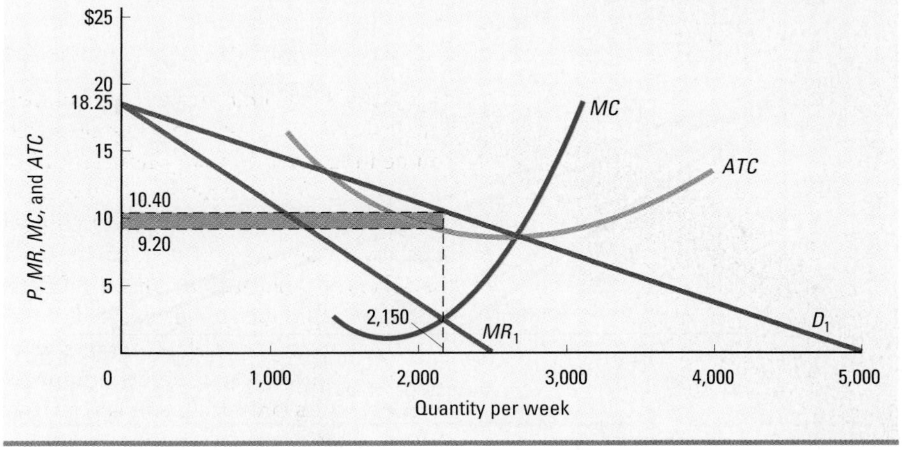

The Long Run We see in Exhibit 11-1 that Mama's Pizza is earning an economic profit. If Mama's experience is typical, then other firms in the market are also earning returns that exceed what their owners could be earning in some related activity. Positive economic profits will encourage new firms to enter Mama's market.

As new firms enter, the availability of substitutes for Mama's pizzas will increase, which will reduce the demand facing Mama's Pizza and make the demand curve for Mama's Pizza more elastic. Its demand curve will shift to the left. Any shift in a demand curve shifts the marginal revenue curve as well. New firms will continue to enter, shifting the demand curves for existing firms to the left, until pizza firms such as Mama's no longer make an economic profit. The zero-profit solution occurs where Mama's demand curve is tangent to its average total cost curve—at point A in Exhibit 11-2. Mama's price will fall to $10 per pizza and its output will fall to 2,000 pizzas per week. Mama's will just cover its opportunity costs. Hence it will earn zero economic profit. At any other price, the firm's cost per unit would be greater than the price at which a pizza could be sold, and the firm would sustain an economic loss. Thus, the firm and the industry are in long-run equilibrium. There is no incentive for firms to either enter or leave the industry.

Had Mama's Pizza and other similar restaurants been incurring economic losses, the process of moving to long-run equilibrium would work in reverse. Some firms would exit. With fewer substitutes available, the demand curve faced by each remaining firm would shift to the right. Price and output at each restaurant would rise. Exit would continue until the industry was in long-run equilibrium, with the typical firm earning zero economic profit.

Such comings and goings are typical of monopolistic competition. Because entry and exit are easy, favorable economic conditions in the industry encourage start-ups. New firms hope that they can differentiate their products enough to make a go of it. Some will; others will not. Competitors to Mama's may try to improve the ambience, play different music, offer pizzas of different sizes and shapes. It might take a while for other restaurants to come up with just the right product to pull customers and profits away from Mama's. But as long as Mama's continues to earn economic profits, there will be incentives for other firms to try.

Excess Capacity: The Price of Variety

The long-run equilibrium solution in monopolistic competition always produces zero economic profit at a point to the left of the minimum of the average total cost curve. The firm thus produces less than the output at which it would minimize average total cost. A firm that operates to the left of the lowest point on its average total cost curve has **excess capacity.**

Because monopolistically competitive firms charge prices that exceed marginal cost, monopolistic competition is inefficient. The marginal benefit consumers receive from an additional unit of the good is given by its price. Since the benefit of an additional unit of output is greater than the marginal cost, consumers would be better off if output were expanded. Furthermore, an expansion of output would reduce average total cost. But monopolistically competitive firms will not voluntarily increase output, since for them, the marginal revenue would be less than the marginal cost.

One can thus criticize a monopolistically competitive industry for falling short of the efficiency standards of perfect competition. But monopolistic competition is inefficient because of product differentiation. Think about a monopolistically competitive activity in your area. Would consumers be better off if all the firms in this industry produced identical products so that they could match the assumptions of perfect competition? If identical products are impossible, would consumers be better off if some of the firms were ordered to shut down on grounds the model pre-

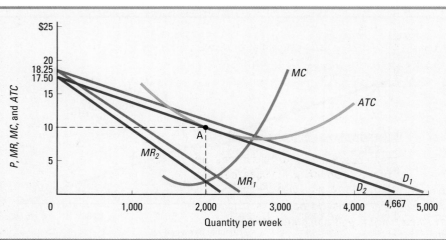

Exhibit 11-2

Monopolistic Competition in the Long Run

The existence of economic profits in a monopolistically competitive industry will induce entry in the long run. As new firms enter, the demand curve D_1 and marginal revenue curve MR_1 facing a typical firm will shift to the left, to D_2 and MR_2. Eventually this shift produces a profit-maximizing solution at zero economic profit, where D_2 is tangent to the average total cost curve *ATC* (point A). The long-run equilibrium solution here is an output of 2,000 units per week at a price of $10 per unit.

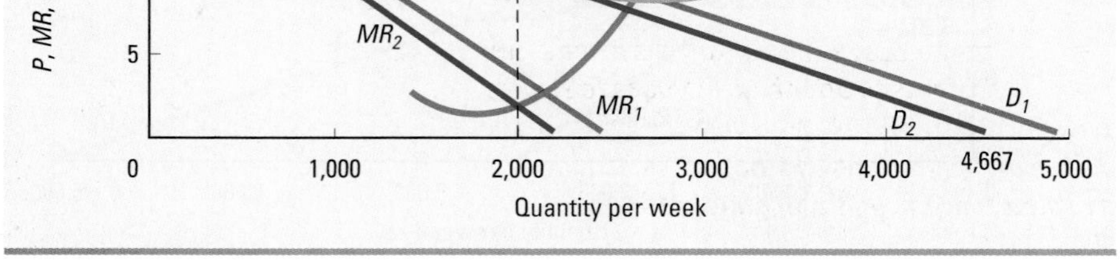

Caution!

The term "monopolistic competition" is easy to confuse with the term "monopoly." Remember, however, that the two models are characterized by quite different market conditions. A monopoly is a single firm with high barriers to entry. Monopolistic competition implies an industry with many firms, differentiated products, and easy entry and exit.

Why is the term monopolistic competition used to describe this type of market structure? The reason is that it bears some similarities to both perfect competition and to monopoly. Monopolistic competition is similar to perfect competition in that in both of these market structures many firms make up the industry and entry and exit are fairly easy. Monopolistic competition is similar to monopoly in that, like monopoly firms, monopolistically competitive firms have at least some discretion when it comes to setting prices. However, because monopolistically competitive firms produce goods that are close substitutes for those of rival firms, the degree of monopoly power that monopolistically competitive firms possess is very low.

dicts there will be "too many" firms? The inefficiency of monopolistic competition may be a small price to pay for a wide range of product choices. Furthermore, remember that perfect competition is merely a model. It isn't a goal toward which an economy might strive as an alternative to monopolistic competition.

Checklist

- A monopolistically competitive industry features some of the same characteristics as perfect competition: a large number of firms and easy entry and exit.
- The characteristic that distinguishes monopolistic competition from perfect competition is differentiated products; each firm is a price setter and thus faces a downward-sloping demand curve.
- Short-run equilibrium for a monopolistically competitive firm is identical to that of a monopoly firm. The firm produces an output at which marginal revenue equals marginal cost and sets its price according to its demand curve.
- In the long run in monopolistic competition any economic profits or losses will be eliminated by entry or by exit, leaving firms with zero economic profit.
- A monopolistically competitive industry will have some excess capacity; this may be viewed as the cost of the product diversity that this market structure produces.

Try It Yourself 11-1

Suppose the monopolistically competitive restaurant industry in your town is in long-run equilibrium, when difficulties in hiring cause restaurants to offer higher wages to servers and dishwashers. Using graphs similar to Exhibits 11-1 and 11-2, explain the effect of the wage increase on the industry in the short run and in the long run. Be sure to include in your answer an explanation of what happens to price, output, and economic profit.

Oligopoly: Competition Among the Few

A new marketing strategy introduced by General Motors is likely to affect Toyota; Toyota is likely to respond. It may develop a new marketing strategy of its own, for example, or it may respond by lowering the prices of its cars or offering new financing terms. Whatever Toyota's response is, it will affect the outcome of the new GM strategy. A decision by Procter & Gamble to lower the price of Crest toothpaste may elicit a response from Colgate-Palmolive, and that response will affect the sales of Crest. In an **oligopoly**, the fourth and final market structure that we will study, the market is dominated by a few firms, each of which recognizes that its own actions will produce a response from its rivals and that those responses will affect it.

The firms that dominate an oligopoly recognize that they are interdependent: What one firm does affects each of the others. This interdependence stands in sharp contrast to the models of perfect competition and monopolistic competition, where we assume that each firm is so small that it assumes the rest of the market will, in effect, ignore what it does. A perfectly competitive firm responds to the market, not to the actions of any other firm. A monopolistically competitive firm responds to its own demand, not to the actions of specific rivals. These presumptions greatly simplify the analysis of perfect competition and monopolistic competition. We do not have that luxury in oligopoly, where the interdependence of firms is the defining characteristic of the market.

Some oligopoly industries make standardized products: steel, aluminum, wire, and industrial tools. Others make differentiated products: cigarettes, automobiles, computers, ready-to-eat breakfast cereal, and soft drinks.

Measuring Concentration in Oligopoly

Oligopoly means that a few firms dominate an industry. But how many is "a few," and how large a share of industry output does it take to "dominate" the industry?

Compare, for example, the ready-to-eat breakfast cereal industry and the ice cream industry. The $7 billion per year cereal market is dominated by two firms, Kellogg's and General Mills, which together captured about 63 percent of market sales in the United States in 1998.[1] This oligopoly operates in a highly concentrated market. The market for ice cream, where the four largest firms accounted for just 24 percent of output in 1992, is much less concentrated.

One way to measure the degree to which output in an industry is concentrated among a few firms is to use a **concentration ratio**, which reports the percentage of output accounted for by the largest firms in an industry. The higher the concentration ratio, the more the firms in the industry take account of their rivals' behavior. The lower the concentration ratio, the more the industry reflects the characteristics of monopolistic competition or perfect competition.

The U.S. Census Bureau, based on surveys it conducts of manufacturing firms every 5 years, reports concentration ratios. These surveys show concentration ratios for the largest 4, 8, 20, and 50 firms in each industry category. Some concentration ratios from the 1992 survey (the latest data available) are reported in Exhibit 11-3. Notice that the four-firm concentration ratio for breakfast cereals is 85 percent; for ice cream it is 24 percent.

An alternative measure of concentration is found by squaring the percentage share of each firm in an industry, then summing these squared market shares to derive a **Herfindahl–Hirschman Index (HHI)**. The largest HHI possible is the case of monopoly, where one firm has 100 percent of the market; the index is 100^2, or 10,000. An industry with two firms, each with 50 percent of total output, has an HHI of 5,000 ($50^2 + 50^2$). In an industry with 10,000 firms that have 0.01 percent of the market each, the HHI is 1. Herfindahl–Hirschmann Indexes reported by the Census Bureau are also given in Exhibit 11-3. Notice that the HHI

[1] "Kellogg Faces Crunch As Rival Overtakes It," [London] *Sunday Times* 10 January 1999, p. B8.

is 2,253 for breakfast cereals and only 293 for ice cream.

In some cases, the census data understate the degree to which a few firms dominate the market. One problem is that industry categories may be too broad to capture significant cases of industry dominance. The sporting goods industry, for example, appears to be highly competitive if we look just at measures of concentration, but markets for individual goods, such as golf clubs, running shoes, and tennis rackets, tend to be dominated by a few firms. Further, the data reflect shares of the national market. A tendency for regional domination doesn't show up. For example, the concrete industry appears to be highly competitive. But concrete is produced in local markets—it's too expensive to ship it very far—and many of these local markets are dominated by a handful of firms.

The census data can also overstate the degree of actual concentration. The "motor vehicles and auto bodies" category, for example, has a four-firm concentration ratio that suggests the industry is strongly dominated by four large firms (in fact, U.S. production is dominated by three: General Motors, Ford, and DaimlerChrysler). Those firms hardly account for all car sales in the United States, however, as other foreign producers have captured a large portion of the domestic market. Including those foreign competitors suggests a far less concentrated industry than the census data imply.

Percentage of 1992 Value of Industry Shipments

Industry	Largest 4 firms	Largest 8 firms	Largest 20 firms	Largest 50 firms	HHI
Ice cream	24	40	68	87	293
Breakfast cereal	85	98	99+	100	2,253
Cigarettes	93	D*			D*
Men's and boy's shirts	28	42	60	78	315
Women's, misses', and juniors' blouses and shirts	12	20	35	55	87
Motor vehicles and passenger car bodies	84	91	99	99	2,676
Athletic and sporting goods, except clothing, footwear, small arms, and ammunition	14	23	39	57	103
Medicinal chemicals and botanical products	76	84	91	97	2,999
Special dies and tools, die sets, jigs and fixtures, industrial	3	5	10	17	7

*D, data withheld by the government to avoid revealing information about specific firms.

Source: The table contains selected statistics from the 1992 *Census of Manufactures* MC92-S-2, Table 3, "Concentration Ratios in Manufacturing." For 1992, this report has not been released in printed format.

Exhibit 11-3

Concentration Ratios and Herfindahl–Hirschmann Indexes

Two measures of industry concentration are reported by the Census Bureau: concentration ratios and the Herfindahl–Hirschmann Index (HHI).

The Collusion Model

There is no single model of profit-maximizing oligopoly behavior that corresponds to economists' models of perfect competition, monopoly, and monopolistic competition. Uncertainty about the interaction of rival firms makes specification of a single model of oligopoly impossible. Instead, economists have devised a variety of models that deal with the uncertain nature of rivals' responses in different ways. In this section we review one type of oligopoly model, the collusion model. After examining this traditional approach to the analysis of oligopoly behavior, we shall turn to another method of examining oligopolistic interaction: game theory.

Firms in any industry could achieve the maximum profit attainable if they all agreed to select the monopoly price and output and to share the profits. One approach to the analysis of oligopoly is to assume that firms in the industry collude, selecting the monopoly solution.

Suppose an industry is a **duopoly**, an industry with two firms. Exhibit 11-4 shows a case in which the two firms are identical. They sell identical products and face identical demand and cost conditions. To simplify the analysis, let's assume that each has a horizontal marginal cost curve *MC*. The demand and marginal revenue curves are the same for both firms. We find the combined demand curve for the two firms, D_{combined}, by adding the individual demand curves together. Because one firm's demand curve, D_{firm}, represents one-half of market demand, it is the same as the combined marginal revenue curve for the two firms. If these two firms act as a monopoly, together they produce Q_{m} and charge a price P_{m}. This result is achieved if each firm selects its profit-maximizing output, which equals ½ Q_{m}. This solution

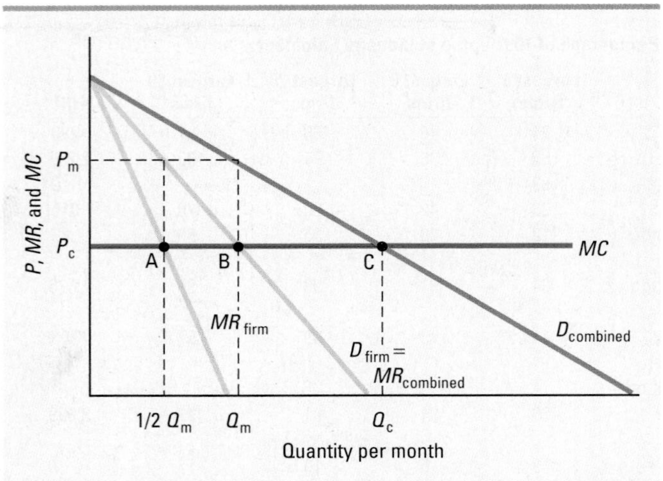

Exhibit 11-4

Monopoly Through Collusion

Two identical firms have the same horizontal marginal cost curve *MC*. Their demand curves D_{firm} and marginal revenue curves MR_{firm} are also identical. The combined demand curve is $D_{combined}$; the combined marginal revenue curve is $MR_{combined}$. The profits of the two firms are maximized if each produces ½ Q_m at point A. Industry output at point B is thus Q_m and the price is P_m. At point C, the efficient solution output would be Q_c, and the price would equal *MC*.

is inefficient; the efficient solution is price P_c and output Q_c, found where the combined market demand curve $D_{combined}$ and the marginal cost curve *MC* intersect.

In the simplest form of collusion, **overt collusion,** firms openly agree on price, output, and other decisions aimed at achieving monopoly profits. Firms that coordinate their activities through overt collusion and by forming collusive coordinating mechanisms make up a **cartel.**

Firms form a cartel to gain monopoly power. A successful cartel can earn large profits, but there are several problems with forming and maintaining one. First, in many countries, including the United States, cartels are generally illegal.[2] They are banned because their purpose is to raise prices and restrict output. Second, the cartel may not succeed in inducing all firms in the industry to join. Firms that remain outside the cartel can compete by lowering price, and thus they prevent the cartel from achieving the monopoly solution. Third, there is always an incentive for individual members to cheat on cartel agreements. Suppose the members of a cartel have agreed to impose the monopoly price in their market and to limit their output accordingly. Any one firm might calculate that it could charge slightly less than the cartel price and thus capture a larger share of the market for itself. Cheating firms expand output and drive prices down below the level originally chosen.

The Organization of Petroleum Exporting Countries (OPEC), perhaps the best-known cartel, is made up of 13 oil-producing countries. In the 1970s, OPEC successfully acted like a monopoly by restricting output and raising prices. By the mid-1980s, however, the monopoly power of the cartel had been weakened by expansion of output by nonmember producers such as Mexico and Norway and by cheating among the cartel members.

An alternative to overt collusion is **tacit collusion,** an unwritten, unspoken understanding through which firms agree to limit their competition. Firms may, for example, begin following the price leadership of a particular firm, raising or lowering their prices when the leader makes such a change. The price leader may be the largest firm in the industry, or it may be a firm that has been particularly good at assessing changes in demand or cost. At various times, tacit collusion has been alleged to occur in a wide range of industries, including steel, cars, and breakfast cereals.

It is difficult to know how common tacit collusion is. The fact that one firm changes its price shortly after another one does cannot prove that a tacit conspiracy exists. After all, we expect to see the prices of all firms in a perfectly competitive industry moving together in response to changes in demand or production costs.

Game Theory and Oligopoly Behavior

Oligopoly presents a problem in which decisionmakers must select strategies by taking into account the responses of their rivals, which they cannot know for sure in advance. A choice based on the recognition that the actions of others will affect the outcome of the choice and that takes these possible actions into account is called a **strategic choice. Game theory** is an analytical approach through which strategic choices can be assessed.

Among the strategic choices available to an oligopoly firm are pricing choices, marketing strategies, and product-development efforts. An airline's decision to raise or lower its fares—

[2]One legal cartel is the NCAA, which many economists regard as a successful device through which member firms (colleges and universities) collude on a wide range of rules through which they produce sports.

Case in Point The Matzo Fix

The three conspirators spoke guardedly at Ratner's Restaurant on Manhattan's Lower East Side. Millions of dollars were at stake in their negotiations, and stiff fines or even a jail sentence awaited them if they were caught.

They met each fall at Ratner's to fix the price of matzo, a flat, unleavened bread eaten primarily by Jews at Passover. The conspirators came from the nation's biggest matzo producers: Manischewitz, Aron Streit, and Horowitz. The Manischewitz executive would tell the representatives of the other two firms about its plans for price and output for the next Passover; Aron Streit and Horowitz would agree to charge the same price.

Federal prosecutors indicted Manischewitz in 1990 for violating the Sherman Antitrust Act, a federal statute that prohibits such conspiracies. The other two firms were named as unindicted co-conspirators. Manischewitz pleaded no contest to the charges and was slapped with a $1 million fine. Federal Judge Harold Ackerman, in levying the fine, said "Nothing less than $1 million would be fair and just."

In addition to the fine, Manischewitz was sued by many of its major customers, who charged they had been harmed by the monopoly price. The firm settled one suit by paying $500,000 and agreeing to provide $2 million worth of kosher food to a charity.

In the end, however, Manischewitz was able to continue its market dominance in a different guise—it purchased Horowitz.

Sources: Christopher Kilbourne, "Judge Urged to Throw Book at Matzo Maker Manischewitz Calls $1 M Fine Excessive," [Bergen, New Jersey] *Record,* 16 May 1991, p. A1; "Matzo Maker Fined For Price-Fixing," [Louisville, Kentucky] *Courier-Journal,* 18 May 1991, p. A6.

or to leave them unchanged—is a strategic choice. The other airlines' decision to match or ignore their rival's price change is also a strategic choice. Wendy's used its former chief executive officer, Dave Thomas, as a spokesperson; this was a strategic marketing decision. IBM boosted its share in the highly competitive personal computer market in large part because a strategic product-development strategy accelerated the firm's introduction of new products.

Once a firm implements a strategic decision, there will be an outcome. The outcome of a strategic decision is called a **payoff.** In general, the payoff in an oligopoly game is the change in economic profit to each firm. The firm's payoff depends partly on the strategic choice it makes and partly on the strategic choices of its rivals. Firms in the airline industry, for example, raised their fares in 1993, expecting to enjoy increased profits as a result. They changed their strategic choices when Northwest chose to slash its fares, and all firms ended up with a payoff of lower profits.

We shall use two applications to examine the basic concepts of game theory. The first examines a classic game theory problem called the prisoners' dilemma. The second deals with strategic choices by two firms in a duopoly.

The Prisoners' Dilemma Suppose a local district attorney (DA) is certain that two individuals, Frankie and Johnny, have committed a burglary, but she has no evidence that would be admissible in court.

The DA arrests the two. On being searched, each is discovered to have a substantial amount of marijuana. The DA now has a sure conviction on a possession of marijuana charge, but she will get a conviction on the burglary charge only if at least one of the prisoners confesses and implicates the other.

The DA decides on a strategy designed to elicit confessions. She separates the two prisoners and then offers each the following deal: "If you confess and your partner doesn't, you'll get the minimum sentence of 1 year in jail on the possession and burglary charges. If you both confess, your sentence will be 3 years in jail. If your partner confesses and you don't, the plea bargain is off and you'll get 6 years in prison. If neither of you confess, you'll each get 2 years in prison on the drug charge."

The two prisoners each face a dilemma; they can choose to confess or not confess. Because the prisoners are separated, they can't plot a joint strategy. Each must make a strategic choice in isolation.

The outcomes of these strategic choices, as outlined by the DA, depend on the strategic choice made by the other prisoner. The payoff matrix for this game is given in Exhibit 11-5. The two rows represent Frankie's strategic choices; she may confess or not confess. The two columns represent Johnny's strategic choices; he may confess or not confess. There are four possible outcomes: Frankie and Johnny both confess (cell A), Frankie confesses but Johnny doesn't (cell B), Frankie doesn't confess but Johnny does (cell C), and neither Frankie nor Johnny confesses (cell D). The portion at the lower left in each cell shows Frankie's payoff; the shaded portion at the upper right shows Johnny's payoff.

If Johnny confesses, Frankie's best choice is to confess—she'll get a 3-year sentence rather than the 6-year sentence she'd get if she didn't confess. If Johnny does not confess, Frankie's best strategy is still to confess—she'll get a 1-year rather than a 2-year sentence. In this game, Frankie's best strategy is to confess, regardless of what Johnny does. When a player's best strategy is the same regardless of the action of the other player, that strategy is said to be a **dominant strategy.** Frankie's dominant strategy is to confess to the burglary.

For Johnny, the best strategy to follow if Frankie confesses is to confess. The best strategy to follow if Frankie doesn't confess is also to confess. Confessing is a dominant strategy for Johnny as well. A game in which there is a dominant strategy for each player is called a **dominant strategy equilibrium.** Here, the dominant strategy equilibrium is for both prisoners to confess; the payoff will be given by cell A in the payoff matrix.

From the point of view of the two prisoners together, a payoff in cell D would have been preferable. Had they both denied participation in the robbery, their combined sentence would have been 4 years in prison—2 years each. Indeed, cell D offers the lowest combined prison time of any of the outcomes in the payoff matrix. But because the prisoners can't communicate, each is likely to make a strategic choice that results in a more costly outcome. Of course, the outcome of the game depends on the way the payoff matrix is structured.

Exhibit 11-5

Payoff Matrix for the Prisoners' Dilemma

The four cells represent each of the possible outcomes of the prisoners' game.

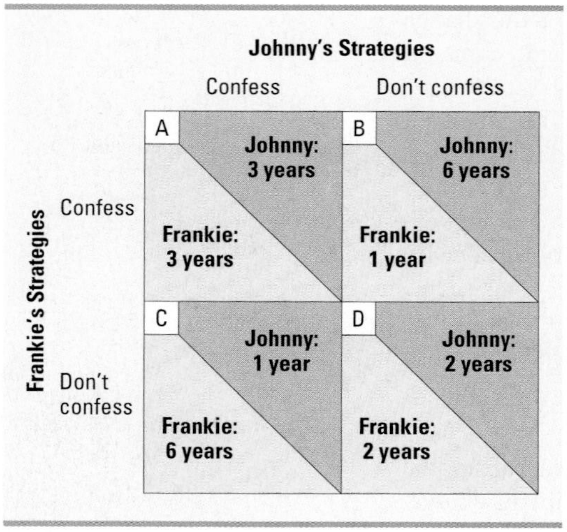

Johnny's Strategies
Confess
Don't confess
Frankie's Strategies
Confess
Don't confess
A
Johnny: 3 years
Frankie: 3 years
B
Johnny: 6 years
Frankie: 1 year
C
Johnny: 1 year
Frankie: 6 years
D
Johnny: 2 years
Frankie: 2 years

Repeated Oligopoly Games The prisoners' dilemma was played once, by two players. The players were given a payoff matrix; each could make one choice, and the game ended after the first round of choices.

The real world of oligopoly has as many players as there are firms in the industry. They play round after round: a firm raises its price, another firm introduces a new product, the first firm cuts its price, a third firm introduces a new marketing strategy, and so on. An oligopoly game is a bit like a baseball game with an unlimited number of innings—one firm may come out ahead after one round, but another will emerge on top another day. In the computer industry game, the introduction of personal computers changed the rules. IBM, which had won the mainframe game quite handily, struggles to keep up in a world in which rivals continue to slash prices and improve quality.

Oligopoly games may have more than two players, so the games are more complex, but this doesn't change their basic structure. The fact that the games are repeated introduces new strategic considerations. A player must consider not just the ways in which its choices will affect its rivals now but how its choices will affect them in the future as well.

Let's keep the game simple, however, and consider a duopoly game. The two firms have colluded, either tacitly or overtly, to create a monopoly solution. As long as each player upholds the agreement, the two firms will earn the maximum economic profit possible in the enterprise.

There will, however, be a powerful incentive for each firm to cheat. The monopoly solution may generate the maximum economic profit possible for the two firms combined, but what if one firm captures some of the other firm's profit? Suppose, for example, that two equipment rental firms, Quick Rent and Speedy Rent, operate in a community. Given the economies of scale in the business and the size of the community, it isn't likely that another firm will enter. Each firm has about half the market, and they have agreed to charge the prices that would be chosen if the two combined as a single firm. Each earns economic profits of $20,000 per month.

Quick and Speedy could cheat on their arrangement in several ways. One of the firms could slash prices, introduce a new line of rental products, or launch an advertising blitz. This approach wouldn't be likely to increase the total profitability of the two firms, but if one firm could take the other by surprise, it might profit at the expense of its rival, at least for a while.

Let's focus on the strategy of cutting prices, which we'll call a strategy of cheating on the duopoly agreement. The alternative is not to cheat on the agreement. Cheating increases a firm's profits *if* its rival doesn't respond. Exhibit 11-6 shows the payoff matrix facing the two firms at a particular time. As in the prisoners' dilemma matrix, the four cells list the payoffs for the two firms. If neither firm cheats (cell D), profits remain unchanged.

This game has a dominant strategy equilibrium. Quick's preferred strategy, regardless of what Speedy does, is to cheat. Speedy's best strategy, regardless of what Quick does, is to cheat. The result is that the two firms will select a strategy that lowers their combined profits!

Quick Rent and Speedy Rent face an unpleasant dilemma. They both want to maximize profit, yet each is likely to choose a strategy inconsistent with that goal. If they continue the game as it now exists, each will continue to cut prices, eventually driving prices down to the point where price equals average total cost (presumably, the price-cutting will stop there). But that would leave the two firms with zero economic profits.

Both firms have an interest in maintaining the status quo of their collusive agreement. Overt collusion is one device through which the monopoly outcome may be maintained, but that is illegal. One way for the firms to encourage each other not to cheat is to use a tit-for-tat strategy. In a **tit-for-tat strategy** a firm responds to cheating by cheating, and it responds to cooperative behavior by cooperating. As each firm learns that its rival will respond to cheating by cheating, and to cooperation by cooperating, cheating on agreements becomes less and less likely.

Still another way firms may seek to force rivals to behave cooperatively rather than competitively is to use a **trigger strategy**, in which a firm makes clear that it is willing and able to respond to cheating by permanently revoking an agreement. A firm might, for example, make a credible threat to cut prices down to the level of average total cost—and leave them there—in response to any price-cutting by a rival. A trigger strategy is calculated to impose huge costs on any firm that cheats—and on the firm that threatens to invoke the trigger. A firm might threaten to invoke a trigger in hopes that the threat will forestall any cheating by its rivals.

Game theory has proved to be an enormously fruitful approach to the analysis of a wide range of problems. Corporations use it to map out strategies and to anticipate rivals' responses. Governments use it in developing foreign-policy strategies. Military leaders play war games on computers

Exhibit 11-6

To Cheat or Not to Cheat: Game Theory in Oligopoly

Two rental firms, Quick Rent and Speedy Rent, operate in a duopoly market. They have colluded in the past, achieving a monopoly solution. Cutting prices means cheating on the arrangement; not cheating means maintaining current prices. The payoffs are changes in monthly profits, in thousands of dollars. If neither firm cheats, then neither firm's profits will change. In this game, cheating is a dominant strategy equilibrium.

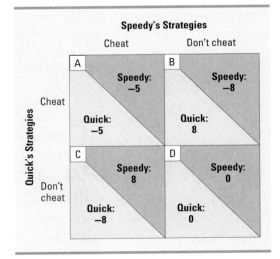

Quick's Strategies	Speedy's Strategies: Cheat	Speedy's Strategies: Don't cheat
Cheat	A — Speedy: −5; Quick: −5	B — Speedy: −8; Quick: 8
Don't cheat	C — Speedy: 8; Quick: −8	D — Speedy: 0; Quick: 0

using the basic ideas of game theory. Any situation in which rivals make strategic choices to which competitors will respond can be assessed using game theory analysis.

One rather chilly application of game theory analysis can be found in the period of the Cold War when the United States and the Soviet Union upheld a nuclear weapons policy that was described by the acronym MAD, which stood for *m*utually *a*ssured *d*estruction. Both countries had enough nuclear weapons to destroy the other several times over, and each threatened to launch sufficient nuclear weapons to destroy the other country if the other country launched a nuclear attack against it or any of its allies. On its face, the MAD doctrine seems, well, mad. It was, after all, a commitment by each nation to respond to any nuclear attack with a counterattack that many scientists expected would end human life on earth. As crazy as it seemed, however, it worked. For 40 years, the two nations did not go to war. While the collapse of the Soviet Union in 1991 ended the need for a MAD doctrine, during the time that the two countries were rivals, MAD was a very effective trigger indeed.

Check*list*

- The key characteristics of oligopoly are a recognition that the actions of one firm will produce a response from rivals and that these responses will affect it. Each firm is uncertain what its rivals' responses might be.
- The degree to which a few firms dominate an industry can be measured using a concentration ratio or a Herfindahl-Hirschmann Index.
- One way to avoid the uncertainty firms face in oligopoly is through collusion. Collusion may be overt, as in the case of a cartel, or tacit, as in the case of price leadership.
- Game theory is a tool that can be used to understand strategic choices by firms.
- Firms can use tit-for-tat and trigger strategies to encourage cooperative behavior by rivals.

Try It Yourself 11-2

Which model of oligopoly would seem to be most appropriate for analyzing firms' behavior in each of the situations given below?

1. *When South Airlines lowers its fare between Miami and New York City, North Airlines lowers its fare between the two cities. When South Airlines raises its fare, North Airlines does too.*
2. *Whenever Bank A raises interest rates on car loans, other banks in the area do too.*
3. *In 1986, Saudi Arabia intentionally flooded the market with oil in order to punish fellow OPEC members for cheating on their production quotas.*
4. *In July 1998, Saudi Arabia floated a proposal in which a group of eight or nine major oil-exporting countries (including OPEC members and some nonmembers, such as Mexico) would manage world oil prices by adjusting their production.*

Extensions of Imperfect Competition: Advertising and Price Discrimination

The models of monopoly and of imperfectly competitive markets allow us to explain two commonly observed features of many markets: advertising and price discrimination. Firms in markets that are not perfectly competitive try to influence the positions of the demand curves they face, and hence profits, through advertising. Profits may also be enhanced by charging different customers different prices. In this section we'll discuss these aspects of the behavior of firms in markets that are not perfectly competitive.

Advertising

Firms in monopoly, monopolistic competition, and oligopoly use advertising when they expect it to increase their profits. We see the results of these expenditures in a daily barrage of advertising on television, radio, newspapers, magazines, billboards, passing buses, park benches, the mail, home telephones—in virtually every medium imaginable. Is all this advertising good for the economy?

We've already seen that a perfectly competitive economy with fully defined and easily transferable property rights will achieve an efficient allocation of resources. There is no role for advertising in such an economy, because everyone knows that firms in each industry produce identical products. Furthermore, buyers already have complete information about the alternatives available to them in the market.

But perfect competition contrasts sharply with imperfect competition. Imperfect competition can lead to a price greater than marginal cost and thus generate an inefficient allocation of resources. Firms in an imperfectly competitive market may advertise heavily. Does advertising cause inefficiency, or is it part of the solution? Does advertising insulate imperfectly competitive firms from competition and allow them to raise their prices even higher, or does it encourage greater competition and push prices down?

There are two ways in which advertising could lead to higher prices to consumers. First, the advertising itself is costly; in 1997, U.S. firms spent $188 billion on advertising, an amount equal to 2.3 percent of the value of all goods and services produced that year. By pushing up production costs, advertising may push up prices. If the advertising serves no socially useful purpose, these costs represent a waste of resources in the economy. Second, firms may be able to use advertising to manipulate demand and create barriers to entry. If a few firms in a particular market have developed intense brand loyalty, it may be difficult for new firms to enter—the advertising creates a kind of barrier to entry. By maintaining barriers to entry, firms may be able to sustain high prices.

But advertising has its defenders. They argue that advertising provides consumers with useful information and encourages price competition. Without advertising, these defenders argue, it would be impossible for new firms to enter an industry. Advertising, they say, promotes competition, lowers prices, and encourages a greater range of choice for consumers.

Advertising, like all other economic phenomena, has benefits as well as costs. To assess those benefits and costs, let's examine the impact of advertising on the economy.

Advertising and Information Advertising does inform us about products and their prices. Even critics of advertising generally agree that when advertising advises consumers about the availability of new products, or when it provides price information, it serves a useful function. But much of the information provided by advertising appears to be of limited value. Hearing that "Pepsi is the right one, baby" or "Coors is the right one now" may not be among the most edifying lessons consumers could learn.

Some economists argue, however, that even advertising that seems to tell us nothing may provide useful information. They note that a consumer is unlikely to make a repeat purchase of a product that turns out to be a dud. Advertising an inferior product is likely to have little payoff; people who do try it aren't likely to try it again. It isn't likely a firm could profit by going to great expense to launch a product that produced only unhappy consumers. Thus, if a product is heavily advertised, its producer is likely to be confident that many consumers will be satisfied with it and make repeat purchases. If this is the case, then the fact that the product is advertised, regardless of the content of that advertising, signals consumers that at least its producer is confident that the product will satisfy them.

Advertising and Competition If advertising creates consumer loyalty to a particular brand, then that loyalty may serve as a barrier to entry to other firms. Some brands of household products, such as laundry detergents, are so well established they may make it difficult for other firms to enter the market.

In general, there is a positive relationship between the degree of concentration of market power and the fraction of total costs devoted to advertising. This relationship, critics argue, is a causal one; the high expenditures on advertising are the cause of the concentration. To the extent that advertising increases industry concentration, it is likely to result in higher prices to consumers and lower levels of output. The higher prices associated with advertising are not simply the result of passing on the cost of the advertising itself to consumers; higher prices also derive from the monopoly power the advertising creates.

But advertising may encourage competition as well. By providing information to consumers about prices, for example, it may encourage price competition. Suppose a firm in a world of no advertising wants to increase its sales. One way to do that is to lower price. But without advertising, it is extremely difficult to inform potential customers of this new policy. The likely result is that there would be little response, and the price experiment would probably fail. Price competition would thus be discouraged in a world without advertising.

Empirical studies of markets in which advertising is not allowed have confirmed that advertising encourages price competition. One of the most famous studies of the effects of advertising looked at pricing for prescription eyeglasses. In the early 1970s, about half the states in the United States banned advertising by firms making prescription eyeglasses; the other half allowed it. A comparison of prices in the two groups of states by economist Lee Benham showed that the cost of prescription eyeglasses was far lower in states that allowed advertising than in states that banned it.[3] Mr. Benham's research proved quite influential—virtually all states have since revoked their bans on such advertising.

Advertising may also allow more entry by new firms. When Kia, a South Korean automobile manufacturer, entered the U.S. low-cost compact car market in 1994, it flooded the airwaves with advertising. Suppose such advertising had not been possible. Could Kia have entered the market in the United States? It seems highly unlikely that any new product could be launched without advertising. The absence of advertising would thus be a barrier to entry that would increase the degree of monopoly power in the economy. A greater degree of monopoly power would, over time, translate into higher prices and reduced output.

Advertising is thus a two-edged sword. On the one hand, the existence of established and heavily advertised rivals may make it difficult for a new firm to enter a market. On the other hand, entry into most industries would be virtually impossible without advertising.

Economists don't agree on whether advertising helps or hurts competition in particular markets, but one general observation can safely be made—a world with advertising is more competitive than a world without advertising would be. The important policy question is more limited—and more difficult to answer: Would a world with *less* advertising be more competitive than a world with more?

Price Discrimination

Throughout the text up to this point, we have assumed that firms sold all units of output at the same price. In some cases, however, firms can charge different prices to different consumers. If such an opportunity exists, the firm can increase profits further.

[3]Lee Benham, "The Effect of Advertising on the Price of Eyeglasses," *Journal of Law and Economics* 15(2) (1972): 337–352.

Case in Point The Ban on Cigarette Advertising

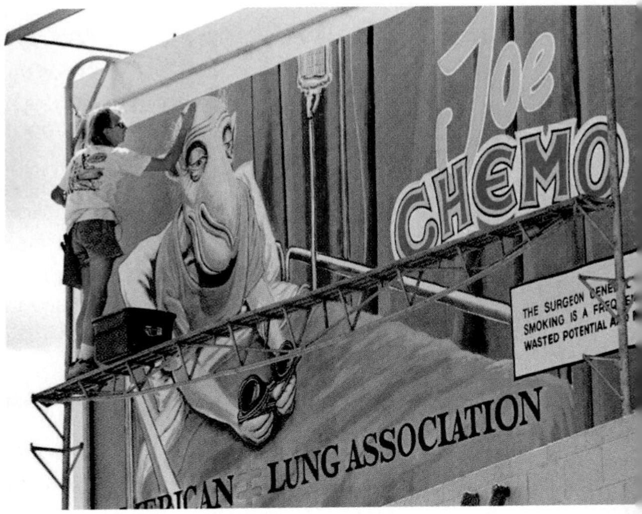

Cigarettes were once one of the most heavily advertised products on television, but radio and television advertising of the product were banned by the federal government in 1970 because of health problems associated with smoking. The ban provided a partial test of how advertising restrictions might affect the market for a widely promoted consumer good.

The ban does not appear to have had any particular effect on cigarette sales. Indeed, per capita cigarette consumption had been falling before the ban was imposed; it rose after the ban!

Economist Woodrow Eckard of the University of Colorado at Denver has examined the impact of the ban on the competitiveness of the cigarette industry. If advertising makes industries less competitive, then limiting advertising should have made the cigarette industry more competitive. If advertising encourages competition, then a ban on a major form of advertising should have reduced competition. That would tend to boost profits of cigarette firms.

Mr. Eckard's findings were consistent with the hypothesis that advertising encourages competition. He found that the market shares of the leading cigarette producers had been declining, but stabilized or increased after the ban was imposed. New brand entry virtually stopped for four years after the ban. Profit margins of tobacco companies increased.

The tobacco industry protested when President Clinton proposed new restrictions on cigarette advertising in 1995. But privately, some industry executives said that the restrictions might boost the profits of leading firms. "Whenever you put on competitive restraints, the bigger get bigger and the smaller players get knocked out," a Philip Morris executive told *The Wall Street Journal.*

In 1999, cigarette advertising could once again be seen on television, but with messages designed to discourage consumers and potential consumers, especially teens, from smoking. Using an expected $200 billion settlement paid by tobacco companies to states that had sued to recover the costs of smoking-related illnesses and deaths suffered by residents, state governments began running ads illustrating graphically the health consequences of smoking. Whether this negative advertising will have its desired effect remains to be seen.

Sources: Woodrow Eckard, "Competition and the Cigarette TV Advertising Ban," *Economic Inquiry* 29(1) (January 1991), pp. 119–133; Suein L. Hwang, "Clinton Ad Ban Could Strengthen Philip Morris," *Wall Street Journal,* 21 August 1995, p. B1.

When a firm charges different prices for the same good or service to different consumers, even though there is no difference in the cost to the firm of supplying these consumers, the firm is engaging in **price discrimination.** Except for a few situations of price discrimination that have been declared illegal, such as manufacturers selling their goods to distributors at different prices when there are no differences in cost, price discrimination is generally legal.

The potential for price discrimination exists in all market structures except perfect competition. As long as a firm faces a downward-sloping demand curve and thus has some degree of monopoly power, it may be able to engage in price discrimination. But monopoly power alone is not enough to allow a firm to price discriminate. Monopoly power is one of three conditions that must be met:

1. ***A Price-Setting Firm*** The firm must have some degree of monopoly power—it must be a price setter. A price-taking firm can only take the market price as given—it isn't in a position to make price choices of any kind. Thus, firms in perfectly competitive markets will not engage in price discrimination. Firms in monopoly, monopolistically competitive, or oligopolistic markets may engage in price discrimination.

2. ***Distinguishable Customers*** The market must be capable of being fairly easily segmented—separated so that customers with different elasticities of demand can be identified and treated differently.

3. ***Prevention of Resale*** The various market segments must be isolated in some way from one another to prevent customers who are offered a lower price from selling to customers who are charged a higher price. If consumers can easily resell a product, then discrimination is unlikely to be successful. Resale may be particularly difficult for certain services, such as dental checkups.

Examples of price discrimination abound. Senior citizens and students are often offered discount fares on city buses. Children receive discount prices for movie theater tickets and entrance fees at zoos and theme parks. Faculty and staff at colleges and universities might receive discounts at the campus bookstore. Airlines give discount prices to customers who are willing to stay over a Saturday night. Physicians might charge wealthy patients more than poor ones. In all these cases a firm charges different prices to different customers for what is essentially the same product.

Not every instance of firms charging different prices to different customers constitutes price discrimination. Differences in prices may reflect different costs associated with providing the product. One buyer might require special billing practices, another might require delivery on a particular day of the week, and yet another might require special packaging. Price differentials based on differences in production costs are not examples of price discrimination.

Why would a firm charge different prices to different consumers? The answer can be found in the marginal decision rule and in the relationship between marginal revenue and elasticity.

Suppose an airline has found that its long-run profit-maximizing solution for a flight between Minneapolis and Cleveland, when it charges the same price to all passengers, is to carry 300 passengers at $200 per ticket. The airline has a degree of monopoly power, so it faces a downward-sloping demand curve. The airline has noticed that there are essentially two groups of customers on each flight: people who are traveling for business reasons and people who are traveling for personal reasons (visiting family or friends or taking a vacation). We'll call this latter group tourists. Of the 300 passengers, 200 are business travelers and 100 are tourists. The airline's revenue from business travelers is therefore currently $40,000 ($200 times 200 business travelers) and from tourists is currently $20,000 ($200 times 100 tourists).

It seems likely that the price elasticities of demand of these two groups for a particular flight will differ. Tourists may have a wide range of substitutes: They could take their trips at a different time, they could vacation in a different area, or they could easily choose not to go at all. Business travelers, however, might be attending meetings or conferences at a particular time and in a particular city. They have options, of course, but the range of options is likely to be more limited than the range of options facing tourists. Given all this, tourists are likely to have more elastic demand than business travelers for a particular flight.

The difference in elasticities suggests the airline could increase its profit by adjusting its pricing. To simplify, suppose that at a price of about $200 per ticket, demand by tourists is price elastic and by business travelers is price inelastic. Also suppose that the marginal cost of additional passengers is zero between 300 and 350 passengers. It is plausible that the marginal cost is likely to be quite low, since the number of crewmembers will not vary and no food is served on short flights. Thus, if the airline can increase its revenue, its profits will increase. Suppose the airline lowers the price for tourists to $190. The lower price encourages 10 more tourists to take the flight. Of course, the airline can't charge different prices to different tourists; rather it charges $190 to all, now 110, tourists. Still, the airline's revenue from tourist passengers increases from $20,000 to $20,900

($190 times 110 tourists). Suppose it charges $250 to its business travelers. As a result, only 195 business travelers take the flight. The airline's revenue from business travelers still rises from $40,000 to $48,750 ($250 times 195 business travelers). The airline will continue to change the mix of passengers, and increase the number of passengers, so long as doing so increases its profit. Because tourist demand is elastic, relatively small reductions in price will attract relatively large numbers of additional tourists. Because business demand is inelastic, relatively large increases in price will discourage relatively small numbers of business travelers from making the trip. The airline will continue to reduce its price to tourists and raise its price to business travelers as long as it gains profit from doing so.

Of course, the airline can impose a discriminatory fare structure only if it can distinguish tourists from business travelers. Airlines typically do this by looking at the travel plans of their customers. Trips that involve a stay over a weekend, for example, are more likely to be tourist related, whereas trips that begin and end during the workweek are likely to be business trips. Thus, airlines charge much lower fares for trips that extend through a weekend than for trips that begin and end on weekdays.

In general, price-discrimination strategies are based on differences in elasticity among groups of customers and the differences in marginal revenue that result. A firm will seek a price structure that offers customers with more elastic demand a lower price and offers customers with relatively less elastic demand a higher price.

It is always in the interest of a firm to discriminate. Yet most of the goods and services that we buy are not offered on a discriminatory basis. A grocery store doesn't charge a higher price for vegetables to vegetarians, whose demand is likely to be less elastic than that of its omnivorous customers. An audio store doesn't charge a different price for Pearl Jam's compact disks to collectors seeking a complete collection than it charges to casual fans who could easily substitute a disk from another performer. In these cases, firms lack a mechanism for knowing the different demands of their customers and for preventing resale.

Check list

- If advertising reduces competition, it tends to raise prices and reduce quantities produced. If it enhances competition, it tends to lower prices and increase quantities produced.
- In order to engage in price discrimination, a firm must be a price setter, must be able to identify consumers whose elasticities differ, and must be able to prevent resale of the good or service among consumers.
- The price discriminating firm will adjust its prices so that customers with more elastic demand pay lower prices than customers with less elastic demand.

Try It Yourself 11-3

Explain why price discrimination is often found in each of the following settings. Does it make sense in terms of price elasticity of demand?

1. *Senior citizen discounts for travel.*
2. *Food sold cheaper if the customer has a coupon for the item.*
3. *College scholarships to students with the best academic records or to students with special athletic, musical, or other skills.*

A Look Back

This chapter examined the world of imperfect competition that exists between the idealized extremes of perfect competition and monopoly. Imperfectly competitive markets exist whenever there is more than one seller in a market and at least one seller has some degree of control over price.

We discussed two general types of imperfectly competitive markets: monopolistic competition and oligopoly. Monopolistic competition is characterized by many firms producing similar but differentiated goods and services in a market with easy entry and exit. Oligopoly is characterized by relatively few firms producing either standardized or differentiated products. There may be substantial barriers to entry and exit.

In the short run, a monopolistically competitive firm's pricing and output decisions are the same as those of a monopoly. In the long run, economic profits will be whittled away by the entry of new firms and new products that increase the number of close substitutes. An industry dominated by a few firms is an oligopoly. Each oligopolist is aware of its interdependence with other firms in the industry and is constantly aware of the behavior of its rivals. Oligopolists engage in strategic decisionmaking in order to determine their best output and pricing strategies as well as the best forms of nonprice competition.

Advertising in imperfectly competitive markets can increase the degree of competitiveness by encouraging price competition and promoting entry. It can also decrease competition by establishing brand loyalty and thus creating barriers to entry.

Where conditions permit, a firm can increase its profits by price discrimination, charging different prices to customers with different elasticities of demand. To practice price discrimination, a price-setting firm must be able to segment customers that have different elasticities of demand and must be able to prevent resale among its customers.

A Look Ahead Our discussion in this chapter of the implications of imperfect competition in product markets concludes our examination of product market structure. In the next part of this textbook, we turn our attention to markets for factors of production.

Terms and Concepts for Review

imperfect competition, **224**
monopolistic competition, **224**
excess capacity, **226**
oligopoly, **228**
concentration ratio, **228**
Herfindahl–Hirschmann Index, **228**
duopoly, **229**
overt collusion, **230**
cartel, **230**
tacit collusion, **230**
strategic choice, **230**
game theory, **230**
payoff, **231**
dominant strategy, **232**
dominant strategy equilibrium, **232**
tit-for-tat strategy, **233**
trigger strategy, **233**
price discrimination, **237**

For Discussion

1. What are the major distinctions between a monopolistically competitive industry and an oligopolistic industry?
2. What is the difference between a price taker and a price setter?
3. Suppose a city experiences substantial population growth. What is likely to happen to profits in the short run and in the long run in the market for haircuts, a monopolistically competitive market?
4. Some professors grade students on the basis of an absolute percentage of the highest score earned on each test given during the semester. All students who get within a certain percentage of the highest score earned

get an A. Why don't these professors worry that the students will get together and collude in such a way as to keep the high score in the class equal to a very low total?

5. Your parents probably told you to avoid tit-for-tat behavior. Why does it make sense for firms to do it?
6. What model of oligopoly behavior were the matzo producers discussed in the Case in Point following? How might the matzo producers have achieved their goal and still stayed within the law?
7. What conditions are necessary for a firm to be able to practice price discrimination?
8. Restaurants typically charge much higher prices for dinner than for lunch, despite the fact that the cost of serving these meals is about the same. Why do you think this is the case? (*Hint:* Think about the primary consumers of these meals and their respective elasticities.)
9. What effect do you think advertising to discourage cigarette smoking will have on teens? On adults? What changes might occur in the cigarette market as a result?

Problems

1. Suppose the monopolistically competitive barber shop industry in a community is in long-run equilibrium. Incomes rise. Illustrate the short-run and long-run effects of the change on the price and output of a typical firm in the market.
2. Consider the same industry as in Problem 1. Suppose the market is in long-run equilibrium and that an annual license fee is imposed on barber shops. How does this affect price and output in the short run and in the long run?
3. Industry A consists of four firms, each of which has an equal share of the market. Industry B consists of two firms, each of which has an equal share of the market. Compare the four-firm concentration ratios and the Herfindahl–Hirschmann Indexes for the two industries.
4. Given the payoff matrix (shown at right) for a duopoly in which each firm is considering an expanded advertising campaign, determine whether each firm has a dominant strategy. Is there a dominant strategy equilibrium? All figures in the payoff matrix reflect changes in annual profits (in millions of dollars).

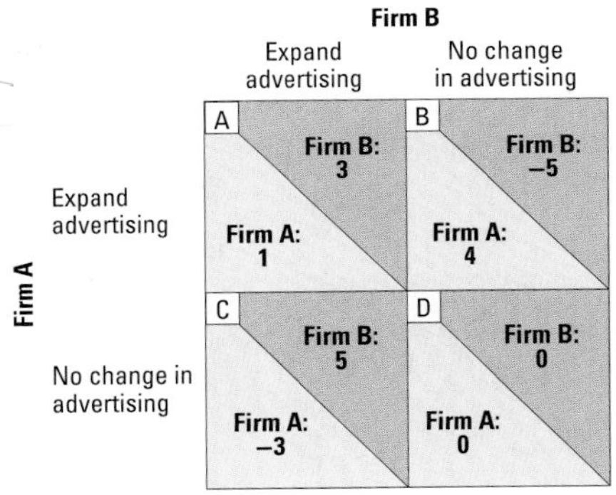

Answers to Try It Yourself Problems

Try It Yourself 11-1

As shown in Panel (a), higher wages would cause both MC and ATC to increase. The upward shift in MC from MC_1 to MC_2 would cause the profit-maximizing level of output (number of meals served per week, in this case) to fall from q_1 to q_2 and price to increase from P_1 to P_2. The increase in ATC from ATC_1 to ATC_2 would mean that some restaurants would be earning negative economic profits, as shown by the shaded area.

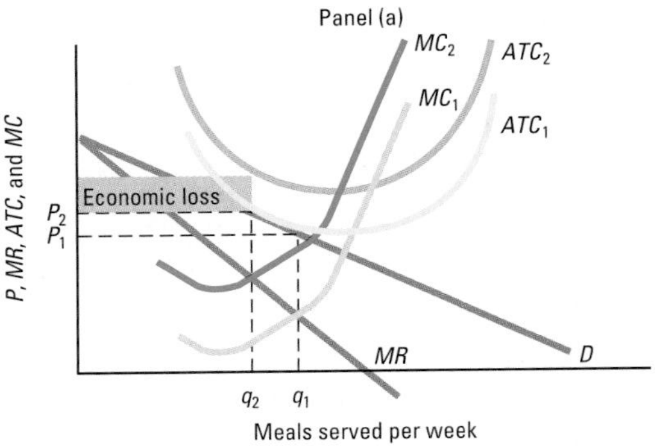

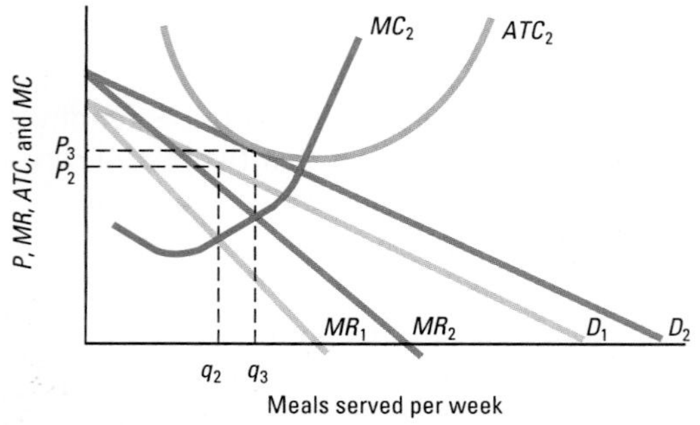

As shown in Panel (b), in the long run, as some restaurants close down, the demand curve faced by the typical remaining restaurant would shift to the right from D to D'. The demand curve shift leads to a corresponding shift in marginal revenue from MR to MR'. Price would increase further from P_2 to P_3, and output would increase to q_3, above q_2. In the new long-run equilibrium, restaurants would again be earning zero economic profit.

Try It Yourself 11-2

1. North Airlines seems to be practicing a price strategy known in game theory as tit-for-tat.
2. The banks could be engaged in tacit collusion, with Bank A as the price leader.
3. Saudi Arabia appears to have used a trigger strategy, another aspect of game theory. In general, of course, participants hope they will never have to "pull" the trigger, because doing so harms all participants. After years of cheating by other OPEC members, Saudi Arabia did undertake a policy that hurt all members of OPEC, including itself; OPEC has never since regained the prominent role it played in oil markets.
4. Saudi Arabia seems to be trying to create another oil cartel, a form of overt collusion.

Try It Yourself 11-3

1. Senior citizens are (usually!) easy to identify, and for travel, preventing resale is usually quite easy as well. For example, a picture ID is required to board an airplane. Airlines might be expected to oppose implementing the rule since it is costly for them. The fact that they support the rule can be explained by how it aids them in practicing price discrimination, by preventing the resale of discount tickets, which now can easily be matched to the purchasing customers. The demand for air travel by senior citizens is likely to be more elastic than it is for other passengers, especially business travelers, since the purpose of their travel is largely discretionary (often touristic in nature) and since their time is likely to be less costly, making them more willing to seek out information on travel alternatives than the rest of the population.
2. Since the customer must present the coupon at the point of sale, identification is easy. Willingness to search for and cut out coupons suggests a high degree of price consciousness and thus a greater price elasticity of demand.
3. Such students are likely to have more choices of where to attend college. As we learned in Chapter 5, demand is likely to be more elastic when substitutes are available for it. Enrollment procedures make identification and prevention of resale very easy.

12 Wages and Employment in Perfect Competition

Getting Started: College Pays

Workers with a college degree generally earn more than workers with only a high school education. One way of measuring the payoff from college is to compare the extent to which the wages of college-trained workers exceed the wages of high-school-trained workers. Viewed in that context, the payoff from college has soared over the last 20 years.

In 1979, male college graduates between 25 and 34 years old earned 28 percent more than male high school graduates in the same age bracket. By 1997 the gap had more than doubled—young male college graduates earned a stunning 57 percent more than young male high school graduates. Female college graduates gained as well. Young female college graduates earned 54 percent more than their high-school-educated counterparts in 1979; that gap increased to 75 percent by 1996.

The dramatic widening of the wage gap between workers with different levels of education reflected the operation of demand and supply in the market for labor. For reasons we'll explore in this chapter, the demand for college graduates was increasing while the demand for high school graduates—particularly male high school graduates—was slumping.

Why would the demand curves for different kinds of labor shift? What determines the demand for labor? What about the supply? How do changes in demand and supply affect wages and employment? In this chapter we'll apply what we've learned so far about production, profit maximization, and utility maximization to answer those questions in the context of a perfectly competitive market for labor.

This is the first of three chapters focusing on factor markets, that is, on markets in which households supply factors of production—labor, capital, and natural resources—demanded by firms. Look back at the circular flow model introduced in Chapter 3 and shown in Exhibit 3-13 (page 78). The bottom half of the circular flow model shows that households earn income from firms by supplying factors of production to them. The total income earned by households thus equals the total income earned by the labor, capital, and natural resources supplied to firms. Our focus in this chapter is on labor markets that operate in a competitive environment in which the individual buyers and sellers of labor are assumed to be price takers. We'll examine competitive markets for capital and for natural resources in the next chapter. The final chapter in this part on factor markets examines imperfectly competitive markets for labor and for other factors of production.

Labor generates considerably more income in the economy than all other factors of production combined. Exhibit 12-1 shows the share of total income earned annually by workers in the United States since 1959. Labor accounts for roughly 80 percent of the income earned in the U.S. economy. The rest is generated by owners of capital and of natural resources.

We calculate the total income earned by workers by multiplying their wage times the number of workers employed. We can view the labor market as a single market, as suggested in Panel (a) of Exhibit 12-2. Here we assume that all workers are identical, that there is a single market for them, and that they all

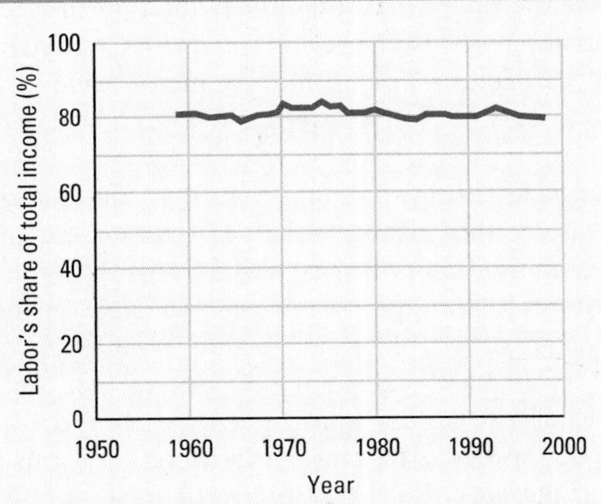

Exhibit 12-1

Labor's Share of U.S. Income, 1959–1997

Workers have accounted for roughly 80 percent of all the income earned in the United States since 1959. The remaining income was generated by capital and natural resources.

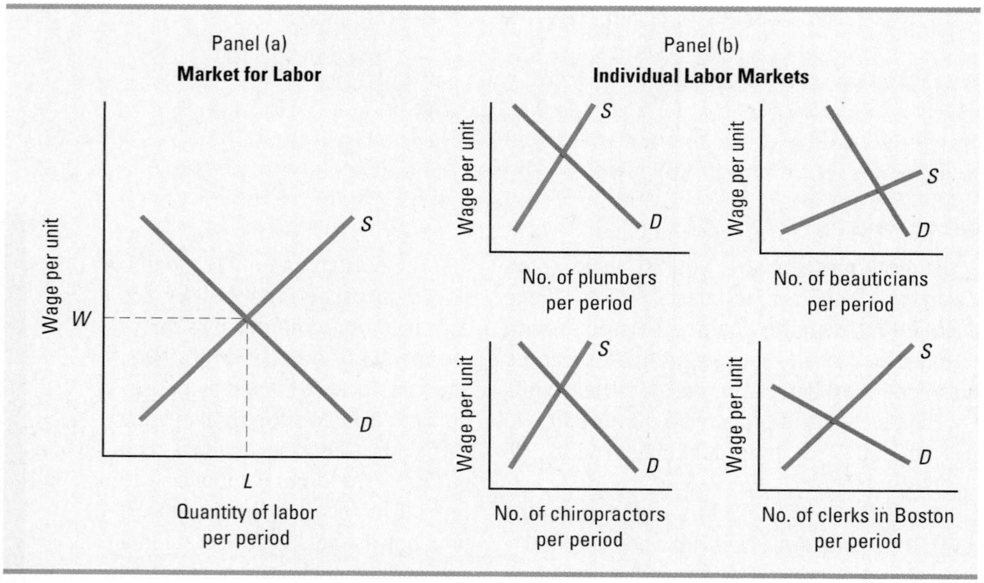

Exhibit 12-2

Alternative Views of the Labor Market

One way to analyze the labor market is to assume that it is a single market with identical workers, as in Panel (a). Alternatively, we could examine specific pieces of the market, focusing on particular job categories or even on job categories in particular regions, as the graphs in Panel (b) suggest.

earn the same wage, *W;* the level of employment is *L*. Although the assumption of a single labor market flies wildly in the face of reality, economists often use it to highlight broad trends in the market. For example, if we want to show the impact of an increase in the demand for labor throughout the economy, we can show labor as a single market in which the increase in demand raises wages and employment.

But we can also use demand and supply analysis to focus on the market for a particular group of workers. We might examine the market for plumbers, beauticians, or chiropractors. We might even want to focus on the market for, say, clerical workers in the Boston area. In such cases, we would examine the demand for and the supply of a particular segment of workers, as suggested by the graphs in Panel (b) of Exhibit 12-2.

Macroeconomic analysis typically makes use of the highly aggregated approach to labor-market analysis illustrated in Panel (a), where labor is viewed as a single market. Microeconomic analysis typically assesses particular markets for labor, as suggested in Panel (b).

When we use the model of demand and supply to analyze the determination of wages and employment, we are assuming that market forces, not individuals, determine wages in the economy. The model says that equilibrium wages are determined by the intersection of the demand and supply curves for labor in a particular market. Workers and firms in the market are thus price takers; they take the market-determined wage as given and respond to it. We are, in this instance, assuming that perfect competition prevails in the labor market. Just as there are some situations in the analysis of markets for goods and services for which such an assumption is inappropriate, so there are some cases in which the assumption is inappropriate for labor markets. We'll turn to such cases in Chapter 14. In this chapter, however, we'll find that the assumption of perfect competition can give us important insights into the forces that determine wages and employment levels for workers.

We'll begin our analysis of labor markets in the next section by looking at the forces that influence the demand for labor. In the following section we'll turn to supply. In the final section, we'll use what we've learned to look at labor markets at work.

The Demand for Labor

A firm must have labor to produce goods and services. But how much labor will the firm employ? A profit-maximizing firm will base its decision to hire additional units of labor on the marginal decision rule: If the extra output that is produced by hiring one more unit of labor adds more to total revenue than it adds to total cost, the firm will increase profit by increasing its use of labor. It will continue to hire more and more labor up to the point that the extra revenue generated by the additional labor no longer exceeds the extra cost of the labor.

For example, if a computer software company could increase its annual total revenue by \$40,000 by hiring a programmer at a cost of \$39,000 per year, the marginal decision rule says that it should do so. Since the programmer will add \$39,000 to total cost and \$40,000 to total revenue, hiring the programmer will increase the company's profit by \$1,000. If still another programmer would increase annual total revenue by \$38,000 but would also add \$39,000 to the firm's total cost, that programmer should not be hired because he or she would add less to total revenue than to total cost and would reduce profit.

Marginal Revenue Product and Marginal Factor Cost

The amount that an additional unit of a factor adds to a firm's total revenue during a period is called the **marginal revenue product (*MRP*)** of the factor. An additional unit of a factor of production adds to a firm's revenue in a two-step process: First, it increases the firm's output. Second, the increased output increases the firm's total revenue. We find marginal revenue product by multiplying the marginal product (*MP*) of the factor by the marginal revenue (*MR*).

$$MRP = MP \times MR \qquad (1)$$

In a perfectly competitive market the marginal revenue a firm receives equals the market-determined price *P*. Therefore, for firms in perfect competition, we can express marginal revenue product as follows:

$$\text{In perfect competition, } MRP = MP \times P \qquad (2)$$

The marginal revenue product of labor (MRP_L) is the marginal product of labor (MP_L) times the marginal revenue (which is the same as price under perfect competition) the firm obtains from additional units of output that result from hiring the additional unit of labor. If an additional worker adds 4 units of output per day to a firm's production, and if each of those 4 units sells for \$20, then the worker's marginal revenue product is \$80 per day. With perfect competition, the marginal revenue product for labor, MRP_L, equals the marginal product of labor, MP_L, times the price, *P*, of the good or service the labor produces:

$$\text{In perfect competition, } MRP_L = MP_L \times P \qquad (3)$$

The law of diminishing marginal returns tells us that if the quantity of a factor is increased while other inputs are held constant, its marginal product will eventually decline. If marginal product is falling, marginal revenue product must be falling as well.

Suppose that an accountant, Stephanie Lancaster, has started an evening call-in tax advisory service. Between the hours of 7 and 10 P.M., customers can call and get advice on their income taxes. Ms. Lancaster's firm, TeleTax, is one of several firms offering similar advice; the going market price is \$10 per call. Ms. Lancaster's business has expanded, so she hires other accountants to handle the calls. She must determine how many accountants to hire.

Exhibit 12-3

Marginal Product and Marginal Revenue Product

The table gives the relationship between the number of accountants employed by TeleTax each evening and the total number of calls handled. From these values we derive the marginal product and marginal revenue product curves.

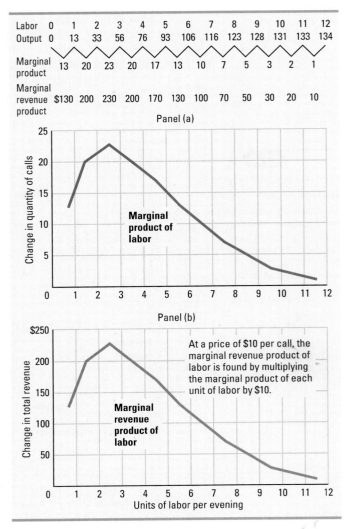

Labor	0	1	2	3	4	5	6	7	8	9	10	11	12
Output	0	13	33	56	76	93	106	116	123	128	131	133	134
Marginal product		13	20	23	20	17	13	10	7	5	3	2	1
Marginal revenue product		\$130	200	230	200	170	130	100	70	50	30	20	10

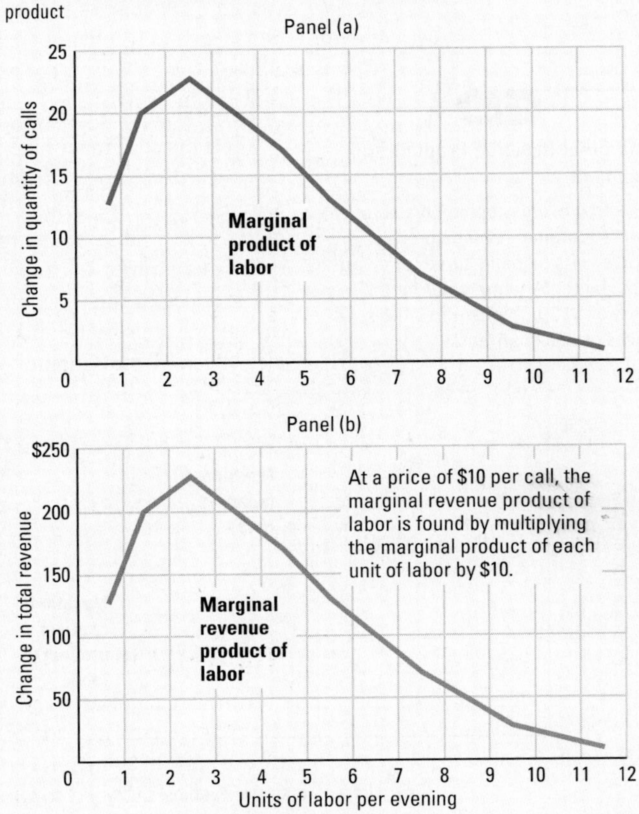

As Ms. Lancaster adds accountants, her service can take more calls. The table in Exhibit 12-3 gives the relationship between the number of accountants available to answer calls each evening and the number of calls TeleTax handles. Panel (a) shows the increase in the number of calls handled by each additional accountant—that accountant's marginal product. The first accountant can handle 13 calls per evening. Adding a second accountant increases the number of calls handled by 20. With two accountants, a degree of specialization is possible if each accountant takes calls dealing with questions about which he or she has particular expertise. Hiring the third accountant increases TeleTax's output per evening by 23 calls.

Suppose the accountants share a fixed facility for screening and routing calls. They also share a stock of reference materials to use in answering calls. As more accountants are added, the firm will begin to experience diminishing marginal returns. The fourth accountant increases output by 20 calls. The marginal product of additional accountants continues to decline after that. The marginal product curve shown in Panel (a) of Exhibit 12-3 thus rises and then falls.

Each call TeleTax handles increases the firm's revenues by $10. To obtain marginal revenue product, we multiply the marginal product of each accountant by $10; the marginal revenue product curve is shown in Panel (b) of Exhibit 12-3.

We can use Ms. Lancaster's marginal revenue product curve to determine the quantity of labor she will hire. Suppose accountants in her area are available to offer tax advice for a nightly fee of $150. Each additional accountant Ms. Lancaster hires thus adds $150 per night to her total cost. The amount a factor adds to a firm's total cost per period is called its **marginal factor cost (*MFC*).** Marginal factor cost (*MFC*) is the change in total cost (ΔTC) divided by the change in the quantity of the factor (Δf):

$$MFC = \frac{\Delta TC}{\Delta f} \qquad (4)$$

Exhibit 12-4

Marginal Revenue Product and Demand

The downward-sloping portion of a firm's marginal revenue product curve is its demand curve for a variable factor. At a marginal factor cost of $150, TeleTax hires the services of 5 accountants.

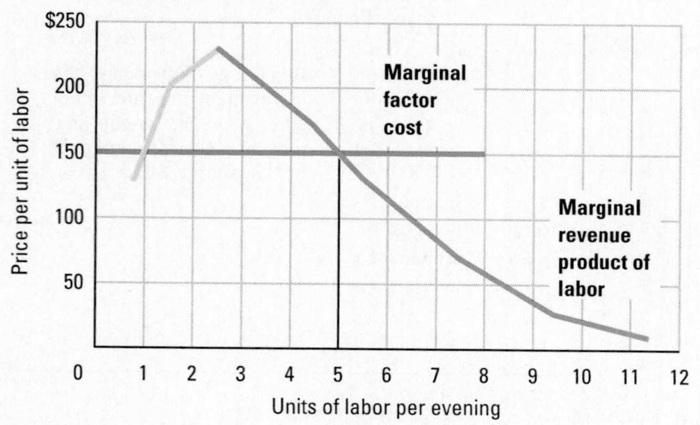

The marginal factor cost to TeleTax of additional accountants ($150 per night) is shown as a horizontal line in Exhibit 12-4. It is simply the market wage.

TeleTax will maximize profit by hiring additional units of labor up to the point where the downward-sloping portion of the marginal revenue product curve intersects the marginal factor cost curve; we see in Exhibit 12-4 that it will hire 5 accountants. Based on the information given in the table in Exhibit 12-3, we know that the 5 accountants will handle a total of 93 calls per evening; TeleTax will earn a total revenue of $930 per evening. The firm pays $750 for the services of the 5 accountants—that leaves $180 to apply to the fixed cost associated with the tax advice service and the implicit cost of Stephanie Lancaster's effort in organizing the service. Recall from Chapter 9 that these implicit costs include the income forgone (that is, opportunity cost) by not shifting her resources, including her own labor, to her next best alternative.

If TeleTax had to pay a higher price for accountants, it would face a higher marginal factor cost curve and would hire fewer accountants. If the price were lower, TeleTax would hire more accountants. The downward-sloping portion of TeleTax's marginal revenue product curve shows the number of accountants it will hire at each price for accountants; it is thus the firm's demand curve for accountants. It is the portion of the curve that exhibits diminishing returns, and a firm will always seek to operate in the range of diminishing returns to the factors it uses.

It may seem counterintuitive that firms don't operate in the range of increasing returns, which would correspond to the upward-sloping portion of the marginal revenue

Caution!

The Two Rules Lead to the Same Outcome In Chapter 9 on competitive output markets we learned that profit-maximizing firms will increase output so long as doing so adds more to revenue than to cost, or up to the point where marginal revenue, which in perfect competition is the same as the market-determined price, equals marginal cost. In this chapter we have learned that profit-maximizing firms will hire labor up to the point where marginal revenue product equals marginal factor cost. Is it possible that a firm that follows the marginal decision rule for hiring labor would end up producing a different quantity of output compared to if it followed the marginal decision rule for deciding directly how much output to produce? Is there a conflict between these two marginal decision rules?

The answer is no. These two marginal decision rules are really just two ways of saying the same thing: One rule is in terms of quantity of output and the other in terms of the quantity of factors required to produce that quantity of output. Hiring an additional unit of a factor means producing a certain amount of additional output.

Using the example of Teletax, at \$150 per accountant per night, we found that Ms. Lancaster maximizes profit by hiring 5 accountants. The MP_L of the fifth accountant is ΔQ; it is 17. At 5 accountants, the marginal cost of a call is $\Delta TC/\Delta Q$ = \$150/17 = \$8.82, which is less than the price of \$10 per call, so hiring that accountant adds to her profit. At 6 accountants, the marginal cost of a call would be \$150/13 = \$11.54, which is greater than the \$10 price, so hiring a sixth accountant would lower profit. The profit-maximizing output of 93 calls, found by comparing marginal cost and price, is thus consistent with the profit-maximizing quantity of labor of 5 accountants, found by comparing marginal revenue product and marginal factor cost.

product curve. However, to do so would forgo profit-enhancing opportunities. For example, in Exhibit 12-4, adding the second accountant adds \$200 to revenue but only \$150 to cost, so hiring that accountant clearly adds to profit. But why stop there? What about hiring a third accountant? That additional hire adds even more to revenue (\$230) than to cost. In the region of increasing returns, marginal revenue product rises. With marginal factor cost constant, not to continue onto the downward-sloping part of the marginal revenue curve would be to miss out on profit-enhancing opportunities. The firm continues adding accountants until doing so no longer adds more to revenue than to cost, and that occurs where the marginal revenue product curve slopes downward.

In general, then, we can interpret the downward-sloping portion of a firm's marginal revenue product curve for a factor as its demand curve for that factor.[1] We find the market demand for labor by adding the demand curves for individual firms, just as we added supply curves for individual firms, shown in Exhibit 9-8, to obtain an industry supply curve for a good or service.

Shifts in Labor Demand

The fact that a firm's demand curve for labor is given by the downward-sloping portion of its marginal revenue product of labor curve provides a guide to the factors that will shift the curve. In perfect competition, marginal revenue product equals the marginal product of labor times the price of the good that the labor is involved in producing; anything that changes

[1]Strictly speaking, it is only that part of the downward-sloping portion over which variable costs are at least covered. This is the flip-side of what you learned about a firm's supply curve in Chapter 9: Only the portion of the rising marginal cost curve that lies above the minimum point of the average variable cost curve constitutes the supply curve of a perfectly competitive firm.

either of those two variables will shift the curve. The marginal revenue product of labor will change when there is a change in the quantities of other factors employed. It will also change as a result of a change in technology, a change in the price of the good being produced, or a change in the number of firms hiring the labor.

Changes in the Use of Other Factors of Production As a firm changes the quantities of different factors of production it uses, the marginal product of labor may change. Having more reference manuals, for example, is likely to make additional accountants more productive—it will increase their marginal product. That increase in their marginal product would increase the demand for accountants. When an increase in the use of one factor of production increases the demand for another, the two factors are **complementary factors of production.**

One important complement of labor is human capital, the set of skills and abilities workers bring to the production of goods and services. When workers gain additional human capital, their marginal product rises. The demand for them by firms thus increases. This is perhaps one reason why you have decided to pursue a college education.

Other inputs may be regarded as substitutes for each other. A robot, for example, may substitute for some kinds of assembly-line labor. Two factors are **substitute factors of production** if the increased use of one lowers the demand for the other.

Changes in Technology Technological changes can increase the demand for some workers and reduce the demand for others. The production of a more powerful computer chip, for example, may increase the demand for software engineers. It may also allow other production processes to be computerized and thus reduce the demand for workers who had been employed in those processes.

Technological changes have significantly increased the economy's output over the past century. The application of sophisticated technologies to production processes has boosted the marginal products of workers who have the skills these technologies require. That has increased the demand for skilled workers. The same technologies have been a substitute for less-skilled workers, and the demand for those workers has fallen. As the Case in Point on the banking industry implies, envisioning the impact of technological change on demand for different kinds of labor may be something to keep in mind as you consider educational options. As you consider your major, for example, you should keep in mind that some occupations may benefit from technological changes; others may not.

Changes in Product Demand A change in demand for a final product changes its price, at least in the short run. An increase in the demand for a product increases its price and increases the demand for factors that produce the product. A reduction in demand for a product reduces its price and reduces the demand for the factors used in producing it. Because the demand for factors that produce a product depends on the demand for the product itself, factor demand is said to be **derived demand.** That is, factor demand is derived from the demand for the product that uses the factor in its production.

Suppose, for example, that the demand for computers increases. The price and quantity of computers available will go up. A higher price for computers increases the marginal revenue product of labor of computer-assembly workers and thus increases the demand for these workers.

Just as increases in the demand for particular goods or services increase the demand for the workers that produce them, so reductions in demand for particular goods or services will reduce the demand for the workers that produce them. An example is the relationship between the demand for train travel and the demand for conductors. Over the years, the fall in demand for train travel has reduced the demand for railroad conductors.

Case in Point Where Have All the Tellers Gone?

In the late 1990s, despite an expanding U.S. economy and despite expansion of the banking industry in particular, employment in banking decreased substantially since it peaked in 1989. By 1996, employment in banking had fallen in excess of 6 percent from its 1989 peak and some expect a decline of 20 percent by the year 2010.

Ben Craig, an economist at the Federal Reserve Bank of Cleveland, has studied the reasons for the decline in bank employment. He considered three possible reasons for the employment decline: (1) a decrease in demand for banking services, (2) a decrease in the price of a substitute factor of production, and (3) a decrease in the number of banks.

A decline in demand for banking services can be readily dismissed. Indeed, the industry grew by about 15 percent between 1988 and 1995. Other things held constant, expansion of the industry would be expected to cause an increase, not a decrease, in employment.

On the other hand, the second reason—increased use of a substitute factor of production—seems to explain much of the employment decline. The automatic teller machine (ATM) is essentially the robot version of the human bank teller, and a change in the price of ATMs will affect the demand for tellers. Mr. Craig estimated the cross price elasticity of labor demand with respect to the price of capital within a bank to be about 0.1. In other words, a 10 percent decrease in the price of capital—the various machines used by banks—lowers employment at a bank by about 1 percent. Capital and labor are, at banks, substitute factors of production.

The number of transactions completed via ATM has exploded in recent years. There were 3.5 billion transactions by ATM in 1985; in 1995, there were 10 billion ATM transactions. In terms of value, in 1985 the ATM transactions totaled $200 billion; in 1995, such transactions totaled $650 billion.

Other less-visible substitutions of machines for humans have also occurred. For example, electronic check scanners have eliminated the need for workers to enter the information on a check by hand, and computer programs can analyze eligibility for loans.

The third possible reason—a decline in the number of banks—has also contributed to job loss in the industry. Mergers and acquisitions reduced the number of banks by more than 20 percent between 1988 and 1995. This consolidation resulted in elimination of duplicate departments and offices, but also created new employment opportunities. For example, two small banks might not have a research department, but the larger merged institution might. Mr. Craig estimated that the overall effect on employment decline due to this factor is minimal—about 1 or 2 percent.

Mr. Craig concluded that the main reason for job loss in banking has been the substitution of capital for labor.

Source: Title and content from Ben Craig, "Where Have All the Tellers Gone?" *Federal Reserve Bank of Cleveland Economic Commentary* (April 15, 1997): 1–4; Ben Craig, "The Long-Run Demand for Labor in the Banking Industry," *Federal Reserve Bank of Cleveland Economic Review* 33(3) (Quarter 3, 1997): 23–33.

Changes in the Number of Firms We can determine the demand curve for any factor by adding the demand for that factor by each of the firms using it. If more firms employ the factor, the demand curve shifts to the right. A reduction in the number of firms shifts the demand curve to the left. For example, if the number of restaurants in an area increases, the demand for waiters and waitresses in the area goes up. We expect to see local wages for these workers rise as a result.

Checklist

- In using the model of demand and supply to examine labor markets, we assume in this chapter that perfect competition exists—that all workers and employers are price takers.
- A firm's demand curve for a factor is the downward-sloping portion of the marginal revenue product curve of the factor.
- The market demand for labor is found by adding the demand curves for labor of individual firms.
- The market demand for labor will change as a result of a change in the use of a complementary input or a substitute input, a change in technology, a change in the price of the good produced by labor, or a change in the number of firms that employ the labor.

Try It Yourself 12-1

How would each of the following affect the demand for labor by the accounting advice service, TeleTax, described in this chapter?

a. A reduction in the market price for a tax advice call.

b. An increase in the market fee for the accountants that Teletax hires.

c. An increase in the marginal product of each accountant due to an expansion of the facility for screening and routing calls and an increase in the number of reference materials available to the accountants.

The Supply of Labor

The demand curve for labor is one determinant of the equilibrium wage and quantity of labor in a perfectly competitive market. The supply curve, of course, is the other.

Economists think of the supply of labor as a problem in which individuals weigh the opportunity cost of various activities that can fill an available amount of time and choose how to allocate it. Everyone has 24 hours in a day. There are lots of uses to which we can put our time: We can raise children, work, sleep, play, or participate in volunteer efforts. To simplify our analysis, let us assume that there are two ways in which an individual can spend his or her time: in work or in leisure. Leisure is a type of consumption good; individuals gain utility directly from it. Work provides income that, in turn, can be used to purchase goods and services that generate utility.

The more work a person does, the greater his or her income, but the smaller the amount of leisure time available. An individual who chooses more leisure time will earn less income than would otherwise be possible. There is thus a tradeoff between leisure and the income that can be earned from work. We can think of the supply of labor as the flip side of the demand for leisure. The more leisure people demand, the less labor they supply.

Two aspects of the demand for leisure play a key role in understanding the supply of labor. First, leisure is a normal good. All other things unchanged, an increase in income will increase the demand for leisure. Second, the opportunity cost or "price" of leisure is the wage an individual can earn. A worker who can earn $10 per hour gives up $10 in income by consuming an extra hour of leisure. The $10 wage is thus the price of an hour of leisure. A worker who can earn $20 an hour faces a higher price of leisure.

Income and Substitution Effects

Suppose wages rise. The higher wage increases the price of leisure. We saw in Chapter 7 that consumers substitute more of other goods for a good whose price has risen. The substitution effect of a higher wage causes the consumer to substitute labor for leisure. To put it another way, the higher wage induces the individual to supply a greater quantity of labor.

We can see the logic of this substitution effect in terms of the marginal decision rule. Suppose an individual is considering a choice between extra leisure and the additional income from more work. Let MU_{Le} denote the marginal utility of an extra hour of leisure. What is the price of an extra hour of leisure? It is the wage W that the individual forgoes by not working for an hour. The extra utility of \$1 worth of leisure is thus given by MU_{Le}/W.

Suppose, for example, that the marginal utility of an extra hour of leisure is 20 and the wage is \$10 per hour. Then MU_{Le}/W equals 20/10, or 2. That means that the individual gains 2 units of utility by spending an additional \$1 worth of time on leisure. For a person facing a wage of \$10 per hour, \$1 worth of leisure would be the equivalent of 6 minutes of leisure time.

Let MU_Y be the marginal utility of an additional \$1 of income (Y is the abbreviation economists generally assign to income). The price of \$1 of income is just \$1, so the price of income P_Y is always \$1. Utility is maximized by allocating time between work and leisure so that

$$\frac{MU_Y}{P_Y} = \frac{MU_{Le}}{W} \qquad (5)$$

Now suppose the wage rises. That reduces the marginal utility of \$1 worth of leisure, MU_{Le}/W, so that the extra utility of earning \$1 will now be greater than the extra utility of \$1 worth of leisure:

$$\frac{MU_Y}{P_Y} > \frac{MU_{Le}}{W} \qquad (6)$$

Faced with the inequality in Equation 6, an individual will give up some leisure time and spend more time working. As the individual does so, however, the marginal utility of the remaining leisure time rises and the marginal utility of the income earned will fall. The individual will continue to make the substitution until the two sides of the equation are again equal. For a worker, the substitution effect of a wage increase always reduces the amount of leisure time consumed and increases the amount of time spent working. A higher wage thus produces a positive substitution effect on labor supply.

But the higher wage also has an income effect. An increased wage means a higher income, and since leisure is a normal good, the quantity of leisure demanded will go up. And that means a *reduction* in the quantity of labor supplied.

For labor supply problems, then, the substitution effect is always positive; a higher wage induces a greater quantity of labor supplied. But the income effect is always negative; a higher wage implies a higher income, and a higher income implies a greater demand for leisure, and more leisure means

Exhibit 12-5

The Substitution and Income Effects of a Wage Change

The substitution and income effects influence Meredith Wilson's supply of labor when she gets a pay raise. At a wage of \$10 per hour, she supplies 42 hours of work per week (point A). At \$15 per hour, the substitution effect pulls in the direction of an increased quantity of labor supplied, and the income effect pulls in the opposite direction.

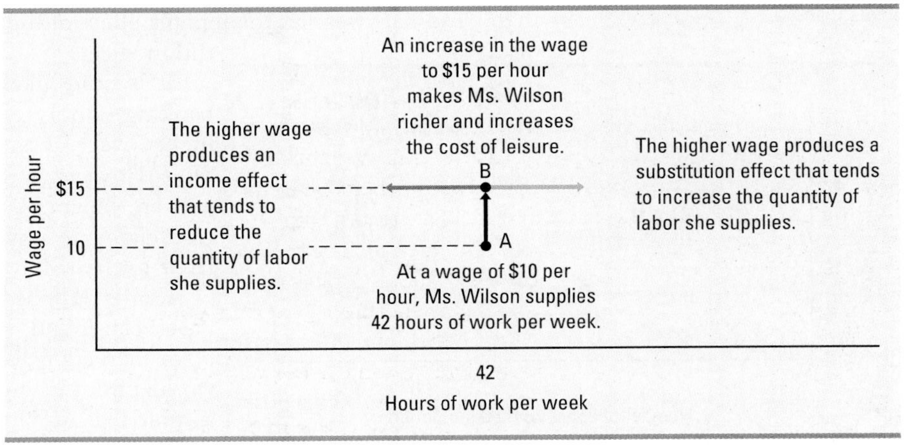

a lower quantity of labor supplied. With the substitution and income effects working in opposite directions, it isn't clear whether a wage increase will increase or decrease the quantity of labor supplied—or leave it unchanged.

Exhibit 12-5 illustrates the opposite pull of the substitution and income effects of a wage change facing an individual worker. A locksmith, Meredith Wilson, earns $10 per hour. She now works 42 hours per week, on average, earning $420.

Now suppose Ms. Wilson receives a $5 raise to $15 per hour. As shown in Exhibit 12-5, the substitution effect of the wage change induces her to increase the quantity of labor she supplies; she substitutes some of her leisure time for additional hours of work. But she's richer now; she can afford more leisure. At a wage of $10 per hour, she was earning $420 per week. She could earn that same amount at the higher wage in just 28 hours. With her higher income, she can certainly afford more leisure time. The income effect of the wage change is thus negative; the quantity of labor supplied falls. The effect of the wage increase on the quantity of labor Ms. Wilson supplies depends on the relative strength of the substitution and income effects of the wage change. We'll see what Ms. Wilson decides to do in the next section.

Wage Changes and the Slope of the Supply Curve

What would any one individual's supply curve for labor look like? One possibility is that over some range of labor hours supplied, the substitution effect will dominate. Because the marginal utility of leisure is relatively low when little labor is supplied (that is, when most time is devoted to leisure), it takes only a small increase in wages to induce the individual to substitute more labor for less leisure. Further, because few hours are worked, the income effect of those wage changes will be small.

Exhibit 12-6 shows Meredith Wilson's supply curve for labor. At a wage of $10 per hour, she supplies 42 hours of work per week (point A). An increase in her wage to $15 per hour boosts her quantity supplied to 48 hours per week (point B). The substitution effect thus dominates the income effect of a higher wage.

It is possible that beyond some wage rate, the negative income effect of a wage increase could just offset the positive substitution effect; over that range, a higher wage would have no effect on the quantity of labor supplied. That's illustrated between points B and C on the supply curve in Exhibit 12-6; Ms. Wilson's supply curve is vertical over that range. As wages continue to rise, the income effect becomes even stronger, and additional increases in the wage reduce the quantity of labor she supplies. The supply curve illustrated here bends backward beyond point C and thus assumes a negative slope. The supply curve for labor can thus slope upward over part of its range, become vertical, and then bend backward as the income effect of higher wages begins to dominate the substitution effect.

Exhibit 12-6

A Backward-Bending Supply Curve for Labor

As the wage rate increases from $10 to $15 per hour, the quantity of labor Meredith Wilson supplies increases from 42 to 48 hours per week. Between points A and B, the positive substitution effect of the wage increase outweighs the negative income effect. As the wage rises above $15, the negative income effect just offsets the substitution effect, and Ms. Wilson's supply curve becomes a vertical line between points B and C. As the wage rises above $20, the income effect becomes stronger than the substitution effect, and the supply curve bends backward between points C and D.

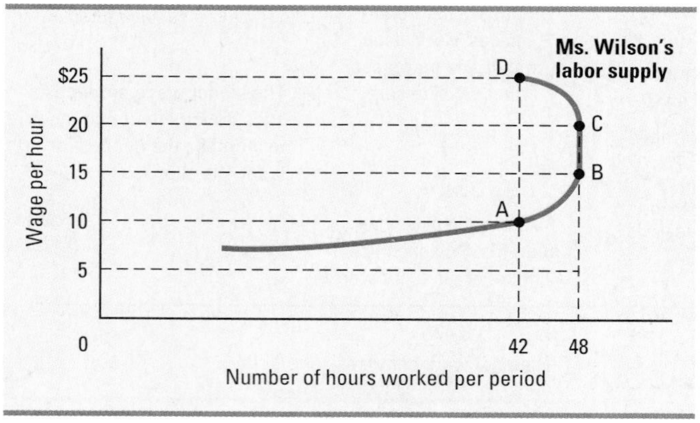

It is quite likely that some individuals have backward-bending supply curves for labor—beyond some point, a higher wage induces those individuals to work less, not more. However, supply curves for labor in specific labor markets are generally upward sloping. As wages in one industry rise relative to wages in other industries, workers shift their labor to the relatively high-wage one. An increased quantity of labor is supplied in that industry. While some exceptions have been found, the mobility of labor between competitive labor markets is likely to prevent the total number of hours worked from falling as the wage rate increases. Thus we shall assume that supply curves for labor in particular markets are upward sloping.

Case in Point Celebrities Supply Check-Cashing Effort

It wasn't exactly a study of labor supply, and it certainly wasn't serious, but *Spy* magazine's July 1990 investigation of the willingness of big celebrities to cash small checks suggests some of the same issues that are involved in conventional estimates of supply.

The magazine set up a corporation that sent letters to 58 rich and famous people explaining that, due to a computer error, they had been overcharged for a recent purchase. A refund check of $1.11 was enclosed with each letter. A decision to cash a check required giving up some time and effort on the part of the celebrity or an assistant in exchange for a little extra money. Within 2 months, 26 rich and famous people had cashed their checks. Michael Douglas and Faye Dunaway were among the celebrities who snapped up the money. For the rest, the chance to pick up $1.11 wasn't worth the effort.

The magazine then sent refund checks for $2 to the 32 holdouts. At this higher price, 6 of the previous holdouts were willing to make the effort to cash their checks—they included Richard Gere and Candice Bergen. The magazine then offered a refund check of a whopping $3.47 to the 26 rich and famous people who had ignored the $2 offer. Two more rich and famous people—designer Halston and opera star Beverly Sills—snapped up the bait.

The magazine's experiment then turned to the 26 celebrities who had cashed their checks for $1.11 to see how much lower they would be willing to go. Those celebrities got checks for $0.64. Offered a lower reward, just 13 made the effort to cash their checks—Cher was among them. These 13 were then sent checks for $0.13. That was enough of a reward to attract just 2 rich and famous people: developer Donald Trump and arms dealer Adnan Khashoggi.

Putting *Spy's* results together, we obtain a supply curve for celebrity check-cashing effort. At $0.13, the magazine had just 2 takers. When the offer went up to $0.64, more celebrities were willing to cash their checks. As the reward went higher, the quantity of check-cashing effort went higher. Finally, at the highest refund check offered, a majority of the original group of 58 couldn't resist. The payments were too small to reflect much of an income effect; this suggests that the higher the "wage" offered, the greater the willingness of rich and famous people (or their assistants) to deposit a check.

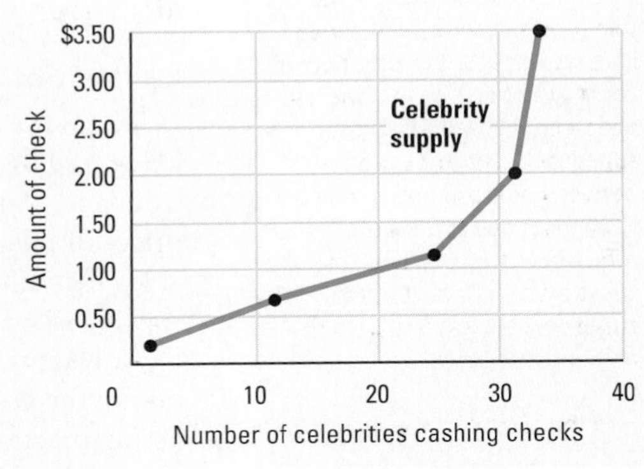

Source: Julius Lowenthal, *Spy*, July 1990.

Shifts in Labor Supply

What events shift the supply curve for labor? People supply labor in order to increase their utility—just as they demand goods and services in order to increase their utility. The supply curve for labor will shift in response to changes in the same set of factors that shift demand curves for goods and services.

Changes in Preferences A change in attitudes toward work and leisure can shift the supply curve for labor. If people decide they value leisure more highly, they will work fewer hours at each wage, and the supply curve for labor will shift to the left. If they decide they want more goods and services, the supply curve is likely to shift to the right.

Changes in Income An increase in income will increase the demand for leisure, reducing the supply of labor. We must be careful here to distinguish movements along the supply curve from shifts of the supply curve itself. An income change resulting from a change in wages is shown by a movement along the curve; it produces the income and substitution effects we already discussed. But suppose income is from some other source: A person marries and has access to a spouse's income, or receives an inheritance, or wins a lottery. Those nonlabor increases in income are likely to reduce the supply of labor, thereby shifting the supply curve for labor of the recipients to the left.

Changes in the Prices of Related Goods and Services Several goods and services are complements of labor. If the cost of child care (a complement to work effort) falls, for example, it becomes cheaper for workers to go to work, and the supply of labor tends to increase. If recreational activities (which are a substitute for work effort) become much cheaper, individuals might choose to consume more leisure time and supply less labor.

Changes in Population An increase in population increases the supply of labor; a reduction lowers it. Labor organizations have generally opposed increases in immigration because their leaders fear that the increased number of workers will shift the supply curve for labor to the right and put downward pressure on wages.

Changes in Expectations One change in expectations that could have an effect on labor supply is life expectancy. Another is confidence in the availability of Social Security. Suppose, for example, that people expect to live longer yet become less optimistic about their likely benefits from Social Security. That could induce an increase in labor supply.

Labor Supply in Specific Markets The supply of labor in particular markets could be affected by changes in any of the variables we've already examined—changes in preferences, incomes, prices of related goods and services, population, and expectations. In addition to these variables that affect the supply of labor in general, there are changes that could affect supply in specific labor markets.

A change in wages in related occupations could affect supply in another. A sharp reduction in the wages of surgeons, for example, could induce more physicians to specialize in, say, family practice, increasing the supply of doctors in that field. Improved job opportunities for women in other fields appear to have decreased the supply of nurses, shifting the supply curve for nurses to the left.

The supply of labor in a particular market could also shift because of a change in entry requirements. Most states, for example, require barbers and beauticians to obtain training before entering the profession. Elimination of such requirements would increase the supply of these workers. Financial planners have, in recent years, sought the introduction of tougher licensing requirements, which would reduce the supply of financial planners.

Worker preferences regarding specific occupations can also affect labor supply. A reduction in willingness to take risks could lower the supply of labor available for risky occupations such as farm work (the most dangerous work in the United States), law enforcement, and fire fighting. An increased desire to work with children could raise the supply of child-care workers, elementary school teachers, and pediatricians.

Checklist

- A higher wage increases the opportunity cost or price of leisure and increases worker incomes. The effects of these two changes pull the quantity of labor supplied in opposite directions.
- A wage increase raises the quantity of labor supplied through the substitution effect, but it reduces the quantity supplied through the income effect. Thus an individual's supply curve of labor may be positively or negatively sloped, or have sections that are positively sloped, sections that are negatively sloped, and vertical sections. While some exceptions have been found, the labor supply curves for specific labor markets are generally upward sloping.
- The supply curve for labor will shift as a result of a change in worker preferences, a change in nonlabor income, a change in the prices of related goods and services, a change in population, or a change in expectations.
- In addition to the effects on labor supply of the variables just cited, other factors that can change the supply of labor in particular markets are changes in wages in related markets or changes in entry requirements.

Try It Yourself 12-2

Economists Laura Duberstein and Karen Oppenheim Mason analyzed the labor-supply decisions of 1,383 mothers with preschool-aged children in the Detroit Metropolitan area. They found that respondents were more likely to work the higher the wage, less likely to work if they preferred a traditional family structure with a husband as the primary breadwinner, less likely to work if they felt that care provided by others was strongly inferior to a mother's care, and less likely to work if child-care costs were higher.[2] Given these findings, explain how each of the following would affect the labor supply of mothers with preschool-aged children.

a. An increase in the wage.

b. An increase in the preference for a traditional family structure.

c. An increased sense that child care is inferior to a mother's care.

d. An increase in the cost of child care.

(Remember to distinguish between movements along the curve and shifts of the curve.) Is the labor supply curve positively or negatively sloped? Does the substitution effect or income effect dominate?

Labor Markets at Work

We've seen that a firm's demand for labor depends on the marginal product of labor and the price of the good the firm produces. We add the demand curves of individual firms to obtain the market demand curve for labor. The supply curve for labor depends on variables such as population and worker preferences. Supply in a particular market depends on variables such as worker preferences, the skills and training a job requires, and wages available in alternative occupations. Wages are determined by the intersection of demand and supply.

[2]Laura Duberstein and Karen Oppenheim Mason, "Do Child Care Costs Influence Women's Work Plans? Analysis for a Metropolitan Area," Research Report, Population Studies Center, University of Michigan, Ann Arbor, July 1991.

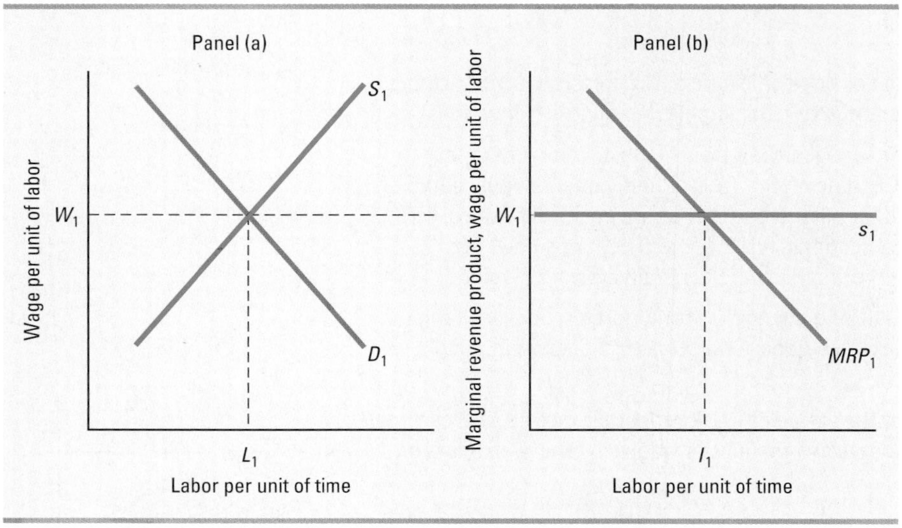

Exhibit 12-7

Wage Determination and Employment in Perfect Competition

Wages in perfect competition are determined by the intersection of demand and supply in Panel (a). An individual firm takes the wage W_1 as given. It faces a horizontal supply curve for labor at the market wage, as shown in Panel (b). This supply curve s_1 is also the marginal factor cost curve for labor. The firm responds to the wage by employing l_1 units of labor, a quantity determined by the intersection of its marginal revenue product curve MRP_1 and its supply curve s_1.

Once the wage in a particular market has been established, individual firms in perfect competition take it as given. Because each firm is a price taker, it faces a horizontal supply curve for labor at the market wage. For one firm, changing the quantity of labor it hires does not change the wage. In Chapter 14 we'll consider cases in which an individual firm's choices do affect the wage it pays. In the context of the model of perfect competition, however, buyers and sellers are price takers. That means that a firm's choices in hiring labor do not affect the wage.

The operation of labor markets in perfect competition is illustrated in Exhibit 12-7. The wage W_1 is determined by the intersection of demand and supply in Panel (a). Employment equals L_1. An individual firm takes that wage as given; it is the supply curve s_1 facing the firm. This wage also equals the firm's marginal factor cost. The firm hires l_1 units of labor, a quantity determined by the intersection of its marginal revenue product curve for labor MRP_1 and the supply curve s_1. We use lowercase letters to show quantity for a single firm and uppercase letters to show quantity in the market.

Changes in Demand and Supply

If wages are determined by demand and supply, then changes in demand and supply should affect wages. An increase in demand or a reduction in supply will raise wages; an increase in supply or a reduction in demand will lower them.

Panel (a) of Exhibit 12-8 shows how an increase in the demand for labor affects wages and employment. The shift in demand to D_2 pushes the wage to W_2 and boosts employment to L_2. Such an increase implies that the marginal product of labor has increased, that the number of firms has risen, or that the price of the good the labor produces has gone up. As we've seen, the marginal product of labor could rise because of an increase in the use of other factors of production, an improvement in technology, or an increase in human capital.

Clearly, a rising demand for labor has been the dominant trend in the market for U.S. labor through most of the nation's history. Wages and employment have generally risen as the availability of capital and other factors of production has increased, as technology has advanced, and as human capital has increased. All have increased the productivity of labor, and all have acted to increase wages.

Panel (b) of Exhibit 12-8 shows a reduction in the demand for labor to D_2. Wages and employment both fall. Given that the demand for labor in the aggregate is generally increasing, reduced labor demand is most often found in specific labor markets. For example, a slump in construction activity in a particular community can lower the demand for construction workers. Technological changes can reduce as well as increase demand. The Case in Point on wages and technology suggests that technological changes since the late 1970s have tended to reduce the demand for workers with only a high school education while increasing the demand for those with college degrees.

Panel (c) of Exhibit 12-8 shows the impact of an increase in the supply of labor. The supply curve shifts to S_2, pushing employment to L_2 and cutting the wage to W_2. For labor markets as a whole, such a supply increase could occur because of an increase in population or an increase in the amount of work people are willing to do. For individual labor markets, supply will increase as people move into a particular market.

Just as the demand for labor has increased throughout much of the history of the United States, so has the supply of labor. Population has risen both through immigration and through natural increases. Such increases tend, all other determinants of wages unchanged, to reduce wages. The fact that wages have tended to rise suggests that demand has, in general, increased more rapidly than supply. Still, the more supply rises, the smaller the increase in wages will be, even if demand is rising. For example, U.S. wages have increased much more slowly since the early 1970s than they did during the previous two decades. One reason for this was increased participation in the labor force by women, which tended to shift the supply curve for labor to the right.

Finally, Panel (d) of Exhibit 12-8 shows the impact of a reduction in labor supply. One dramatic example of a drop in the labor supply was caused by a reduction in population after the outbreak of bubonic plague in Europe in 1348—the so-called Black Death. The plague killed about one-third of the people of Europe within a few years, shifting the supply curve for labor sharply to the left. Wages doubled during the period.[3]

The fact that a reduction in the supply of labor tends to increase wages explains efforts by some employee groups to reduce labor supply. Members of certain professions have successfully promoted strict licensing requirements to limit the number of people who can enter the profession—U.S. physicians have been particularly successful in this effort. Unions often seek restrictions in immigration in an effort to reduce the supply of labor and thereby boost wages. We'll examine such efforts to restrict supply more carefully in Chapter 14.

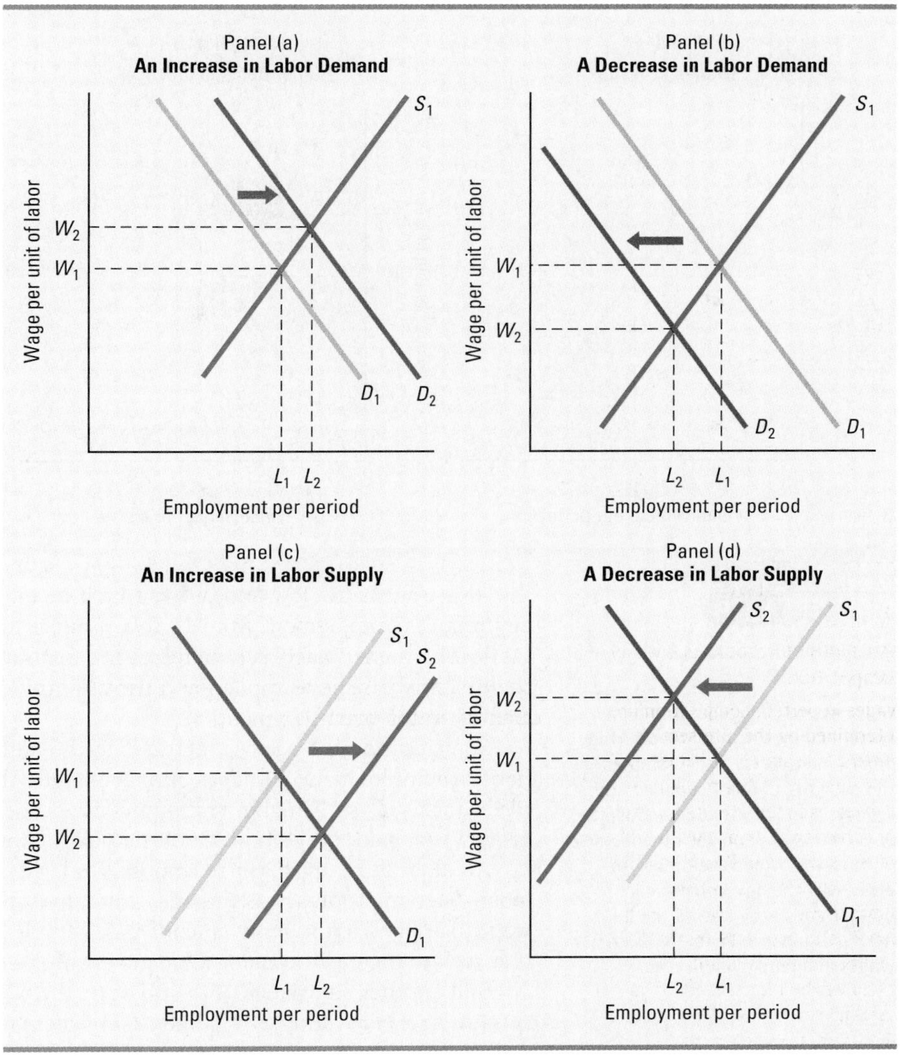

Exhibit 12-8

Changes in the Demand for and Supply of Labor

Panel (a) shows an increase in demand for labor; the wage rises to W_2 and employment rises to L_2. A reduction in labor demand, shown in Panel (b), reduces employment and the wage level. An increase in the supply of labor, shown in Panel (c), reduces the wage to W_2 and increases employment to L_2. Panel (d) shows the effect of a reduction in the supply of labor; wages rise and employment falls.

Competitive Labor Markets and the Minimum Wage

The Case in Point on technology and the wage gap points to an important social problem. Changes in technology boost the demand for highly educated workers. In turn, the resulting wage premium for more highly educated workers is a signal that encourages people to acquire more education. The market is an extremely powerful mechanism for moving resources

[3]Carlo M. Cipolla, *Before the Industrial Revolution: European Society and Economy, 1000–1700,* 2nd ed. (New York: Norton, 1980), pp. 200–202. The doubling in wages was a doubling in real terms, meaning that the purchasing power of an average worker's wage doubled.

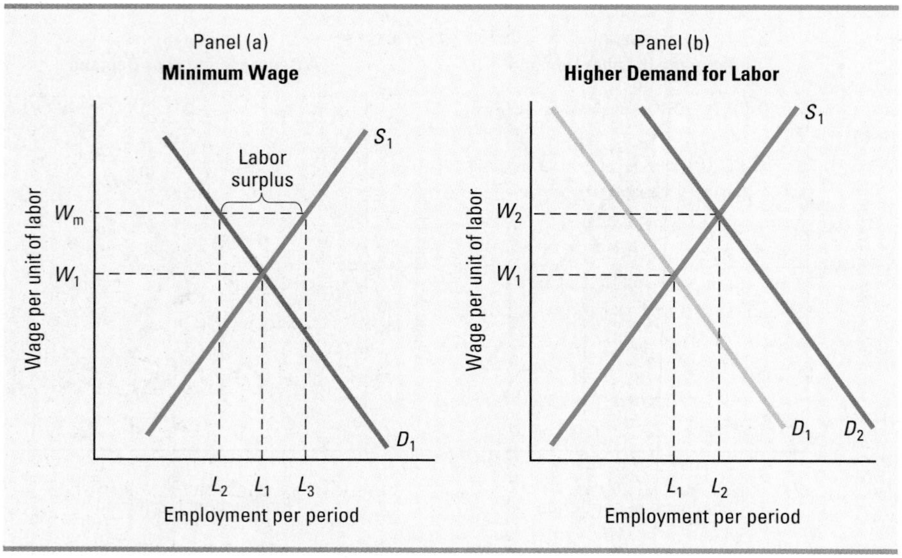

Exhibit 12-9

Alternative Responses to Low Wages

Government can respond to a low wage by imposing a minimum wage of W_m in Panel (a). This increases the quantity of labor supplied and reduces the quantity demanded. It does, however, increase the income of those who keep their jobs. Another way the government can boost wages is by raising the demand for labor in Panel (b). Both wages and employment rise.

to the areas of highest demand. At the same time, however, changes in technology seem to be leaving less educated workers behind. What will happen to people who lack the opportunity to develop the skills that the market values highly or who are unable to do so?

In order to raise wages of workers whose wages are relatively low governments around the world have imposed minimum wages. A minimum wage works like other price floors discussed in Chapter 4. The impact of a minimum wage is shown in Panel (a) of Exhibit 12-9. Suppose the current equilibrium wage of unskilled workers is W_1, determined by the intersection of the demand and supply curves of these workers. The government determines that this wage is too low and orders that it be increased to W_m, a minimum wage. This strategy reduces employment from L_1 to L_2, but it raises the incomes of those who continue to work. The higher wage also increases the quantity of labor supplied to L_3. The gap between the quantity of labor supplied and the quantity demanded, $L_3 - L_2$, is a surplus—a surplus that increases unemployment.

Some economists oppose increases in the minimum wage on grounds that such increases boost unemployment. Other economists argue that the demand for unskilled labor is relatively inelastic, so a higher minimum wage boosts the incomes of unskilled workers as a group. That gain, they say, justifies the policy, even if it increases unemployment.

An alternative approach to imposing a legal minimum is to try to boost the demand for labor. Such an approach is illustrated in Panel (b). An increase in demand to D_2 pushes the wage to W_2 and at the same time increases employment to L_2. Public sector training programs that seek to increase human capital are examples of this policy.

Still another alternative is to subsidize the wages of workers whose incomes fall below a certain level. Providing government subsidies—either to employers who agree to hire unskilled workers or to workers themselves in the form of transfer payments—enables people who lack the skills—and the ability to acquire the skills—needed to earn a higher wage to earn more without the loss of jobs implied by a higher minimum wage. Such programs can be costly. They also reduce the incentive for low-skilled workers to develop the skills that are in greater demand in the marketplace.

Checklist

- Wages in a competitive market are determined by demand and supply.
- An increase in demand or a reduction in supply will increase the equilibrium wage. A reduction in demand or an increase in supply will reduce the equilibrium wage.
- The government may respond to low wages for some workers by imposing the minimum wage, by attempting to increase the demand for those workers, or by subsidizing the wages of workers whose incomes fall below a certain level.

Case in Point Technology, Capital, and the Wage Gap

The introduction to this chapter noted the dramatic change in relative wages of college-educated versus high-school-educated workers in the 1980s. Adjusted for inflation, the wages of workers with college degrees rose, while the wages of workers with only a high school education fell, widening the gap between the wages of the two groups. The 1980s also saw a sharp increase in the wages of women relative to men.

Economists John Bound and George Johnson of the University of Michigan have examined explanations for the increased educational wage gap. One possible explanation lies on the supply side. If the supply of high-school-educated workers increased more than the supply of college-educated workers during the period, that would account for the gap. But the reverse was true: The supply of college-educated workers increased more than the supply of high-school-educated workers. The explanation of the increased gap had to lie in changes in demand.

One reason factor demand might change is that product demand can change. Bound and Johnson found that product demand shifts during the period tended to hurt college-educated workers more than their high-school-educated counterparts. They concluded that changes in product demand had actually tended to lower the wages of college-educated relative to high-school-educated workers.

The economists also examined the possibility that a shift by some firms to the use of foreign workers had increased the gap. During the 1980s, U.S. firms in some industries shifted a substantial share of their manufacturing activity to foreign plants, reducing the demand for U.S. labor. Because those shifts involved primarily unskilled workers, they contributed to the widening wage gap. But Mr. Bound says that it can't fully explain that gap: "The wage gap widened in a broad range of industries, including the service sector, and that can't be explained by a shift in international trade," he says. "For example, the gap between wages of high-school-educated and college-educated workers widened in hospitals, and they aren't affected by foreign production."

Having ruled out other factors, the economists concluded that technological changes accounted for the widened wage gap. The primary source of that change, they argue, has been the computer revolution. "It's not just computers sitting on someone's desk," Mr. Bound says. "It's the use of computer applications in all phases of production." As computers are integrated into more and more production processes, firms require relatively more workers with higher education—and relatively

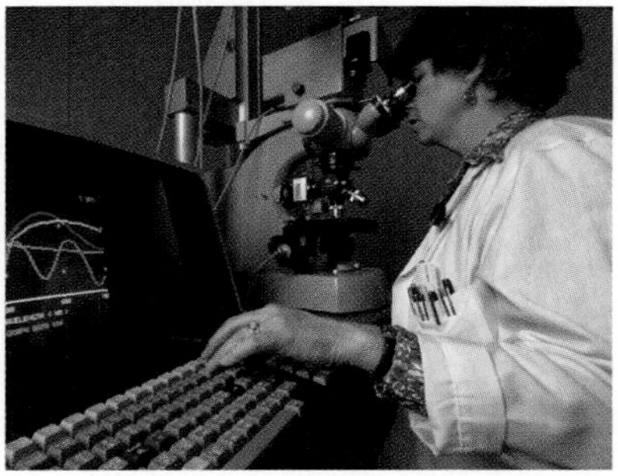

fewer workers with less education.

Increases in the use of high-tech capital, the Michigan economists argue, have increased the demand for college-educated workers. They have also increased the demand for women relative to men, since women tend to be concentrated in occupations requiring greater intellectual skills, while men tend to be concentrated in occupations that emphasize physical skills. Thus, the shift to more sophisticated production not only widened the high school–college wage gap—it also narrowed slightly the male–female wage gap. Bound and Johnson found that the average wage gap between men and women was 30 percent in 1979. In 1996, the wage gap between men and women was about 26 percent.

Source: John Bound and George Johnson, "What Are the Causes of Rising Wage Inequality in the United States?" *Economic Policy Review, Federal Reserve Bank of New York,* 1(1) (January 1995): 9–17; and personal interview.

Try It Yourself 12-3

Assuming that the market for construction workers is perfectly competitive, illustrate graphically how each of the following would affect the demand or supply for construction workers. What would be the impact on wages and on the number of construction workers employed?

a. The demand for new housing increases as more people move into the community.

b. Changes in societal attitudes lead to more women wanting to work in construction.

c. Improved training makes construction workers more productive.

d. New technology allows much of the framing used in housing construction to be built by robots at a factory and then shipped to construction sites.

A Look Back

In this chapter we have extended our understanding of the operation of perfectly competitive markets by looking at the market for labor. We found that the common sense embodied in the marginal decision rule is alive and well. A firm should hire additional labor up to the point at which the marginal benefit of doing so equals the marginal cost.

The demand curve for labor is given by the downward-sloping portion of the marginal revenue product (*MRP*) curve of labor. A profit-maximizing firm will hire labor up to the point at which its marginal revenue product equals its marginal factor cost. The demand for labor shifts whenever there is a change in (1) related factors of production, including investment in human capital; (2) technology; (3) product demand; and (4) the number of firms.

The quantity of labor supplied is closely linked to the demand for leisure. As more hours are worked, income goes up, but the marginal cost of work, measured in terms of forgone leisure, also increases. We saw that the substitution effect of a wage increase always increases the quantity supplied. But the income effect of a wage increase reduces the quantity of labor supplied. It is possible that, above some wage, the income effect more than offsets the substitution effect. At or above that wage, an individual's supply curve for labor is backward bending. Supply curves for labor in individual markets, however, are likely to be upward sloping.

Because competitive labor markets generate wages equal to marginal revenue product, workers who add little to the value of a firm's output will receive low wages. The public sector can institute a minimum wage, seek to improve these workers' human capital, or subsidize their wages.

A Look Ahead In Chapter 13 we'll examine competitive markets for two other factors of production—capital and natural resources.

Terms and Concepts for Review

marginal revenue product, **245**
marginal factor cost, **246**
complementary factors of production, **249**
substitute factors of production, **249**
derived demand, **249**

For Discussion

1. Explain the difference between the marginal product of a factor and the marginal revenue product of a factor.
2. In perfectly competitive input markets, the factor price and the marginal factor cost are the same. True or false? Explain.
3. Many high school vocational education programs are beginning to shift from an emphasis on training students to perform specific tasks to training students to learn new tasks. Students are taught, for example, how to read computer manuals so that they can more easily learn new systems. Why has this change occurred? Do you think the change is desirable?
4. How would an increase in the prices of so-called truck crops—crops of fresh produce that must be brought immediately to market—affect the wages of workers who harvest those crops?
5. If individual labor supply curves of all individuals are backward bending, does this mean that a market supply curve for labor in a particular industry will also be backward bending?
6. There was an unprecedented wave of immigration to the United States during the latter third of the nineteenth century. Wages, however, rose at a rapid rate throughout the period. Why was the increase in wages surprising in light of rising immigration, and what probably caused it?

7. Suppose you were the economic adviser to the president of a small underdeveloped country. What advice would you give him or her with respect to how the country could raise the productivity of its labor force? (*Hint:* What factors increase labor productivity?)
8. The text argues that the effect of a minimum wage on the incomes of workers depends on whether the demand for their services is elastic or inelastic. Explain why.
9. How would a successful effort to increase the human capital of unskilled workers affect their wage? Why?
10. Does the Case in Point on ATMs and employment of bank tellers suggest that the two factors are substitutes or complements? Explain.
11. The Case in Point on celebrity check cashing suggests that no income effect was involved in the experiment by *Spy* magazine. Why not? Is the supply curve shown consistent with the theory of substitution effects? Why or why not?
12. Given the evidence cited in the Case in Point on the increasing wage gap between workers with college degrees and those who have only completed high school, how has the greater use by firms of high-tech capital affected the marginal products of workers with college degrees? How has it affected their marginal revenue product?

Problems

1. Felicia Alvarez, the bakery manager introduced in the appendix to Chapter 1, faces the total product curve shown, which gives the relationship between the number of bakers she hires each day and the number of loaves of bread she produces, assuming all other factors of production are given.

Number of bakers per day	Loaves of bread per day
0	0
1	400
2	700
3	900
4	1,025
5	1,100
6	1,150

Assume that bakers in the area receive a wage of $100 per day and that the price of bread is $1.00 per loaf. Plot the bakery's marginal revenue product and marginal factor cost curves (remember that marginal values are plotted at the midpoints of the intervals). How many bakers will Ms. Alvarez employ per day?

2. Suppose that wooden boxes are produced under conditions of perfect competition and that the price of a box is $10. The demand and supply curves for the workers who make these boxes are given in the table.

Wage per day	Workers demanded	Workers supplied
$100	6,000	12,000
80	7,000	10,000
60	8,000	8,000
40	9,000	6,000
20	10,000	4,000

Plot the demand and supply curves for labor, and determine the equilibrium wage for box makers.

3. Assume that the market for nurses is perfectly competitive. Illustrate graphically how each of the following events will affect the demand or supply for nurses. State the impact on wages and on the number of nurses employed.
   a. New hospital instruments reduce the amount of time physicians must spend with patients in intensive care and increase the care that nurses can provide.
   b. The number of doctors increases.
   c. Changes in the labor market lead to greater demand for the services of women in a wide range of occupations. The demand for nurses, however, does not change.
   d. New legislation establishes primary-care facilities in which nurses care for patients with minor medical problems. No supervision by physicians is required in the facilities.
   e. The wage for nurses rises.
4. Plot the supply curves for labor implied by each of the following statements:
   a. "I'm sorry, kids, but now that I'm earning more, I just can't afford to come home early in the afternoon, so I won't be there when you get home from school."
   b. "They can pay me a lot or they can pay me a little. I'll still put in my 8 hours a day."
   c. "Wow! With the raise the boss just gave me, I can afford to knock off early each day."

Answers to Try It Yourself Problems

Try It Yourself 12-1

a. A reduction in market price would decrease the marginal revenue product of labor. Since the demand for labor is the downward-sloping portion of the marginal revenue product curve, the demand for labor by TeleTax would shift to the left.
b. An increase in the market fee that TeleTax pays the accountants it hires corresponds to an increase in marginal factor cost. TeleTax's demand curve would not shift; rather Teletax would move up along its same demand curve for accountants. As a result, Teletax would hire fewer accountants.
c. An increase in the marginal product of each accountant corresponds to a rightward shift in the marginal revenue product curve and hence a rightward shift in TeleTax's demand curve for accountants.

Try It Yourself 12-2

The first question is about willingness to work as the wage rate changes. It thus refers to movement along the labor supply curve. That mothers of preschool-age children are more willing to work the higher the wage implies an upward-sloping labor supply curve. When the labor supply curve is upward sloping, the substitution effect dominates the income effect. The other three questions refer to factors that cause the labor supply curve to shift. In all three cases, the circumstances imply that the labor supply curve would shift to the left.

Try It Yourself 12-3

a. An increase in the demand for new housing would shift the demand curve for construction workers to the right, as shown in Exhibit 12-8, Panel (a). Both the wage rate and the employment in construction rise.
b. A larger number of women wanting to work in construction means an increase in labor supply, as shown in Exhibit 12-8, Panel (c). An increase in the supply of labor reduces the wage rate and increases employment.
c. Improved training would increase the marginal revenue product of construction workers and hence increase demand for them. Wages and employment would rise, as shown in Exhibit 12-8, Panel (a).
d. The robots are likely to serve as a substitute for labor. That will reduce demand, wages, and employment of construction workers, as shown in Panel (b).

13

Interest Rates and the Markets for Capital and Natural Resources

Getting Started: Building the "Internet in the Sky"

The race is on to build the "Internet in the Sky." Current telecommunication systems transport information using a combination of high-altitude, geostationary earth-orbiting (GEO) satellites and ground linkages, but in a few years this complex network will be replaced by low earth-orbiting (LEO) satellites. LEO satellites will allow information to be sent and received instantaneously anywhere on the face of the globe. At least that's the plan.

Are such projects technically feasible? Will users be willing to pay for the service? Or is the "Internet in the Sky" just pie in the sky?

Craig McCaw, who made a fortune developing and then selling to AT&T the world's largest cellular phone network, is now chair of Teledesic, the company he formed to build a LEO satellite system. Betting that it will be a winner, Mr. McCaw has put up millions of dollars to fund the project, as has Microsoft's Bill Gates and Prince Alwaleed Bin Talal Bin Abdulaziz of Saudi Arabia. Boeing, Motorola, and Matra Marconi Space, Europe's leading satellite manufacturer, are corporate partners.

Even if the project is successful, the rewards to the companies and to the individuals that put their financial capital into the venture will be a long time in coming. The first launch is scheduled for 2002 and commercial service is to begin in 2003. When there will be enough customers for Teledesic to start earning a profit is a guess, but some analysts are estimating the industry will generate about $21 billion in revenues by 2005. And there are competitors to worry about as well.

Teledesic's venture is bigger than most capital projects, but it shares some basic characteristics with any acquisition of capital by firms. As we saw in Chapter 2, the production of capital—the goods used in producing other goods and services—requires sacrificing consumption. The returns to capital will be spread over the period in which the capital is used. The choice to acquire capital is thus a choice to give up consumption today in hopes of returns in the future. Because those returns are far from certain, the choice to acquire capital is inevitably a risky one.

For all its special characteristics, however, capital is a factor of production. As we investigate the market for capital, the concepts of marginal revenue product and marginal factor cost that we developed in the last chapter will continue to serve us. The big difference is that the benefits and costs of holding capital are distributed over time.

We'll also examine markets for natural resources in this chapter. Like decisions involving capital, choices in the allocation of natural resources have lasting effects. For potentially exhaustible natural resources such as oil, the effects of those choices last forever.

For the analysis of capital and natural resources, we shift from the examination of outcomes in the current period to the analysis of outcomes distributed over many periods. Interest rates, which link the values of payments that occur at different times, will be central to our analysis.

Time and Interest Rates

Time, the saying goes, is nature's way of keeping everything from happening all at once. And the fact that everything doesn't happen at once introduces an important complication in economic analysis.

Teledesic has decided to use funds to install capital that won't begin to produce income for several years, so it needs a way to compare the significance of funds spent now to income earned later. It must find a way to compensate financial investors who give up the use of their funds for several years, until the project begins to pay off. How can payments that are distributed across time be linked to one another? Interest rates are the linkage mechanism; we shall investigate how they achieve that linkage in this section.

The Nature of Interest Rates

Let's consider a delightful problem of choice. Your Aunt Carmen offers to give you $10,000 now or $10,000 in one year. Which would you pick?

Most people would choose to take the payment now. One reason for that choice is that the average level of prices is likely to rise over the next year. The purchasing power of $10,000 today is thus greater than the purchasing power of $10,000 a year hence. There's also a question of whether you can count on receiving the payment. If you take it now, you've got it. It's risky to wait a year; who knows what will happen?

Let's eliminate both of these problems. Suppose that you're confident that the average level of prices won't change during the year, and you're absolutely certain that if you choose to wait for the payment, you and it will both be available. Will you take the payment now or wait?

Chances are you'd *still* want to take the payment now. Perhaps there are some things you'd like to purchase with it, and you'd like them sooner rather than later. Moreover, if you wait a year to get the payment, you won't be able to use it while you're waiting. If you take it now, you can choose to spend it now or wait.

Now suppose Aunt Carmen wants to induce you to wait and changes the terms of her gift. She offers you $10,000 now or $11,000 in one year. In effect, she's offering you a $1,000 bonus if you'll wait a year. If you agree to wait a year to receive Aunt Carmen's payment, you'll be accepting her promise to provide funds instead of the funds themselves. Either will increase your **wealth,** which is the sum of all your assets less all your liabilities. **Assets** are anything you have that is of value; **liabilities** are obligations to make future payments. Both a $10,000 payment from Aunt Carmen now and her promise of $10,000 in a year are examples of assets. The alternative to holding wealth is to consume it. You could, for example, take Aunt Carmen's $10,000 and spend it for a trip to Europe, thus reducing your wealth. By making a better offer—$11,000 instead of $10,000—Aunt Carmen is trying to induce you to accept an asset you won't be able to consume during the year.

The $1,000 bonus Aunt Carmen is offering if you'll wait a year for her payment is interest. In general, **interest** is a payment made to people who agree to postpone their use of wealth. The **interest rate** represents the opportunity cost of using wealth today, expressed as a percentage of the amount of wealth whose use is postponed. Aunt Carmen is offering you $1,000 if you'll pass up the $10,000 today. She's thus offering you an interest rate of 10 percent ($1,000/$10,000 = 0.1 = 10%).

Suppose you tell Aunt Carmen that, given the two options, you'd still rather have the $10,000 today. She now offers you $11,500 if you'll wait a year for the payment—an interest rate of 15 percent. The more she pays for waiting, the higher the interest rate.

You are probably familiar with the role of interest rates in loans. In a loan, the borrower obtains a payment now in exchange for promising to repay the loan in the future. The lender thus must postpone his or her use of wealth until the time of repayment. To induce lenders to postpone their use of their wealth, borrowers offer interest. Borrowers are willing to pay interest because it allows them to acquire the sum now rather than having to wait for it. And lenders require interest payments to compensate them for postponing their own use of their wealth.

Interest Rates and Present Value

We saw in the previous section that people generally prefer to receive a payment of some amount today rather than wait to receive that same amount later. We may conclude that the value today of a payment in the future is less than the dollar value of the future payment. An important application of interest rates is to show the relationship between the current and future values of a particular payment.

To see how we can calculate the current value of a future payment, let's consider an example similar to Aunt Carmen's offer. This time you have $1,000 and you deposit it in a bank, where it earns interest at the rate of 10 percent per year.

How much will you have in your bank account at the end of 1 year? You'll have the original $1,000 plus 10 percent of $1,000, or $1,100:

$$\$1{,}000 + (0.10)(\$1{,}000) = \$1{,}100$$

More generally, if we let P_0 equal the amount you deposit today, r the percentage rate of interest, and P_1 the balance of your deposit at the end of 1 year, then we can write

$$P_0 + rP_0 = P_1 \tag{1}$$

Factoring out the P_0 term on the left-hand side of Equation 1, we have

$$P_0\,(1 + r) = P_1 \tag{2}$$

Equation 2 shows how to determine the future value of a payment or deposit made today. Now let's turn the question around. We can ask what P_1, an amount that will be available 1 year from now, is worth today. We solve for this by dividing both sides of Equation 2 by $(1 + r)$ to obtain

$$P_0 = \frac{P_1}{1 + r} \tag{3}$$

Equation 3 suggests how we can compute the value today, P_0, of an amount P_1 that will be paid a year hence. An amount that would equal a particular future value if deposited today at a specific interest rate is called the **present value** of that future value.

More generally, the present value of any payment to be received n periods from now is

$$P_0 = \frac{P_n}{(1 + r)^n} \tag{4}$$

Suppose, for example, that your Aunt Carmen offers you the option of $1,000 now or $15,000 in 30 years. We can use Equation 4 to help you decide which sum to take. The present value of $15,000 to be received in 30 years, assuming an interest rate of 10 percent, is

$$P_0 = \frac{P_{30}}{(1 + r)^{30}} = \frac{\$15{,}000}{(1 + 0.10)^{30}} = \$859.63$$

Assuming that you could earn that 10 percent return with certainty, you'd be better off taking Aunt Carmen's $1,000 now; it's greater than the present value, at an interest rate of 10 percent, of the $15,000 she would give you in 30 years. The $1,000 she gives you now, assuming an interest rate of 10 percent, in 30 years will grow to

$$\$1{,}000\,(1 + 0.10)^{30} = \$17{,}449.40$$

The present value of some future payment depends on three things.

1. **The Size of the Payment Itself.** The bigger the future payment, the greater its present value.
2. **The Length of the Period Until Payment.** The present value depends on how long a period will elapse before the payment is made. The present value of $15,000 in 30 years, at an interest rate of 10 percent, is $859.63. But that same sum, if paid in 20 years, has a present value of $2,229.65. And if paid in 10 years, its present value is more than twice as great: $5,783.15. The longer the time period before a payment is to be made, the lower its present value.
3. **The Rate of Interest.** The present value of a payment of $15,000 to be made in 20 years is $2,229.65 if the interest rate is 10 percent; it rises to $5,653.34 at an interest rate of 5

Present Value of $15,000

Interest rate (%)	Time until payment: 5 years	10 years	15 years	20 years
5	$11,752.89	$9,208.70	$7,215.26	$5,653.34
10	9,313.82	5,783.15	3,590.88	2,229.65
15	7,457.65	3,707.77	1,843.42	916.50
20	6,028.16	2,422.58	973.58	391.26

Exhibit 13-1

Time, Interest Rates, and Present Value

The higher the interest rate and the longer the time until payment is made, the lower the present value of a future payment. The table shows the present value of a future payment of $15,000 under different conditions. The present value of $15,000 to be paid in 5 years is $11,752.89 if the interest rate is 5 percent. Its present value is just $391.26 if it is to be paid in 20 years and the interest rate is 20 percent.

percent. The lower the interest rate, the higher the present value of a future payment. Exhibit 13-1 gives present values of a payment of $15,000 at various interest rates and for various time periods.

The concept of present value can also be applied to a series of future payments. Suppose you've been promised $1,000 at the end of each of the next 5 years. Because each payment will occur at a different time, we calculate the present value of the series of payments by taking the value of each payment separately and adding them together. At an interest rate of 10 percent, the present value P_0 is

$$P_0 = \frac{\$1{,}000}{1.10} + \frac{\$1{,}000}{1.10^2} + \frac{\$1{,}000}{1.10^3} + \frac{\$1{,}000}{1.10^4} + \frac{\$1{,}000}{1.10^5} = \$3{,}790.78$$

Interest rates can thus be used to compare the values of payments that will occur at different times. Choices concerning capital and natural resources require such comparisons, so you'll find applications of the concept of present value throughout this chapter, but the concept of present value applies whenever costs and benefits do not all take place in the current period.

State lottery winners often have a choice between a single large payment now or smaller payments paid out over a 25- or 30-year period. Comparing the single payment now to the present value of the future payments allows winners to make informed decisions. For example, in April 1999 Maria Grasso, of Braintree, Massachusetts, became the winner of the world's biggest lottery ever won by one person. Given the alternative of claiming the $197 million jackpot in 26 annual payments of $7.58 million or taking $104 million in a lump sum, she chose the latter. Holding all other considerations that must have been going through her mind unchanged, she must have thought her best rate of return would be 6 percent or more. Why 6 percent? Using an interest rate of 6 percent, $104 million is equal to the present value of the 26-year stream of payments. At all interest rates greater than 6 percent, the present value of the stream of benefits would be less than $104 million. At all interest rates less than 6 percent, the present value of the stream of payments would be more than $104 million. Our present value analysis suggests that if she thought the interest rate she could earn was more than 6 percent, she should take the lump sum payment, which she did.

Checklist

- People generally prefer to receive a payment now rather than to wait and receive it later.
- Interest is a payment made to people who agree to postpone their use of wealth.
- We compute the present value, P_0, of a sum to be received in n years, P_n, as $P_0 = P_n/(1 + r)^n$.
- The present value of a future payment will be greater the larger the payment, the sooner it is due, and the lower the rate of interest.

Try It Yourself 13-1

Suppose your friend Sara asks you to lend her $5,000 so she can buy a used car. She tells you she can pay you back $5,200 in a year. Reliable Sara always keeps her word! Suppose the interest rate you could earn by putting the $5,000 in a savings account is 5 percent. What is the present value of her offer? Is it a good deal for you or not? What if the interest rate on your savings account is only 3 percent?

Case in Point Waiting, AIDS, and Life Insurance

It is a tale of the 1990s that has become all too familiar.

Call him Roger Johnson. He has AIDS, a disease that will almost certainly kill him. Mr. Johnson is unable to work and his financial burdens compound his tragic medical situation. He's mortgaged his house and sold his other assets in a desperate effort to get his hands on the cash he needs for care, for food, and for shelter. He has a life insurance policy, but it will pay off only when he dies. If only he could get some cash sooner. . . .

The problem facing Mr. Johnson spawned a market solution—companies that buy the life insurance policies of the terminally ill. Mr. Johnson can sell his policy to one of these companies and collect the purchase price. The company takes over his premium payments. When Mr. Johnson dies, the company will collect the proceeds of the policy.

The new industry is called the viatical industry. (The term *viatical* comes from viaticum, a Christian sacrament given to a dying person.) It provides the terminally ill with access to quick cash while they're alive; it provides financial investors a healthy interest premium on their funds.

It's a grisly business. Potential buyers pore over patients' medical histories, studying T-cell counts and other indicators of how soon the patient will die. From the buyer's point of view, a speedy death is desirable. A patient with a life expectancy of less than 6 months can typically sell his or her life insurance policy for 80 percent of its face value; a $200,000 policy would thus fetch $160,000. A person with a better prognosis will collect less. Patients expected to live 2 years, for example, typically get only 60 percent of the face value of their policies.

Life Partners, Inc., in Waco, Texas, is a leader in the viatical settlements industry. It reports that it arranges purchases of more than $250 million in policies per year—and that the number is growing fast. The firm says that its clients, the financial investors who put up the funds that Life Partners uses to buy insurance policies, earn an interest return of 25 percent per year on their financial investments.

Kim D. Orr, an agent for the firm, says that the firm's activities make for a win-win situation. "Some years ago I had a cousin who died of AIDS. He was, at the end, destitute, and had to rely totally on his family for support. Today, there's a broad market, with lots of participants, and a patient can realize a high fraction of the face value of a policy on selling it. The market helps buyers and patients alike."

Source: Personal interview and information obtained from the web site of Life Partners, Inc. (www.lifepartnersinc.com).

Interest Rates and Capital

The quantity of capital that firms employ in their production of goods and services has enormously important implications for economic activity and for the standard of living people in the economy enjoy. Increases in capital increase the marginal product of labor and boost wages at the same time they boost total output. An increase in the stock of capital therefore tends to raise incomes and improve the standard of living in the economy.

Capital is often a fixed factor of production in the short run. A firm can't quickly retool an assembly line or add a new office building. Determining the quantity of capital a firm will use is likely to involve long-run choices.

The Demand for Capital

A firm uses additional units of a factor until marginal revenue product equals marginal factor cost. Capital is no different from other factors of production, save for the fact that the revenues and costs it generates are distributed over time. As the first step in assessing a firm's demand for capital, we determine the present value of marginal revenue products and marginal factor costs.

Capital and Net Present Value Suppose Carol Stein is considering the purchase of a new $95,000 tractor for her farm. Ms. Stein expects to use the tractor for 5 years and then sell it; she expects that it will sell for $22,000 at the end of the 5-year period. She has the $95,000 on hand now; her alternative to purchasing the tractor could be to put $95,000 in a bank account earning 7 percent annual interest.

Ms. Stein expects that the tractor will bring in additional revenue of $50,000 but will cost $30,000 per year to operate, for a net revenue of $20,000 annually. For simplicity, we shall suppose that this net revenue accrues at the end of each year.

Should she buy the tractor? We can answer this question by computing the tractor's **net present value (NPV),** which is equal to the present value of all the revenues expected from an asset minus the present value of all the costs associated with it. We thus measure the difference between the present value of marginal revenue products and the present value of marginal factor costs. If *NPV* is greater than zero, purchase of the asset will increase the profitability of the firm. A negative *NPV* implies that the funds for the asset would yield a higher return if used to purchase an interest-bearing asset. A firm will maximize profits by acquiring additional capital up to the point that the present value of capital's marginal revenue product equals the present value of marginal factor cost.

If the revenues generated by an asset in period t equal R_t and the costs in period t equal C_t, then the net present value NPV_0 of an asset expected to last for n years is

$$NPV_0 = R_0 - C_0 + \frac{R_1 - C_1}{1 + r} + \dots + \frac{R_n - C_n}{(1 + r)^n} \qquad (5)$$

To purchase the tractor, Ms. Stein pays $95,000. She will receive additional revenues of $50,000 per year from increased planting and more efficient harvesting, less the operating cost per year of $30,000, plus the $22,000 she expects to get by selling the tractor at the end of 5 years. The net present value of the tractor, NPV_0, is thus given by

$$NPV_0 = -\$95{,}000 + \frac{\$20{,}000}{1.07} + \frac{\$20{,}000}{1.07^2} + \frac{\$20{,}000}{1.07^3} + \frac{\$20{,}000}{1.07^4} + \frac{\$42{,}000}{1.07^5} = \$2{,}690$$

Given the cost of the tractor, the net returns Ms. Stein projects, and an interest rate of 7 percent, Ms. Stein will increase her profits by purchasing the tractor. The tractor will yield a return whose present value is $2,690 greater than the return that could be obtained by the alternative of putting the $95,000 in a bank account.

Ms. Stein's acquisition of the tractor is called investment. Economists define **investment** as an addition to capital stock. Any acquisition of new capital goods therefore qualifies as investment.

The Demand Curve for Capital Our analysis of Carol Stein's decision regarding the purchase of a new tractor suggests the forces at work in determining the economy's demand for capital. In deciding to purchase the tractor, Ms. Stein considered the price she would have to pay to obtain the tractor, the costs of operating it, the marginal revenue product she would receive by owning it, and the price she could get by selling the tractor when she expects to be done with it. Notice that with the exception of the purchase price of the tractor, *all* those figures were projections. Her decision to purchase the tractor depends almost entirely on the costs and benefits she *expects* will be associated with its use.

Finally, Ms. Stein converted all those figures to a net present value based on the interest rate prevailing at the time she made her choice. A positive *NPV* means that her profits will be increased by purchasing the tractor. That result, of course, depends on the prevailing interest rate. At an interest rate of 7 percent, the *NPV* is positive. At an interest rate of 8 percent, the *NPV* would be negative. At that interest rate, Ms. Stein would do better to put her funds elsewhere.

At any one time, millions of choices like that of Ms. Stein concerning the acquisition of capital will be under consideration. Each decision will hinge on the price of a particular piece of capital, the expected cost of its use, its expected marginal revenue product, its expected scrap value, and the interest rate. Not only will firms be considering the acquisition of new capital, they will be considering retaining existing capital as well. Ms. Stein, for example, may have other tractors. Should she continue to use them, or should she sell them? If she keeps them, she'll experience a stream of revenues and costs over the next several periods; if she sells them, she'll have funds now that she could use for something else. To decide whether a firm should keep the capital it already has, we need an estimate of the *NPV* of each unit of capital. Such decisions are always affected by the interest rate. At higher rates of interest, it makes sense to sell some capital rather than hold it. At lower rates of interest, the *NPV* of holding capital will rise.

Because firms' choices to acquire new capital and to hold existing capital depend on the interest rate, the **demand curve for capital** in Exhibit 13-2, which shows the quantity of capital firms intend to hold at each interest rate, is downward sloping. At point A, we see that at an interest rate of 10 percent, $8 trillion worth of capital is demanded in the economy. At point B, a reduction in the interest rate to 7 percent increases the quantity of capital demanded to $9 trillion. At point C, at an interest rate of 4 percent, the quantity of capital demanded is $10 trillion. A reduction in the interest rate increases the quantity of capital demanded.

The demand curve for capital for the economy is found by summing the demand curves of all holders of capital. Ms. Stein's demand curve, for example, might show that at an interest rate of 8 percent, she'll demand the capital she already has—suppose it's $600,000 worth of equipment. If the interest rate drops to 7 percent, she'll add the tractor; the quantity of capital she demands rises to $695,000. At interest rates greater than 8 percent, she might decide to reduce her maintenance efforts for some of the capital she already has; the quantity of capital she demands would fall below $600,000. As with the demand for capital in the economy, we can expect individual firms to demand a smaller quantity of capital when the interest rate is higher.

Shifts in the Demand for Capital Why might the demand for capital change? Because the demand for capital reflects the marginal revenue product of capital, anything that changes the marginal revenue product of capital will shift the demand for capital. Our search for demand shifters must thus focus on factors that change the marginal product of capital, the prices of the goods capital produces, and the costs of acquiring and holding capital. Let's discuss some factors that could affect these variables and thus shift the demand for capital.

Changes in Expectations Choices concerning capital are always based on expectations. Net present value is computed from the expected revenues and costs over the expected life of an asset. If firms' expectations change, their demand for capital will change. If something causes firms to revise their sales expectations upward (such as stronger than expected sales in the recent past), it is likely to increase their demand for capital. Similarly, an event that dampens firms' expectations (such as recent weak sales) is likely to reduce their demand for capital.

Technological Change Technological changes can boost the marginal product of capital and thus boost the demand for capital. The discovery of new ways to integrate computers into production processes, for example, has dramatically increased the demand for capital in the last few years. Many universities are adding new classroom buildings or renovating old ones so they can better use computers in instruction, and businesses use computers in nearly every facet of operations.

Changing Demand for Goods and Services Ultimately, the source of demand for factors of production is the demand for the goods and services produced by those factors. As population and incomes expand, we can expect greater demand for goods and services, a change that will boost the demand for capital.

Exhibit 13-2

The Demand Curve for Capital

The quantity of capital firms will want to hold depends on the interest rate. The higher the interest rate, the less capital firms demand.

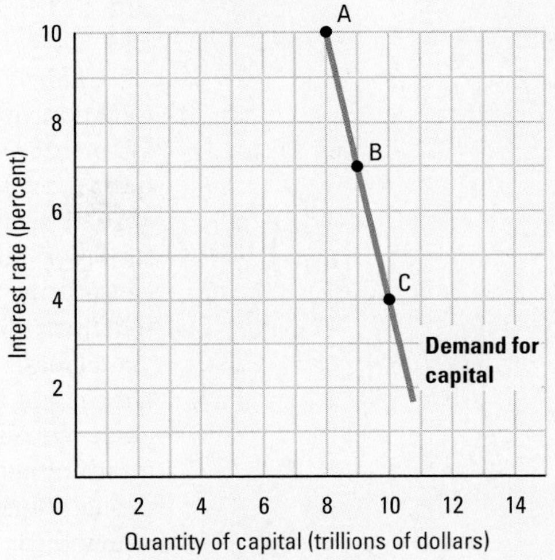

Case in Point The Net Present Value of an MBA

An investment in human capital differs little from an investment in capital—one acquires an asset that will produce additional income over the life of the asset. One's education produces—or it can be expected to produce—additional income over one's working career.

Ronald Yeaple, a professor at the University of Rochester business school, has estimated the net present value (*NPV*) of an MBA obtained from each of 20 top business schools. The costs of attending each school include tuition and forgone income. To estimate the marginal revenue products of a degree, Mr. Yeaple started with survey data showing what graduates of each school were earning 5 years after obtaining their MBAs. He then estimated what students with the savvy to attend those schools would have been earning without an MBA. The estimated marginal revenue product for each year is the difference between the salary students earned with a degree versus what they would have earned without it. The *NPV* is then computed using Equation 5.

The estimates given here show the *NPV* of an MBA over the first 7 years of work after receiving the degree. They suggest that an MBA from 15 of the schools ranked is a good investment—but that a degree at the other schools might not be. Mr. Yeaple says that extending income projections beyond 7 years wouldn't significantly affect the analysis, because present values of projected income differentials with and without an MBA become very small. Of course, Mr. Yeaple's calculations only include financial aspects of the investment and do not cover any psychic benefits that MBA recipients may incur from perhaps more interesting work or prestige or simply being more attuned to the nightly business reports broadcast on television.

School	Net present value, first 7 years of work	School	Net present value, first 7 years of work
Harvard	$148,378	Virginia	30,046
Chicago	106,847	Dartmouth	22,509
Stanford	97,462	Michigan	21,502
MIT	85,736	Carnegie-Mellon	18,679
Yale	83,775	Texas	17,459
Wharton	59,486	Rochester	−307
UCLA	55,088	Indiana	−3,315
Berkeley	54,101	NYU	−3,749
Northwestern	53,562	North Carolina	−4,565
Cornell	30,874	Duke	−17,631

Source: "The MBA Cost-Benefit Analysis," *The Economist*, 6 August 1994, p. 58. © 1994 The Economist Newspaper Group, Inc. Table reprinted with permission. Further reproduction prohibited.

Changes in Relative Factor Prices Firms achieve the greatest possible output for a given total cost by operating where the ratios of marginal product to factor price are equal for all factors of production. For a firm that uses capital (K) and labor (L), for example, this requires that $MP_L/P_L = MP_K/P_K$. Suppose these equalities hold and the price of labor rises. The ratio of the marginal product of labor to its price goes down, and the firm substitutes capital for labor. Similarly, an increase in the price of capital, all other things unchanged, would cause firms to substitute other factors of production for capital. The demand for capital, therefore, would fall.

Change in Tax Policy Government can indirectly affect the price of capital through changes in tax policy. For example, suppose the government enacts an investment tax credit for businesses, that is, a deduction of a certain percentage of their spending on capital from their profits before paying taxes. Such a policy would effectively lower the price of capital, causing firms to substitute capital for other factors of production and increasing the demand for capital. The repeal of an investment tax credit would lead to a decrease in the demand for capital.

The Market for Loanable Funds

When a firm decides to expand its capital stock, it can finance its purchase of capital in several ways. It might already have the funds on hand. It can also raise funds by selling shares of stock, as discussed in Chapter 4. When a firm sells stock, it is selling shares of ownership of the firm. It can borrow the funds for the capital from a bank. Another option is to issue and sell its own bonds. A **bond** is a promise to pay back a certain amount at a certain time. When a firm borrows from a bank or sells bonds, of course, it accepts a liability—it must make interest payments to the bank or the owners of its bonds as they come due.

Regardless of the method of financing chosen, a critical factor in the firm's decision on whether to acquire and hold capital and on how to finance the capital is the interest rate. The role of the interest rate is obvious when the firm issues its own bonds or borrows from a bank. But even when the firm uses its own funds to purchase the capital, it is forgoing the option of lending those funds directly to other firms by buying their bonds or indirectly by putting the funds in bank accounts, thereby allowing the banks to lend the funds. The interest rate gives the opportunity cost of using funds to acquire capital rather than putting the funds to the best alternative use available to the firm.

The interest rate is determined in a market in the same way that the price of potatoes is determined in a market: by the forces of demand and supply. The market in which borrowers (demanders of funds) and lenders (suppliers of funds) meet is the **loanable funds market.**

We will simplify our model of the role that the interest rate plays in the demand for capital by ignoring differences in actual interest rates that specific consumers and firms face in the economy. For example, the interest rate on credit cards is higher than the mortgage rate of interest, and large, established companies can borrow funds or issue bonds at lower interest rates than new, start-up companies can. Interest rates that firms face depend on a variety of factors, such as riskiness of the loan, the duration of the loan, and the costs of administering the loan. However, since we will focus on general tendencies that cause interest rates to rise or fall and since the various interest rates in the economy tend to move up and down together, the conclusions we reach about the market for loanable funds and how firms and consumers respond to interest rate changes will still be valid.

The Demand for Loanable Funds In the previous section we learned that a firm's decision to acquire and keep capital depends on the net present value of the capital in question, which in turn depends on the interest rate. The lower the interest rate, the greater the amount of capital that firms will want to acquire and hold, since lower interest rates translate into more capital with positive net present values. The desire for more capital means, in turn, a desire for more loanable funds. Similarly, at higher interest rates, less capital will be demanded, because more of the capital in question will have negative net present values. Higher interest rates therefore mean less funding demanded.

Thus the demand for loanable funds is downward sloping, like the demand for potatoes, as shown in Exhibit 13-3. The lower the interest rate, the more capital firms will demand. The more capital that firms demand, the greater the funding that is required to finance it.

The Supply of Loanable Funds Lenders are consumers or firms that determine that they are willing to forgo some current use of their funds in order to have more available in the future. Lenders supply funds to the loanable funds market. In general, higher interest rates make the lending option more attractive.

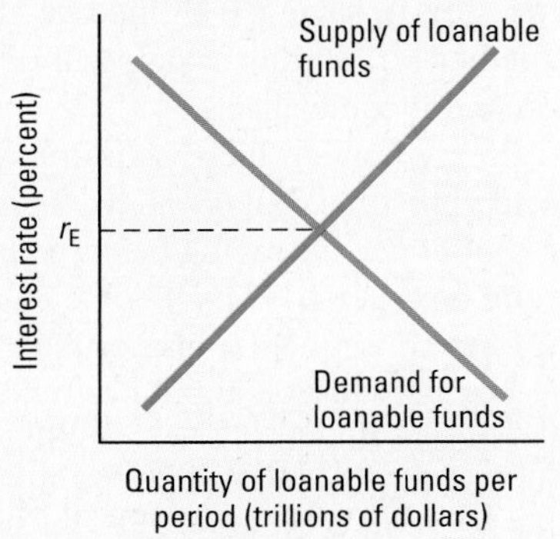

Exhibit 13-3

The Demand and Supply of Loanable Funds

At lower interest rates, firms demand more capital and therefore more loanable funds. The demand for loanable funds is downward sloping. The supply of loanable funds is generally upward sloping. The equilibrium interest rate, r_E, will be found where the two curves intersect.

Caution!

Notice that in Exhibit 13-2 the demand for capital is shown as a function of the interest rate, not the price of capital. Because the value on the vertical axis is the interest rate, as the interest rate changes, the quantity of capital demanded changes. A change in the price of capital (for example, an increase in the price of Ms. Stein's tractor) causes the demand curve to shift.

Of course, if we were to express the demand for capital as a function of the price of capital goods (which would then be the value on the vertical axis), a change in price would lead to a change in quantity demanded. In that case, a change in the interest rate would cause the demand curve to shift.

As you will see, putting the interest rate on the vertical axis allows us to relate the demand for capital to how the capital is financed.

For consumers, however, the decision is a bit more complicated than it is for firms. In examining consump-tion choices across time, economists think of consumers as having an expected stream of income over their lifetimes. It is that expected income that defines their consumption possibilities. The problem for consumers is to determine when to consume this income. They can spend less of their projected income now and thus have more available in the future. Alternatively, they can boost their current spending by borrowing against their future income.

Saving is income not spent on consumption. (We shall ignore taxes in this analysis.) **Dissaving** occurs when consumption exceeds income during a period. Dissaving means that the individual's saving is negative. Dissaving can be financed either by borrowing or by using past savings. Many people, for example, save in preparation for retirement and then dissave during their retirement years.

Saving adds to a household's wealth. Dissaving reduces it. Indeed, a household's wealth is the sum of the value of all past saving less all past dissaving.

We can think of saving as a choice to postpone consumption. Because interest rates are a payment paid to people who postpone their use of wealth, interest rates are a kind of reward paid to savers. Will higher interest rates encourage the behavior they reward? The answer is a resounding "maybe." Just as higher wages might not increase the quantity of labor supplied, higher interest rates might not increase saving. The problem, once again, lies in the fact that the income and substitution effects of a change in interest rates will pull in opposite directions.

Consider a hypothetical consumer, Tom Smith. Let us simplify the analysis of Mr. Smith's choices concerning the timing of consumption by assuming that there are only two periods: the present period is period 0, and the next is period 1. Suppose the interest rate is 8 percent and his income in both periods is expected to be $30,000.

Mr. Smith could, of course, spend $30,000 in period 0 and $30,000 in period 1. In that case, his saving equals zero in both periods. But he has alternatives. He could, for example, spend more than $30,000 in period 0 by borrowing against his income for period 1. Alternatively, he could spend less than $30,000 in period 0 and use his saving—and the interest he earns on that saving—to boost his consumption in period 1. If, for example, he spends $20,000 in period 0, his saving in period 0 equals $10,000. He'll earn $800 interest on that saving, so he'll have $40,800 to spend in the next period.

Suppose the interest rate rises to 10 percent. The increase in the interest rate has boosted the price of current consumption. Now for every $1 he spends in period 0 he gives up $1.10 in consumption in period 1, instead of $1.08, which was the amount that would have been given up in consumption in period 1 when the interest rate was 8 percent. A higher price produces a substitution effect that reduces an activity—Mr. Smith will spend less in the current period due to the substitution effect. The substitution effect of a higher interest rate thus boosts saving. But the higher interest rate also means that he earns more income on his saving. Consumption in the current period is a normal good, so an increase in income can be expected to increase current consumption. But an increase in current consumption implies a reduction in saving. The income effect of a higher interest rate thus tends to reduce saving. Whether Mr. Smith's saving will rise or fall depends on the relative strengths of the substitution and income effects.

To see how an increase in interest rates might reduce saving, imagine that Mr. Smith has decided that his goal is to have $40,800 to spend in period 1. At an interest rate of 10 percent, he can reduce his saving below $10,000 and still achieve his goal of having $40,800 to spend in the next period. The income effect of the increase in the interest rate has reduced his saving, and consequently his desire to supply funds to the loanable funds market.

Because changes in interest rates produce substitution and income effects that pull saving in opposite directions, we can't be sure what will happen to saving if interest rates change. The combined effect of all consumers' and firms' decisions, however, generally leads to an upward-sloping supply curve for loanable funds, as shown in Exhibit 13-3. That is, the substitution effect usually dominates the income effect.

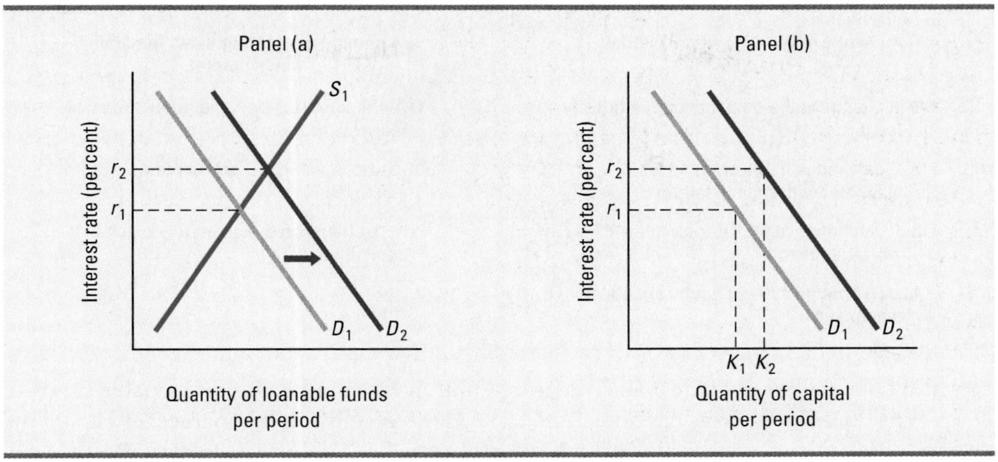

Exhibit 13-4

Loanable Funds and the Demand for Capital

The interest rate is determined in the loanable funds market and the quantity of capital demanded varies with the interest rate. Thus events in the loanable funds market and the demand for capital are interrelated. If the demand for capital increases to D_2 in Panel (b), the demand for loanable funds is likely to increase as well. Panel (a) shows the result in the loanable funds market—a shift in the demand curve for loanable funds from D_1 to D_2 and an increase in the interest rate from r_1 to r_2. At r_2, the quantity of capital demanded will be K_2, as shown in Panel (b).

The equilibrium interest rate is determined by the intersection of the demand and supply curves.

Capital and the Loanable Funds Market

If the quantity of capital demanded varies inversely with the interest rate, and if the interest rate is determined in the loanable funds market, then it follows that the demand for capital and the loanable funds market are interrelated. Because the acquisition of new capital is generally financed in the loanable funds market, a change in the demand for capital leads to a change in the demand for loanable funds—and that affects the interest rate. A change in the interest rate, in turn, affects the quantity of capital demanded on any demand curve.

The relationship between the demand for capital and the loanable funds market thus goes both ways. Changes in the demand for capital affect the loanable funds market, and changes in the loanable funds market can affect the quantity of capital demanded.

Changes in the Demand for Capital and the Loanable Funds Market Exhibit 13-4 suggests how an increased demand for capital by firms will affect the loanable funds market, and thus the quantity of capital firms will demand. In Panel (a) the initial interest rate is r_1. At r_1 in Panel (b) K_1 units of capital are demanded (on curve D_1). Now suppose an improvement in technology increases the marginal product of capital, shifting the demand curve for capital in Panel (b) to the right to D_2. Firms can be expected to finance the increased acquisition of

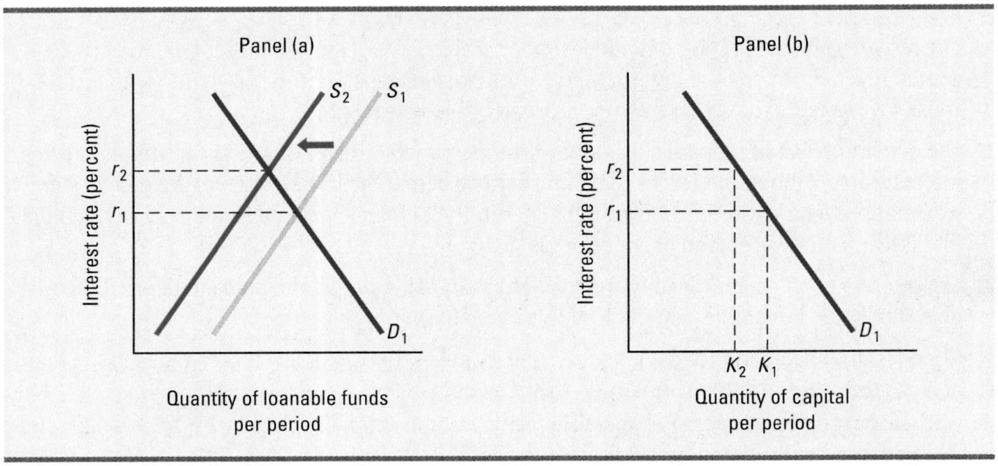

Exhibit 13-5

A Change in the Loanable Funds Market and the Quantity of Capital Demanded

A change that begins in the loanable funds market can affect the quantity of capital firms demand. Here, a decrease in consumer saving causes a shift in the supply of loanable funds from S_1 to S_2 in Panel (a). Assuming there is no change in the demand for capital, the quantity of capital demanded falls from K_1 to K_2 in Panel (b).

Exhibit 13-6

Two Routes to Changes in the Quantity of Capital Demanded

A change in the quantity of capital that firms demand can begin with a change in the demand for capital or with a change in the demand for or supply of loanable funds.

A change originating in the capital market	A change originating in the loanable funds market
1. A change in the demand for capital leads to . . .	1. A change in the demand for or supply of loanable funds leads to . . .
2. . . . a change in the demand for loanable funds, which leads to . . .	2. . . . a change in the interest rate, which leads to . . .
3. . . . a change in the interest rate, which leads to . . .	3. . . . a change in the quantity of capital demanded.
4. . . . a change in the quantity of capital demanded.	

capital by demanding more loanable funds, shifting the demand curve for loanable funds to D_2 in Panel (a). The interest rate thus rises to r_2. Consequently, in the market for capital the demand for capital is greater and the interest rate is higher. The new quantity of capital demanded is K_2 on demand curve D_2.

Changes in the Loanable Funds Market and the Demand for Capital Events in the loanable funds market can also affect the quantity of capital firms will hold. Suppose, for example, that consumers decide to increase current consumption and thus to supply fewer funds to the loanable funds market at any interest rate. This change in consumer preferences shifts the supply curve for loanable funds in Panel (a) of Exhibit 13-5 from S_1 to S_2 and raises the interest rate to r_2. If there is no change in the demand for capital D_1, the quantity of capital firms demand falls to K_2 in Panel (b).

Our model of the relationship between the demand for capital and the loanable funds market thus assumes that the interest rate is determined in the market for loanable funds. Given the demand curve for capital, that interest rate then determines the quantity of capital firms demand.

Exhibit 13-6 shows that a change in the quantity of capital that firms demand can begin with a change in the demand for capital or with a change in the demand for or supply of loanable funds. A change in the demand for capital affects the demand for loanable funds and hence the interest rate in the loanable funds market. The change in the interest rate leads to a change in the quantity of capital demanded. Alternatively, a change in the loanable funds market, which leads to a change in the interest rate, causes a change in quantity of capital demanded.

Checklist

- The net present value (*NPV*) of an investment project is equal to the present value of its expected revenues minus the present value of its expected costs. Firms will want to undertake those investments for which the *NPV* is greater than or equal to zero.
- The demand curve for capital shows that firms demand a greater quantity of capital at lower interest rates. Among the forces that can shift the demand curve for capital are changes in expectations, changes in technology, changes in the demands for goods and services, changes in relative factor prices, and changes in tax policy.
- The interest rate is determined in the market for loanable funds. The demand curve for loanable funds has a negative slope; the supply curve has a positive slope.
- Changes in the demand for capital affect the loanable funds market, and changes in the loanable funds market affect the quantity of capital demanded.

Try It Yourself 13-2

Suppose that baby boomers become increasingly concerned about whether or not the government will really have the funds to make Social Security payments to them over their retirement years. As a result, they boost saving now. How would their decisions affect the market for loanable funds and the demand curve for capital?

Natural Resources and Conservation

Natural resources are the gifts of nature. They include everything from oil to fish in the sea to magnificent scenic vistas. The stock of a natural resource is the quantity of the resource with which the earth is endowed. For example, a certain amount of oil lies in the earth, a certain population of fish live in the sea, and a certain number of acres make up an area such as Yellowstone National Park or Manhattan. These stocks of natural resources, in turn, can be used to produce a flow of goods and services. Each year, we can extract a certain quantity of oil, harvest a certain quantity of fish, and enjoy a certain number of visits to Yellowstone.

As with capital, we examine the allocation of natural resources among alternative uses across time. By definition, natural resources cannot be produced. Our consumption of the services of natural resources in one period can affect their availability in future periods. We must thus consider the extent to which the expected demands of future generations should be taken into account when we allocate natural resources.

Natural resources often present problems of property rights in their allocation. We saw in Chapter 6 that a resource for which exclusive property rights have not been defined will be allocated as a common property resource. In such a case, we expect that the marketplace will not generate incentives to use the resource efficiently. In the absence of government intervention, natural resources that are common property may be destroyed. In this section, we shall consider natural resources for which exclusive property rights have been defined. The public sector's role in the allocation of common property resources is investigated in Chapter 18.

We can distinguish two categories of natural resources, those that are renewable and those that are not. A **renewable natural resource** is one whose services can be used in one period without necessarily reducing the stock of the resource that will be available in subsequent periods. The fact that they *can* be used in such a manner does not mean that they *will* be; renewable natural resources can be depleted. Wilderness areas, land, and water are renewable natural resources. The consumption of the services of an **exhaustible natural resource,** on the other hand, necessarily reduces the stock of the resource. Oil and coal are exhaustible natural resources.

Exhaustible Natural Resources

Owners of exhaustible natural resources can be expected to take the interests of future as well as current consumers into account in their extraction decisions. The greater the expected future demand for an exhaustible natural resource, the greater will be the quantity preserved for future use.

Expectations and Resource Extraction Suppose you are the exclusive owner of a deposit of oil in Wyoming. You know that any oil you pump from this deposit and sell cannot be replaced. You are aware that this is true of all the world's oil; the consumption of oil inevitably reduces the stock of this resource.

If the quantity of oil in the earth is declining and the demand for this oil is increasing, then it's likely that the price of oil will rise in the future. Suppose you expect the price of oil to increase at an annual rate of 15 percent.

Exhibit 13-7

Future Generations and Exhaustible Natural Resources

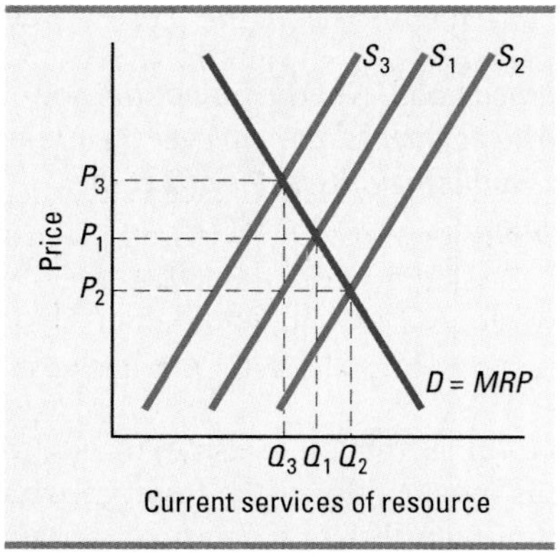

The current demand D for services of an exhaustible resource is given by its marginal revenue product (*MRP*). S_1 reflects the current marginal cost of extracting the resource, the prevailing interest rate, and expectations of future demand for the resource. The level of current consumption is thus at Q_1. If the interest rate rises, the supply curve shifts to S_2, causing the price of the resource to fall to P_2 and the quantity consumed to rise to Q_2. A drop in the interest rate shifts the supply curve to S_3, leading to a higher price of P_3 and a decrease in consumption to Q_3.

Given your expectation, should you pump some of your oil out of the ground and sell it? To answer that question, you need to know the interest rate. If the interest rate is 10 percent, then your best alternative is to leave your oil in the ground. With oil prices expected to rise 15 percent per year, the dollar value of your oil will increase faster if you leave it in the ground than if you pump it out, sell it, and purchase an interest-earning asset. If the market interest rate were greater than 15 percent, however, it would make sense to pump the oil and sell it now and use the revenue to purchase an interest-bearing asset. The return from the interest-earning asset, say 16 percent, would exceed the 15-percent rate at which you expect the value of your oil to increase. Higher interest rates thus reduce the willingness of resource owners to preserve these resources for future use.

The supply of an exhaustible resource such as oil is thus governed by its current price, its expected future price, and the interest rate. An increase in the expected future price—or a reduction in the interest rate—reduces the supply of oil today, preserving more for future use. If owners of oil expect lower prices in the future, or if the interest rate rises, they will supply more oil today and conserve less for future use. This relationship is illustrated in Exhibit 13-7. The current demand D for these services is given by their marginal revenue product (*MRP*). Suppose S_1 reflects the current marginal cost of extracting the resource, the prevailing interest rate, and expectations of future demand for the resource. If the interest rate increases, owners will be willing to supply more of the natural resource at each price, thereby shifting the supply curve to the right to S_2. The current price of the resource will

Exhibit 13-8

Natural Resource Prices, 1890–1997

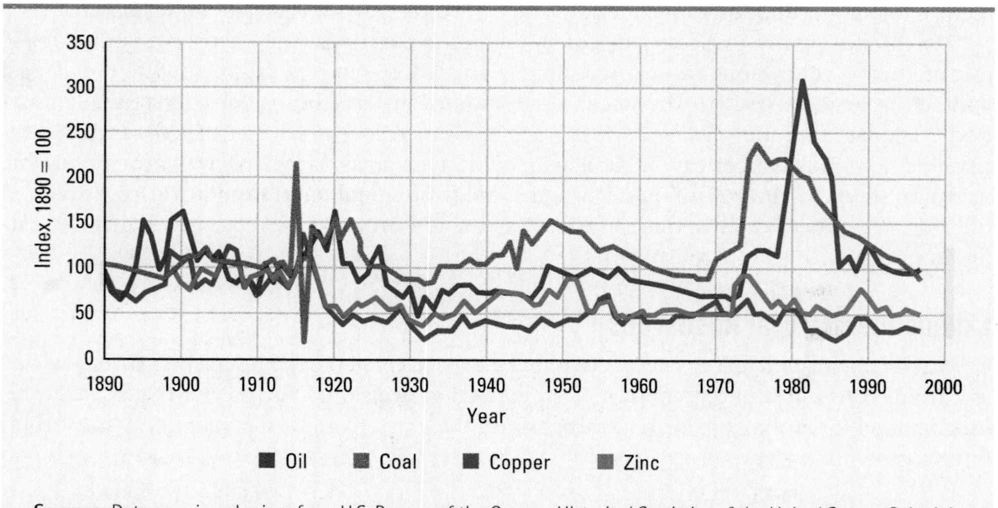

The chart shows changes in the prices of four exhaustible resources—oil, coal, copper, and zinc, from 1890 to 1996. Here, all prices have been adjusted for inflation; for example, if the inflation rate in a particular period is 5 percent and the price of a natural resource rises 6 percent, then the price increase recorded is 1 percent. All prices have been converted to an index number by setting them equal to 100 in 1890. We see that the inflation-adjusted prices of oil and coal are about the same as they were a century ago, while the prices of zinc and copper have fallen by more than half.

Sources: Data on mineral prices from U.S. Bureau of the Census, *Historical Statistics of the United States: Colonial Times to the Present,* Part 1 (Washington, DC: U.S. Government Printing Office, 1975); U.S. Bureau of the Census, *Statistical Abstract of the United States,* various volumes (Washington, DC: U.S. Government Printing Office); and Louis M. Irwin, *Economic Indicators of Mineral Scarcity: A Time Series Analysis of Mineral Prices* (Boulder: University of Colorado, 1989) (Master's Thesis). All price data are adjusted by the GDP deflator; values from 1890 to 1928 are from Robert J. Gordon, *Macroeconomics,* 6th edition (New York: Harper Collins, 1993), table A–1; data from 1929 to 1992 are from U.S. Council of Economic Advisers, *Economic Report of the President 1999* (Washington, DC: U.S. Government Printing Office, 1995), table B–3.

fall. If the interest rate falls, the supply curve for the resource will shift to the left to S_3 as more owners of the resource decide to leave more of the resource in the ground. As a result, the current price rises.

Resource Prices Over Time Since using nonrenewable resources would seem to mean exhausting a fixed supply, then one would expect the prices of exhaustible natural resources to rise over time as the resources become more and more scarce. During the past century, however, actual prices of most exhaustible natural resources have fallen. Exhibit 13-8 shows the prices of four major natural resources over the past century. Prices have been adjusted for inflation to reflect the prices of these resources relative to other prices.

Why have the prices of exhaustible natural resources generally fallen during the last century? In setting their expectations, people in the marketplace must anticipate not only future demand but future supply as well. Demand in future periods could fall short of expectations if new technologies produce goods and services using less of a natural resource. That has clearly happened. The quantity of energy—which is generally produced using exhaustible fossil fuels—used to produce a unit of output has fallen by more than half in the last two decades. Supply increases when

Case in Point The Doomsday Bet

Virtually everything we produce—and thus everything we consume—requires the use of some exhaustible natural resource. There's only so much oil, so much coal, so much copper, so much molybdenum—so much of any of a host of resources vital to economic activity. Our continued use of these resources must therefore mean that we're running out of them.

If our activities require natural resources, and if we inevitably have less and less of them, then it would seem that we must be headed for trouble. And trouble is just what many scientists think inevitably awaits us. An influential study, *Limits to Growth,* predicted in 1971 that, barring major discoveries or changes in policy, the earth was likely to run out of oil, copper, gold, lead, mercury, natural gas, silver, tin, and zinc by the end of the twentieth century. The authors of *Limits* argued that resource scarcity would make economic activity increasingly difficult and that even under the most optimistic assumptions, massive starvation and global depression would set in by the middle of the twenty-first century.

Economists, armed with a theoretical framework that suggests that rising prices of some factors will lead firms to make substitutions and to seek new technologies, have generally argued against the doomsday view. Indeed, the constant effort to cut current and expected costs by reducing resource use can reduce natural resource prices. The history of the last century suggests that factor substitution, technological change, and discoveries of additional resource deposits have combined to make resources *less* scarce.

Economist Julian Simon (who died in 1998), impressed by the evidence that resources have become relatively less scarce over the past century, issued an open challenge to doomsayers in 1981. He told them to pick any five exhaustible natural resources. If their average price, adjusted for inflation, rose over the next decade, Simon would pay $1,000. If their price fell, however, Mr. Simon would get the $1,000.

Only one of the doomsayers, biologist Paul Ehrlich of Stanford University, took Mr. Simon up on his offer. Mr. Ehrlich, the author of a 1968 book, *The Population Bomb,* that argued resource

scarcity would lead to the starvation of hundreds of millions of people by 1990, is one of the leading proponents of the view that humankind faces a grim future.

The average inflation-adjusted price of the five resources Mr. Ehrlich chose (chromium, copper, nickel, tin, and tungsten) fell during the 1980s—just as did the prices of exhaustible resources generally. Mr. Ehrlich paid the $1,000.

Source: Personal interviews with Paul Ehrlich and Julian Simon.

Exhibit 13-9

An Explanation for Falling Resource Prices

Demand for resources has increased over time from D_1 to D_2, but this shift in demand is less than it would have been (D_3) if technologies for producing goods and services using less resource per unit of output had not been developed. Supply of resources has increased from S_1 to S_2, due to discoveries of previously unknown deposits of natural resources and development of new technologies for extracting and refining resources. As a result, prices of many natural resources have fallen.

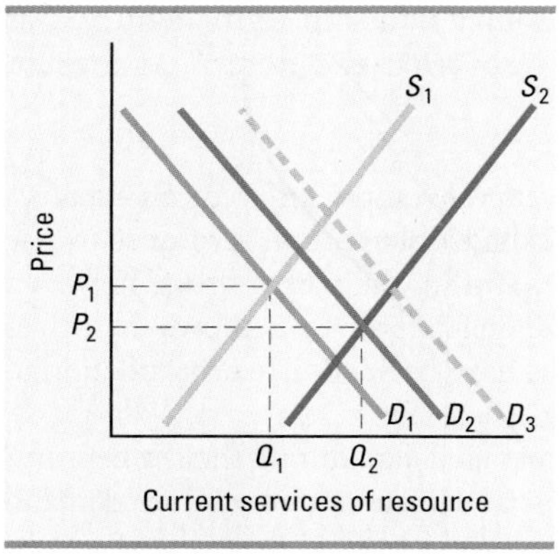

previously unknown deposits of natural resources are discovered and when technologies are developed to extract and refine resources more cheaply. Exhibit 13-9 shows that discoveries that reduce the demand below expectations and increase the supply of natural resources can push prices down in a way that people in previous periods might not have anticipated.

Will we ever run out of exhaustible natural resources? Past experience suggests that we won't. If no new technologies or discoveries that reduce demand or increase supply occur, then resource prices will rise. As they rise, consumers of these resources will demand lower quantities of these resources. Eventually, the price of a particular resource could rise so high that the quantity demanded would fall to zero. At that point, no more of the resource would be used. There would still be some of the resource in the earth—it simply wouldn't be practical to use more of it. The market simply won't allow us to "run out" of exhaustible natural resources.

New technologies and the discovery of additional deposits of exhaustible resources tend to pull resource prices down. They prolong the life of natural resources. Over the last century, discoveries and new technologies have dominated in this tug-of-war, and resource prices have fallen.

Renewable Natural Resources

As is the case with exhaustible natural resources, our consumption of the services of renewable natural resources can affect future generations. Unlike exhaustible resources, however, renewable resources can be consumed in a way that does not diminish their stocks.

Exhibit 13-10

Future Generations and Renewable Resources

The efficient quantity of services to consume is determined by the intersection of the supply curve S_1 and the demand curve D. This intersection occurs at point E, at a quantity of Q_1. This lies below the carrying capacity of the resource, Q_{cap}. An increase in interest rates, however, shifts the supply curve to S_2. The efficient level of current consumption rises to Q_2, which now exceeds the carrying capacity of the resource.

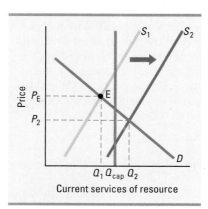

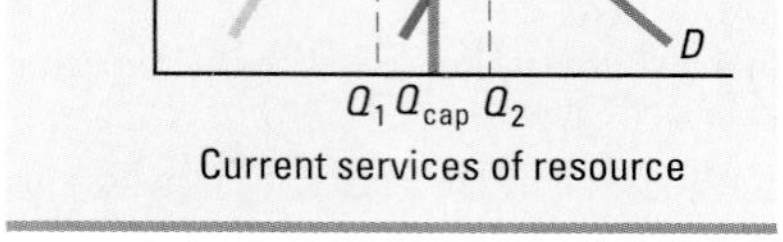

Carrying Capacity and Future Generations The quantity of a renewable natural resource that can be consumed in any period without reducing the stock of the resource available in the next period is its **carrying capacity.** Suppose, for example, that a school of 10 million fish increases by 1 million fish each year. The carrying capacity of the school is therefore 1 million fish per year—the harvest of 1 million fish each year will leave the size of the population unchanged. Harvests that exceed a resource's carrying capacity reduce the stock of the resource; harvests that fall short of it increase that stock.

As is the case with exhaustible natural resources, future generations have a stake in current consumption of a renewable resource. Exhibit 13-10 shows the efficient level of consumption of such a resource. Suppose Q_{cap} is the carrying capacity of a particular resource and S_1 is the supply curve that reflects the current marginal cost of utilizing the resource, including costs for the labor and capital required to make its services available, given the interest rate and expected future demand. The efficient level of consumption in the current period is found at point E, at the intersection of the current period's demand and the supply curves. Notice that in the case shown, current consumption at Q_1 is less than the carrying capacity of the resource. A larger stock of this resource will be available in subsequent periods than is available now.

Now suppose interest rates increase. As with nonrenewable resources, higher interest rates shift the supply curve to the right, as shown by S_2. The result is an increase in current consumption to Q_2. Now consumption exceeds the carrying capacity, and the stock of the resource available to future generations will be reduced. While this solution may be efficient, the resource will not be sustained over time at current levels.

If society is concerned about a reduction in the amount of the resource available in the future, further steps may be required to preserve it. For example, if trees are being cut down faster than they are being replenished in a particular location, such as the Amazon in Brazil, a desire to maintain biological diversity might lead to conservation efforts.

Economic Rent and the Market for Land We turn finally to the case of land that is used solely for the space it affords for other activities—parks, buildings, golf courses, and so forth. We shall assume that the carrying capacity of such land equals its quantity.

The supply of land is a vertical line. Although draining lakes and using refuse or other material to create landfills may increase the amount of land, the quantity of land in a particular location is fixed. Suppose, for example, that the price of a 1-acre parcel of land is zero. At a price of zero, there is still 1 acre of land; quantity is unaffected by price. If the price were to rise, there would still be only 1 acre in the parcel. That means that the price of the parcel exceeds the minimum price—zero—at which the land would be available. The amount by which any price exceeds the minimum price necessary to make a resource available is called **economic rent.** If our 1-acre parcel (perhaps representing Wall Street in lower Manhattan) in Exhibit 13-11 commands a price *P* per acre, the entire amount is economic rent.

The concept of economic rent can be applied to any factor of production that is in fixed supply above a certain price. In this sense, much of the salary received by Brad Pitt constitutes economic rent. At a low enough salary, he might choose to leave the entertainment industry. How low would depend on what he could earn in a best alternative occupation. If he earns $30 million now but could earn $100,000 in a best alternative occupation, then $29.9 million of his salary is economic rent. Most of his current earnings are in the form of economic rent, because his salary substantially exceeds the minimum price necessary to keep him supplying his resources to current purposes.

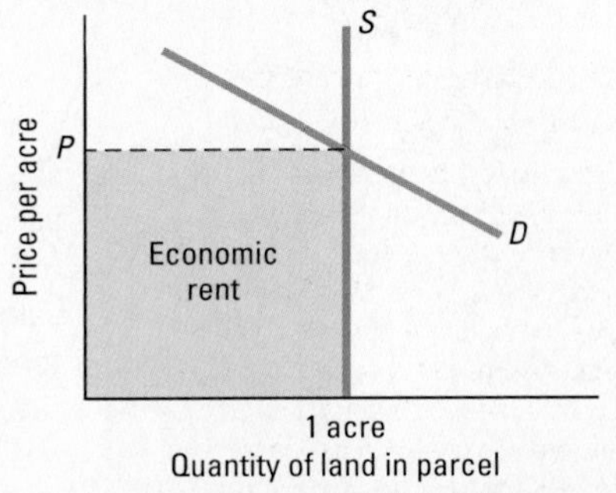

Exhibit 13-11

The Market for Land

The price of a 1-acre parcel of land is determined by the intersection of a vertical supply curve and the demand for a parcel. The sum paid for the parcel, shown by the shaded area, is economic rent.

Checklist

- Natural resources are either exhaustible or renewable.
- The demand for the services of a natural resource in any period is given by the marginal revenue product of those services.
- Owners of natural resources have an incentive to take into account the current price, the expected future demands for them, and the interest rate when making choices about resource supply.
- The services of a renewable natural resource may be consumed at levels that are below or greater than the carrying capacity of the resource.
- The payment for a resource above the minimum price necessary to make the resource available is economic rent.

Try It Yourself 13-3

You've just inherited a small oil well in Texas from good old Aunt Carmen. The current price of oil is $25 per barrel, and it is estimated that your oil deposit contains about 10,000 barrels of oil. For simplicity, assume that it doesn't cost anything to extract the oil and get it to market and that you must decide whether to empty the well now or wait until next year. Suppose the interest rate is 10 percent and the expected price of oil next year and the year after is $30 per barrel. What should you do? Would your decision change if the choice were to empty the well now or in 2 years?

A Look Back

Time is the complicating factor when we analyze capital and natural resources. Because current choices affect the future stocks of both resources, we must take those future consequences into account. And because a payment in the future is worth less than an equal payment today, we need to convert the dollar value of future consequences to present value. We determine the present value of a future payment by dividing the amount of that payment by $(1 + r)^n$, where r is the interest rate and n is the number of years until the payment will occur. The present value of a given future value is smaller at higher values of n and at higher interest rates.

Interest rates are determined in the market for loanable funds. The demand for loanable funds is derived from the demand for capital. At lower interest rates, the quantity of capital demanded increases. This, in turn, leads to an increase in the demand for loanable funds. In aggregate, the supply curve of loanable funds is likely to be upward sloping.

We assume that firms determine whether to acquire an additional unit of capital by examining the net present value (*NPV*) of the asset. When *NPV* equals zero, the present value of capital's marginal revenue product equals the present value of its marginal factor cost. The demand curve for capital shows the quantity of capital demanded at each interest rate. Among the factors that shift the demand curve for capital are changes in expectations, new technology, change in demands for goods and services, and change in relative factor prices.

Markets for natural resources are distinguished according to whether the resources are exhaustible or renewable. Owners of natural resources have an incentive to consider future as well as present demands for these resources. Land, when it has a vertical supply curve, generates a return that consists entirely of rent. In general, economic rent is return to a resource in excess of the minimum price necessary to make that resource available.

A Look Ahead In the next chapter, we'll look at imperfectly competitive markets for factors of production, that is, at situations where either the buyer or seller of the factor has some degree of monopoly power.

Terms and Concepts for Review

wealth, **264**
assets, **264**
liabilities, **264**
interest, **264**
interest rate, **264**
present value, **265**
net present value, **268**
investment, **268**
demand curve for capital, **269**
bond, **271**
loanable funds market, **271**
saving, **272**
dissaving, **272**
renewable natural resource, **275**
exhaustible natural resource, **275**
carrying capacity, **278**
economic rent, **279**

For Discussion

1. The charging of interest rates is often viewed with contempt. Do interest rates serve any useful purpose?
2. How does an increase in interest rates affect the present value of a future payment?
3. How does an increase in the size of a future payment affect the present value of the future payment?
4. Two payments of $1,000 are to be made. One of them will be paid 1 year from today and the other will be paid 2 years from today. Which has the greater present value? Why?
5. The Case in Point on the viatical settlements industry suggests that investors pay only 80 percent of the face value of a life insurance policy that's expected to be paid off in

6 months. Why? Wouldn't it be more fair if investors paid the full value?

6. How would each of the following events affect the demand curve for capital?

   a. A prospective cut in taxes imposed on business firms
   b. A reduction in the price of labor
   c. An improvement in technology that increases capital's marginal product
   d. An increase in interest rates

7. If developed and made practical, fusion technology would allow the production of virtually unlimited quantities of cheap, pollution-free energy. Some scientists predict that the technology for fusion will be developed within the next few decades. How does an expectation that fusion will be developed affect the market for oil today?

8. Is the rent paid for an apartment economic rent? Explain.

9. Suppose you own a ranch, and that commercial and residential development start to take place around your ranch. How will this affect the value of your property? What will happen to the quantity of land? What kind of return will you earn?

10. Explain why higher interest rates tend to increase the current use of natural resources.

Problems

Use the tables at the right to answer Problems 1–3. Table (a) gives the present value of $1 at the end of different time periods, given different interest rates. For example, at an interest rate of 10 percent, the present value of $1 to be paid in 20 years is $0.149. At 10 percent interest, the present value of $1,000 to be paid in 20 years equals $1,000 times $0.149, or $149. Table (b) gives the present value of a stream of payments of $1 to be made at the end of each period for a given number of periods. For example, at 10 percent interest, the present value of a series of $1 payments, made at the end of each year for the next 10 years, is $6.145. Using that same interest rate, the present value of a series of 10 payments of $1,000 each is $1,000 times $6.145, or $6,145.

1. Your Uncle Arthur, not to be outdone by Aunt Carmen, offers you a choice. You can have $10,000 now or $30,000 in 15 years. If you took the payment now, you could put it in a fund or bank account earning 8 percent interest. Use present value analysis to determine which alternative is better.

2. Remember Carol Stein's tractor? We saw that at an interest rate of 7 percent, a decision to purchase the tractor would pay off; its net present value is positive. Suppose the tractor is still expected to yield $20,000 in net revenue per year for each of the next 5 years and to sell at the end of 5 years for $22,000; and the purchase price of the tractor still equals $95,000. Use Tables (a) and (b) to compute the net present value of the tractor at an interest rate of 8 percent.

Table (a)

Present Value of $1 to Be Received at the End of a Given Number of Periods

	Percent interest									
Period	**2**	**4**	**6**	**8**	**10**	**12**	**14**	**16**	**18**	**20**
1	0.980	0.962	0.943	0.926	0.909	0.893	0.877	0.862	0.847	0.833
2	0.961	0.925	0.890	0.857	0.826	0.797	0.769	0.743	0.718	0.694
3	0.942	0.889	0.840	0.794	0.751	0.712	0.675	0.641	0.609	0.579
4	0.924	0.855	0.792	0.735	0.683	0.636	0.592	0.552	0.515	0.842
5	0.906	0.822	0.747	0.681	0.621	0.567	0.519	0.476	0.437	0.402
10	0.820	0.676	0.558	0.463	0.386	0.322	0.270	0.227	0.191	0.162
15	0.743	0.555	0.417	0.315	0.239	0.183	0.140	0.180	0.084	0.065
20	0.673	0.456	0.312	0.215	0.149	0.104	0.073	0.051	0.037	0.026
25	0.610	0.375	0.233	0.146	0.092	0.059	0.038	0.024	0.016	0.010
30	0.552	0.308	0.174	0.099	0.057	0.033	0.020	0.012	0.007	0.004
40	0.453	0.208	0.097	0.046	0.022	0.011	0.005	0.003	0.001	0.001
50	0.372	0.141	0.054	0.021	0.009	0.003	0.001	0.001	0	0

Table (b)

Present Value of $1 to Be Received at the End of Each Period for a Given Number of Periods

	Percent interest									
Period	**2**	**4**	**6**	**8**	**10**	**12**	**14**	**16**	**18**	**20**
1	0.980	0.962	0.943	0.926	0.909	0.893	0.877	0.862	0.847	0.833
2	1.942	1.886	1.833	1.783	1.736	1.690	1.647	1.605	1.566	1.528
3	2.884	2.775	2.673	2.577	2.487	2.402	2.322	2.246	2.174	2.106
4	3.808	3.630	3.465	3.312	3.170	3.037	2.322	2.246	2.174	2.106
5	4.713	4.452	4.212	3.993	3.791	3.605	3.433	3.274	3.127	2.991
10	8.983	8.111	7.360	6.710	6.145	5.650	5.216	4.833	4.494	4.192
15	12.849	11.118	9.712	8.559	7.606	6.811	6.142	5.575	5.092	4.675
20	16.351	13.590	11.470	9.818	8.514	7.469	6.623	5.929	5.353	4.870
25	19.523	15.622	12.783	10.675	9.077	7.843	6.873	6.097	5.467	4.948
30	22.396	17.292	13.765	11.258	9.427	8.055	7.003	6.177	5.517	4.979
40	27.355	19.793	15.046	11.925	9.779	8.244	7.105	6.233	5.548	4.997
50	31.424	21.482	15.762	12.233	9.915	8.304	7.133	6.246	5.554	4.999

3. Mark Jones is thinking about going to college. If he goes, he'll earn nothing for the next 4 years and, in addition, will have to pay tuition and fees totaling $10,000 per year. He also wouldn't earn the $25,000 per year he could make by working full time during the next 4 years. After his 4 years of college, he expects that his income, both while working and in retirement, will be $20,000 per year more, over the next 50 years, than it would have been had he not attended college. Should he go to college? Assume that the interest rate is 6 percent and that each payment for college and dollar of income earned occur at the end of the years in which they occur. Ignore possible income taxes in making your calculations.
4. You own several barrels of wine; over the years, the value of this wine has risen at an average rate of 10 percent per year. It is expected to continue to rise in value, but at a slower and slower rate. Assuming your goal is to maximize your revenue from the wine, at what point will you sell it?

Answers to Try It Yourself Problems

Try It Yourself 13-1

The present value of $5,200 payable in a year with an interest rate of 5 percent is

$$P_0 = \frac{\$5{,}200}{(1 + 0.05)^1} = \$4{,}952.38$$

Since the present value of $5,200 is less than the $5,000 Sara has asked you to lend her, you'd be better off refusing to make the loan. Another way of evaluating the loan is that Sara is offering a return on your $5,000 of 200/5,000 = 4 percent, while the bank is offering you a 5 percent return. On the other hand, if the interest rate that your bank is paying is 3 percent, then the present value of what Sara will pay you in a year is

$$P_0 = \frac{\$5{,}200}{(1 + 0.03)^1} = \$5{,}048.54$$

With your bank only paying a 3 percent return, Sara's offer looks like a good deal.

Try It Yourself 13-2

An increase in saving at each interest rate implies a rightward shift in the supply curve of loanable funds. As a result, the equilibrium interest rate falls. With the lower interest rate, there is movement downward to the right along the demand-for-capital curve, as shown.

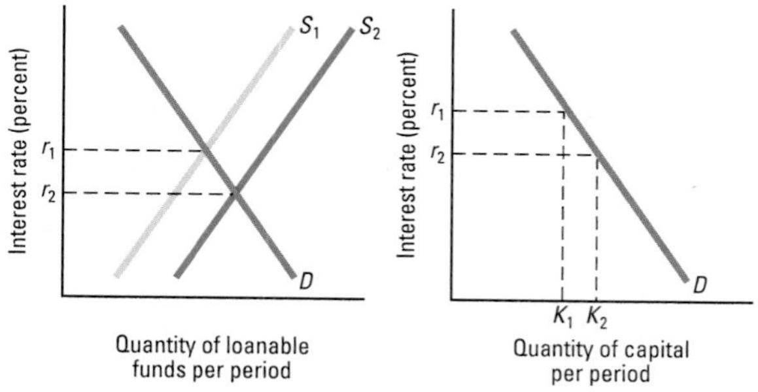

Try It Yourself 13-3

Since oil prices are expected to rise (\$30 – \$25)/\$25 = 20 percent and the interest rate is only 10 percent, you'd be better off waiting a year before emptying the well. Another way of seeing this is to compute the present value of the oil a year from now:

$$P_0 = \frac{(\$30 \times 10{,}000)}{(1 + 0.10)^1} = \$272{,}727.00$$

Since \$272,727 is greater than the \$25 × 10,000 = \$250,000 you could earn by emptying the well now, the present value calculation shows the rewards of waiting a year.

If the choice is to empty the well now or in 2 years, however, you'd be better off emptying it now, since the present value is only \$247,933.88:

$$P_0 = \frac{(\$30 \times 10{,}000)}{(1 + 0.10)^2} = \$247{,}933.88$$

14 Imperfectly Competitive Markets for Factors of Production

Getting Started: Not Playing Ball

In 1994 major league baseball players, whose salaries averaged more than $1 million per year, walked off their jobs and shut down the 1994 season. They were protesting a plan by their employers, the owners of baseball teams, to impose a limit on how much each team spent on player salaries. The players have thus far succeeded; no caps have been imposed, and player salaries have continued to rise.

More recently, when the owners of professional National Basketball Association (NBA) teams could not get the players to accept a limit on the percent of revenues that would go to salaries, they imposed a lockout. Almost 40 percent of the 1998–1999 NBA season was canceled. The average player's salary for the prior season stood at $2.24 million. The season resumed only after the two sides agreed that there would be no limit on salaries for 3 years. Limits would take effect in the fourth year of the 7-year agreement.

Were the players simply being greedy? Or were the owners the bad guys? After all, the owners of other types of firms don't band together to limit their payrolls. There's no salary cap on computer programmers or carpenters. Why should the owners of sports teams be allowed to combine for the purpose of keeping wages down?

For economists, greed is not the issue. All individuals are assumed to act in their own self-interest. In both cases, the showdown between players and owners illustrates an intriguing battle over the rules of the game of salary determination. Revolutionary changes in the rules that govern relations between owners of sports teams and the players they seek to hire have produced textbook examples of the economic forces at work in the determination of wages in imperfectly competitive markets.

Markets for labor and for other factors of production can diverge from the conditions of perfect competition in several ways, all of which involve price-setting behavior. Firms that purchase inputs may be price setters. Suppliers of inputs may have market power as well: a firm may have monopoly control over some key input, or input suppliers may band together to achieve market power. Workers may organize unions. Suppliers of services, such as physicians or hairdressers, may form associations that exert power in the marketplace.

This chapter puts the marginal decision rule to work in the analysis of imperfectly competitive markets for labor and other factors of production. Imperfect competition in these markets generally results in a reduction in the quantity of an input used, relative to the competitive equilibrium. The price of the input, however, could be higher or lower than in perfect competition, depending on the nature of the market structure involved.

Price-Setting Buyers: The Case of Monopsony

We have seen that market power in product markets exists when firms have the ability to set the prices they charge, at least within the limits of the demand curves for their products. Depending on the factor supply curve, firms may also have some power to set the prices they pay in factor markets.

A firm can set price in a factor market if instead of a market-determined price it faces an upward-sloping supply curve for the factor. This fact creates a fundamental difference between price-taking and price-setting firms in factor markets. A price-taking firm can hire any amount of the factor at the market price; it faces a horizontal supply curve for the factor at the market-determined price, as shown in Panel (a) of Exhibit 14-1. A price-setting firm facing supply curve S in Panel (b) obtains Q_1 units of the factor when it sets the price P_1. To obtain a larger quantity, such as Q_2, it must offer a higher price, P_2.

Consider a situation in which one firm is the only buyer of a particular factor. An example might be an isolated mining town where the mine is the single employer. A market in which there is a single buyer of a good, service, or factor of production is called a **monopsony**. Monopsony is the buyer's counterpart of monopoly. Monopoly implies a single seller; monopsony implies a single buyer.

Assume that the suppliers of a factor in a monopsony market are price takers; there is perfect competition in factor supply. But a single firm constitutes the entire market for the factor. That means that the monopsony firm faces the upward-sloping market supply curve for the factor. Such a case is illustrated in Exhibit 14-2, where the price and quantity combinations on the supply curve for the factor are given in the table.

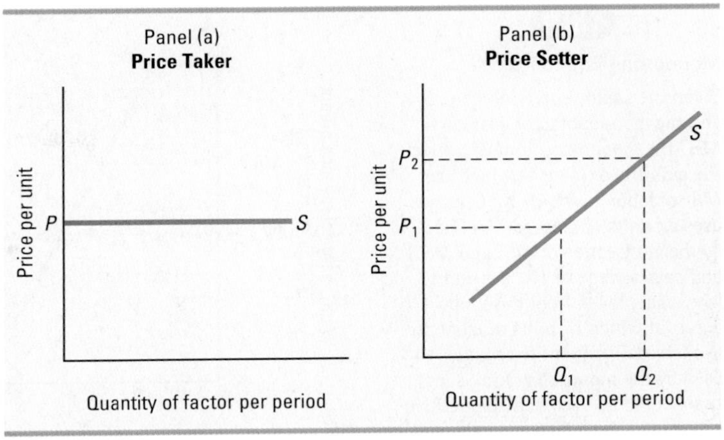

Exhibit 14-1

Factor Market Price Setters and Price Takers

A price-taking firm faces the market-determined price, *P*, for the factor in Panel (a) and can purchase any quantity it wants at that price. A price-setting firm faces an upward-sloping supply curve *S* in Panel (b). The price-setting firm sets the price consistent with the quantity of the factor it wants to obtain. Here, the firm can obtain Q_1 units at a price P_1, but it must pay a higher price per unit, P_2, to obtain Q_2 units.

Suppose the monopsony firm is now using 3 units of the factor at a price of $6 per unit. Its total factor cost for this factor is $18. Now suppose the firm is considering adding 1 unit of the factor. Given the supply curve, the only way the firm can obtain 4 units of the factor rather than 3 is to offer a higher price of $8 for all four units of the factor. That would increase the firm's total factor cost from $18 to $32. The marginal factor cost of the fourth unit of the factor is thus $14. It includes the $8 the firm pays for the fourth unit plus an additional $2 for each of the 3 units the firm was already using, since it has increased the price for the factor to $8 from $6. The marginal factor cost (*MFC*) thus exceeds the price of the factor. We can plot the *MFC* for each increase in the quantity of the factor the firm uses; notice in Exhibit 14-2 that the *MFC* curve lies above the supply curve. As always in plotting marginal values, we plot the $14 midway between units 3 and 4 because it is the increase in factor cost as the firm goes from 3 to 4 units.

Monopsony Equilibrium and the Marginal Decision Rule

The marginal decision rule, as it applies to a firm's use of factors, calls for the firm to add more units of a factor up to the point that the factor's *MRP* is equal to its *MFC*. Exhibit 14-3 illustrates this solution for a firm that is the only buyer of labor in a particular market.

The firm faces the supply curve for labor, *S*, and the marginal factor cost curve for labor, *MFC*. The profit-maximizing quantity is determined by the intersection of the *MRP* and *MFC* curves—the firm will hire L_m units of labor. The wage at which the firm can obtain L_m units of labor is given by the supply curve for labor; it is W_m. Labor receives a wage that is less than its *MRP*.

If the monopsony firm were broken up into a large number of small firms and all other conditions in the market re-

Price	$0	2	4	6	8	10
Quantity supplied	0	1	2	3	4	5
Total factor cost	$0	2	8	18	32	50

MFC	$2	6	10	14	18

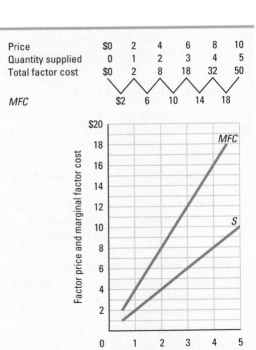

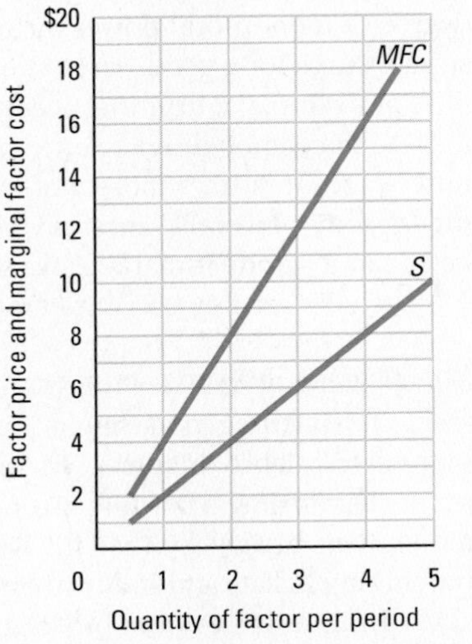

Exhibit 14-2

Supply and Marginal Factor Cost

The table gives prices and quantities for the factor supply curve plotted in the graph. Notice that the marginal factor cost curve lies above the supply curve.

Exhibit 14-3

Monopsony Equilibrium

Given the supply curve for labor, *S*, and the marginal factor cost curve *MFC*, the monopsony firm will select the quantity of labor at which the *MRP* of labor equals its *MFC*. It thus uses L_m units of labor (determined by the intersection of *MRP* and *MFC*) and pays a wage of W_m per unit (the wage, taken from the supply curve, at which L_m units of labor are available). The quantity of labor used by the monopsony firm is less than would be used in a competitive market (L_c), and the wage paid by the monopsony firm is less than the competitive wage (W_c).

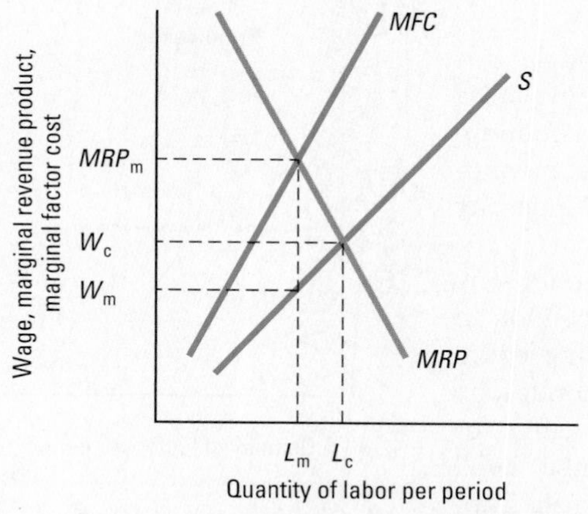

mained unchanged, then the sum of the *MRP* curves for individual firms would be the market demand for labor. The equilibrium wage would be W_c, and the quantity of labor demanded would be L_c. Thus, compared to a competitive market, a monopsony solution generates a lower factor price and a smaller quantity of the factor demanded.

Monopoly and Monopsony: A Comparison

There is a close relationship between the models of monopoly and monopsony. A clear understanding of this relationship will help to clarify both models.

Exhibit 14-4 compares the monopoly and monopsony equilibrium solutions. Both types of firms are price setters: The monopoly is a price setter in its product market, and the monopsony is a price setter in the factor market in which it has monopsony power. Both firms must change price to change quantity: The monopoly must lower its product price to sell an additional unit of output, and the monopsony must pay more to hire an additional unit of the factor. Because both types of firms must adjust prices to change quantities, the marginal consequences of their choices are not given by the prices they charge (for products) or pay (for factors). For a monopoly, marginal revenue is less than price; for a monopsony, marginal factor cost is greater than price.

Both types of firms follow the marginal decision rule: A monopoly produces a quantity of product at which marginal revenue equals marginal cost, and a monopsony employs a quantity of factor at which marginal revenue product equals marginal factor cost. Both firms set prices at which they can sell or purchase the profit-maximizing quantity. The monopoly sets its product price based on the demand curve it faces; the monopsony sets its factor price based on the factor supply curve it faces.

Monopsony in the Real World

Although cases of pure monopsony are rare, there are many situations in which buyers have a degree of monopsony power. A buyer has **monopsony power** if it faces an upward-sloping supply curve for a good, service, or factor of production.

For example, a firm that accounts for a large share of employment in a small community may be large enough relative to the labor market that it is not a price taker. Instead, it must raise wages to attract more workers. It thus faces an upward-sloping supply curve and has monopsony power. Because buyers are more likely to have monopsony power in factor markets than in product markets, we shall focus on those.

The next section examines monopsony power in professional sports.

Monopsonies in Sports Professional sports provide something close to a laboratory experiment in which economists can test theories of wage determination in competitive versus monopsony labor markets. In their analyses, economists assume professional teams are profit-maximizing firms that hire labor (athletes and other workers) to produce a product: entertainment bought by the fans who watch their games. Fans influence revenues directly by purchasing tickets and indirectly by generating the ratings that determine television and radio advertising revenues from broadcasts of games.

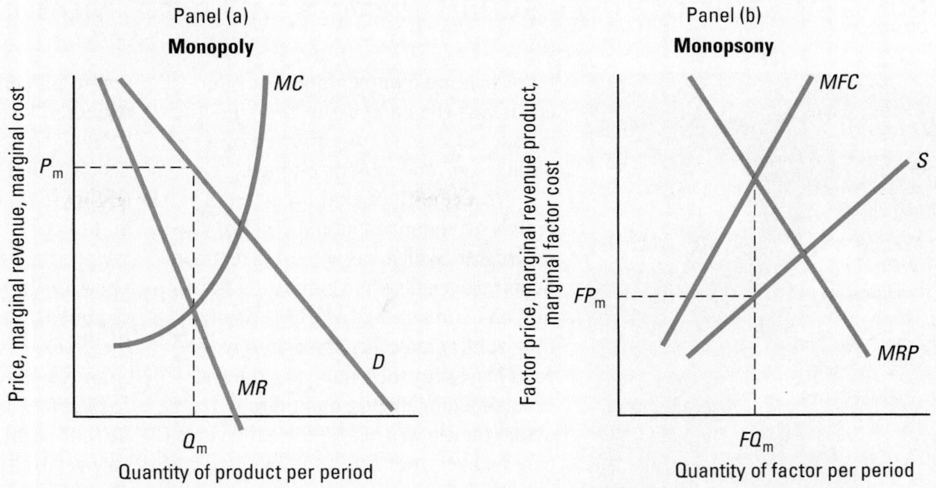

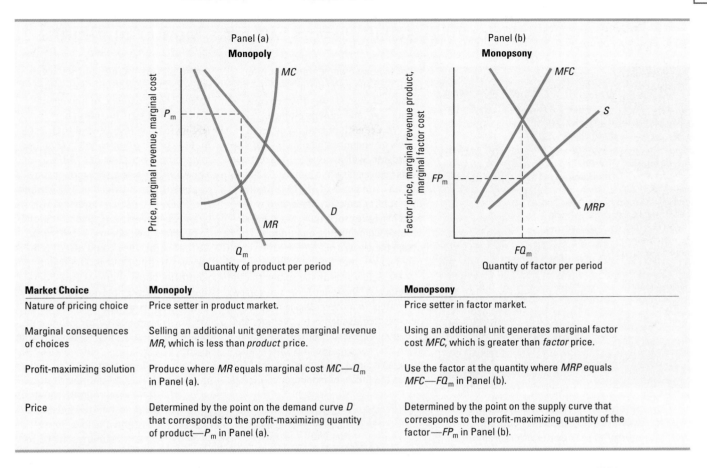

Market Choice	Monopoly	Monopsony
Nature of pricing choice	Price setter in product market.	Price setter in factor market.
Marginal consequences of choices	Selling an additional unit generates marginal revenue *MR*, which is less than *product* price.	Using an additional unit generates marginal factor cost *MFC*, which is greater than *factor* price.
Profit-maximizing solution	Produce where *MR* equals marginal cost *MC*—Q_m in Panel (a).	Use the factor at the quantity where *MRP* equals *MFC*—FQ_m in Panel (b).
Price	Determined by the point on the demand curve *D* that corresponds to the profit-maximizing quantity of product—P_m in Panel (a).	Determined by the point on the supply curve that corresponds to the profit-maximizing quantity of the factor—FP_m in Panel (b).

Exhibit 14-4

Monopoly and Monopsony

The graphs and the table provide a comparison of monopoly and monopsony.

In a competitive system, a player should receive a wage equal to his or her *MRP*—the increase in team revenues the player is able to produce. As New York Yankee owner George Steinbrenner once put it, "You measure the value of a ballplayer by how many fannies he puts in the seats."

The monopsony model, however, predicts that players facing monopsony employers will receive wages that are less than their *MRP*s. A test of monopsony theory, then, would be to determine whether players in competitive markets receive wages equal to their *MRP*s and whether players in monopsony markets receive less.

Since the late 1970s, there has been a major shift in the rules that govern relations between professional athletes and owners of sports teams. The shift has turned the once monopsonistic market for professional athletes into a competitive one. Before 1977, for example, professional baseball players in the United States labored under the terms of the "reserve clause," which specified that a player was "owned" by his team. Once a team had acquired a player's contract, the team could sell, trade, retain, or dismiss the player. Unless the team dismissed him, the player was unable to offer his services for competitive bidding by other teams. Moreover, players entered major league baseball through a draft that was structured so that only one team had the right to bid for any one player. Throughout a player's career, then, there was always only one team that could bid on him—each player faced a monopsony purchaser for his services to major league baseball.

Conditions were similar in other professional sports. Many studies have shown that the salaries of professional athletes in various team sports fell short of their *MRP*s while monopsony prevailed.

Case in Point: Salaries of Baseball Players Surge as Monopsony Ends

Professional baseball players have not always enjoyed the freedom they have today to seek better offers from other teams. Before 1977, they could deal only with the team that owned their contract—one that "reserved" the player to that team. This reserve clause gave teams monopsony power over the players they employed.

Gerald Scully, an economist at the University of Texas at Dallas, estimated the impact of the reserve clause on baseball player salaries. He sought to demonstrate whether player salaries fell short of *MRP.* Mr. Scully estimated the *MRP* of players in a two-step process. First, he studied the determinants of team attendance. He found that in addition to factors such as population and income in a team's home city, the team's win–loss record had a strong effect on attendance. Second, he examined the player characteristics that determined win–loss records. He found that for hitters, batting average was the variable most closely associated with a team's winning percentage. For pitchers, it was the earned-run average—the number of earned runs allowed by a pitcher per nine innings pitched.

With equations that predicted a team's attendance and its win–loss record, Mr. Scully was able to take a particular player, describe him by his statistics, and compute his *MRP.* Mr. Scully then subtracted costs associated with each player for such things as transportation, lodging, meals, and uniforms to obtain the player's net *MRP.* He then compared players' net *MRPs* to their wages.

Mr. Scully's results, displayed in the table below, show net *MRP* and salary, estimated on a career basis, for players he classified as mediocre, average, and star-quality, based on their individual statistics. For average and star-quality players, salaries fell far below net *MRP,* just as the theory of monopsony suggests.

	Career Net *MRP*	Career Salary	Salary as Percentage of Net *MRP*
Hitters			
Mediocre	–$129,300	$60,800	
Average	906,700	196,200	22
Star	3,139,100	477,200	15
Pitchers			
Mediocre	–$53,600	$54,800	
Average	1,119,200	222,500	20
Star	3,969,600	612,500	15

The fact that mediocre players with negative net *MRPs* received salaries presents something of a puzzle. One explanation could be that when they were signed to contracts, these players were expected to perform well, so their salaries reflected their expected contributions to team revenues. Their actual performance fell short, so their wages exceeded their *MRPs.* Another explanation could be that teams paid young players more than they were expected to contribute to revenues early in their careers. In any event, Scully found that the costs of mediocre players exceeded their estimated contribution to team revenues, giving them negative net *MRPs.*

A further test of the monopsony argument was provided in 1977, when the reserve clause arrangement was changed. Players were given the right to become "free agents" after 6 years. At that point, they could offer their services to other teams. The results were striking. Economists Paul Sommers and Noel Quinton of Middlebury College, using an approach similar to Mr. Scully's, estimated the *MRPs* and salaries of 14 players who became free agents in 1977. They found that hitters' salaries increased to about half of their net *MRPs.* Pitchers' salaries rose to a level roughly equal to their estimated net *MRPs,* as shown below. Subsequent estimates of the relationship between salaries of baseball players and their net *MRPs* suggest that the gap between the salaries and net *MRPs* of hitters has continued to close as the monopsony power of baseball teams has weakened.

Pitcher	Net *MRP*	1977 Salary
Doyle Alexander	$166,203	$166,677
Bill Campbell	205,639	210,000
Rollie Fingers	303,511	332,000
Wayne Garland	282,091	230,000
Don Gullett	340,846	349,333

Sources: Gerald Scully, "Pay and Performance in Major League Baseball," *American Economic Review* 64(2) (Dec. 1974): 915–930. Paul Sommers and Noel Quinton, "Pay and Performance in Major League Baseball: The Case of the First Family of Free Agents," *Journal of Human Resources* 17(3) (Summer 1982): 426–436.

When the reserve clauses were abandoned, however, as economic theory predicts, players' salaries shot up. Because players could offer their services to any number of teams, owners began to bid for their services. Profit-maximizing owners were willing to pay athletes their *MRPs*. Average annual salaries for baseball players rose from about $50,000 in 1975 to nearly $1.4 million in 1997. Average annual player salaries in men's basketball rose from $109,000 in 1976 to $2.24 million in 1998. Football players worked under an almost pure form of monopsony until 1989, when a few players were allowed free agency status each year. In 1993, when 484 players were released to the market as free agents, those players received pay increases averaging more than 100 percent. Under the NFL collective bargaining agreement in effect in 1998, players could become unrestricted free agents if they had been playing for 4 years. There were 305 unrestricted free agents (out of a total player pool of approximately 1,700) that year. About half signed new contracts with their old teams, while the other half signed with new teams. The Case in Point shows how dramatically salaries of major league baseball players rose with the demise of the reserve clause.

Given the dramatic impact on player salaries of more competitive markets for athletes, events such as the 1994–1995 strike in major league baseball or the 1998–1999 lockout in basketball came as no surprise. Under the reserve clause, teams were able to obtain the services of players at wages far below their players' *MRPs*. With free agency and a more competitive market, player salaries appear to be roughly equal to *MRPs*. The proposals by the owners of baseball teams in 1994 and by owners of basketball teams in 1998 to limit the total payroll of each team were attempts to reinstate some of the old monopsony power of the owners. Players had a huge financial stake in resisting such attempts. The battle between owners and players over how salaries are determined will continue.

Monopsony in Other Labor Markets A firm that has a dominant position in a local labor market may have monopsony power in that market. Even if a firm does not dominate the total labor market, it may have monopsony power over certain types of labor. For example, a hospital may be the only large employer of nurses in a local market, and it may have monopsony power in employing them.

Colleges and universities generally pay part-time instructors considerably less for teaching a particular course than they pay full-time instructors. In part, the difference reflects the fact that full-time faculty members are expected to have more training and are expected to contribute far more in other areas. But the monopsony model suggests an additional explanation.

Part-time instructors are likely to have other regular employment. A university hiring a local accountant to teach a section of accounting doesn't have to worry that that person will go to another state to find a better offer as a part-time instructor. For part-time teaching, then, the university may be the only employer in town—and thus able to exert monopsony power to drive the part-time instructor's wage below the instructor's *MRP*.

Monopsony in Other Factor Markets Monopsony power may also exist in markets for factors other than labor. The U.S. Department of Defense, for example, has considerable monopsony power in the market for sophisticated military goods. Major retailers often have some monopsony power with respect to some of their suppliers. Sears, for example, is the only wholesale buyer of Craftsman brand tools. One major development in medical care in recent years has been the emergence of managed care organizations that contract with a large number of employers to purchase medical services on behalf of employees. These organizations may then have sufficient monopsony power to force down the prices charged by providers such as drug companies, physicians, and hospitals.

Whatever the source of monopsony power, the expected result is the same. Buyers with monopsony power are likely to pay a lower price and to buy a smaller quantity of a particular factor than buyers who operate in a more competitive environment.

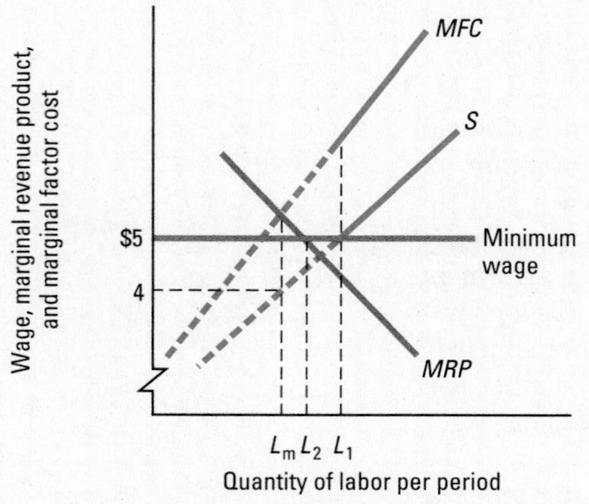

Exhibit 14-5

Minimum Wage and Monopsony

A monopsony employer faces a supply curve *S*, a marginal factor cost curve *MFC*, and a marginal revenue product curve *MRP*. It maximizes profit by employing L_m units of labor and paying a wage of $4 per hour. The imposition of a minimum wage of $5 per hour makes the dashed sections of the supply and *MFC* curves irrelevant. The marginal factor cost curve is thus a horizontal line at $5 up to L_1 units of labor. *MRP* and *MFC* now intersect at L_2 so that employment increases.

Monopsony and the Minimum Wage

We've seen that wages will be lower in monopsony than in otherwise similar competitive labor markets. In a competitive market, workers receive wages equal to their *MRP*s. Workers employed by monopsony firms receive wages that are less than *MRP*. This fact suggests sharply different conclusions for the analysis of minimum wages and competitive versus monopsony conditions.

In a competitive market, the imposition of a minimum wage above the equilibrium wage necessarily reduces employment, as we learned in Chapter 12. In a monopsony market, however, a minimum wage above the equilibrium wage could increase employment at the same time as it boosts wages!

Exhibit 14-5 shows a monopsony employer that faces a supply curve, *S*, from which we derive the marginal factor cost curve, *MFC*. The firm maximizes profit by employing L_m units of labor and paying a wage of $4 per hour. The wage is below the firm's *MRP*.

Now suppose the government imposes a minimum wage of $5 per hour; it is illegal for firms to pay less. At this minimum wage, L_1 units of labor are supplied. To obtain any smaller quantity of labor, the firm must pay the minimum wage. That means that the section of the supply curve showing quantities of labor supplied at wages below $5 is irrelevant; the firm can't pay those wages. Notice that the section of the supply curve below $5 is shown as a dashed line. If the firm wants to hire more than L_1 units of labor, it must pay wages given by the supply curve.

Marginal factor cost is affected by the minimum wage. To hire additional units of labor up to L_1, the firm pays the minimum wage. The additional cost of labor beyond L_1 continues to be given by the original *MFC* curve. The *MFC* curve thus has two segments, a horizontal segment at the minimum wage for quantities up to L_1 and the solid portion of the *MFC* curve for quantities beyond that.

The firm will still employ labor up to the point that *MFC* equals *MRP*. In the case shown in Exhibit 14-5, that occurs at L_2. The firm thus increases its employment of labor in response to the minimum wage.

Checklist

- In the monopsony model there is one buyer for a good, service, or factor of production. A monopsony firm is a price setter in the market in which it has monopsony power.
- The monopsony buyer selects a profit-maximizing solution by employing the quantity of factor at which marginal factor cost (*MFC*) equals marginal revenue product (*MRP*) and paying the price on the factor supply curve corresponding to that quantity.
- A degree of monopsony power exists whenever a firm faces an upward-sloping supply curve for a factor.
- A minimum wage could increase employment in a monopsony labor market.

Try It Yourself 14-1

Suppose a firm is the only employer of labor in an isolated area and faces the supply curve for labor suggested by the following table. Plot the supply curve. To compute the marginal factor cost curve, compute total factor cost and then the values for the marginal factor cost curve (remember to plot marginal values at the midpoints of the respective intervals). (Hint: *Follow the example of Exhibit 14-2.)*

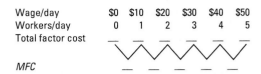

Wage/day	$0	$10	$20	$30	$40	$50
Workers/day	0	1	2	3	4	5
Total factor cost	__	__	__	__	__	__
MFC		__	__	__	__	__

Now suppose you are given the following data for the firm's total product at each quantity of labor. Compute marginal product. Assume the firm sells its product for $10 per unit in a perfectly competitive market. Compute MRP and plot the MRP curve on the same graph on which you've plotted supply and MFC. Remember to plot marginal values at the midpoints of the respective axes.

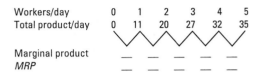

Workers/day	0	1	2	3	4	5
Total product/day	0	11	20	27	32	35
Marginal product		__	__	__	__	__
MRP		__	__	__	__	__

How much labor will the firm employ? What wage will it pay? Now suppose a minimum wage of $40 per day is imposed. How will this affect the firm's use of labor? Its wage?

Price Setters on the Supply Side

Buyers aren't the only agents capable of exercising market power in factor-pricing choices. Suppliers of factor services can exercise market power and act as price setters themselves, in two ways. First, a supplier may be a monopoly or have a degree of monopoly power in the supply of a factor. In that case, economists analyze the firm's choices as they would analyze those of any other imperfectly competitive firm. Second, individual suppliers of a factor of production may band together in an association to gain clout in the marketplace. Farmers, for example, often join forces to offset what they perceive as unfair market power on the part of buyers of their products. Each case is discussed below.

Monopoly Suppliers

A firm with monopoly power over a particular factor can be expected to behave like any other monopoly. It will set marginal revenue equal to marginal cost and charge a price taken from its demand curve.

De Beers has a virtual monopoly in the diamond market; it sells these diamonds as factors to jewelers and to industrial users of diamonds. In 1999, Intel produced roughly 90 percent of the microprocessors used in personal computers, and Microsoft produced about 90 percent of the operating software for personal computers with Intel processors. These firms weren't pure monopolies, but they certainly had a high degree of monopoly power in supplying key components of personal computers.

A monopoly supplier of a factor faces a demand curve that represents the *MRP* of the factor. This situation is illustrated in Exhibit 14-6. The firm will charge a price P_m equal to the *MRP* of the factor and sell Q_m units of the factor.

Exhibit 14-6

Monopoly Supply and Competitive Demand

A monopoly supplier of a factor maximizes profit just like any other monopolist. It selects an output at which marginal revenue *MR* equals marginal cost *MC* and charges a price determined by its demand curve. Since the demand curve is marginal revenue product (*MRP*), the monopoly factor supplier receives a price equal to *MRP*. Relative to the perfectly competitive solution—a price of P_c and a quantity of Q_c—a monopoly supplier restricts output to Q_m and raises price to P_m.

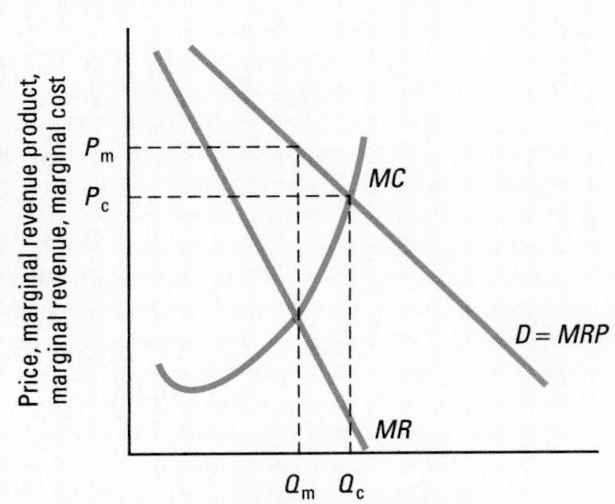

Unions

Workers in a competitive market receive a wage equal to their *MRP*. If they face monopsony power, they get less. Regardless of the market structure, workers are likely to seek higher wages and better working conditions. One way they can try to improve their economic status is to organize into a **labor union,** an association of workers that seeks to raise wages and to improve working conditions. Unions represent their members in **collective bargaining,** a process of negotiation of worker contracts between unions and employers. To strengthen its position, a union may threaten a strike—a refusal by union members to work—unless its demands are met.

A Brief History of Unions in the United States Workers have united to try to better their lot at least since the Middle Ages, when the first professional guilds were formed. In the United States, "workingmen's societies" sprang up in the late eighteenth century. These organizations were **craft unions** uniting skilled workers in the same trade in an attempt to increase wages, shorten working hours, and regulate working conditions for their members.

One goal unions consistently sought was a **closed shop,** where only union members can be hired—an arrangement that gives unions monopoly power in the supply of labor. A second objective was to gain greater political and economic strength by joining together associations of different crafts. Union goals went largely unfulfilled until the twentieth century, when the courts began to favor collective bargaining between workers and employers in disputes over wages and working conditions. Closed-shop arrangements are illegal in the United States today, but many states permit **union-shop** arrangements, in which a firm is allowed to hire nonunion workers who are required to join the union within a specified period. About 20 states have **right-to-work laws** which prohibit union-shop rules.

The development of the **industrial union,** a form of union that represents the employees of a particular industry, regardless of their craft, also aided the growth of the labor movement. The largest industrial union in the United States, the AFL-CIO, was formed in 1955, when unions accounted for just over 35 percent of the labor force. The AFL-CIO remains an important economic and political force, but union strength has fallen since its peak in the 1950s; in 1997, only slightly more than 14 percent of U.S. workers belonged to unions.

Part of the reason for the failure of unions to represent a larger share of workers lies in the market forces that govern wages. As the marginal revenue product of workers rose throughout the economy, their wages increased as well—whether they belonged to a union or not. Impressive economy-wide wage gains over the last two centuries may be one reason why the attraction of unions has remained weak.

Higher Wages and Other Union Goals Higher wages once dominated the list of union objectives, but more recent agreements have also focused on nonwage issues involving job security, health insurance, provision of child care, and job safety. Unions such as the United Auto Workers have negotiated contracts under which members who are laid off will continue to receive payments nearly equal to the wages they earned while on the job. They have also pushed hard for retirement pensions and for greater worker involvement in management decisions.

Union efforts to obtain higher wages have different effects on workers depending on the nature of the labor market. When unions confront an employer with monopsony power, their task is clear: They seek a wage closer to *MRP* than the employer is paying. If the labor market is a competitive one in which wages are determined by demand and supply, the union's task is more difficult. Increasing the wage requires either increasing the demand for labor or reducing the supply. If the union merely achieves a higher wage in the absence of an increase in demand or a reduction in supply, then the higher wage will create a surplus of labor, or unemployment.

Increasing Demand The demand for labor in a competitive market is found by summing the *MRP* curves of individual firms. Increasing demand thus requires increasing the marginal product of labor or raising the price of the good produced by labor.

One way that unions can increase the marginal product of their members is by encouraging investment in their human capital. Consequently unions may pressure firms to implement training programs. Some unions conduct training efforts themselves.

Another way to increase the *MRP* of a factor is to reduce the use by firms of substitute factors. Unions generally represent skilled workers, and they are vigorous proponents of minimum wage laws that make unskilled workers more expensive. A higher minimum wage induces firms to substitute skilled for unskilled labor, and thus increases the demand for the skilled workers unions represent.

Still another way to increase the *MRP* of labor is to increase the demand for the products labor produces. The form this union activity generally takes is in the promotion of "Made in the U.S.A." goods. Unions have also promoted restrictive trade legislation aimed at reducing the supply of foreign goods and thus increasing the demand for domestic ones.

Reducing Supply Unions can restrict the supply of labor in two ways. First, they can seek to slow the growth of the labor force; unions from the earliest times have aggressively opposed immigration. Union support for Social Security also cut the labor supply by encouraging workers to retire early. Second, unions can promote policies that make it difficult for workers to enter a particular craft. Unions representing plumbers and electrical workers, for example, have restricted the number of people who can enter these crafts in some areas by requiring that workers belong to a union but limiting the union's membership.

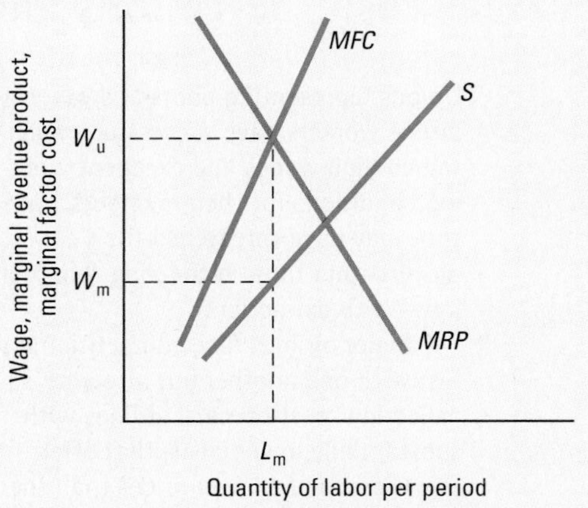

Exhibit 14-7

Bilateral Monopoly

If a union has monopoly power over the supply of labor and faces a monopsony purchaser of this labor, the wage negotiated between the two will be indeterminate. The employer wants a wage W_m on the supply curve *S*. The union will seek a wage close to the maximum the employer would be willing to pay for this quantity, W_u, at the intersection of the marginal revenue product (*MRP*) and marginal factor cost (*MFC*) curves. The actual wage is likely to be somewhere between these two amounts.

Bilateral Monopoly Suppose a union has negotiated a closed-shop arrangement (in a country where such arrangements are legal) with an employer that possesses monopsony power in its labor market. The union has a kind of monopoly in the supply of labor. A situation in which a monopsony buyer faces a monopoly seller is called **bilateral monopoly.** Wages in this model are indeterminate, with the actual wage falling somewhere between the pure monopoly and pure monopsony outcomes.

Exhibit 14-7 shows the same monopsony situation in a labor market that was shown in Exhibit 14-3. The employer will seek to pay a wage W_m for a quantity of labor L_m. The union will seek W_u, the highest wage the employer would be willing to pay for that quantity of labor. This wage is found on the *MRP* curve. The model of bilateral monopoly does not tell us the wage that will emerge. Whether the final wage will be closer to what the union seeks or closer to what the employer seeks will depend on the bargaining strength of the union and of the employer.

Unions and the Economy: An Assessment Where unions operate effectively in otherwise competitive markets, they may reduce economic efficiency. Efforts to increase demand for American workers through restricting imports or to increase demand for skilled workers by restricting opportunities for unskilled workers almost certainly reduce economic efficiency. Artificial restrictions on the supply of labor reduce efficiency as well. In each case, the wage gain will increase the cost of producing a good or service and thus shift its supply curve to the left. Such efforts, if successful, increase the earnings of union members by creating higher prices and smaller quantities for consumers. They may also reduce the profitability of their employers.

Other attempts by unions to raise wages by increasing the demand for their members are not likely to create inefficiency. For example, union efforts to increase worker productivity or to encourage consumers to buy products made by union members do not reduce economic efficiency.

In the case of bilateral monopoly, the amount of labor employed is restricted by the monopsony firm to a quantity that falls short of the efficient level. In effect, the efficiency damage has already been done. The labor union seeks merely to offset the monopsony firm's ability to restrict the wage.

Are unions successful in their primary goal of increasing wages? Wages for union members in 1997 were 34 percent higher, on average, than nonunion wages. This figure by itself does not accurately reflect the impact of unions, however, because there are other factors

Case in Point Unions and the Airline Industry

Unions representing pilots and other airline workers have successfully maintained high wages and excellent working conditions for their members, but they may have threatened their employers—and thus, in the long run, their jobs—with extinction.

Major airlines face competition not just with one another but also with so-called low-cost carriers, airlines with substantially lower costs, that offer their passengers lower prices than the major airlines. Part of the secret of low-cost operations has been to hire nonunion employees.

Frank J. Dooley, an economist at North Dakota State University, has compared average labor cost for Southwest Airlines, one of the low-cost carriers, with those of major airlines such as American Airlines and United Airlines. He estimates that Southwest's labor costs are 38 percent lower than those of the major airlines.

Southwest's labor cost advantage, Mr. Dooley says, comes from union work rules that keep the productivity of the major carriers well below that achieved by Southwest. Southwest's pilots, for example, fly for an average of 63.7 hours per month, versus 48.3 hours for pilots at the major airlines. Productivity differences give low-cost carriers a sharp advantage. For the 620-mile flight between Baltimore and Chicago, for example, average labor costs for major airlines are $1,200 per flight higher than for low-cost carriers.

Some of the major airlines are swapping union concessions for a share in the company. United's employees, for example, accepted pay cuts and changes in work rules as part of a deal giving them a majority interest in the company. Those concessions were valued at $5 billion, but Mr. Dooley says that unions and the major airlines will have to go even further to compete effectively.

Source: Frank J. Dooley, "Deja Vu for Airline Industrial Relations," *Journal of Labor Research* 15(2) (Spring 1994): 169–191.

(such as differences between union and nonunion workers in age, educational level, and occupation) that also contribute to wage differences. Adjusting for such factors, unions appear to raise wages for their members by less than 15 percent on average.[1]

Other Suppliers and Monopoly Power

Just as workers can unionize to gain a degree of monopoly power in the marketplace, so other suppliers can organize with a similar goal. Two of the most important types of organizations aimed at garnering market power are professional associations and producers' cooperatives.

Professional Associations Professional people generally belong to organizations that represent their interests. For example, physicians in the United States belong to the American Medical Association (AMA), and lawyers belong to the American Bar Association. Both organizations work vigorously to advance the economic interests of their members.

Professional organizations often lobby for legislation that protects their members. They may seek to restrict competition by limiting the number of individuals who can be licensed to practice a particular profession. The AMA has been very successful in limiting the number of physicians, thus maintaining higher salaries than would otherwise exist. The American Bar Association has fought legal reforms aimed at limiting awards to plaintiffs who win damage suits; such reforms would be likely to reduce the incomes of lawyers.

[1]George J. Borjas, *Labor Economics* (New York: McGraw Hill, 1996), p. 385.

Producers' Cooperatives Independent producers sometimes band together into a cooperative for the purpose of selling their products. The cooperative sets the price and assigns production quotas to individual firms. In effect, a cooperative acts as a legal cartel.

Because they violate the provisions of laws that outlaw such arrangements in most industries, producers' cooperatives must be authorized by Congress. Farmers have sometimes been given such rights when they are confronted by monopsony buyers. For example, Congress granted dairy farmers the right to form cooperatives in the 1920s because they faced monopsony buyers. High transportation costs for fresh milk, together with economies of scale in processing milk, generally left only one dairy processor to buy raw milk from dairy farmers in a particular area. By forming a cooperative, farmers could counter the monopsony power of a processor with monopoly power of their own, creating a bilateral monopoly.

Checklist

- A firm that has monopoly power in the supply of a factor makes choices in the same manner as any other monopoly firm; it maximizes profit by selecting a level of output at which marginal revenue equals marginal cost and selling that output at a price determined by the demand curve.
- Unions have traditionally sought to raise wages and to improve working conditions by exerting market power over the supply of labor.
- In bilateral monopoly, a monopsony buyer faces a monopoly seller. Prices in the model are indeterminate.
- Professional associations often seek market power through their influence on government policy.
- Producers' cooperatives, a form of legal cartel, have been organized in some agricultural markets in an effort to offset the perceived monopsony power of some buyers of agricultural products.

Try It Yourself 14-2

Consider the case of bilateral monopoly illustrated in Exhibit 14-7. Over what range of wages will employment be higher than it would have been if there were a monopsony buyer of labor but no monopoly in the supply of labor?

A Look Back

Factor markets diverge from perfect competition whenever buyers and/or sellers are price setters rather than price takers. A firm that is the sole purchaser of a factor is a monopsony. The distinguishing feature of the application of the marginal decision rule to monopsony is that the *MFC* of the factor exceeds its price. Less of the factor is used than would be the case if the factor were demanded by many firms. The price paid by the monopsony firm is determined from the factor supply curve; it is less than the competitive price would be. The lower quantity and lower price that occur in a monopsony factor market arise from features of the market that are directly analogous to the higher product price and lower product quantity chosen in monopoly markets. A price floor (e.g., a minimum wage) can induce a monopsony to increase its use of a factor.

Sellers can also exercise power to set price. A factor can be sold by a monopoly firm, which is likely to behave in a way that corresponds to the monopoly model discussed in Chapter 10.

When there are large numbers of sellers, they may band together in an organization that seeks to exert a degree of market power on their behalf. Workers (sellers of labor), for example, have organized unions to seek better wages and working conditions. This goal can be accomplished by restricting the available supply or by increasing the demand for labor. When a union represents all of a monopsony firm's workers, a bilateral monopoly exists. A bilateral monopoly results in a kind of price-setters' standoff, in which the firm seeks a low wage and the union a high one.

Professional associations may seek to improve the economic position of their members by supporting legislation that reduces supply or raises demand. Some agricultural producers join producers' cooperatives to exert some power over price and output. Agricultural cooperatives must be authorized by Congress; otherwise they would violate laws against collusion in the marketplace.

A Look Ahead In the next chapter we shall turn from the examination of the choices of individuals in the marketplace to the choices of individuals in the political arena. We shall explore the role of the public sector in a market economy and investigate the kinds of choices made.

Terms and Concepts for Review

monopsony, **285**
monopsony power, **286**
labor union, **292**
collective bargaining, **292**
craft unions, **292**
closed shop, **292**
union shop, **292**
right-to-work laws, **292**
industrial union, **292**
bilateral monopoly, **293**

For Discussion

1. Unions have generally advocated restrictions on foreign competition. Why?
2. There is a growing tendency in the United States for hospitals to merge, reducing competition in local markets. How are such mergers likely to affect the market for nurses?
3. When a town has a single university, the university may have monopsony power in the hiring of part-time faculty. But what about the hiring of full-time faculty? (*Hint:* The market for full-time faculty is a national one.)
4. David Letterman earns more than $10 million per year from CBS. Why do you suppose he earns so much? Is there any reason to believe he is underpaid?
5. Suppose a union obtains a union-shop agreement with firms in a particular industry. Is there any limit to the wages the union can achieve for its workers?
6. It is illegal for firms in most industries to join together in a producers' cooperative. Yet such arrangements are common in agriculture. Why?
7. In proposing an increase in the minimum wage in 1999, the Clinton administration argued that in some markets, a higher minimum wage could actually increase employment for unskilled workers. How could this happen?
8. In 1998 the average salary of professional basketball players in the women's American Basketball Association (ABA) stood at $80,000, while the average professional NBA basketball player's salary was $2.24 million. Why was there such a large discrepancy?
9. The Case in Point on baseball suggests that baseball players now receive salaries equal to their marginal revenue products. These are typically quite high. Are such high salaries fair? Why or why not?
10. The Case in Point on the airline industry suggested that nonunion airlines such as Southwest enjoy substantial cost advantages over airlines that employ union members. Why is this the case? Are such advantages fair?

Problems

Suppose a firm faces the following supply schedule for labor by unskilled workers:

Wage per day	Number of workers
$80	10
72	9
64	8
56	7
48	6
40	5
32	4
24	3
16	2
8	1
0	0

1. In terms of its demand for labor, what sort of firm is this? Explain. Prepare a table of values for the firm's marginal factor cost curve.
2. Plot the supply and marginal factor cost curves for this firm. Remember to plot marginal values at the midpoints of the intervals.
3. Suppose the firm faces the following total product schedule for labor:

Number of workers	Output per day
0	0
1	92
2	176
3	252
4	320
5	380
6	432
7	476
8	512
9	540
10	560

Compute the schedules for the firm's marginal product and marginal revenue product curves, assuming the price of the good the firm produces is $1 and that the firm operates in a perfectly competitive product market.

4. Add the marginal revenue product curve from Problem 3 to your graph in Problem 2, and determine the number of workers the firm will employ and the wage it will pay.
5. Now suppose the firm is required to pay a minimum wage of $48 per day. Show what will happen to the quantity of labor the firm will hire and the wage it will pay.

Answers to Try It Yourself Problems

Try It Yourself 14-1

The completed tables are shown in Panel (a). Drawing the supply (*S*), *MFC*, and *MRP* curves, we have Panel (b). The monopsony firm will employ 3 units of labor per day (the quantity at which *MRP* = *MFC*) and will pay a wage taken from the supply curve: $30 per day. The imposition of a minimum wage of $40 per day makes the *MFC* curve a horizontal line at $40, up to the *S* curve. In this case, the firm adds a fourth worker and pays the required wage, $40.

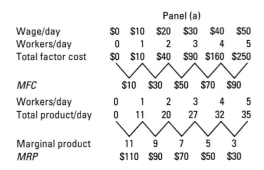

Panel (a)

Wage/day	$0	$10	$20	$30	$40	$50
Workers/day	0	1	2	3	4	5
Total factor cost	$0	$10	$40	$90	$160	$250
MFC		$10	$30	$50	$70	$90
Workers/day	0	1	2	3	4	5
Total product/day	0	11	20	27	32	35
Marginal product		11	9	7	5	3
MRP		$110	$90	$70	$50	$30

Panel (b)

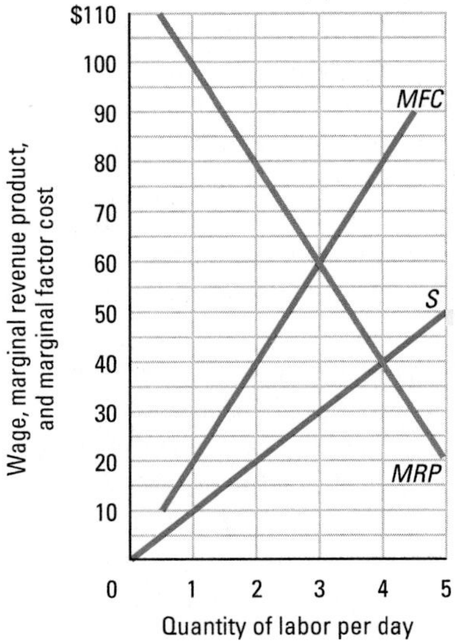

Try It Yourself 14-2

Any wage negotiated between the monopsony (the firm hiring the labor) and the monopoly (the union representing the labor) that falls between W_m and W_u will lead to a quantity of labor employed that is greater than L_m. The portion of the supply curve below the negotiated wage becomes irrelevant since the firm can't hire workers for those wages. The supply curve thus becomes a horizontal line at the negotiated wage until the negotiated wage intersects the supply curve; at wages higher than the negotiated wage, the existing supply curve is operative. Up to the quantity of labor at the intersection of the negotiated wage and the supply curve, the wage and *MFC* are the same. At any wage between W_m and W_u, the firm will maximize profit by employing labor where *MRP* and *MFC* are equal, and this will occur at a quantity of labor that is greater than L_m.

15 Public Finance and Public Choice

Getting Started: Where Your Tax Dollars Go

You pay sales taxes on most of the goods you purchase. If you smoke or drink or drive a car, you pay taxes on cigarettes, alcohol, or gasoline. If you work, you may pay income and payroll taxes.

What does the government do with the taxes it collects? If you go to a public school, you are a consumer of public sector services. You also consume the services of the public sector when you drive on a public street or go to a public park. You consume public sector services because you are protected by law enforcement agencies and by the armed forces. And the production of everything else you consume is affected by regulations imposed by local, state, or federal agencies.

The public sector is a crucially important segment of the economy, due in part to its size. The nearly 90,000 government jurisdictions in the United States, from local fire protection districts to the federal government, either produce or purchase nearly one-fifth of all domestic goods and services. The U.S. government is the largest single purchaser of goods and services in the world.

This chapter examines the role of government in a market economy and the ways in which the taxes that support government affect economic behavior. The study of government expenditure and tax policy and of their impact on the economy is called **public finance.**

We'll also explore the economics of public sector choices. Economists put the notions of self-interest and the marginal decision rule to work in the analysis of choices made by people in the public sector—voters, government employees, interest groups, and politicians.

The Demand for Government Services

What do we want from our government? One answer is that we want a great deal more than we did several decades ago. The role of government has expanded dramatically in the last 70 years. In 1929 (the year the Commerce Department began keeping annual data on macroeconomic performance in the United States), government expenditures at all levels (state, local, and federal) were less than 10 percent of the nation's total output, which is called gross domestic product (GDP). By 1998, that share had tripled. Total government spending per capita, adjusted for inflation, has increased more than sixfold since 1929.

Exhibit 15-1 shows total government expenditures and revenues as a percentage of GDP from 1929 to 1998. All levels of government are included. **Government expenditures** include all spending by government agencies. **Government revenues** include all funds received by government agencies. The primary component of government revenues is taxes; revenue also includes miscellaneous revenues from fees, fines, and other sources. We'll look at types of government revenues and expenditures later in this chapter.

Exhibit 15-1 also shows government purchases as a percentage of GDP. **Government purchases** occur when a government agency purchases or produces a good or a service. We measure government purchases to suggest the opportunity cost of government. Whether a government agency purchases a good or service or produces it, factors of production are being used for public sector, rather than private sector, activities. A city police department's purchase of new cars is an example of a government purchase. Spending for public education is another example.

Source: U.S. Council of Economic Advisers, *Economic Report of the President 1999* (Washington, D.C.: U.S. Government Printing Office, February 1999), tables B-1 and B-84. Data prior to 1959 are taken from earlier issues of the report.

Exhibit 15-1

Government Revenues, Expenditures, and Purchases as a Percentage of GDP, 1929–1998

The chart shows total expenditures, revenues, and purchases for all levels of government as a percentage of the economy's total output, as measured by gross domestic product (GDP). The shaded bars mark periods of war.

Government expenditures and purchases aren't equal because much government spending is not for the purchase of goods and services. The primary source of the gap is **transfer payments,** payments made by government agencies to individuals in the form of grants rather than in return for labor or other services. Transfer payments represent government expenditures but not government purchases. Governments engage in transfer payments in order to redistribute income from one group to another. The various welfare programs for low-income people are examples of transfer payments. Social Security is the largest transfer payment program in the United States. This program transfers income from people who are working (by taxing their pay) to people who have retired. Interest payments on government debt, which are also a form of expenditure, are another example of an expenditure that is not counted as a government purchase.

Several points about Exhibit 15-1 bear special attention. Note first the path of government purchases. Government purchases relative to GDP rose dramatically during World War II, then dropped back to about their prewar level almost immediately afterward. Government purchases rose again, though less sharply, during the Korean War. This time, however, they didn't drop back very far after the war. It was during this period that military spending rose to meet the challenge posed by the Soviet Union and other communist states. Government purchases have ranged between 15 and 20 percent of GDP ever since. Neither the Vietnam War nor the Persian Gulf War had the impact on purchases that characterized World War II or even the Korean War. A second development, the widening gap between expenditures and purchases, has occurred since the 1960s. This reflects the growth of federal transfer programs, principally Social Security, programs to help people pay for health-care costs, and aid to low-income people. We will discuss these programs later in this chapter.

Finally, note the relationship between expenditures and receipts. When a government's revenues equal its expenditures for a particular period, it has a **balanced budget.** A **budget surplus** occurs if a government's revenues exceed its expenditures, while a **budget deficit** exists if government expenditures exceed revenues.

Prior to 1980, revenues roughly matched expenditures for the public sector as a whole, except during World War II. But expenditures remained consistently higher than revenues between 1980 and 1996. The federal government generated very large deficits during this period, deficits that exceeded surpluses that typically occur at the state and local levels of government. The largest increases in spending came from Social Security and increased health-care spending at the federal level. Efforts by the federal government to reduce and ultimately eliminate its deficit, together with surpluses among state and local governments, put the combined budget for the public sector in surplus beginning in 1997. As of 1999, the Congressional Budget Office was predicting that increased federal revenues produced by a growing economy would continue to produce budget surpluses well into the twenty-first century.

The evidence presented in Exhibit 15-1 doesn't fully capture the rise in demand for public sector services. In addition to a government that spends more, people in the United States have clearly chosen a government that does more. The scope of regulatory activity conducted by governments at all levels, for example, has risen sharply in the last several decades. Regulations designed to prevent discrimination, to protect consumers, and to protect the environment are all part of the response to a rising demand for public services, as are federal programs in health care and education.

Exhibit 15-2 summarizes the main revenue sources and types of expenditures for the federal government in 1998. Most federal revenues came from personal income taxes and from payroll taxes. Most expenditures were for transfer payments to individuals. Federal purchases were primarily for national defense; the "other purchases" category includes things such as spending for transportation projects and for the space program. Interest payments on the national debt and grants by the federal government to state and local governments were the other major expenditures.

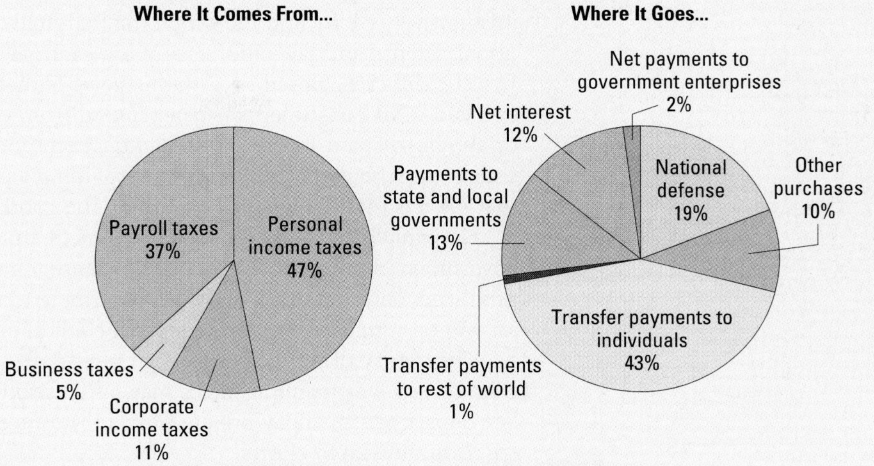

Source: *Survey of Current Business National Data*, June 1999, Tables 3.2 and 3.7

Exhibit 15-2

Federal Revenues and Expenditures, 1998

The principal sources of federal revenues are personal income and payroll taxes. Transfer payments account for more spending than any other category. Federal purchases go primarily to national defense.

To understand the role of government, it will be useful to distinguish four broad types of government involvement in the economy. First, the government attempts to respond when the market fails to allocate resources efficiently. In a particular market, efficiency means that the quantity produced is determined by the intersection of a demand curve that reflects all the benefits of consuming a particular good or service and a supply curve that reflects the opportunity costs of producing it. Second, government agencies act to encourage or discourage the consumption of certain goods and services. The prohibition of drugs such as heroin and cocaine is an example of government seeking to discourage consumption of these drugs. Third, the government redistributes income through programs such as welfare and Social Security. Fourth, the government can use its spending and tax policies to influence the level of economic activity and the price level.

We'll examine the first three of these aspects of government involvement in the economy in this chapter. The fourth, efforts to influence the level of economic activity and the price level, falls within the province of macroeconomics.

Responding to Market Failure

In Chapter 6, we learned that a market maximizes net benefit by achieving a level of output at which marginal benefit equals marginal cost. That is the efficient solution. In most cases, we expect that markets will come close to achieving this result—that's the important lesson of Adam Smith's idea of the market as an invisible hand, guiding the economy's scarce factors of production to their best uses. That is not always the case, however.

We've studied several situations in which markets are unlikely to achieve efficient solutions. In Chapter 6, we saw that private markets are likely to produce less than the efficient quantities of public goods such as national defense. They may produce too much of goods that generate external costs and too little of goods that generate external benefits. In cases of imperfect competition, we've seen that the market's output of goods and services is likely to fall short of the efficient level. In all these cases, it's possible that government intervention will move production levels closer to their efficient quantities. In the next three sections, we shall review how a government could improve efficiency in the cases of public goods, external costs and benefits, and imperfect competition.

Public Goods A public good, defined in Chapter 6, is a good or service for which exclusion is prohibitively costly and for which the marginal cost of adding another consumer is zero. National defense and law enforcement are examples of public goods.

The difficulty posed by a public good is that if a firm produces it, it is freely available to everyone. No consumer can be excluded from consumption of the good on grounds that he or she hasn't paid for it. Consequently, each consumer has an incentive to be a free rider in consuming the good, and the firms providing a public good don't get a signal from consumers that reflects their benefit of consuming the good.

Certainly we can expect some benefits of a public good to be revealed in the market. If the government did not provide national defense, for example, we would expect some defense to be produced, and some people would contribute to its production. But because free-riding behavior will be common, the market's production of public goods will fall short of the efficient level.

The theory of public goods is an important argument for government involvement in the economy. Government agencies may either produce public goods themselves, as do local police departments, or pay private firms to produce them, as is the case with many government-sponsored research efforts.

External Costs and Benefits External costs are imposed when an action by one person or firm harms another, outside of any market exchange. The **social cost** of producing a good or service equals the private cost plus the external cost of producing it. In the case of external costs, private costs are less than social costs.

Similarly, external benefits are created when an action by one person or firm benefits another, outside of any market exchange. The **social benefit** of an activity equals the private benefit revealed in the market plus external benefits. When an activity creates external benefits, its social benefit will be greater than its private benefit.

Case in Point Providing Education: Should Government Buy It or Produce It?

Traditionally, local school districts have provided education by producing it; schools are owned and operated by the public sector. But some school districts are now beginning to experiment with private sector production of education.

An alternative advocated by some economists is the provision of vouchers similar to food stamps. An annual voucher good for, say, $3,500 would be provided for each child. Parents could then choose to send their children to private schools or to public schools; the schools would get the vouchers and cash them in with the government agency that issued them. In 1998, voucher systems were operating in only a few school districts in the United States.

Another approach to the production of education is charter schools. A charter school is organized privately and then contracts with a local school district to provide education for children in the area who choose to attend the charter school. Funding for charter schools comes from the school district, not the parents. There were 1,000 charter schools operating in 1998; a bill passed by Congress that year will provide federal funding to induce school districts to provide more such schools. In signing the bill, President Bill Clinton set a goal of increasing the number of these schools to 3,000 by 2002.

The goal of such alternatives is to provide parents with more choices for their children's education. The theory is that if parents have more choices, schools will be more responsive to their preferences. Critics of such alternatives argue that parents may not make wise choices and that providing choice weakens public schools.

The lack of a market transaction means that the person or firm responsible for the external cost or benefit doesn't face the full cost or benefit of the choice involved. We expect markets to produce more than the efficient quantity of goods or services that generate external costs and less than the efficient quantity of goods or services that generate external benefits.

Consider the case of firms that produce memory chips for computers. The production of these chips generates water pollution. The cost of this pollution is an external cost; the firms that generate it do not face it. These firms thus face some, but not all, of the costs of their production choices. We can expect the market price of chips to be lower, and the quantity produced greater, than the efficient level.

Inoculations against infectious diseases create external benefits. A person getting a flu shot, for example, receives private benefits; he or she is less likely to get the flu. But there will be external benefits as well: Other people will also be less likely to get the flu because the person getting the shot is less likely to have the flu. Because this latter benefit is external, the social benefit of flu shots exceeds the private benefit, and the market is likely to produce less than the efficient quantity of flu shots.

Imperfect Competition In a perfectly competitive market, price equals marginal cost. If competition is imperfect, however, individual firms face downward-sloping demand curves and will charge prices greater than marginal cost. Consumers in such markets will be faced by prices that exceed marginal cost, and the allocation of resources will be inefficient.

An imperfectly competitive private market will therefore produce less of a good than is efficient. As we saw in Chapter 10, government agencies seek to prohibit monopoly in most markets and to regulate the prices charged by those monopolies that are permitted. Government policy toward monopoly is discussed more fully in Chapter 17.

Assessing Government Responses to Market Failure In each of the models of market failure we've reviewed here—public goods, external costs and benefits, and imperfect competition—the market may fail to achieve the efficient result. There is a potential for government intervention to move inefficient markets closer to the efficient solution.

Exhibit 15-3 reviews the potential gain from government intervention in cases of market failure. In each case, the potential gain is the deadweight loss resulting from market failure; government intervention may prevent or limit this deadweight loss. In each panel, the deadweight loss resulting from market failure is shown as a shaded triangle.

Panel (a) of Exhibit 15-3 illustrates the case of a public good. The market will produce some of the public good; suppose it produces the quantity Q_m. But the demand curve that reflects the social benefits of the public good, D_1, intersects the supply curve at Q_e; that is, the efficient quantity of the good. Public sector provision of a public good may move the quantity closer to the efficient level.

Panel (b) shows a good that generates external costs. Absent government intervention, these costs will not be reflected in the market solution. The supply curve, S_1, will be based only on the private costs associated with the good. The market will produce Q_m units of the good at a price P_1. If the government were to confront producers with the external cost of the good, perhaps with a tax on the activity that creates the cost, the supply curve would shift to S_2 and reflect the social cost of the good. The quantity would fall to the efficient level, Q_e, and the price would rise to P_2.

Panel (c) gives the case of a good that generates external benefits. The demand curve revealed in the market, D_1, reflects only the private benefits of the good. Incorporating the external benefits of the good gives us the demand curve D_2 that reflects the social benefit of the good. The market's output of Q_m units of the good falls short of the efficient level Q_e. The government may seek to move the market solution toward the efficient level through subsidies or other measures to encourage the activity that creates the external benefit.

Exhibit 15-3

Correcting Market Failure

In each panel, the potential gain from government intervention to correct market failure is shown by the deadweight loss avoided, as given by the shaded triangle. In Panel (a), we assume that a private market produces Q_m units of a public good. The efficient level, Q_e, is defined by the intersection of the demand curve (D_1) for the public good and the supply curve S_1. Panel (b) shows that if the production of a good generates an external cost, the supply curve S_1 reflects only the private cost of the good. The market will produce Q_m units of the good at price P_1. If the public sector finds a way to confront producers with the social cost of their production, then the supply curve shifts to S_2 and production falls to the efficient level Q_e. Panel (c) shows the case of a good that generates external benefits. Purchasers of the good base their choices on the private benefit, and the market demand curve is D_1. The market quantity is Q_m. A demand curve D_2 that reflects the social benefit of the good achieves the efficient quantity Q_e. In Panel (d), an imperfectly competitive firm produces Q_m units and charges price P_1. The efficient level of output is Q_e.

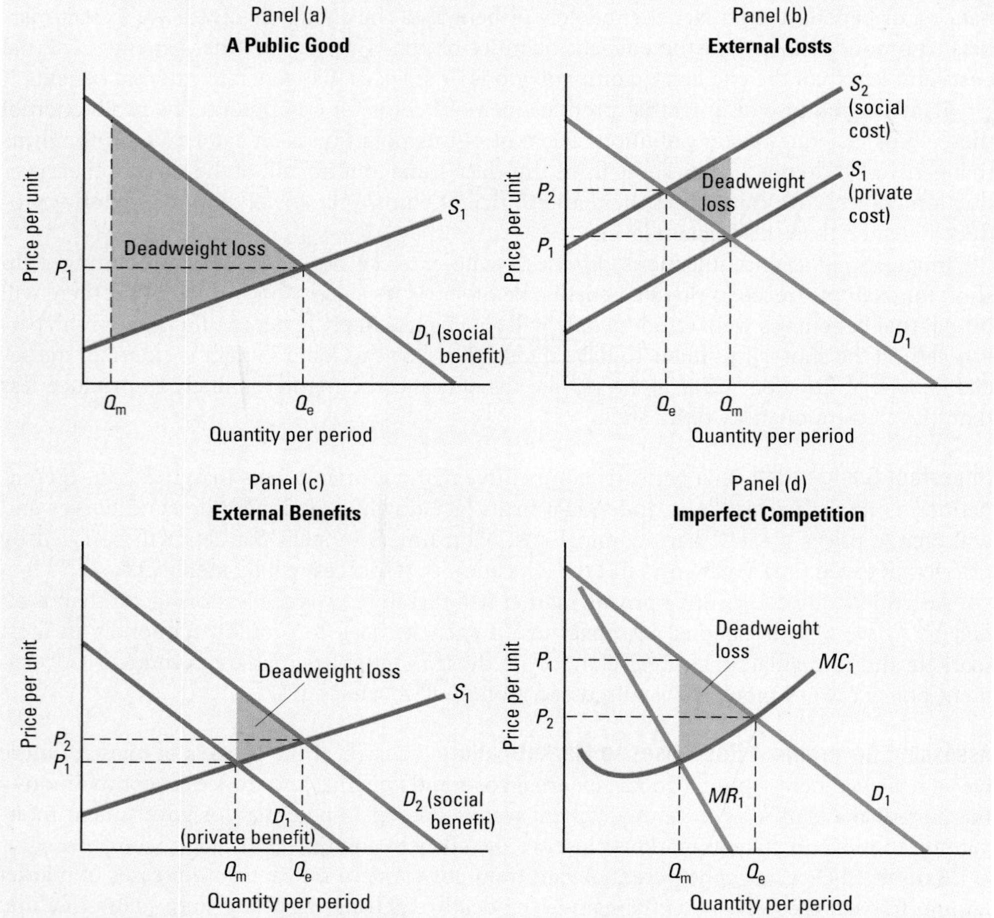

Finally, Panel (d) shows the case of imperfect competition. A firm facing a downward-sloping demand curve such as D_1 will select the output Q_m at which the marginal cost curve MC_1 intersects the marginal revenue curve MR_1. The government may seek to move the solution closer to the efficient level, defined by the intersection of the marginal cost and demand curves.

While it is important to recognize the potential gains from government intervention to correct market failure, we must recognize the difficulties inherent in such efforts. Government officials may lack the information they need to select the efficient solution. Even if they have the information, they may have goals other than the efficient allocation of resources. Each instance of government intervention involves an interaction with utility-maximizing consumers and profit-maximizing firms, none of whom can be assumed to be passive participants in the process. So, while the potential exists for improved resource allocation in cases of market failure, government intervention may not always achieve it.

The late George Stigler, winner of the Nobel Prize for economics in 1982, once remarked that people who advocate government intervention to correct every case of market failure reminded him of the judge at an amateur singing contest who, upon hearing the first contestant, awarded first prize to the second. Stigler's point was that even though the market is often an inefficient allocator of resources, so is the government likely to be. Government may improve on what the market does; it can also make it worse. The choice between the market's allocation and an allocation with government intervention is always a choice between imperfect alternatives. We'll examine the nature of public sector choices later in this chapter and explore an economic explanation of why government intervention may fail to move market solutions closer to their efficient levels.

Merit and Demerit Goods

In some cases, the public sector makes a determination that people should consume more of some goods and services and less of others, even in the absence of market failure. This is a normative judgment, one that presumes that consumers aren't always the best judges of what's good, or bad, for them.

Merit goods are goods whose consumption the public sector promotes, based on a presumption that many individuals don't adequately weigh the benefits of the good and should thus be induced to consume more than they otherwise would. Many local governments support symphony concerts, for example, on grounds that the private market would not provide an adequate level of these cultural activities.

Indeed, government provision of some merit goods is difficult to explain. Why, for example, do many local governments provide tennis courts but not bowling alleys, golf courses but not auto racetracks, symphony halls but not movie theaters? One possible explanation is that some consumers—those with a fondness for tennis, golf, and classical music—have been more successful than others in persuading their fellow citizens to assist in funding their preferred activities.

Demerit goods are goods whose consumption the public sector discourages, based on a presumption that individuals don't adequately weigh all the costs of these goods and thus should be induced to consume less than they otherwise would. The consumption of such goods may be prohibited, as in the case of illegal drugs, or taxed heavily, as in the case of cigarettes and alcohol.

Income Redistribution

The proposition that a private market will allocate resources efficiently if the efficiency condition introduced in Chapter 6 is met always comes with a qualification: The allocation of resources will be efficient given the initial distribution of income. If 5 percent of the people receive 95 percent of the income, it might be efficient to allocate roughly 95 percent of the goods and services produced to them. But many people (perhaps 95 percent of them!) might argue that such a distribution of income is undesirable and that the allocation of resources that emerges from it is undesirable as well.

There are several reasons to believe that the distribution of income generated by a private economy might not be satisfactory. For example, the incomes people can earn are in part due to luck. Much income results from inherited wealth and thus depends on the family into which one happens to have been born. Likewise, talent is distributed in unequal measure. Many people suffer handicaps that limit their earning potential. Changes in demand and supply can produce huge changes in the values—and the incomes—the market assigns to particular skills. Given all this, many people argue that incomes should not be determined solely by the marketplace.

A more fundamental reason for concern about income distribution is that people care about the welfare of others. People with higher incomes often have a desire to help people with lower incomes. This preference is demonstrated in voluntary contributions to charity and in support of government programs to redistribute income.

A public goods argument can be made for government programs that redistribute income. Suppose that people of all income levels feel better off knowing that financial assistance is being provided to the poor and that they experience this sense of well-being whether or not they are the ones who provide the assistance. In this case, helping the poor is a public good. When the poor are better off, other people feel better off; this benefit is nonexclusive. One could thus

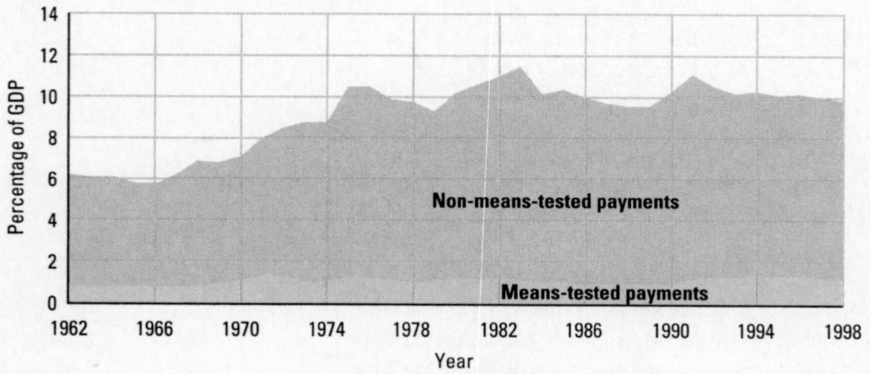

Source: Congressional Budget Office, *The Economic and Budget Outlook: Fiscal Years 2000–2009* (Washington, D.C.: U.S. Government Printing Office, 1999), table F-13.

Exhibit 15-4

Federal Transfer Payment Spending

This chart shows federal means-tested and non-means-tested transfer payment spending as a percentage of GDP in the United States since 1962.

argue that leaving private charity to the marketplace is inefficient and that the government should participate in income redistribution. Whatever the underlying basis for redistribution, it certainly occurs. The governments of every country in the world make some effort to redistribute income.

Programs to redistribute income can be divided into two categories. One transfers income to poor people; the other transfers income based on some other criterion. A **means-tested transfer payment** is one for which the recipient qualifies on the basis of income; means-tested programs transfer income from people who have more to people who have less. The largest means-tested program in the United States is Medicaid, which provides health care to the poor. Other means-tested programs include Temporary Assistance to Needy Families (TANF) and food stamps. A **non-means-tested transfer payment** is one for which income is not a qualifying factor. Social Security, a program that taxes workers and their employers and transfers this money to retired workers, is the largest non-means-tested transfer program. Indeed, it is the largest transfer program in the United States. Other non-means-tested transfer programs include Medicare, unemployment compensation, and programs that aid farmers.

Exhibit 15-4 shows federal spending on means-tested and non-means-tested programs as a percentage of GDP, the total value of output, since 1962. As the chart suggests, the bulk of income redistribution efforts in the United States are non-means-tested programs.

The fact that most transfer payments in the United States are not means-tested leads to something of a paradox: Some transfer payments go from people whose incomes are relatively low to people whose incomes are relatively high. Social Security, for example, transfers income from people who are working to people who have retired. But many retired people enjoy higher incomes than working people in the United States. Aid to farmers, another form of non-means-tested payments, transfers income to farmers, who on average are wealthier than the rest of the population. These situations have come about because of policy decisions, which we discuss later in the chapter.

Check*list*

- One role of government is to correct problems of market failure associated with public goods, external costs and benefits, and imperfect competition.
- Government intervention to correct market failure always has the potential to move market solutions closer to efficient solutions, and thus reduce deadweight losses. There is, however, no guarantee that such gains will be achieved.
- Governments may seek to alter the level of provision of certain goods and services, based on a normative judgment that consumers will consume too much or too little of the goods. Goods for which such judgments have been made are called merit or demerit goods.
- Governments redistribute income. Such redistribution often goes from people with higher incomes to people with lower incomes, but other transfer payments go to people who are relatively better off.

Try It Yourself 15-1

Here is a list of actual and proposed government programs. Each is a response to one of the justifications for government activity described in the text: correction of market failure (due to public goods, external costs, external benefits, or imperfect competition), encouragement or discouragement of the consumption of merit or demerit goods, and redistribution of income. In each case, identify the source of demand for the activity described.

a. *The Justice Department sought to prevent Microsoft Corporation from releasing Windows '98, arguing that the system's built-in internet browser represented an attempt by Microsoft to monopolize the market for browsers.*
b. *In 1999 Congress considered measures that would sharply increase the federal tax on cigarettes and require tobacco companies to take action to reduce smoking by children.*
c. *The federal government engages in research to locate asteroids that might hit the earth, and studies how impacts from asteroids could be prevented.*
d. *The federal government increases spending for food stamps for people whose incomes fall below a certain level.*
e. *The federal government increases benefits for recipients of Social Security.*
f. *The Environmental Protection Agency tightens standards for limiting the emission of pollutants into the air.*
g. *A state utilities commission regulates the prices charged by utilities that provide natural gas to homes and businesses.*

Financing Government

If government services are to be provided, they must be paid for. The primary source of government revenue is taxes. In this section we examine the principles of taxation, compare alternative types of taxes, and consider the question of who actually bears the burden of taxes.

In addition to imposing taxes, governments obtain revenue by charging **user fees**, which are charges levied on consumers of government-provided services. The tuition and other fees charged by public universities and colleges are user fees, as are entrance fees at national parks. Finally, government agencies might obtain revenue by selling assets or by holding bonds on which they earn interest.

Principles of Taxation

Virtually anything can be taxed, but what should be taxed? Are there principles to guide us in choosing a system of taxes?

Jean-Baptiste Colbert, a minister of finance in seventeenth-century France, is generally credited with one of the most famous principles of taxation:

> The art of taxation consists in so plucking the goose as to obtain the largest possible amount of feathers with the smallest possible amount of hissing.

Economists, who typically don't deal with geese, cite two criteria for designing a tax system. The first is based on the ability of people to pay taxes, and the second focuses on the benefits they receive from government services.

Ability to Pay The **ability-to-pay principle** holds that people with more income should pay more taxes. As income rises, the doctrine asserts, people are able to pay more for public services; a tax system should therefore be constructed so that taxes rise too. Wealth, the total of assets less liabilities, is sometimes used as well as income as a measure of ability to pay.

The ability-to-pay doctrine lies at the heart of tax systems that link taxes paid to income received. The relationship between taxes and income may take one of three forms: taxes can be regressive, proportional, or progressive.

Regressive Tax A **regressive tax** is one that takes a lower percentage of income as income rises. Taxes on cigarettes, for example, are regressive. Cigarettes are an inferior good—their consumption falls as incomes rise. Thus, people with lower incomes spend more on cigarettes than do people with higher incomes. The cigarette taxes paid by low-income people represent a larger share of their income than do the cigarette taxes paid by high-income people.

Proportional Tax A **proportional tax** is one that takes a fixed percentage of income. Total taxes rise as income rises, but taxes are equal to the same percentage no matter what the level of income. Some people argue that the U.S. income tax system should be changed into a so-called flat tax system, a tax that would take the same percentage of income from all taxpayers. Such a tax would be a proportional tax.

Progressive Tax A **progressive tax** is one that takes a higher percentage of income as income rises. The federal income tax is an example of a progressive tax. Exhibit 15-5 shows federal income tax rates for various brackets of income for a family of four in 1998. Such a family paid no income tax at all if its income fell below $17,000. At higher income levels, families faced a higher percentage tax rate. Any income over $288,500, for example, was taxed at a rate of 39.6 percent.

1998 adjusted gross income (family of four)	Personal income tax rate applied to bracket
Less than $17,000	Zero (family may receive earned income credit)
$17,000–$60,250	15 percent
$60,250–$120,200	28 percent
$120,200–$173,850	31 percent
$173,850–$296,350	36 percent
Greater than $296,350	39.6 percent

Exhibit 15-5

Federal Income Tax Brackets, 1998.

While a pure flat tax would be proportional, most proposals for such a tax would exempt some income from taxation. Suppose, for example, that households paid a "flat" tax of 20 percent on all income over $40,000 per year. This tax would be progressive. A household with an income of $25,000 per year would pay no tax. One with an income of $50,000 per year would pay a tax of $2,000, or 4 percent of its income. A household with an income of $100,000 per year would pay a tax of $12,000 per year, or 12 percent of its income. A flat tax with an income exemption is thus a progressive tax.

Benefits Received An alternative criterion for establishing a tax structure is the **benefits-received principle,** which holds that a tax should be based on the benefits received from the government services funded by the tax.

Local governments rely heavily on taxes on property, in large part because the benefits of many local services, including schools, streets, and the provision of drainage for wastewater, are reflected in higher property values. Suppose, for example, that public schools in a particular area are especially good. People are willing to pay more for houses served by those schools, so property values are higher; property owners benefit from better schools. The greater their benefit, the greater the property tax they pay. The property tax can thus be viewed as a tax on benefits received from some local services.

Fees charged for government services apply the benefits-received principle directly. A student paying tuition, a visitor paying an entrance fee at a national park, and a motorist paying a highway toll are all paying to consume a publicly provided service; they are thus paying directly for something from which they expect to benefit. Such fees can be used only for goods for which exclusion is possible; a user fee could not be applied to a service such as national defense.

Taxes to finance public goods may satisfy both the ability-to-pay and benefits-received principles. The demand for public goods generally rises with income. Thus, people with higher incomes benefit more from public goods. The benefits-received principle thus suggests that taxes should rise with income, just as the ability-to-pay principle does. Consider, for example, an effort financed through income taxes by the federal government to clean up the environment. People with higher incomes will pay more for the cleanup than people with lower incomes, consistent with the ability-to-pay principle. But studies by economists consistently show that people with higher incomes have a greater demand for environmental improvement than do people with lower incomes—a clean environment is a normal good. Requiring people with higher incomes to pay more for the cleanup can thus be justified on the benefits-received principle as well.

Certainly taxes can't respond precisely to benefits received. Neither the ability-to-pay nor the benefits-received doctrine gives us a recipe for determining just what each person "should" pay in taxes, but these doctrines give us a framework for thinking about the justification for particular taxes.

Types of Taxes

It's hard to imagine anything that hasn't been taxed at one time or another. Windows, closets, buttons, junk food, salt, death—all have been singled out for special taxes. In general, taxes fall into one of four primary categories. Income taxes are imposed on the income earned by a person or firm; property taxes are imposed on assets; sales taxes are imposed on the value of goods sold; and excise taxes are imposed on specific goods or services. Exhibit 15-6 shows the major types of taxes financing all levels of government in the United States.

Personal Income Taxes The federal personal income tax is the largest single source of tax revenue in the United States; most states and many cities tax income as well. All income tax systems apply a variety of exclusions to a taxpayer's total income before arriving at taxable income, the amount of income that is actually subject to the tax. In the U.S. federal income tax system, for example, a family deducted $2,650 from total income earned in 1997 for each member of the family as part of its computation of taxable income.

Income taxes can be structured to be regressive, proportional, or progressive. Income tax systems in use today are progressive.

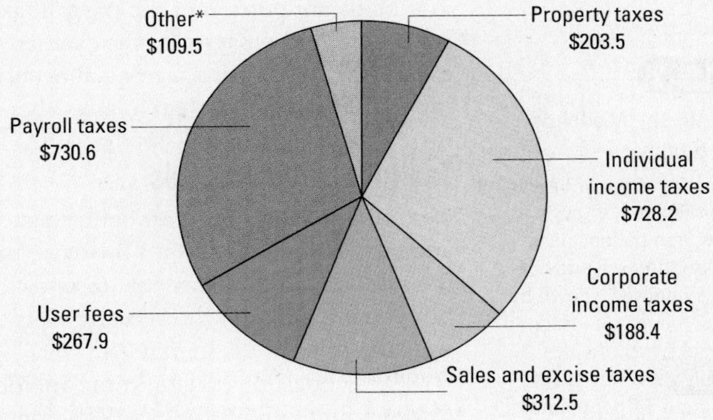

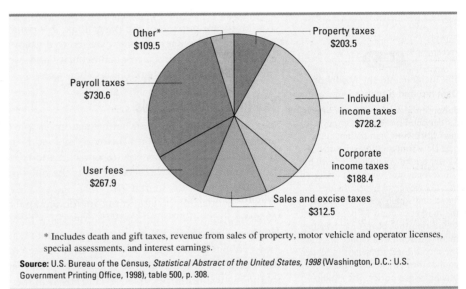

* Includes death and gift taxes, revenue from sales of property, motor vehicle and operator licenses, special assessments, and interest earnings.

Source: U.S. Bureau of the Census, *Statistical Abstract of the United States, 1998* (Washington, D.C.: U.S. Government Printing Office, 1998), table 500, p. 308.

Exhibit 15-6

Sources of Government Revenue, 1995

The chart shows sources of revenue for federal, state, and local governments in the United States. The data omit revenues from government-owned utilities and liquor stores (all figures in billions of dollars).

In analyzing the impact of a progressive tax system on taxpayer choice, economists focus on the **marginal tax rate.** This is the tax rate that would apply to an additional $1 of taxable income received by a household. A family of four with a 1998 adjusted gross income of $79,900 paid federal income taxes of $11,451, or 14.7 percent of adjusted gross income. If the taxpayer were to receive $100 more of taxable income, however, that $100 would be taxed at a rate of 28 percent, the rate that applied in 1997 to adjusted gross incomes between $60,250 and $120,000 for families of four using the standard deduction. That family thus faced a marginal tax rate of 28 percent.

Economists argue that choices are made at the margin; it is thus the marginal tax rate that is most likely to affect decisions. Say that the head of household in our family is considering taking on additional work that would increase the family's income to $70,000 per year. With a marginal tax rate of 28 percent, the family would keep $7,200 of the additional $10,000 earned. It is that $7,200 that the family will weigh against the opportunity cost in forgone leisure in deciding whether to do the extra work.

Property Taxes Property taxes are imposed on assets. Local governments, for example, generally impose a property tax on business and personal property. A government official (typically a local assessor) determines the property's value, and a proportional tax rate is then applied to that value.

Property ownership tends to be concentrated among higher income groups; economists generally view property taxes as progressive. That conclusion, however, rests on assumptions about who actually pays the tax, an issue examined later in this chapter.

Sales Taxes Sales taxes are imposed as a fixed percentage of firms' sales and are generally imposed on retail sales. Some items, such as food, are often exempted from sales taxation.

People with lower incomes generally devote a larger share of their incomes to consumption of goods covered by sales taxes than do people with higher incomes. Sales taxes are thus likely to be regressive.

Excise Taxes An excise tax is imposed on specific items. In some cases, excise taxes are justified as a way of discouraging the consumption of demerit goods, such as cigarettes and alcoholic beverages. In other cases, an excise tax is a kind of benefits-received tax. Excise taxes on gasoline, for example, are typically earmarked for use in building and maintaining highways, so that those who pay the tax are the ones who benefit from the service provided.

The most important excise tax in the United States is the payroll tax imposed on workers' earnings. In 1998, the payroll tax was 15.3 percent and was levied on incomes up to $68,400. The Medicare portion of the payroll tax, 2.9 percent, was levied on all earned wages without limit. Half of the payroll tax is charged to employers, half to employees. The proceeds of this excise on payrolls finance Social Security and Medicare benefits. Most U.S. households pay more in payroll taxes than in any other taxes.

Tax Incidence Analysis

Next time you purchase an item at a store, notice the sales tax imposed by your state, county, and city. The clerk rings up the total, then adds up the tax. The store is the entity that "pays" the sales tax, in the sense that it sends the money to the government agencies that imposed it, but you are the one who actually foots the bill—or are you? Is it possible that the sales tax affects the price of the item itself?

These questions relate to **tax incidence analysis,** a type of economic analysis that seeks to determine where the actual burden of a tax rests. Does the burden fall on consumers, workers, owners of capital, owners of natural resources, or owners of other assets in the economy? When a tax imposed on a good or service increases the price by the amount of the tax, the burden of the tax falls on consumers. If instead it lowers wages or lowers prices for some of the natural resources (such as land) used in the production of the good or service taxed, the burden of the tax falls on owners of these factors. If the tax doesn't change the product's price or factor prices, the burden falls on the owner of the firm—the owner of capital. If prices adjust by a fraction of the tax, the burden is shared.

Exhibit 15-7 gives an example of tax incidence analysis. Suppose D_1 and S_1 are the demand and supply curves for beef. The equilibrium price is $3 per pound; the equilibrium quantity is 3 million pounds of beef per day. Now suppose an excise tax of $2 per pound of beef is imposed. It doesn't matter whether the tax is levied on buyers or on sellers of beef; the important thing to see is that the tax drives a $2 per pound "wedge" between the price buyers pay and the price sellers receive. This tax is shown as the vertical green line in the exhibit; its height is $2.

We insert our tax "wedge" between the demand and supply curves. In our example, the price paid by buyers rises to $4 per pound. The price received by sellers falls to $2 per pound; the other $2 goes to the government. The quantity of beef demanded and supplied falls to 2 million pounds per day. In this case, we conclude that buyers bear half the burden of the tax (the price they pay rises by $1 per pound), and sellers bear the other half (the price they receive falls by $1 per pound). In addition to the change in price, a further burden of the tax

Exhibit 15-7

Tax Incidence in the Model of Demand and Supply

Suppose the market price of beef is $3 per pound; the equilibrium quantity is 3 million pounds per day. Now suppose an excise tax of $2 per pound is imposed, shown by the vertical green line. We insert this tax wedge between the demand and supply curves. It raises the market price to $4 per pound, suggesting that buyers pay half the tax in the form of a higher price. The amount left for sellers is $2 per pound; they pay half the tax by receiving a lower price. The equilibrium quantity falls to 2 million pounds per day.

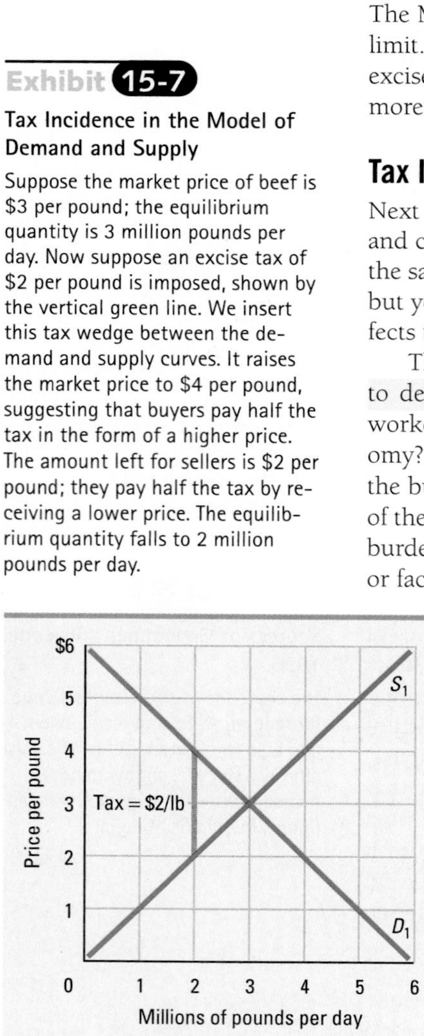

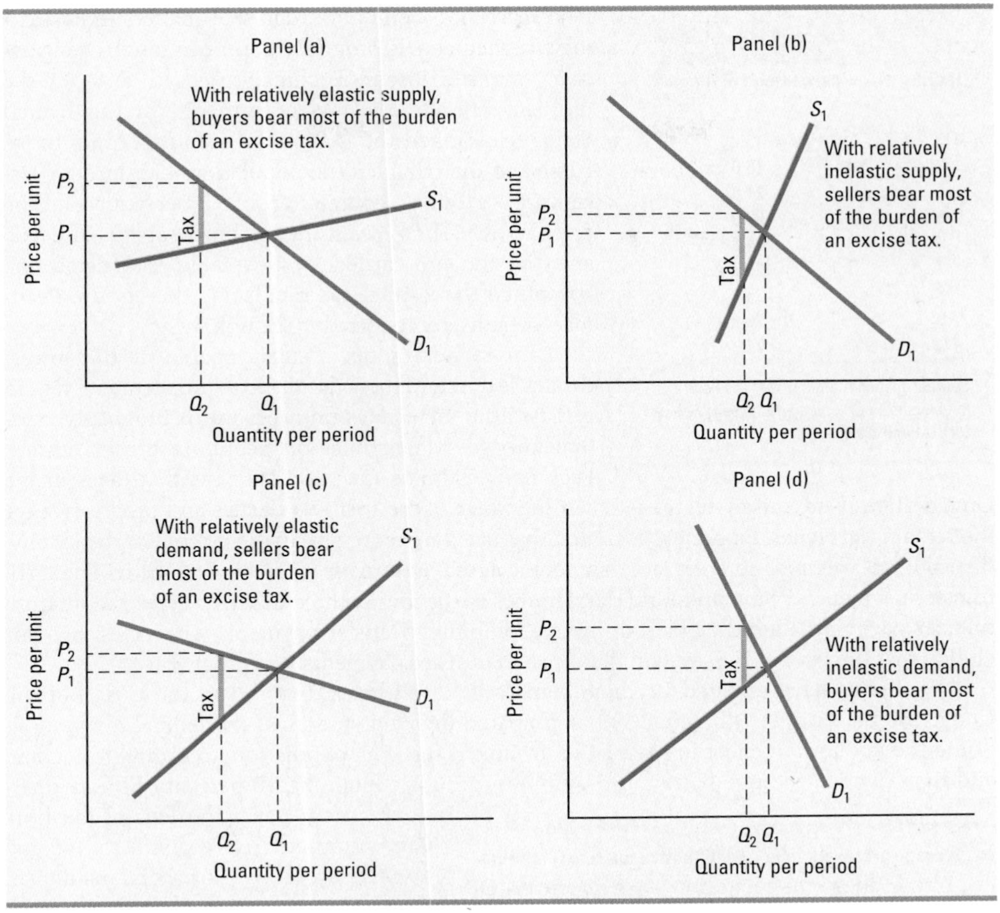

Exhibit 15-8

Tax Incidence and the Elasticity of Demand and of Supply

We show the effect of an excise tax, given by the vertical green line, in the same way that we did in Exhibit 15-7. We see that buyers bear most of the burden of such a tax in cases of relatively elastic supply (Panel (a)) and of relatively inelastic demand (Panel (d)). Sellers bear most of the burden in cases of relatively inelastic supply (Panel (b)) and of relatively elastic demand (Panel (c)).

results from the reduction in consumer and in producer surplus. We have not shown this reduction in the graph.

Exhibit 15-8 shows how tax incidence varies with the relative elasticities of demand and supply. All four panels show markets with the same initial price, P_1, determined by the intersection of demand D_1 and supply S_1. We impose an excise tax, given by the vertical green line. As before, we insert this tax wedge between the demand and supply curves. We assume the amount of the tax per unit is the same in each of the four markets.

In Panel (a), we have a market with a relatively elastic supply curve S_1. When we insert our tax wedge, the price rises to P_2; the price increase is nearly as great as the amount of the tax. In Panel (b), we have the same demand curve as in Panel (a), but with a relatively inelastic supply curve S_2. This time the price paid by buyers barely rises; sellers bear most of the burden of the tax. When the supply curve is relatively elastic, the bulk of the tax burden is borne by buyers. When supply is relatively inelastic, the bulk of the burden is borne by sellers.

Panels (c) and (d) of the exhibit show the same tax imposed in markets with identical supply curves S_1. With a relatively elastic demand curve D_1 in Panel (c) (notice that we are in the upper half, that is, the elastic portion of the curve), most of the tax burden is borne by sellers. With a relatively inelastic demand curve D_2 in Panel (d) (notice that we are in the lower half, that is, the inelastic portion of the curve), most of the burden is borne by buyers. If demand is relatively elastic, then sellers bear more of the burden of the tax. If demand is relatively inelastic, then buyers bear more of the burden.

Exhibit 15-9

Assessing the U.S. Tax Structure

Based on his estimate of how tax burdens were distributed in 1988, Joseph Pechman estimated the degree of progressivity of the U.S. tax system. Each decile represents 10 percent of the population, with deciles ranked from lowest to highest in terms of income. His conclusion was that taxes in the United States were generally progressive.

Decile	Effective federal, state, and local taxes as a percentage of income
1	16.4
2	15.8
3	18.0
4	21.5
5	23.9
6	24.3
7	25.2
8	25.6
9	26.8
10	27.7

Source: Joseph A. Pechman, "The Future of the Income Tax," *American Economic Review* 80(1) (March 1990): 1–20.

Clearly, it's the final burden that matters in evaluating whether a tax is progressive, proportional, or regressive. The late Joseph Pechman tried to sort out the ultimate burden of all taxes imposed in the United States. He ranked the U.S. population according to income and then divided the population into deciles (percentage groups containing 10 percent of the population). Then, given the tax burden on each decile and the income earned by people in that decile, he computed the average tax rate facing that group. Pechman's results are reported in Exhibit 15-9.

In a regressive tax system, people in the lowest deciles face the highest tax rates. A proportional system imposes the same rates on everyone; a progressive system imposes higher rates on people in higher deciles. Pechman's estimate for 1988 suggests that taxes in the United States were mildly regressive over the range of the first two deciles and progressive for the remaining deciles. Before we conclude that taxes are regressive at the bottom of the income distribution, we must note the fact that people at the bottom are more likely to be recipients of transfer payments. Pechman found that families in the lowest three deciles received more from transfer payments than they paid in taxes. Combining transfer payments with taxes, he concluded that the overall U.S. system of taxes and transfer payments was progressive.

No studies have updated Pechman's analysis for all taxes imposed in the U.S., but the Congressional Budget Office (CBO) has prepared detailed studies of the federal tax system. Using the tax laws in effect in May 1998, it ranked the U.S. population according to income and then divided the population into quintiles (groups containing 20 percent of the population). Then, given the federal tax burden imposed by individual income taxes, payroll taxes for social insurance, corporate income taxes, and excise taxes on each quintile and the income earned by people in that quintile, it computed the average tax rate facing that group in 1999. The CBO's results, showing strong progressivity in federal taxes, are reported in Exhibit 15-10.

Cash income	People (millions)	Average pretax income	Effective tax rate (percent)
Lowest	51.1	$ 9,880	8.0
Second	54.7	$ 26,100	15.6
Middle	54.6	$ 44,300	20.3
Fourth	54.5	$ 68,200	23.1
Highest	54.5	$174,000	29.1
All quintiles	272.7	$ 54,700	24.2

Source: CBO, *Estimates of Federal Tax Liabilities for Individuals and Families by Income Category and Family Type for 1995 and 1999*, May 1998, Table 11. Numbers of people do not add up to total because of excluded categories.

Exhibit 15-10

Effective Federal Tax Rates by Quintiles of Cash Income, All Individuals and Families, Projections for 1999

An analysis of the incidence of taxes levied by the federal government suggested that the burden of these taxes was sharply progressive in 1999.

Checklist

- The primary principles of taxation are the ability-to-pay and benefits-received principles.
- The fraction of income taken by a regressive tax falls as income rises. A proportional tax takes a constant fraction of income; a progressive tax takes a fraction that rises as income rises.
- Tax incidence analysis seeks to determine who ultimately bears the burden of taxes.
- Buyers bear most of the burden of an excise tax when supply is relatively elastic and when demand is relatively inelastic; sellers bear most of the burden when supply is relatively inelastic and when demand is relatively elastic.
- Overall, the tax burden in the United States appears to be generally progressive. Federal taxes are strongly progressive.

Case in Point Who Pays the Payroll Tax?

If you work for pay, you know that part of your wage—7.65 percent of it in 1998—is sent by your employer to the government as your Social Security and Medicare contribution. In addition to sending the government "your" payroll tax, your employer must send in an additional 7.65 percent, for a total of 15.3 percent. The 6.2 percent Social Security portion of tax is imposed on the first $68,400 in annual earnings for any one worker; both the firm and the worker continue to pay the 1.45 percent Medicare tax on earnings above that amount. But who actually bears the burden of the tax?

Economic analysis suggests that the elaborate charade of having the firm pay half the tax and the worker the other half has no effect on who really bears the burden of the tax. The payroll tax introduces a 15.3 percent gap between the cost of labor to the firm and the wage received by the worker. Whether firms or workers bear the primary burden of the tax depends on the relative elasticities of the demand and supply curves.

In the absence of a tax, the wage would be determined by supply and demand. The tax opens a gap between the wage paid by the employer and the wage received by the worker. We saw in Exhibit 15-8 that the degree to which such a tax raises the price (in this case the wage) depends on the relative elasticities of demand and supply. If the wage rises by roughly the amount of the tax, then workers bear little of the burden of the tax. If, however, the wage rises by very little, then the tax is borne largely by workers.

Panel (b) of Exhibit 15-8 shows that, with a relatively inelastic supply curve, the increase in price resulting from a payroll tax is slight. Workers bear the burden of the tax. Empirical evidence generally supports the view that the supply curve for labor is, in fact, relatively inelastic. We can conclude that workers bear most of the burden of the payroll tax.

Try It Yourself 15-2

*Consider three goods, A, B, and C. The prices of all three goods are determined by demand and supply (that is, the three industries are perfectly competitive) and equal $100. The supply curve for good A is perfectly elastic; the supply curve for good B is a typical, upward-sloping curve; and the supply curve for good C is perfectly inelastic. Suppose the federal government imposes a tax of $20 per unit on suppliers of each good. Explain and illustrate graphically how the tax will affect the price of each good in the short run. Show whether the equilibrium quantity will rise, fall, or remain unchanged. Who bears the burden of the tax on each good in the short run? (*Hint: *Review Chapter 5 for a discussion of perfectly elastic and perfectly inelastic supply curves; remember that the tax increases variable cost by $20 per unit.)*

Choices in the Public Sector

How are choices made in the public sector? This section examines two perspectives on public sector choice. The first is driven by our examination of market failure. Choices in the public sector are a matter of locating problems of market failure, determining the efficient solution, and finding ways to achieve it. This approach, called the **public interest theory** of government, assumes that the goal of government is to seek an efficient allocation of resources. An alternative approach treats public sector choices like private sector choices. The body of economic thought based on the assumption that individuals involved in public sector choices make those choices to maximize their own utility is called **public choice theory.** Public choice theory argues that individuals in the public sector make choices that maximize their utility—whether as voters, politicians, or bureaucrats, people seek solutions consistent with their self-interest. People who operate business firms may try to influence public sector choices to increase the profits of their firms. The effort to influence public choices to advance one's own self-interest is called **rent-seeking behavior.**

Public Interest Theory

In the public interest approach to the analysis of public sector choices, decisionmaking is a technical matter. The task of government officials is to locate the efficient solution and find a way to move the economy to that point.

For a public good, the efficient solution occurs where the demand curve that reflects social benefits intersects the supply curve for producing the good; that is, the solution given in Panel (a) of Exhibit 15-3. Because this demand curve for a public good isn't revealed in the market, the task for government officials is to find a way to estimate these curves and then to arrange for the production of the optimum quantity. For this purpose, economists have developed an approach called **cost-benefit analysis,** which seeks to quantify the costs and benefits of an activity. Public officials can use cost-benefit analysis to try to locate the efficient solution. In general, the efficient solution occurs where the net benefit of the activity is maximized.

Public sector intervention to correct market failure presumes that market prices do not reflect the benefits and costs of a particular activity. If those prices are generated by a market that we can regard as perfectly competitive, then the failure of prices to convey information about costs or benefits suggests that there is a free-rider problem on the demand side or an external cost problem on the supply side. In either case, it is necessary to estimate costs or benefits that are not revealed in the marketplace.

The public interest perspective suggests an approach in which policymakers identify instances of potential market failure and then look for ways to correct them. Public choice theory instead looks at what motivates the people making those policy choices.

The Public Choice Perspective

Public choice theory discards the notion that people in the public sector seek to maximize net benefits to society as a whole. Rather, it assumes that each participant in the public sector seeks to maximize his or her own utility. This section introduces the flavor of the public choice approach by examining two of its more important conclusions: that many people will rationally abstain from voting, and that legislative choices are likely to serve special interests.

Economics and Voting: The Rational Abstention Problem Public choice theory argues that individuals don't leave their self-interests behind when they enter the voting booth—or even when they're thinking about whether to go to the voting booth. The assumption of utility maximization by voters helps us to understand why most people don't vote in most elections.

Suppose your state is about to hold a referendum on expanded support for state recreation areas, to be financed by an increase in the state sales tax. Given your own likely use of these areas and the way in which you expect to be affected by the tax, you estimate that you will be better off if the program passes. In fact, you've calculated that the present value of your net benefits from the program is $1,000. Will you vote?

As a utility maximizer, you will vote if the marginal benefits to you of voting exceed the marginal costs. One benefit of voting is the possibility that your vote will cause the measure to be passed. That would be worth $1,000 to you. But $1,000 is a benefit to you of voting only if it is your vote that determines the outcome.

The probability that any statewide election will be decided by a single vote is, effectively, zero. State elections that are decided by as many as a few hundred votes are likely to be subject to several recounts, each of which is likely to produce a different result. The outcomes of extremely close elections are ordinarily decided in the courts or in legislative bodies; there is virtually no chance that one vote would, in fact, determine the outcome. Thus, the $1,000 benefit that you expect to receive may not be a factor in your decision about whether to vote. The other likely benefit of voting is the satisfaction you receive from performing your duty as a citizen in a free society. There may be additional personal benefits as well from the chance to visit with other people in your precinct. The opportunity cost of voting would be the value of the best alternative use of your time, together with possible transportation costs.

The fact that no one vote is likely to determine the outcome means that a decision about whether to vote is likely to rest on individual assessments of the satisfactions versus the costs of voting. Most people, in making such decisions, find the costs are greater. In most elections, most people who are eligible to vote don't vote. Public choice analysis suggests that such a choice is rational; a decision not to vote because the marginal costs outweigh the marginal benefits is called **rational abstention.**

Rational abstention suggests there is a public sector problem of external benefits. Elections are a way of assessing voter preferences regarding alternative outcomes. An election is likely to do a better job of reflecting voter preferences when more people vote. But the benefits of an outcome that reflects the preferences of the electorate do not accrue directly to any one voter; a voter faces only some of the benefits of voting and essentially all of the costs. Voter turnouts are thus likely to be lower than is economically efficient.

In the 1996 presidential election, for example, slightly less than half of the voting-age population actually cast votes. President Clinton won 49.2 percent of the votes cast, so it follows that he was elected president through the expressed support of less than one-fourth of the adult population. State and local elections typically have even lower turnouts.

Legislative Choice and Special Interests One alternative to having the general public vote on issues is to elect representatives who will make choices on their behalf. Public choice theory suggests that there are some difficulties with this option as well.

Suppose legislators seek to maximize the probability that they will be reelected. That requires that a legislator appeal to a majority of voters in his or her district. Suppose that each legislator can, at zero cost, learn the preferences of every voter in his or her district. Further, suppose that every voter knows, at zero cost, precisely how every government program will affect him or her.

In this imaginary world of costless information and ambitious legislators, each representative would support programs designed to appeal to a majority of voters. Organized groups would play no special role. Each legislator would already know how every voter feels about every issue, and every voter would already know how every program will affect him or her. A world of costless information would have no lobbyists, no pressure groups seeking a particular legislative agenda. No voter would be more important than any other.

Case in Point: Council Election Was in the Cards

Gary Chemistreck eked out a narrow victory in the 1999 city council race in Edgewood, New Mexico. He drew the highest card.

Mr. Chemistreck received 55 votes for an at-large position on Edgewood's council, the same number of votes received by two other candidates. New Mexico law calls for elections that result in a tie to be decided by a game of chance. Traditionally, tying candidates draw for high card.

Edgewood mayor Lawrence Keaty (who won running unopposed in the same election) says that only about one-quarter of the town's 610 registered voters voted in the election. That means that any one of the majority of Edgewood's citizens who didn't vote missed a rare opportunity: determining the outcome of an election. A single vote for any of the three candidates who tied would have tipped the victory to that candidate.

Opportunities to determine election outcomes occur only if the outcome is determined by a single vote. In elections involving a large number of voters, errors in compiling vote totals and disputes over the eligibility of some voters result in different outcomes with each recount. If one vote *did* affect the outcome, that fact would never be known. The winner would be chosen by some legislative body or by a court.

A single vote could determine the outcome of a race in a city like Edgewood. It is inconceivable that it would in a city like Los Angeles or in any statewide race.

Source: Personal interviews.

Now let us drop the assumption that information is costless but retain the assumption that each legislator's goal is to be reelected. Legislators no longer know how people in the district feel about each issue. Furthermore, voters may not be sure how particular programs will affect them. People can obtain this information, but it is costly.

In this more realistic world of costly information, special-interest groups suddenly play an important role. A legislator who doesn't know how elderly voters in his or her district feel about a certain issue may find a conversation with a representative of the American Association of Retired Persons (AARP) to be a useful source of information. A chat with a lobbyist for the AFL-CIO may reveal something about the views of workers in the district. These groups also may be able to influence voter preferences through speeches and through public information and political action efforts.

A legislator in a world of costly information thus relies on special-interest groups for information and for support. To ensure his or her reelection, the legislator might try to fashion a program that appeals not to a majority of individuals but to a coalition of special-interest groups capable of delivering the support of a majority of voters. These groups are likely to demand something in exchange for their support of a particular candidate; they are likely to seek special programs to benefit their members. The role of special-interest groups is thus inevitable, given the cost of information and the desire of politicians to win elections. In the real world, it is not individual voters who count but well-organized groups that can deliver the support of voters to a candidate.

Public choice theorists argue that the inevitable importance of special-interest groups explains many choices the public sector makes. Consider, for example, the fact noted earlier in this chapter that a great many U.S. transfer payments go to groups, many of whose members are richer than the population as a whole. In the public choice perspective, the creation of a federal transfer program, even one that is intended to help poor people, will lead to competition among interest groups to be at the receiving end of the transfers. To win at this competition, a group needs money and organization—things poor people are not likely to have. In the competition for federal transfers, then, it is the nonpoor who often win.

The perception of growing power of special-interest groups in the United States has led to proposals for reform. One is the imposition of term limits, which restrict the number of terms a legislator can serve. Term limits were first established in Colorado in 1990; over 75 percent of the states had imposed some form of term limits by 1999. One argument for term limits from the public choice perspective is that over time, incumbent legislators establish such close relationships with interest groups that they are virtually assured reelection; limiting terms may weaken these relationships and weaken special interests. The Supreme Court ruled in 1995 that individual states could not impose term limits on members of Congress. If such limits are to prevail at the federal level, a constitutional amendment will be required.

A second type of reform effort is a proposal that campaigns for seats in Congress be federally funded. If candidates did not need to seek funding from special interests, it is argued, the influence of these groups would wane.

Check *list*

- Public interest theory examines government as an institution that seeks to maximize public well-being or net social benefit. It assumes government will seek the efficient solution to market failure problems.
- Public choice theory assumes that individuals engage in rent-seeking behavior by pursuing their self-interest in their dealings with the public sector; they continue to try to maximize utility or profit.

- It may be rational for eligible voters to abstain from voting, according to public choice theory.
- Public choice theory suggests that politicians seeking reelection will try to appeal to coalitions of special-interest groups.

Try It Yourself 15-3

Here is a list of possible explanations for government programs and policies. In each case, identify whether the explanation reflects the public interest theory or the public choice theory of government action.

a. *"It is possible to explain much government activity by investigating the public's demand for government services, but one shouldn't ignore the incentives for increased supply of government services."*

b. *"Through careful application of cost-benefit analysis, we can identify the amount of a public good that should be provided by the government."*

c. *"The determination of what are merit or demerit goods is inherently political rather than scientific and more often than not can be traced to the efforts of groups with an ax to grind or some private motive to pursue."*

d. *"While it is possible that policymakers follow some well-reasoned-out application of ability-to-pay or benefit-received principles, it is more credible to recognize that many of the taxes in this country reflect the fact that groups find it in their interest to organize to get tax burdens shifted to others."*

e. *"It is in the public interest to correct the market failure caused by monopoly firms. Therefore, it behooves us to do so."*

A Look Back

In this chapter we examined the role of the public sector in the market economy. Since 1929, both the size and scope of government activities in the market have expanded considerably in the United States.

People demand government participation in three areas of economic activity. First, people may want correction of market failure involving public goods, external costs and benefits, and inefficient allocation created by imperfect competition. In each case of market failure, the shift from an inefficient allocation to an efficient one has the potential to eliminate or reduce deadweight losses. Second, people may seek government intervention to expand consumption of merit goods and to reduce consumption of demerit goods. Third, people often want government to participate in the transfer of income. Programs to transfer income have grown dramatically in the United States within the past few decades. The bulk of transfer payment spending is not means-tested.

Government activity is financed primarily by taxes. Two principles of taxation are the ability-to-pay principle, which holds that tax payments should rise with income, and the benefits-received principle, which holds that tax payments should be based on the benefits each taxpayer receives. Taxes may be regressive, proportional, or progressive. The major types of taxes in the United States are income taxes, sales and excise taxes, and property taxes. Economists seek to determine who bears the burden of a tax by examining its incidence. Taxes may be borne by buyers or sellers, depending on the relative elasticities of demand and supply.

Two broad perspectives are used to examine choices in the public sector. One is the public interest approach, which uses cost-benefit analysis to find the efficient solution to resource allocation problems. It assumes that the goal of the public sector is to maximize net social benefits. Cost-benefit analysis requires the estimation of benefits and costs when these curves are not revealed in the marketplace. The second approach to the analysis of the public sector is public choice theory, which assumes utility-maximizing and rent-seeking behavior on the part of participants in the public sector and those trying to influence it. We examined two conclusions of public choice theory, the problem of rational abstention from voting and the role of special interests.

A Look Ahead In Chapter 16, we'll turn to an examination of two specific areas of public sector activity: antitrust policy and regulation.

Terms and Concepts for Review

public finance, **299**
government expenditures, **299**
government revenues, **299**
government purchases, **299**
transfer payments, **300**
balanced budget, **300**
budget surplus, **300**
budget deficit, **300**
social cost, **302**
social benefit, **302**
merit goods, **305**
demerit goods, **305**
means-tested transfer payments, **306**
non-means-tested transfer payments, **306**
user fees, **307**
ability-to-pay principle, **307**
regressive tax, **308**
proportional tax, **308**
progressive tax, **308**
benefits-received principle, **308**
marginal tax rate, **309**
tax incidence analysis, **310**
public interest theory, **313**
public choice theory, **313**
rent-seeking behavior, **313**
cost-benefit analysis, **314**
rational abstention, **315**

For Discussion

1. Identify each of the following government programs as efforts to correct market failure, to promote or discourage the consumption of merit or demerit goods, or to transfer income.
   a. Head Start, a preschool program for low-income children
   b. Sports leagues for children sponsored by local governments
   c. A program to limit air pollution generated by power plants
   d. Species preservation efforts by the government
2. Public Broadcasting System (PBS) stations regularly solicit contributions from viewers. Yet only about 11 percent of these viewers, who on average have much higher incomes than the rest of the population, ever contribute. Why?
3. Do you expect to benefit from the research efforts sponsored by the American Cancer Society? Do you contribute? If you answered "Yes," then "No," does this make you a free rider?
4. Suppose the population of the United States increases. What will happen to the demand curve for national defense? What will happen to the efficient quantity of defense?
5. How could a program that redistributes income from rich to poor be considered a public good?
6. We noted that local governments typically supply tennis courts but not bowling alleys. Can you give a public choice explanation for this phenomenon?
7. Find out the turnout at the most recent election for student body president at your school. Does the turnout indicate student apathy?
8. Some welfare programs reduce benefits by $1 for every $1 that recipients earn; in effect, this is a tax of 100 percent on recipient earnings. Who pays the tax?
9. Suppose the quality of elementary education is a public good. How might we infer the demand for elementary school quality from residential property values?
10. V.I. Lenin, founder of the former Soviet Union, wrote that "the State is a machine for the oppression of one class by

another." Explain whether Lenin's view typifies the public interest or the public choice school of public sector choice.

11. Sugar prices in the United States are several times higher than the world price of sugar. This disparity results from a federal government program that keeps enough foreign-produced sugar out of the United States to hold U.S. sugar prices at a high level. The program raises the price of all sweetened foods produced in the United States; it boosts food costs for the average household by more than a hundred dollars per year. Who benefits from the program? Why do you suppose it exists?

Problems

1. In an effort to beautify their neighborhood, four households are considering leasing a small section of vacant land for a park. For a monthly leasing fee, the owner of the vacant land is willing to arrange for some of the maintenance and to make the park available only to the four households. The demand curves for the four households (D_A, D_B, D_C, and D_D) wanting parkland are as follows (all demand curves are linear):

	Acres per Month of Parkland Demanded			
Price per month	D_A	D_B	D_C	D_D
$100	0			
75	1	0		
50	2	1⅓	0	
25	3	2⅔	2	0
0	4	4	4	4

Draw the demand curves for the four neighbors, and show the neighborhood demand curve for parkland.

2. Suppose the owner of the vacant land will provide for and maintain a neighborhood park at a fee of $125 per acre; the neighbors may lease up to 5 acres of land per month. Add this information to the graph you drew in Problem 1, and show the efficient solution. Are the neighbors likely to achieve this solution? Explain the problems involved in achieving it.

3. The perfectly competitive compact disc industry is in long-run equilibrium, selling discs for $5 apiece. Now the government imposes an excise tax of $2 per disc produced. Show what happens to the price and output of discs in the short run and in the long run. Who pays the tax? (*Note:* Show quantities as Q_1, Q_2, etc.)

4. Zounds! A monopoly firm has just taken over the compact-disc industry. There have been technological advances that have lowered cost, but the monopoly firm charges a price greater than average total cost, even in the long run. As it turns out, the firm is still selling compact discs for $5. The government imposes an excise tax of $2 per disc produced. What happens to price and output? Compare your results to your answer in Problem 3 and explain.

5. The following hypothetical data give annual spending on various goods and services for households at different income levels. Assume that an excise tax on any of these would, in the long run, be shifted fully to consumers. Determine whether a tax on any of these goods would be progressive, proportional, or regressive.

Income range	Average income	Food	Clothing	Entertainment
$0– 25,000	$20,000	$5,000	$1,000	$500
25,000– 50,000	40,000	8,000	2,000	2,000
50,000– 75,000	65,000	9,750	3,250	5,200
75,000–100,000	80,000	10,000	4,000	8,000
>100,000	200,000	16,000	10,000	30,000

Answers to Try It Yourself Problems

Try It Yourself 15-1

a. This is an attempt to deal with monopoly, so it's a response to imperfect competition.
b. Cigarettes are treated as a demerit good.
c. Protecting the earth from such a calamity is an example of a public good.
d. Food Stamps is a means-tested program to redistribute income.
e. Social Security is an example of a non-means-tested income redistribution program.
f. This is a response to external costs.
g. This is a response to monopoly, so it falls under the imperfect competition heading.

Try It Yourself 15-2

The tax adds a \$20 wedge between the price paid by buyers and received by sellers. In Panel (a), the price rises to \$120; the entire burden is borne by buyers. In panel (c), the price remains \$100; sellers receive just \$80. Therefore, sellers bear the burden of the tax. In Panel (b), the price rises by less than \$20, and the burden is shared by buyers and sellers. The relative elasticities of demand and supply determine whether the tax is borne primarily by buyers or sellers, or shared equally by both groups.

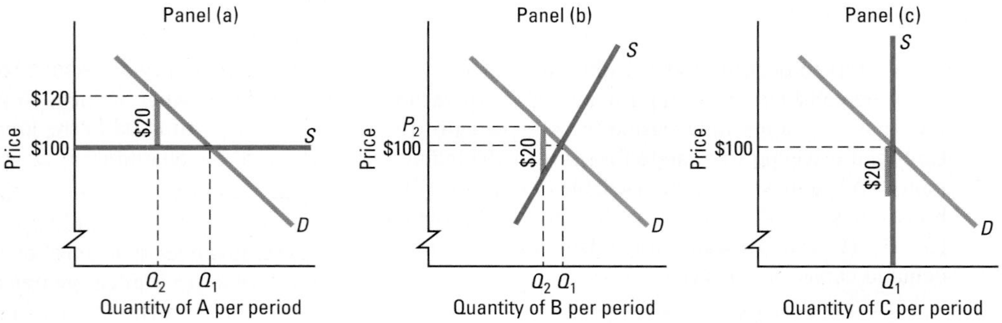

Try It Yourself 15-3

Statements (b) and (e) reflect a public interest perspective. Statements (a), (c), and (d) reflect a public choice perspective.

16 Antitrust Policy and Business Regulation

Getting Started: The Browser War

On May 18, 1998, the U.S. Department of Justice charged Microsoft with violations of the Sherman Antitrust Act because of the way it bundled its internet browser, Internet Explorer, with its Windows operating system. According to the Department of Justice, Microsoft used its dominant market position to bully its distributors, primarily the computer companies that sell their PCs preloaded with Windows 98, to exclude other web browsers from the desktop. These actions allegedly prevented Netscape and other potential rivals from competing in the browser market.

Is Microsoft a monopoly? According to data presented by the Justice Department, Microsoft's Windows operating system has a market share of 95 percent. But the Justice Department has defined the market to include only single-user computers with Intel microprocessors. Is this definition of the market reasonable? It excludes all Apple computers, which use Motorola microprocessors, as well as Sun's networked workstations. Microsoft Windows operating system certainly dominates the market, but its share is much lower when those other systems are included.

Did Microsoft bully computer makers into excluding other products? Were there other ways for rivals in the browser market to distribute their browsers? Or did customers choose Microsoft's browser because it was better?

Is it legal for Microsoft to bundle its browser into Windows? Is Microsoft just providing the integrated package users want? Or is it illegally tying a product consumers want (the Windows operating system) with another (the Internet Explorer browser) that they may not want?

Have Microsoft's actions harmed consumers? If it puts out a continual stream of ever-improving products at lower and lower prices, it's hard to argue that consumers have been harmed. But without Microsoft's allegedly unfair practices, would prices have fallen even faster?

If Microsoft is found guilty, what's the appropriate remedy? A fine? A breakup of the company? Regardless of the outcome (*Microeconomics* went to press before the trial ended), the issues this case brings out have been with us throughout the twentieth century and will remain with us for many years to come.

In this chapter we'll examine some of the limits government imposes on the actions of private firms. The first part of the chapter considers the effort by the U.S. government to limit firms' monopoly power and to encourage competition in the marketplace. The second part looks at those policies in the context of the global economy. In the third part of the chapter we'll consider other regulation of business firms, including regulations that seek to enhance worker and consumer safety, as well as deregulation efforts over the last 20 years.

Antitrust Laws and Their Interpretation

In the decades after the Civil War, giant corporations and cartels began to dominate railroads, oil, banking, meat packing, and a dozen other industries. These businesses were led by entrepreneurs who, rightly or wrongly, came to be thought of as "robber barons" out to crush their competitors, monopolize their markets, and gouge their customers. The term "robber baron" was associated with such names as J.P. Morgan and Andrew Carnegie in the steel industry, Philip Armour and Gustavas and Edwin Swift in meat packing, James P. Duke in tobacco, and John D. Rockefeller in the oil industry. They gained their market power through cartels and other business agreements aimed at restricting competition. Some formed *trusts,* a combination of corporations designed to consolidate, coordinate, and control the operations and policies of several companies. It was in response to the rise of these cartels and giant firms that antitrust policy was created in the United States. **Antitrust policy** refers to government attempts to prevent the acquisition and exercise of monopoly power and to encourage competition in the marketplace.

A Brief History of Antitrust Policy

The final third of the nineteenth century saw two major economic transitions. The first was industrialization—a period in which U.S. firms became far more capital intensive. The second was the emergence of huge firms able to dominate whole industries. In the oil industry, for example, Standard Oil of Ohio (after 1899, the Standard Oil Company of New Jersey) began acquiring smaller firms, eventually controlling 90 percent of U.S. oil-refining capacity. American Tobacco gained control of up to 90 percent of the market for most tobacco products, excluding cigars.

Public concern about the monopoly power of these giants led to a major shift in U.S. policy. What had been an economic environment in which the government rarely intervened in the affairs of private firms was gradually transformed into an environment in which government agencies took on a much more vigorous role. The first arena of intervention was antitrust policy, which authorized the federal government to challenge the monopoly power of firms head-on. The application of this policy, however, has followed a wandering and rocky road.

The Sherman Antitrust Act (1890) The Sherman Antitrust Act of 1890, the first U.S. antitrust legislation, remains the cornerstone of its antitrust policy. The Sherman Act outlawed contracts, combinations, and conspiracies in restraint of trade.

An important issue in the interpretation of the Sherman Act concerns which actions by firms are **illegal per se**, meaning illegal in and of itself without regard to the circumstances under which it occurs. Shoplifting, for example, is illegal per se; courts don't inquire whether shoplifters have a good reason for stealing something in determining whether their acts are illegal. One key question of interpretation is whether it is illegal per se to control a large share of a market. Another is whether a merger that is likely to produce substantial monopoly power is illegal per se.

Two landmark Supreme Court cases in 1911 in which the Sherman Act was effectively used to break up Standard Oil and American Tobacco enunciated the **rule of reason**, which holds that whether or not a particular business practice is illegal depends on the circumstances surrounding the action. In both cases, the companies held dominant market positions, but the Court made it clear that it was their specific "unreasonable" behaviors that the breakups were intended to punish. In determining what was illegal and what was not, emphasis was placed on the conduct, not the structure or size, of the firms.

emphasize conduct

In the next 10 years, the Court threw out antitrust suits brought by government prosecutors against Eastman Kodak, International Harvester, United Shoe Machinery, and United States Steel. The Court determined that none of them had used unreasonable means to achieve their dominant positions in the industry. Rather, they had successfully exploited economies of scale to reduce costs below competitors' costs and had used reasonable means of competition to reap the rewards of efficiency.

The rule of reason suggests that "bigness" is no offense if it has been achieved through legitimate business practices. This precedent, however, was challenged in 1945 when the U.S. Court of Appeals ruled against the Aluminum Company of America (Alcoa). The court acknowledged that Alcoa had been able to capture over 90 percent of the aluminum industry through reasonable business practices. Nevertheless, the court held that by sheer size alone, Alcoa was in violation of the prohibition against monopoly.

In a landmark 1962 court case involving a proposed merger between Brown Shoe Company and one of its competitors, the Supreme Court blocked the merger because the resulting firm would have been so efficient that it could have undersold all of its competitors. The Court recognized that lower shoe prices would have benefited consumers, but chose to protect competitors instead.

The Alcoa case and the Brown Shoe case, along with many other antitrust cases in the 1950s and 1960s, added confusion and uncertainty to the antitrust environment by appearing to reinvoke the doctrine of per se illegality. For example, part of the Justice Department's recent case against Microsoft suggested that Windows' dominance of the market for operating systems was a per se violation of the antitrust laws. But most of the case focused on Microsoft's defense argument that its behavior satisfied the rule of reason. Although the Microsoft case was unresolved at press time, the rule of reason has generally prevailed since the 1970s.

The Sherman Act also aimed, in part, to prevent **price-fixing**, in which two or more firms agree to set prices or to coordinate their pricing policies. For example, in the 1950s General Electric, Westinghouse, and several other manufacturers colluded to fix prices. They agreed to assign market segments in which one firm would sell at a lower price than the others. In 1961, the General Electric–Westinghouse agreement was declared illegal. The companies paid a multimillion-dollar fine, and their officers served brief jail sentences. In May 1999, F. Hoffman-LaRoche, the Swiss pharmaceutical company, and BASF, a German company, were fined $500 million and $225 million, respectively, for conspiring to raise and fix the prices of vitamins. These were the largest fines ever levied for violations under the Sherman Act.

Case in Point "Supermarket to the World" Caught in Price-Fixing Scandal

The multibillion-dollar Archer Daniels Midland (ADM) Company, a distributor of agricultural products, advertises itself as the "Supermarket to the World." The $100 million criminal fine it was assessed in 1996 for price fixing, $100 million in additional payments to its customers in civil lawsuits, as well as the conviction of three of its top executives, provided it with some unwanted advertising.

Secret tape recordings and an informer within the company (who lost his immunity from prosecution because it turned out he was also stealing from the company) simplified the Justice Department's case against ADM. Two former top ADM executives were fined $350,000 each and sentenced to 2 years in prison. A third, who was already serving a 9-year prison term for embezzling ADM, received 20 more months. He spoke to the judge by speaker phone during the sentencing: "Life in prison has actually been better than life at ADM."

ADM's "friendly" competitors were several foreign companies who also pleaded guilty to price-fixing and were fined. Its "enemy" customers were farmers, food manufacturers, and consumers that bought its lysine and citric acid. Lysine is an additive used to spur growth in pigs and chickens. Citric acid is used in many food and beverage products to enhance flavor.

The companies involved colluded to raise prices and divide the market. A videotape of a 1993 meeting shows an ADM executive talking about the lysine market to the executive of a supposedly competing Japanese company, saying, "They can each have 2,000 tons more [of lysine] in 1994 and we get the rest between you and us."

ADM pleaded guilty in 1996 and agreed to pay the $100 million fine. Three top ADM executives were separately charged and convicted. The maximum penalty for individuals is three years' imprisonment and a $350,000 fine. The penalty phase of the trial was indefinitely postponed in May 1999 to provide the judge more time to determine the actual economic effect and damages caused by the price-fixing actions of the conspirators.

Sources: Kurt Eichenwald, "Former Archer Daniels Executives Are Found Guilty of Price Fixing," *New York Times*, 18 September 1998, p. A1; Greg Burns, "Has Success Spoiled ADM? 3 Price-Fixing Convictions Add to Image Woes," *Chicago Tribune*, 18 September 1998, Business p. 1; Scott Kilman, "ADM Ex-Officials Get 2 Years in Jail in Sign of Tougher Antitrust Penalties," *Wall Street Journal*, 12 July 1999, p. A4.

Other Antitrust Legislation Concerned about the continued growth of monopoly power, in 1914 Congress created the Federal Trade Commission (FTC), a five-member commission that, along with the antitrust division of the Justice Department, has the power to investigate firms that use illegal business practices. The FTC still plays a key role in antitrust enforcement.

In addition to establishing the FTC, Congress enacted new antitrust laws intended to strengthen the Sherman Act. The Clayton Act (1914) clarifies the illegal per se provision of the Sherman Act by prohibiting the purchase of a rival firm if the purchase would substantially decrease competition, and outlawing interlocking directorates, in which there are common members sitting on the boards of directors of competing firms. More significantly, the act prohibits price discrimination that is designed to lessen competition or that tends to create a monopoly and exempts labor unions from antitrust laws.

The Sherman and Clayton acts, like other early antitrust legislation, were aimed at preventing mergers that reduce the number of firms in a single industry. The consolidation of two or more producers of the same good or service is called a **horizontal merger**. Such mergers increase concentration and, therefore, the likelihood of collusion among the remaining firms.

The Celler–Kefauver Act of 1950 extended the antitrust provisions of earlier legislation by blocking **vertical mergers**, which are mergers between firms at different stages in the production and distribution of a product if a reduction in competition will result. For example, the acquisition by Ford Motor Company of a firm that supplies it with steel would be a vertical merger.

U.S. Antitrust Policy Today

The "bigness is badness" doctrine dominated antitrust policy from 1945 to the 1970s. But the doctrine always had its critics. If a firm is more efficient than its competitors, why should it be punished? Critics of the antitrust laws point to the fact that of the 500 largest companies in the United States in 1950, over 100 no longer exist. New firms, including such giants as IBM, Microsoft, and Federal Express, have taken their place. The critics argue that the emergence of these new firms is evidence of the dynamism and competitive nature of the modern corporate scene.

There is no evidence to suggest, for example, that the degree of concentration across all industries has increased over the past 20 years. Global competition and the use of the internet as a marketing tool have increased the competitiveness of a wide range of industries. Moreover, critics of antitrust policy argue that it is not necessary that an industry be perfectly competitive to achieve the benefits of competition. It need merely be contestable—open to entry by potential rivals. A large firm may be able to prevent small firms from competing, but other equally large firms may enter the industry in pursuit of the extraordinary profits earned by the initial large firm. For example, AT&T, primarily a competitor in the long-distance telephone market, has in recent years become a main competitor in the cable television market and may even enter the local phone service market.

Exhibit 16-1

Department of Justice and Federal Trade Commission Merger Guidelines

If the postmerger Herfindahl–Hirschman Index is found to be . . .	then the Justice Department will likely take the following action:
Unconcentrated (< 1,000)	No challenge
Moderately concentrated (1,000–1,800)	Challenge if postmerger index changes by more than 100 points
Highly concentrated (> 1,800)	Challenge if postmerger index changes by more than 50 points

Source: U.S. Department of Justice and Federal Trade Commission, *1992 Horizontal Merger Guidelines.*

Currently, the Justice Department follows guidelines based on the Herfindahl–Hirschman Index (HHI). The HHI, introduced in Chapter 11, is calculated by summing the squared percentage market shares of all firms in an industry. The higher the value of the index, the greater the degree of concentration. Possible values of the index range from 0 in the case of perfect competition to 10,000 ($= 100^2$) in the case of monopoly.

Guidelines issued in 1984 and 1992 stipulate that any industry with an HHI under 1,000 is unconcentrated. Except in unusual circumstances, mergers of firms with a postmerger index under 1,000 will not be challenged. The Justice Department has said it would challenge proposed mergers with a postmerger HHI between 1,000 and 1,800 if the index increased by more than 100 points. Industries with an index greater than 1,800 are deemed highly concentrated, and the Justice Department has said it would seek to block mergers in these industries if the postmerger index would increase by 50 points or more. Exhibit 16-1 summarizes the use of the HHI by the Justice Department.

In the 1980s both the courts and the Justice Department held that bigness did not necessarily translate into badness, and corporate mergers proliferated. In the period 1982–1989 there were almost 200 mergers and acquisitions of firms whose value exceeded $1 billion. The total value of these companies was nearly half a trillion dollars.

Megamergers continued in the 1990s. The FTC reported at the end of federal fiscal year 1998 that there was a record number of sizable mergers that year, an increase of 28 percent from 1997 and three times more than occurred in 1991. "The United States is in the midst of a merger wave of unprecedented proportions, with mergers exceeding $1 trillion over the past 12 months," according to William J. Baer, Director of the FTC's Bureau of Competition.[1] Exhibit 16-2 shows some of the biggest mergers of calendar year 1998 (completed and pending). Thousands of horizontal and vertical mergers of smaller firms also took place during the 1980s and 1990s.

Corporate mergers	Value (billions)
Exxon/Mobil*	$77.2
Bell Atlantic/GTE*	72.6
SBC Communications/Ameritech*	69.9
British Petroleum PLC/Amoco*	58.8
NationsBank/BankAmerica	41.5
Worldcom/MCI Communications	37.0
Travelers Group/Citicorp	36.9
Daimler-Benz/Chrysler	32.8
AT&T/Telecommunications*	32.8
Wells Fargo & Co./Norwest	31.7

*Deal pending. Value based on closing stock prices as of November 30, 1998.
Source: Robert F. Bukay, The Associated Press, *Ogden Standard Examiner*, 1 December 1998: p.1A.

Exhibit 16-2
Top Corporate Mergers Involving U.S. Companies, 1998

Checklist

- The government uses antitrust policies to maintain competitive markets in the economy.
- The Sherman Antitrust Act of 1890 and subsequent legislation define illegal business practices, but these acts are subject to widely varying interpretation by government agencies and the courts.
- Although price-fixing is illegal per se, most business practices that may lessen competition are interpreted under the rule of reason.
- The Justice Department uses the Herfindahl–Hirschman Index to determine which industries are so concentrated that mergers and acquisitions within them should be prohibited.

Try It Yourself 16-1

According to what basic principle did the Supreme Court find Eastman Kodak not guilty of violating antitrust laws? According to what basic principle did the U.S. Court find Alcoa guilty of such violations?

Antitrust and Competitiveness in a Global Economy

In the early 1980s U.S. imports from foreign firms rose faster than U.S. exports. In 1986 the trade deficit reached a record level. Antitrust laws played a relatively minor role in increasing the deficit, but business interests and politicians pressed for the relaxation of antitrust policy in order to make U.S. firms more competitive against multinational companies headquartered in other countries.

Antitrust enforcement was altered in the late 1980s so that horizontally competitive U.S. firms could cooperate in research and development (R&D) ventures aimed at innovation, cost-cutting technological advances, and new product development. In an antitrust context,

[1]Federal Trade Commission, Press Release, "FTC Wraps up Record Year in Antitrust Enforcement," October 8, 1998, http:www.ftc.gov/opa/1998/9810/compar.htm

joint ventures refer to cooperative arrangements between two or more firms that otherwise would violate antitrust laws. Proponents of the change argued that foreign multinational firms were not subject to stringent antitrust restrictions and therefore had a competitive advantage over U.S. firms. The International Competition Policy Advisory Committee (ICPAC) was formed in the Department of Justice in 1997 in recognition of the dramatic increases in both international commerce and international anticompetitive activity. Composed of a panel of business, industrial relations, academic, economic, and legal experts, ICPAC is to provide advice and information to the department on international antitrust issues such as transnational cartels and international anticompetitive business practices.

Cooperative Ventures Abroad

Policymakers who revised U.S. antitrust restrictions on joint ventures pointed out that Japanese and European firms are encouraged to cooperate and to collude not only in basic R&D projects, but in production and marketing as well.

The evidence is difficult to interpret, but in Japan, for example, a substantial percentage of research projects are sponsored jointly by firms in the same market. Moreover, the evidence is fairly clear that Japan allows horizontal consolidations and mergers in moderately concentrated markets where antitrust policy would be applied in the United States. Mergers that create substantial monopoly power in Japan are not typically prosecuted by the government.

In Europe, the potential competitive threat to U.S. firms is twofold. First, as the European Union (EU) moved toward economic unification in 1992, it relaxed antitrust enforcement for mergers between firms in different nations, even though they would become a single transnational firm in the near future. In 1984, for example, the European Community (EC), the forerunner of the EU, adopted a regulation that provided blanket exemptions from antitrust provisions against collusion in R&D for firms whose total market share did not exceed 20 percent. This exemption included horizontal R&D and extended to production and distribution to the point of final sale. Moreover, firms that had a market share greater than 20 percent could apply for an exemption based on a case-by-case examination.

The U.S. government has relaxed antitrust restrictions in some cases in an effort to make domestic firms more competitive in global competition. For example, producers of semiconductors were allowed to form a research consortium, Sematech, in order to promote the U.S. semiconductor industry. This type of joint venture was formerly prohibited.

Antitrust Policy and U.S. Competitiveness

In the 1980s Congress passed several laws that relaxed the antitrust prohibition against cooperation among U.S. firms, including the National Cooperative Research Act of 1984 (NCRA) and the Omnibus Trade and Competitiveness Act (OTCA).

The NCRA provided a simple registration procedure for joint ventures in R&D. The NCRA protects members of registered joint ventures from punitive antitrust penalties if the venture is later found to illegally reduce competition or otherwise act in restraint of trade. Between 1984 and 1990 over 200 research joint ventures were registered, substantially more than were formed over the same period within the EC.

Congress passed the OTCA in 1988. The OTCA made unfair methods of competition by foreign firms and importers punishable under the U.S. antitrust laws. It also changed the wording of existing laws concerning "dumping" (selling below cost) by foreign firms. In the past, a domestic firm that claimed injury from a foreign competitor had to prove that the foreign firm was "undercutting" the U.S. market prices. The OTCA changed this provision to the much less restrictive term "underselling" and specifically stated that the domestic firm did not have to prove predatory intent. This legislation opened the door for U.S. competitors to use antitrust laws to *prevent* competition from foreigners, quite the opposite of the laws' original purpose. Dumping is discussed further in the next chapter.

In another policy shift, the Justice Department announced in 1988 that the rule of reason would replace per se illegality in analysis of joint ventures that would increase U.S. competitiveness. The Justice Department uses the domestic guidelines and the Herfindahl–Hirschman Index to determine whether a proposed joint venture would increase concentration and thereby lessen competition. In making that assessment, the Justice Department also looks at (1) whether the firms directly compete in other markets, (2) the possible impact on vertical markets, and (3) whether any offsetting efficiency benefits outweigh the anticompetitiveness of the joint venture. Although mergers between two firms in a moderately or highly concentrated industry are prohibited, joint ventures between them may be allowed.

The major antitrust issues to be resolved in the first decade of the twenty-first century go beyond joint R&D ventures. The World Trade Organization, the international organization created in 1995 to supervise world trade, has established a group to study issues relating to the interaction between trade and competition policy, including anticompetitive practices. Nations currently have quite different antitrust laws, as the Case in Point on Boeing versus Airbus illustrates. The United States has argued against any internationalization of antitrust issues that would reduce its ability to apply U.S. laws. On the other hand, the United States, via the 1994 International Antitrust Enforcement Assistance Act, is negotiating bilateral agreements that allow antitrust agencies in different countries to exchange information for use

Case in Point The United States of Boeing Versus the European Union of Airbus

The European Union's initial reaction to the proposed merger of Boeing and McDonnell Douglas in 1997 was to threaten to impose tariffs on Boeing planes entering the continent if the deal went through. The issue brought the United States and its European partners to the brink of a trade war.

President Bill Clinton responded to the EU's threat by saying, "I'm concerned about what appears to be the reasons for the objection to the Boeing–McDonnell Douglas merger by the European Union and we have some options ourselves when actions are taken in this regard." The president seemed to be suggesting retaliatory trade sanctions, such as U.S. tariffs on European-made planes.

At the last minute, the EU allowed the merger on two conditions: that Boeing give up its exclusive supply deals and agree to license to its competitors (meaning Airbus) McDonnell technology that had been developed with U.S. governmental support.

In the press, the incident was reported as an incipient trade war. Europe was trying to protect its own airplane industry, the United States its own. According to New York University professor Eleanor Fox, though, the dispute stemmed not from countries trying to protect their own companies but from differing antitrust laws.

Ms. Fox argues that U.S. antitrust law is consumer oriented. The question for the U.S. Federal Trade Commission was whether the merger made consumers worse off by raising the price of jets to airlines. The FTC reasoned that McDonnell Douglas had no reasonable chance of making and selling new fleets on its own and thus did not constitute a competitive force in the marketplace. With McDonnell Douglas deemed competitively insignificant, the merger was permissible.

However, EU laws consider not only consumers but also unfair competitive advantages of dominant firms. Because Boeing held 20-year exclusive contracts with three airlines that represent more than 10 percent of the market for airplane manufacture, from the EU point of view the merger magnified Boeing's unfair competitive advantage over other firms (primarily Airbus) that sell aircraft. The conditions that the EU imposed thus made the merger consistent with its antitrust laws.

The issue of how national antitrust policies affect other countries and what to do about it is an area that is likely to receive much attention in coming years.

Source: Eleanor M. Fox, "Antitrust Regulation Across National Borders," *The Brookings Review* 16, Issue 1 (Winter 1998): 30–32.

in antitrust enforcement. The issue of how to deal with anticompetitive practices on a worldwide basis remains unresolved, and this area of antitrust practice and policy will be closely watched and studied by economists.

Checklist

- A joint venture, in the context of antitrust policy, is a cooperative project between firms that otherwise would not be allowed to merge or collude under existing antitrust guidelines.
- A rising trade deficit in the 1980s and concerns about U.S. competitiveness led to relaxation of antitrust enforcement against firms that cooperate in joint ventures, particularly in R&D projects.
- Since 1988, the Justice Department has applied the Herfindahl–Hirschman Index and the rule of reason in determining what mergers and joint ventures are allowed among U.S. firms threatened by competition from foreign firms.

Regulation: Protecting People from the Market

Antitrust policies are primarily concerned with limiting the accumulation and use of market power. Government **regulation** is used to control the choices of private firms or individuals. Regulation may constrain the freedom of firms to enter or exit markets, to establish prices, to determine product design and safety, and to make other business decisions. It may also limit the choices made by individuals.

In general terms, there are two types of regulatory agencies. One group attempts to protect consumers by limiting the possible abuse of market power by firms. The other attempts to influence business decisions that affect consumer and worker safety. Regulation is carried out by more than 50 federal agencies that interpret the applicable laws and apply them in the specific situations they find in real-world markets. Exhibit 16-3 lists some of the major federal regulatory agencies, many of which are duplicated at the state level.

Theories of Regulation

Competing explanations for why there is so much regulation range from theories that suggest regulation protects the public interest to those that argue regulation protects the producers or serves the interests of the regulators. The distinction corresponds to our discussion in the last chapter of the public interest versus the public choice understanding of government policy in general.

The Public Interest Theory of Regulation The public interest theory of regulation holds that regulators seek to find market solutions that are economically efficient. It argues that the market power of firms in imperfectly competitive markets must be controlled. In the case of natural monopolies (discussed in Chapter 10), regulation is viewed as necessary to lower prices and increase output. In the case of oligopolistic industries, regulation is often advocated to prevent cutthroat competition.

The public interest theory of regulation also holds that firms may have to be regulated in order to guarantee the availability of certain goods and services—such as electricity, medical facilities, and telephone service—that otherwise would not be profitable enough to induce unregulated firms to provide them in a given community. Firms providing such goods and services are often granted licenses and franchises that prevent competition. The regulatory authority allows the firm to set prices above average cost in the protected market in order to

Exhibit 16-3

Selected Federal Regulatory Agencies and Their Missions

Financial Markets	
Federal Reserve Board	Regulates banks and other financial institutions
Federal Deposit Insurance Corporation	Regulates and insures banks and other financial institutions
Securities and Exchange Commission	Regulates and requires full disclosure in the securities (stock) markets
Commodity Futures Trading Commission	Regulates trading in futures markets
Product Markets	
Department of Justice, Antitrust Division	Enforces antitrust laws
Federal Communications Commission	Regulates broadcasting and telephone industries
Federal Trade Commission	Focuses efforts on consumer protection, false advertising, and unfair trade practices
Federal Maritime Commission	Regulates international shipping
Surface Transportation Board	Regulates railroads, trucking, and noncontiguous domestic water transportation
Federal Energy Regulatory Commission	Regulates pipelines
Health and Safety	
Occupational Health and Safety Administration	Regulates health and safety in the workplace
National Highway Traffic Safety Administration	Regulates and sets standards for motor vehicles
Federal Aviation Administration	Regulates air traffic and aviation safety
Food and Drug Administration	Regulates food and drug producers; emphasis on purity, labeling, and product safety
Consumer Product Safety Commission	Regulates product design and labeling to reduce risk of consumer injury
Energy and the Environment	
Environmental Protection Agency	Sets standards for air, water, toxic waste, and noise pollution
Department of Energy	Sets national energy policy
Nuclear Regulatory Commission	Regulates nuclear power plants
Corps of Engineers	Sets policies on construction near rivers, harbors, and waterways
Labor Markets	
Equal Employment Opportunity Commission	Enforces antidiscrimination laws in the workplace
National Labor Relations Board	Enforces rules and regulations governing contract bargaining and labor relations between companies and unions

cover losses in the target community. In this way, the firms are allowed to earn, indeed are guaranteed, a reasonable rate of return overall.

Proponents of the public interest theory also justify regulation of firms by pointing to externalities, such as pollution, that are not taken into consideration when unregulated firms make their decisions. As we saw in Chapters 6 and 15, in the absence of property rights that force the firms to consider all of the costs and benefits of their decisions, the market may fail to allocate resources efficiently.

The Public Choice Theory of Regulation The public interest theory of regulation assumes that regulations serve the interests of consumers by restricting the harmful actions of business firms. That assumption, however, is now widely challenged by advocates of the public choice theory of regulation, which rests on the premise that all individuals, including public servants, are driven by self-interest. They prefer the **capture theory of regulation**, which holds that government regulations often end up serving the regulated firms rather than their customers.

Competing firms always have an incentive to collude or operate as a cartel. The public is protected from such collusion by a pervasive incentive for firms to cheat. Capture theory asserts that firms seek licensing and other regulatory provisions to prevent other firms from entering the market. Firms seek price regulation to prevent price competition. In this view, the regulators take over the role of policing cartel pricing schemes; individual firms in a cartel would be incapable of doing so themselves.

Because it is practically impossible for the regulatory authorities to have as much information as the firms they are regulating, and because these authorities often rely on information provided by those firms, the firms find ways to get the regulators to enforce regulations that protect profits. The regulators get "captured" by the very firms they are supposed to be regulating.

In addition to its use of the capture theory, the public choice theory of regulation argues that employees of regulatory agencies are not an exception to the rule that people are driven by self-interest. They maximize their own satisfaction, not the public interest. This insight suggests that regulatory agencies seek to expand their bureaucratic structure in order to serve the interests of the bureaucrats. As the people in control of providing government protection from the rigors of the market, bureaucrats respond favorably to lobbyists and special interests. Murray Weidenbaum, Director of the Center for the Study of American Business, argues, for example, that the budget of the Environmental Protection Agency (EPA)

> is more tied to dramatic news events than to public health risks or shortcomings in the marketplace. Thus, EPA spending rises with reports of leaking dumpsites for toxic wastes. The Coast Guard Budget benefits from oil spills. Food and Drug Administration outlays rise in response to shortcomings in approving generic drugs. The Securities and Exchange Commission grows following insider trading abuses and other Wall Street scandals.[2]

Public choice theory views the regulatory process as one in which various groups jockey to pursue their respective interests. Firms might exploit regulation to limit competition. Consumers might seek lower prices or changes in products. Regulators themselves might pursue their own interests in expanding their prestige or incomes. The abstract goal of economic efficiency is unlikely to serve the interest of any one group; public choice theory does not predict that efficiency will be a goal of the regulatory process. Regulation might improve on inefficient outcomes, but it might not.

Consumer Protection

Every day we come into contact with regulations designed to protect consumers from unsafe products, unscrupulous sellers, or our own carelessness. Seat belts are mandated in cars and airplanes; drivers must provide proof of liability insurance; deceptive advertising is illegal; firms cannot run "going out of business" sales forever; electrical and plumbing systems in new construction must be inspected and approved; packaged and prepared foods must carry certain information on their labels; cigarette packages must warn users of the dangers involved in smoking; gasoline stations must prevent gas spillage; used-car odometers must be certified as accurate. The list of regulations is seemingly endless.

There are very good reasons behind consumer protection regulation, and most economists accept such regulation as a legitimate role and function of government agencies. But there are costs as well as benefits to consumer protection.

The Benefits of Consumer Protection Consumer protection laws are generally based on one of two conceptual arguments. The first holds that consumers don't always know what's best for them. This is the view underlying government efforts to encourage the use of merit goods and discourage the use of demerit goods. The second suggests that consumers simply don't have sufficient information to make appropriate choices.

Laws prohibiting the use of certain products are generally based on the presumption that not all consumers make appropriate choices. Drugs such as cocaine and heroin are illegal for this reason. Children are barred from using products such as cigarettes and alcohol on grounds they are incapable of making choices in their own best interest.

[2]Murray Weidenbaum, "The New Wave of Business Regulation," Contemporary Issues Series 40, December 1990 (St. Louis: Center for the Study of American Business, Washington University), p. 3. Reprinted with permission.

Other regulations presume that consumers are rational but may not have adequate information to make choices. Rather than expect consumers to determine whether a particular prescription drug is safe and effective, for example, federal regulations require the Food and Drug Administration to make that determination for them.

The benefit of consumer protection occurs when consumers are prevented from making choices they'd regret if they had more information. A consumer who purchases a drug that proves ineffective or possibly even dangerous will presumably stop using it. By preventing the purchase in the first place, the government may save the consumer the cost of learning that lesson.

One problem in assessing the benefits of consumer protection is that the laws themselves often induce behavioral changes that work against the intent of the legislation. For example, requirements for greater safety in cars appear to have encouraged drivers to drive more recklessly. Requirements for childproof medicine containers appear to have made people more careless with medicines. Requirements that mattresses be flame-resistant appear to have made people more careless about smoking in bed. In some cases, then, the behavioral changes attributed to consumer protection laws may actually worsen the problem the laws seek to correct. In any event, these "unintended" behavioral changes certainly reduce the benefits achieved by these laws.[3]

The Cost of Consumer Protection Regulation aimed at protecting consumers can benefit them, but it can also impose costs. It adds to the cost of producing goods and services and thus boosts prices. It also restricts the freedom of choice of individuals, some of whom are willing to take more risks than others.

Those who demand, and are willing to pay the price for, high-quality, safe, warranted products can do so. But some argue that people who demand and prefer to pay (presumably) lower prices for lower-quality products that may have risks associated with their use should also be allowed to exercise this preference. By increasing the costs of goods, consumer protection laws may adversely affect the poor, who are forced to purchase higher-quality products; the rich would presumably buy higher-quality products in the first place.

To assess whether a particular piece of consumer protection is desirable requires a careful look at how it stacks up against the marginal decision rule. The approach of economics is to attempt to determine how the costs compare to the benefits of a particular regulation.

Deregulating the Economy

Concern that regulation might sometimes fail to serve the public interest prompted a push to deregulate some industries, beginning in the late 1970s. In 1978, for example, Congress passed the Airline Deregulation Act, which removed many of the regulations that had prevented competition in the airline industry. Safety regulations were not affected. The results of deregulation included a substantial reduction in airfares, the merger and consolidation of airlines, and the emergence of frequent flier plans and other marketing schemes designed to increase passenger miles. Not all the consequences of deregulation were applauded, however. Many airlines, unused to the demands of a competitive, unprotected, and unregulated environment, went bankrupt or were taken over by other airlines. Large airlines abandoned service to small and midsized cities, and although most of these routes were picked up by smaller regional airlines, some consumers complained about inadequate service. Nevertheless, the more competitive airline system today is probably an improvement over the highly regulated industry that existed in the 1970s. It is certainly cheaper.

[3]See, for example, Kip Viscusi, "The Lulling Effect: The Impact of Protective Bottlecaps on Aspirin and Analgesic Poisonings," *American Economic Review* 74(2) (1984): 324–327.

Case in Point Consumers Benefit Substantially from Deregulation

Deregulation in some markets has produced enormous benefits for consumers. But achieving deregulation, and realizing those benefits, takes time.

"Economic deregulation does not happen overnight. It takes time for lawmakers and regulators to dismantle regulatory regimes, and then it takes more time for the deregulated industries to adjust to their new competitive environment," writes Clifford Winston, a senior fellow at the Brookings Institution and a longtime analyst of the impact of economic deregulation.

Mr. Winston contends that policymakers in a democracy tend to focus on the short-term impacts of policies they introduce, impacts that will occur while they're in office. Because they tend to have short time horizons, the benefits of deregulation, which happen over a long period, are often undervalued. Moreover, possible immediate impacts of policy changes, such as short-term price increases, may lead policymakers to backtrack, as they did in deregulating cable television in 1984 and then reregulating it in 1992. Banking deregulation was put at risk by a savings and loan crisis in the 1980s.

However, Mr. Winston argues that in fact banking deregulation was only partly responsible for the savings and loan crisis, and cites previous regulation, lax supervision by agencies that oversee banking, and other factors as sharing the blame. Today the industry is healthy because policymakers stuck with deregulation.

In analyzing the impact of deregulation in five U.S. industries—airlines, trucking, railroads, banking, and natural gas—Mr. Winston found overwhelming evidence of dramatic benefits, as the table shows. Regulatory reform of these industries began in the mid-1970s. According to Mr. Winston, substantial portions of the declines in price over the last 20 years are due directly to deregulation.

Based on common patterns of benefits that these industries produced, Mr. Winston predicts that current deregulation efforts that appear to be slow in gaining steam, such as the deregulation of local telephone service, are likely to be quite successful over time. Moreover, he advocates looking for other industries to deregulate. The industries that have been deregulated so far are different in many ways, but they share a common characteristic: When deregulated, they have improved consumer welfare, and the improvements have increased over time.

Improvements in Consumer Welfare

Industry	Improvements
Airlines	Average fares are roughly 33 percent lower in real terms since deregulation, and service frequency has improved significantly.
Less-than-truckload trucking	Average rates per vehicle mile have declined at least 35 percent in real terms since deregulation, and service times have improved significantly.
Truckload trucking	Average rates per vehicle mile have declined at least 75 percent in real terms since deregulation, and, because of the emergence of "Advanced Truckload" carriers, service times have also improved significantly.
Railroads	Average rates per ton mile have declined more than 50 percent in real terms since deregulation, average transit time has fallen more than 20 percent.
Banking	Consumers have benefitted from higher interest rates on deposits, from better opportunities to manage risk, and from more banking offices and automated teller machines.
Natural gas	Average prices for residential customers have declined at least 30 percent in real terms since deregulation, and average prices for commercial and industrial customers have declined more than 30 percent. In addition, service has been more reliable as shortages have been almost completely eliminated.

Source: Clifford Winston, "U.S. Industry Adjustment to Economic Deregulation," *Journal of Economic Perspectives* 12(3) (Summer 1998): 89–110.

Long-distance telephone service has also been deregulated, and it is also a lot cheaper today than it was when AT&T was the only provider. Until 1984, AT&T had a virtual monopoly for local and long-distance telephone service. At the end of an antitrust suit against the company, AT&T agreed to divest itself of its local phone companies. Since then, the competition in long-distance has taken off. Rates have plummeted and options for consumers have soared. The court ruling, however, did nothing to promote competition for local telephone service. Rather, the regional phone companies, so-called Baby Bells, were spun off from AT&T, but became monopolies in their various regional markets. The Telecommunications Act of 1996 was designed to increase competition in the local telephone service market. As discussed in Chapter 10, competition for local telephone service has proceeded quite slowly.

But there are forces working in the opposite direction as well. Many businesses continue to turn to the government for protection from competition. Public choice theory suggests that more, not less, regulation is often demanded by firms threatened with competition at home and abroad. More and more people seem to demand environmental protection, including clear air, clean water, and regulation of hazardous waste and toxic waste. And there is little reason to expect less demand for regulations in the areas of civil rights, handicapped rights, gay rights, medical care, and elderly care.

The basic test of rationality—that marginal benefits exceed marginal costs—should guide the formulation of regulations. While economists often disagree about which, if any, consumer protection regulations are warranted, they do tend to agree that market incentives ought to be used when appropriate and that the most cost-effective policies should be pursued.

Check*list*

- Federal, state, and local governments regulate business practices. The rationale for such regulation is to protect consumers by (1) limiting the exercise of monopoly power, and (2) influencing business decisions that affect consumer and worker safety.
- The idea that business regulations serve the public interest is now widely challenged. One school of thought suggests that regulations are imposed because firms seek protection from competitors. Another suggests that bureaucratic interests, not the interests of the public, are served by regulation.
- Consumer protection laws may be necessary, but such protection has costs. Economists search for the most efficient way to achieve the objective of consumer protection and emphasize market incentives rather than bureaucratic mandates and regulations.

Try It Yourself 16-2

The deregulation of the airline industry has generally led to lower fares and increased quantities produced. Use the model of demand and supply to show this change. What has happened to consumer surplus in the market? (Hint: *You may want to refer back to Exhibit 6-8.)*

A Look Back

This chapter has shown that government intervention in markets takes the form of antitrust action to prevent the abuse of market power and regulations aimed at achieving socially desired objectives that are not or cannot be provided by an unregulated market system.

We saw that antitrust policy has evolved from a view that big business was bad business to an attempt to assess how the behavior of firms and the structure of markets affect social welfare and the public interest. The rule of reason rather than per se illegality guides most antitrust policy today, but because there is considerable debate concerning the appropriate role of government antitrust policy and regulation, application of the rule of reason in specific cases is uneven. Prosecution and enforcement of the nation's antitrust laws has varied over time.

The rising role of a global economy in the last half of the twentieth century reduced the degree of market power held by domestic firms. Policymakers are reconsidering antitrust policy and what types of joint ventures and cooperation among competing firms should be allowed. Antitrust policy has not been abandoned, but since the early 1980s it has been applied with greater consideration of its implications for the competitiveness of U.S. businesses against Asian, European, and other firms. Whether or not antitrust laws among nations will be made more compatible with each other is an issue for the future.

We saw that there are many different schools of thought concerning regulation. One group believes that regulation serves the public interest. Another believes that much current regulation protects regulated firms from competitive market forces and that the regulators are captured by the firms they are supposed to regulate. Yet another group points out that the regulators may do little more than serve their own interests, which include increasing the bureaucratic reach of their agencies.

Finally, the chapter looked at the complex issues surrounding consumer protection regulations. Consumer protection legislation has costs, borne by consumers and taxpayers. Economists are not in agreement concerning which, if any, consumer protection regulations are warranted. They do agree, however, that market incentives ought to be used when appropriate and that the most cost-effective policies should be pursued.

A Look Ahead This chapter concludes Part Five, which has focused on the role of government in the economy. As we move on to the next part that deals with a number of microeconomic issues, ranging from trade policies to environmental issues, the role of government in regulating the private economy will be very much a part of the discussion.

Terms and Concepts for Review

antitrust policy, **322**
illegal per se, **322**
rule of reason, **322**
price-fixing, **323**
horizontal merger, **324**
vertical merger, **324**
joint ventures, **326**
regulation, **328**
capture theory of regulation, **329**

For Discussion

1. Apex Manufacturing charges Zenith Manufacturing with predatory pricing (that is, selling below cost). What do you think the antitrust authorities will want to consider before they determine whether to prosecute Zenith for unfair practices in restraint of trade?
2. Some states require firms to close on Sunday. What types of firms support these laws? Why? What types of firms do not support these laws? Why?
3. Individual taxis in New York and Chicago must have permits, but there are only a fixed number of permits. Who benefits from such a regulation?
4. What do you predict is the impact on workers' wages of safety regulations in the workplace if the labor market is competitive?
5. Many states require barbers and beauticians to be licensed. Using the public interest theory of regulation as a base, what, if any, arguments could you make to support such a regulation? Do you think consumers gain from such regulations? Why not just allow anyone to open up a barber shop or beauty salon?
6. Suppose a landowner is required to refrain from developing his or her land in order to preserve the habitat of an endangered species. The restriction reduces the value of the land by 50 percent, to $1 million. Under present law, the landowner does not have to be compensated. Several proposals considered by Congress would require that this landowner be compensated. How does this affect the cost of the regulation?
7. A study by the Federal Trade Commission compared the prices of legal services in cities that allowed advertising by lawyers to prices of those same services in cities that didn't. It found that the prices of simple wills with trust provisions

were 11 percent higher in cities that did not allow advertising than they were in cities that did.[4] This, presumably, suggests the cost of such regulation. What might be the benefits? Do you think that such advertising should be restricted?

8. Economist Kip Viscusi studied the effects of federal regulations that require certain medicines be sold in childproof containers. He found that such requirements tended to increase the number of deaths from children ingesting these medications. How could this be? (*Hint:* Think in terms of the effect of the requirement on the cost of closing aspirin bottles and other medicine containers, and then apply the law of demand.)[5]

9. Explain how licensing requirements for providers of particular services result in higher prices for such services. Are such requirements justified? Why or why not?

10. What's so bad about price-fixing? Why does the government prohibit it?

11. In a 1956 antitrust case against DuPont, the Justice Department argued that the firm held a near monopoly in the cellophane market. DuPont argued that the definition of the market should be changed to include all wrapping paper. Why is this issue of market definition important? (DuPont's position prevailed.)

Problems

In 1986, Pepsi announced its intention to buy 7-Up, and Coca-Cola proposed buying Dr Pepper. The table below shows the market shares held by the soft-drink firms in 1986. Assume that the remaining 15 percent of the market is composed of 15 firms, each with a market share of 1 percent.

Company	Market share (percent)
Coca-Cola	39
PepsiCo	28
Dr Pepper	7
7-Up	6
R. J. Reynolds (Canada Dry and Sunkist)	5

1. Calculate the Herfindahl–Hirschman Index (HHI) for the industry as it was structured in 1986. (Refer to Chapter 11 to refresh your memory, if necessary.)
2. Calculate the postmerger HHI if only PepsiCo had bought 7-Up.
3. Calculate the postmerger HHI if only Coca-Cola had bought Dr Pepper.
4. How would you expect the Justice Department to respond to each merger considered separately? To both?

(By the way, the proposed mergers *were* challenged, and neither was completed.)

Answers to Try It Yourself Problems

Try It Yourself 16-1

In the case of Eastman Kodak, the Supreme Court argued that the rule of reason be applied. Even though the company held a dominant position in the film industry, its conduct was deemed reasonable. In the case of Alcoa, the U.S. Court of Appeals based its decision on the structure of the industry and argued that Alcoa's dominant position constituted a per se violation of the Sherman Act.

Try It Yourself 16-2

The fact that price (fares) fell and quantity rose tells us that the supply curve shifted to the right, from S_1 to S_2. Consumer surplus is the difference between the total benefit received by consumers and total expenditure by consumers. Before deregulation, when the price was B and the quantity was Q_1, the consumer surplus was BCD. The lower rates following deregulation reduced the price to consumers to, say, F, and increased the quantity to Q_2 on the graph, thereby increasing consumer surplus to FCG.

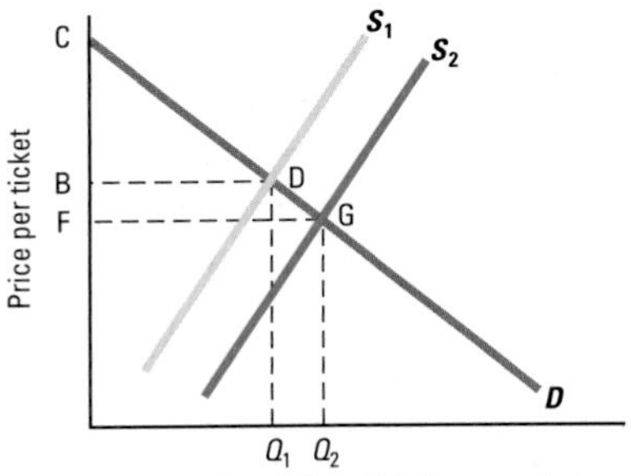

[4]See Carolyn Cox and Susan Foster, "The Costs and Benefits of Occupational Regulation," Federal Trade Commission, October 1990, p. 31.

[5]Viscusi, "The Lulling Effect: . . ." (see footnote 3).

17 International Trade

Getting Started: Trade Winds

Recent increases in the flow of goods and services between vastly different nations and cultures have changed what people eat, how they dress, and even how they communicate with one another. For you, increased trade has meant greater choice of what to buy and often lower prices. Look through your room. Chances are it is full of items from all around the world. The relatively free trade that exists today provides you with expanded choices. No one forced you to buy that shirt from India or that CD player from Japan. Presumably you bought them because you preferred them to other shirts and CD players you might have bought, perhaps because they had certain characteristics—style, color, perceived quality, or price—that you preferred.

Your gains are being experienced worldwide because the winds of international trade have blown generally freer in the past decade. Nations all over the world have dramatically lowered the barriers they impose on the products of other countries.

One region that was once closed to virtually all trade but is now open is Eastern Europe and the countries that made up the former Soviet Union. A key part of these countries' struggles to create market capitalist economic systems has been the opening of their borders to international trade.

In Western Europe, the members of the European Union (EU) have eliminated virtually every restriction on the free flow of goods and services among them. A truckload of electronic equipment from Italy now passes through France on its way to Spain with no more restrictions than would be encountered by a truck delivering goods from Michigan to Illinois. The purchase of the equipment can even be arranged using a new currency, the euro, which has been adopted by most EU nations.

Canada, Mexico, and the United States, while not adopting a common currency, have created a similar free trade area, the North American Free Trade Agreement (NAFTA). In addition, the 18 member nations of the Asian-Pacific Economic Cooperation organization (APEC) agreed in 1994 to forge a free trade area among industrialized nations such as the United States and Japan by 2010. Other member nations such as Mexico and China agreed to participate by 2020.

In 1995, the World Trade Organization (WTO) was established to "help trade flow smoothly, freely, fairly and predictably" among member nations. It now has more than 130 members and many other nations are clamoring to join. Since World War II, the General Agreement on Tariffs and Trade (GATT)—WTO's predecessor—and WTO have generated a series of agreements that slashed trade restraints among members. These agreements have helped propel trade, which in 1997 was 14 times its level in 1950.

Why have so many countries moved to make trade freer? What are the effects of free trade? Why do efforts to eliminate trade restrictions meet with resistance? Why do many nations continue to impose barriers against some foreign goods and services? How do such barriers affect the economy? How do such barriers affect *you?*

This chapter will answer these questions by developing a model of international trade based on the idea of comparative advantage, introduced in Chapter 2. The model predicts that free international trade will benefit the countries that participate in it. Free trade does not benefit everyone, however. Most people benefit from free trade, but some are hurt. We will then look at the phenomenon of two-way trade, in which countries both import and export the same goods. The last part of the chapter examines the effects of trade restrictions and evaluates the arguments made for such restrictions. Economists tend to be skeptical of their validity.

The Gains from Trade

To model the effects of trade, we begin by looking at a hypothetical country that does not engage in trade and then see how its production and consumption change when it does engage in trade.

Production and Consumption Without International Trade

Suppose the country of Roadway is completely isolated from the rest of the world. It neither exports nor imports goods and services. We shall use the production possibilities model to analyze Roadway's ability to produce goods and services.

A production possibilities curve illustrates the production choices available to an economy. Recall from Chapter 2 that the production possibilities curve for a particular country is determined by the factors of production and the technology available to it.

Exhibit 17-1 shows a production possibilities curve for Roadway that produces only two goods—trucks and boats. Roadway must be operating somewhere on its production possibilities curve or it will be wasting resources; it will be engaging in inefficient production. If it were operating inside the curve at a point such as D, then a combination on the curve, such as B, would provide more of both goods (Roadway produces 3,000 more trucks and 3,000 more boats per year at B than at D). At any point inside the curve, Roadway's production would not be efficient. Point E suggests an even higher level of output than points A, B, or C, but because point E lies outside Roadway's production possibilities curve, it cannot be attained.

We saw in Chapter 2 that the absolute value of the slope of a production possibilities curve at any point gives the quantity of the good on the vertical axis that must be given up to produce an additional unit of the good on the horizontal axis. It thus gives the opportunity cost of producing another unit of the good on the horizontal axis.

Exhibit 17-2 shows the opportunity cost of producing boats at points A, B, and C. Recall that the slope of a curve at any point is equal to the slope of a line drawn tangent to the curve at that point. The slope of a line tangent to the production possibilities curve at point B, for example, is −1. The opportunity cost of producing one more boat is thus 1; at point B, one truck must be given up to produce an additional boat. As the law of increasing opportunity costs predicts, in order to produce more boats, Roadway must give up more and more trucks for each additional boat. Roadway's opportunity cost of producing boats increases as we travel to the right on its production possibilities curve.

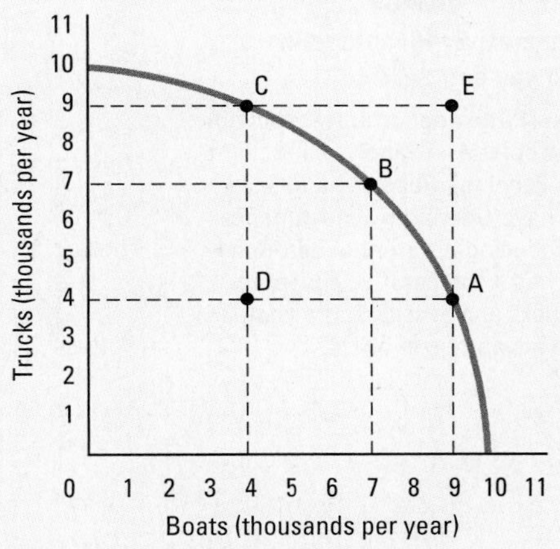

Exhibit 17-1

Roadway's Production Possibilities Curve

The production possibilities curve for Roadway shows the combinations of trucks and boats that it can produce, given the factors of production and technology available to it. To maximize the value of total production, Roadway must operate somewhere along this curve. Production at point D implies that Roadway is failing to use its resources fully and efficiently; production at point E is unattainable.

Comparative Advantage

People participate in international trade because they make themselves better off by doing so. In this section we'll find that countries that participate in international trade are able to consume more of all goods and services than they could consume while producing in isolation from the rest of the world.

Suppose the world consists of two countries, Roadway and Seaside. Their production possibilities curves are given in Exhibit 17-3. Roadway's production

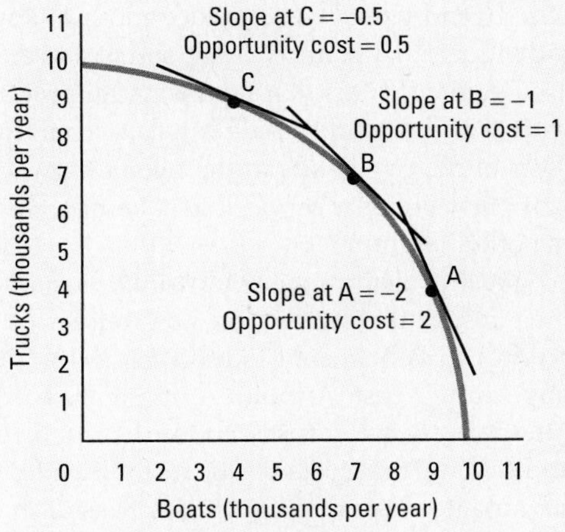

Exhibit 17-2

Measuring Opportunity Cost in Roadway

The slope of the production possibilities curve at any point is equal to the slope of a line tangent to the curve at that point. The absolute value of that slope equals the opportunity cost of increased boat production. Moving down and to the right along its production possibilities curve, the opportunity cost of boat production increases; this is an application of the law of increasing cost introduced in Chapter 2.

Exhibit 17-3

Comparative Advantage in Roadway and Seaside

Because their opportunity costs differ at point A in Panel (a) and point A′ in Panel (b), Roadway and Seaside have comparative advantages in producing different goods. Roadway has a comparative advantage in trucks and Seaside has a comparative advantage in boats.

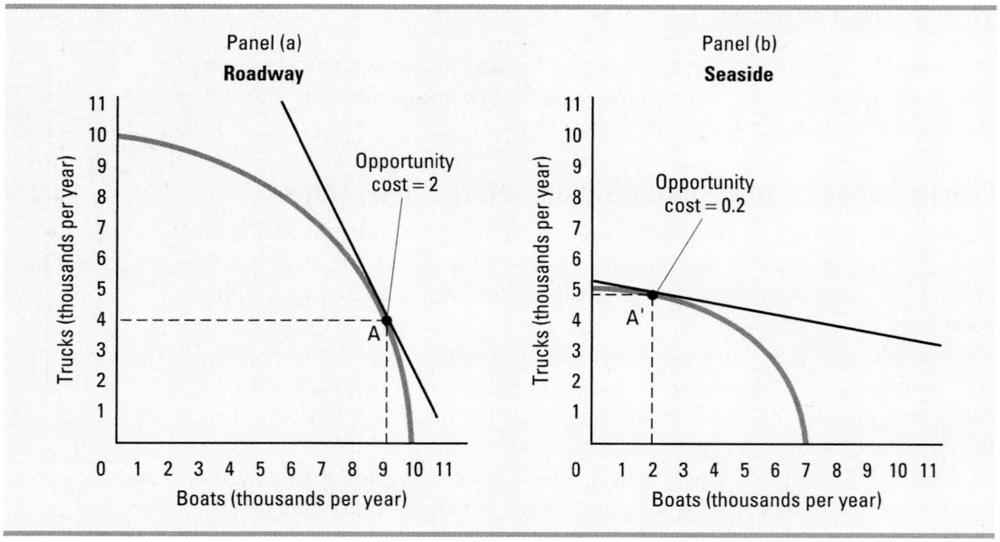

possibilities curve in Panel (a) is the same as the one in Exhibits 17-1 and 17-2. Seaside's curve is given in Panel (b).

Each country produces two goods, boats and trucks. Suppose no trade occurs between the two countries and that they are each currently operating on their production possibilities curves at points A and A′ in Exhibit 17-3. We'll assume that the two countries have chosen to operate at these points through the workings of demand and supply. That is, resources have been guided to their current uses as producers have responded to the demands of consumers in the two countries.

The two countries differ in their respective abilities to produce trucks and boats. As we can see by looking at the intersection of the production possibilities curves with the vertical axes in Exhibit 17-3, Roadway is able to produce more trucks than Seaside. If Roadway concentrated all of its resources on the production of trucks, it could produce 10,000 trucks per year. Seaside could produce only 5,000. Now look at the intersection of the production possibilities curves with the horizontal axes. If Roadway concentrated all of its resources on the production of boats, it could produce 10,000 boats. Seaside could produce only 7,000 boats. Because Roadway is capable of producing more of both goods, we can infer that it has more resources or is able to use its labor resources more productively than Seaside. When an economy or individual can produce more of any good per unit of labor than another country or individual, that country or person is said to have an **absolute advantage.**

Despite the fact that Roadway can produce more of both goods, it can still gain from trade with Seaside—and Seaside can gain from trade with Roadway. The key lies in the opportunity costs of the two goods in the two countries. The country with a lower opportunity cost for a particular good or service has a comparative advantage in producing it and will export it to the other country.

We can determine opportunity costs in the two countries by comparing the slopes of their respective production possibilities curves at the points where they are producing. At point A in Panel (a) of Exhibit 17-3, 1 additional boat costs 2 trucks in Roadway; that is its opportunity cost. At point A′ in Panel (b), 1 additional boat in Seaside costs only 0.2 truck. Alternatively, we can ask about the opportunity cost of an additional truck. In Roadway, an additional truck costs 0.5 boat. In Seaside, it costs 5 boats. Roadway thus has a comparative advantage in producing trucks; Seaside has a comparative advantage in producing boats. This situation is suggested pictorially in Exhibit 17-4.

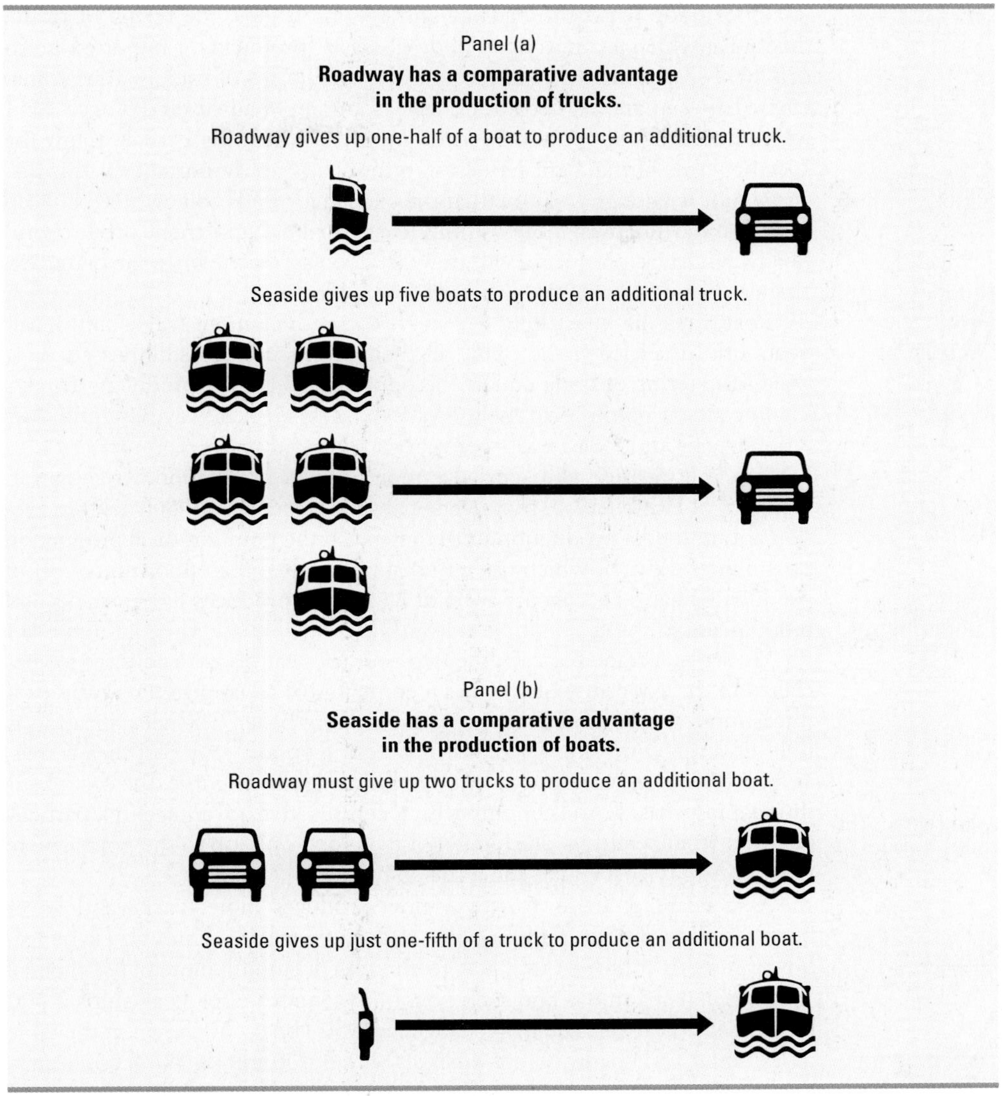

Panel (a)
Roadway has a comparative advantage in the production of trucks.
Roadway gives up one-half of a boat to produce an additional truck.
Seaside gives up five boats to produce an additional truck.
Panel (b)
Seaside has a comparative advantage in the production of boats.
Roadway must give up two trucks to produce an additional boat.
Seaside gives up just one-fifth of a truck to produce an additional boat.

Exhibit 17-4

A Picture of Comparative Advantage in Roadway and Seaside

The exhibit gives a picture of Roadway's comparative advantage in trucks and Seaside's comparative advantage in boats.

Specialization and the Gains from Trade

We have so far assumed that no trade occurs between Roadway and Seaside. Now let us assume that trade opens up. The fact that the opportunity costs differ between the two countries suggests the possibility for mutually advantageous trade. The opportunities created by trade will induce a greater degree of specialization in both countries, specialization that reflects comparative advantage.

Trade and Specialization Before trade, truck producers in Roadway could exchange a truck for half a boat. In Seaside, however, a truck could be exchanged for 5 boats. Once trade opens between the two countries, truck producers in Roadway will rush to export trucks to Seaside.

Boat producers in Seaside enjoy a similar bonanza. Before trade, one of their boats could be exchanged for one-fifth of a truck. By shipping their boats to Roadway, they can get more trucks for each boat. Boat producers in Seaside will rush to export boats to Roadway.

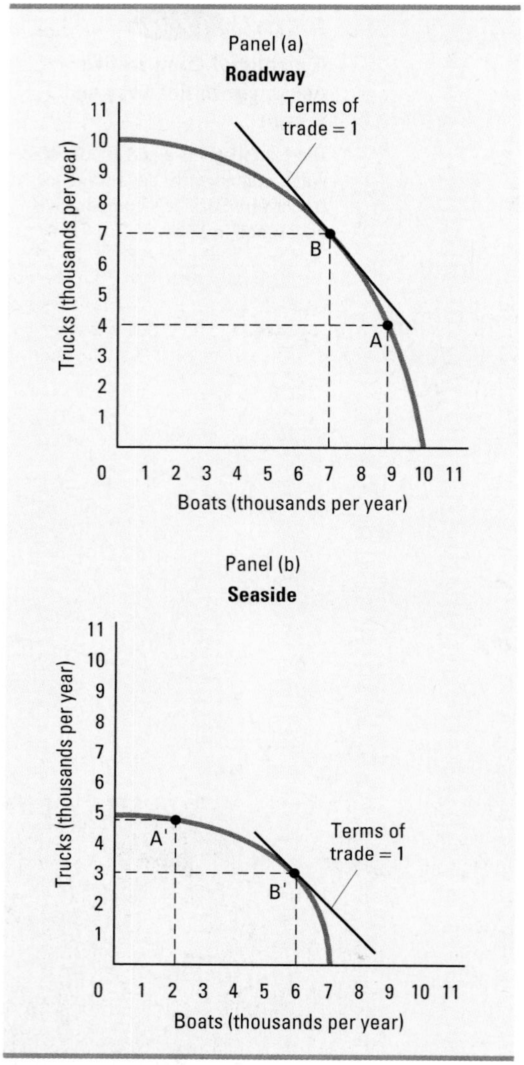

Exhibit 17-5

International Trade Induces Greater Specialization

Before trade, Roadway is producing at point A in Panel (a) and Seaside is producing at point A′ in Panel (b). The terms of trade are 1, meaning that 1 boat exchanges for 1 truck. Each country moves along its production possibilities curve to the point that has a slope of −1. Roadway moves to point B, producing more trucks and fewer boats. Seaside moves to point B′, producing more boats and fewer trucks. Trade leads each country to a greater degree of specialization in the good in which it has a comparative advantage.

Once trade between Roadway and Seaside begins, **the terms of trade**, the rate at which a country can trade domestic products for imported products, will seek a market equilibrium. The final terms of trade will be somewhere between one-half boat for 1 truck found in Roadway and 5 boats for 1 truck in Seaside. Suppose the terms of trade is 1 boat for 1 truck. (How the specific terms of trade are actually determined is not important for this discussion. It is enough to know that the exchange rate is somewhere between Seaside's and Roadway's opportunity costs for boat and truck production.) Roadway's truck producers will now get 1 boat per truck—a far better exchange than was available to them before trade.

Roadway's manufacturers will move to produce more trucks and fewer boats until they reach the point on their production possibilities curve at which the terms of trade equals the opportunity cost of producing trucks. That occurs at point B in Panel (a) of Exhibit 17-5; Roadway now produces 7,000 trucks and 7,000 boats per year.

Similarly, Seaside will specialize more in boat production. As shown in Panel (b) of Exhibit 17-5, producers will shift resources out of truck production and into boat production until they reach the point on their production possibilities curve at which the terms of trade equal the opportunity cost of producing boats. This occurs at point B'; Seaside produces 3,000 trucks and 6,000 boats per year.

We see that trade between the two countries causes each country to specialize in the good in which it has a comparative advantage. Roadway produces more trucks, and Seaside produces more boats. The specialization is not, however, complete. The law of increasing opportunity cost means that, as an economy moves along its production possibilities curve, the cost of additional units rises. An economy with a comparative advantage in a particular good will expand its production of that good only up to the point where its opportunity cost equals the terms of trade.

As a result of trade, Roadway now produces more trucks and fewer boats. Seaside produces more boats and fewer trucks. Through exchange, however, both countries are likely to end up consuming more of *both* goods.

Exhibit 17-6 shows one such possibility. Suppose Roadway ships 2,500 trucks per year to Seaside in exchange for 2,500 boats, as shown in the table in Exhibit 17-6. Roadway thus emerges with 4,500 trucks (the 7,000 it produces at B minus the 2,500 it ships) and 9,500 boats. It has 500 more of each good than it did before trade.

How does Seaside fare? When trade began, factors of production shifted into boat production, in which Seaside had a comparative advantage. Seaside tripled its production of boats—from 2,000 per year to 6,000 per year. It sends 2,500 of those boats to Roadway, so it ends up with 3,500 boats per year. It reduces its production of trucks to 3,000 per year, but receives 2,500 more from Roadway. That leaves it with 5,500. Seaside emerges from the opening of trade with 1,500 more boats and 1,500 more trucks than it had before trade.

As Roadway trades trucks for boats, its production remains at point B. But it now consumes combination C; it has more of both goods than it had at A, the solution before trade. Seaside's production remains at point B', but it now consumes at point C', where it has more trucks and more boats than it had before trade.

Although all countries can increase their consumption through trade, not everyone in those countries will be happy with the result. In the case of Roadway and Seaside, for example, some boat producers in Roadway will be displaced as cheaper boats arrive from Seaside. Some truck producers in Seaside will be displaced as cheaper trucks arrive from Roadway. The production possibilities model suggests that the resources displaced will ultimately find more pro-

Production and Consumption of Trucks and Boats

	Roadway				Seaside			
	Production		Consumption		Production		Consumption	
	BT	AT	BT	AT	BT	AT	BT	AT
Trucks	4,000	7,000	4,000	4,500	4,750	3,000	4,750	5,500
Boats	9,000	7,000	9,000	9,500	2,000	6,000	2,000	3,500

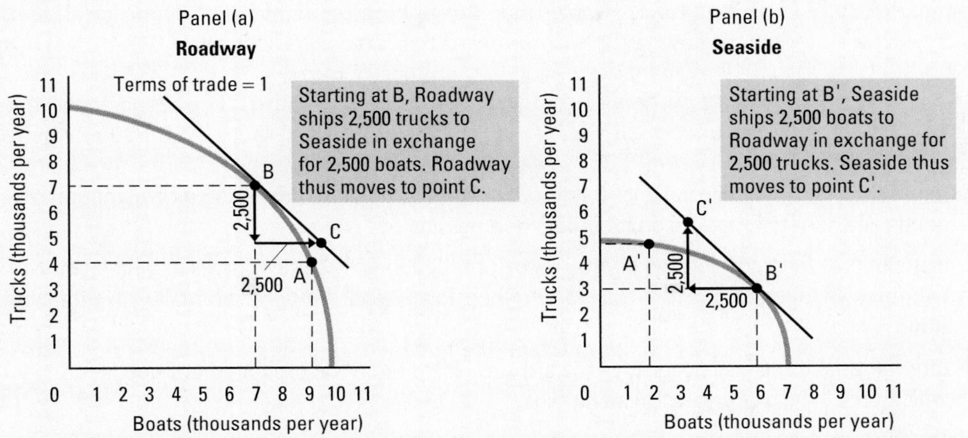

Exhibit 17-6

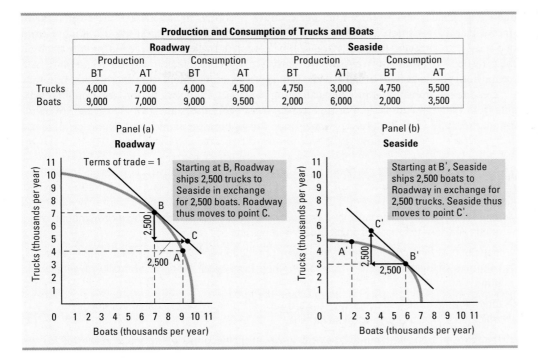

The Mutual Benefits of Trade

Roadway and Seaside each consume more of both goods when there is trade between them. The table shows values of production and consumption for each country before trade (BT) and after trade (AT). Here, the terms of trade are 1 truck in exchange for 1 boat. Roadway exports 2,500 trucks to Seaside in exchange for 2,500 boats and ends up at point C; Seaside ends up at point C'.

Case in Point America's Shifting Comparative Advantage

What is America's comparative advantage? A look at the country from an airplane on a cross-country flight suggests one answer. Its vast open spaces give the United States a comparative advantage in the production of agricultural products. But this traditional answer is outdated—agricultural goods account for only a small share of U.S. exports.

Doomsayers suggest that our comparative advantage in the twenty-first century will lie in flipping hamburgers and sweeping the floors around Japanese computers. This forecast makes for good jokes, but it hardly squares with the facts. America's comparative advantage now lies largely in the production of high-tech capital equipment.

In 1960, only 20 percent of the capital goods produced in the United States were exported; by 1997 over 43 percent were. Capital goods now account for more than half of the goods exported by the United States.

Tom Saponas, a plant manager for Hewlett-Packard, which manufactures electronic capital goods, suggests that the source of the U.S. advantage lies in what might be called a climate of innovation. "The Japanese are generally superior to us in high-volume production," he says. "Where we excel is in producing difficult-to-make, low-volume things—the kinds of capital firms often need. I think that's a result of a greater emphasis here on entrepreneurial effort and problem solving. It fosters more flexibility and an ability to respond more quickly to technological change."

The emergence of the United States as a world leader in capital goods production puts it atop two rising global tides. First, the world is becoming more capital-intensive generally. In the last 20 years, the share of world output devoted to capital goods has risen to 26 percent from 22 percent. Second, firms all over the world are demanding more and more high-tech capital, a segment of the capital goods sector in which the United States is particularly dominant. The effort of other countries to acquire

more capital—and especially more high-tech capital—has become a bonanza for the United States. Economist Lawrence Lindsey, a former member of the Board of Governors of the United States Federal Reserve System, says that each 1 percent rise in world investment spending translates into a 1.5 percent boost in U.S. exports of capital goods.

Sources: Lawrence B. Lindsey, "America's Growing Lead," *Wall Street Journal,* 7 February 1992; Department of Commerce data; personal interview with Tom Saponas.

ductive uses. They will produce trucks in Roadway and boats in Seaside. *But* there will be a period of painful transition as workers and owners of capital and natural resources move from one activity to another. That transition will be completed when the two countries are back on their respective production possibilities curves. Full employment will be restored, which means both countries will be back at the same level of employment they had before trade.

Despite the transitional problems affecting some factors of production, the potential benefits from free trade are large. For this reason, most economists are strongly in favor of opening markets and extending international trade throughout the world. The economic case has been a powerful force in moving the world toward freer trade.

Checklist

- In order to maximize the value of its output, a country must be producing a combination of goods and services that lies on its production possibilities curve.
- If the opportunity costs at the points on the production possibilities curves at which two countries are operating before trade differ, there is an opportunity for mutually advantageous trade.
- International trade leads countries toward specialization in the production of goods for which they have a comparative advantage.
- The terms of trade determine the extent to which each country will specialize. Each will increase production of the good or service in which it has a comparative advantage up to the point where the opportunity cost of producing it equals the terms of trade.
- Free international trade can increase the availability of all goods and services in all the countries that participate in it.

Try It Yourself 17-1

Suppose the world consists of two countries, Alpha and Beta. Both produce only two goods, computers and washing machines. Suppose that Beta is much more populous than Alpha, but because workers in Alpha have more physical and human capital, Alpha is able to produce more of both goods than Beta.

Specifically, suppose that if Alpha devotes all its factors of production to computers, it is able to produce 10,000 per month, and if it devotes all its factors to washing machines, it is able to produce 10,000 per month. Suppose the equivalent amounts for Beta are 8,000 computers and 8,000 washing machines per month. Sketch typical, bowed-out production possibilities curves for the two countries. (You only have numbers for the end points of the production possibilities curves. Use them to sketch curves of a typical shape.)

Assume the computers and washing machines produced in the two countries are identical. Assume that no trade occurs between the two countries. In Alpha, at the point on its production possibilities curve at which it is operating, the opportunity cost of an additional washing machine is 0.5 computer. At the point on its production possibilities curve at which it is operating, the opportunity cost of an additional washing machine in Beta is 3.5 computers. How many computers exchange for a washing machine in Alpha? Beta?

Now suppose trade occurs, and the terms of trade are 1.5. How will the production of the two goods be affected in each economy?

Two-Way Trade

The model of trade presented thus far assumed that countries specialize in producing the good in which they have a comparative advantage and, therefore, engage in one-way trade. **One-way (or interindustry) trade** occurs when countries specialize in producing the goods in which they have a comparative advantage and then export those goods so they can import the goods in which they do not have a comparative advantage.

However, when we look at world trade, we also see countries exchanging the same goods or goods in the same industry category. For example, the United States may both export construction materials to Canada and import them from Canada. American car buyers can choose Chevrolets, Fords, and Chryslers. They can also choose imported cars such as Toyotas. Japanese car buyers may choose to purchase Toyotas—or imported cars such as Chevrolets, Fords, and Chryslers. The United States imports cars from Japan and exports cars to it. Conversely, Japan imports cars from the United States and exports cars to it. International trade in which countries both import and export the same or similar goods is called **two-way (or intraindustry) trade.**

Two reasons why countries import and export the same goods are variations in transportation costs and seasonal effects. In the example of the United States and Canada both importing and exporting construction materials, transportation costs are the likely explanation. It may be cheaper for a contractor in northern Maine to import construction materials from the eastern part of Canada than to buy them in the United States. For a contractor in Vancouver, it may be cheaper to import construction materials from somewhere in the western part of the United States than to buy them in Canada. By engaging in trade, both the American and Canadian contractors save on transportation costs. Seasonal factors explain why the United States both imports fruit from and exports fruit to Chile.

Another explanation of two-way trade in similar goods lies in recognizing that not all goods are produced under conditions of perfect competition. Once this assumption is relaxed, we can explain two-way trade in terms of a key feature of monopolistic competition and some cases of oligopoly: product differentiation. Suppose two countries have similar endowments of factors of production and technologies available to them, but their products are differentiated—clocks produced by different manufacturers, for example, are different. Consumers in the United States buy some clocks produced in Switzerland, just as consumers in Switzerland purchase some clocks produced in the United States. Indeed, if two countries are similar in their relative endowments of factors of production and in the technologies available to them, two-way trade based on product differentiation is likely to be more significant than one-way trade based on comparative advantage. For example, one study showed that two-way trade made up two-thirds of the volume of trade between the United States and other high-income countries, whereas between the United States and lower-income countries nearly two-thirds of trade was one-way trade.[1]

In comparison to the expansion of one-way trade based on comparative advantage, expansion of two-way trade may entail lower adjustment costs. In the case of two-way trade, there is specialization within industries rather than movement of factors of production out of industries that compete with newly imported goods and into export industries. Such adjustments are likely to be faster and less painful for labor and for the owners of the capital and natural resources involved.

The fact that two-way trade dominates among the countries of the European Union may be one reason for its success in removing trade barriers. Exhibit 17-7 indicates the extent and growth of two-way trade in the European Union. It shows the tendency for two-way trade to dominate among countries at high levels of per capita income. Only for Greece, the poorest country in the European Union, is two-way trade rather limited.

[1]Claudy Culem and Lars Lundberg, "The Product Pattern of Two-Way Trade: Stability Among Countries over Time," *Weltwirtschaftliches Archiv* 122(1)(1986):113–130.

Country	Percentage of Total Trade 1970	1980	1987	1995	1996	1997
Belgium–Luxembourg	69	76	77	77	80	81
Denmark	41	52	57	65	65	67
Germany	73	78	76	80	80	80
Greece	22	24	31	27	27	27
Spain	35	57	64	72	73	72
France	76	83	83	86	86	87
Ireland	35	61	62	53	53	53
Italy	63	55	57	61	60	61
Netherlands	67	73	76	61	60	61
Austria	na	na	na	71	71	75
Portugal	23	32	37	52	55	55
Finland	na	na	na	51	48	55
Sweden	na	na	na	69	69	70
United Kingdom	74	81	77	80	80	80

na = not available.

Source: European Commission, "Economic Reform: Report on the Functioning of Community Product and Capital Markets," 1999, Figure A-1 at http://europa.eu.int/comm/dg15en/update/econ/cardiffenpdf

Because two-way trade occurs in the context of imperfect competition, we cannot expect it to meet the efficiency standards of one-way trade based on comparative advantage and the underlying assumption of perfectly competitive markets. But, as we discussed in Chapter 11, the inefficiency must be weighed against the benefits derived from product differentiation. People in the United States are not limited to buying only the kinds of cars produced in the United States, just as people in Japan are not limited to buying only cars produced in Japan.

Exhibit 17-7

Two-Way Trade in the European Union (percentage of total trade)

Two-way trade now accounts for the bulk of trade among the countries of the European Union.

Checklist

- Specialization and trade according to comparative advantage leads to one-way trade.
- A large percentage of trade among countries with similar factor endowments is two-way trade, in which countries import and export the same or similar goods.
- Two-way trade in the same goods is often explained by variations in transportation costs and seasonal factors; in similar goods it often occurs in the context of models of imperfect competition.
- Adjustment costs associated with expansion of two-way trade may be lower than for expansion of one-way trade.

Case in Point: Two-Way Trade in Water?

Water is an export of the United States to Russia; it is also an import from Russia to the United States.

Both are traded through Seattle-based Thomas International Inc. Owner Thomas Wilbur admits that American-made Talking Rain and Siberian-made Monastirskaya are nearly identical in content and are similarly processed before bottling. However, they convey different messages to consumers in the different countries. According to Mr. Wilbur, Monastirskaya seems to Americans to be blessed. It comes from a 132-foot well near a Russian Orthodox monastery located in the Siberian forests. The label on the bottle pictures 34 monks who live in the monastery. In Russia, Talking Rain has the aura of America.

Most trade between Russia and the United States is one-way, with the United States buying natural resources from its relatively poor trading partner and Russia buying agricultural products and manufactured goods from the United States. According to Mr. Wilbur, "We're one of the first to bring in a finished product from the Russian Far East into the U.S." That the transaction is part of a two-way trade makes it even more unusual.

Source: *Puget Sound Business Journal* 18, Issue 21 (3–9 October 1997): 2.

Restrictions on International Trade

In spite of the strong theoretical case that can be made for free international trade, every country in the world has erected at least some barriers to trade. Trade restrictions are typically undertaken in an effort to protect companies and workers in the home economy from competition by foreign firms. A **protectionist policy** is one in which a country restricts the importation of goods and services produced in foreign countries. The United States, for example, uses protectionist policies to limit the quantity of foreign-produced sugar coming into the United States. The effect of this policy is to reduce the supply of sugar in the U.S. market and increase the price of sugar, thus reducing the quantity consumed. In general, protectionist policies imposed for a particular good always reduce its supply, raise its price, and reduce the equilibrium quantity, as shown in Exhibit 17-8. Protection often takes the form of an import tax or a limit on the amount that can be imported, but it can also come in the form of voluntary export restrictions and other barriers.

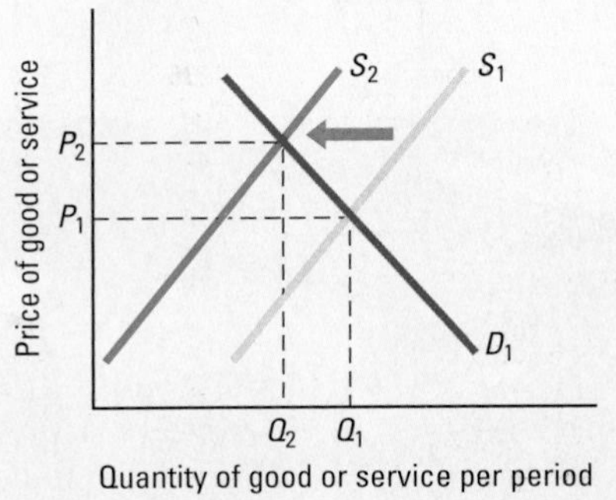

Exhibit 17-8

The Impact of Protectionist Policies

Protectionist policies reduce the quantities of foreign goods and services supplied to the country that imposes the restriction. As a result, such policies shift the supply curve to the left for the good or service whose imports are restricted. In the case shown, the supply curve shifts to S_2, the equilibrium price rises to P_2, and the equilibrium quantity falls to Q_2.

Tariffs

A **tariff** is a tax on imported goods and services. The average tariff on dutiable imports in the United States (that is, those imports on which a tariff is imposed) is about 4 percent. Some imports have much higher tariffs. For example, the U.S. tariff on imported frozen orange juice is 35 cents per gallon (which amounts to about 40 percent of value). The tariff on imported canned tuna is 35 percent, and the tariff on imported shoes ranges between 2 and 48 percent.

A tariff raises the cost of selling imported goods. It thus shifts the supply curve for goods to the left, as in Exhibit 17-8. The price of the protected good rises and the quantity available to consumers falls.

Quotas

A **quota** is a direct restriction on the total quantity of a good or service that may be imported during a specified period. Quotas restrict total supply and therefore increase the domestic price of the good or service on which they are imposed. Quotas generally specify that an exporting country's share of a domestic market may not exceed a certain limit.

In some cases, quotas are set to raise the domestic price to a particular level. Congress requires the Department of Agriculture, for example, to impose quotas on imported sugar to keep the wholesale price in the United States above 22 cents per pound. The world price is typically less than 10 cents per pound.

A quota restricting the quantity of a particular good imported into an economy shifts the supply curve to the left, as in Exhibit 17-8. It raises price and reduces quantity.

An important distinction between quotas and tariffs is that quotas don't increase costs to foreign producers; tariffs do. In the short run, a tariff will reduce the profits of foreign exporters of a good or service. A quota, however, raises price but not costs of production and thus may increase profits. Because the quota imposes a limit on quantity, any profits it creates in other countries won't induce the entry of new firms that ordinarily eliminates profits in perfect competition.

Voluntary Export Restrictions

Voluntary export restrictions are a form of trade barrier by which foreign firms agree to limit the quantity of goods exported to a particular country. They came to prominence in the United States in the 1980s, when the U.S. government persuaded foreign exporters of automobiles and steel to agree to limit their exports to the United States.

Although such restrictions are called voluntary, they typically are agreed to only after pressure is applied by the country whose industries they protect. The United States, for

Case in Point The Quota Bonanza for Japanese Automakers

The U.S. government pressured Japanese automakers in 1981 to accept voluntary restrictions on their exports of cars to the United States. The restrictions proved to be a bonanza for Japanese as well as for American automakers.

The restriction shifted the supply curve of foreign cars to the left. Prices of Japanese cars in the United States rose by about $2,500. The higher prices for a substitute increased the demand for American-produced cars. The prices of American cars rose by about the same amount. But higher prices weren't the only result of the export restriction.

The agreement set a limit on the *number* of vehicles Japan could export to the United States. When it was imposed, virtually all of Japan's export autos were compact cars. But Japanese automakers began shifting to production of midsize and luxury cars like the Lexus, for which their accounting profit per car is higher.

Although the restrictions boosted profits for Japanese companies, each individual company had an incentive to raise profits even more by finding ways to avoid the restriction. The easiest way to do that was to establish production plants in the United States. Cars built in the United States by Japanese-owned firms aren't counted as Japanese exports. Honda Motor Company opened the first of these "transplants" in the United States in 1982. Toyota's "transplants" employ more than 25,000 people in the United States, and in 1999 more than half the Toyotas sold in the United States were built in the United States. The export limitation agreement has played an important role in shifting Japanese production to the United States.

example, has succeeded in pressuring many other countries to accept quotas limiting their exports of goods ranging from sweaters to steel.

A voluntary export restriction works precisely like an ordinary quota. It raises prices for the domestic product and reduces the quantity consumed of the good or service affected by the quota. It can also increase the profits of the firms that agree to the quota, because it raises the price they receive for their products.

Other Barriers

In addition to tariffs and quotas, measures such as safety standards, labeling requirements, pollution controls, and quality restrictions all may have the effect of restricting imports.

Many restrictions aimed at protecting consumers in the domestic market create barriers as a purely unintended, and probably desirable, side effect. For example, limitations on insecticide levels in foods are often more stringent in the United States than in other countries. These standards tend to discourage the import of foreign goods, but their primary purpose appears to be to protect consumers from harmful chemicals, not to restrict trade. But other nontariff barriers seem to serve no purpose other than to keep foreign goods out. Tomatoes produced in Mexico, for example, compete with those produced in the United States. But Mexican tomatoes tend to be smaller than U.S. tomatoes. The United States has long imposed size restrictions to "protect" U.S. *consumers* from small tomatoes. The result is a highly effective trade barrier that protects U.S. *producers* and raises U.S. tomato prices.

Justifications for Trade Restriction: An Evaluation

The conceptual justification for free trade is one of the oldest arguments in economics; there is no disputing the logic of the argument that free trade increases global production, worldwide consumption, and international efficiency. But critics stress that the argument is a theoretical one. In the real world, they say, there are several arguments that can be made to justify protectionist measures.

Infant Industries One argument for trade barriers is that they serve as a kind of buffer to protect fledgling domestic industries. Initially, firms in a new industry may be too small to achieve significant economies of scale and could be clobbered by established firms in other countries. A new domestic industry with potential economies of scale is called an **infant industry.**

Consider the situation in which firms in a country are attempting to enter a new industry in which many large firms already exist in the international arena. The foreign firms have taken advantage of economies of scale and have therefore achieved relatively low levels of production costs. New firms, facing low levels of output and higher average costs, may find it difficult to compete. The infant industry argument suggests that by offering protection during an industry's formative years, a tariff or quota may allow the new industry to develop and prosper.

The infant industry argument played a major role in tariff policy in the early years of U.S. development. Exhibit 17-9 shows average tariff rates on dutiable imports in the United States since 1820. The high tariffs of the early nineteenth century were typically justified as being necessary to allow U.S. firms to gain a competitive foothold in the world economy. As domestic industries became established, tariff rates fell. Subsequent increases in tariffs were a response in part to internal crises: the Civil War and the Great Depression. Tariff rates have fallen dramatically since 1930.

Critics of the infant industry argument say that once protection is in place, it may be very difficult to remove. Inefficient firms, they contend, may be able to survive for long periods under the umbrella of infant industry protection.

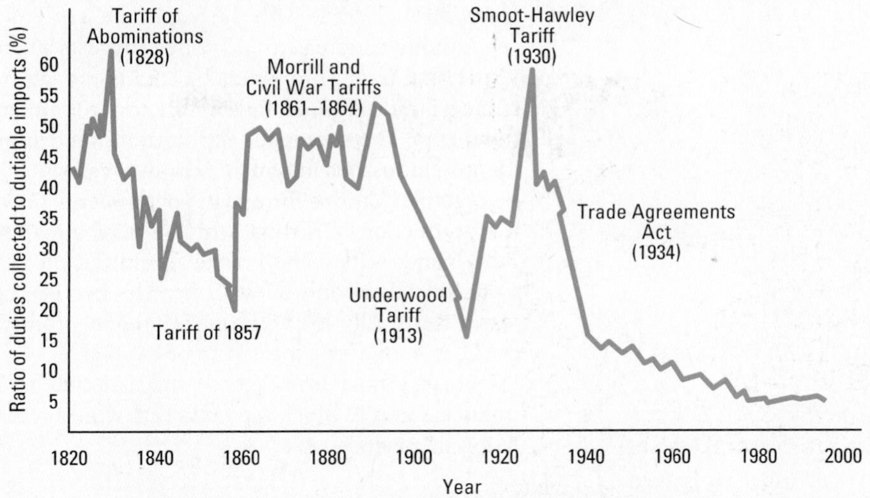

Source: *Historical Statistics, Colonial Times to 1970; Statistical Abstract of the United States, 1998,* Table no. 1325; *Statistical Abstract of the United States, 1990.*

Exhibit 17-9

Average U.S. Tariff Rates, 1820–1996

The average U.S. tariff on dutiable (taxable) imports was high early in the nineteenth century; then it fell. It rose again during the Civil War and the Great Depression. Tariff rates have fallen quite sharply since 1930.

Strategic Trade Policy A new version of the infant industry argument has been used in the past few years as technological developments have spawned whole new industries and transformed existing ones. The new version of the infant industry argument assumes an imperfectly competitive market.

Suppose technological change has given rise to a new industry. Given the economies of scale in this industry, only a few firms are likely to dominate it worldwide—it will likely emerge as an oligopoly. The firms that dominate the industry are likely to earn economic profits that will persist. Furthermore, because there will be only a few firms, they will be located in only a few countries. Their governments could conceivably impose taxes on these firms' profits that would enhance economic well being within the country. The potential for such gains may justify government efforts to assist firms seeking to acquire a dominant position in the new industry.

Government aid could take the form of protectionist trade policies aimed at allowing these firms to expand in the face of foreign competition, assistance with research and development efforts, programs to provide workers with special skills needed by the industry, or subsidies in the form of direct payments or special tax treatment. Any such policy aimed at promoting the development of key industries that may increase a country's domestic well-being through trade with the rest of the world is known as a **strategic trade policy.**

Although strategic trade policy suggests a conceptually positive role for government in international trade, proponents of the approach note that it has dangers. Firms might use the strategic trade argument even if their development were unlikely to offer the gains specified in the theory. The successful application of the approach requires that the government correctly identify industries in which a country can, in fact, gain dominance—something that may not be possible. Various European governments provided subsidies to firms that were involved in the production of Airbus, which is now a major competitor in the airplane industry. On the other hand, Britain and France subsidized the development of the supersonic plane called the Concorde. After only a few Concordes had been produced, it became obvious that the aircraft was a financially losing proposition and production was halted. A few Concordes fly today, but they are never expected to be profitable.

Finally, those firms whose success strategic trade policy promotes might have sufficient political clout to block the taxes that would redistribute the gains of the policies to the population in general.

National Security It is sometimes argued that the security of the United States would be threatened if this country depended on foreign powers as the primary source of strategic materials. In time of war, the United States might be cut off from sources of foreign supply and lose some of the materials upon which U.S. industry depends.

One area where the national security argument is applied is the oil industry. Given the volatility of the political situation in the Middle East, some people say, the United States should protect the domestic oil industry in order to ensure adequate production capability in the event Middle Eastern supplies are cut off.

An alternative to tariff protection of strategic commodities is to stockpile those commodities for use in time of crisis. For example, the United States maintains a strategic petroleum reserve for use in case of a cutoff in foreign supplies.

Job Protection The desire to maintain existing jobs threatened by foreign competition is probably the single most important source of today's protectionist policies. Some industries that at one time had a comparative advantage are no longer among the world's lowest-cost producers; they struggle to stay afloat. Cost cutting leads to layoffs, and layoffs lead to demands for protection.

The model of international trade in perfect competition suggests that trade will threaten some industries. As countries specialize in activities in which they have a comparative advantage, sectors in which they don't have this advantage will shrink. Maintaining those sectors through trade barriers blocks a nation from enjoying the gains possible from free trade.

A further difficulty with the use of trade barriers to shore up employment in a particular sector is that it can be an enormously expensive strategy. Suppose enough of a foreign good is kept out of the United States to save one U.S. job. That shifts the supply curve slightly to the left, raising prices for U.S. consumers and reducing their consumer surplus. The loss to consumers is the cost per job saved. Estimates of the cost of saving *one* job in the steel industry through restrictions on steel imports, for example, go as high as $800,000 per year.

Cheap Foreign Labor One reason often given for the perceived need to protect American workers against free international trade is that workers must be protected against cheap foreign labor. This is an extension of the job protection argument in the previous section. From a theoretical point of view, of course, if foreign countries can produce a good at lower cost than we can, it is in our collective interest to obtain it from them. But workers counter by saying that the low wages of foreign workers means that foreign workers are exploited. To compete with foreign workers, American workers would have to submit themselves to similar exploitation. This objection, however, fails to recognize that differences in wage rates generally reflect differences in worker productivity.

Consider the following example: Suppose U.S. workers in the tool industry earn $20 per hour while Indonesian workers in the tool industry earn only $2 per hour. If we assume that the tool industry is competitive, then the wages in both countries are based on the marginal revenue product of the workers. The higher wage of U.S. workers must mean that they have a higher marginal product—they are more productive. The higher wage of U.S. workers need not mean that labor costs are higher in the United States than in Indonesia.

Further, we have seen that what matters for trade is comparative advantage, not comparative labor costs. When each nation specializes in goods and services in which it has a comparative advantage—measured in the amounts of other goods and services given up to produce them—then world production, and therefore world consumption, rises. By definition, each nation will have a comparative advantage in *something*.

Retaliation Against Dumping Foreign producers of goods and services are often accused of "dumping" their goods in the U.S. market. **Dumping** means selling goods in a foreign market at a price below production cost.

In the United States, domestic firms can file charges with the Commerce Department, accusing foreign competitors of dumping. If Commerce finds that foreign firms have sold goods in U.S. markets below their cost of production, it imposes higher tariffs against the countries in which the firms are located. In 1993, for example, the U.S. Commerce Department slapped duties of up to 73 percent on steel produced by 19 different nations whose firms were found guilty of dumping steel in the United States.

The Commerce Department evaluates charges of dumping by estimating the actual cost a foreign firm incurs in producing goods. In estimating these costs, Commerce assumes that the firm "should" earn a certain profit rate. In the steel ruling, for example, it assumed that foreign firms should earn a profit rate equal to 8 percent of total sales—about double the actual rate earned by U.S. corporations. Imposing this rule often results in a finding that foreign firms are selling below cost.

One difficulty with tariffs imposed in retaliation against dumping, then, is that the charge is often based on an arbitrary assessment of a firm's costs. Another objection, of course, is that the retaliation imposes high costs on U.S. consumers of the goods and services affected.

Differences in Environmental Standards Another justification for protectionist measures is that free trade is unfair if it pits domestic firms against foreign rivals who do not have to adhere to the same regulatory standards. In the debate over NAFTA, for example, critics warned that Mexican firms, facing relatively lax pollution control standards, would have an unfair advantage over U.S. firms if restraints on trade between the two countries were removed.

Economic theory suggests, however, that differences in pollution-control policies can be an important source of comparative advantage. In general, the demand for environmental quality is positively related to income. People in higher-income countries demand higher environmental quality than do people in lower-income countries. That means that pollution has a lower cost in poorer than in richer countries. If an industry generates a great deal of pollution, it may be more efficient to locate it in a poor country than in a rich country. In effect, a poor country's lower demand for environmental quality gives it a comparative advantage in production of goods that generate a great deal of pollution.

Provided the benefits of pollution exceed the costs in the poor country, with the costs computed based on the preferences and incomes of people in that country, it makes sense for more of the good to be produced in the poor country and less in the rich country. Such an allocation leaves people in both countries better off than they would be otherwise. Then, as freer trade leads to higher incomes in the poorer countries, people there will also demand improvements in environmental quality.

Do economists support *any* restriction on free international trade? Nearly all economists would say no. The gains from trade are so large, and the costs of restraining it so high, that it's hard to find any satisfactory reason to limit trade.

Checklist

- Protectionist policies restrict the importation of goods and services produced in foreign countries and shift the supply curves for those goods and services to the left in the country imposing the protection.
- Tariffs are taxes on imported goods and services. Quotas are limitations on the quantity that can be imported. Both tariffs and quotas decrease the equilibrium quantity and raise the equilibrium price of the goods and services on which they are imposed. Voluntary export restrictions have the same economic effect as quotas.
- Regulations, such as safety standards and pollution controls, can also be used as protectionist policies.
- Arguments in favor of protectionist policies include the infant industry argument, strategic trade policy, the national security argument, the job protection argument, the cheap foreign labor argument, the retaliation against dumping argument, and the environmental standards argument. Economists generally agree that these arguments rarely, if ever, justify protectionist measures.

Try It Yourself 17-2

Suppose the United States imposes a quota reducing its imports of imported shoes by one-half (roughly 85–90% of the shoes now sold in the United States are imported). Assume that shoes are produced under conditions of perfect competition and that the equilibrium price of shoes is now $50 per pair. Illustrate and explain how this quota will affect the price and output of shoes in the United States.

A Look Back

In this chapter we have seen how international trade makes it possible for countries to improve on their domestic production possibilities.

A country that is operating on its production possibilities curve can obtain more of all goods by opening its markets to free international trade. Free trade allows nations to consume goods beyond their domestic production possibilities curves. If nations specialize in the production of goods and services in which they have a comparative advantage, total output increases. Free trade enhances production possibilities on a worldwide scale. It does not benefit everyone, however. Some workers and owners of other factors of production will be hurt by free trade, at least in the short run.

Contrary to the implication of the model of specialization based on comparative advantage, not all trade is one-way trade. Two-way trade in the *same* goods may arise from variations in transportation costs and seasonal influences. Two-way trade in *similar* goods is often the result of imperfect competition. Much trade among high-income countries is two-way trade.

The imposition of a tariff, quota, or voluntary export restriction raises the equilibrium price and reduces the equilibrium quantity of the restricted good. Although there are many arguments in favor of such restrictions on free trade, economists generally agree that none of them justifies protectionist measures.

A Look Ahead International trade is the first chapter in this part of the book in which we apply the tools and models of microeconomic analysis to a series of issues. The next chapter focuses on how economists look at environmental problems.

Terms and Concepts for Review

absolute advantage, **338**
terms of trade, **340**
one-way (or interindustry) trade, **343**
two-way (or intraindustry) trade, **343**
protectionist policy, **345**
tariff, **345**
quota, **345**
voluntary export restrictions, **345**
infant industry, **347**
strategic trade policy, **348**
dumping, **349**

For Discussion

1. Explain how through trade a country can consume at levels beyond the reach of its production possibilities.
2. Why do countries place restrictions on international trade?
3. What's the difference between a tariff and a quota?
4. The Case in Point on America's shifting comparative advantage suggests that the United States may have a comparative advantage over other countries in the production of high-tech capital goods. What do you think might be the sources of this advantage?
5. "I know a lawyer who can type 100 words per minute but pays a secretary $10 per hour to type court briefs. But the secretary can only type 50 words per minute. I have told my lawyer friend a hundred times she'd be better off doing the typing herself, but she just won't listen." Who has the better part of this disagreement, the lawyer or the friend? Explain.
6. Which individuals in the United States might benefit from a tariff placed on the importation of shoes? Who might lose?
7. Explain why economists argue that protectionist policies lead to the misallocation of resources in the domestic economy.
8. Tomatoes grow well in Kansas. Why do the people of Kansas buy most of their tomatoes from Florida, Mexico, and California?
9. Under what circumstances will a country both export and import the products of the same industry?
10. Suppose the United States imposes a quota on copper imports. Who might be helped? Who might be hurt?
11. Some people argue that international trade is fine, but that firms in different countries should play on a "level playing field." They argue that if a good can be produced more cheaply abroad than at home, tariffs should be imposed on the good so that the costs of producing it are the same everywhere. What do you think of this argument?
12. Suppose wages in the Philippines are one-tenth of wages in the United States. Why don't all U.S. firms just move production to the Philippines?

Problems

1. Argentina and New Zealand each produce wheat and mutton, as shown on the accompanying production possibilities curves.

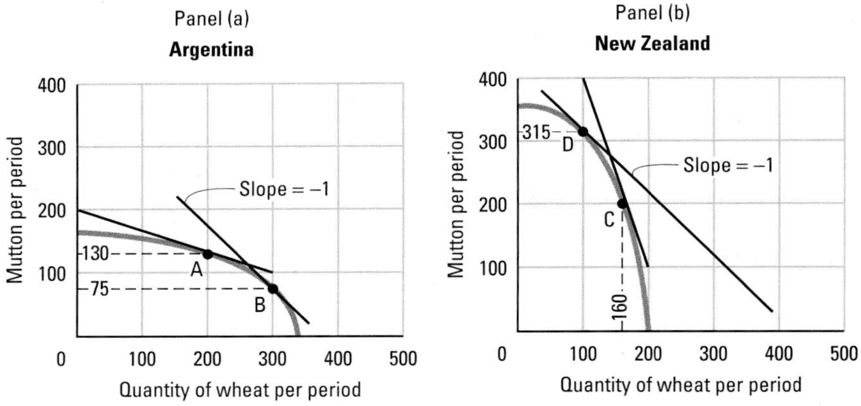

Assume that there is no trade between the two countries and that Argentina is now producing at A and New Zealand at C. What is the opportunity cost of producing each good in each country? Which country has a comparative advantage in which good? Explain.

2. Assume that trade opens between Argentina and New Zealand and that, with trade, a unit of mutton exchanges for a unit of wheat. Before trade, Argentina produced at A and New Zealand produced at C. Argentina moves to point B, while New Zealand moves to point D. Calculate and illustrate graphically an exchange between Argentina and New Zealand that would leave both countries with more of both goods than they had before trade.

Answers to Try It Yourself Problems

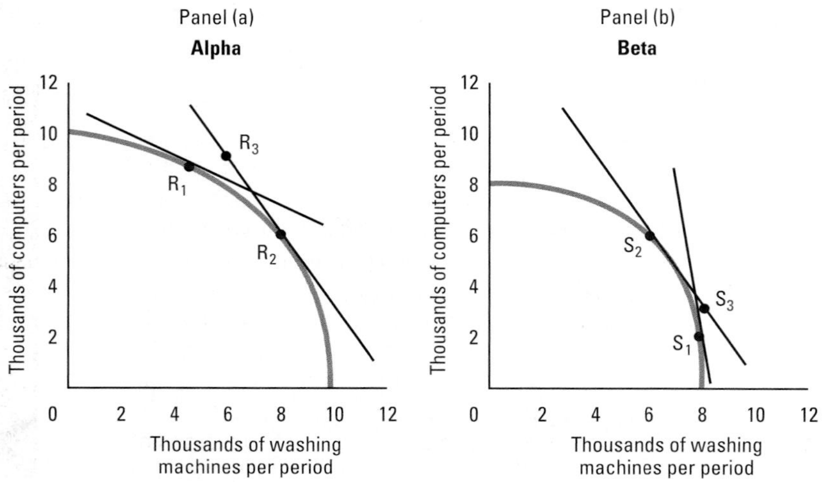

Try It Yourself 17-1

Here are sketches of possible production possibilities curves. Alpha is operating at a point such as R_1, while Beta is operating at a point such as S_1. In Alpha, 1 computer trades for 2 washing machines; in Beta, 3.5 computers trade for a washing machine. If trade opens between the two economies and the terms of trade are 1.5, then Alpha will produce more washing machines and fewer computers (moving to a point such as R_2), while Beta will produce more computers and fewer washing machines (moving to a point such as S_2). Though you weren't asked to do this, the graphs demonstrate that it is possible that trade will result in both countries having more of both goods. If, for example, Alpha ships 2,000 washing machines to Beta in exchange for 3,000 computers, then the two economies will move to points R_3 and S_3, respectively, consuming more of both goods than they had before trade. There are many points along the tangent lines drawn at points R_2 and S_2 that are up to the right and therefore contain more of both goods. We have chosen points R_3 and S_3 at specific points, but any point along the tangent line that is up to the right from R_1 and S_1 would suffice.

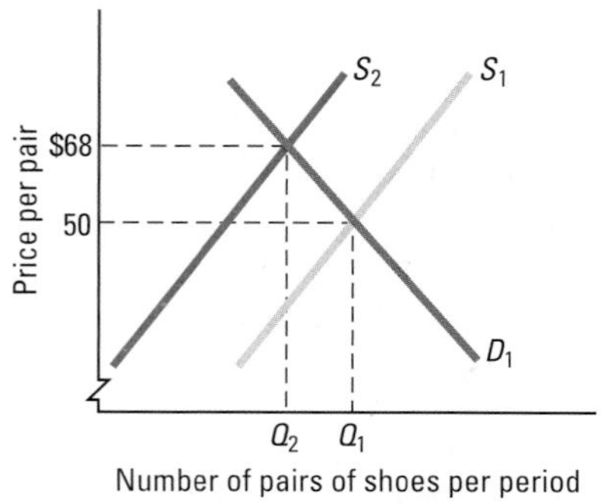

Try It Yourself 17-2

The quota shifts the supply curve to the left, increasing the price of shoes in the United States and reducing the equilibrium quantity. In the case shown, the price rises to $68. Because you aren't given the precise positions of the demand and supply curves, you can only conclude that price rises; your graph may suggest a different price. The important thing is that the new price is greater than $50.

18 The Economics of the Environment

Getting Started: Selling the Right to Pollute

Wisconsin Power and Light, a Madison utility company, wrote a new page in the history of environmental policy in 1992 when it sold the right to dump 15,000 tons of airborne sulfur dioxide (SO_2) to Duquesne Light, a Pittsburgh utility.

Federal legislation passed in 1990 set tough new standards for the dumping of sulfur dioxide, a pollutant associated with acid rain. The standards, which went into effect in 1995, specify the maximum quantity of sulfur dioxide each utility can dump per year. Utilities that dump less than that quantity are permitted to sell rights to other firms, allowing them to dump more than their allotment. Duquesne Light calculated that it would be cheaper to buy additional rights than to cut its emissions further. Wisconsin Power and Light, for its part, had an aggressive program in place to cut its emissions well below its ceiling; it could boost its profits by selling some of its rights.

Almost no one was opposed to the objective of reducing SO_2 emissions nationwide. While the people in Pittsburgh may have preferred an outright reduction in Duquesne Light's emissions, we'll see that from a national perspective, the trading of pollution rights helped achieve the national objective of lower total emissions at the lowest possible opportunity cost.

Wisconsin Power and Light's sale was the first under the new program. Today, rights to dump sulfur dioxide are traded at the Chicago Board of Trade, where commodities such as pork bellies and gold are exchanged. The effort represents a new thrust in environmental policy—the use of markets to solve environmental problems. The development of a market for pollution rights puts market forces to work in an effort to reduce the problem of acid rain. The Case in Point later in this chapter provides a preliminary evaluation of the trading program in SO_2 pollution rights.

In this chapter we shall put the analytical tools we've developed to work on the problems of the environment, with a focus on air and water pollution. While we emphasize air and water pollution, the approach can be applied to other environmental issues, such as protecting endangered species and controlling noise around airports.

We'll look particularly at alternative regulatory approaches to such problems. Direct controls, in which government agencies tell polluters what they must do to reduce pollution, remain the primary means of government regulation. Persuasion, seeking voluntary compliance with pollution reduction efforts, is also used. Two alternatives that economists advocate are taxes on pollutants and marketable pollution rights; such systems are gaining in importance.

Maximizing the Net Benefits of Pollution

We all pollute the environment. We do so not because we get some perverse satisfaction from polluting, but because activities that give us utility inevitably pollute. We do not drive our cars in order to dump carbon monoxide into the air but because we gain utility from the transportation and convenience cars provide. Firms pollute the environment if doing so allows them to produce goods and services at lower cost.

The benefits we derive from pollution are indirect. We obtain them from the other activities that generate pollution. But that's not unusual—there are lots of things we do because of the other benefits they produce. Firms benefit from hiring labor not because their owners enjoy hiring workers but because those workers produce greater profits. We purchase electricity not because we enjoy the feeling of having the stuff racing through wires in the house but because the electricity produces light, heat, and other services more cheaply than would alternatives such as candles or fires. We pollute in the process of obtaining more of other goods and services we enjoy. We thus benefit from our pollution.

Of course, we suffer from the pollution we all generate as well. Smog-choked air damages our health and robs us of scenic views. We may not be able to fish or swim in polluted rivers. Just as the generation of pollution makes many of the activities we pursue less expensive, the fact that we have pollution increases many costs. Polluted rivers increase the cost of producing drinking water. Polluted air requires us to spend more on health care and to paint our buildings more often. Polluted soils produce less food.

Like any other activity, then, pollution has benefits as well as costs. The difficulty with pollution problems is that decisionmakers experience the benefits of their own choices to pollute the environment, but the costs spill over to everyone who breathes the air or consumes the water. These costs are examples of external costs. Recall from Chapter 6 that external costs produce one type of market failure and that market failures lead to inefficiency in the

Case in Point Environmental Problems Even Worse Under Command Socialist Systems

One might have expected that the absence of private, profit-seeking firms under command socialist systems would have led to better treatment of the environment than has been the case under market capitalism, but the evidence from the former Soviet Union and Soviet Bloc countries of Eastern Europe reveals quite the opposite. These nations had acute environmental problems.

A comparison of countries along the East–West divide in the early 1990s, following the fall of the Berlin Wall when information on them became more readily available, revealed, for example, that East Germany's sulfur dioxide emissions per person were 15 times those of West Germany. The concentration of smoke in Poland's industrial Upper Silesia exceeded Western European standards by 600 percent. In Bohemia, part of what was then Czechoslovakia, 70 percent of wastewater went untreated and half the forests were declared dead or dying. These countries also reported very high rates of birth defects and illnesses, such as leukemia, tuberculosis, and heart disease, that were suspected of being pollution-related.

Why was the environment so abused? One factor was that government planners in these countries emphasized heavy industries, such as steel and chemicals, that tend to be more polluting than agriculture or light industry. Moreover, Eastern European countries relied on their own high-sulfur coal, as well as oil and gas bought from the Soviet Union at prices far below world levels. Because energy was so cheap, they had little incentive to improve energy efficiency. Energy use in Eastern Europe per dollar of output was two to three times that of Western Europe. Finally, their governments did little to provide incentives for firms to take into account the externalities generated by production. Laws on the books were routinely ignored. If in theory their governments owned the land, air, and water in the same way that they owned the factories and farms, they did not in any substantial way exert their property rights over these resources. Emphasizing production targets, they allowed firms to treat the environment as a free resource.

Has the switch to market capitalism in the 1990s helped the environment? There have been some improvements in the former Soviet Bloc countries of Eastern Europe. For example, dust emissions fell from 1.5 million tons in 1989 to about a half million in 1994, and sulfur dioxide emissions fell from 2.8 million tons to 1.7 million tons. Some of the improvement is the result of privatized firms having to pay world prices for the energy they use; the higher prices have caused them to cut back on the intensity of energy use and to consider alternative production methods. Some of the improvement is due to the closure of highly polluting factories whose products are no longer in demand.

Sources: Stanley J. Kabala, "The Environmental Morass in Eastern Europe," *Current History* 90, Issue 559 (November 1991): 384–389; Jane Perlez, "Global Warming: Around the Globe, Big Worries and Small Signs of Progress; Poland's Pollution Drops Even as Economy Rises," *New York Times*, 1 December 1997, p. F9.

allocation of resources. The environment presents us with an allocation problem in which decisionmakers aren't faced with all the benefits and costs of their choices. Environmental resources will not, in such cases, be allocated efficiently. Economists who examine and analyze environmental problems try to determine what an efficient allocation of the environment would most likely be—one that maximizes the difference between the total benefits and total costs of our pollution.

A second task of environmental economics is to find ways to get from where we are, typically with more pollution than is efficient, to the efficient solution. We learned in Chapter 6 that private markets often fail to achieve efficient solutions to environmental problems because property rights are difficult to define and to exchange. We'll see, however, that environmental economists have devised innovative ways to introduce property rights to environmental policy and to harness market forces to improve rather than degrade environmental quality.

Pollution and Scarcity

Pollution exists whenever human activity generates a sufficient concentration of a substance in the environment to cause harm to people or to resources valued by people. Many potentially harmful substances are natural features of the environment, but they are not generally regarded as pollutants. Pollutants are the products of people, not nature.

Pollution implies scarcity. If an activity emits harmless by-products into the environment, then the emission of the by-products isn't an alternative to some other activity. A scarcity problem exists at the point where harm occurs. A campfire in the wilderness whose smoke goes unnoticed doesn't suggest a scarcity problem. But when there are other campers who will be harmed by the smoke, then one person's enjoyment of a campfire becomes an alternative to another person's enjoyment of fresh air. Fresh air has become scarce, and pollution has become an economic problem.

Economists generally argue that pollution that harms plants or animals imposes a cost if the plants or animals are valued by people. When a farmer uses a pesticide that damages another farmer's crop, for example, a pollution problem occurs. If an oil spill in the ocean damages sea animals that people care about, there is a pollution problem. It is, after all, people who make the choices that lead to pollution. It is people who can choose to limit their pollution. Economists therefore examine pollution problems from the perspective of the preferences of people.

The Efficient Level of Pollution

The efficient level of pollution is the quantity at which its total benefits exceed its total costs by the greatest possible amount. This occurs where the marginal benefit of an additional unit of pollution equals its marginal cost.

Exhibit 18-1 shows how we can determine an efficient quantity of pollution. Suppose two individuals, Mary and John, generate air pollution that harms two other individuals, Sarah and Richard, who live downwind. We shall assume that Mary and John are the only polluters and that Sarah and Richard are the only people harmed by the pollution.

Suppose, as is often the case, that no mechanism exists to charge Mary and John for their emissions; they can pollute all they want and never have to compensate society (that is, pay Sarah and Richard) for the damage they do. Alternatively, suppose there is no mechanism for Sarah and Richard to pay Mary and John to get them to reduce their pollution. In either situation, the pollution generated by Mary and John imposes an external cost on Sarah and Richard. Mary and John will pollute up to the point that the marginal benefit of additional pollution to them has reached zero—that is, up to the point where the marginal benefit matches their marginal cost. They ignore the external costs they impose on "society"—Sarah and Richard.

Mary's and John's demand curves for pollution are shown in Panel (a). These demand curves, D_M and D_J, show the quantities of emissions each generates at each possible price,

Exhibit 18-1

Determining the Efficient Level of Pollution

In Panel (a), we add the demand curves for emissions for Mary (D_M) and John (D_J) to get the total demand D_T for emitting the pollutant. At a price of $13 per unit, the quantity of emissions per period equals 34; at a price of zero, it is 60. In Panel (b), we see the effects of the pollution on Sarah and Richard; we add their marginal cost curves MC_S and MC_R vertically to obtain total marginal cost MC_T. The curves for total demand and total marginal cost are shown in Panel (c); the efficient solution is 34 units of pollutant emitted per period.

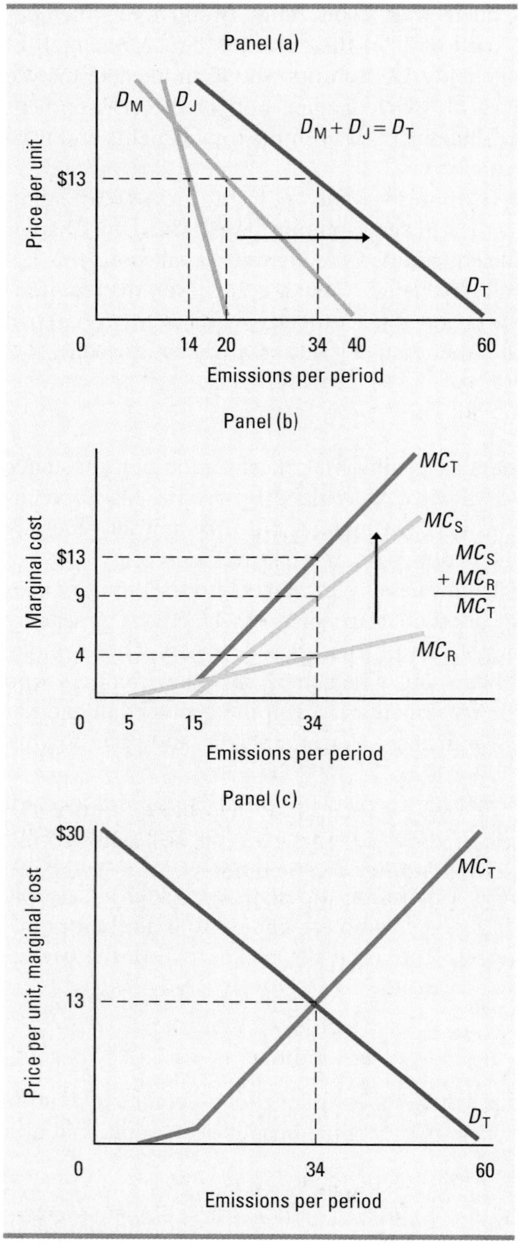

assuming such a fee were assessed. At a price of $13 per unit, for example, Mary will emit 20 units of pollutant per period, and John will emit 14. Total emissions at a price of $13 would be 34 units per period. If the price of emissions were zero, total emissions would be 60 units per period. Whatever the price they face, Mary and John will emit additional units of the pollutant up to the point that their marginal benefit equals that price. We can therefore interpret their demand curves as their marginal benefit curves for emissions. Their combined demand curve D_T gives the marginal benefit to society (that is, to Mary and John) of pollution.

In Panel (b) we see how much Sarah and Richard are harmed; the marginal cost curves MC_S and MC_R show their respective valuations of the harm imposed on them by each additional unit of emissions. Notice that over a limited range, some emissions generate no harm. At very low levels, neither Sarah nor Richard is even aware of the emissions. Richard begins to experience harm as the quantity of emissions goes above 5; it is here that pollution begins to occur. As emissions increase, the additional harm each unit creates becomes larger and larger—the marginal cost curves are upward sloping. The first traces of pollution may be only a minor inconvenience, but as pollution goes up, the problems it creates become more serious—and its marginal cost rises.

Because the same emissions affect both Sarah and Richard, we add their marginal cost curves vertically to obtain their combined marginal cost curve MC_T. The 34th unit of emissions, for example, imposes an additional cost of $9 on Sarah and $4 on Richard. It thus imposes a total marginal cost of $13.

The efficient quantity of emissions is found at the intersection of the demand (D_T) and marginal cost (MC_T) curves in Panel (c) of Exhibit 18-1, with 34 units of the pollutant emitted. The marginal benefit of the 34th unit of emissions, as measured by the demand curve D_T, equals its marginal cost MC_T. The solution at which marginal benefit equals marginal cost maximizes the net benefit of an activity.

We've already seen that in the absence of a mechanism to charge Mary and John for their emissions, they face a price of zero and would emit 60 units of pollutant per period. But that level of pollution is inefficient. Indeed, as long as the marginal cost of an additional unit of pollution exceeds its marginal benefit, as measured by the demand curve, there is too much pollution; the net benefit of emissions would be greater with a lower level of the activity.

Just as too much pollution is inefficient, so is too little. Suppose Mary and John aren't allowed to pollute; emissions equal zero. We see in Panel (c) that the marginal benefit of dumping the first unit of pollution is quite high; the marginal cost it imposes on Sarah and Richard is zero. Because the marginal benefit of additional pollution exceeds its marginal cost, the net benefit to society would be increased by increasing the level of pollution. That's true at any level of pollution below 34 units, the efficient solution.

The notion that too little pollution could be inefficient may strike you as strange. To see the logic of this idea, imagine that the pollutant involved is carbon monoxide, a pollutant emitted whenever combustion occurs. It is, for example, emitted when you drive a car. Now suppose that no emissions of carbon monoxide are allowed. Among other things, this would require a ban on driving. Surely the benefits of some driving would exceed the cost of the pollution created. The problem in pollution policy from an economic perspective is to find the quantity of pollution at which total benefits exceed total costs by the greatest possible amount—the solution at which marginal benefit equals marginal cost.

Property Rights and the Coase Theorem

The problem of getting the efficient amount of pollution arises because no one owns the right to the air. If someone did, then that owner could decide how to use it. If a nonowner didn't like the way the owner was using it, then he or she could try to pay the owner to change the way the air was being used.

In our earlier example, if Mary and John own the right to the air, but Sarah and Richard don't like how much Mary and John are polluting it, Sarah and Richard can offer to pay Mary and John to cut back on the amount they are polluting. Alternatively, if Sarah and Richard own the air, then in order to pollute it, Mary and John would have to compensate the owners. Bargaining among the affected parties, if costless, would lead to the efficient amount of pollution.

Specifically, suppose Mary and John own the right to the air and had been emitting 60 units of pollution per period. If Sarah and Richard offer to pay them $13 for each unit of pollutant they cut back, Mary and John will reduce their pollution to 34 units, since the marginal benefit to them of the 35th to 60th unit is less than $13. Sarah and Richard are better off since the marginal cost of those last 26 units of pollution is greater than $13 per unit. The efficient outcome of 34 units of pollution is thus achieved.

Suppose instead that Sarah and Richard own the right to the air. They could charge Mary and John $13 per unit of pollution emitted. Mary and John would willingly pay for the right to emit 34 units of pollution, but not for any more, since beyond that amount the marginal benefit of each unit of pollution emitted is less than $13. Sarah and Richard would willingly accept payments for 34 units of pollution at $13 each since the marginal cost to them for each of those units is less than $13.

While the well-being of the affected parties is not independent of who owns the property right (each would be better off owning than not owning the right), the establishment of who owns the air leads to a solution that solves the externality problem and leads to an efficient market outcome. The proposition that if property rights are well defined and if bargaining is costless, then the private market can achieve an efficient outcome regardless of which of the affected parties holds the property rights is known as the **Coase theorem,** named for the Nobel-Prize-winning economist Ronald Coase who discovered this idea.

In many instances, however, the conditions for private parties to achieve an efficient outcome on their own are not present. Property rights may not be defined. Even if one party owns a right, enforcement may be difficult. Suppose Sarah and Richard own the right to clean air but many people, not just two as in our example, contribute to polluting it. Would each producer that pollutes have to strike a deal with Sarah and Richard? Could the government enforce all those deals? And what if there are many owners as well? Enforcement becomes increasingly difficult and striking deals becomes more and more costly.

Nonetheless, it is the insight that the Coase theorem provides that has led economists to consider solutions to environmental problems that attempt to use the establishment of property rights and market mechanisms in various ways to bring about the efficient market outcome. Before considering alternative ways of controlling pollution, we look first at how the benefits and costs might be measured so that we have a better sense of what the efficient solution is.

The Measurement of Benefits and Costs

Saying that the efficient level of pollution occurs at a certain rate of emissions, as we have done so far, is one thing. Determining the actual positions of the demand and marginal cost curves that define that efficient solution is quite another. Economists have devised a variety of methods for measuring these curves.

Benefits: The Demand for Emissions A demand curve for emitting pollutants shows the quantity of emissions at each price. It can, as we've seen, be taken as a marginal benefit curve for emitting pollutants.

The general approach to estimating demand curves involves observing quantities demanded at various prices, together with the values of other determinants of demand. In most pollution problems, however, the price charged for emitting pollutants has always been zero—we simply don't know how the quantity of emissions demanded will vary with price.

One approach to estimating the demand curve for pollution utilizes the fact that this demand occurs because pollution makes other activities cheaper. If we know how much the emission of 1 more unit of a pollutant saves, then we can infer how much consumers or firms would pay to dump it.

Suppose, for example, that there is no program to control automobile emissions—motorists face a price of zero for each unit of pollution their cars emit. Suppose that a particular motorist's car emits an average of 10 pounds of carbon monoxide per week. Its owner could reduce emissions to 9 pounds per week at a cost of $1. This $1 is the marginal cost of reducing emissions from 10 to 9 pounds per week. It's also the maximum price the motorist would pay to increase emissions from 9 to 10 pounds per week—it's the marginal benefit of the 10th pound of pollution. We say it is the maximum price because if asked to pay more, the motorist would choose to reduce emissions at a cost of $1 instead.

Now suppose that emissions have been reduced to 9 pounds per week and that the motorist could reduce them to 8 at an additional cost of $2 per week. The marginal cost of reducing emissions from 9 to 8 pounds per week is $2. Alternatively, this is the maximum price the motorist would be willing to pay to increase emissions from 8 to 9 pounds; it is the marginal benefit of the 9th pound of pollution. Again, if asked to pay more than $2, the motorist would choose to reduce emissions to 8 pounds per week instead.

We can thus think of the marginal benefit of an additional unit of pollution as the added cost of not emitting it. It is the saving a polluter enjoys by dumping additional pollution rather than going to the cost of preventing its emission. Exhibit 18-2 shows this dual interpretation of cost and benefit. Initially, our motorist emits 10 pounds of carbon monoxide per week. Reading from right to left, the curve measures the marginal costs of pollution abatement (MC_A). We see that the marginal cost of abatement rises as emissions are reduced. That makes sense; the first reductions in emissions will be achieved through relatively simple measures such as getting more frequent tune-ups. Further reductions, however, might require burning more expensive fuels or installing more expensive pollution-control equipment.

Read from left to right, the curve in Exhibit 18-2 shows the marginal benefit of additional emissions (MB_E). Its negative slope suggests that the first units of pollution emitted have very high marginal benefits, because the cost of not emitting them would be very high. As more of a pollutant is emitted, however, its marginal benefit falls—the cost of preventing these units of pollution becomes quite low.

Economists have also measured demand curves for emissions by using surveys in which polluters are asked to report the costs to them of reducing their emissions. In cases in which polluters are charged for the emissions they create, the marginal benefit curve can be observed directly.

As we saw in Exhibit 18-1, the marginal benefit curves of individual polluters are added horizontally to obtain a market demand curve for pollution. This curve measures the additional benefit to society of each additional unit of pollution.

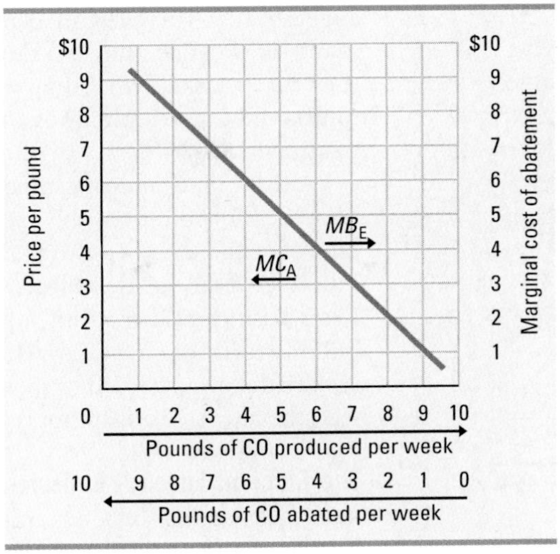

Exhibit 18-2

Abatement Costs and Demand

A car emits an average of 10 pounds of carbon monoxide per week when no restrictions are imposed—when the price of emissions is zero. The marginal cost of abatement (MC_A) is the cost of eliminating a unit of emissions. The same curve can be read from left to right as the marginal benefit of emissions (MB_E).

The Marginal Cost of Emissions Pollutants harm people and the resources they value. The marginal cost curve for a pollutant shows the additional cost imposed by each unit of the pollutant. As we saw in Exhibit 18-1, the marginal cost curves for all the individuals harmed by a particular pollutant are added vertically to obtain the marginal cost curve for the pollutant.

Like the marginal benefit curve for emissions, the marginal cost curve can be interpreted in two ways, as suggested in Exhibit 18-3. When read from left to right, the curve measures the marginal cost of additional units of emissions (MC_E). If increasing the motorists' emissions from 4 pounds of carbon monoxide per week to 5 pounds of carbon monoxide per week imposes an external cost of $2, though, the marginal benefit of not being exposed to that unit of pollutant must be $2. The marginal cost curve can thus be read from right to left as a marginal benefit curve for abating emissions (MB_A). This marginal benefit curve is, in effect, the demand curve for cleaner air.

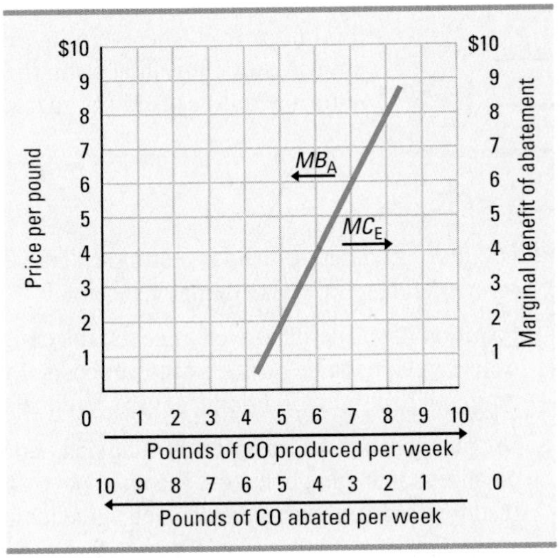

Exhibit 18-3

The Marginal Cost of Emissions

The marginal cost curve for emissions (MC_E) is found by adding individual marginal cost curves vertically. It can be read from right to left as the marginal benefit curve for obtaining emissions (MB_A), or the demand curve for cleaner air.

Economists estimate the marginal cost curve of pollution in several ways. One is to infer it from the demand for goods for which environmental quality is a complement. Another is to survey people, asking them what pollution costs—or what they would pay to reduce it. Still another is to determine the costs of damages created by pollution directly.

For example, environmental quality is a complement of housing. The demand for houses in areas with cleaner air is greater than the demand for houses in areas that are more polluted. By observing the relationship between house prices and air quality, economists can learn the value people place on cleaner air—and thus the cost of dirtier air. Studies have been conducted in cities all over the United States to determine the relationship between air quality and house prices so that a measure of the demand for cleaner air can be made. They show that increased pollution levels result in lower house values.[1]

Surveys are also used to assess the marginal cost of emissions. The fact that the marginal cost of an additional unit of emissions is the marginal benefit of avoiding the emissions

[1]For a summary of studies of house values and pollution levels, see Barry C. Field, *Environmental Economics* (New York: McGraw-Hill, 1994).

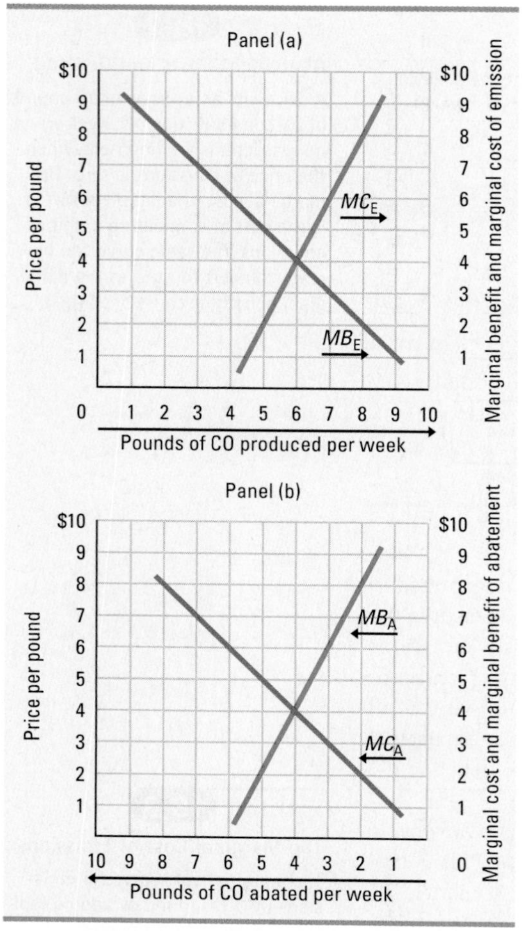

Exhibit 18-4

The Efficient Level of Emissions and Pollution Abatement

In Panel (a) we combine the marginal benefit and marginal cost of emissions curves. In Panel (b) we combine the marginal benefit and marginal cost of abatement curves. The efficient level of emissions is 6 pounds of CO per week, as shown in Panel (a). That corresponds to an efficient level of abatement of 4 pounds of CO per week, as shown in Panel (b).

suggests that surveys can be designed in two ways. Respondents can be asked how much they would be harmed by an increase in emissions, or they can be asked what they would pay for a reduction in emissions. Economists often use both kinds of questions in surveys designed to determine marginal costs.

A third kind of cost estimate is based on objects damaged by pollution. Increases in pollution, for example, require buildings to be painted more often; the increased cost of painting is one measure of the cost of added pollution. A study of the effects of air pollutants on agriculture in the Ohio River basin found that air pollution in the region would destroy about $7 billion worth of soybeans, wheat, and corn during the final quarter of the twentieth century.[2] While each of these attempts to measure cost is imperfect, the alternative is to not try to quantify cost at all.

The Efficient Level of Emissions and Abatement Whether economists measure the marginal benefits and marginal costs of emissions or the marginal benefits and marginal costs of abatement, the policy implications are the same from an economic perspective. As shown in Panel (a) of Exhibit 18-4, applying the marginal decision rule in the case of emissions suggests that the efficient level of pollution occurs at 6 pounds of CO produced per week. At any lower level, the marginal benefits of the pollution would outweigh the marginal costs. At a higher level, the marginal costs of the pollution would outweigh the benefits.

As shown in Panel (b) of Exhibit 18-4, application of the marginal decision rule suggests that the efficient level of abatement effort is to reduce pollution by 4 pounds of CO produced per week. That is, reduce the level of pollution from the 10 units that would occur at a zero price to 6 units. For any greater effort at abating the pollution, the marginal cost of the abatement efforts would exceed the marginal benefit.

Checklist

- Pollution is related to the concept of scarcity. The existence of pollution implies that an environmental resource has alternative uses.
- Pollution has benefits as well as costs; the emission of pollutants benefits people by allowing other activities to be pursued at lower costs. The efficient rate of emissions occurs where the marginal benefit of additional emissions equals the marginal cost they impose.
- The marginal benefit curve for emitting pollutants can also be read from right to left as the marginal cost of abating pollution. The marginal cost curve for increased pollution levels can also be read from right to left as the demand curve for improved environmental quality.
- The Coase theorem suggests that if property rights are well-defined and if bargaining is costless, then the private market may achieve an efficient outcome. These conditions, however, may not be present.
- Surveys are sometimes used to measure the marginal benefit curves for emissions and the marginal cost curves for increased pollution levels. Marginal cost curves may also be inferred from other relationships. Two that are commonly used are the demand for houses and the relationship between pollution and production.

[2]Walter P. Page et al., "Estimation of Economic Losses to the Agricultural Sector from Airborne Residuals in the Ohio River Basin," *Journal of the Air Pollution Control Association* 32(2) (February 1982): 151–154.

Try It Yourself 18-1

The table at right shows the marginal benefit to a paper mill of polluting a river and the marginal cost to residents who live downstream. In this problem assume that the marginal benefits and marginal costs are measured at *(not* between*) the specific quantities shown.*

Plot the marginal benefit and marginal cost curves. What is the efficient quantity of pollution? Explain why neither 1 ton nor 5 tons is an efficient quantity of pollution. In the absence of pollution fees or taxes, how many units of pollution do you expect the paper mill will choose to produce? Why?

Quantity of pollution (tons per week)	Marginal benefit	Marginal cost
0	110	0
1	100	20
2	90	20
3	80	35
4	70	70
5	60	150
6	0	300

Alternatives in Pollution Control

Suppose that the goal of public policy is to reduce the level of emissions. Three types of policy alternatives could be applied. The first is persuasion—people can be exhorted to reduce their emissions. The second relies on direct controls, and the third uses incentives to induce reductions in emissions.

Moral Suasion

Smokey the Bear asks us to be careful with fire. Signs everywhere remind us not to litter. Some communities have mounted campaigns that admonish us to "Give a hoot—don't pollute."

These efforts to influence our choices are examples of **moral suasion,** an effort to change people's behavior by appealing to their sense of moral values. Moral suasion is widely used as a tactic in attempting to reduce pollution. It has, for example, been fairly successful in campaigns against littering, which can be considered a kind of pollution. Efforts at moral suasion are not generally successful in reducing activities that pollute the air and water. Pleas that people refrain from driving on certain days, for example, achieve virtually no compliance.

Moral suasion appears to be most effective in altering behaviors that are not already widespread and for which the cost of compliance is low. It's easy to be careful with one's fires or to avoid littering.

Moral suasion does not, however, appear to lead to significant changes in behavior when compliance costs are high or when the activity is already widely practiced. It is therefore not likely to be an effective tool for reducing most forms of pollution.

Command and Control

In the most widely used regulatory approach to environmental pollution, a government agency tells a polluting agent how much pollution it can emit or requires the agent to use a particular production method aimed at reducing emissions. This method, in which the government agency tells a firm or individual how much or by what method emissions must be adjusted, is called the **command-and-control-approach.**

Economists are generally critical of the command-and-control approach for two reasons. First, it achieves a given level of emissions reduction at a higher cost than what would be required to achieve that amount of reduction if market incentives (discussed below) were implemented. Second, it gives polluters no incentive to explore technological and other changes that might reduce the demand for emissions.

Suppose two firms, A and B, each dump 500 tons of a certain pollutant per month, and that there is no fee imposed (that is, the price for their emissions equals zero). Total emissions for the two firms thus equal 1,000 tons per month. The EPA decides to cut this in half and orders each firm to reduce its emissions to 250 tons per month, for a total reduction of 500 tons. This is a command-and-control regulation because it specifies the amount of reduction each firm must make. Although it may seem fair to require equal reductions by the two firms, this approach is likely to generate excessive costs.

Suppose that Firm A is quite old and that the reduction in emissions to 250 tons per period would be extremely costly. Suppose that removing the 251st ton costs this firm $1,000 per month. Put another way, the marginal benefit to Firm A of emitting the 251st ton would be $1,000.

Suppose Firm B, a much newer firm, already has some pollution-control equipment in place. Reducing its emissions to 250 tons imposes a cost, but a much lower cost than to Firm A. Indeed, suppose Firm B could reduce its emissions to 249 tons at an additional cost of $100; the marginal benefit to Firm B of emitting the 250th ton is $100.

If two firms have different marginal benefits of emissions, the allocation of resources is inefficient. The same level of emissions could be achieved at a lower cost. Suppose, for example, Firm A is permitted to increase its emissions to 251 tons while Firm B reduces emissions to 249. Firm A saves $1,000, while the cost to Firm B is just $100. Society achieves a net gain of $900, and the level of emissions remains at 500 tons per month.

As long as Firm A's marginal benefit of emissions exceeds Firm B's, a saving is realized by shifting emissions from B to A. At the point at which their marginal benefits are equal, no further reduction in the cost of achieving a given level of emissions is possible, and the allocation of emissions is efficient. When a given reduction in emissions is achieved so that the marginal benefit of an additional unit of emissions is the same for all polluters, it is a **least-cost reduction in emissions.** A command-and-control approach is unlikely to achieve a least-cost reduction in emissions.

The inefficiency of command-and-control regulation is important for two reasons. First, of course, it wastes scarce resources. If the same level of air or water quality could be achieved at a far lower cost, then surely it makes sense to use the cheaper method. Perhaps even more significant, reliance on command-and-control regulation makes environmental quality far more expensive than it needs to be—and that's likely to result in an unwillingness to achieve the improvements that would be economically efficient.

Incentive Approaches

Markets allocate resources efficiently when the price system confronts decisionmakers with the costs and benefits of their decisions. Prices create incentives—they give producers an incentive to produce more and consumers an incentive to economize. Regulatory efforts that seek to create market-like incentives to encourage reductions in pollution, but that allow individual decisionmakers to determine how much to pollute, are called **incentive approaches.**

Emissions Taxes One incentive approach to pollution control relies on taxes. If a tax is imposed on each unit of emissions, polluters will reduce their emissions until the marginal benefit of emissions equals the tax, and a least-cost reduction in emissions is achieved.

Emissions taxes are widely used in Europe. France, for example, has enacted taxes on the sulfur dioxide and nitrous oxide emissions of power plants and other industrial firms. Spain has recently imposed taxes on the dumping of pollutants into the country's waterways. Emissions taxes have long been imposed on firms that dump pollutants into some river systems in Europe. Such taxes have not been widely used in the United States.

An emissions tax requires, of course, that a polluter's emissions be monitored. The polluter is then charged a tax equal to the tax per unit times the quantity of emissions. The tax clearly gives the polluter an incentive to reduce emissions. It also ensures that reductions will be accomplished by those polluters that can achieve them at the lowest cost. Polluters for whom reductions are most costly will generally find it cheaper to pay the emissions tax.

In cases where it is difficult to monitor emissions, a tax could be imposed indirectly. Consider, for example, farmers' use of fertilizers and pesticides. Rain may wash some of these materials into local rivers, polluting the water. Clearly, it would be virtually impossible to monitor this runoff and assess responsible farmers a charge for their emissions. But it would be possible to levy a tax on these materials when they are sold, confronting farmers with a rough measure of the cost of the pollution their use of these materials imposes.

Marketable Pollution Permits An alternative to emissions taxes is marketable pollution permits, which allow their owners to emit a certain quantity of pollution during a particular period. The introduction to this chapter dealt with an example of marketable pollution permits; each of the permits that Duquesne Light purchased from Wisconsin Power and Light allowed the owner to dump 1 ton of sulfur dioxide per year.

To see how this works, suppose that Firms A and B are again told that they must reduce their emissions to 250 tons per month. This time, however, they are given 250 permits each—1 permit allows the emission of 1 ton per month. They can trade their permits; a firm that emits less than its allotted 250 tons can sell some of its permits to another firm that wants to emit more.

We saw that Firm B can reduce its emissions below 250 tons for a much lower cost than Firm A. For example, it could reduce its emissions to 249 tons for $100. Firm A would be willing to pay $1,000 for the right to emit the 251st ton of emissions. Clearly, a mutually profitable exchange is possible. In fact, as long as their marginal benefits of pollution differ, the firms can profit from exchange. Equilibrium will be achieved at the least-cost solution at which the marginal benefits for both firms are equal.

Wisconsin Power and Light sold rights to dump 15,000 tons of sulfur dioxide to Duquesne Light, applying the concept of marketable pollution permits. The sulfur dioxide emitted from coal-burning power plants is thought to be a major cause of acid rain. The EPA regards acid rain as an international problem and a reduction in sulfur dioxide emissions as a national goal, hence its willingness to allow emissions rights to be traded across state lines. This decision emphasizes the overall well-being of the population rather than that of people in particular locations. The impact of this program has been studied; the results are provided in the Case in Point.

One virtue of using marketable permits is that this approach represents only a modest departure from traditional command-and-control regulation. Once a polluter has been told to reduce its emissions to a certain quantity, it has a right to emit that quantity. Polluters will exchange rights only if doing so increases their utility or profits—allowing rights to be exchanged can only make them better off. The greatest benefit, of course, is that such exchanges allow a shift from the inefficient allocation created by command-and-control regulation to an efficient allocation in which pollution is reduced at the lowest possible cost.

Merits of Incentive Approaches Incentive systems, either emissions taxes or tradable permits, can achieve reductions in emissions at a far lower cost than command-and-control regulation. Even more important, however, are the long-run incentives they create for technological change. A firm that is ordered to reduce its emissions to a certain level has no incentive to do better, whereas a firm facing an emissions tax has a constant incentive to seek out new ways to lower its emissions and thus lower its taxes. Similarly, a firm faces a cost for using an emissions permit—the price that could be obtained from selling the permit—so it will seek ways to reduce emissions. As firms discover new ways to lower their costs of reducing emissions, the demand for emissions permits will fall, lowering the efficient quantity of emissions—and improving environmental quality even further.

Public Policy and Pollution: The Record

Federal efforts to control air and water pollution in the United States have produced mixed results. Air quality has generally improved; water quality has improved in some respects but deteriorated in other ways.

Case in Point Trading Pollution Rights

The 1990 Clean Air Act Amendments established the first large-scale pollution-control program that relied on tradable pollution permits. Its goal is to reduce sulfur dioxide (SO_2) emissions, a major ingredient in acid rain, from electric generating plants to about half their 1980 level. There are two phases to the program. Phase I, running from 1995 through 1999, put a cap on emissions from the 263 dirtiest large generating units. Phase II, from 2000 on, puts a cap on all coal-burning electric generating units in the continental United States.

The program works by giving all affected units a fixed number of tradable permits called "allowances," each year. Each allowance entitles the holder to emit one ton of SO_2. The Environmental Protection Agency (EPA) also auctions off a small number of additional allowances. Each year owners must show the EPA valid allowances covering their emissions or face penalties. The annual cost of monitoring emissions has been about $124,000 per electric generating unit. Permits can be traded anywhere in the continental United States, and allowances not used in the year they were issued can be banked for use in later years.

Unlike the traditional command-and-control approach to reducing environmental damage, which prescribes abatement methods and standards, this approach directly limits total emissions. It also allows owners to decide whether to reduce emissions by switching to low-sulfur fuels or by employing scrubbing technologies.

Richard Shmalensee and four other economists have done a preliminary evaluation of the program. Emissions in 1995 and 1996 were not only lower than they would have been had no program been in place, they were more than 30 percent below the limits established by the program, reflecting owners' decisions to bank a share of their allowances for future years.

The researchers estimated that the allowance program has saved 25 to 34 percent as compared to a program that would not allow trading of pollution rights. The savings would be even higher if compared to a purely command-and-control approach. They concluded their study:

Economists have argued for decades that, where the tradable permit approach can be used, it is superior to command-and-control environment regulation. The U.S. acid rain program appears to prove this argument correct in practice. Not only did Title IV more than achieve the SO_2 emissions goal established for Phase I, it did so on time, without extensive litigation, and at costs lower than had been projected. Some of the credit must be attributed to the lower rail rates that widened the area within which low-sulfur Powder River Basin coal could be economically used. Nonetheless, it is important to note that few command-and-control environmental programs, if any, have ever succeeded on all these dimensions.

Source: Richard Schmalensee et al., "An Interim Evaluation of Sulfur Dioxide Emissions Trading," *Journal of Economic Perspectives* 12: 3 (Summer 1998): 53–68.

Exhibit 18-5 shows how annual average concentrations of airborne pollutants in major U.S. cities have declined since 1975. Lead concentrations have dropped most dramatically, largely because of the increased use of unleaded gasoline.

Public policy has generally stressed command-and-control approaches to air and water pollution. To reduce air pollution, the EPA sets air quality standards that regions must achieve, then tells polluters what adjustments they must make in order to meet the standards. For water pollution, the EPA has set emissions limits based on the technologies it considers reasonable to require of polluters. If the implementation of a particular technology will reduce a polluter's emissions by 20 percent, for example, the EPA will require a 20 percent reduction in emissions. National standards have been imposed; no effort has been made to consider the benefits and costs of pollution in individual streams. Further, the EPA's technology-based approach pays little attention to actual water quality—and has produced few gains.

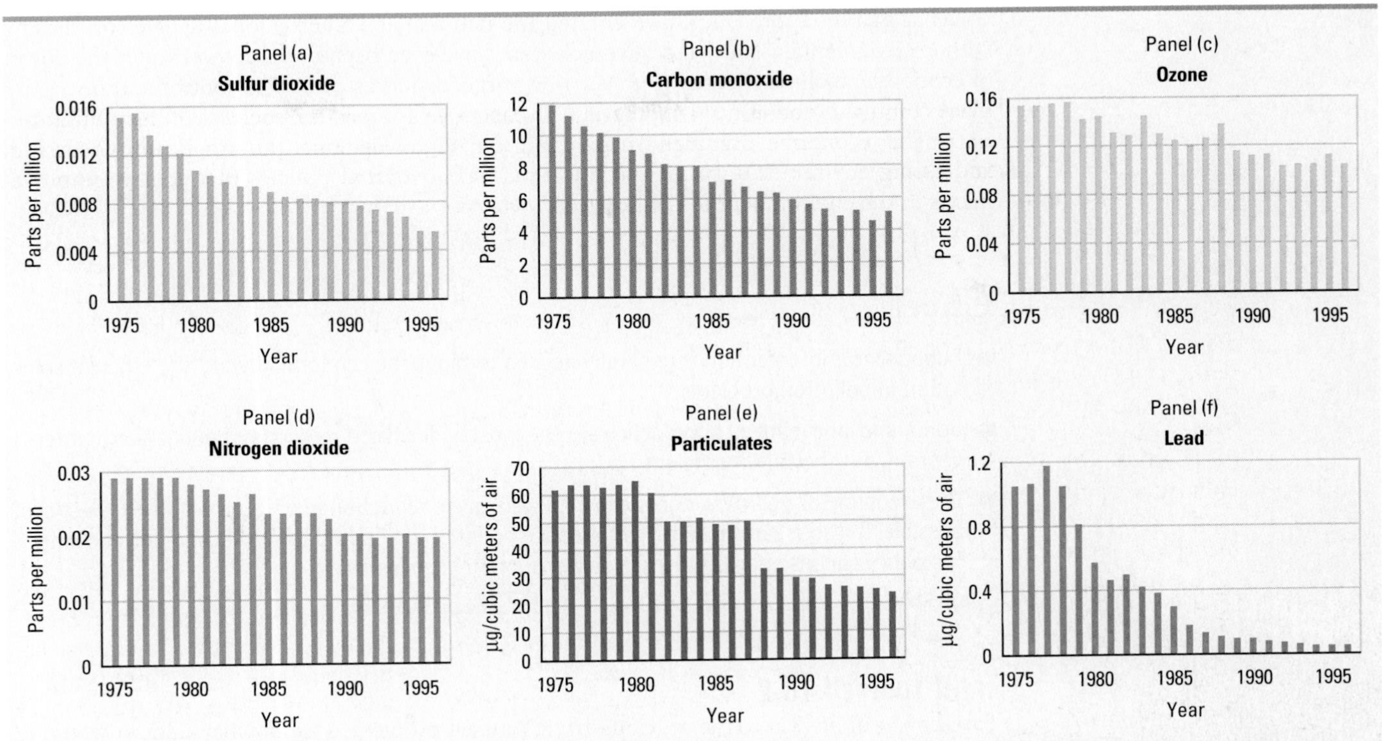

Source: U.S. Bureau of the Census, *Statistical Abstract of the United States, 1998* (Washington, D.C.: U.S. Government Printing Office, 1998), table 398, p. 242. Observations before 1990 are taken from previous volumes of the abstract.

Exhibit 18-5

Progress Against Pollution

Panels (a) through (f) give average concentration levels of major pollutants in U.S. cities from 1975 to 1996. Levels have generally fallen over that period.

Moreover, environmental problems go beyond national borders. For example, sulfur dioxide emitted from plants in the United States can result in acid rain in Canada and elsewhere. Another possible pollution problem that extends across national borders is suggested by the global warming hypothesis.

Many scientists have argued that increasing emissions of carbon dioxide, caused primarily by the burning of fossil fuels, trap ever more of the sun's energy and make the planet warmer. Global warming, they argue, could lead to flooding of coastal areas, losses in agricultural production, and the elimination of many species. If this global warming hypothesis is correct, then carbon dioxide is a pollutant with global implications, one that calls for a global solution.

At the 1997 United Nations conference in Kyoto, Japan, the industrialized countries agreed to cuts in carbon dioxide emissions of 5 percent below the 1990 level by 2010. At the 1998 conference in Buenos Aires, Argentina, 170 countries agreed on a two-year action plan for designing mechanisms to reduce emissions and procedures to encourage transfers of new energy technologies to developing countries.

Debates at these conferences have been over the extent to which developing countries should be required to reduce their emissions and over the role that market mechanisms should play. Developing countries argue that their share in total emissions is fairly small and that it is unfair to ask them to give up economic growth, given their lower income levels. As for how emissions reductions will be achieved, the United States has been the strongest advocate for emissions trading in which each country would receive a certain number of tradable emissions rights.

While the delegates to the conferences sign the various protocols, countries are not bound by them until ratified by appropriate governmental bodies. By mid-1999, only a few dozen countries had ratified the Kyoto protocols; the United States was not one of them.

That market approaches have entered the national and international debates on dealing with environmental issues, and to some extent have even been used, demonstrates the power of economic analysis. Economists have long argued that as pollution-control authorities replace command-and-control strategies with incentive approaches, society will reap huge savings. The economic argument has rested on acknowledging the opportunity costs of addressing environmental concerns and thus has advocated policies that achieve improvements in the environment in the least costly ways.

Checklist

- Public sector intervention is generally needed to move the economy toward the efficient solution in pollution problems.
- Command-and-control approaches are the most widely used methods of public sector intervention, but they are inefficient.
- The exchange of pollution rights can achieve a given reduction in emissions at the lowest cost possible. It also creates incentives to reduce pollution demand through technological change. Tax policy can also achieve a least-cost reduction in emissions.

Try It Yourself 18-2

Based on your answer to the previous Try It Yourself problem, a tax of what amount would result in the efficient quantity of pollution?

A Look Back

Pollution is a by-product of human activity. It occurs when the environment becomes scarce—when dumping garbage imposes a cost. There are benefits as well as costs to pollution; the efficient quantity of pollution occurs where the difference between total benefits and total costs is maximized. This solution is achieved where the marginal benefit of additional pollution equals the marginal cost. It is also achieved where the marginal benefit of pollution abatement equals the marginal cost of abatement.

Economists measure the benefits of pollution in terms of the costs of not dumping the pollution. The same curve can be read from left to right as the marginal benefit curve for emissions and from right to left as the marginal cost curve for abatement.

The costs of pollution are measured in two ways. One is through direct surveys. Respondents can be asked how much compensation they would be willing to accept in exchange for a reduction in environmental pollution; alternatively, they can be asked how much they would pay for an improvement in environmental quality. A second approach infers the marginal cost of increased pollution from other relationships. The effects of pollution on house prices, for example, allow economists to estimate the value people place on environmental quality. Pollution costs can also be estimated on the basis of the costs they impose on firms in production.

Three types of policies are available to reduce pollution. Moral suasion is sometimes used, but it is effective only under limited conditions. Command-and-control regulation is used most commonly, but it is likely to be inefficient. It also fails to provide incentives for technological change in the long run. The most promising policies are the incentive approaches, which include emissions taxes and marketable pollution permits. Both can be designed to reduce emissions at the lowest cost possible, and both create an incentive for firms to search out new and cheaper ways to reduce emissions.

Although public policy has stressed command-and-control methods in the past, pollution rights exchanges are now being introduced. Past policies may have been inefficient, but they have succeeded in improving air quality, at least in the nation's cities.

A Look Ahead In the next chapter, we'll turn to another set of public policy issues that can be assessed using economic analysis: the problems of poverty and discrimination. We'll look at the sources of poverty and discrimination and examine alternative public sector responses to these problems.

Terms and Concepts for Review

pollution, **355**
Coase theorem, **357**
moral suasion, **361**
command-and-control approach, **361**
least-cost reduction in emissions, **362**
incentive approaches, **362**

For Discussion

1. We noted that economists consider the benefits and costs of pollution from the perspective of people's preferences. Some critics argue, however, that the interests of plants and animals should be considered: for example, if pollution is harming trees, the trees have a right to protection. Do you think that's a good idea? How would it be implemented?
2. List five choices you make that result in pollution. What price do you pay to pollute the environment? Does that price affect your choices?
3. In any urban area, what group is likely to be exposed to a greater level of pollution—rich people or poor people? (*Hint:* Utilize the findings of economists concerning the relationship between house prices and pollution levels.)
4. Suppose the accompanying graph shows the demand and marginal cost curves, *D* and *MC*, for a pollutant in a particular area. How do you think future economic and population growth will affect the efficient rate of emissions per period, *Q*, and thus the level of pollution?

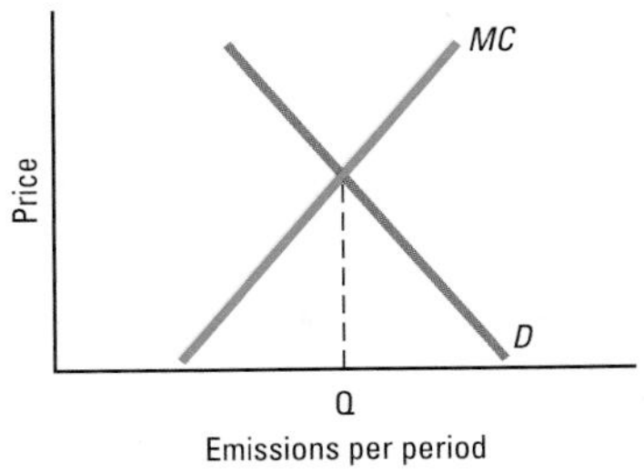

5. "Environmental quality is not just a matter of technical efficiency; it's about how people relate to nature. Economists are completely off base in their analysis of the benefits and costs of pollution." Comment.
6. Campaigns that exhort us to "Give a hoot—don't pollute" imply that anyone who pollutes the environment is uncaring—that people who are concerned about environmental quality would not be dumping garbage into the environment. Is that true?
7. We've seen that a system of marketable pollution permits achieves the same solution as a system of emissions taxes. Which do you think would be more fair? Why?
8. Many environmentalists are horrified by the notion of marketable pollution permits advocated by economists. These environmentalists insist that pollution is wrong, and that no one should be able to buy the right to pollute the environment. What do you think?
9. Some people object that charging firms for their emissions will do no good—firms will simply raise their prices and go on doing what they were doing before. Comment on this objection to emissions taxes.
10. Suppose firms in a perfectly competitive industry generate water pollution as a by-product of their production, and they aren't charged for this. Who benefits from their free use of the environment as a dumping ground? If an emissions tax is imposed, costs to these firms increase and emissions drop. Who will bear the burden of this tax? Is that fair?
11. The Case in Point on pollution in countries that were once command socialist suggests that these countries had terrible pollution problems. Do you think that a transformation of these countries to market capitalist systems would correct these problems? Why or why not?

Problems

1. Suppose the dry-cleaning industry is perfectly competitive. The process of dry cleaning generates emissions that pollute the air, and firms now emit this pollution at no cost. If the long-run equilibrium price for dry cleaning a typical item is $3 and a pollution-control program increases the marginal cost by $1 per item, how will the pollution-control program affect the price and output of dry-cleaning services in the short run and in the long run? Explain and illustrate graphically. Who pays for pollution control in the industry? Explain.
2. Suppose local government regulations allow only a single firm to provide dry-cleaning services to a local community, and this firm generates pollution as in Problem 1. The firm initially charges a price of $4 per item. Now a pollution-control program is imposed, increasing the firm's marginal and average total costs by $1 per item. Explain and illustrate graphically how the program will affect the firm's price and output. Who pays for the pollution-control program?
3. Suppose the marginal benefit (*MB*) and marginal cost (*MC*) curves for emitting particulate matter are given by the following schedules, where *E* is the quantity of emissions per period. The marginal benefits and costs are measured at the quantities of emissions shown.

E	*MB*	*MC*
0	$230	$–10
200	190	10
400	150	30
600	110	50
800	70	70
1,000	30	90

   a. Plot the marginal benefit and marginal cost curves and state the efficient quantity of emissions per period.
   b. What quantity of emissions will occur when the price of emissions is zero?
   c. What tax rate would achieve the efficient rate of emissions?

4. Now suppose that rising incomes increase marginal cost as follows:

E	New *MC*
0	$–10
200	30
400	70
600	110
800	150
1,000	190

   a. Plot the new marginal cost curve in the graph you drew in Problem 3. What is the new efficient quantity of emissions per period?
   b. What quantity of emissions will occur when the price of emissions is zero?
   c. What tax rate would achieve the efficient rate of emissions?

Answers to Try It Yourself Problems

Try It Yourself 18-1

The efficient quantity of pollution is 4 tons per week. At 1 ton of pollution, the marginal benefit exceeds the marginal cost. If the paper mill expands production, the additional pollution generated leads to additional benefits for it that are greater than the additional cost to the residents nearby. At 5 tons, the marginal cost of polluting exceeds the marginal benefit. Reducing production, and hence pollution, brings the marginal costs and benefits closer.

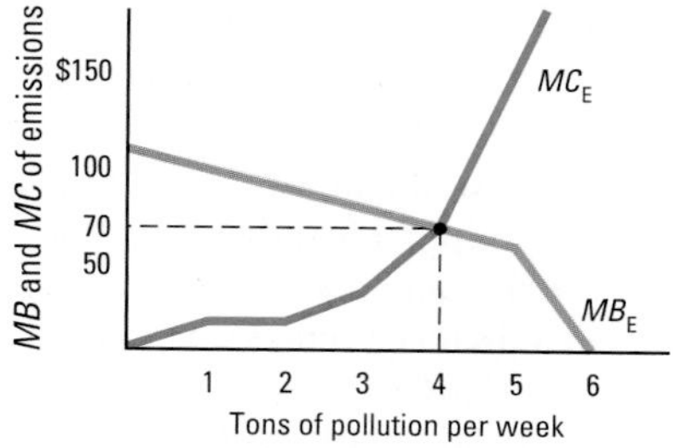

In the absence of any fees, taxes, or other charges for its pollution, the paper mill will likely choose to generate 6 tons per week, where the marginal benefit has fallen to zero.

Try It Yourself 18-2

The paper mill will reduce its pollution until the marginal benefit of polluting equals the tax. In this case a tax of $70 would cause the paper mill to reduce its pollution to 4 tons, the efficient level. At pollution levels below that amount, the marginal benefit of polluting exceeds the tax, and so the paper mill is better off polluting and paying the tax. At pollution levels greater than that amount, the marginal benefit of polluting is less than the tax.

19 Inequality, Poverty, and Discrimination

Getting Started: Fighting Poverty

It was January 8, 1964. President Lyndon B. Johnson stood before the Congress of the United States to make his first State of the Union address and to declare a new kind of war, a War on Poverty. "This administration today here and now declares unconditional war on poverty in America," the president said. "Our aim is not only to relieve the symptoms of poverty but to cure it; and, above all, to prevent it." In the United States that year, 35.1 million people, about 22 percent of the population, were, by the official definition, poor.

The president's plan included stepped-up federal aid to low-income people, an expanded health-care program for the poor, new housing subsidies, expanded federal aid to education, and job training programs. The proposal became law later that same year.

More than three decades and trillions of dollars in federal antipoverty spending later, the nation seems to have made little progress toward the president's goal. While the percentage of the population defined as poor by the federal government has declined to less than 14 percent, the number of people in poverty is essentially the same as it was when the president launched his program to eliminate poverty.

With a growing sense of frustration in the nation that the very programs that were designed to reduce poverty were contributing to it, Congress and President Clinton agreed on major changes in federal programs to help low-income people. Welfare reform in 1996 eliminated the entitlement aspect of welfare programs and emphasized moving individuals out of welfare and into work.

A year later, President Clinton proclaimed the effort a success. In his 1998 State of the Union address, he declared that the welfare reform goal of moving 2 million Americans off of welfare by the year 2000 was "two full years ahead of schedule."

Moving people off welfare, however, does not mean that will also move them out of poverty. Even with recent welfare successes, the percentage of people in the United States who are classified as poor remains higher than that of any other industrialized nation. Many people who are working still do not earn enough to lift themselves out of poverty.

Moreover, over the past three decades, the distribution of income has also become more skewed. The share of income going to the rich has risen, while the share going to the poor has fallen.

In this chapter we shall analyze three issues related to the question of fairness. We begin by looking at income inequality and explanations of why the distribution of income has grown more unequal in recent years. We shall then analyze poverty. We shall examine government programs designed to alleviate poverty and explore why so little progress appears to have been made toward eliminating it after all these years.

We shall also explore the problem of discrimination. Being at the lower end of the income distribution and being poor are more prevalent among racial minorities and among women than among white males. To a degree, this situation reflects discrimination. We shall investigate the economics of discrimination and its consequences for the victims and for the economy. We shall also assess efforts by the public sector to eliminate discrimination.

Questions of fairness often accompany discussions of income inequality, poverty, and discrimination. Answering them ultimately involves value judgments; they are normative questions, not positive ones. You must decide for yourself if a particular distribution of income is fair or if society has made adequate progress toward reducing poverty or discrimination. The material in this chapter will not answer those questions for you; rather, in order for you to have a more informed basis for making your own value judgments, it will shed light on what economists have learned about these issues through study and testing of hypotheses.

Income Inequality

We shall learn in this section how the degree of inequality can be measured, and we'll see how inequality has risen in the United States since 1968. We shall examine the sources of rising inequality and consider what policy measures, if any, are suggested.

A Changing Distribution of Income

This section describes a graphical approach to measuring the equality, or inequality, of the distribution of income.

Measuring Inequality The primary evidence of growing inequality is provided by census data. Households are asked to report their income, and they are ranked from the household with the lowest income to the household with the highest income. The Census Bureau then reports the percentage of total income earned by those households ranked among the bottom 20 percent, the next 20 percent, and so on, up to the top 20 percent. Each 20 percent of households is called a quintile. The bureau also reports the share of income going to the top 5 percent of households.

The tables in Exhibit 19-1 report the census data on income shares in 1968 and 1997, the mean income level for each quintile, and the income level at which each quintile ends. The data, adjusted for inflation and expressed in dollars of 1997 purchasing power, clearly show growing inequality since 1968. The share of income going to the bottom quintile of households fell from 4.2 percent in 1968 to 3.6 percent in 1997. The share of income going to those in the top quintile rose from 42.8 percent to 49.4 percent. The shares received by the middle three quintiles fell from 53.1 percent to 47.1 percent. The Census Bureau reported that in 1997 the lowest household in the top 5 percent had $126,550 in income, more than 8 times that of the household at the top of the lowest quintile ($15,400), while in 1968 the lowest household in the top 5 percent had just under 6 times the income of the household at the top of the lowest quintile.

Income distribution data can be presented graphically using a **Lorenz curve,** a curve that shows cumulative shares of income received by individuals or groups. To plot the curve, we begin with the lowest quintile and mark a point to show the percentage of total income those households received. We then add the next quintile and its share and mark a point to show the share of the lowest 40 percent of households. Since the share of income received by all the quintiles will be 100 percent, the last point on the curve always shows that 100 percent of households receive 100 percent of the income.

If every household in the United States received the same income, the Lorenz curve would coincide with the 45-degree line drawn in Exhibit 19-1. The bottom 20 percent of households would receive 20 percent of income, the bottom 40 percent would receive 40 percent, and so on. If the distribution of income were perfectly unequal, with one household receiving

Exhibit 19-1

The Distribution of U.S. Income, 1968 and 1997

The distribution of income among households in the United States became more unequal from 1968 to 1997. The Lorenz curve for 1997 was more bowed out than the 1968 curve. (Mean income adjusted for inflation and reported in 1997 dollars; percentages may not sum to 100% due to rounding.)

Quintile	1968 mean income	1968 income share	1997 mean income	1997 income share
Lowest 20%	$7,799	4.2	$8,872	3.6
Second 20%	20,614	11.1	22,098	8.9
Third 20%	32,692	17.5	37,177	15.0
Fourth 20%	45,608	24.5	57,582	23.2
Highest 20%	79,875	42.8	122,764	49.4
Top 5 percent		16.6		21.7

Household income at selected percentiles	1968	1997
Lowest 20% — upper limit	$14,147	$15,400
Second 20% — upper limit	26,821	29,200
Third 20% — upper limit	38,443	46,000
Fourth 20% — upper limit	54,017	71,500
Top 5%—lower limit	84,507	126,550

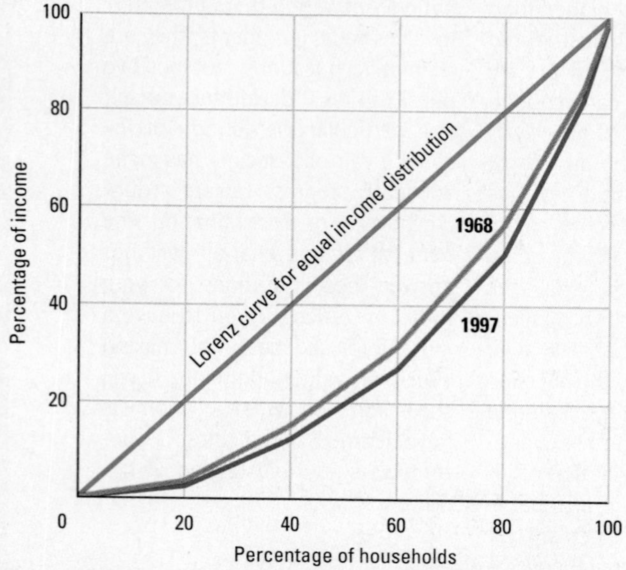

Source: U.S. Bureau of the Census, *Current Population Reports, P60–200, Money Income in the United States: 1997* (Washington, D.C.: U.S. Government Printing Office, 1998), Table B-3.

all the income and the rest zero, then the Lorenz curve would be shaped like a backward L, with a horizontal line across the bottom of the graph at 0 percent of income and a vertical line up the right-hand side. The vertical line would show, as always, that 100 percent of families still receive 100 percent of income. Actual Lorenz curves lie between these extremes. The closer a Lorenz curve lies to the 45-degree line, the more equal the distribution. The more bowed out the curve, the less equal the distribution. We see that the Lorenz curve became more bowed out between 1968 and 1997.

Mobility and Income Distribution When we speak of the bottom 20 percent or the middle 20 percent of families, we aren't speaking of a static group. Some families who are in the bottom quintile one year move up to higher quintiles in subsequent years; some families move down.

Addressing the question of mobility requires that researchers follow a specific group of families over a long period of time. Since 1968, the Panel Survey of Income Dynamics at the University of Michigan has followed 5,000 families. The effort has produced a much deeper understanding of changes in income inequality than it is possible to obtain from census data, which simply take a snapshot of incomes at a particular time.

Based on the University of Michigan's data, Professor Peter Gottschalk of Boston University[1] reported that over the 17-year period from 1974 to 1991, nearly three-fifths of those who were in the lowest quintile in 1974 had moved to a higher quintile in 1991, with most moving to the second-lowest quintile. Just under half of those starting the period in the top quintile had fallen to a lower quintile at the end of the period. Because people move up and down the distribution, we get a quite different picture of income change when we look at the incomes of a fixed set of persons over time rather than comparing average incomes for a particular quintile at a particular point in time, as was done in Exhibit 19-1. An important reason for the sharp gains in income over time for people at the bottom of the income distribution is that many who start out at the bottom are young; they tend to achieve substantial gains as they age.

Explaining Inequality

Everyone agrees that the distribution of income in the United States generally became more equal during the first two decades after World War II and that it has become more unequal since 1968. While some people conclude that this increase in inequality suggests the latter period was unfair, others want to know why the distribution changed. Let's examine some of the explanations.

Family Structure Clearly an important source of rising inequality since 1968 has been the sharp increase in the percentage of families headed by women. In 1997, the median income of families headed by married couples was 2.5 times that of families headed by women with no husband present. The percentage of families headed by women with no husband present has more than doubled since 1968.

Technological and Managerial Change Technological change has affected the demand for labor. One of the most dramatic changes since the late 1970s has been an increase in the demand for skilled labor and a reduction in the demand for unskilled labor.

The result has been an increase in the gap between the wages of skilled and unskilled workers. That has produced a widening gap between college- and high-school-trained workers. That gap more than doubled in percentage terms during the 1980s and 1990s and thus contributed to rising inequality.

[1]Peter Gottschalk, "Inequality, Income Growth, and Mobility: The Basic Facts," *Journal of Economic Perspectives* 11 (2) (Spring 1997): 21–40.

Technological change has meant the integration of computers into virtually every aspect of production. And that has increased the demand for workers with the knowledge to put new methods to work—and to adapt to the even more dramatic changes in production likely to come. At the same time, the demand for workers who don't have that knowledge has fallen.

Along with new technologies that require greater technical expertise, firms are adopting new management styles that require stronger communication skills. The use of production teams, for example, shifts decisionmaking authority to small groups of assembly-line workers. That means those workers need more than the manual dexterity that was required of them in the past. They need strong communication skills. They must write effectively, speak

Case in Point Brainy, Poor Kids Miss Out on College

One explanation for growing income inequality is the widening wage gap between the college educated and those with high school educations or less. More education is one way for people from lower income brackets to move up on the income scale. Yet, unfortunately, according to a study by Mathtech, Inc. in Princeton, New Jersey, for the Department of Education, academically talented students from low-income families are less likely to go to college than students from high-income families.

The findings are based on a survey of 13,000 students who were followed from when they were in eighth grade in 1988 through the second year after high school. To analyze the survey, the researchers divided participants into nine groups: low, medium, and high scorers on a standardized test from low-, medium-, and high-income families. Students were put into the low-income group if their families earned less than $25,000, into the middle-income group if their families earned between $25,000 and $50,000, and into the high-income group if their families earned more than $50,000.

The study found that students from the low-income families were about half as likely to pursue higher education as students from high-income families (44 percent compared to 86 percent), and that high scorers from the low-income group were less likely to attend college than *all* students from the top income group (75 percent compared to 86 percent). Even after controlling for family characteristics (such as parental education and family size), student characteristics (such as gender and race), kinds of courses taken (college prep or vocational), type of school (urban, suburban, or rural), and behavioral characteristics (such as drug use and number of hours spent on homework and watching TV), students from low-income families were 32 percent less likely to pursue post-secondary education than were students from middle-income families. Compared to middle-income families and controlling for the various factors just mentioned, students from the high-income families were 44 percent more likely to pursue post-secondary education than were students from the middle-income group.

Trying to figure out the reason for the discrepancies in college attendance statistics by income group, the researchers discovered that there was also a substantial discrepancy in percentages of parents of the then eighth graders who were knowledgeable about financial aid resources. About a quarter of the parents of the top-performing, low-income students reported that they had little information on financial aid. In contrast, less than 18 percent of *all* parents in the top income group were similarly uninformed. Another noted discrepancy was that students from low-income families were less likely to take college-prep courses.

The report stresses two policies that might reduce these discrepancies: keeping low-income students, especially those in the high-scoring group, in the college-prep track and informing them and their parents early on about financial aid opportunities. According to Karen Akerhielm, one of the study's authors, "Students and parents in the low-income group don't seem to realize that going to college is a realistic option for them."

The suggested policy changes could enhance mobility in the income distribution, as well as improve the efficiency and growth of the economy.

Source: Karen Akerhielm, Jacqueline Berger, Marianne Hooker, and Donald Wise, *Factors Related to College Enrollment* (Washington, D.C., 1998: U.S. Government Printing Office), and personal interview.

effectively, and interact effectively with other workers. Workers who can't do so simply aren't in demand to the degree they once were.

The "intellectual wage gap" seems likely to widen even further in the twenty-first century. That's likely to lead to an even higher degree of inequality and to pose a challenge to public policy for decades to come. Increasing education and training could lead to reductions in inequality. Indeed, individuals seem to have already begun to respond to this changing market situation, since the percentage who graduate from high school and college is rising.

Tax Policy Did tax policy contribute to rising inequality over the past quarter century? The tax changes most often cited in the fairness debate are the Reagan tax cuts introduced in 1981. When President Reagan came to office, the top tax rate for the rich was 70 percent. When he left, it was 28 percent. While the reductions in the top tax rate were most dramatic, taxes were reduced at all income levels. The Tax Reform Act of 1986, which lowered the top rate to 28 percent, also exempted millions of people at the bottom of the income distribution from paying any federal income tax. The top tax rate now stands at 39.6 percent.

The theory behind these reductions in marginal tax rates was to stimulate people to become more productive, earn more income, and thus in the end pay more taxes. The policy appears to have worked; taxpayers at the top of the income distribution increased not only the amount of taxes they paid but their share of total income taxes. In 1980, the top 5 percent of income earners paid 37 percent of all federal income taxes. In 1995, their share had increased to 48.9 percent. To the extent that tax policy encouraged people at the upper end of the income distribution to be more productive and earn higher incomes, it could be said to have increased the degree of inequality. On the other hand, this same tax policy left people at the upper end of the income distribution paying a much higher share of income taxes.

Check*list*

- The distribution of income has become more unequal since 1968.
- There is considerable mobility among quintiles of the distribution of income, with many families moving from lower to higher quintiles and others moving from higher to lower quintiles.
- Among the possible factors contributing to increased inequality have been changes in family structure, technological change, and tax policy.

Try It Yourself 19-1

The accompanying Lorenz curves show the distribution of income in a country before taxes and welfare benefits are taken into account (curve A) and after taxes and welfare benefits are taken into account (curve B). Do taxes and benefits serve to make the distribution of income in the country more equal or more unequal?

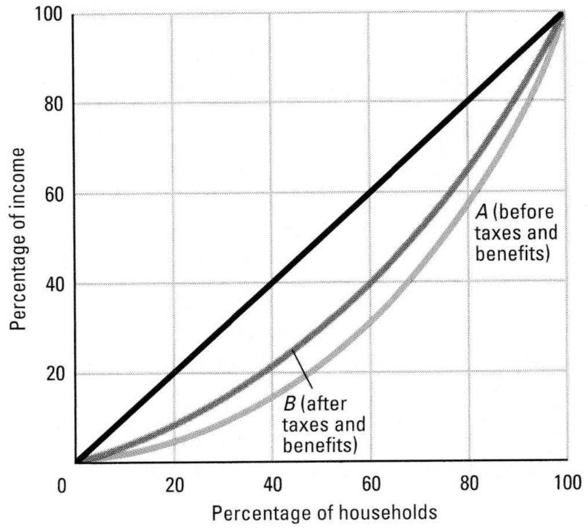

The Economics of Poverty

Poverty in the United States is something of a paradox. Per capita incomes in this country are among the highest on earth. How can a nation that is so rich have so many people who are poor?

There is no single answer to the question of why so many people are poor. But we shall see that there are economic factors at work that help to explain poverty. We shall also examine the nature of the government's response to poverty and the impact that response has. First, however, we shall examine the definition of poverty and look at some characteristics of the poor in the United States.

Defining Poverty

Suppose you were asked to determine whether a particular family was poor or not poor. How would you do it?

You might begin by listing the goods and services that would be needed to provide a minimum standard of living and then finding out if the family's income was enough to purchase those items. If it weren't, you might conclude that the family was poor. Alternatively, you might examine the family's income relative to the incomes of other families in the community or in the nation. If the family was on the low end of the income scale, you might classify it as poor.

These two approaches represent two bases on which poverty is defined. The first is an **absolute income test,** which sets a specific income level and defines a person as poor if his or her income falls below that level. The second is a **relative income test,** in which people whose incomes fall at the bottom of the income distribution are considered poor. For example, we could rank households according to income as we did in the previous section on income inequality and define the lowest one-fifth of households as poor. In 1997, any U.S. household with an annual income below $15,400 fell in this category.

In contrast, to determine who is poor according to the absolute income test, we define a specific level of income, independent of how many households fall above or below it. The federal government defines a household as poor if the household's annual income falls below a dollar figure called the **poverty line.** In 1997, the poverty line for a family of four was an income of $16,400. Exhibit 19-2 shows the poverty line for various family sizes.

The concept of a poverty line grew out of a Department of Agriculture study in 1955 that found families spending one-third of their incomes on food. With the one-third figure as a guide, the department then selected four food plans that met the minimum daily nutritional requirements established by the federal government. The cost of the least expensive plan for each household size was multiplied by 3 to determine the income below which a household would be considered poor. The government used this method to count the number of poor people from 1959 to 1969. The poverty line was adjusted each year as food prices changed. Beginning in 1969, the poverty line was adjusted annually by the average percentage price change for all consumer goods, not just changes in the price of food.

There is little to be said for this methodology for defining poverty. No attempt is made to establish an income at which a household could purchase basic

Exhibit 19-2

The Poverty Line and Household Size in the United States, 1997

The poverty line varies with household size. Figures are adjusted each year by the rate of inflation.

Number of people in household	Poverty line
1	$ 8,183
2	10,473
3	12,802
4	16,400
5	19,380
6	21,886
7	24,802
8	27,593
9 or more	32,566

Source: Joseph Dalaker and Mary Naifeh, U.S. Bureau of the Census, *Current Population Reports, Series P60-201, Poverty in the United States: 1997* (Washington, D.C.: U.S. Government Printing Office, 1998), table A-2, p. A-4.

necessities. Indeed, no attempt is made in the definition to establish what such necessities might be. The day has long passed when the average household devoted one-third of its income to food purchases; today such purchases account for less than one-fifth of household income. Still, it's useful to have some threshold that is consistent from one year to the next so that progress—or the lack thereof—in the fight against poverty can be assessed.

The percentage of the population that falls below the poverty line is called the **poverty rate.** Exhibit 19-3 shows both the number of people and the percentage of the population that fell below the poverty line each year since 1959.

Despite its shortcomings, measuring poverty using an absolute measure allows for the possibility of progress in reducing it; using a relative measure of poverty does not, since there will always be a lowest one-fifth of the population. But relative measures do make an important point: Poverty is in large measure a relative concept. In the United States, poor people have much higher incomes than most of the world's people or even than average Americans did as recently as the early 1970s. By international and historical standards, poor people in the United States are rich! The material possessions of America's poor would be considered lavish in another time and in another place. For example, in 1995 about 40 percent of poor households in the United States owned their own homes, 70 percent owned a car, and 75 percent owned a VCR. About two-thirds of poor households had air conditioning. Thirty years ago, only 36 percent of the entire population in the United States had air conditioning.[2]

But people judge their incomes relative to incomes of people around them, not relative to people everywhere on the planet or to people in years past. You may feel poor when you compare yourself to some of your classmates, who may have fancier cars or better clothes. And a family of four in a Los Angeles slum with an annual income of $13,000 surely does not feel rich because its income is many times higher than the average family income in Ethiopia or

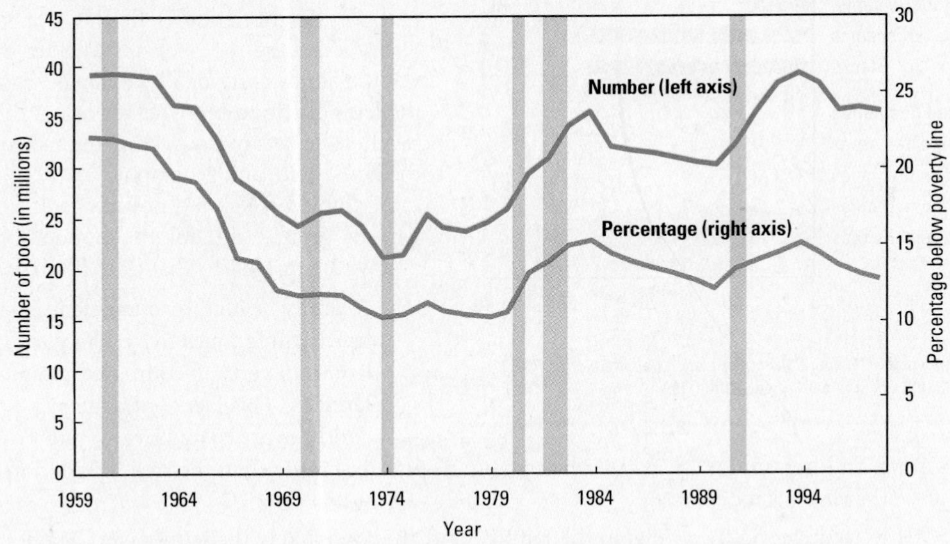

Source: Joseph Dalaker and Mary Naifeh, U.S. Bureau of the Census, *Current Population Reports, Series P60-201, Poverty in the United States: 1997* (Washington, D.C.: U.S. Government Printing Office, 1998), table C-1, p. C-2.

Exhibit 19-3

The Poverty Rate

The poverty rate has generally risen during periods of economic recession (shown as shaded areas in the chart).

[2]Robert Rector, "The Myth of Widespread American Poverty," *The Heritage Foundation Backgrounder,* No. 1221 (September 18, 1998).

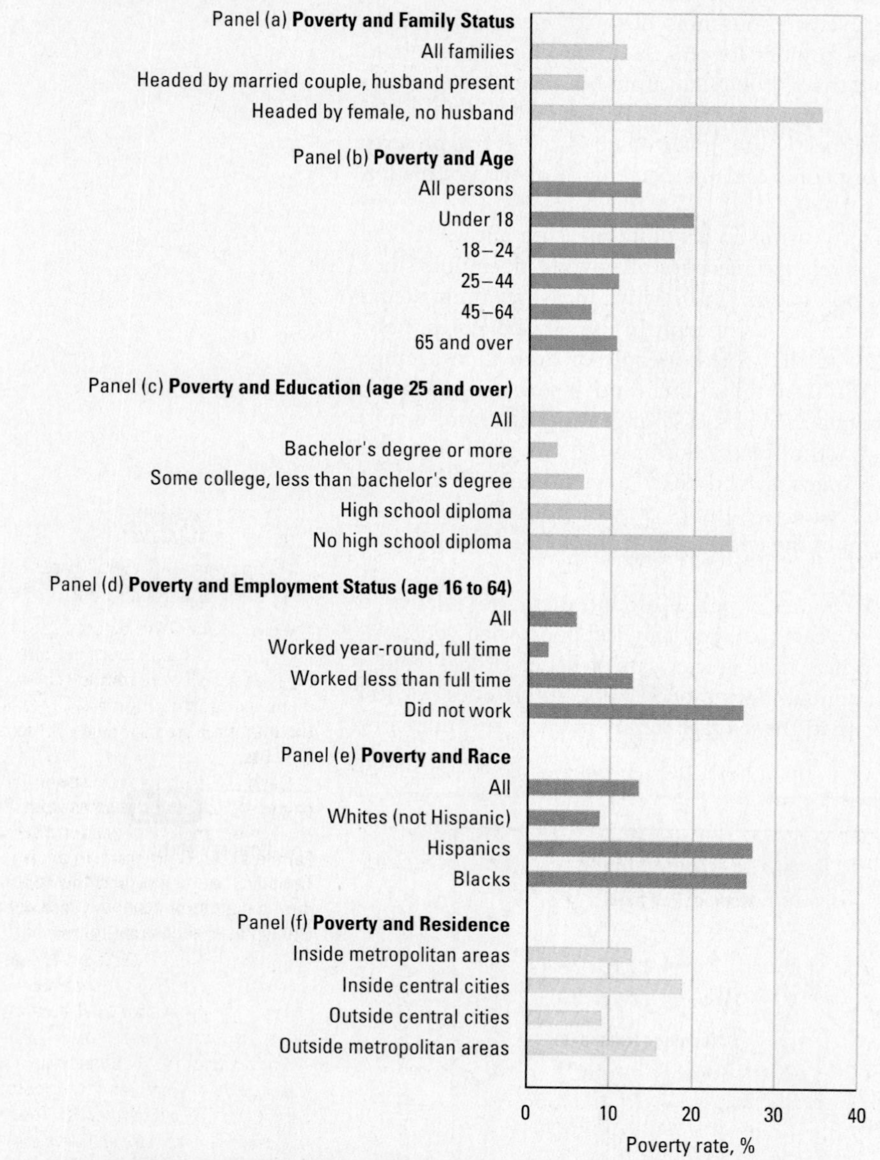

Source: Joseph Dalaker and Mary Naifeh, U.S. Bureau of the Census, *Current Population Reports, Series P60-201, Poverty in the United States: 1997* (Washington, D.C.: U.S. Government Printing Office, 1998).

Exhibit 19-4

Demographic Characteristics Affecting Poverty Rates, 1997

Panels (a) through (f) compare poverty rates among different groups of the U.S. population.

than Americans of a few decades ago. While the material possessions of poor Americans are vast by Ethiopian standards, they are low in comparison to how the average American lives. What we think of as poverty clearly depends more on what people around us are earning than on some absolute measure of income.

Both the absolute and relative income approaches are used in discussions of the poverty problem. When we speak of the number of poor people, we are typically using an absolute income test of poverty. When we speak of the problems of those at the bottom of the income distribution, we are speaking in terms of a relative income test. In the rest of this section, we focus on the absolute income test of poverty.

The Demographics of Poverty

There is no iron law of poverty that dictates that a household with certain characteristics will be poor. Nonetheless, poverty is much more highly concentrated among some groups than among others. The six characteristics of families that are important for describing who in the United States constitute the poor are whether or not the family is headed by a female, age, the level of education, whether or not the head of the family is working, the race of the household, and geography.

Exhibit 19-4 shows poverty rates for various groups and for the population as a whole in 1997. What does it tell us?

1. A family headed by a female is nearly three times more likely to live in poverty as compared to all families. This fact contributes to child poverty. The poverty rate among children under 18 in 1997 was about 20 percent higher than the rate reported in any other age category.
2. The less education the adults in the family have, the more likely the family is to be poor. A college education is an almost sure ticket out of poverty; the poverty rate for college graduates is about 3 percent.
3. The poverty rate is higher among those who do not work than among those who do. The poverty rate for people who didn't work was about 7 times the poverty rate of those who worked full time.
4. The prevalence of poverty varies by race and ethnicity. Specifically, the poverty rate in 1997 for whites (non-Hispanic origin) was less than half that for Hispanics or blacks.

5. The poverty rate in central cities was more than twice that of people living in "suburbs" (metropolitan areas outside central cities).

The incidence of poverty soars for families when several of these demographic factors associated with poverty are combined. For example, the poverty rate for families with children that are headed by women who lack a high school education is higher than 50 percent.

Government Policy and Poverty

Consider a young single parent with three small children. The parent is not employed and has no support from other relatives. What does the government provide for the family?

The primary form of cash assistance is likely to come from a program called Temporary Assistance for Needy Families (TANF). This program began with the passage of the Personal Responsibility and Work Opportunity Reconciliation Act of 1996. It replaced Aid to Families with Dependent Children (AFDC). TANF is funded by the federal government but administered through the states. Eligibility is limited to 2 years of continuous payments and to 5 years in a person's lifetime, although 20 percent of a state's caseload may be exempted from this requirement.

In addition to this assistance, the family is likely to qualify for food stamps, which are vouchers that can be exchanged for food at the grocery store. The family may also receive rent vouchers, which can be used as payment for private housing. The family may qualify for Medicaid, a program that pays for physician and hospital care as well as for prescription drugs.

A host of other programs provide help ranging from counseling in nutrition to job placement services. The parent may qualify for federal assistance in attending college. The children may participate in the Head Start program, a program of preschool education designed primarily for low-income children. If the poverty rate in the area is unusually high, local public schools the children attend may receive extra federal aid. **Welfare programs** are the array of programs that government provides to alleviate poverty.

In addition to public sector support, a wide range of help is available from private sector charities. These may provide scholarships for education, employment assistance, and other aid.

Exhibit 19-5 shows participation rates in the major federal programs to help the poor.

Not all people whose incomes fall below the poverty line receive aid. In 1997, 73 percent of those counted as poor received some form of aid. But as shown by Exhibit 19-5, the percentages who were helped by individual programs were much lower. Only 34 percent of

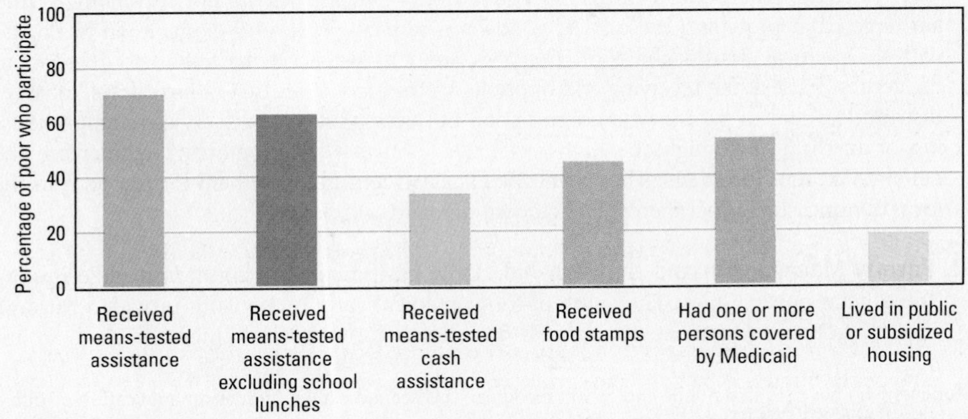

Source: U.S. Bureau of the Census, *Current Population Survey, Annual Demographic Survey 1998,* (March Supplement), Table 3 (http://ferret.bls.census.gov/macro/031998/pov/3_001.htm).

Exhibit 19-5

Participation in Public Sector Programs to Aid the Poor

The chart shows the percentage of poor people who received various types of assistance from government-sponsored programs. Some of the major programs include these benefits.

Cash The primary source of payments to families comes from the Temporary Assistance for Needy Families (TANF) program. In addition, disabled people and the dependents of deceased workers receive payments from Social Security.

Medical Care Medicaid acts as a kind of government insurance program that pays for health care for many low-income people.

Food Benefits Food stamps, vouchers distributed to low-income people, can be exchanged for food at grocery stores. Low-income children also qualify for subsidized meals at school.

Housing The federal government owns housing and provides it at a fraction of cost to low-income people. It also has a program that provides rent vouchers, which can be used as payment for rent.

Education (not shown) The federal government provides funds to school districts with a high percentage of people below the poverty line. Other educational programs include Head Start for preschool children and Pell Grants, Stafford Loans, and work-study grants for college aid.

people below the poverty line received some form of cash assistance in 1997. Less than half received food stamps and slightly more than half lived in a household in which one or more people received medical services through Medicaid. Only about one-fifth of the people living in poverty received some form of housing aid.

Although for the most part poverty programs are federally funded, individual states set eligibility standards and administer the programs. Allowing states to establish their own programs was a hallmark feature of the 1996 welfare reform. As state budgets have come under greater pressure, many states have tightened standards.

Cash Versus Noncash Assistance Aid provided to people falls into two broad categories: cash and noncash assistance. **Cash assistance** is a money payment that a recipient can spend as he or she wishes. **Noncash assistance** is the provision of specific goods and services, such as food or medical services, job training, or subsidized child care rather than cash.

Noncash assistance is the most important form of aid to the poor. The large share of noncash relative to cash assistance raises two issues. First, since the poor would be better off (that is, reach a higher level of satisfaction) with cash rather than noncash assistance, why is noncash aid such a large percentage of total aid to the poor? Second, the importance of noncash assistance raises an important issue concerning the methodology by which the poverty rate is measured in the United States. We examine these issues in turn.

1. **Why Noncash Aid?** Suppose you had a choice between receiving $515 or a television set worth $515. Neither gift is taxable. Which would you take?

   Given a choice between cash and an equivalent value in merchandise, you'd probably take the cash. Unless the television set happened to be exactly what you would purchase with the $515, you could find some other set of goods and services that you would prefer to the TV set. The same is true of funds that you can spend on anything versus funds whose spending is restricted. Given a choice of $515 that you could spend on anything and $515 that you could spend only on food, which would you choose? A given pool of funds allows consumers a greater degree of satisfaction than does a specific set of goods and services.

   We can conclude that poor people who receive government aid would be better off from their own perspectives with cash grants than with noncash aid. Why, then, is most government aid given as noncash benefits?

   Economists have suggested two explanations. The first is based on the preferences of donors. Recipients might prefer cash, but the preferences of donors matter also. The donors, in this case, are taxpayers. Suppose they want poor people to have specific things—perhaps food, housing, and medical care. Given such donor preferences, it's not surprising to find aid targeted at providing these basic goods and services. A second explanation has to do with the political clout of the poor. The poor are not likely to be successful competitors in the contest to be at the receiving end of public sector income redistribution efforts; most redistribution goes to people who are not poor. But firms that provide services such as housing or medical care might be highly effective lobbyists for programs that increase the demand for their products. They could be expected to seek more help for the poor in the form of noncash aid that increases their own demand and profits.[3]

2. **Poverty Management and Noncash Aid.** Only cash income is counted in determining the official poverty rate. The value of food, medical care, or housing provided through various noncash assistance programs is not included in household income. That's an im-

[3]Students who have studied public choice will recognize this second explanation as an application of public choice theory.

portant omission, because most government aid is noncash aid. Data for the official poverty rate thus do not reflect the full extent to which government programs act to reduce poverty.

The Census Bureau estimates the impact of noncash assistance on poverty. If a typical household would prefer, say, $515 in cash to $515 in food stamps, then $515 worth of food stamps is not valued at $515 in cash. Economists at the Census Bureau adjust the value of noncash aid downward to reflect an estimate of its lesser value to households. Suppose, for example, that given the choice between $515 in food stamps and $475 in cash, a household reports that it is indifferent between the two—either would be equally satisfactory. That implies that $515 in food stamps generates satisfaction equal to $475 in cash; the food stamps are thus "worth" $475 to the household.

Each year, the Census Bureau reports alternative estimates of the poverty rate that correct for this and some other problems. Exhibit 19-6 shows the official poverty rate for 1997, 13.3 percent. Incorporating the value of noncash assistance, along with adjusting for some other measurement problems, reduces it to 8.8 percent.

Welfare Reform

The welfare system in the United States came under increasing attack in the 1980s and early 1990s. It was perceived to be expensive, and it had clearly failed to eliminate poverty. Many observers worried that welfare was becoming a way of life for people who had withdrawn from the labor force, and that existing welfare programs did not provide an incentive for people to work. President Clinton made welfare reform one of the key issues in the 1992 presidential campaign.

The Personal Responsibility and Work Opportunity Reconciliation Act of 1996 was designed to move people from welfare to work. It eliminated the entitlement aspect of welfare by defining a maximum period of eligibility. It gave states considerable scope in designing their own programs. In the first two years following welfare reform, the number of people on welfare dropped by several million.

Advocates of welfare reform proclaimed victory, while critics pointed to the booming economy, the tight labor market, and the general increase in the number of jobs over the same period. The critics also pointed out that the most employable welfare recipients (those with a high school education, no school-aged children living at home, fewer personal problems) were the first to find jobs. The remaining welfare recipients, the critics argue, will have a harder time doing so. Moreover, having a job is not synonymous with getting out of poverty. Though some cities and states have reported notable successes (see the Case in Point on Experimental Welfare Programs), more experience is required before a final verdict can be reached.

Exhibit 19-6

Alternative Measures of the Poverty Rate

The poverty rate falls from the official level of 13.3 percent in 1997 to 8.8 percent when noncash assistance is counted. (Correction to inflation rate also included.)

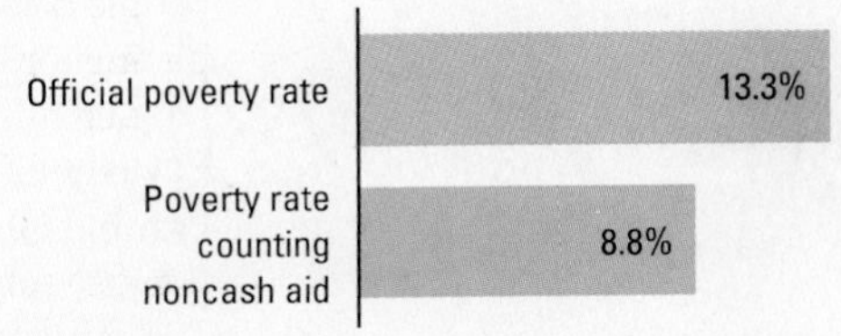

Source: Joseph Dalaker and Mary Naifeh, U.S. Bureau of the Census, *Current Population Reports, Series P60-201, Poverty in the United States: 1997* (Washington, D.C.: U.S. Government Printing Office, 1998).

Explaining Poverty

Just as the increase in income inequality begs for explanation, so does the question of why poverty seems so persistent. Shouldn't the long periods of economic growth in the 1980s and 1990s have substantially reduced poverty? Have the various government programs been ineffective?

Clearly, some of the same factors that have contributed to rising income inequality have also contributed to the persistence of poverty. In particular, the increase in households headed by females and the growing gaps in wages between skilled and unskilled workers have been major contributors.

On the other hand, tax policy changes have reduced the extent of poverty. In addition to general reductions in tax rates, the Earned Income Tax Credit, which began in 1975 and was expanded in the 1990s, provides

Case in Point Experimental Welfare Programs Show Early Successes

In Portland, Oregon, a former welfare client (right) found full-time work as an office manager after participating in an experimental program to place welfare recipients in jobs.

Even before the 1996 welfare reform act went into effect, states were experimenting with almost every means they could think of to pare down their welfare rolls, and with notable success. Since 1996, the number of experiments has multiplied. By 1998, nearly every state had some type of welfare program in effect that at the start of the decade would have seemed radical.

Indeed, the number of people receiving TANF declined dramatically between 1996 and 1998. Two experiments—one in Portland, Oregon, and the other in Los Angeles, California—give grounds for cautious optimism that welfare reform programs may be having a positive effect. In both cases, Manpower Demonstration Research Corporation, a New York based research company, compared welfare clients who were served through a more traditional program to those who were served by an experimental program over the same period.

The experimental Portland program allowed clients 6 to 9 months for basic education, job training, motivational training, self-esteem courses, drug and alcohol treatment, and subsidized work experiences. Besides these "carrots," the program also had a "stick": Recipients could lose part of their checks for noncompliance with the program. Researchers found that about 20 percent had lost part of their welfare checks for an average length of penalty of 5 months. The 3-year study found that those in the experimental program had a higher employment rate (72 percent versus 61 percent) and higher wages ($7.34 an hour compared to $6.48 an hour) than those in the traditional program. (Traditional programs simply allowed anyone who applied and met the eligibility criteria to receive payments.) Costs to the government were about $1,200 per person lower.

The Los Angeles experimental program required welfare recipients to attend job orientation sessions, to look for work, to participate in job clubs, and to work with job counselors. The study of the Los Angeles experimental program covered a shorter period than that of the Portland program, but the findings pointed in the same direction. Those in the experimental program had a higher employment rate (43 percent versus 32 percent) and higher monthly earnings ($1,286 versus $879 in the first six months) than those in traditional programs. The Los Angeles findings are particularly encouraging because welfare rolls in large cities have been shrinking more slowly than those in small urban, suburban, and rural areas. Also, most of those included in the Los Angeles experiment were "difficult" cases consisting of people without high school diplomas and with limited proficiency in English.

Whether these early signs of success will continue or not is an open question. Will the newly employed keep working, especially when job growth slows or turns negative? Also, despite being employed, many continue to receive various forms of welfare because their incomes are still low.

Sources: Judith Haveman, "Study Praises Oregon Welfare Reform Results," *Washington Post,* 24 June 1998, p. A3, and Judith Havemann, "Welfare Reform Success Cited in Los Angeles," *Washington Post,* 20 August 1998, p. A1.

people below a certain income level with a supplement for each dollar of income earned. This supplement, roughly 30 cents for every dollar earned, is received as a tax refund at the end of the year.

Poverty and Economic Growth To see what role economic growth has played, look back at Exhibit 19-3. Notice that in the past, periods of economic expansion tended to reduce the poverty rate, but recently that relationship has broken down. The economic expansion of the 1980s, a long one by the standards of U.S. economic history, brought a reduction in the poverty rate of just 2.2 percentage points. From 1989 to 1998, the poverty rate actually increased 0.2 percent, despite the longest peacetime expansion in U.S. history. In contrast, the expansion of the 1960s reduced the rate by nearly 10 percentage points. Economic growth does not appear to pack the antipoverty wallop it once did. Why not?

One answer appears in Exhibit 19-4. Many of the poor are children or adults who do not work. That suggests one explanation for the weak relationship between poverty and economic growth in recent years. A growing economy reduces poverty by creating more jobs and higher incomes. Neither of those will reach those who, for various reasons, are not in the labor force.

Look at Exhibit 19-7. Of the nation's 35.6 million poor people in 1997, only about 9.9 million could be considered available to participate in the labor market. The rest were either too young, retired, sick or disabled, or they were students or people who were unavailable for work because of their family situations, such as responsibility for caring for disabled family members.

Of the nearly 10 million poor people available for work, about two-thirds were already working full time; only about a third were available for work in 1997, but were not working. Exhibit 19-7 summarizes this information; it shows that most of the nation's poor people are unlikely to be available for work in an expanding economy.

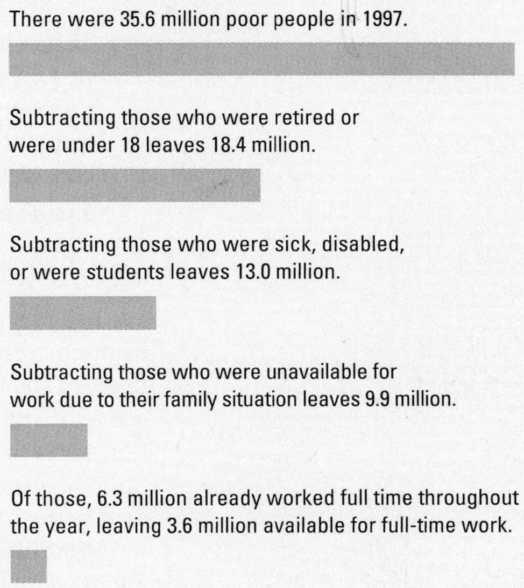

There were 35.6 million poor people in 1997.
Subtracting those who were retired or were under 18 leaves 18.4 million.
Subtracting those who were sick, disabled, or were students leaves 13.0 million.
Subtracting those who were unavailable for work due to their family situation leaves 9.9 million.
Of those, 6.3 million already worked full time throughout the year, leaving 3.6 million available for full-time work.

Source: Joseph Dalaker and Mary Naifeh, U.S. Bureau of the Census, *Current Population Reports, Series P60-201,Poverty in the United States: 1997,* U.S.Government Printing Office, Washington, DC, 1998 and Current Population Survey, Annual Demographic Survey (March Supplement), Table 13 (http://ferret.bls.census.gov/macro/031998/pov/13_000.htm).

Exhibit 19-7

Employment Status of the Nation's Poor

Most poor people are, for reasons of age, physical condition, or family or school status, unavailable for work at any one time.

Poverty and Welfare Programs How effective have government programs been in alleviating poverty? Here, it is important to distinguish between the poverty rate and the degree of poverty. Cash programs might reduce the degree of poverty, but might not affect a family's income enough to actually move that family above the poverty line. Thus, even though the gap between the family's income and the poverty line is lessened, the family is still classified as poor and would thus still be included in the poverty-rate figures. The data in Exhibit 19-7 show that significant gains in work participation will be difficult to achieve.

Empirical studies prior to federal welfare reform generally showed that welfare payments discouraged work effort, but the effect was fairly small.[4] Evaluation of the effect of the federal welfare reform program on work participation, particularly over the long term, and on poverty continues.

Checklist

- Poverty can be defined in both absolute and relative terms. The standard definition of poverty is based on the concept of the poverty line, an absolute test.
- Poverty is concentrated among families headed by women, families in which the adults have little education and/or do not participate in the labor force, the young, and racial minorities. The poverty rate is higher in central cities than elsewhere.
- Most welfare aid is given in the form of noncash assistance.
- The official poverty rate is based on estimates of household money income only; it does not count the value of noncash benefits. A calculation of the rate incorporating the value of noncash benefits suggests a much lower poverty rate than the official measure.
- Welfare reform in 1996 was designed to move people out of welfare and into work. It also limited the number of years that individuals are allowed to receive welfare payments.

[4]For a review of the literature, see Rebecca M. Blank, *It Takes a Nation* (New York: Russell Sage Foundation: 1997).

Try It Yourself 19-2

The Smiths, a family of four, have an income of $16,000 in 1997. Using the absolute income test approach and the data given in the chapter, determine if this family is poor. Use the relative income test to determine if this family is poor. Suppose the family receives various forms of noncash assistance valued at $2,000. Including such assistance, would it still be considered poor? If so, according to which income test(s)?

The Economics of Discrimination

We have just seen that being a female head of household or being a member of a racial minority increases the likelihood of being at the low end of the income distribution and of being poor. In the real world, we know that on average women and members of racial minorities receive different wages from white male workers, even though they may have similar qualifications and backgrounds. They might be charged different prices or denied employment opportunities. This section examines the economic forces that create such discrimination, as well as the measures that can be used to address it.

Discrimination occurs when people with similar economic characteristics experience different economic outcomes because of their race, sex, or other noneconomic characteristics. A black worker whose skills and experience are identical to those of a white worker but who receives a lower wage is a victim of discrimination. A woman denied a job opportunity solely on the basis of her gender is the victim of discrimination. To the extent that discrimination exists, a country will not be allocating resources efficiently; the economy will be operating inside its production possibilities curve.

Discrimination in the Marketplace: A Model

Pioneering work on the economics of discrimination was done by Gary S. Becker, an economist at the University of Chicago who won the Nobel Prize in economics in 1992. He suggested that discrimination occurs because of people's preferences or attitudes. If enough people have prejudices against certain racial groups, or against women, or against people with any particular characteristic, the market will respond to those preferences.

In Mr. Becker's model, discriminatory preferences drive a wedge between the outcomes experienced by different groups. Discriminatory preferences can make salespeople less willing to sell to one group than to another or make consumers less willing to buy from the members of one group than from another.

Let's explore Mr. Becker's model by examining labor-market discrimination against black workers. We begin by assuming that no discriminatory preferences or attitudes exist. For simplicity, suppose that the supply curves of black and white workers are identical; they are shown as a single curve in Exhibit 19-8. Suppose further that all workers have identical marginal products; they are equally productive. In the absence of racial preferences, the demand for workers of both races would be D. Black and white workers would each receive a wage W per unit of labor. A total of L black workers and L white workers would be employed.

Now suppose that employers have discriminatory attitudes that cause them to assume that a black worker is less productive than an otherwise similar white worker. Now employers have a lower demand, D_B, for black than for white workers. Employers pay black workers a lower wage, W_B, and employ fewer of them, L_B instead of L, than they would in the absence of discrimination.

Exhibit 19-8

A Model of Discrimination

Assuming that black and white workers have the same supply curve $S_{B,W}$, these two groups have identical marginal products, and employers have no discriminatory preferences. Both black and white workers face the same demand curve D. Both groups earn the same wage W and experience the same level of employment L. If discriminatory preferences or attitudes confront blacks with a lower demand D_B, they will receive a lower wage W_B. Employment among black workers will fall to L_B.

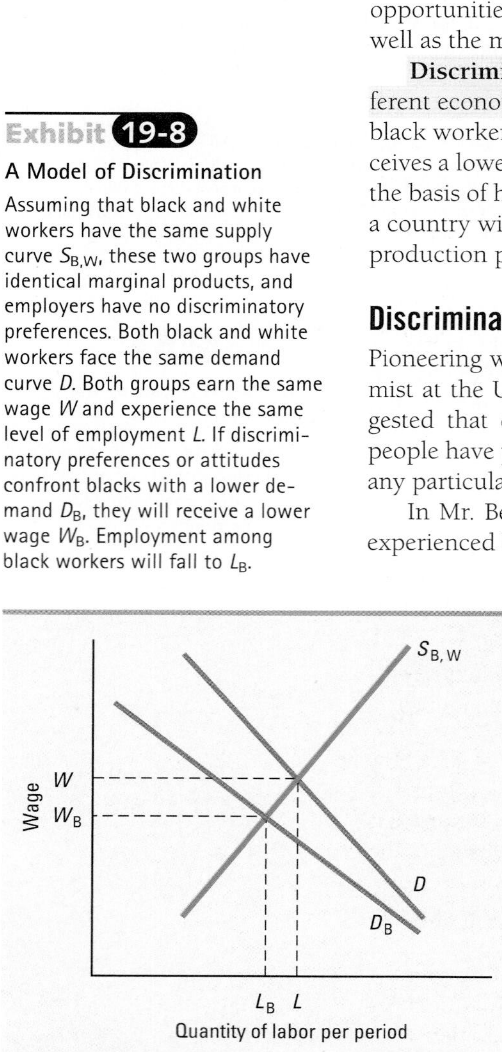

Sources of Discrimination

As illustrated in Exhibit 19-8, racial prejudices on the part of employers produce discrimination against black workers, who receive lower wages and have fewer employment opportunities than white workers. Discrimination can result from prejudices among other groups in the economy as well.

One source of discriminatory prejudices is other workers. Suppose, for example, that white workers prefer not to work with black workers and require a wage premium for doing so. Such preferences would, in effect, raise the cost to the firm of hiring black workers. Firms would respond by demanding fewer of them, and wages for black workers would fall.

Another source of discrimination against black workers could come from customers. If the buyers of a firm's product prefer not to deal with black employees, the firm might respond by demanding fewer of them. In effect, prejudice on the part of consumers would lower the revenue that firms can generate from the output of black workers.

Whether discriminatory preferences exist among employers, employees, or consumers, the impact on the group discriminated against will be the same. Fewer members of that group will be employed, and their wages will be lower than the wages of other workers whose skills and experience are otherwise similar.

Race and sex aren't the only characteristics that affect hiring and wages. Some studies have found that people who are short, overweight, or physically unattractive also suffer from discrimination, and charges of discrimination have been voiced by disabled people and by homosexuals. Whenever discrimination occurs, it implies that employers, workers, or customers have discriminatory preferences. For the effects of such preferences to be felt in the marketplace, they must be widely shared.

There are, however, market pressures that can serve to lessen discrimination. For example, if some employers hold discriminatory preferences but others do not, it will be profit enhancing for those who do not to hire workers from the group being discriminated against. Because workers from this group are less expensive to hire, costs for the nondiscriminating firms will be lower. If the market is at least somewhat competitive, firms who continue to discriminate may be driven out of business.

Discrimination in the United States Today

The federal government has waged a long and vigorous battle against discrimination. In 1954, the U.S. Supreme Court rendered its decision that so-called separate but equal schools for black and white children were inherently unequal, and the Court ordered that racially segregated schools be integrated. The Equal Pay Act of 1963 requires employers to pay the same wages to men and women who do substantially the same work. Federal legislation was passed in 1965 to ensure that minorities were not denied the right to vote.

Congress passed the most important federal legislation against discrimination in 1964. The Civil Rights Act barred discrimination on the basis of race, sex, or ethnicity in pay, promotion, hiring, firing, and training. An Executive Order issued by President Lyndon Johnson in 1967 required federal contractors to implement affirmative action programs to ensure that members of minority groups and women were given equal opportunities in employment. The practical effect of the order was to require that these employers increase the percentage of women and minorities in their work forces. Affirmative action programs at most colleges and universities for minorities followed.

What has been the outcome of these efforts to reduce discrimination? A starting point is to look at wage differences among different groups. Gaps in wages between males and females and between blacks and whites have fallen over time. In 1955, the wages of black men were about 60 percent of those of white men; in 1997, they were 73 percent of those of white men.

For black men, the reduction in the wage gap occurred primarily between 1965 and 1975. In contrast, the gap between the wages of black women and white men closed more substantially, and progress in closing the gap continued after 1975, albeit at a slower rate. Specifically, the wages of black women were about 35 percent of those of white men in 1955, 58 percent in 1975, and 63 percent in the 1997. For white women, the pattern of gain is still different. The wages of white women were about 65 percent of those of white men in 1955, and fell to about 60 percent from the mid-1960s to the late 1970s. The wages of white females relative to white males did improve, however, over the last 20 years. In 1997, white female wages were 75 percent of white male wages. While there has been improvement in wage gaps between black men, black women, and white women vis-à-vis white men, a substantial gap still remains. Exhibit 19-9 shows the wage differences for the period 1969–1997.

Exhibit 19-9

Ratio of Median Earnings by Gender and Race

While there has been a reduction in wage gaps between black men, black women, and white women vis-à-vis white men, a substantial gap still remains. (For black men, the reduction in the wage gap occurred primarily between 1965 and 1975.)

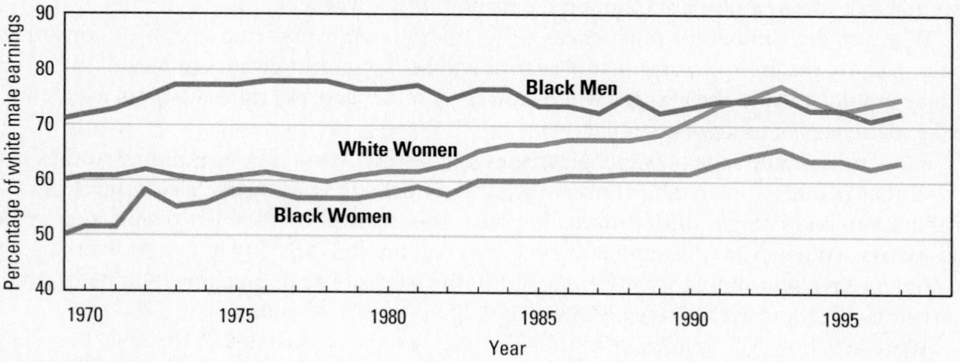

One question that economists try to answer is the extent to which the gaps are due to discrimination per se and the extent to which they reflect other factors, such as differences in education, job experience, or choices that dividuals in particular groups make about labor-force participation. Once these factors are accounted for, the amount of the remaining wage differential due to discrimination is less than the raw differentials presented in Exhibit 19-9 would seem to indicate.

There is evidence as well that the wage differential due to discrimination against women and blacks, as measured by empirical studies, has declined over time. For example, a number of studies have concluded that black men in the 1980s and 1990s experienced a 12 to 15 percent loss in earnings due to labor-market discrimination.[5] University of Chicago economist James Heckman denies that the entire 12 to 15 percent differential is due to racial discrimination, pointing to problems inherent in measuring and comparing human capital among individuals. Nevertheless, he reports that the earnings loss due to discrimination similarly measured would have been between 30 and 40 percent in 1940 and still over 20 percent in 1970.[6]

Can civil rights legislation take credit for the reductions in labor-market discrimination over time? To some extent, yes. A study by Heckman and John J. Donohue III, a law professor at Northwestern University, concluded that the landmark 1964 Civil Rights Act, as well as other civil rights activity leading up to the act, had the greatest positive impact on blacks in the South during the decade following its passage. Evidence of wage gains by black men in

[5]William A. Darity and Patrick L. Mason, "Evidence on Discrimination in Employment," *Journal of Economic Perspectives* 12:2 (Spring 1998): 63–90.

[6]James, J. Heckman, "Detecting Discrimination," *Journal of Economic Perspectives* 12:2 (Spring 1998): 101-116.

Case in Point Discrimination in Home Mortgage Lending

Besides jobs and wages, another potential source of economic discrimination is in the area of access to credit. The 1990 Home Mortgage Disclosure Act requires banks to disclose information on the numbers of home-loan applications they accept and reject by race, sex, and income. Ever since, the annual report has shown that the home mortgage rejection rate for blacks and Hispanics is higher than the rejection rate for whites. The 1991 report showed that the rejection rate for white applicants was 14.4 percent, compared to 33.9 percent for black applicants and 21.4 percent for Hispanics. The 1997 report showed rejection rates of 26 percent, 53 percent, and 38 percent, for white, black, and Hispanic applicants, respectively.

While these data appear to suggest discrimination on the part of lending institutions, it is also possible that the differences in rejection rates could be justified on other grounds. The profitability of a mortgage depends not only on the interest rate charged, but also on the probability that the borrower will default. If there are reasons why minority applicants are more likely than white applicants to default on their mortgages, due to such factors as the applicant's ratio of debt payments to income, past credit problems, instability of employment, or other aspects of creditworthiness, then the differential loan rejection rates could be attributed to the desire of lending institutions to maximize profits and not to discrimination per se.

To test the extent to which such legitimate factors explain the difference in loan rejection rates by race, then Council of Economic Advisors member Alicia Munnell and Federal Reserve Bank of Boston researchers Geoffrey Tootell, Lynn Browne, and James McEneany conducted a detailed study of the Boston housing market. After accounting for additional variables that lending institutions deem important in making lending decisions, they concluded that race still played an important, though lesser, role in the mortgage-lending decision. Controlling for applicant and property characteristics reduced the discrepancy in the mortgage rejection rate from 18 percentage points to 8 percentage points—smaller but still significant. While recognizing that their results could still be challenged due to failure to control for some other legitimate factors in mortgage evaluation, the authors conclude that "The results of this study suggest that, given the same property and personal characteristics, white applicants may enjoy a general presumption of creditworthiness that black and Hispanic applicants do not" (p. 26).

Source: Alicia H. Munnell, Geoffrey M. B. Tootell, Lynn E. Browne, and James McEneany, "Mortgage Lending in Boston: Interpreting HMDA Data," *American Economic Review* 86 (1) (March 1996): 25–53.

other regions of the country was, however, minimal. Most federal activity was directed toward the South, and the civil rights effort shattered an entire way of life that had subjugated black Americans and had separated them from mainstream life.[7]

In recent years, affirmative action programs have been under attack. Proposition 209, passed in California in 1996, and Initiative 200, passed in Washington State in 1998, bar preferential treatment due to race in admission to public colleges and universities in those states. The 1996 Hopwood case against the University of Texas, decided by the United States Court of Appeals for the Fifth Circuit, eliminated the use of race in university admissions, both public and private, in Texas, Louisiana, and Mississippi.

Controversial research by two former Ivy League university presidents, political scientist Derek Bok of Harvard University and economist William G. Bowen of Princeton University,

[7]John J. Donohue III and James Heckman, "Continuous Versus Episodic Change: The Impact of Civil Rights Policy on the Economic Status of Blacks," *Journal of Economic Literature* 29 (December 1991): 1603–1643.

concluded that affirmative action policies have created the backbone of the black middle class and taught white students the value of integration. The study focused on affirmative action at 28 elite colleges and universities. It found that while blacks enter those institutions with lower test scores and grades than those of whites, receive lower grades, and graduate at a lower rate, after graduation blacks earn advanced degrees at rates identical to those of their former white classmates and are more active in civic affairs.[8]

While stricter enforcement of civil rights laws or new programs designed to reduce labor-market discrimination may serve to further improve earnings of groups that have been historically discriminated against, wage gaps between groups also reflect differences in choices and in "premarket" conditions, such as family environment and early education. Some of these premarket conditions may themselves be the result of discrimination.

The narrowing in wage differentials may reflect the dynamics of the Becker model at work. As people's preferences change, or are forced to change due to competitive forces and changes in the legal environment, discrimination against various groups will decrease. However, it may be a long time before discrimination disappears from the labor market, not only due to remaining discriminatory preferences but also because the human capital and work characteristics that people bring to the labor market are decades in the making.

Checklist

- Discrimination occurs when people with similar economic characteristics experience dissimilar economic outcomes because of a characteristic such as race or sex.
- An economic model suggests that discrimination is a response to discriminatory preferences on the part of individual employers, consumers, or employees.
- Discriminatory preferences cause some groups to experience lower wages and fewer employment opportunities and to pay higher prices than others.
- Wage gaps between women and blacks on the one hand, and white males on the other hand, have fallen since the 1950s, though for black males, most of the reduction occurred between 1965 and 1975. Much of the declining wage gap is due to acquisition of human capital by women and blacks, but some of the reduction also reflects a reduction in discrimination.

Try It Yourself 19-3

Use a production possibilities curve (introduced in Chapter 2) to illustrate the impact of discrimination on the production of goods and services in the economy. Label the horizontal axis as consumer goods per year. Label the vertical axis as capital goods per year. Label a point A *that shows an illustrative bundle of the two which can be produced given the existence of discrimination. Label another point* B *that lies on the production possibilities curve above and to the right of point* A*. Use these two points to describe the outcome that might be expected if discrimination were eliminated.*

[8]Derek Bok and William G. Bowen, *The Shape of the River: Long-Term Consequences of Considering Race in College and University Admissions* (Princeton N.J.: Princeton University Press, 1998).

A Look Back

In this chapter, we looked at three issues related to the question of fairness: income inequality, poverty, and discrimination.

The distribution of income in the United States has become more unequal in the last three decades. Among the factors contributing to increased inequality have been changes in family structure, technological change, and tax policy. While rising inequality can be a concern, there is a good deal of movement of families up and down the distribution of income.

Poverty can be measured using an absolute or a relative income standard. The official measure of poverty in the United States relies on an absolute standard. This measure tends to overstate the poverty rate because it does not count noncash welfare aid as income. Poverty is concentrated among female-headed households, minorities, people with relatively little education, and people who are not in the labor force. Children have a particularly high poverty rate.

Welfare reform in 1996 focused on moving people off welfare and into work. It limits the number of years that individuals can receive welfare payments and allows states to design the specific parameters of their own welfare programs. Between 1996 and 1998, the number of people on welfare fell dramatically. Whether this reduction is due to the booming economy of that time or to reforms in the programs that states run awaits further analysis.

Federal legislation bans discrimination. Affirmative action programs, though controversial, are designed to enhance opportunities for minorities and women. Wage gaps between women and white males and between blacks and white males have declined since the 1950s. For black males, however, most of the reduction occurred between 1965 and 1975. Much of the decrease in wage gaps is due to acquisition of human capital by women and blacks, but some of the decrease also reflects a reduction in discrimination.

Terms and Concepts for Review

Lorenz curve, **370**
absolute income test, **374**
relative income test, **374**
poverty line, **374**
poverty rate, **375**
welfare programs, **377**
cash assistance, **378**
noncash assistance, **378**
discrimination, **382**

For Discussion

1. Explain how rising demand for college-educated workers and falling demand for high-school-educated workers contributes to increased inequality of the distribution of income.
2. Discuss the advantages and disadvantages of the following three alternatives for dealing with the rising inequality of wages.
   a. Increase the minimum wage each year so that wages for unskilled workers rise as fast as wages for skilled workers.
   b. Subsidize the wages of unskilled workers.
   c. Do nothing.
3. How would you define poverty? How would you determine whether a particular family is poor? Is the test you have proposed an absolute or a relative test?
4. Why does the failure to adjust the poverty line for regional differences in living costs lead to an understatement of poverty in some states and an overstatement of poverty in others?
5. The text argues that welfare recipients could achieve higher levels of satisfaction if they received cash rather than in-kind aid. Use the same argument to make a case that gifts given at Christmas should be in cash rather than specific items. Why do you suppose they usually are not?

6. Suppose a welfare program provides a basic grant of $10,000 per year to poor families but reduces the grant by $1 for every $1 of income earned. How would such a program affect a household's incentive to work?
7. Welfare reform calls for a 2-year limit on welfare payments, after which recipients must go to work. Suppose a recipient with children declines work offers. Should aid be cut? What about the children?
8. How would you tackle the welfare problem? State the goals you would seek, and explain how the measures you propose would work to meet those goals.
9. Suppose a common but unfounded belief held that people with blue eyes were not as smart as people with brown eyes. What would we expect to happen to the relative wages of the two groups? Suppose you were an entrepreneur who knew that the common belief was wrong. What could you do to enhance your profits?

Problems

1. Here are income distribution data for three countries, from the *World Development Report 1998/99*, table 5. Plot the Lorenz curves for each in a single graph, and compare the degree of inequality for the three countries. (Don't forget to convert the data to cumulative shares; e.g., the lowest 40 percent of the population in Panama receives 8.3 percent of total income.) Compare your results to the Lorenz curve given in the text for the United States. Which country in your chart appears closest to the United States in terms of its income distribution?

	Quintiles					
	Lowest	2nd	3rd	4th	Highest 20%	Highest 10%
Panama	2.0	6.3	11.3	20.3	60.1	42.5
Hungary	9.7	13.9	16.9	21.4	38.1	24
France	7.2	12.7	17.1	22.8	40.1	24.9

2. Suppose black workers are receiving a wage of W_B as in Exhibit 19-8, while white workers receive *W*. Now suppose a regulation is imposed that requires that black workers be paid *W* also. How does this affect the employment, wages, and total incomes of black workers?

Answers to Try It Yourself Problems

Try It Yourself 19-1

The Lorenz curve showing the distribution of income after taxes and benefits are taken into account is less bowed out than the Lorenz curve showing the distribution of income before taxes and benefits are taken into account.Thus, income is more equally distributed after taking them into account.

Try It Yourself 19-2

According to the absolute income test, the Smiths are poor because their income of $16,000 falls below the 1997 poverty threshold of $16,400. According to the relative income test, they are not poor because their $16,000 income is above the upper limit of the lowest quintile, $15,400. If the Smiths received $2,000 in noncash assistance, they would still be considered poor under the absolute income test, because the "official" estimates do not adjust for such assistance. However, given the adjustment process discussed in Exhibit 19-6, it is likely that they would move above the "adjusted" poverty threshold using an absolute income test.

Try It Yourself 19-3

Discrimination leads to an inefficient allocation of resources and results in production levels that lie inside the production possibilities curve (*PPC*) (point A). If discrimination were eliminated, the economy could increase production to a point on the *PPC*, such as B.

20 Socialist Economies in Transition

Getting Started: The Collapse of Socialism

It's hard, even in retrospect, to appreciate how swiftly the collapse came. Command socialism, which had reigned supreme in Russia for more than 70 years and in much of the rest of the world for more than 40 years, had come to seem a permanent institution. Indeed, many observers had expected its influence to increase by the end of the twentieth century. But in the span of 5 months in 1989, command socialist systems fell in six Eastern European nations. The Soviet Union broke up in 1991.

The start of the collapse can be dated to 1980. The government of Poland, a command socialist state that was part of the Soviet bloc, raised meat prices. The price boosts led to widespread protests and to the organization of Solidarity, the first independent labor union permitted in a Soviet bloc state. After 9 years of political clashes, Solidarity won an agreement from the Polish government for wide-ranging economic reforms and for free elections. Solidarity-backed candidates swept the elections in June 1989, and a new government, pledged to democracy and to market capitalism, came to power in August.

Command socialist governments in the rest of the Soviet bloc disappeared quickly in the wake of Poland's transformation. Hungary's government fell in October. East Germany opened the Berlin Wall in November, and the old regime, for which that wall had been a symbol, collapsed. Bulgaria and Czechoslovakia kicked out their command socialist leaders the same month. Romania's dictator, Nicolae Ceausescu, was executed after a bloody uprising in December. Ultimately, every nation in the Warsaw Pact, the bloc making up the Soviet Union and its Eastern European satellite nations, announced its intention to discard the old system of command socialism. The collapse of the command socialist regimes of the former Soviet bloc precipitated an often painful process of transition as countries tried to put in place the institutions of a market capitalist economy.

Meanwhile, a very different process of transition has been under way in China. The Chinese began a gradual process of transition toward a market economy in 1979. It has been a process marked by spectacular economic gain.

In this chapter we'll examine the rise of command socialist systems and explore their ideological roots. Then we'll see how these economic systems operated and trace the sources of their collapse. Finally, we'll investigate the problems and prospects for the transition from command socialism to market capitalism.

The Theory and Practice of Socialism

Socialism has a very long history. The earliest recorded socialist society is described in the Book of Acts in the Bible. Following the crucifixion of Jesus, Christians in Jerusalem established a system in which all property was owned in common.

There have been other socialist experiments in which all property was held in common, effectively creating socialist societies. Early in the nineteenth century, such reformers as Robert Owen, Count Claude-Henri de Rouvroy de Saint-Simon, and Charles Fourier established almost 200 communities in which workers shared in the proceeds of their labor. These men, while operating independently, shared a common ideal—that in the appropriate economic environment, people will strive for the good of the community rather than for their own self-interest. Although some of these communities enjoyed a degree of early success, none survived.

Socialism as the organizing principle for a national economy is in large part the product of the revolutionary ideas of one man, Karl Marx. His analysis of what he saw as the inevitable collapse of market capitalist economies provided a rallying spark for the national socialist movements of the twentieth century. Another important contributor to socialist thought was Vladimir Ilyich Lenin, who modified many of Marx's theories for application to the Soviet Union. Lenin put his ideas into practice as dictator of that country from 1917 until his death in 1924. We shall examine the ideas of Marx and Lenin and investigate the operation of the economic systems based upon them.

The Economics of Karl Marx

Marx is perhaps best known for the revolutionary ideas expressed in the ringing phrases of the *Communist Manifesto,* such as those shown in the Case in Point. Written with Friedrich Engels in 1848, the *Manifesto* was a call to arms. But it was Marx's exhaustive, detailed theoretical analysis of market capitalism, *Das Kapital (Capital),* that was his most important effort. This four-volume work, most of which was published after Marx's death, examines a theoretical economy that we would now describe as perfect competition. In this context, Marx outlined a dynamic process that would, he argued, inevitably result in the collapse of capitalism.

Marx stressed a historical approach to the analysis of economics. Indeed, he was sharply critical of his contemporaries, complaining that their work was wholly lacking in historical perspective. To Marx, capitalism was merely a stage in the development of economic systems. He explained how feudalism would tend to give way to capitalism and how capitalism would give way to socialism. Marx's conclusions stemmed from his labor theory of value and from his perception of the role of profit in a capitalist economy.

The Labor Theory of Value and Surplus Value In *The Wealth of Nations,* Adam Smith proposed the idea of the **labor theory of value,** which states that the relative values of different goods are ultimately determined by the relative amounts of labor used in their production. This idea was widely accepted at the time Marx was writing. Economists recognized the roles of demand and supply but argued that these would affect prices only in the short run. In the long run, it was labor that determined value.

Marx attached normative implications to the ideas of the labor theory of value. Not only was labor the ultimate determinant of value, it was the only *legitimate* determinant of value. The price of a good in Marx's system equaled the sum of the labor and capital costs of its production, plus profit to the capitalist. Marx argued that capital costs were determined by the amount of labor used to produce the capital, so the price of a good equaled a return to labor plus profit. Marx defined profit as **surplus value,** the difference between the price of a good or service and the labor cost of producing it. Marx insisted that surplus value was unjustified and represented exploitation of workers.

Marx accepted another piece of conventional economic wisdom of the nineteenth century, the concept of subsistence wages. This idea held that wages would, in the long run, tend toward their subsistence level, a level just sufficient to keep workers alive. Any increase in wages above their subsistence level would simply attract more workers, forcing wages back down. Marx suggested that unemployed workers were important in this process; they represented a surplus of labor that acted to push wages down.

Capital Accumulation and Capitalist Crises The concepts of surplus value and subsistence wages provide the essential dynamics of Marx's system. He said that capitalists, in an effort to increase surplus value, would seek to acquire more capital. But as they expanded capital, their profit rates, expressed as a percentage of the capital they held, would fall. In a desperate effort to push profit rates up, capitalists would acquire still more capital, which would only push their rate of return down further.

A further implication of Marx's scheme was that as capitalists increased their use of capital, the wages received by workers would become a smaller share of the total value of goods.

Marx assumed that capitalists used all their funds to acquire more capital. Only workers, then, could be counted on for consumption. But their wages equaled only a fraction of the value of the output they produced—they could not possibly buy all of it. The result, Marx said, would be a series of crises in which capitalists throughout the economy, unable to sell their output, would cut back production. This would cause still more reductions in demand, exacerbating the downturn in economic activity. Crises would drive the weakest capitalists out of business; they would become unemployed and thus push wages down further. The economy could recover from such crises, but each one would weaken the capitalist system.

Faced with declining surplus values and reeling from occasional crises, capitalists would seek out markets in other countries. As they extended their reach throughout the world, Marx said, the scope of their exploitation of workers would expand. Although capitalists could make temporary gains by opening up international markets, their continuing acquisition of capital meant that profit rates would resume their downward trend. Capitalist crises would now become global affairs.

According to Marx, another result of capitalists' doomed efforts to boost surplus value would be increased solidarity among the working class. At home, capitalist acquisition of capital meant workers would be crowded into factories, building their sense of class identity. As capitalists extended their exploitation worldwide, workers would gain a sense of solidarity with fellow workers all over the planet. Marx argued that workers would recognize that they were the victims of exploitation by capitalists.

Marx wasn't clear about precisely what forces would combine to bring about the downfall of capitalism. He suggested other theories of crisis in addition to the one based on insufficient demand for the goods and services produced by capitalists. Indeed, modern theories of the business cycle owe much to Marx's discussion of the possible sources of economic downturns. Although Marx spoke sometimes of bloody revolution, it isn't clear that this was the mechanism he thought would bring on the demise of capitalism. Whatever the precise mechanism, Marx was confident that capitalism would fall, that its collapse would be worldwide, and that socialism would replace it.

Marx's Theory: An Assessment To a large degree, Marx's analysis of a capitalist economy was a logical outgrowth of widely accepted economic doctrines of his time. As we've seen, the labor theory of value was conventional wisdom, as was the notion that workers would receive only a subsistence wage. The notion that profit rates would fall over time was widely accepted. Doctrines similar to Marx's notion of recurring crises had been developed by several economists of the period.

What was different about Marx was his tracing of the dynamics of a system in which values would be determined by the quantity of labor, wages would tend toward the subsistence level, profit rates would fall, and crises would occur from time to time. Marx saw these forces as leading inevitably to the fall of capitalism and its replacement with a socialist economic system. Other economists of the period generally argued that economies would stagnate; they did not anticipate the collapse predicted by Marx.

Marx's predictions have turned out to be wildly off the mark. Profit rates have not declined; they have remained relatively stable. Wages have not tended downward toward their subsistence level; they have risen. Labor's share of total income in market economies hasn't fallen; it has increased. Most important, the predicted collapse of capitalist economies hasn't occurred.

Revolutions aimed at establishing socialism have been rare. Perhaps most important, none has occurred in a market capitalist economy. In Cuba and Nicaragua, economies that had some elements of market capitalism in them, but which also had features of command systems as well,[1] were overthrown and socialist systems were established. In other cases where

[1]While resources in these countries were generally privately owned, the government had broad powers to dictate their use.

Case in Point The Powerful Images in the *Communist Manifesto* Turn 150

The year 1998 marked the 150th anniversary of the *Communist Manifesto* by Karl Marx and Friedrich Engels. It was orginally published in London in 1848, a year in which there were a number of uprisings across Europe that at the time could have been interpreted as the beginning of the end of capitalism. This relatively short (12,000 words) document was thus more than an analysis of the process of historical change, in which class struggles propel societies from one type of economic system to the next, and a prediction about how capitalism would evolve and why it would end. It was also a call to action. It contains powerful images that cannot be easily forgotten. It begins,

> A specter is haunting Europe—the specter of communism. All the Powers of old Europe have entered into a holy alliance to exorcise this specter: Pope and Czar, Metternich and Guizot, French Radicals and German police-spies.

Its description of history begins, "The history of all hitherto existing society is the history of class struggles. Freeman and slave, patrician and plebeian, lord and serf, guild-master and journeyman, in a word, oppressor and oppressed, stood in constant opposition to one another . . .". In capitalism, the divisions are yet more stark: "Society as a whole is more and more splitting up into two great hostile camps, into two great classes directly facing each other: Bourgeoisie and Proletariat."

Foreshadowing the globalization of capitalism, Marx and Engels wrote,

> The bourgeoisie, by the rapid improvement of all instruments of production, by the immensely facilitated means of communication, draws all, even the most barbarian, nations into civilization. The cheap prices of its commodities are the heavy artillery with which it batters down all Chinese walls, with which it forces the barbarians' intensely obstinate hatred of foreigners to capitulate. It compels all nations, on pain of extinction, to adopt the bourgeois mode of production: it compels them to introduce what it calls civilization into their midst. . . . In one word, it creates a world after its own image.

But the system, like all other class-based systems before it, brings about its own demise: "The weapons with which the bourgeoisie felled feudalism to the ground are now turned against the bourgeoisie itself. . . . Masses of laborers, crowded into the factory, are organized like soldiers. . . . It was just

this contact that was needed to centralize the numerous local struggles, all of the same character, into one national struggle between classes." The national struggles eventually become an international struggle in which "What the bourgeoisie, therefore, produces, above all, is its own gravediggers." The *Manifesto* ends,

> Let the ruling classes tremble at a Communistic revolution. The proletarians have nothing to lose but their chains. They have a world to win. WORKING MEN OF ALL COUNTRIES, UNITE!

socialism has been established through revolution it has replaced systems that could best be described as feudal. The Russian Revolution of 1917 that established the Soviet Union and the revolution that established the People's Republic of China in 1949 are the most important examples of this form of revolution. In the countries of Eastern Europe, socialism was imposed by the former Soviet Union in the wake of World War II.

Whatever the shortcomings of Marx's economic prognostications, his ideas have had enormous influence. Politically, his concept of the inevitable emergence of socialism promoted the proliferation of socialist-leaning governments during the middle third of the twentieth century. Before socialist systems began collapsing in 1989, fully one-third of the earth's population lived in countries that had adopted Marx's ideas. Ideologically, his vision of a market capitalist system in which one class exploits another has had enormous influence.

Checklist

- Marx's theory, based on the labor theory of value and the presumption that wages would approach the subsistence level, predicted the inevitable collapse of capitalism and its replacement by socialist regimes.
- Lenin modified many of Marx's theories for application to the Soviet Union and put his ideas into practice as dictator of that country from 1917 until his death in 1924.
- Before socialist systems began collapsing in 1989, fully one-third of the earth's population lived in countries that had adopted Marx's ideas.

Try It Yourself 20-1

Distinguish between a market capitalist economy and a command socialist economy. These terms were introduced in Chapter 2. It is a good idea to refresh your memory before proceeding.

Socialist Systems in Action

The most important example of socialism was the economy of the Union of Soviet Socialist Republics, the Soviet Union. The Russian Revolution succeeded in 1917 in overthrowing the czarist regime that had ruled the Russian Empire for centuries. Leaders of the revolution created the Soviet Union in its place and sought to establish a socialist state based on the ideas of Karl Marx.

The leaders of the Soviet Union faced a difficulty in using Marx's writings as a foundation for a socialist system. He had sought to explain why capitalism would collapse; he had little to say about how the socialist system that would replace it would function. He did suggest the utopian notion that, over time, there would be less and less need for a government and the state would wither away. But his writings did not provide much of a blueprint for running a socialist economic system.

Lacking a guide for establishing a socialist economy, the leaders of the new regime in Russia struggled to invent one. In 1917, Lenin attempted to establish what he called "war communism." The national government declared its ownership of most firms and forced peasants to turn over a share of their output to the government. The program sought to eliminate the market as an allocative mechanism; government would control production and distribution. The program of war communism devastated the economy. In 1921, Lenin declared a New Economic Policy. It returned private ownership to some sectors of the economy and reinstituted the market as an allocative mechanism.

Lenin's death in 1924 precipitated a power struggle from which Joseph Stalin emerged victorious. It was under Stalin that the Soviet economic system was created. Because that system served as a model for most of the other command socialist systems that emerged, we shall examine it in some detail. We shall also examine an intriguing alternative version of socialism that was created in Yugoslavia after World War II.

Command Socialism in the Soviet Union

Stalin began by seizing virtually all remaining privately owned capital and natural resources in the country. The seizure was a brutal affair; he eliminated opposition to his measures through mass executions, forced starvation of whole regions, and deportation of political opponents to prison camps. Estimates of the number of people killed during Stalin's centralization of power range in the tens of millions. With the state in control of the means of production, Stalin established a rigid system in which a central administration in Moscow determined what would be produced.

The justification for the brutality of Soviet rule lay in the quest to develop "socialist man." Leaders of the Soviet Union argued that the tendency of people to behave in their own self-interest was a by-product of capitalism, not an inherent characteristic of human beings. A successful socialist state required that the preferences of people be transformed so that they would be motivated by the collective interests of society, not their own self-interest. Propaganda was widely used to reinforce a collective identity. Those individuals who were deemed beyond reform were likely to be locked up or executed.

The political arm of command socialism was the Communist party. Party officials participated in every aspect of Soviet life in an effort to promote the concept of socialist man and to control individual behavior. Party leaders were represented in every firm and in every government agency. Party officials charted the general course for the economy as well.

A planning agency, Gosplan, determined the quantities of output that key firms would produce each year and the prices that would be charged. Other government agencies set output levels for smaller firms. These determinations were made in a series of plans. A 1-year plan specified production targets for that year. Soviet planners also developed 5-year and 20-year plans.

Managers of state-owned firms were rewarded on the basis of their ability to meet the annual quotas set by the Gosplan. The system of quotas and rewards created inefficiency in several ways. First, no central planning agency could incorporate preferences of consumers and costs of factors of production in its decisions concerning the quantity of each good to produce. Decisions about what to produce were made by political leaders; they were not a response to market forces. Further, planners could not select prices at which quantities produced would clear their respective markets. In a market economy, prices adjust to changes in demand and supply. Given that demand and supply are always changing, it is inconceivable that central planners could ever select market-clearing prices. Soviet central planners typically selected prices for consumer goods that were below market-clearing levels, causing shortages throughout the economy. Changes in prices were rare.

Plant managers had a powerful incentive for meeting their quotas; they could expect bonuses equal to about 35 percent of their base salary for producing the quantities required of their firms. Those who exceeded their quotas could boost this to 50 percent. In addition, successful managers were given vacations, better apartments, better medical care, and a host of other perquisites. Managers thus had a direct interest in meeting their quotas; they had no incentive to select efficient production techniques or to reduce costs.

Perhaps most important, there was no incentive for plant managers to adopt new technologies. A plant implementing a new technology risked start-up delays that could cause it to fall short of its quota. If a plant did succeed in boosting output, it was likely to be forced to accept even larger quotas in the future. A plant manager who introduced a successful technology would only be slapped with tougher quotas; if the technology failed, he or she would lose a bonus. With little to gain and a great deal to lose, Soviet plant managers were extremely reluctant to adopt new technologies. Soviet production was, as a result, characterized by outdated technologies. When the system fell in 1991, Soviet manufacturers were using production methods that had been obsolete for decades in other countries.

Centrally controlled systems often generated impressive numbers for total output but failed in satisfying consumer demands. Gosplan officials, recognizing that Soviet capital was not very productive, ordered up a lot of it. The result was a heavy emphasis on unproductive capital goods and relatively little production of consumer goods. On the eve of the collapse of the Soviet Union, Soviet economists estimated that per capita consumption was less than one-sixth of the U.S. level.

The Soviet system also generated severe environmental problems. In principle, a socialist system should have an advantage over a capitalist system in allocating environmental resources for which private property rights are difficult to define. Because a socialist government owns all capital and natural resources, the ownership problem is solved. The problem in the Soviet system, however, came from the labor theory of value. Since natural resources aren't produced by labor, the value assigned to them was zero. Soviet plant managers thus had no incentive to limit their exploitation of environmental resources, and terrible environmental tragedies were common.

Systems similar to that created in the Soviet Union were established in other Soviet bloc countries as well. The most important exceptions were Yugoslavia, which is discussed in the next section, and China, which started with a Soviet-style system and then moved away from it. The Chinese case is examined later in this chapter.

Yugoslavia: Another Socialist Experiment

Although the Soviet Union was able to impose a system of command socialism on nearly all the Eastern European countries it controlled after World War II, Yugoslavia managed to forge its own path. Yugoslavia's communist leader, Marshal Tito, charted an independent course,

Case in Point Socialist Cartoons

These cartoons came from the Soviet press. Soviet citizens were clearly aware of many of the problems of their planned system.

"But where is the equipment that was sent to us?" "Which year are you talking about?"

"Why are they sending us new technology when the old still works?"

"But Santa, it's winter, so we asked for boots for our son!"
"I know, but the only thing available in the state store was a pair of sandals."

accepting aid from Western nations such as the United States and establishing a unique form of socialism that made greater use of markets than the Soviet-style systems did. Most important, however, Tito quickly moved away from the centralized management style of the Soviet Union to a decentralized system in which workers exercised considerable autonomy.

In the Yugoslav system, firms with five or more employees were owned by the state but made their own decisions concerning what to produce and what prices to charge. Workers in these firms elected their managers and established their own systems for sharing revenues. Each firm paid a fee for the use of its state-owned capital. In effect, firms operated as labor cooperatives. Firms with fewer than five employees could be privately owned and operated.

Economic performance in Yugoslavia was impressive. Living standards there were generally higher than those in other Soviet bloc countries. The distribution of income was similar to that of command socialist economies; it was generally more equal than distributions achieved in market capitalist economies. The Yugoslav economy was plagued, however, by persistent unemployment, high inflation, and increasing disparities in regional income levels.

Yugoslavia began breaking up shortly after command socialist systems began falling in Eastern Europe. It had been a country of republics and provinces with uneasy relationships among them. Tito had been the glue that held them together. After his death, the groups began to move apart. In 1991, Croatia, Bosnia and Herzegovina, and Slovenia declared their independence from Yugoslavia; Macedonia followed suit in 1992. In 1999, hostilities between ethnic Albanians living in Yugoslavia's Kosovo province (Kosovars) and Serbs led to NATO bombings of the country on behalf of the Kosovars. The country's intriguing experiment with its version of socialism has been lost to a series of bloody ethnic struggles.

Exhibit 20-1

Per Capita Output in Former Soviet Bloc States and in the United States, 1995

Per capita output was far lower in the former republics of the Soviet Union and in Warsaw Pact countries in 1995 than in the United States. All values are measured in units of equivalent purchasing power.

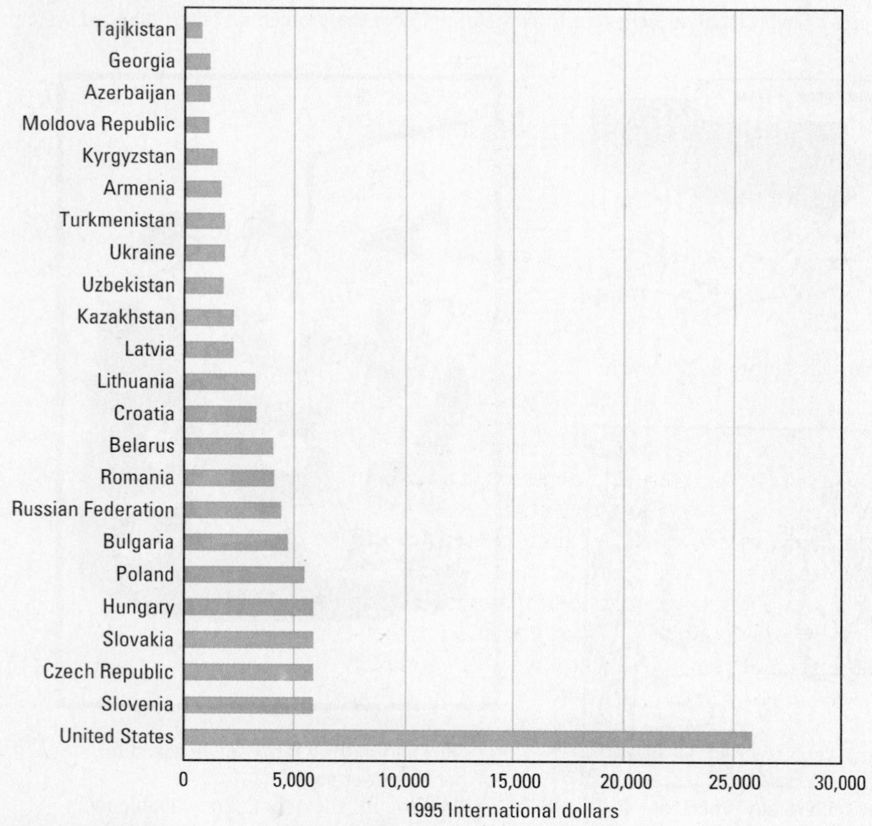

Source: United Nations, *Human Development Report*, 1998.

Evaluating Economic Performance Under Socialism

Soviet leaders placed great emphasis on Marx's concept of the inevitable collapse of capitalism. While they downplayed the likelihood of a global revolution, they argued that the inherent superiority of socialism would gradually become apparent. Countries would adopt the socialist model in order to improve their living standards, and socialism would gradually assert itself as the dominant world system.

One key to achieving the goal of a socialist world was to outperform the United States economically. Stalin promised in the 1930s that the Soviet economy would surpass that of the United States within a few decades. The goal was clearly not achieved. Indeed, it was the gradual realization that the command socialist system could not deliver high living standards that led to the collapse of the old system.

Exhibit 20-1 shows the World Bank's estimates of per capita output, measured in dollars of 1995 purchasing power, for the republics that made up the Soviet Union, for the Warsaw Pact nations of Eastern Europe for which data are available, and for the United States in 1995. Nations that had operated within the old Soviet system had quite low levels of per capita output. Living standards were lower still, given that these nations devoted much higher shares of total output to investment and to defense than did the United States.

Ultimately, it was the failure of the Soviet system to deliver living standards on a par with those achieved by market capitalist economies that brought the system down. We saw in Chapter 2 that market capitalist economic systems create incentives to allocate resources efficiently; socialist systems do not. Of course, a society may decide that other attributes of a socialist system make it worth retaining. But the lesson of the 1980s was that few that had lived under command socialist systems wanted to continue to do so.

Checklist

- In the Soviet Union a central planning agency, Gosplan, set output quotas for enterprises and determined prices.
- The Soviet central planning system was highly inefficient. Sources of this inefficiency included failure to incorporate consumer preferences into decisions about what to produce, failure to take into account costs of factors of production, setting of prices without regard to market equilibrium, lack of incentives for incorporating new technologies, overemphasis on capital goods production, and inattention to environmental problems.
- Yugoslavia developed an alternative system of socialism in which firms were run by their workers as labor cooperatives.
- It was the realization that command socialist systems could not deliver high living standards that contributed to their collapse.

Try It Yourself 20-2

What specific problem of a command socialist system does each of the cartoons in the Case in Point parodying that system highlight?

Economies in Transition: China and Russia

Just as leaders of the Soviet Union had to create their own command socialist systems, so leaders of the economies making the transition to market capitalist economies must find their own paths to new economic systems. It is a task without historical precedent.

In this section we'll examine two countries and the strategies they have chosen for the transition. China was the first socialist nation to begin the process, and in many ways it has been the most successful. Russia was the dominant republic in the old Soviet Union; whether its transition is successful will be crucially important. Before turning to the transition process in these two countries, we shall consider some general problems common to all countries seeking to establish market capitalism in the wake of command socialism.

Problems in Transition

Establishing a system of market capitalism in a command socialist economy is a daunting task. It's also a task no nation has yet completed; the nations making the attempt must invent the process as they go along. Each of them, though, faces similar problems. Former command socialist economies must establish systems of property rights, establish banking systems, deal with the problem of inflation, and work through a long tradition of ideological antipathy toward the basic nature of a capitalist system.

Property Rights A market system requires property rights before it can function. A property right details what one can and cannot do with a particular asset. A market system requires laws that specify the actions that are permitted and those that are proscribed, and it also requires institutions for the enforcement of agreements dealing with property rights. These include a court system and lawyers trained in property law and contract law. For the system to work effectively, there must be widespread understanding of the basic nature of private property and of the transactions through which it is allocated.

Command socialist economies possess virtually none of these prerequisites for market capitalism. When the state owned virtually all capital and natural resources, there was little need to develop a legal system that would spell out individual property rights. Governments were largely free to do as they wished.

Countries seeking a transition from command socialism to market capitalism must develop a legal system comparable to those that have evolved in market capitalist countries over centuries. The problem of creating a system of property rights and the institutions necessary to support it is a large hurdle for economies making the transition to a market economy.

One manifestation of the difficulties inherent in establishing clear and widely recognized property rights in formerly socialist countries is widespread criminal activity. Newly established private firms must contend with racketeers who offer protection at a price. Firms that refuse to pay the price may find their property destroyed or some of their managers killed. Criminal activity has been rampant in economies struggling toward a market capitalist system.

Banking Banks in command socialist countries were operated by the state. There was no tradition of banking practices as they are understood in market capitalist countries.

In a market capitalist economy, a privately owned bank accepts deposits from customers and lends these deposits to borrowers. These borrowers are typically firms or consumers. Banks in command socialist economies generally accepted saving deposits, but checking accounts for private individuals were virtually unknown. Decisions to advance money to firms were made through the economic planning process, not by individual banks. Banks didn't have an opportunity to assess the profitability of individual enterprises; such considerations were irrelevant in the old command socialist systems. Bankers in these economies were thus unaccustomed to the roles that would be required of them in a market capitalist system.

Inflation One particularly vexing problem facing transitional economies is inflation. Under command socialist systems, the government set prices; it could abolish inflation by decree. But such systems were characterized by chronic shortages of consumer goods. Consumers, unable to find the goods they wanted to buy, simply accumulated money. As command socialist economies began their transitions, there was typically a very large quantity of money available for consumers to spend. A first step in transitions was the freeing of prices. Because the old state-determined prices were generally below equilibrium levels, prices typically surged in the early stages of transition. Prices in Poland, for example, shot up 400 percent within a few months of price decontrol. Prices in Russia went up tenfold within 6 months.

One dilemma facing transitional economies has been the plight of bankrupt state enterprises. In a market capitalist economy, firms unable to generate revenues that exceed their costs go out of business. In command socialist economies, the central bank simply wrote checks to cover their deficits. As these economies have begun the transition toward market capitalism, they have generally declared their intention to end these bailouts and to let failing firms fail. But the phenomenon of state firms earning negative profits is so pervasive that allowing all of them to fail at once could cause massive disruption.

The practical alternative to allowing firms to fail has been continued bailouts. But in transitional economies, that has meant issuing money to failed firms. This practice increases the money supply and contributes to continuing inflation. Most transition economies experienced high inflation in the initial transition years, but were subsequently able to reduce it.

Ideology Soviet citizens, and their counterparts in other command socialist economies, have been told for decades that market capitalism is an evil institution, that it fosters greed and human misery. They've been told that some people become rich in the system, but that they do so only at the expense of others who become poorer.

In the context of a competitive market, this view of market processes as a zero-sum game—one in which the gains for one person come only as a result of losses for another—is wrong. In market transactions, one person gains only by making others better off. But the zero-sum view runs deep, and it is a source of lingering hostility toward market forces.

Countries seeking to transform their economies from command socialist to more market-oriented systems face daunting challenges. Given these challenges, it is remarkable that they have persisted in the effort. There are a thousand reasons for economic reform to fail, but the reform effort has, in general, continued to move forward.

China: A Gradual Transition

China is a giant by virtually any standard. Larger than the continental United States, it is home to more than 1.4 billion people—more than one-fifth of the earth's population. Although China is desperately poor, its economy has been among the fastest growing in the world since 1980. That rapid growth is the result of a gradual shift toward a market capitalist economy. The Chinese have pursued their transition in a manner quite different from the paths taken by former Soviet bloc nations.

Recent History China was invaded by Japan during World War II. After Japan's defeat, civil war broke out between Chinese communists, led by Mao Zedong, and nationalists. The communists prevailed, and the People's Republic of China was proclaimed in 1949.

Mao set about immediately to create a socialist state in China. He nationalized firms and redistributed land to peasants. Many of those who had owned land under the old regime were executed. China's entry into the Korean War in 1950 led to much closer ties to the Soviet Union, which helped China to establish a command socialist economy.

China's first 5-year plan, launched in 1953, followed the tradition of Soviet economic development. It stressed capital-intensive production and the development of heavy industry. But China had far less capital and a great many more people than did the Soviet Union. Capital-intensive development made little sense. In 1958, Mao declared a uniquely Chinese approach to development, which he dubbed the Great Leap Forward. It focused on labor-intensive development and the organization of small productive units. Indeed, households were encouraged to form their own productive units under the slogan "An iron and steel foundry in every backyard." The Great Leap repudiated the bonuses and other material incentives stressed by the Soviets; motivation was to come from revolutionary zeal, not self-interest.

In agriculture, the new plan placed greater emphasis on collectivization. Farmers were organized into communes containing several thousand households each. Small private plots of land, which had been permitted earlier, were abolished. China's adoption of the plan was a victory for radical leaders in the government.

The Great Leap was an economic disaster. Output plunged. Moderate leaders then took over, and the economy got back to its 1957 level of output by the mid-1960s.

Power shifted back and forth between radicals and moderates during the next 15 years. China remained a command socialist economy throughout this period; the two groups differed primarily on the nature of the incentives that the system would offer. Changes in economic policy at the center, however, contributed to greater autonomy at regional levels. Another factor promoting regional autonomy was Chinese geography. The country is vast, and transportation across it difficult. The eighth-century poet Li Bao once remarked that it was more difficult to get to Sichuan, a province in south-central China, than to get to heaven. Difficulty in travel and the lack of a good communications system contributed to a high degree of regional autonomy in China. That autonomy, in turn, played a key role in China's reform process.

China's Reforms In 1978 Zhao Ziyang, first secretary of the Communist party in Sichuan province, expressed his frustration with the Chinese economic system, likening China's economy to a silkworm locked in the cocoon of central planning. He issued an order freeing six state enterprises in Sichuan from control by the planning system and directed the firms to operate independently. They could determine their own output, set their own prices, and keep the profits they earned. Within 2 years, 6,600 firms had been unleashed. Zhao became China's head of state, and China was launched on a course that would take it closer to a market capitalist economy.

The initial impetus for reform thus came from a provincial leader. That was also true of agricultural reform, which has been the most impressive success story in the Chinese experience. Reform in China was thus a bottom-up process, one that began in the provinces and then became national policy. That's quite different from the top-down reform process of other transitional economies, in which the central government commits to reform and then orders local government officials to go along. Given the high level of autonomy of local leaders in China's system, a bottom-up approach to reform was probably the only one that could succeed.

Beginning in 1979, many Chinese provincial leaders instituted a system called *bao gan dao hu*—"contracting all decisions to the household." Under the system, provincial officials contracted the responsibility for operating collectively owned farmland to individual households. Government officials gave households production quotas they were required to meet and purchased that output at prices set by central planners. But farmers were free to sell any additional output they could produce at whatever prices they could get in the marketplace and to keep the profits for themselves.

The shift to household quotas from the old system of quotas that had been set for each collective was officially banned by China's central government in 1979. The ban, however, carried little weight. By 1984, 93 percent of China's agricultural land had been contracted to individual households.

The new system of household contracting was an immediate success. Crop output had increased at only a 2.5 percent rate between 1953 and 1978, a slower pace than the rate of population growth. From 1979 to 1984, it grew at a 6.8 percent rate. The central government finally withdrew its official opposition and sanctioned the program in 1984.

Urban industrial reform, which had been pursued on a limited basis since Zhao's directive in 1978, became national policy in 1984. State firms were told to meet their quotas and then were free to engage in additional production for sale in free markets.

In effect, China has two tiers of economic systems, a command system and a market system operating at the margin. By leaving the state system in place, the Chinese avoided the disruptions that have plagued the transition process in other countries. Chinese officials refer to the approach as "changing a big earthquake into a thousand tremors."

How well has the gradual approach to transition worked? Between 1980 and 1998, China had one of the fastest-growing economies in the world. Its per capita output, measured in dollars of constant purchasing power, more than doubled. The country, once one of the poorest in the world, now ranks eighth among low-income countries, according to the World Bank. Exhibit 20-2 compares growth rates in China to those achieved by Japan and the United States and to the average annual growth rate of all world economies between 1985 and 1997.

Where will China's reforms lead? While the Chinese leadership has continued to be repressive politically, it has generally supported the reform process. The result has been continued expansion of the free economy and a relative shrinking of the state-run sector. Given the rapid progress China has achieved with its gradual approach to reform, it's hard to imagine that the country would reverse course. Given the course it's on, China seems likely to become a market capitalist economy—and a prosperous one—within a few decades.

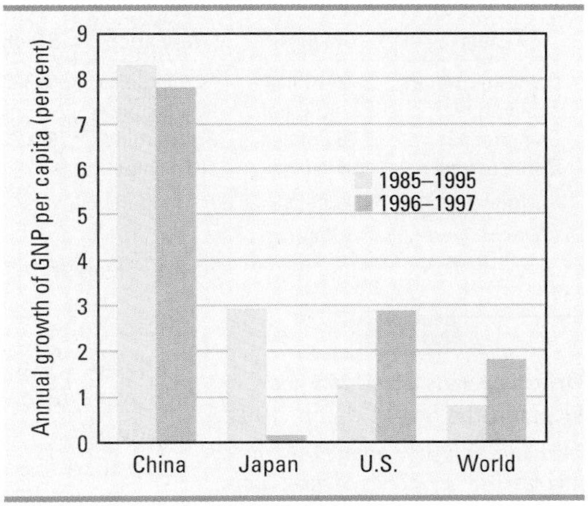

Exhibit 20-2

Soaring Output in China

China's growth in per capita output from 1985 to 1997 greatly exceeded rates recorded for Japan, the United States, or the average of all nations.

Russia: An Uncertain Path to Reform

Russia dominated the former Soviet Union. It contained more than half the Soviet people and more than three-fourths of the nation's land area. Russia's capital, Moscow, was the capital and center of power for the entire country.

Today, Russia retains control over the bulk of the military power that had been accumulated by the former Soviet Union. While it is now an ally of the United States, Russia still possesses the nuclear capability to destroy life on earth. Its success in making the transition to market capitalism and joining as a full partner in the world community thus has special significance for peace.

Recent History Russia's shift toward market capitalism has its roots in a reform process initiated during the final years of the existence of the Soviet Union. That effort presaged many of the difficulties that have continued to plague Russia.

The Soviet Union, as we have already seen, had a well-established system of command socialism. Leading Soviet economists, however, began arguing as early as the 1970s that the old system could never deliver living standards comparable to those achieved in market capitalist economies. The first political leader to embrace the idea of radical reform was Mikhail Gorbachev, who became General Secretary of the Communist party—the highest leadership post in the Soviet Union—in 1985.

Mr. Gorbachev instituted political reforms that allowed Soviet citizens to speak out, and even to demonstrate, against their government. Economically, he called for much greater autonomy for state enterprises and a system in which workers' wages would be tied to productivity. The new policy, dubbed *perestroika*, or "restructuring," appeared to be an effort to move the system toward a mixed economy.

But Mr. Gorbachev's economic advisers wanted to go much further. A small group of economists, which included his top economic adviser, met in August 1990 to draft a radical plan to transform the economy to a market capitalist system—and to do it in 500 days. Stanislav Shatalin, a Soviet economist, led the group. Mr. Gorbachev endorsed the Shatalin plan the following month, and it appeared that the Soviet Union was on its way to a new system. The new plan, however, threatened the Soviet power elite. It called for sharply reduced funding for the military and for the Soviet Union's secret police force, the KGB. It would have stripped central planners, who were very powerful, of their authority. The new plan called for nothing less than the destruction of the old system—and the elimination of the power base of most government officials.

Top Soviet bureaucrats and military leaders reacted to the Shatalin plan with predictable rage. They delivered an ultimatum to Mr. Gorbachev: Dump the Shatalin plan or be kicked out.

Caught between advisers who had persuaded him of the necessity for radical reform and Communist party leaders who would have none of it, Mr. Gorbachev chose to leave the command system in place and to seek modest reforms. He announced a new plan that retained control over most prices but allowed prices for roughly 30 percent of Soviet output to be negotiated between firms that produced the goods and firms that purchased them. He left in place the state's ownership of enterprises. In an effort to deal with shortages of other goods, he ordered sharp price increases early in 1991.

These measures, however, accomplished little. Black market prices for basic consumer goods were typically 10 to 20 times the level of state prices. Those prices, which respond to

Item	Old price	New price	Black market price
Children's shoes	2–10 rubles	10–50 rubles	50–300 rubles
Toilet paper	32–40 kopeks	60–75 kopeks	2–3 rubles
Compact car	7,000 rubles	35,000 rubles	70,000–100,000 rubles
Bottle of vodka	10.5 rubles	10.5 rubles	30–35 rubles

Note: 1 ruble = 100 kopeks = $0.60 at the official exchange rate in 1991.

Source: *Komsomolskaya Pravda.*

Exhibit 20-3

Official Versus Black Market Prices in the Soviet Union, 1991

Mikhail Gorbachev ordered sharp increases in the prices of most consumer goods early in 1991 in an effort to eliminate shortages. As the table shows, however, a large gap remained between official and black market prices.

demand and supply, may be taken as a rough gauge of equilibrium prices. People were willing to pay the higher black market prices because they simply couldn't find goods at the state-decreed prices. Mr. Gorbachev's order to double and even triple some state prices narrowed the gap between official and equilibrium prices, but did not close it. Exhibit 20-3 shows some of the price changes imposed and compares them to black market prices.

Perhaps the most important problem for Mr. Gorbachev's price hikes was that there was no reason for state-owned firms to respond to them by increasing their output. The managers and workers in these firms, after all, were government employees receiving government-determined salaries. There was no mechanism through which they would gain from higher prices. A private firm could be expected to increase its quantity supplied in response to a higher price. State-owned firms did not.

The Soviet people faced the worst of economic worlds in 1991. Soviet output plunged sharply, prices were up dramatically, and there was no relief from severe shortages. A small group of government officials opposed to economic reform staged a coup in the fall of 1991, putting Mr. Gorbachev under house arrest. The coup produced massive protests throughout the country and failed within a few days. Chaos within the central government created an opportunity for the republics of the Soviet Union to declare their independence, and they did. These defections resulted in the collapse of the Soviet Union late in 1991.

The Reform Effort Boris Yeltsin, the president of Russia, had been a leading proponent of market capitalism even before the Soviet Union collapsed. He had supported the Shatalin plan and had been sharply critical of Mr. Gorbachev's failure to implement it. Once Russia became an independent republic, Mr. Yeltsin sought a rapid transition to market capitalism.

Mr. Yeltsin's reform efforts, however, have been slowed by Russian legislators, most of them former Communist officials who were appointed to their posts under the old regime. They fought reform and have repeatedly sought to impeach Mr. Yeltsin.

Despite the hurdles, Russian reformers have accomplished a great deal. Prices of most goods have been freed from state controls. Most state-owned firms have been privatized, and most of Russia's output of goods and services is now produced by the private sector.

To privatize state firms, Russian citizens were issued vouchers that could be used to purchase state enterprises. Under this plan, state enterprises were auctioned off. Individuals, or groups of individuals, could use their vouchers to bid on them. Russian officials auctioned 5 percent of state enterprises in the spring of 1993; by 1995 most state enterprises in Russia had been privatized.

While Russia has taken major steps toward transforming itself into a market economy, it has not been able to institute its reforms in a coherent manner. For example, despite privatization, restructuring of Russian firms to increase efficiency has been slow. Establishment and enforcement of rules and laws that undergird modern, market-based systems have been lacking in Russia. Most notable has been the inability of the federal government to enforce tax collection. As a result, it has chronically been unable to meet its obligations to pay government workers and pensioners on time. Corruption has become endemic.

To be fair, some of Russia's problems stem from declining world oil prices, since oil is an important export for Russia. Overall, though, most would argue that Russian transition policies have made a difficult situation worse. The August 1998 decision of the government to delay payments on its outstanding debts was a clear sign that the transition process was in trouble. What new policies the Russian government would choose were quite uncertain throughout the rest of 1998 and 1999.

Why has the transition in Russia been so difficult? One reason may be that Russians lived with command socialism longer than did any other country. In addition Russia had no historical

Case in Point Contrasting Attitudes Toward Entrepreneurship in Russia and Poland

August 1998 saw a severe setback in reform efforts in Russia. The value of the ruble fell dramatically, as did the value of Russia's stocks and bonds. The government announced a moratorium on repaying its debts. The Russian economic scene was chaotic. Prices throughout the economy rose nearly 70 percent in a little more than a month. Total output for the year was expected to decline 6 percent.

This description gives the broad overview of Russia's faltering attempt at economic transition. Negotiations between Russia and the International Monetary Fund have focused on macroeconomic policies to control the price level, to improve government spending and taxing policies, and to restore and then to increase aggregate production levels.

The underlying cause of these macrolevel problems, however, can perhaps be found in Russia's reluctance to promote and accept entrepreneurship. Initially, following the collapse of the Soviet Union, Russians were encouraged to set up kiosks, roadside stands, and other types of small businesses. There was very little government control and these small businesses flourished.

As time went on, though, Russian authorities cracked down on what was perceived to be noisy, messy street activity. Local governments imposed licensing and other requirements on these new businesses. Whereas in the early 1990s, the number of start-up businesses in Russia was growing, by 1994 this sector of the Russian economy was stagnating. Anders Aslund, a former adviser to the Russian government who is now at the Carnegie Institute for International Peace, estimates that in Russia there is only 1 business for every 55 people. In typical capitalist countries the ratio is 1 in 10.

In contrast, Poland welcomed start-ups (photo at left). This seemed to break the power of state-owned enterprises, to offer job opportunities to Poles outside the state sector, and to deny organized crime easy opportunities. For most of the 1990s, Poland has been the fastest growing of the transition economies of Europe.

Overcoming ideological hostility toward market capitalism is difficult for Russia following its 70-year experience with command socialism. Poland was lucky to have gotten out after 40 years.

Source: Michael M. Weinstein, "Russia Is Not Poland, and That's Too Bad," *New York Times*, Section 5, 30 August 1998, p. 5.

experience with market capitalism. In countries that did have it, such as the Czech Republic, the switch back to capitalism has gone far more smoothly and has met with far more success.

There is much at stake for the world in helping Russia's success in the transition process. The outcome is still very much in doubt.

Try It Yourself 20-3

Exhibit 20-3 shows three prices for various goods in the Soviet Union in 1991. Illustrate the market for compact cars using a demand and supply diagram. On your diagram, show the old price, the new price, and the black market price.

A Look Back

Socialism, a system in which factors of production are owned in common or by the public sector, is a very old idea. The impetus for installing it as a national economic system came from the writings of Karl Marx.

Marx argued that capitalism would inevitably collapse and give way to socialism. He argued that under capitalism workers would receive only a subsistence wage. Capitalists would extract the difference between what workers receive and what they produce as surplus value, a concept roughly equivalent to profit. As capitalists struggled to maintain surplus value, the degree and extent of exploitation of workers would rise. Capitalist systems would suffer through a series of crises in which firms cut back their output. The suffering of workers would increase, and the capitalist class would be weakened. Ultimately, workers would overthrow the market capitalist system and establish socialism in its place.

Marx's predictions about capitalist development have not come to fruition, but his ideas have been enormously influential. By the 1980s, roughly one-third of the world's people lived in economies built on the basis of his ideas.

The most important command socialist economy was the Soviet Union. In this economy, central planners determined what would be produced and at what price. Quotas were given to each state-owned firm. The system, which was emulated in most socialist nations, failed to deliver living standards on a par with those achieved by market economies. This failure ultimately brought down the system.

A very different approach to socialism was pioneered by Yugoslavia. State-owned firms were managed by their workers, who shared in their profits. Yugoslavia's economic system fell apart as the country broke up and suffered from ethnic strife and civil war.

As the governments of command socialist nations fell in 1989 and early in the 1990s, new governments launched efforts to achieve transition to market capitalism. We examined two cases of transition. China's gradual strategy has produced rapid growth, but in a politically repressive regime. As this book went to press, China continued to be one of the fastest growing economies in the world.

Russia's transition has met opposition from officials who held power under the old system and whose continued power is threatened by reforms. While Russia has taken some steps to create a market-based system, most notably by privatizing a large portion of its firms, the transition process has been notable for its lack of coherence and for the inability of the Russian government to enforce the rules and laws that support modern, market-based systems. Russia's financial crisis in 1998 increased uncertainty about the future of Russia's reform efforts. As this book went to press, the outcome was very much in doubt.

Terms and Concepts for Review

labor theory of value, **392**

surplus value, **392**

For Discussion

1. There is a gap between what workers receive and the value of what workers produce in a market capitalist system. Why? Does this constitute exploitation? Does it create the kinds of crises Marx anticipated? Why or why not?
2. What is meant by the labor theory of value? What are the shortcomings of the theory?
3. What would you say is the theory of value offered in this book? How does it differ from the labor theory of value?

Illustration Credits

Chapter 1

p. 4: Stephen J. Krasemann/DRK Photos.
p. 10: Left, courtesy Lucinda Vargas, Federal Reserve Bank of Dallas, El Paso Branch; right, R. E. Ilg. **p. 11:** Courtesy Wendy Stock, Kansas State University. **p. 14:** The Everett Collection.

Chapter 2

p. 41: Courtesy Chevron Corporation.
p. 48: National Archives/Photo Researchers.
p. 51: Robert Trippett/Sipa Press.

Chapter 3

p. 65: L.M. Otero/ AP/Wide World Photos.
p. 71: Jim Noelker.

Chapter 4

p. 89: Hollyman/ Liaison Agency. **p. 91:** David R. Frazier/Photo Researchers. **p. 97:** Corbis/Warren Morgan. **p. 109:** John Eastcott/Yva Momatiuk/The Image Works.

Chapter 5

p. 112: David J. Phillip/ AP/Wide World Photos.
p. 116: Daniel Hulshizer/ AP/Wide World Photos.

Chapter 6

p. 130: Natalie Fobes/Tony Stone Images.
p. 133: AP/Wide World Photos. **p. 140:** Bill Pugliano/ Liaison Agency.

Chapter 7

p. 147: Rob Gage/FPG International.
p. 154: Bob Gomel, Houston, Texas.

Chapter 8

p. 171: Chris Harvey/Tony Stone Images.
p. 179: Jim Tynan/ Impact Visuals/ PNI.
p. 180: Will and Deni McIntyre/Photo Researchers.

Chapter 9

p. 195: Rick Romanenko. **p. 202:** Rick Bowner/ AP/Wide World Photos.

Chapter 10

p. 210: Corbis/Werner Forman.
p. 217: Rohan/Tony Stone Images.
p. 221: Rick Romanenko.

Chapter 11

p. 231: Treë. **p. 237:** M. Krakowski/ AP/Wide World Photos.

Chapter 12

p. 248: C. Bennett/ AP/Wide World Photos.
p. 253: Left and right, Corbis/Mitchell Gerber.
p. 259: Bill Gallery/ Stock, Boston/ PNI.

Chapter 13

p. 269: Elena Rooraid/PhotoEdit.
p. 277: Photri.

Chapter 14

p. 288: Corbis/Kevin Fleming. **p. 294:** Craig Schmittman/Tony Stone Images.

Chapter 15

p. 302: Jeffry W. Myers/The Stock Market.

Chapter 16

p. 323: Corbis/James Warren. **p. 327:** Left, trademark provided courtesy The Boeing Company; © 1999 The Boeing Company, Seattle, Washington; BOEING ® is a registered trademark of The Boeing Company; right, courtesy Airbus Industrie, AINA Holdings, Inc., Virginia.

Chapter 17

p. 341: J. Plunkett/ AP/Wide World Photos.
p. 344: Rick Romanenko. **p. 346:** Renato Rotolo/ Liaison Agency.

Chapter 18

p. 354: Michael St. Maur Sheil/ Black Star.
p. 364: J. Carl Ganter/ Contact Press Images.

Chapter 19

p. 372: Mark Richards/ PhotoEdit. **p. 380:** Shane Young/AP/Wide World Photos. **p. 385:** Photo, Tom Croke/ Liaison Agency; EOL logo, courtesy Equal Housing Opportunity.

Chapter 20

p. 394: Corbis/Archivo Iconografico, S. A.
p. 397: Top left, from Ekonomicheskaia gazeta, January 1986, no. 5, p. 11; bottom left, from Ekonomicheskaia gazeta, January 1986, no. 25, p. 24; right, from Krododil, January 1986.
p. 405: A. Keplicz/ AP/Wide World Photos.

Index

Note: Page numbers in boldface type indicate pages where terms are defined; those followed by n indicate notes.

Dictionary of Economic Terms

Ability-to-pay principle holds that people with more income should pay more taxes.

Absolute advantage exists when an economy or individual can produce more per unit of labor than another in the production of the good under consideration.

Absolute income test defines a person as poor if his or her income falls below a specific level.

Accounting profit is profit using only explicit costs in the calculation.

Aggregate demand is the relationship between the total quantity of goods and services demanded and the price level, all other determinants of spending being unchanged.

Aggregate demand curve is a graphical representation of aggregate demand.

Aggregate production function relates the total output of an economy to the total amount of labor employed in the economy, all other determinants of production (which include capital, natural resources, and technology) being unchanged.

Antitrust policy refers to government attempts to prevent the acquisition and exercise of monopoly power and to encourage competition in the marketplace.

Arc elasticity is computed by calculating percentage changes relative to the average value of each variable between two points.

Asset is anything that is of value.

Automatic stabilizers are government programs that tend to reduce fluctuations in GDP automatically.

Average fixed cost is total fixed cost divided by quantity.

Average product is the output per unit of variable factor.

Average product of labor is the ratio of output to the quantity of labor.

Average revenue is total revenue divided by quantity.

Average total cost is total cost divided by quantity; it is the firm's total cost per unit of output and is the sum of average variable cost and average fixed cost.

Average variable cost is the firm's total variable cost per unit of output; it is total variable cost divided by quantity.

Balance of payments is the balance between spending flowing into a country from other countries and spending flowing out of that country to other countries.

Balance on capital account is the sum of credits and debits in the capital account.

Balance on current account is the sum of credit and debit items in a country's current account.

Balance sheet is a form of financial statement showing assets, liabilities, and net worth.

Balanced budget means that a government's revenues equal its expenditures for a particular period.

Balanced budget occurs if the surplus equals zero.

Bank is a financial institution that accepts deposits, makes loans, and offers checking accounts.

Barriers to entry are market conditions that prevent the entry of new firms in a monopoly market.

Barter occurs when goods are exchanged directly for one another.

Base period is a time period against which costs of the market basket in other periods will be compared in computing a price index.

Benefits-received principle holds that a tax should be based on the benefits received from the government services funded by the tax.

Bilateral monopoly is a situation in which a monopsony buyer faces a monopoly seller.

Bond is a promise by the issuer of the bond to make a series of payments to the owner of the bond on specific dates.

Bond is a promise to pay back a certain amount of money at a certain time.

Budget constraint restricts a consumer's spending to the total budget available to the consumer.

Budget deficit exists if a government's expenditures exceed its revenues.

Budget deficit is a negative surplus; it occurs when expenditures exceed revenues.

Budget line shows graphically the combinations of two goods a consumer can buy with a given budget.

Budget surplus occurs if a government's revenues exceed its expenditures.

Budget surplus occurs when revenues exceed expenditures.

Business cycle is a pattern of expansion, then contraction, then expansion again of real GDP.

Capacity utilization rate measures the percentage of the capital stock in use.

Capital is a factor of production that has been produced for use in the production of other goods and services.

Capital account is a statement of spending flows into and out of the country during a particular period for purchases of assets.

Capital account deficit exists if the balance on capital account is negative.

Capital account surplus exists if the balance on capital account is positive.

Capital intensive describes a firm or country when it increases the ratio of capital to labor that it uses.

Capture theory of regulation holds that government regulations often end up serving the regulated firms rather than their customers.

Carrying capacity of a resource is the quantity of its services that can be consumed in one period without reducing the stock of the resource in subsequent years.

Cartel is a group of firms engaged in overt collusion.

Cash assistance is a money payment that a recipient can spend as he or she deems appropriate.

Central bank oversees the banking system in a nation by acting as a banker to the central government and to other banks, by regulating banks, and by setting monetary policy.

Ceteris paribus is a Latin phrase that means "all other things unchanged."

Change in aggregate demand is a change in the aggregate quantity of goods and services demanded at each price level.

Change in aggregate quantity of goods and services supplied is a movement along the short-run aggregate supply curve in response to a change in the price level.

Change in demand is a shift in the demand curve.

Change in quantity demanded is a movement along the demand curve; it results from a change in the price of a good or service.

Change in quantity supplied is a movement along the supply curve; it results from a change in the price of a good or service.

Change in short-run aggregate supply is a change in the aggregate quantity of goods and services supplied at every price level in the short run.

Change in supply is a shift in the supply curve.

Change in the aggregate quantity of goods and services demanded is a movement along the aggregate demand curve.

Check is a legal document used to transfer the ownership of a checkable deposit.

Checkable deposit is a bank deposit whose ownership can be transferred with a check.

Choice at the margin is a decision whether to do a little more or a little less of something.

Circular flow model provides an overview of how markets work and how they are related to each other. It shows flows of spending and income through the economy.

Classical economics is the body of macroeconomic thought associated primarily with 19th century British economist David Ricardo.

Closed shop is a firm in which workers must belong to a union before they can gain employment.

Coase theorem is the proposition that if property rights are well defined and if bargaining is costless, then the private market can achieve an efficient outcome regardless of which of the affected parties holds the property rights.

Collective bargaining is a process of negotiation of worker contracts between unions and employers.

Command-and-control approach is one in which a government agency specifies how much or by what method a polluting agent must adjust its emissions.

Command socialist economy is one in which the government is the primary owner of capital and natural resources and has broad power to allocate the use of factors of production.

Commodity money is money that has a value apart from its use as money.

Common property resource is a resource for which no exclusive property rights exist.

Comparative advantage in producing a good or service occurs for an economy if the opportunity cost of producing that good or service is lower for that economy than for any other.

Complementary factors of production are those for which an increase in the use of one increases the demand for the other.

Complements are two goods related in such a way that a reduction in the price of one increases the demand for the other.

Concentration ratio reports the percentage of total industry output accounted for by the largest firms in the industry.

Constant is something whose value doesn't change.

Constant returns to scale occur when long-run average cost stays the same over an output range.

Constant-cost industry exists when expansion or contraction doesn't affect price in the markets for inputs the industry uses in the long run.

Constraint is a boundary that limits the range of choices that can be made.

Consumer price index (CPI) is a price index whose movement reflects changes in the prices of goods and services typically purchased by consumers.

Consumer surplus is the amount by which the total benefit to consumers exceeds their total expenditure.

Contractionary policy is a stabilization policy designed to decrease real GDP.

Corporate stocks are shares in the ownership of a corporation.

Corporation is a firm owned by a number of persons who own shares of corporate stock.

Cost-benefit analysis seeks to quantify the costs and benefits of an activity.

Coupon rate is a percentage of the face value of a bond that will be paid periodically to its owner.

Craft unions unite skilled workers in the same trade.

Cross price elasticity of demand for one good or service equals the percentage in demand at a specific price for that good or service divided by the percentage change in price of a related good or service, all other things unchanged.

Crowding out is the tendency for an expansionary fiscal policy to reduce other components of aggregate demand.

Currency is paper money and coin issued by a government.

Current account is a statement of spending flows into and out of the nation during a particular period for exports and imports, together with the flow of payments to owners of foreign assets and transfer payments that flow across international borders.

Current account deficit exists if the balance on current account is negative.

Current account surplus exists if the balance on current account is positive.

Cyclical unemployment is unemployment in excess of the unemployment that exists at the natural level of employment.

Cyclically adjusted budget shows what federal expenditures and revenues would be if the economy were operating at its potential output.

Deadweight loss is the net benefit sacrificed by not choosing the solution at which marginal benefit equals marginal cost.

Decreasing-cost industry exists when expansion (contraction) decreases (increases) inputs prices and thus decreases (increases) production costs in the long run.

Deflation is a decrease in the average level of prices.

Demand curve is a graphical representation of a demand schedule. It shows the relationship between the price and quantity demanded of a good or service during a particular period, all other things unchanged.

Demand curve for capital is the quantity of capital firms intend to hold at each interest rate.

Demand curve for money shows the quantity of money demanded at each interest rate, all other things unchanged.

Demand for money is the relationship between the quantity of money people want to hold and the factors that determine that quantity.

Demand schedule is a table that shows the quantities of a good or service demanded at different prices during a particular period, all other things unchanged.

Demand shifter is a variable that can change the quantity of a good or service demanded at each price.

Demerit goods are goods whose consumption the public sector discourages, based on a presumption that individuals don't adequately weigh all the costs of these goods and should thus be induced to consume less than they otherwise would.

Demographic transition is a process in which population growth rises with a fall in death rates and then falls with a reduction in birth rates.

Dependency theory is a body of economic theory that concludes that the poverty found in the less developed nations is primarily caused by the inability of the developing nations to free themselves from dependence on the industrialized nations.

Dependent variable is one that changes in response to a change in another variable.

Deposit multiplier (m_d) equals the ratio of the maximum possible change in checkable deposits divided by the change in reserves that created it.

Depreciation is a measure of the amount of capital that wears out or becomes obsolete during a period.

Derived demand is said to be because the demand for factors that produce a product depends on the demand for the product itself.

Developing countries are those that are not among the high-income nations of the world.

Diminishing marginal returns occur when additional units of a variable factor add less and less to total output, given constant quantities of other factors.

Diminishing marginal returns to a factor of production occur when the marginal product of the factor is positive but falling as more of it is used, given a constant level of all other factors.

Discount rate is the interest rate the Fed charges to banks when it lends reserves to them.

Discrimination occurs when people with similar economic characteristics experience different economic outcomes because of their race, sex, or other noneconomic characteristics.

Diseconomies of scale are experienced by a firm when long-run average cost rises as the firm expands its output.

Disposable personal income equals the income households have available to spend on goods and services.

Dissaving is negative saving; it occurs when consumption during a period exceeds income during the period.

Dominant strategy is one that is the same regardless of the action of the other player in a game.

Dominant strategy equilibrium occurs in a game if every player has a dominant strategy.

Dumping occurs when an exporter sells goods in a foreign market at a price below its own production cost.

Duopoly is an industry that consists of two firms.

Economic development is a process that produces sustained and widely shared gains in per capita real GDP.

Economic growth is the process through which an economy achieves an outward shift in its production possibilities curve.

Economic loss (negative economic profit) is incurred if total cost exceeds total revenue. It equals total revenue less total cost, and is a negative number.

Economic profit is the difference between a firm's total revenues and its total costs.

Economic profit per unit is the difference between price and average total cost.

Economic rent is the amount by which the current price of a resource exceeds the minimum price necessary to make the resource available.

Economic system is the set of rules that define how an economy's resources are to be owned and how decisions about their use are to be made.

Economics is a social science that examines how people choose among the alternatives available to them.

Economies of scale are experienced by a firm when long-run average cost declines as the firm expands its output.

Efficiency condition requires a competitive market with well-defined and transferable property rights.

Efficiency-wage theory holds that firms may try to increase productivity by paying a wage in excess of the market-clearing wage.

Efficient allocation of resources is one that maximizes the net benefit of all activities.

Efficient production is achieved when an economy is operating on its production possibilities curve.

Elasticity is the percentage change in a dependent variable divided by the percentage change in an independent variable, all other things unchanged.

Entrepreneur is a person who seeks to earn profits by finding new ways to organize factors of production.

Equation of exchange states that the money supply times its velocity equals nominal GDP.

Equilibrium price is the price at which the quantity demanded equals the quantity supplied.

Equilibrium quantity is the quantity demanded and supplied at the equilibrium price.

Excess capacity exists when the profit-maximizing level of output is less than the output associated with the minimum possible average total cost of production.

Excess reserves are any reserves banks hold in excess of required reserves.

Exchange rate is the price of a currency in terms of another currency or currencies.

Exclusive property right is one that allows its owner to prevent others from using the resource.

Exhaustible natural resource is one for which consumption of its services necessarily reduces the stock of the resource.

Expansion is a period in which real GDP is rising.

Expansionary policy is a policy designed to increase real GDP.

Explicit costs include charges that must be paid for factors of production such as labor and capital, together with an estimate of depreciation.

Exponential growth is what a quantity experiences when it grows at a given percentage rate.

Exports are sales of a country's goods and services to buyers in the rest of the world during a particular time period.

External benefit is a benefit received by others as a result of an action by a person or firm in the absence of any market agreement.

External cost is a cost imposed on others outside of any market exchange.

Face value of a bond is the amount that will be paid to the holder of the bond when it matures.

Factor markets are markets in which households supply factors of production demanded by firms.

Factors of production are the resources available to an economy for the production of goods and services.

Fallacy of false cause is the incorrect conclusion that one event causes another because the two events tend to occur together.

Federal funds market is a market in which banks lend reserves to one another.

Federal funds rate is the rate of interest charged for reserves in the federal funds market.

Fiat money is money that some authority has ordered be accepted as money.

Financial capital includes money and other "paper" assets (such as stocks and bonds) that represent claims on future payments.

Financial intermediary is an institution that amasses funds from one group and makes them available to another.

Financial markets are markets where funds accumulated by one group are made available to another group.

Firms are organizations that produce goods and services.

Fiscal policy is the use of government purchases, transfer payment, and taxes to influence the level of economic activity.

Fixed costs are the costs associated with the use of fixed factors of production.

Fixed factor of production is a factor whose quantity cannot be changed during a particular period.

Flow variable is a variable that occurs over a specific period of time.

Foreign exchange market is a market in which currencies of different countries are traded for one another.

Fractional reserve banking system is one in which banks hold reserves whose value is less than the sum of claims on those reserves.

Free-floating exchange rate system is one in which governments and central banks do not participate in the currency market.

Free good is one for which the choice of one use does not require that we give up another.

Free riders are people or firms that consume a public good without paying for it.

Frictional unemployment is unemployment that occurs because it takes time for employers looking for workers and workers looking for work to find each other.

Full employment occurs if all the factors of production that are available for use under current market conditions are being utilized.

Game theory is an analytical framework used in the analysis of strategic choices.

Government expenditures include all spending by government agencies.

Government purchases are the sum of purchases of goods and services from firms by government agencies plus the total value of output produced by government agencies themselves during a time period.

Government purchases occur when a government agency purchases or produces a good or a service.

Government revenues include all funds received by government agencies.

Graph is a pictorial representation of a relationship between two or more variables.

Gross domestic income (GDI) measures the total income generated in an economy by the production of final goods and services during a particular period.

Gross national product (GNP) is the total value of final goods and services produced during a particular period with factors of production owned by the residents of a particular area.

Gross private domestic investment is the official measure of private investment in the economy. It includes three flows that add to the nation's capital stock: expenditures by business firms on new buildings, plants, tools, and equipment that will be used in the production of goods and services; expenditures on new residential housing; and changes in business inventories.

Herfindahl–Hirschmann Index is an alternative measure of concentration, found by squaring the percentage share of each firm in an industry, then summing these squared market shares.

Horizontal merger is the consolidation of firms that compete in the same industry or product line.

Human capital is the set of skills a worker has as a result of education, training, or experience that can be used in production.

Hyperinflation is an inflation rate in excess of 200 percent per year.

Hypothesis is a testable assertion of a relationship between two or more variables that could be proven to be false.

Illegal per se refers to a business practice that violates the law, and no consideration is given to the circumstances under which it occurs.

Impact lag is the lag between the time a policy goes into effect and the time the policy has its impact on the economy.

Imperfect competition exists in an industry with more than one firm and in which at least one firm is a price setter.

Implementation lag is the delay between the time at which a problem is recognized and the time at which a policy to deal with it is enacted.

Implicit cost is one that is included in the economic concept of opportunity cost but that is not an explicit cost.

Implicit price deflator is a price index for all final goods and services produced. It is computed as the ratio of nominal GDP to real GDP.

Import substitution refers to a developing nation's policy to restrict importation of consumer and capital goods, substituting domestically produced items.

Imports are purchases of foreign-produced goods and services by a country's residents during a period.

Incentive approaches to pollution regulation create market-like incentives to encourage reductions in pollution but allow individual decisionmakers to decide how much to pollute.

Income effect of a price change is the amount by which a consumer changes his or her consumption of a good or service in response to the implicit change in income caused by a change in the good's price.

Income elasticity of demand (e_Y) is the percentage change in demand at a specific price divided by the percentage in income, all other things unchanged.

Income-compensated price change is an imaginary exercise in which we assume that when the price of a good or service changes, the consumer's income is adjusted so that he or she has just enough to purchase the original combination of goods and services at the new set of prices.

Increasing-cost industry exists when expansion (contraction) increases (decreases) inputs prices and thus increases (decreases) production costs in the long run.

Increasing marginal returns to a factor of production occur when the marginal product of the factor is rising as more of it is used, given a constant level of all other factors.

Independent variable is a variable that induces a change in a dependent variable.

Indifference curve shows the combinations of two goods that yield equal levels of utility.

Indirect business taxes are taxes imposed on the production or sale of goods and services or on other business activity.

Industrial unions represent the employees of a particular industry, regardless of their craft.

Inefficient production results when an economy is operating inside its production possibilities curve.

Infant industry is a new domestic industry with potential economies of scale.

Inferior good is a good for which demand decreases when income increases.

Inflation is an increase in the average level of prices.

Inflationary gap is the difference between the level of real GDP and potential output, when real GDP is greater than potential.

Inflation-unemployment cycle is the pattern of a Phillips phase, stagflation phase, and recovery phase observed in the relationship between inflation and unemployment.

Intercept is the point at which a curve intersects an axis.

Intercept of the curves is the point at which a curve intersects an axis.

Interest is a premium paid to people who agree to postpone their use of wealth.

Interest rate is a premium paid for the use of wealth, expressed as a percentage of the amount of wealth involved.

Interest rate is the payment made for the use of money, expressed as a percentage of the amount borrowed.

Interest rate effect is the tendency for a change in the price level to affect the interest rate and thus to affect the quantity of investment demanded.

International finance is the study of the economic implications of the financial flows associated with international trade.

International trade effect is the tendency for a change in the price level to affect net exports.

Investment is an addition to capital stock.

Investment demand curve is a curve that shows the quantity of investment demanded at each interest rate, with all other determinants of investment unchanged.

Joint ventures are cooperative projects carried out by two or more firms. In the context of antitrust, joint ventures involve collusion that otherwise would be prohibited.

Keynesian economics asserts that changes in aggregate demand can create gaps between the actual and natural levels of real GDP, and that such gaps can be prolonged.

Labor is the human effort that can be applied to the production of goods and services.

Labor force is the number of people working plus the number of people unemployed.

Labor intensive describes a firm or country when it reduces the ratio of capital to labor that it uses.

Labor theory of value holds that the relative values of goods and services are ultimately determined by the quantities of labor required in their production.

Labor union is an association of workers that seeks to increase wages and to improve working conditions for its members.

Law is a theory that has won virtually universal acceptance.

Law of demand holds that, for virtually all goods and services, a higher price induces a reduction in quantity demanded and a lower price induces an increase in quantity demanded, all other things unchanged.

Law of diminishing marginal returns holds that the marginal product of any variable factor of production will eventually decline, assuming the quantities of other factors of production are unchanged.

Law of diminishing marginal utility is the tendency of marginal utility to decline beyond some level of consumption during a period.

Law of increasing opportunity cost holds that as an economy moves along its production possibilities curve in the direction of producing more of a particular good, the opportunity cost of additional units of that good will increase.

Least-cost reduction in emissions is one in which emissions are reduced so that the marginal benefit of an additional unit of pollution is the same for all polluters.

Liability is a financial obligation to make future payments to another party.

Liability is an obligation to another party.

Linear curve is a curve with constant slope.

Linear relationship between two variables is one for which the slope of the curve describing the relationship is constant.

Liquidity of an asset reflects the ease with which it can be converted to money.

Liquidity trap is said to exist when a change in monetary policy has no effect on interest rates.

Loanable funds market is the market in which borrowers (demanders of funds) and lenders (suppliers of funds) meet.

Loaned up is the situation when a bank holds no excess reserves.

Long run in macroeconomic analysis is a period in which wages and prices are flexible.

Long run in microeconomics is the planning period over which a firm can consider all factors of production as variable.

Long-run aggregate supply curve relates the level of output produced by firms to the price level in the long run.

Long-run average cost curve shows the firm's cost per unit at each level of output, assuming all factors of production are variable and that the firm has chosen the optimal factor mix for producing any level of output.

Long-run industry supply curve relates the price of a good or service to the quantity produced after all long-run adjustments to a price change have been completed.

Lorenz curve shows the cumulative shares of income received by individuals or groups.

M1 includes currency in circulation plus checkable deposits plus traveler's checks.

M2 includes M1 as well as other deposits, such as small time deposits, savings accounts, and money market mutual funds, that are easily converted to checkable deposits.

Macroeconomics is the branch of economics that focuses on the impact of choices on the total, or aggregate, level of economic activity.

Malthusian trap is reached when population increases beyond the ability of the earth to feed it; starvation holds subsequent population in check.

Margin is the current level of activity.

Marginal benefit is the amount by which an additional unit of an activity increases its total benefit.

Marginal cost is the amount by which an additional unit of an activity increases its total cost.

Marginal decision rule is a principle of decisionmaking that holds that if the marginal benefit of an additional unit of an activity exceeds its marginal cost, the quantity of the activity should be increased. If the marginal benefit is less than the marginal cost, the quantity should be reduced. Net benefit is maximized at the point at which marginal benefit equals marginal cost.

Marginal factor cost (MFC) is the change in total cost when one more unit of a factor of production is added.

Marginal product is the amount by which output rises with an additional unit of a variable factor, the quantity of all other factors held constant. It is the ratio of the change in output to the change in quantity of a variable factor.

Marginal product of labor is the amount by which output rises with an additional unit of labor, the quantity of all other factors held constant. It is the ratio of the change in output to the change in the quantity of labor.

Marginal rate of substitution is the maximum amount of one good or service a consumer would be willing to give up in order to obtain an additional unit of another.

Marginal rate of technical substitution of capital for labor is the rate at which capital can be substituted for labor without affecting output; it is the negative of the slope of the isoquant curve.

Marginal revenue is the increase in total revenue from a 1-unit increase in quantity.

Marginal revenue product (MRP) is the amount by which an additional unit of a factor increases a firm's total revenue during a period.

Marginal tax rate is the tax rate that would apply to an additional $1 of taxable income received by a household.

Marginal utility is the amount by which total utility rises with consumption of an additional unit of a good, service, or activity, all other things unchanged.

Market capitalist economy is one in which resources are generally owned by private individuals who have the power to make decisions about their use.

Market failure occurs when private decisions do not result in an efficient allocation of scarce resources.

Maturity date of a bond is the date on which the issuer promises to pay the face value.

Means-tested transfer payments are payments for which the recipient qualifies on the basis of income.

Medium of exchange is anything that is widely accepted as a means of payment.

Merit goods are goods whose consumption the public sector promotes, based on a presumption that many individuals don't adequately weigh the benefits of the good and should thus be induced to consume more than they otherwise would.

Microeconomics is the branch of economics that focuses on the choices made by consumers and firms and the impacts those choices have on individual markets.

Mixed economies are economies that combine elements of market capitalist and of command socialist economic systems.

Model is a set of simplifying assumptions about some aspect of the real world.

Model of demand and supply uses demand and supply curves to explain the determination of price and output in a market.

Monetarist school holds that changes in the money supply are the primary cause of changes in nominal GDP.

Monetary policy is the use of central bank policies to influence the level of economic activity.

Money is anything that serves as a medium of exchange.

Money market is the interaction among institutions through which money is supplied to individuals, firms, and other institutions that demand money.

Money market equilibrium occurs at the interest rate at which the quantity of money demanded is equal to the quantity of money supplied.

Money supply is the total quantity of money in the economy at any one time.

Monopolistic competition is characterized by many firms producing differentiated products in a market with easy entry and exit.

Monopoly is a firm that is the only producer of a good or service for which there are no close substitutes and for which entry by potential rivals is prohibitively difficult.

Monopoly power is the power a firm has to act as a price setter.

Monopsony is a market in which there is a single buyer of a good, service, or factor of production.

Monopsony power is held by a buyer facing an upward-sloping supply curve for a good, service, or factor of production.

Moral suasion is an effort to change people's behavior by appealing to their sense of moral values.

Movement along a curve is a change from one point on the curve to another that occurs when the dependent variable changes in response to a change in the independent variable.

Multiplier is the ratio of the change in the quantity of real GDP demanded at each price level to the initial change in one or more components of aggregate demand that produced it.

National debt is the sum of all past federal deficits minus any surpluses.

Natural level of employment is the level of employment at which the quantity of labor demanded equals the quantity supplied.

Natural monopoly exists whenever a single firm confronts economies of scale over the entire range of production that is relevant to its market.

Natural rate of unemployment is the unemployment rate consistent with employment at the natural level.

Natural resources are the resources of nature that can be used for the production of goods and services.

Negative marginal returns to a factor of production occur when the marginal product of the factor is negative and total output falls as more of it is used, given a constant level of all other factors.

Negative relationship is one in which two variables move in opposite directions.

Net benefit is an activity's total benefit minus its opportunity cost.

Net exports are equal to imports minus exports.

Net present value (NPV) of an asset equals the present value of the revenues minus the present value of the costs associated with an asset.

Net worth equals assets less liabilities.

Network effects arise when a firm has a patent on a product that becomes more useful the larger the number of users of the product with the same standard.

New classical economics is the approach to macroeconomic analysis built from an analysis of individual maximizing choices.

New Keynesian economics is a body of macroeconomic thought that stresses the stickiness of prices and the need for activist stabilization policies to keep the economy operating close to its natural level through the manipulation of aggregate demand.

Nominal GDP is the GDP for a period valued at prices in that period (see **gross domestic product**).

Nominal value is a value measured in dollars of current purchasing power.

Noncash assistance is the provision of specific goods and services rather than cash.

Nonintervention policy is a policy choice to take no action to try to close a recessionary or an inflationary gap, but to allow the economy to adjust on its own to its potential output.

Nonlinear curve is a curve whose slope changes as the value of one of the variables changes.

Nonlinear relationship between two variables is one for which the slope of the curve showing the relationship changes as the value of one of the variables changes.

Non-means-tested transfer payments are payments for which income is not a qualifying factor.

Normal good is a good for which demand increases when income increases.

Normative statement is one that makes a value judgement.

Oligopoly is a market dominated by a few firms; each of those firms recognizes that its own choices will affect the choices of its rivals and that its rivals' choices will affect it.

One-way (or interindustry) trade occurs when countries specialize in producing the goods in which they have a comparative advantage and then export those goods so they can import the goods in which they do not have a comparative advantage.

Open-market operations are transactions in which the Fed buys or sells federal government bonds.

Opportunity cost is the value of the best alternative forgone in making any choice.

Origin of the graph is the point at which the axes intersect.

Output per capita for an economy equals real GDP per person.

Overt collusion means that firms agree openly on price, output, and other decisions aimed at achieving monopoly profits.

Partnership is a firm owned by several individuals.

Payoff is the outcome of a strategic choice.

Peak of a business cycle is reached when real GDP stops rising and begins falling.

Per capita real GNP equals a country's real GNP divided by its population.

Perfect Competition is a model of the market based on the assumption that a large number of firms produce identical goods consumed by a large number of buyers.

Perfectly elastic If price elasticity of demand is infinite, demand is perfectly elastic.

Perfectly inelastic If price elasticity of demand is equal to 0, demand is perfectly inelastic.

Personal consumption measures the value of goods and services that are purchased by households during a time period.

Phillips curve implies a negative relationship between inflation and unemployment.

Phillips phase is a period in which the inflation rate rises and the unemployment falls.

Pollution exists when human activity produces a sufficient concentration of a substance in the environment to cause harm to people or to resources valued by people.

Positive relationship between two variables is one in which both variables move in the same direction.

Positive statement is a statement of fact or a hypothesis.

Potential output is the level of output an economy can achieve when labor is employed at its natural level. It is also called the natural level of real GDP.

Poverty line is an annual income level that marks the dividing line between poor households and those that are not poor.

Poverty rate is the percentage of the population living in households whose income falls below the poverty line.

Precautionary demand for money is the money people and firms hold for contingencies that may occur.

Present value of a specific future value is the amount that would, if deposited today at some interest rate, equal the future value.

Price ceiling is a maximum allowable price.

Price discrimination means charging different prices to different customers for the same good or service even though the cost of supplying those customers is the same.

Price elastic If the absolute value of the price elasticity of demand is greater than 1, demand is price elastic.

Price elasticity of demand is the percentage change in the quantity demanded divided by the percentage change in price, all other things unchanged.

Price elasticity of supply is the ratio of the percentage change in the quantity supplied to the percentage change in price, all other things unchanged.

Price floor is a minimum allowable price.

Price index is a number whose movement reflects movement in the average level of prices.

Price inelastic If the absolute value of the price elasticity of demand is less than 1, demand is price inelastic.

Price setter is a firm that sets or picks price based on its output decision.

Price takers are individuals (or firms) who must take the market price as given.

Price-fixing is an agreement between two or more firms to collude in order to establish a price and not to compete on the basis of price.

Private goods are goods for which exclusion is possible and for which the marginal cost of another user is positive.

Private investment includes the value of all goods produced by firms during a period for use in the production by firms of goods and services.

Producer surplus is the difference between the total revenue received by sellers and their total cost.

Product markets are markets in which firms supply goods and services demanded by households.

Production function is the relationship between factors of production and the output of a firm.

Production possibilities curve is a graphical illustration of the alternative combinations of goods and services an economy can produce.

Production possibilities model shows the goods and services that an economy is capable of producing given the resources it has available.

Productivity is the amount of output per worker.

Progressive tax is one that takes a higher percentage of income as income rises.

Property rights are a set of rules that specify the ways in which an owner can use a resource.

Proportional tax is one that takes a fixed percentage of income.

Protectionist policy is one in which a country restricts the importation of goods and services produced in foreign countries.

Public choice theory is the body of economic thought based on the assumption that individuals involved in public sector choices make those choices to maximize their own utility.

Public finance is the study of government expenditure and tax policy and of their impact on the economy.

Public goods are goods for which the costs of exclusion are prohibitive and for which the marginal cost of an additional user is zero.

Public interest theory of government assumes that the goal of government is to seek an efficient allocation of resources.

Quantity demanded of a good or service is the quantity buyers are willing and able to buy at a particular price during a particular period, all other things unchanged.

Quantity supplied of a good or service is the quantity sellers are willing to sell at a particular price during a particular period, all other things unchanged.

Quantity theory of money holds that the price level moves in proportion with changes in the money supply.

Quota is a ceiling imposed by a country on the quantity of a good or service it will import.

Quota is a direct restriction on the total quantity of a good or service that may be imported during a specified period.

Rational abstention is a decision not to vote because the marginal costs outweigh the marginal benefits.

Rational expectations hypothesis assumes that individuals form expectations about the future based on the information available to them, and that they act on those expectations.

Rational expectations hypothesis is that people use all available information to make forecasts about future economic activity and the price level, and that they adjust their behavior to these forecasts.

Real gross domestic product (real GDP) is the total value of final goods and services produced during a particular year or period, adjusted to eliminate the effects of changes in prices.

Real value is a value measured in dollars of constant purchasing power.

Recession is a period in which real GDP is falling.

Recessionary gap is the difference between the level of real GDP and potential output, when real GDP is less than potential.

Recognition lag is a lag between the time a macroeconomic problem arises and the time at which policymakers become aware of it.

Recovery phase is a period in which inflation and unemployment decline.

Regressive tax is one that takes a lower percentage of income as income rises.

Regulation is an effort by government agencies to control the choices of private firms or individuals.

Relative income test defines people as poor if their incomes fall at the bottom of the distribution of income.

Renewable natural resource is one whose services can be consumed without potentially reducing the stock of the resource.

Rent-seeking behavior is the effort to influence public choices to advance one's own self-interest.

Repudiation of the debt is the declaration by a government that it will no longer honor its debt.

Required reserve ratio is the ratio of reserves to checkable deposits banks are required to maintain.

Required reserves are the quantity of reserves banks are required to hold.

Reservation wage is the lowest wage that, if offered, an unemployed worker would accept.

Reserves equal the cash a bank has in its vault plus deposits the bank maintains with the Fed.

Right-to-work laws prohibit union-shop rules.

Rotation of a curve occurs when we change its slope, with one point on the curve fixed.

Rule of reason holds that whether or not a particular business practice is illegal depends upon the circumstances surrounding the action.

Rule of 72 states that the approximate doubling time of a variable growing at some exponential rate equals 72 divided by the growth rate, stated as a whole number.

Saving is income not spent on consumption.

Scarce good is one for which the choice of one alternative use requires that another use be given up.

Scarcity is the condition of having to choose among alternatives due to limited resources.

Scatter diagram shows individual points relating values of the variable on one axis to values of the variable on the other.

Scientific method is a systematic set of procedures, including the formulation and testing of hypotheses, through which knowledge is created.

Shift in a curve implies new values of one variable at each value of the other variable.

Short run in macroeconomic analysis is a period in which wages and some other prices are sticky.

Short run in microeconomics is a planning period over which the managers of a firm must consider one or more of their factors of production as fixed in quantity.

Short-run aggregate supply curve is a graphical representation of the relationship between production and the price level in the short run.

Shortage is the amount by which the quantity demanded exceeds the quantity supplied at the current price.

Shutdown point is the minimum level of average variable cost, which occurs at the intersection of the marginal cost curve and the average variable cost curve.

Slope of a curve is the ratio of the change in the variable on the vertical axis to the change in the variable on the horizontal axis, measured between two points on the curve.

Social benefit of an activity equals its private plus its external benefit.

Social cost of an activity equals its private cost plus its external cost.

Sole proprietorship is a firm owned by one individual.

Specialization implies an economy is producing the goods and services in which it has a comparative advantage.

Speculative demand for money is the money households and firms hold because of a concern that bond prices and the prices of other financial assets might change.

Stabilization policy is a policy in which the government or central bank acts to move the economy to its potential output.

Stagflation phase is a period in which inflation remains high while unemployment increases.

Sticky price is a price that is slow to adjust to its equilibrium level, creating sustained periods of shortage or surplus.

Stock market is the set of institutions in which shares of stock are bought and sold.

Stock variable is a variable that is independent of time.

Store of value is the ability to hold value over time; a necessary property of money.

Strategic choice is based on the recognition that the actions of others will affect the outcome of the choice, and it takes these actions into account.

Strategic trade policy is one aimed at promoting the development of key industries within a country.

Structural unemployment is unemployment that results from a mismatch between worker qualifications and employer requirements.

Substitute factors of production are those for which the increased use of one lowers the demand for the other.

Substitutes are two goods related in such a way that a reduction in the price of one reduces the demand for the other.

Substitution effect of a price change is the change in a consumer's consumption of a good or service in response to an income-compensated price change.

Sunk cost is an expenditure that has already been made that cannot be recovered.

Supply curve is a graphical representation of a supply schedule. It shows the relationship between the price and quantity supplied of a good or service during a particular period, all other things unchanged.

Supply curve of money relates the quantity of money supplied to the interest rate.

Supply schedule is a table that shows the quantities of a good or service supplied at different prices during a particular period, all other things unchanged.

Supply shifter is a variable that can change the quantity of a good or service supplied at each price.

Supply-side economics is the notion that fiscal policy can be used to stimulate long-run aggregate supply.

Surplus is the amount by which the quantity supplied exceeds the quantity demanded at the current price

Surplus value is the difference between the price of a good or service and its labor cost.

Tacit collusion is an unwritten, unspoken agreement through which firms limit competition among themselves.

Tangent line is a straight line that touches, but does not intersect, a nonlinear curve at only one point.

Tariff is a tax imposed by a country on an imported good or service.

Tariff is a tax on imported goods and services.

Tax incidence analysis is economic analysis that seeks to determine where the actual burden of a tax rests.

Technology is knowledge that can be applied to the production of goods and services.

Terms of trade is the rate at which a country can trade domestic products for imported products.

Theory is a hypothesis that has not been rejected after widespread testing and that has won widespread acceptance.

Third-party payer is an agent other than the seller or the buyer who pays part of the price of a good or service

Time-series graph shows how the value of a particular variable or variables has changed over some period of time.

Tit-for-tat strategy is one in which a firm responds to cheating by a rival by cheating and to cooperation by a rival by cooperating.

Total cost is the sum of total variable cost and total fixed cost.

Total fixed cost is cost that does not vary with output.

Total product curve shows the quantities of output that can be obtained from different quantities of a variable factor of production, assuming other factors of production are fixed.

Total revenue for a firm is found by multiplying its output by the price at which it sells that output.

Total revenue is price per unit times the number of units sold.

Total utility is the number of units of utility that a consumer gains from consuming a given quantity of a good, service, or activity during a particular period.

Total variable cost is cost that varies with the level of output.

Trade deficit implies negative net exports.

Trade surplus occurs when exports exceed imports.

Trade-weighted exchange rate is an index of exchange rates.

Transactions demand for money is the money households and firms hold to pay for goods and services they anticipate buying.

Transfer payments are payments made by governments to individuals as grants rather than in return for labor or other services.

Transfer payments are payments that do not require that the recipient produce a good or service in order to receive them.

Transferable property right is one that allows the owner of a resource to sell or lease it to someone else.

Trigger strategy is a threat to respond to a rival's cheating by permanently revoking an agreement.

Trough of a business cycle is reached when real GDP stops falling and begins rising.

Two-way (or intraindustry) trade involves international exchanges in which countries both import and export the same or similar goods.

Unemployment is measured as the number of people not working who are looking and are available for work at any one time.

Unemployment rate is the percentage of the labor force who are unemployed.

Union shop is a firm that can hire union as well as nonunion workers, but nonunion workers are required to join the union within a specified period of time.

Unit of account is a consistent means of measuring the value of things.

User fees are charges levied on consumers of government-provided goods or services.

Utility-maximizing condition requires that total outlays equal the budget and that the ratios of marginal utilities to prices are equal for all goods and services.

Utility is the value or satisfaction that people derive from the goods and services they consume and the activities they pursue.

Value added is the amount by which the value of a firm's products exceeds the value of the goods and services the firm purchases from other firms at each stage of production.

Variable is something whose value can change.

Variable costs are the costs associated with the use of variable factors of production.

Variable factor of production is a factor whose quantity can be changed during a particular period.

Velocity of money is the number of times the money supply is spent for the goods and services that make up GDP during a particular period.

Vertical merger is the consolidation of firms that participate in the production of a given product line, but at different stages of the production process.

Voluntary export restrictions are a form of trade barrier by which foreign firms agree to limit the quantity of goods exported to a particular country.

Wealth is the total of assets less liabilities.

Wealth effect is the tendency for a change in the price level to affect real wealth and thus alter consumption.

Welfare programs are the array of programs that government provides to alleviate poverty.

Zero-coupon bond is a bond that does not carry a coupon rate.